DARK HORSE

Kenneth D. Ackerman

DARK HORSE

*The Surprise Election
and Political Murder of
President James A. Garfield*

VIRAL HISTORY PRESS, LLC
FALLS CHURCH, VIRGINIA

Dark Horse
*The Surprise Election and Political Murder
of President James A. Garfield*

Viral History Press, LLC
Falls Church, VA 22044
www.viralhistorypress.com

Copyright © 2011 Kenneth D. Ackerman

First Carroll & Graf edition 2003
First Carroll & Graf trade paperback edition 2004

Library of Congress Cataloging-in-Publication Data is available.

ISBN-13: 978-1-61945-000-4

Designed by Zaccarine Design, Inc.
Printed in the United States of America

Dedicated to my father, William Ackerman,
loved and missed by his large family,
who taught me that politicians
should always stand for justice.

❖ ❖ ❖ ❖ ❖

CONTENTS

THE FEUD
• APRIL 1866 •

Starting soon after the Civil War, a Great Feud between two ambitious men would drive American politics for the next twenty years, splitting the Republican Party, shaping three presidential elections, and proximately causing one president to be shot in the back by an assassin, before ruining the careers of both rivals. They were still young when the feud began, in their mid-thirties, but close to emerging as the two dominant political personalities of their time. They would attract legions of followers, known as "Stalwarts" and "Half-Breeds," who would wage great passionate wars on their behalf. For good and ill, their struggle would comprise the politics of the Gilded Age.

Fittingly, the spark that ignited the Great Feud was a matter so small, petty, and avoidable that, had it not been for the contention caused, it would have been soon forgotten. As is, it became legend.

Washington, D.C.—April 1866

"I move to strike out section twenty of the bill."[1]

The House of Representatives had been debating the Military Bill for four tedious hours when Roscoe Conkling, Congressman from Utica, New York, rose to speak in a clear, loud voice easily heard in every corner. Congressmen in the chamber dropped their chatter. A ripple of attention crossed the visitor's gallery above. Conkling cut a striking figure. Self-consciously vain, he stood six foot, three inches tall, with an athletic build, erect posture, and well-muscled arms and shoulders from daily exercise at the punching bag. Conkling enjoyed frequent rides on horseback through Rock Creek Park or along the Potomac River and wore garish ties, trousers, and waistcoats. His sharp eyes looked out from beneath waves of sandy-blond hair, a single curl laid carefully across his forehead. A full beard accentuated a handsome face.

1

"My objection to this section is that it creates an unnecessary office for an undeserving public servant," Conkling continued. "It fastens an incubus upon the country"—he stressed the Latin pronunciation *IN-cu-bus*—"a hateful instrument of war, which deserves no place in a free government in time of peace." Conkling punctuated his words with sharp jabs of his hands and sweeping waves of his arms, gestures he practiced before a mirror. Only in his third term, the 36-year-old Congressman had made himself a favorite with ladies in the galleries, newspaper men, and sightseers. He peppered his talk with arrogant sarcasm that made opponents wilt.

Section twenty of the Military Bill, which Conkling proposed to delete, authorized the salary and staff of the Provost Marshal General, an obscure Army officer who'd been saddled with recruiting soldiers for the Union war effort— the hated Conscription. President Lincoln's military draft had sparked riots in New York and other cities during the War. Ugly, drunk mobs had burned, looted, and killed dozens of police and black bystanders. Recruitment bonuses for volunteer soldiers ended up lining pockets of thieves and deserters.

Conkling himself, under contract to the War Department, had prosecuted recruitment frauds in upstate New York in 1864. He had won his cases, and had learned to hate the officer in charge, Provost Marshal General James Barnet Fry. Now he would abolish General Fry's office. Conkling on the warpath made good copy. Newspaper men in the gallery opened their notebooks and readied for drama.

Just twelve months after Robert E. Lee's surrender to Ulysses Grant at Appomattox Court House had ended the great Civil War, almost every family, North and South, still grieved for lost husbands, fathers, and brothers— the 400,000 killed and millions injured on the blood-soaked battlefields of Virginia, Georgia, and the West. Many Congressmen wore blue Union army uniforms as they milled about the House chamber, joking, smoking cigars, writing letters, spitting into gold spittoons, having no offices beyond the tops of their congressional desks. The chamber, lit by gas-lamps and sky-lights, stank of mold and tobacco amid its marble elegance. Military titles of General, Colonel, or Lieutenant still carried more social grace in Washington, D.C. than did Congressman, Senator, or even President.

The Capitol Building itself looked down over a City of swamps, mud streets, and dank field hospitals. At the far end of Pennsylvania Avenue, Andrew Johnson, the current occupant of the White House, a Tennessee Democrat, was a sad contrast to the martyred Abraham Lincoln. Northern Congressmen despised Johnson's brazen southern sympathies so soon after the War and were fast clipping his wings. They had passed a civil rights bill over Johnson's veto and were finalizing a Constitutional amendment guaranteeing freed slaves the right to vote as citizens, all of which Johnson opposed.

Impeachment against the president would start within the year.

On Capitol Hill, hard-line "radicals" dominated. All eleven defeated Confederate states had sent members to the 39th Congress, elected in 1865 under President Johnson's liberal "reconstruction" terms. The unrepentant, all-white delegations included four Confederate Generals, several Colonels and Lieutenants, and even Alexander Stephens, the Confederacy's Vice President under Jefferson Davis. These recent warriors now expected co-equal seats in Congress, as if an ocean of blood hadn't been spilled to squash their rebellion. To Union eyes, they were criminals, rebels with fresh murder on their hands and treason in their hearts.

Hard-liners would have none of it. When Congress had convened in December 1865, Republican radicals simply locked the rebels out, deleting their names from the House roll call. As a result, Roscoe Conkling now addressed a House with 191 members, of whom three quarters were Republicans. The majority could impose a "reconstruction" with teeth and finish the work of the War.

So now, in April 1866, heads turned in the House chamber as Conkling laid out his case against General James Barnet Fry with typical force. General Fry had run an office rife with "coxcombs and thieves," Conkling declared. Honest citizens had been "victimized by constant uncertainty and deception," millions of government dollars had disappeared, criminals on the General's staff had stolen money meant for soldiers at the front. Conkling produced a letter from General Ulysses Grant, now serving as Lieutenant General of the Army in the War Department, calling the Provost Marshal's office unnecessary. Conkling denounced Fry himself for "insolence in office."

Conkling's political roots ran deep. His father, Alfred, had served in Congress during the 1820s, as a Federal Judge from 1825 to 1852, and as United States Minister to Mexico under President Millard Fillmore. His older brother Frederick, a New York financier, had served in Congress during the Civil War. Roscoe himself, born in 1829, was already winning fame in legal circles by 1855 when he married Julia Seymour, younger sister of New York's Democratic Governor (and 1868 presidential candidate) Horatio Seymour.

After that, milestones came quickly: District Attorney of Oneida County, then Mayor of Utica, all the while building his reputation as a master court-room advocate. He had won his first of four elections to Congress in 1858. Since Congress only met about four months each year, he could supplement his $5,000 annual Congressional pay by continuing his private law practice. In presidential election years, Republican leaders had recruited him to stump the countryside, first for John Fremont in 1856, then for Abraham Lincoln in 1860.

During sessions of Congress, Conkling bunked in a local Washington rooming house with other members. Julia stayed home in Utica with their young daughter, Bessie. Roscoe's escapades with other women had begun to strain their marriage.

Once in Congress, Conkling took every occasion to address the House floor, playing to the galleries and the power brokers. People who mattered took notice. House Speaker Schuyler Colfax had recently placed Conkling on the new Reconstruction Committee, which was then beginning its high-profile struggles with President Johnson. Earlier that April, popular New York essayist Theodore Tilton had profiled him as a rising Washington personality. "Roscoe Conkling of New York, is strong, positive, and critical," Tilton wrote in the *New York Independent*. "[A]nd, in many respects, reminds one of Henry Winter Davis, whose grave quenched one of the noblest spirits of these times," he continued, referring to the popular wartime Congressman from Maryland.[2]

New York politicos already courted Conkling for a Senate seat that would be coming open in 1867.

For all his admirers, though, Roscoe Conkling counted few friends in the House of Representatives. His arrogance and bullying, the constant chip on his shoulder, all sat poorly with other members. Conkling had a lifelong aversion to being touched physically that amplified his air of superiority; colleagues resented it. There were whispers. It was bad to cross Roscoe Conkling, they said. He carried grudges.

James B. Fry was learning that lesson today.

So, too, soon would James Gillespie Blaine.

◉ ◉ ◉ ◉ ◉

James G. Blaine, junior Congressman from Maine, was just three months younger than Roscoe Conkling. He, too, was smart, articulate, and widely considered a rising star. Teacher, journalist, lawyer, state legislator, political

"Boss," Blaine had already led Maine's Republican party as state chairman, served as speaker of its state legislature, and edited two of its leading newspapers, the *Kennebec Journal* and *Portland Advertiser*, all before coming to Congress in 1863 on a pledge to support Abraham Lincoln and the War.

Blaine had risen quickly in Washington as well. He had already achieved fame for developing a comprehensive plan to repay state war debts on a national basis, citing "one Country, one Constitution, one Destiny." Politically, he had crossed swords with crusty old Thaddeus Stevens, chairman of the Reconstruction Committee and a leading Radical, in debates on war debts and currency controls, but had kept his friendship. Where Conkling relied on oratory and force, Blaine used charm. Tall, with an easy bearing, blond hair, beard, and prominent eyes, Blaine made friends easily, remembered peoples' names and birthdays, and was quick with a joke or pleasantry.

Born in rural Pennsylvania, raised partly in the home of then-Treasury Secretary Thomas Ewing, the young James Blaine could recite Plutarch from memory at age nine. After earning his degree at Pennsylvania's Washington and Jefferson College, he taught Greek, Latin, and geometry at the Western Military Academy in Kentucky, where he met his wife-to-be, fellow teacher Harriet Stanwood. Then, for two years, he taught mathematics to students at the Pennsylvania Institute for the Blind in Philadelphia while studying law.

His wife's family brought Blaine to Maine in 1854 and helped him purchase a stake in the *Kennebec Journal*. There, Blaine's talent as political *raconteur* made him a celebrity. In small towns throughout New England, people grew to depend on Blaine's weekly columns as their portal to the outside world. He wrote about a wide range of topics, from the Crimean War to Bloody Kansas to fashions in New York and Boston.

Fame made Blaine a political force, with a hand in forming the new Republican Party both statewide and nationally. He became chairman of the Maine state party in 1861, and for the next two decades he exercised wide power in his adopted state: choosing candidates, managing campaigns, controlling patronage, and shaping legislation. Rarely did he use the heavy-handed tactics of other party "Bosses." But James Blaine, the ultimate pragmatist, always kept the option open.

Like most Congressional wives, Harriet stayed home in Augusta during sessions along with their two young sons Walker and William, eleven and nine, and daughter Maggie, six (an eldest son, Stanwood, had died in in-

fancy). Blaine often brought them to Washington for visits, though, and political friends prized invitations to the Blaine household for dinner or drinks.
Their table became known for good conversation and good cheer.

Typically, aging Thaddeus Stevens, after losing one close vote to the upstart Congressman, blamed it on "the House, partaking of the magnetic manner of my friend from Maine."[3] The nickname "magnetic man" would follow
Blaine for life.

As a member of the Military Affairs Committee, Blaine had co-authored
the Military Bill being considered by the House this day. Distracted by a head
cold, he had gone to sit in the House gallery when Roscoe Conkling launched
his attack on General Fry. At first, Blaine could only shrug. Most Americans
hated the wartime draft and the enlistment scandals. If Conkling wanted to
eliminate the office, Blaine had no objection. Besides, Blaine didn't know
General Fry personally. They weren't friends, and Fry was not a constituent.

But as Blaine sat and listened, he bristled at the attack. Why did Roscoe
Conkling have to personalize the issue? Most Congressmen who had dealt
face-to-face with General Fry knew him as a hard-working bureaucrat saddled
with a thankless wartime job. And Fry wasn't here to defend himself. It hardly
seemed honorable to harass him this way.

Blaine had never especially liked Roscoe Conkling. The two had sparred
before on the House floor. According to one account, friction between them
had started months earlier with an argument at a Washington dinner party
over authorship of some lines of poetry. Years later, after their feud had become a national fixture, friends suggested that their starkly different personalities had made the rift inevitable.

Maybe Blaine simply felt jealous that day in April 1866 of Roscoe Conkling's recent good newspaper clippings. Or maybe a colleague had egged him
on, telling him that "Someone ought to take that big-talking New Yorker
down a notch." Whatever the reason, Blaine came down from the gallery to
the House floor and gained recognition. "Though the gentleman from New
York has had some differences with General Fry, yet I take pleasure in saying
that, as I believe, there is not in the American army a more honorable and
high-toned officer than General Fry."[4]

Blaine, too, spoke in a manner that demanded attention. Gesturing with
one hand, he gave his voice an infectious animation and the unassuming
calm of a teacher. Now, sensing his audience's attention, he explained how
section 20 of the Military Bill simply reflected an earlier request from Gen-

eral Grant, nothing more. Roscoe Conkling had had "quarrels" with General
Fry, Blaine explained, "in which quarrels it is generally understood the gentleman came out second best." Conkling's issue was personal, Blaine declared,
and it was hardly "honorable" or "chivalry" for Conkling to raise it here, on
the House floor, without giving Fry a chance to answer.

"When I hear the Gentleman from New York rehearse in this House, all
the details of the recruiting frauds in New York, which General Fry used his
best energies to repress with iron hand," Blaine said, "my personal indignation carries me beyond my personal strength and impels me to denounce such
a course of proceeding."

However much Blaine may have disliked Conkling, Roscoe, for his part,
had no special love for James G. Blaine. Sensing eyes on him from throughout the House chamber, Conkling saw a challenge in Blaine's speech. He was
certainly not going to show the "white feather" to the newspaperman from
New England, not in front of all their colleagues.

"Mr. Speaker, if General Fry is reduced to depending for vindication upon
the Gentleman from Maine, he is to be commiserated certainly," Conkling
said, regaining the floor, assuming his already-familiar imperious tone. Blaine,
seated at his desk, usually enjoyed this verbal jousting, but Conkling's arrogance wore thin. Conkling went on: "If I have fallen to the necessity to taking lessons from that gentleman in the rules of propriety, or of right or wrong,
God help me."

Debates in Congress in the 1860s could be rowdy affairs. Insults, one-up-
smanship, bullying, acerbic humor, all played a part. Then as now, a Congressman needed a thick skin to shrug off attacks while keeping ties to colleagues. Today's enemy could be tomorrow's ally. But "honor" in chivalrous
Nineteenth Century America had a brittle side. Insults often led to actual
bloodshed. Many states still looked the other way at duels. Once a man
showed fear or weakness, he became a "mark."

And as two young public figures who had both avoided military service
in the Civil War, Conkling and Blaine likely felt extra need to prove their
valor.

Conkling now chose to push his edge. "I mean to take no advantage…
of the absence of General Fry," he said. "On the contrary, I am ready to avow
what I have to say anywhere. I am responsible, not only here but elsewhere,
for what I have said and for what I will say of the Provost Marshal General."

Blaine's ears shot up. Had Conkling just threatened him?

Conkling went on, his tone turning acidic. "I say further, that the State-ment made by the Gentleman from Maine with regard to myself personally and my quarrels with General Fry, and their result, is false. He says I can—"

Blaine jumped to his feet. Had Conkling just called him a liar? Here, in front of their House colleagues and the newspaper writers? Maybe it was just Conkling's tone that sounded so offensive. But either way, having staked his position in the arena, Blaine was not about to be pushed out. He interrupted Conkling in mid-sentence. "What does the gentleman mean to say was false?"

"I mean to say that the statement made by the gentleman from Maine is false," Conkling repeated.

"What statement?"

"Does not the gentleman understand what I mean?"

"I call the gentleman to order." Blaine motioned to the presiding officer, House Speaker Schuyler Colfax from Indiana, standing above them at the podium, for a point of order. "I have the parliamentary right. I demand he shall state what was false in what I said."

But Colfax, usually amiable and helpful, sensed danger and refused to in-tervene. "The chair overrules the point of order. The gentleman from New York will proceed," Colfax said.

"One more single word," Blaine insisted.

"I will not yield," Conkling said.

The two men were now shouting at each other across the chamber, their faces red, driven as much by stubbornness and confusion as genuine anger. But public insults, once launched, demand answers.

Roscoe Conkling held the floor. He steadied his stance and continued a long, condescending analysis of Blaine's statement as "erroneous and desti-tute." Blaine tried to interrupt again, but Conkling refused to look at him. "I decline to yield to the Gentleman from Maine," he said, taking his time to finish.

Another Congressman, Rufus Spalding from Ohio, now demanded recog-nition and Speaker Colfax gladly allowed him three minutes, hoping this would give Blaine and Conkling time to calm down. It didn't help.

When Spalding was done, Blaine immediately stood at his desk and re-gained the floor. "When we had gentlemen here from the eleven seceded States," he said, trying once more to win back his audience, "they used to talk about answering 'here and elsewhere,' and it was understood that they meant a duel." The chamber broke into uneasy laughter. Roscoe Conkling stood motionless, glaring at Blaine the entire time. "[The duelist] means that he is willing to receive a note outside of the District of Columbia [where duels were illegal]. Well, now, that is very cheap… When I have to resort to the epithet of 'false' upon this floor, and this cheap swagger… I shall have very little faith in the cause I stand up to maintain."

Then Blaine sat down.

So began the contest. Neither Conkling nor Blaine spoke again on the House floor that day. Cooler heads took over debate on the Military Bill. They dropped Section 20, but the core issue remained. Personal honor had been questioned. A gauntlet had been thrown down. A code of honor demanded that it be taken up.

⊙ ⊙ ⊙ ⊙ ⊙

Around the country, the verbal fireworks between the two junior Congressmen, Blaine of Maine and Conkling of New York, quickly became a sensation. Newspapers in the 1860s regularly reported House floor debates each day, and readers from New York to Chicago to Atlanta to San Francisco awoke the next morning or so to front-page accounts from Washington, D.C. of the "long and acrimonious" exchange where "Mr. Blaine charged Mr. Conkling with indulging in bluster and cheap swagger," (*New York Times*), the "very spicy debate" with its "excited manner, and a scene of considerable interest and confusion," (*Chicago Tribune*), the "desultory discussion" where Blaine and Conkling spoke with "great emphasis." (*Washington Star*).[5]

Tongues wagged all over Washington, but there was no official comment. Some friends hoped that, even now, despite the public embarrassment, a party elder might intervene and stop the feud. If Thaddeus Stevens or Schuyler Colfax, or Lincoln, were he still alive, had taken the two hot-heads, sat them down, and demanded they mend fences to aid the Party, certainly Conkling and Blaine would have complied. After all, despite their bad chemistry, the two still agreed on the dominant issues of the day: reconstruction, civil rights, national expansion, hard money, the tariff. Their votes on key questions matched head to head.

And both, as ambitious politicos, knew enough to follow orders from leadership. But whatever attempt friends did make to bridge the gap failed. Party elders kept.

For several days, the argument simmered. Official Washington turned its attention elsewhere. The spring social season blossomed, the first since 1860 free from shadows of war, replete with balls, receptions, and Sunday boat excursions on the Potomac River. Congress plowed ahead on reconstruction and the Fourteenth Amendment. There was work aplenty for the two young Congressmen, even as they avoided each other about town.

Blaine, meanwhile, quietly explored his options. He contacted General Fry and the War Department to investigate their "quarrel" with Conkling. He studied the New York recruitment scandals and Conkling's role in their prosecution. Blaine felt embarrassed at not having researched his case before confronting Conkling on the House floor. If his charges were wrong, he might have to apologize publicly. What a profound embarrassment that would be!

But as he dug, Blaine found ample evidence and an energetic ally in General Fry, who was eager to clear his own name.

Roscoe Conkling, meanwhile, visited the *Congressional Globe** offices after the flare-up to delete the offensive "here but elsewhere" language from the official record. Blaine noticed the change and attacked Conkling for yet another breach of honor.[6] There was no cooling off between them.

As the days passed, word spread through the Washington grapevine that the Congressman from Maine would soon spring a trap on the arrogant New Yorker. On Monday, April 30, just one week after the first encounter, as members began to debate a routine River and Harbor bill, a large crowd filled the grand marble House chamber. No one, it seemed, wanted to miss Act II of this curious political drama.

Their eyes turned that day as Blaine rose, standing erect on the blue-carpeted floor of the House of Representatives, interrupted pending business, and addressed the chamber: "Mr. Speaker, I hold in my hand a letter from Provost Marshal General Fry, which I ask to have read at the Clerk's desk for the double purpose of vindicating myself from the charge of having stated in debate last week what was false, and also for the purpose… of allowing fair play to an honorable man in the same forum in which he has been assailed."[7]

Blaine, working with General Fry, had developed a point-by-point rebuttal to Roscoe Conkling's earlier assault, along with new counter-punches. Fry had written it up in a long letter, with attached proofs, that he addressed to Blaine. Now, asserting his right to a "personal explanation," Blaine stood

---

* The *Congressional Globe* was the official reporter of House and Senate debates until replaced by the modern *Congressional Record* in 1873.

and demanded the record be set straight. Speaker Colfax, after some delay, had no choice but to allow Blaine to present Fry's letter to the House.

If Roscoe Conkling knew what was coming, he gave no clue. He stepped forward to stand before the Speaker. "I do not object," he announced, "but only ask, if the matter relates to me, to have opportunity to reply."

"I object to the gentleman from New York making a speech," said Lewis Ross, an Illinois Democrat.

"The gentleman does not want a letter to be read relating to a member and then not permit that member to reply?" Conkling asked.

"I withdraw my objection."

For the next full hour, as almost two hundred members of Congress and dozens of newspaper writers and dignitaries in the galleries listened, the House clerk read aloud the long, detailed letter from General Fry. Most damaging were fresh charges of wrongdoing by Roscoe Conkling himself. For one thing, it said, Conkling had improperly drawn a Congressional paycheck during the War while simultaneously receiving a $3,000 government retainer for legal services from the War Department.* For another, it said, Conkling had tried to suppress corruption charges against political friends in Utica. And for another, it said, each of Conkling's charges of dishonesty against Fry and his staff had already been reviewed by the War Department and found wanting.

John Bingham, an Ohio Republican, interrupted at one point and asked the Speaker to speed up the tedious reading, but Conkling objected. "[T]his is personal to me," he said with icy calm. "It is all new to me, and gentlemen will appreciate my desire in having it read."

When the clerk finally finished, Speaker Colfax, trying to maintain decorum, recognized the gentleman from Utica to respond. Conkling sensed the dramatic moment. He took the floor with an air of wounded dignity, standing tall and proudly defiant. "I appreciate the indifference with which the House must listen to an issue such as this," he said, "so personal and individual in its character." He then launched into a detailed rejoinder. He spoke for a full hour, ignoring occasional peppering from Congressman Ross on the double-salary issue. Most House colleagues kept their mouths shut throughout. Conkling insisted on his innocence. He demanded that the House appoint a committee to investigate the charges. This was done.

---

* While Congressmen were still allowed to carry on private law practices during this period and collect fees in addition to their Congressional salaries, double dipping from the government was generally barred.

Blaine too recognized the dramatic flow. He waited until Conkling had spoken nearly his full piece before joining the argument. "I do not know that I have anything to say, and I shall not take very long to say it," he told the room, chiding Conkling for his long-windedness. "[I]t has taken him an hour today to explain that while he and General Fry have been at sword's points for a year, there has been no difficulty at all between them."

By now, Conkling had had his fill of James Blaine and his irritating accusations. He dropped any pretence of courtesy toward his colleague; he physically turned his back on him. A moment later, when Blaine again asked for recognition, Conkling said simply: "No, sir. I do not wish to have anything to do with the member from Maine, not even so much as to yield him the floor."

After answering one last point from Martin Thayer of Pennsylvania, Conkling prepared to finish, but could not stop without settling accounts one last time. He turned and addressed Blaine directly for the first time all afternoon. "[I]f the member from Maine had the least idea how profoundly indifferent I am to his opinion upon the subject which he has been discussing, or upon any other subject personal to me, I think he would hardly take the trouble to rise here and express his opinion," Conkling said. "Ungentlemanly and impertinent, and having nothing whatever to do with the question"—this was his dismissal of Blaine's entire effort.

Conkling sat down and faced the other direction. He busied himself with papers on his desk—as if trying to erase from consciousness any lingering trace of the "Magnetic Man" from Maine.

But Blaine wasn't finished yet, either. This final broadside from Conkling—its arrogance and disdain—had caused him to lose whatever restraint he might have shown a moment before. In his anger, Blaine seemed to forget who and where he was: a U.S. Congressman speaking in formal public session. All he saw, it seemed, was a conceited bully needing to be knocked down.

If any doubts remained about James Blaine's precise feelings toward his New York colleague, he removed them now.

"As for the gentleman's cruel sarcasm," Blaine said, standing, eyes to the galleries, waving back-handedly at his opponent, "I hope he will not be too severe. The contempt of that large-minded gentleman is so wilting; his haughty disdain, his grandiloquent swell, his majestic, supereminent, overpowering, turkey-gobbler strut has been so crushing to myself and all members of this House that I know it was an act of the greatest temerity for me to venture upon a controversy with him."

Blaine felt his oratorical juices flowing. Had he even wanted to stop here, had his better judgment demanded it, he could not. He seized on the recent newspaper article by Theodore Tilton comparing the "strong, positive" Roscoe Conkling with the late Henry Winter Davis, and turned it to ridicule. "The gentleman [Conkling] took it seriously, and it has given his strut additional pomposity. The resemblance is great. It is striking. Hyperiorn to a satyr, Thersites to Hercules, mud to marble, dunghill to diamond, a singed cat to a Bengal tiger, a whining puppy to a roaring lion. Shade of the mighty [Henry Winter] Davis? Forgive the almost profanation of that jocose satire!"

Blaine sat down. There was silence, except for an embarrassed laugh or two that resounded in the chamber. Newsmen wrote furiously.

Today, you can search the *Congressional Record* and *Globe* through two hundred years of debate and never see a member of Congress insult a colleague so directly, brutally, and articulately, on the record, in public, looking directly at him across the room, as Blaine did to Conkling that day. It was one of the best speeches of Blaine's life, utterly spontaneous, memorably colorful, and profoundly destructive.

After the famous outburst, any hope of reconciliation between Conkling and Blaine disappeared. Bruises hardened into scars. The House investigating committee cleared Conkling of any wrong-doing in the affair,*[8] but that hardly mattered. When George Boutwell, a Massachusetts colleague and future Treasury Secretary and Senator, tried to mend fences in the mid-1870s, Conkling brushed him off. "That attack was made without any provocation by me as against Mr. Blaine," he said. "I shall never overlook it."[9]

Such was the new generation of political leadership that was emerging in America after the Civil War.

⊙ ⊙ ⊙ ⊙ ⊙

Fortunately for both, fortune soon separated Roscoe Conkling and James G. Blaine, allowing each to thrive in his own separate garden during the 1870s, Blaine in the House, Conkling in the Senate. Each became the leading figure of his domain.

Blaine's promotion came in 1868. As bitterness sharpened between Congress and President Andrew Johnson over Reconstruction, the public in-

---

* The Special Committee found that while Conkling had taken the alleged legal fees from the War Department, it concluded by lengthy analysis it did not violate any of the legal bars.

creasingly gave its trust to Ulysses Grant, Hero of Appomattox and Savior of the Union. They saw General Grant's stoic silence as battle-won strength. Amid chaos, he signified order.

Republicans in 1868 unanimously chose Grant to carry their party's Presidential banner. Grant, in turn, chose the popular Schuyler Colfax of Indiana as his Vice President. This left the House Speaker's chair vacant, and Blaine's "magnetic" popularity paid dividends as colleagues elected him by a wide margin. Over the next six years, he built a national reputation while presiding over the House, emerging as the Party's leading spokesman for sound finance, national expansion, and civil rights. He and his wife Harriett established their new townhouse on Washington, D.C.'s Fifteenth Street as a social center for the Capitol. From President and Mrs. Grant on down, their dinner parties attracted the political elite of all stripes.

These years would be the happiest in Blaine's life.

When Grant announced his plans to retire in 1876, Blaine, with help from friends across the country, became a natural candidate to replace him in the White House. Robert Ingersoll, the brilliant Illinois orator, nominated him at that year's Republican Convention in Cincinnati with a fiery speech calling Blaine the "plumed knight" for dashing pursuit of Republican causes. Blaine had the most votes among convention delegates and should have won, despite a brewing scandal over the so-called "Mulligan letters"* concerning his personal dealings in railroad stocks.

But another 1876 presidential prospect, Roscoe Conkling of New York, older now and far more powerful, gladly transferred his own delegates to long-shot Ohio favorite son Rutherford Hayes on the Convention's seventh ballot to block Blaine—the first of their three major collisions in Presidential politics.

Roscoe Conkling's opportunity had come in 1867 when the New York legislature chose him to fill the state's open seat in the United States Senate, where Conkling thrived and his eloquence blossomed.** Politically, he became the strongest supporter of President Grant, defending the Silent Soldier during his darkest scandals. Grant recognized Conkling's loyalty by offering

---

* Named for James Mulligan, a former Blaine family clerk, the letters detailed Blaine's suspicious dealings with the Little Rock and Fort Smith Railroad, a scandal that would follow him for life.

** United States Senators were elected by State legislatures, rather than by popular vote of the people, until the adoption of the 17th amendment to the Constitution in 1913.

him the seat of Chief Justice of the U.S. Supreme Court in 1874, but Conkling declined.

Instead, Conkling focused his energies on becoming supreme Boss of New York State's Republican party. He built a powerful machine, using his alliance with President Grant to win patronage for supporters. At its foundation stood the New York Custom House, which employed hundreds of political workers, where Conkling installed his protégé, Chester Alan Arthur, to manage his affairs.

In the late 1870s, Conkling entered a long, bitter contest with the new President, Rutherford Hayes, over Hayes' decision to remove Arthur from the Custom House as a nod to civil service reform. Conkling by then had become the leading Senator, long before such thing as a formal Majority Leader existed. When people visited Washington and explored the Capitol, the first question they usually asked was "Which one is Conkling?" Newspapers spread gossip about his affairs with glamorous women.

Conkling lost his battle to keep Arthur at the Custom House, but he kept the loyalty of his machine. The fight provoked an outburst by Conkling almost as famous as Blaine's toward him a decade earlier. At its height in 1877, Conkling, speaking to the annual New York State Republican Convention in Utica, lashed out against Hayes' "snivel service" reformers, calling them "the man-milliners, the dilettanti, and carpet-knights of politics." He said: "When Dr. Johnson defined patriotism as the last resource of a scoundrel, he was unconscious of the then undeveloped capabilities and uses of the word 're-form.'"[10]

Rutherford Hayes, badly weakened, chose not to seek re-election in 1880.

Meanwhile, the country had changed dramatically in the fifteen years since Appomattox. Prosperity had blossomed; the nation had entered the Industrial Age. The energy of war now was channeled into building railroads, factories, and mines, along with the great mansions and fortunes of a generation of robber barons and capitalists. Settlers crossed the western frontier and added two new states, Nebraska and Colorado. Immigrants helped swell the population by almost 60 percent, from 31 million (free and slave) in 1860 to over 50 million in 1880.

Change caused unrest. Labor unrest and political corruption also grew.

In the old Confederacy, Reconstruction had ended with the removal of Federal troops in 1876. In its wake, the promise of voting rights for freed black slaves and white moderates collapsed under frauds and violence. A divided

North saw itself confronted by a solidly Democratic and assertive South that threatened to resurrect the worst elements of the "lost cause."

As 1880 approached, Roscoe Conkling led a triumvirate of Stalwart senators seeking to return Ulysses Grant to the White House for an unprecedented third term. Grant, still America's most renowned citizen, had recaptured the imaginations of many who wanted a "strong man" as president, notwithstanding the scandals of his past terms. For Conkling, Grant's victory would give him vast influence in a new administration.

James Blaine too eyed 1880 with hope. Elevated to the U.S. Senate in 1867, Blaine built a strong organization of moderate "Half-Breeds"—a term that began as an insult against Republicans who wavered in their loyalty for Grant but became a compliment as Grant's scandals mounted in his second term. Blaine launched a well-organized national campaign that gathered dozens of delegates for the upcoming Republican National Convention, set for Chicago in early June.

By mid-May, 1880, General Grant and Senator Blaine each counted nearly three hundred delegates ready to support them on the first ballot in Chicago, out of the 379 needed to win the Republican nomination. A handful of favorite sons held the balance, the strongest being John Sherman of Ohio, who served as Treasury Secretary in President Hayes' outgoing administration.

As 1880 shaped up as yet another test of wills between Blaine and Conkling and their loyal factions, people wondered. They seemed so similar: two State party Bosses, both stalwart Radicals, both patronage men with the same disdain toward "reform" and with so much to gain by joining forces. Why, then, were they always on opposite sides of every political struggle?

But by then, everyone knew the story of how James G. Blaine had called out Roscoe Conkling on his "turkey gobbler strut" years ago on the floor of the House of Representatives. Knowing the two men, that seemed to explain everything.

PART I

The Great Contest, 1880

❂ ❂ ❂ ❂ ❂

Following tradition, the three main Presidential candidates stayed away from Chicago during the Republican nominating convention, instead leaving their fates in the hands of their political "friends" and managers, led by—

For **General Grant***: Senators Roscoe Conkling of New York, Don Cameron of Pennsylvania, and John "Black Jack" Logan of Illinois (the "triumvirate");*

For **Senator Blaine***: long-time political operative William E. Chandler of New Hampshire, aided by leaders of the Maine delegation; and*

For Treasury Secretary **John Sherman***: the four at-large delegates from Ohio: Governor Charles Foster, Former Governor William Dennison, attorney Warner M. Bateman, and Senator-elect James A. Garfield.*

• 1 •
CHICAGO

Saturday, May 29, 1880
Chicago, Illinois.

GENERAL GARFIELD?"[1]

He moved quickly for a large man. Entering the Grand Pacific Hotel on Jackson Street, he had to push through the lobby crowd, carrying his over-stuffed bag, stopping every few feet to shake a familiar hand or pat a familiar back. James Garfield seemed to know everyone. At the registration desk, he quickly drew a crowd. The reporter recognized him easily, even at a distance. Garfield stood out, with his tall, athletic build and full beard—a profile long familiar to anyone who followed politics in America since the War.

The Republican National Convention's opening gavel was still four days off, but trainload after trainload of delegates, lobbyists, newsmen, dignitaries, and camp-followers already had flooded Chicago, arriving at the Union and Dearborn railway stations from across the states and territories. They clogged the streets around the Exposition Building with parades and banners. From noon to midnight, brass bands led competing carnivals of Blaine men, Grant men, Germans, Ute Indians, Irish... clubs and factions of every description. They held rallies, sang, filled saloons and dancehalls, and kept both the pros-titutes and police busy—all the while talking and speculating and theoriz-ing. Grant "third-termers" waved white silk handkerchiefs proclaiming "Let Us Have Peace." Sherman backers wore red labels on their chests.

For six months, the struggle among Grant, Blaine, and Sherman for the White House had transfixed the nation. Now, this seventh quadrennial Re-

19

publican nominating forum promised to be the greatest American political festival ever.

The reporter already had a book full of interviews from his morning's work, patrolling the railway stations and major hotels, button-holing celebrities and asking the popular questions: Will it be Grant? Or Blaine? Or Sherman? Or a "dark horse"?* What about the third-term? And what about the Bosses and their plan to impose a "unit rule"? A unit rule would allow a state delegation's majority to bind all its members to a single candidate—gagging any dissenters. For the reporter, grabbing Garfield for an interview was a coup. Garfield not only was a leader of the Sherman camp, but also the subject of "dark horse" whispers in his own right.

"General Garfield?" the reporter shouted again, elbowing his way forward. Garfield, after representing Ohio in Congress for the eighteen years since 1863, had recently been elevated by the Ohio legislature to the U.S. Senate for a term starting the next year in 1881. But the reporter knew his protocol. Just fifteen years after Appomattox, a title of "General"—especially one like Garfield's, earned on Civil War battlefields—easily out-ranked "Congressman," "Senator," or even "President."

Just ask the former President, *General* Grant.

Garfield was ready with an evasion for the reporter, who identified himself as representing the *Chicago Tribune*. "I have just arrived. Please don't ask me anything about political matters," he said. "I have not really had time to make an estimate or form an opinion of the situation."[2]

Garfield had just reached Chicago that morning after taking the overnight train from Cleveland. Since leaving Washington, D.C., on Tuesday, he had spent two nights at his family's farm in Mentor, Ohio, near Cleveland, where his wife Lucretia—or "Crete" to the family—was undertaking a major farmhouse renovation. Carpenters, painters, roofers, and furniture movers had worked around them as the family tried to catch up. Their two older sons, James and Harry, fifteen and sixteen years old, had just come home from boarding school in New Hampshire for the week; the younger children, Abram, Irvin, and Mollie, seven, ten, and thirteen years old, played underfoot.[3] Outside, in the mild May sunshine, farm hands worked

---

* The term "dark horse" in U.S. presidential politics is generally seen as beginning with Tennessee's James K. Polk, a non-candidate nominated by Democrats in 1844 on the ninth ballot after front-runners Martin Van Buren and Lewis Cass had deadlocked. Polk then defeated Whig Henry Clay in the general election.

with horse-drawn plows to plant corn and wheat crops under Garfield's direction.

On Friday, James and Lucretia spent the day by themselves in Cleveland picking out furniture, hearths, and mantelpieces for the farmhouse. Then, late in the afternoon, she left him at the railway depot. Rowdy political conventions were no place for proper political wives.

The twelve night hours between Cleveland and Chicago gave Garfield plenty of time to read newspapers, write in his journal, and be alone with his thoughts. Garfield had raised himself from abject poverty of a childhood in the Ohio Western Reserve wilderness. He'd become enamored with reading, worked his way through Williams College, and then taught at and became first president of the new Eclectic University (now Hiram College) in Ohio. Here he'd met and married Lucretia, a one-time Hiram pupil and later a school-teacher herself, after a five-year courtship. For almost twenty years beginning in 1860, Garfield had placed himself at the center of every great national issue, from Civil War to Reconstruction to the Grant scandals to the 1876 election dispute. In Congress, he had chaired the Banking and Appropriations Committees and been elected House Minority Leader. He had fretted about his upcoming promotion to the more formal U.S. Senate, "a place composed of old men whose ideas and opinions are crystalized into fixed and well nigh unchangeable forms," he told a friend, where "personal antagonisms and jealousies prevail to a far greater extent ... than in the House." Longtime colleagues "who have gone from the House to the Senate have been immeasurably lost in its silence," he said. "I may be of that number."[4]

Still, Garfield loved politics, and he loved Washington. That spring, he had slipped away from the Capitol Building between House sessions four different times to watch base-ball games at the old wooden grandstand near the half-finished Washington monument where the Washington Nationals played.* Weeks earlier, he had taken Lucretia to the Ford's Theatre opening of *The Pirates of Penzance*, the sensational new musical play by British writers Gilbert and Sullivan. He then spent an afternoon watching the rowing contest along the Potomac River between Canadian Edward Hanlan and American Charles Courtney.

---

* Washington baseball would move in 1891 to the new National Park Stadium on Georgia Avenue and W street, later named Griffith Stadium, which would house the American League Senators until 1962 when they moved to Robert F. Kennedy Stadium. In 1971, the Senators left Washington altogether for Texas, leaving the nation's capital without a major league baseball team until the return of the Washington Nationals in 2005.

The townhouse on Washington's I Street where he and Lucretia lived when in the Capitol overflowed with happy memories of family and friends—including James G. Blaine, a House colleague for two decades whom he counted among his closest allies.

Garfield had heard the talk about himself as a "dark horse" for the presidency, but he tried to ignore it.[5] He had committed himself publicly to support fellow-Ohioan John Sherman, long-time Senator and now Treasury Secretary under President Hayes. Any hint of disloyalty would spell disaster. Sherman would never forgive Garfield for any betrayal, and would surely avenge himself by sinking any political future Garfield might have. Whatever doubts Garfield held about John Sherman as a candidate, or whatever ambitions he harbored for himself, this week in Chicago he planned to swallow his pride and do his duty.

Besides, the odds against a Garfield nomination were staggering. The eligible "dark horses" already made a long list: former Congressman Elihu Washburne of Illinois, Senators George Edmunds of Vermont and William Windom of Minnesota, even Roscoe Conkling of New York. Besides, James Garfield was only forty-eight years old in 1880. "Few men in our history have ever obtained the Presidency by planning to obtain it," he had written a few years earlier.[6] His time could come later.

As the overnight train made its way across Ohio and Indiana, Garfield walked about the cars and stopped to talk with the few friends he found. He shared some time with Richard C. Parsons, owner of the *Cleveland Herald*, en route to cover the convention. Parsons certainly knew the latest delegate counts, and they probably parsed the numbers and handicapped the possible outcomes. The *Albany Journal* had published a typical one that week showing Blaine with 277 votes, Grant with 314, Sherman with 106, and others with 49—all far short of the 379 needed to win, unless, of course, the Grant side could make mischief with the unit rule. Otherwise, if each held its votes intact, a long deadlock could result. Until one side or the other crumbled, the tension would be tremendous.

"I go with much reluctance," Garfield wrote that night in his journal, "for I dislike the antagonisms and controversies which are likely to blaze out in the convention."[7]

Reaching Chicago early the next morning, Garfield had to marvel at the great city of half a million people he saw rising on the prairie, already America's third largest after New York and Philadelphia. As a young Congressman,

Garfield visited Chicago shortly after the terrible 1871 fire that had inciner-ated the central districts, killing 300, and leaving 90,000 men, women, and children homeless. He had seen "the wonderful ruin," as he put it, and "the exhibition of marvelous energy which is rebuilding the ruined city."[8] Now, just a few years later, he saw startling contrast. From his train window, Garfield saw entire blocks of grand new brick buildings rising from the ashes, hun-dreds of ships lining the Lake Michigan waterfront, railroad lines stretching to every far horizon, and billowing smoke rising from smokestacks of dozens of factories and plants. From the vast animal stock-yards near Peoria Street, to Cyrus McCormick's reaper production works, to the elegant new homes ris-ing on the north side, Chicago burst with energy and industry, like the coun-try itself.

Now, that morning, from the moment he left his railroad car at Dearborn station, people approached Garfield one after another, pulling him aside with talk and gossip. "I arrived here at 8 o'clock, and find the city boiling over with politics," he wrote Lucretia in a letter that day. "Everything is in the vague of vastness and uncertainty."[9]

Most key political leaders had already reached Chicago days before Garfield and set up headquarters in the major hotels, mostly the Palmer House and the Grand Pacific. John Sherman's team had set up at the Grand Pacific and waited impatiently for Garfield to join them. As Garfield started toward the Hotel's new Otis Elevator, the *Chicago Tribune* reporter pulled him back for one more try. "How do you stand on the unit rule?" he asked.[10]

Garfield was ready for the question. The arcane unit rule, which would allow a state delegation's majority to bind all its members to a single candi-date, had come to dominate the pre-convention maneuvering. Unit rule meant control by strong-arm state party bosses, specifically Roscoe Conkling, Don Cameron, and John Logan, the three leading Senators backing General Grant. The "triumvirate" they called themselves—like Roman emperors. The rule would guarantee Grant's third-term nomination by silencing dissenters in the big states, even if an actual majority of delegates opposed it.

Garfield leaned close to give the newsman his well-rehearsed line. "I will give you an answer because I have an opinion on that subject," he said. "[A]ll delegates… are political units, each one of which has a right to express his own political sentiment by his own personal vote…. It is wholly un-Repub-lican for one man to cast another man's vote." The reporter scribbled down the words verbatim. Clear enough, he thought. Garfield, speaking for the

Sherman faction, would fight the rule. But Garfield wasn't quite finished yet. "I regard it as being more important than even the choice of a candidate," he added.

⦿ ⦿ ⦿ ⦿ ⦿

Breaking away from the *Chicago Tribune* writer, Garfield rode the noisy elevator to the hotel's fifth floor. Ohio's suite stood just down the hall from the large, noisy New York delegation. Garfield had to pass their garish "New York Solid for Grant" banner and the brassy hallway "greeters" to reach his own room, number 108. Garfield's parlor opened directly into room 110, where Governor Foster already had set up housekeeping. Garfield knew Charley Foster well from Congress where Foster had served three terms during the 1870s. Son of a wealthy merchant who'd named his Ohio town after himself—Fostoria—the governor held a sizeable fortune and an ego to match. Foster's ears had tingled at whispers that Blaine might pick him for vice president should Sherman drop from the race.

A private telegraph wire ran directly from the Sherman suite to Secretary John Sherman's own Treasury Department office in Washington, D.C. The line was already in heavy use. Garfield found his colleagues tightly huddled in political talk, their faces strained and fatigued, but in high spirits. "Outlook is very encouraging," Warner Bateman, the campaign chief, had telegraphed Sherman in Washington that morning. "All talk is favorable to you." Then later: "Your friends have never felt as confident of success as at present. The defeat of Grant means your nomination."[11]

The convention had reached its first make-or-break crisis. Telegrams shot back and forth across the wires from managers to candidates and to newspaper bureaus around the country. At issue: the "unit rule," and a rumored plan by General Grant's managers to railroad his nomination on the very first day. It had created a unifying point for all the anti-Grant factions. In fact, the immediate decision for Sherman's camp, awaiting Garfield's urgent input, was whether to join forces with Blaine delegates in the emergency.

Garfield barely had time to drop his bags and change clothes before joining the others. He knew these men well—Bateman, Foster, and William Dennison—the Sherman chiefs who sat in the hotel suite plotting strategy. Their ties went back decades. Dennison, the oldest at 65 years, he'd known the longest. As Ohio's wartime Governor, Dennison had launched young James Garfield's military career by appointing him Colonel of the state's newly-formed 42nd volunteer militia in 1861. Garfield, then just 31 years old and already a leading state legislator, university president, and ardent abolitionist, had seized the opportunity and become an early war hero. He 'd led outnumbered troops to victory in Kentucky's Sandy Valley weeks before Colonel Ulysses Grant's first success at Fort Donelson.[12] Garfield's troops then joined the Battle of Shiloh and pursued General Beauregard's retreat. The War Department promoted him to Brigadier General and then assigned him to General William Rosecrans' corps as Chief of Staff, just in time for the disastrous 1863 Chickamauga campaign. Thousands of Union troops died in this Union defeat. Rosecrans lost his command; Garfield salvaged his own reputation only by conspicuous bravery under fire. He was "the most able and prominent of the young politicians who entered the army at the outbreak of the war," wrote Whitelaw Reid, the war correspondent and future publishing mogul.[13]

As Garfield's fame spread, Dennison stepped in again, this time to help engineer Garfield's 1863 election to Congress in *abstentia*. Garfield, reluctant to leave the army at first despite his election, had visited Washington, D.C., and sought advice from Abraham Lincoln himself. Lincoln, tired of incompetent *prima donnas* in uniform, had told the earnest young officer that he "had more commanding Generals around than he knew what to do with." What he needed, he said, was support on the political front.

With Lincoln's blessing, Garfield, wearing his blue Union officer's uniform, entered Congress in late 1863—the same year as Blaine. Dennison had followed him to Washington months later to join Lincoln's cabinet as Postmaster General, a seat he held until 1866.

Still, despite these long-ago friendships, Garfield privately had little hope for John Sherman's 1880 presidential cause. Garfield had known John Sherman for twenty years—a square-jawed, serious man with an iron will and a stern face. On paper, Sherman's claim to the White House made perfect sense. But Garfield knew better. Personality mattered in politics, and, to Garfield, Sherman had well earned his nickname "the Ohio icicle." Square-shouldered, six-foot tall, lanky, with a beard and dark hair, Sherman in private came across as aloof: "reserved, self-contained, affable when approached, a good eater and a moderate drinker," noted a dinner companion. In public, he was "not eloquent, though a graceful speaker, confining himself almost entirely to statements of fact."[14] Still, the 57-year old brother of Civil War General William Tecumseh Sherman had used his twenty-two years in Congress, and four in the Cabinet to build a solid national network. He'd won enormous credit on Wall Street for restoring the nation's finances after the Panic of 1873. By 1878, John Sherman's Treasury Department had resumed backing of U.S. paper currency with gold for the first time since the Civil War. All that, plus quiet backing from President Hayes, had to give him a serious leg up in the contest.

From his office in the Treasury Department in Washington, John Sherman's window looked directly out at the White House just across the street. He saw it every day and was close enough to look longingly and imagine himself inside—and probably doing a better job than the incumbent.

Even in Ohio, his "favorite son" state, Sherman had only lukewarm support. "[M]en are scattered over the country... who will knock a man down for calling you or Blaine a thief," reported Garfield's Ohio friend Charles Henry. "Who ever heard of anyone knocked down for calling Sherman a thief?" When John Sherman had visited the Ohio legislature in Columbus that April to drum up support and shake hands, he was "nowhere greeted with any cheering or enthusiasm," according to one press account, and the reception was "very cold and formal ..., and was soon ended."[15] [16]

Nine of Ohio's own 44 delegates were threatening to bolt for Senator Blaine. Garfield, left to his own devices, might have joined them. "[I]n my District the popular feeling is for Blaine," Garfield had told the *Cincinnati Enquirer* in April, before he'd joined the Sherman crusade. "I rather think Blaine is the favorite among the Republican masses."[17]

Now, though, as the showdown approached, Garfield had to put his doubts aside. He would not sit still for this assault over the "unit rule." He and his Sherman team had to stop it.

Warner Bateman explained the problem. Of everyone in the group, Bateman, a gray-haired Cincinnati lawyer, and one-time Republican leader of the Ohio legislature, felt the most personal loyalty for John Sherman. Bateman had left his family and come to Washington, D.C. in February to head Sherman's National Committee and "literary bureau" which produced campaign pamphlets and circulars. For months, he'd scoured the country lining up Sherman delegates, using the Secretary's Treasury Department patronage to lure allies.[18] As Bateman saw it, the contest now boiled down to numbers. General Grant's managers claimed to control about 360 votes in Chicago, a whisker shy of the 379 needed to crown the nominee. This gave them a commanding position. In fact, Don Cameron had shown Bateman one delegate count giving Grant an outright majority on the first ballot. But this count included "solid" blocks from the three states controlled by Grant's Senate "triumvirate": New York (Conkling) with 70, Illinois (Logan) with 42, and Pennsylvania (Cameron) with 58.

Most people knew better. Revolts had broken out in each of these three Stalwart (pro-Grant) states. As many as 60 dissidents from New York, Illinois, and Pennsylvania altogether had threatened to bolt to other candidates, mostly to Blaine. Roscoe Conkling fumed at this betrayal; he took it as a personal insult—particularly since it was James G. Blaine who would benefit at the expense of his own candidate Grant.

Presidential nominating conventions, begun in the 1840s, had become fixtures for Republicans and Democrats alike by 1880, grand festivals of oratory and intrigue. Instead of having fixed rules, each convention issued its own "call" for delegates. For Republicans in 1880, the "call" gave each local Congressional district two voting members, a system designed to provide a wide diversity of local views. It then allotted each State four at-large delegates, generally for senators, governors, or prominent party elders.

Beginning in January, activists held caucuses and conventions in every local district to pick delegates. State conventions then chose the at-large members.

Pressure, manipulation, and sometimes graft came at every stage. The candidates themselves, through their "friends," competed for each delegate; local machines twisted the outcomes. John Sherman, for instance, had used Treasury Department employees—all political appointees under his control— to pack local caucuses across the South and guarantee a harvest of friendly delegates. Newspapers openly took sides, cheered their favorites at every step.

State-level Bosses used the state conventions to whip delegates into line. At New York's convention in Utica that year, for instance, Grant supporters had held only a slight majority of 217-180, but Roscoe Conkling used it to drive through a resolution instructing that all Chicago delegates support a third term for Grant—ignoring the fact that many had been locally pledged to Blaine.

Conkling told delegates they were "bound by every consideration of honor" to follow the state's direction. To violate it, he guaranteed, meant public censure, personal dishonor, and political revenge.

No one at Utica had the backbone to question Conkling face-to-face. But now, in Chicago, a small faction had declared plans to bolt, violating the instructions and throwing their support to Blaine. Knowing the abuse to expect from Conkling and friends, these dissenters had taken rooms in the Palmer House, several city blocks away from the other New York conventioneers, and started to organize resistance.

Don Cameron had pushed a similar "instruction" through the Pennsylvania state convention, sparking a similar revolt.

Illinois Boss John Logan, though, won the prize for heavy-handed tactics. Faced with locally-elected delegates from Cook County pledged to Blaine and Elihu Washburne, Logan had simply locked them out of the state convention in Springfield and replaced them with his own picks—all "solid" for Grant. The maneuver infuriated the dissenters. "Our people here are as bitter against the action of the Grant Ring at Springfield as it is possible for men to be," one of them wrote to William Chandler.[19]

"Stand by your gun and prevent if possible the nomination of Grant," wrote another. "Not that I love Grant less, but the Party and the Country more."[20]

Republicans never had a formal unit rule allowing a state's majority to force all delegates to vote as a block, thereby silencing the minority.* The Chicago delegates in 1880 certainly would reject one in any open, clean vote. It seemed to violate fair play, and, politically, the anti-Grant delegates could easily unite against it. Only a shrewd trick could impose a unit rule on this convention, and the Grant managers had developed a plan to do it.

For pure muscle, they chose Don Cameron, the Pennsylvania Senator and charter member of the Grant triumvirate. Cameron, by happy coincidence, was also chairman of the Republican National Committee. That last role gave him the absolute right to call the convention to order. On any early procedural vote, he could impose the unit rule by fiat: be it picking a temporary chairman, adopting rules, or resolving credentials. If anyone challenged him, he could squash the protest under a unit rule-driven roll call. The New York and Pennsylvania bolters would never be heard.

People could curse all day long, but so long as Cameron controlled the gavel—either personally or though a puppet chairman—their talk meant nothing.

---

* Individual states had imposed such rules internally in the past, such as Illinois in 1860 which came pledged as a unit to Abraham Lincoln. The Democratic Party had a national "unit rule" in effect until 1968. Also, unlike the Republicans, Democratic conventions until 1936 required a two-thirds majority to nominate a Presidential candidate.

Unfortunately for Cameron, through, his elegant secret plan had leaked. It was now known all over town.

Warner Bateman had already talked it over with William Chandler, leader of Senator Blaine's forces in Chicago. If Cameron stuck to his guns, they agreed, they could only stop him by fighting muscle with muscle—taking away his gavel *before* the convention by removing him as chairman of the RNC. But only if the Blaine and Sherman forces stuck together would they have the votes to do this.

Chandler wanted to fight. The worst risk, he figured, was that one side or the other, Grant or anti-Grant, might walk out, splitting the party into two rival conventions. The bitterness from such a brawl could cripple it in November. But still, Chandler assured his Blaine delegates: "This should not be feared…. If the convention itself is chaotic, it must wash itself clean."[21]

Warner Bateman had a different concern. He still considered John Sherman a strong candidate for President of the United States, and saw the unit rule fight cutting two ways. "I was invited by Logan to go see C[ameron] yesterday," he reported to Sherman and to his friends in the Grand Pacific Hotel suite that day. They "may desire to support you on failure of Grant & fear abandonment of unit rule will strengthen Blaine."[22]

By conspiring with Blaine, Sherman's friends might just ruin their candidate's only slim chance for the nomination by scuttling any down-the-road alliance with Grant. Still, if they let Cameron succeed, Grant could win the prize instantly and abandon them totally. Both major candidates, Blaine and Grant, knew that Sherman's forces held the balance. "Much anxiety displayed by Grant men as to our position toward Blaine," Bateman reported.[23]

James Garfield listened to these pros and cons, but had already made up his mind. Normally cautious, Garfield recognized the time for action. Sitting with his old friends in their Chicago hotel suite that afternoon, Garfield spoke clearly, having thought long and hard about his words. They must defeat the unit rule at all costs. It was "the great question of the Convention," he told them, "far greater than as to nomination, and the fight should be made upon the question without regard to consequences."

"I… urged them to take a bold and aggressive stand" and to "unite with friends of all candidates who take this view," Garfield wrote in his own journal that day. Garfield "is on this matter exceedingly earnest," Bateman reported to Sherman, describing the appeal.[24]

They talked it over, closing the door of their hotel suite against spies or intruders. They telegraphed notes back and forth with Sherman in Washington. Bateman still worried that the strategy might backfire. "I do not... want to lose sight of the fact that you are a candidate for nomination," he telegraphed Sherman during the afternoon. "Garfield may be right,—is doubtless right, but in carrying out his plan neither he nor the balance of us will forget that it ought to be in a mode that does least injury to your interests."[25]

John Sherman, sitting in Washington, D.C., hearing this discussion relayed to him through cryptic telegrams during the day, had to wonder. Whose interest was Garfield really pushing, Sherman's or Garfield's? For months he'd heard the rumors about Garfield as a "dark horse." "It is strange that the two leading papers of his [Congressional] District should be so prominent in their advocacy of Blaine...," he had written to Dennison in March.[26] Back in January, Sherman had insisted that Garfield publicly endorse his presidential bid before Sherman would back Garfield's own quest for a U.S. Senate seat. As final insurance, just that prior Tuesday, Sherman had summoned Garfield to his Treasury Department office and asked him to place his name in nomination in Chicago. Garfield had no choice. He couldn't refuse.

Sherman had tied Garfield to himself as closely and publicly as he possibly could, where he could watch his every move.

Still, Sherman had to admit, Garfield's point on the "unit rule" made good tactical sense. He telegraphed instructions to Bateman: "Say to parties that we cannot waive independent right of each delegate to vote for himself. He must judge for himself the force of instructions. No one can do it for him.... Appeal to Cameron to agree to this. His frank acquiescence would avoid dissension. Opposite course dangerous, suicidal, anti-Republican. Never mind who it benefits or hurts. Show colleagues before conference. John Sherman."[27]

The Republican National Committee, with Don Cameron in the chairman's seat, would meet on Monday night, on the eve of the convention itself. If a blow-up were to come, it would come there.

◎ ◎ ◎ ◎ ◎

That night, Garfield dined at Chicago's Commercial Club with a small circle of business leaders and political friends. During the banquet, he gave a short speech on American art. Afterwards, riding though Chicago streets back to his hotel, he drank in the energizing commotion of the thousands of reveling politicos, teasing, shouting, joking, singing, chanting, marching in parades. Brass bands played in the streets; music floated from dozens of saloons in the downtown district. Along the way, he met friends, colleagues, and old army mates. They joked, told stories, shared gossip, and relished the human carnival.

More quietly, from friend after friend, Garfield heard rising bitterness between the two main factions in Chicago: those ready to ride roughshod to nominate Ulysses Grant for President, and those ready to do anything to stop them: pro-Grant and anti-Grant; the "Stalwarts" and the "Half-breeds."

As darkness fell, he saw luminescent fireworks light the sky with red, orange, and yellow flashes. And he thought about home, the future, and the country.

Alone in his room at the Grand Pacific well past midnight, he took pen in hand. Tired and drawn, he wrote his daily letter to Lucretia: "No definite things appear on the face of this chaos except the fact that the unit rule will be the center of battle and to that I expect to address myself. Whatever fight is in me I will make on that point." Garfield seemed to sense the import of the "unit rule" issue better than James Blaine, John Sherman, U.S. Grant, or any of the politicos who saw it only in tactical terms. Opposing the "unit rule" sent a signal deep and profound. To the body politic of the American nation in 1880, after two decades of civil war, reconstruction, economic boom, civic graft, Ku Klux violence, and partisan rancor, it signaled moderation, tolerance, and inclusion—putting principle and decency before greed and advantage.

Beneath their bluster, the Chicago delegates, like their countrymen, thirsted for leadership to share that vision.

"You know that my heart is with you in your struggle to bring order out of our house of your planning, and I would gladly exchange this turmoil for the smaller and sweeter turmoil of the farm," Garfield wrote, and then turned off the gas-lamp.[28]

Back in Mentor, Ohio, Lucretia too took time from her day, busy with directing farm hands, painters, and carpenters, tending the children, and fending off political callers, to write her husband a short note: "I have time only for a word," she scribbled. "I am well and loving you every moment, and all is going on well. I hope you find the situation no worse than you expected—on the contrary, better. I will write you more tomorrow. Ever your own—Crete."[29]

THE HERO

Saturday, May 29, 1880
Galena, Illinois

JOHN RUSSELL YOUNG, senior editor of the *New York Herald*, got off the train at Galena, Illinois, that Saturday morning. He looked out over the brightly decorated town nestled in the green hills along the Galena River, a stone's throw from the Mississippi, and probably recalled Julia Dent Grant's warm descriptions of it from their countless talks while traveling around the world. "The atmosphere [in Galena] was so cool and dry, the sun shone so brightly, that it gave us the impression of a smiling welcome," she wrote. "Galena, I must say, has always thus welcomed General Grant and his family. She has greeted us with open arms. I have only pleasant, kindly memories of this home."[1]

Galena in 1880 still flourished from its hey-day as lead mining center and largest Mississippi River port between St. Louis and St. Paul, but it sparkled brightest when its most famous citizen came home. Ulysses S. Grant had come here just over twenty years ago, in 1859, to work in his father's store. He and Julia were poor then: she with their four small children; he having left the army with dismal prospects, quarreled with his family, and failed at farming in Missouri. In Galena, Ulysses and Julia Grant found a fresh start, an open community, and new neighbors who would become lifelong friends: Elihu Washburne, the Congressman who would sponsor Grant's promotions during the War; John Rawlins, his future chief-of-staff; William Rowley, a future aide-de-camp, and many others.

Today, colorful flags, bunting, and banners decorated the red brick build-

ings and street lamps. Galena swelled with out-of-towners, newspaper men
and politicos, many hovering about the stately brick home on Bouthillier
Street that townspeople had built for Grant in 1865 as thanks for defeating
Robert E. Lee and saving the American nation—similar to gift homes presented to Grant by wealthy citizens in New York, Philadelphia, and Washington. Today it housed the leading candidate for an unprecedented third
term as President of the United States.

Onlookers instantly recognized John Russell Young. People knew the
round handsome face and dark hair of the journalist who had accompanied
the former president on his great journey and brought the story home to millions of American readers through the *New York Herald* and through his best-
selling leather-bound, illustrated, two-volume book *Around the World with
General Grant*.

Traveling by rail from New York City that week, Young had seen first-
hand how the political contest in Chicago had captured the nation's attention. In every state and city, from Newark to Pittsburgh to Buffalo to Cincinnati, among rich and poor, immigrant and native, black and white, farmers,
coal miners, factory workers, railroad and steamboat men, dress-makers, cowboys, and robber barons, people followed the drama and held strong views—
even those, like women, who weren't allowed to vote. Ulysses Grant, a
healthy 58 years old, had become America's lightning rod once again, his
"half-breed" opponents as passionate as his "stalwart" supporters.

Quiet Galena, just two hours west from Chicago by train, seemed de-
ceptively calm, an eye of the storm.

Ulysses and Julia Grant greeted Young warmly at their front door. Both
looked stouter and grayer now than during their White House years. Their
home buzzed with activity; old friends, neighbors, and supporters talked and
lounged about. Adam Badeau and Horace Porter, two staff aides from the war,
had come for support; Colonel Fred Grant, their eldest son, traveling back
and forth between Galena and Chicago that week to represent his father at
the convention.

Julia especially enjoyed the people and attention. She had first met
Ulysses Grant in 1844 when he was a young officer stationed at the Jefferson
Barracks in St. Louis. Grant, a West Point classmate of her older brother, became a frequent guest at Julia's family's estate in nearby White Haven. He
married her four years later, after the Mexican War. Now, Julia and "Ulys"
shared the easy intimacies of a 30-year partnership in a unique life: the early

hardships, Civil War command, fame, the White House, and now this latest run at the presidency.

The parlor conversation that day touched on their recent trips and old time memories, but never strayed far from politics.[2]

Ulysses Grant never discussed the presidential race publicly. His studied aloofness—cigar in mouth, face firm and with resolute, mild eyes and steady gaze—had become an American fixture. Grant was the man of few words and granite will, who had demanded "unconditional surrender" at Fort Donelson in 1862, proposed to "hold this line if it takes all summer" at Petersburg in 1864, and then offered "let us have peace" as candidate for President in 1868— words that every American school-child could recite by heart. To Grant, the office must seek the man, not he the office. But as the Chicago showdown approached in May 1880, Grant talked freely among private friends. He had become "extremely anxious to receive the nomination," reported Adam Badeau.[3] His managers had ordered a special telegraph wire strung from Chicago to the home of his neighbor, Colonel Rowley, for dispatches.

Running a telegraph to the candidate's own home, as James G. Blaine had done in Washington, D.C., Grant considered distasteful.

Grant "manifested as much anxiety as I ever saw him display on his own account," Badeau noted, struck by the change in character. He "calculated the chances, he counted the delegates, considered how every movement would affect the result, and was pleased or indignant at the conversion of enemies or the defection of friends, just as any other human being," he wrote, "only it was hardly natural to [Grant], who was used to concealing his personal feelings in all things."[4]

Occasionally, a houseguest would step outside to feed the newspaper writers on the sidewalk a confident note. Young took his turn. "Grant does not evidence the slightest anxiety; … he positively refrains from taking any active part in the contest for nomination," he told a *Washington Post* reporter at one point. "He is as calm as a summer morning." And more: Young said he was "confident of Grant's chances, and claims that he has 410 votes," the reporter noted. "He, of course, counts the New York, Pennsylvania, and Illinois delegations solid."[5]

By now, of course, the whole country knew about the "unit rule" fight in Chicago and the revolts in the Stalwart delegations.

Brave words aside, though, John Russell Young had come to Galena that morning on an awkward mission. Backed by certain "friends" in New York and Washington, he had come to ask Grant to withdraw his name from the presidential contest, just days before convention balloting would begin.

John Russell Young had a special tie with Ulysses Grant and these "friends" hoped that Grant might trust him on the issue.

When Grant had left the White House in 1877, he and Julia had decided to travel—as far as $25,000* of savings would take them. This, plus $60,000 from a family investment, took them all around the globe. Leaving from Philadelphia in May that year, they journeyed not just to the usual European capitals but also to places exotic and unique: Cairo and the Pyramids, Jerusalem, Gibraltar, Suez, Bombay and Delhi, Rangoon, Malacca, Singapore, Saigon, Cochin and Shanghai, and Tokyo, to name a few. At every step, Grant received tributes and accolades far beyond that experienced by any prior American visitor.

The *New York Herald* had sent Young to cover the journey. Young, a former Civil War correspondent who had followed the Army of the Potomac from bloodbath to bloodbath, from Bull Run to Chickahominy, had since become the *Herald's* chief European writer. Now, for the next two years, he would send back a stream of engaging tableaus that rekindled America's affection for the old soldier and former president. His stories sparked waves of national pride. Unlike any American president to that time, sitting or retired, Ulysses Grant strode the world stage as equal to England's Queen, Germany's Chancellor, Japan's Emperor, the Pope, or the King of Siam. Commoners, royalty, and heads of state, from Liverpool workmen to Chinese peasants to European dukes and princes, all poured out their cheers and hospitality, celebrating his entourage as embodiments of America.

Grant had come a long way from Shiloh, Cold Harbor, and the Wilderness—let alone "Hardscrabble"—the bare hand-built cabin where Grant and Julia had suffered dire poverty trying to farm in Missouri in the 1850s—and California where Grant's drinking grew out of control in the army.

Along the way, traveling at close quarters, John Russell Young shared all the intimate moments with Julia and Ulysses Grant, both playful and profound. He became a virtual family member, comforting Julia when she became seasick on the Mediterranean and sharing countless cigars and brandies with her husband. From Italy, he captured Ulysses' silly but endearing observation

---

* Comparing sums of money between 1880 and 2002 is highly inexact. As a general rule, multiply the 1880 amount by twenty. Even so, far fewer people in 1880 had $10,000 than have $200,000 today.

that "Venice would be a pretty city if it were only drained." In a Paris museum, he caught Julia inspecting Queen Isabella's crown jewels and joked that he would "telegraph to New York that Mrs. Grant is here in Europe trying on crowns." She laughed. A few weeks later, as their ship steamed down the Suez Canal along Egypt's stark Sinai peninsula, Young found a Bible and read aloud from the book of Exodus as the Grants gazed in wonder at Mount Sinai.[6]

In Peking, Young bore witness as Ulysses received tribute from the "shores [of the Pei-Ho River] lined with thousands and thousands of people. A line of Chinese gunboats was drawn up, dressed, and yards manned. Banners waved and cannon boomed, and it was all magnificent." In Tokyo, he wrote of their splendid reception with the emperor and his masses of subjects.

From this close proximity, John Russell Young clearly saw the logic of a Grant third-term candidacy in 1880. Grant's popularity had soared—a remarkable turnabout from four years earlier when scandals, reconstruction, financial hard times, and eight years of familiarity had all conspired to turn the public against its two-term president. "Grantism" had become an insult, linked to corruption. Many "reformers" had already bolted from Grant in 1872 to support Liberal Republican Horace Greeley; *literati* like Henry Adams and Whitelaw Reid had always disdained the Silent (they would say "inarticulate" or "slow-witted"*) General. Congress, to avoid any possible third term, passed resolutions in early 1876 denouncing the idea, and Ulysses Grant happily agreed. "I do not want to be here [in the White House] another four years," he told Julia at the time. "I do not think I could stand it."[7]

Rutherford Hayes became president in March 1877, though, and the country soon faced a parade of shocks that made people nostalgic for the steady hand of their former chief. Fortunes turned.

Hayes, an Ohio governor whom Henry Adams, unfairly but cogently, described as a "third-rate non-entity, whose only recommendation is that he is obnoxious to no one,"[8] had been backed by the same "reformers" who had enjoyed denigrating Grant. But Hayes' election had reeked from suspicion. Both sides disputed the outcome over alleged frauds in three Southern States—Florida, Louisiana, and South Carolina; a special Electoral Commission had decided the issue by party-line votes. Hayes' inauguration was tainted by whispers of back-room deals to withdraw Federal troops from South Carolina and

---

* Said Henry Adams: "The progress of evolution from President Washington to President Grant, was alone evidence enough to upset Darwin." Adams 266.

Louisiana that would end Reconstruction, while abandoning freed black slaves and white Republican governors elected on the same ballots as Hayes himself—all in exchange for presidential power.

Grant must have enjoyed watching the "reformers" squirm as they now had to defend their new champion, President "Rutherfraud," "his fraudulency," Hayes.

Other Republicans shared the outrage. James G. Blaine, as a U.S. Senator, blasted Hayes from the Senate floor for proposing "to abandon the remnant that is left of the Republican party between the Potomac and the Rio Grande." Blaine, instead, pledged to "stand for southern Union men of both colors," he said. Old anti-slavery stalwarts shook their heads. "No act of President Hayes did so much to create discontent within the ranks of the Republican party," Blaine later wrote.[9]

Then, that summer of 1877, labor strife exploded across America. Workers at the Baltimore and Ohio Railroad, faced with multiple pay cuts, walked off their jobs. Within weeks, the strike had spread from New England to Chicago to California, joined by 40,000 sympathetic coal miners from Pennsylvania and West Virginia. Rail traffic came to a halt; strikers derailed cars and burned buildings. Riots erupted in Martinsburg, Baltimore, Pittsburgh, Chicago, and other cities. Hayes called out Federal troops who fired on workers for the first time ever in America. Over 70 people died in the melees. Afterwards, working men seethed at the harsh Federal response while business leaders feared European-style revolution and social decay.

In 1878, Hayes lost control of Congress. Democrats captured both the House and Senate, backed by a solid South built on widespread frauds, lynchings, intimidations, and bulldozing. Promises that Southern white leaders had made to Hayes in 1876 that their "better classes" would protect the voting rights of freed black slaves—the pretext under which federal troops had been removed—now looked ridiculous. The Southern Democrats used their new power in Congress to blackmail the U.S. army. They loaded the annual Army Appropriations bill with amendments to repeal civil rights Enforcement Acts, forcing Hayes to veto them four times.

Fear spread in the North that, next, the former rebel-Congressmen would demand pensions for Confederate soldiers, payments to former slave-owners, repeal of the Fourteenth Amendment, and legal recognition of "black codes"—laws enacted by many Southern states to define the rights of newly freed slaves in a way "as near to slavery as possible," as one Louisiana legislator put it.[10] To Northerners, by every look, the South had cheated Hayes in his "great compromise" of 1876. Only a solid North could now confront a solid South that based its power on violence and intimidation.

Finally, politically, when Hayes needed support the most, he burned bridges in his own party. He handed plum patronage jobs to Southern Democrats while denying them to Northern Republicans. He fired Roscoe Conkling's protégé Chester Arthur from the Collectorship of the Port of New York in the name of "civil service reform"—prompting Conkling's "snivel service" retort. Republican senators fumed. Even James Blaine held his nose and backed his old enemy Conkling in defense of patronage and Arthur's position in the Custom House.

Rising anger against President Hayes quickly reached the ears of Ulysses Grant traveling in Europe. As early as 1877, Grant's friends in America sent letters decrying the situation. The country needed a "strong man," they said. Newspapers echoed the call. The *St Louis Globe Democrat* demanded a "man of iron" to replace the "man of straw" in the White House.[11] The movement accelerated after Democrats captured Congress. "You cannot realize," Orville Babcock wrote to Adam Badeau, "how deep the Grant sentiment has sunk into the minds of the people of the North."[12]

Ironically to John Russell Young, the world trip itself had now made Ulysses Grant far more qualified for the White House then ever before, with a deeper perspective on world affairs and America's role. To Grant's supporters, the four-year Hayes interlude solved any impediment over a third term for the General.

By this time in his life, Ulysses Grant had developed a unique view toward elective office. In 1868, as Lieutenant General of the Army at his height of fame, Grant had never lifted a finger to win his first presidential election. The politicians had come to him—not unlike George Washington in 1788. Now the same thing seemed about to happen again. Friends advised Grant to bide his time, stay abroad, extend his trip, and plan his return to America—and the expected public outpouring—to coincide with the Chicago Republican convention. Grant would sweep the country like he'd swept the world. "Most every letter I get from the States ... asks me to remain abroad," Grant wrote to Adam Badeau from Rome. "They have designs for me which I do not contemplate for myself."[13] By his very silence, though, Grant signaled the bandwagon to begin.

Perhaps over-eager, he reached American shores ahead of schedule, in

October 1879, seven full months before Chicago, and continued his high-profile travelogue with public "welcome home" celebrations in cities from San Francisco to Philadelphia. After a short rest in Galena, he traveled to Mexico, then Texas, Louisiana, and the South. At each stop, Grant pressed the flesh. He visited the New Orleans and Mobile Cotton Exchanges, watched boat races from the Southern Yacht Club, shook hands with every party leader, and ate the local food.

Wherever he went, people loved him, mobbed him, followed him—while he denied any concern with politics.

While Grant stayed aloof, his self-appointed "friends" took over. Grant never directly approached the three Senate bosses, Conkling, Logan and Cameron, his "triumvirate," for help. During their months of highly public work lining up delegates, though, he never discouraged them. This dance of nods and winks had awkward moments. That May, for instance, after John Logan had nailed down Illinois as "solid for Grant," the candidate had refused to answer telegrams of congratulations. When his local supporters complained, Grant, sitting in Galena, felt compelled to respond. "I assure you that there was no intentional neglect on my part," he wrote to Logan. "I appreciate the action of my friends in the [Illinois] convention as highly probably as if more demonstrative about it."[14]

Julia herself made no secret of wanting back her old station in the White House. By her own account, she never would have allowed Grant to leave at all in 1877 had it been her choice. Julia had put on a proud face for the Hayes inaugural that year, even hosting a White House lunch for the new President and Lucy Hayes. But when she and Ulysses finally boarded a train two weeks later to leave Washington for good, the "floodgates" broke loose. "I bravely stood looking out," she wrote, "waving my scarf as we glided out of the depot, and when we had passed all our friends I quickly sought my stateroom and, in an abandonment of grief, flung myself on the lounge and wept. Wept, oh, so bitterly."[15]

Now, in late May 1880, the Grant canvass looked solid. New York, Pennsylvania, and Illinois led a national phalanx of delegates. If the unit rule went their way, they were sitting within inches of the nomination. Their managers voiced confidence. "Nothing but an act of God could prevent Grant's nomination," Roscoe Conkling had told reporters on reaching Chicago that week.[16] Delegates were committed; plans in place. The champagne and oysters had been ordered for the celebrations.

Time was running out for anyone to stop the party.

But where many saw a juggernaut, others saw a train wreck—including John Russell Young and his "friends." Young had come to try and prevent disaster by persuading Ulysses Grant to withdraw from the race.

Julia herself had grown increasingly nervous. "I did not feel that General Grant would be nominated," she later confided. "I *knew* of the disaffection of more than one of his trusted friends. The General would not believe me, but I saw it plainly." She, like Young, had heard the rumors. Key friends of General Grant had grown soft; some might even defect.[17]

Few spoke openly. Marshall Jewell, Governor of Connecticut and Postmaster General in Grant's own Cabinet, for instance, had refused to be a delegate in Chicago because he felt Grant would lose the election for Republicans. "I don't think he ought to be nominated," he brazenly told the *Chicago Tribune*, knowing his words would reach Galena. "I am very glad to be free from the embarrassment which I should feel as a delegate."[18] Roscoe Conkling, confronted with such talk among his own troops, reportedly lashed out in "most emphatic terms" that "under no consideration would he join in advising Gen. Grant's withdrawal, that he was for him first and last, and had no second choice." Asked if he would support Blaine as a back-up, he said: "Never!" Washburne? "Never!" Sherman? "Never!"

Grant partisans sharply denied the chronic reports that Grant might drop from the race. After all, they said, Grant didn't retreat at Vicksburg or Shiloh despite hails of bullets and cannonball. "Gen. Grant's name has never gone before the public as a candidate for the presidency by any word or act of his own, and he most certainly will not order his name withdrawn," insisted the *Galena Gazette*, its editor a "personal friend of General Grant."[19] But the talk hurt nonetheless.

Now, John Russell Young, seeing both Julia's and Ulysses' anxiety, treaded carefully. He waited to get Grant alone before broaching the issue. He took him aside. Grant still enjoyed horseback rides along the Galena River—his favorite exercise since boyhood—or walks through the nearby mountains. They had "long and repeated conversations," reported Adam Badeau, "usually carried on in [Julia's] absence."

As Ulysses Grant listened, Young laid out the basic reason why Grant should withdraw from the race. Simply put, he would lose, and it would be a terrible embarrassment for the country's most respected citizen. Since his return to America, Grant's public support had waned while his opponents had counter-attacked. Grant had lost ground, especially over the third term issue. Two terms as president had been enough for George Washington, Andrew Jackson, Thomas Jefferson, James Madison, and James Monroe, opponents argued. To a growing number of voters, it looked unseemly for Grant to put himself above those forefathers.

Further, Young argued, the campaign had lost control. Grant's good name was being tarred by heavy-handed tactics of the Senate Bosses—gag rules, delegate lock-outs, unit rule conspiracies. If Grant were elected, Roscoe Conkling and John Logan would demand pay-back: control of patronage, Cabinet seats, vetoes over policy choices. Newspapers vented this talk. Just days earlier, the *Chicago Tribune* had mocked Roscoe Conkling as aspiring to be the "Warwick of the land –the King-maker whose power behind the throne will be greater than that of the occupant." The Bosses would demand control, and Grant, it seemed, was the only one who didn't know it.*

Grant surely recoiled at this last point. Other people might consider Conkling and John Logan "low, coarse men," but Grant appreciated their loyalty. These "practical" men had never betrayed him. Roscoe Conkling had hosted him at his home in Utica and Grant had hosted Conkling at his ocean side cottage in Long Branch, New Jersey. Conkling had always been Grant's favorite, for the Supreme Court in 1874, and even to succeed him as President in 1876. If Roscoe Conkling wanted patronage, let him have it. To Grant, they were friends, and Conkling had well earned the political spoils.

All of Young's arguments had glaring flaws. Grant "could be the means of ending the 'miserable sectional strifes' between the North and South,"[20] the former president argued in his own defense. His candidacy had a larger purpose. Still, Young apparently made an impression. Grant respected his earnest friend and travel mate and whatever "friends" he claimed to represent. He chose a middle ground. After talking with Young, he sat down in the Galena house that weekend, took pen to paper, and wrote a letter to Don Cameron in Chicago. The letter must be kept secret, he said. He didn't keep a copy, and none survives today. But by most accounts, in it he authorized (not demanded) Cameron to withdraw his name from the nomination contest after consulting with his key supporters: Conkling, Logan, and Senator George Boutwell of Massachusetts. The letter may have insisted that Blaine, too,

---

* John Logan's own son saw the problem. "I see that you are rendering your services to Grant," he wrote in a letter. "If he is elected he will be under a load of obligation to you, which he can hardly discharge."

withdraw at the same time—the two acting together to avoid a party split and allow the convention to pick a neutral "dark horse."

Adam Badeau was apoplectic after finding out about it. "This was a most extraordinary influence for any one man to exert with Grant," he wrote. The letter was a "half-way reversal" and "calculated, of course, to dampen the enthusiasm and bewilder the counsels of Grant's most devoted adherents," he wrote, calling it a weak prevarication much "unlike General Grant's ordinary character."

Word leaked quickly. Julia Grant was among the first to hear of the letter, and not from her husband. "Mr. Young was unwise enough to read [it] to me," she later explained, "and I then told him to tell Senator Cameron *not* to use the letter." Julia bristled at the indecision, or, worse, disloyalty. Others might abandon ship, but not she. Grant must not break his word, she insisted. "If General Grant were not nominated, then let it be so, but he must not withdraw his name—no, never."[21]

Nevertheless, with "a large sealed envelope" in hand, John Russell Young left Galena that Monday and raced back to Chicago, where he found the preconvention hoopla well under way. He found Colonel Fred Grant, the General's son, at the Palmer House Hotel fully engaged in the battle, button-holing delegates for the cause. Fred, following his father's instructions, took the envelope from Young, tracked down Conkling, Logan, Cameron, and Boutwell, and shared the message with them. Of the four, only Boutwell left any record of the incident amid the bedlam. He mentioned it in a note to his daughter that day: "Young returned [from Galena] today, and says that Grant directed him to say to Cameron, Logan, Conkling, and Boutwell that he should be satisfied with whatever they may do."[22] By Boutwell's reading, the letter seemed to demand nothing at all and simply gave his managers a free hand—which was perhaps exactly Grant's intent.

By Saturday, June 5, five days later, Roscoe Conkling still found it necessary to issue a public denial through the Western Union newswire of "the report in circulation that he has a letter from Grant asking him to consult with Logan and, if they deem if proper, to withdraw [Grant's] name as a candidate for nomination."[23]

Almost twenty years later, in the 1890s, long after these events, John Russell Young would insist publicly that Conkling, Logan, Boutwell et al, had selfishly betrayed General Grant in Chicago that week by ignoring his written order to withdraw his name from the famous nomination fight. Boutwell and Fred Grant would disagree. By then, Conkling and Grant both would be dead. No original letter fitting the description would appear, and no other "friend" would come forward to settle the argument. Most likely, the message had come simply too late, or been too vague, for the delegates to be "influenced by this phase of irresolution which passed over [General Grant]," as Badeau put it.[24] Or perhaps it was Julia's instruction that carried the day.

John Russell Young himself had had the chance to set the record straight that week in Chicago when an *Albany Evening Journal* reporter confronted him about the letter on the very day that Young[25] had returned with it from Galena. Instead, he chose to lie. "[T]he report that he had gone that far to induce Gen. Grant to write a letter of withdrawal [was] mere fiction," Young told the newsman. The trip "was purely of a personal nature, and had no political significance."

Whatever the truth, whatever Ulysses Grant had truly wanted for himself in May 1880, however strongly he desired or dreaded again to become President of the United States, his "friends" in Chicago, his family, and destiny all seemed to have wants of their own, which none was ready to forego any time soon.

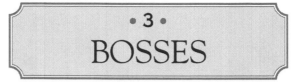

• 3 •

BOSSES

Monday, May 31, 1880
Chicago, Illinois

J. DONALD CAMERON, Senator from Pennsylvania, banged his gavel precisely at seven pm to convene the Republican National Committee for its last meeting before the official opening of the grand Chicago Convention less than twenty-four hours away.[1] Members filled every seat around the long mahogany table in suite 27 of the Palmer House. Aides and clerks crowded the corners.

For days, tensions in Chicago had been building over the "unit rule" with its potential to nail down Ulysses Grant's third-term nomination immediately. Now the issue threatened to explode here in the National Committee.

Cameron, blond-haired, Princeton-educated, his face clean-shaven with thick side-whiskers and mustache, had the well-tailored look of one born to power. His father, 78-year-old Simon Cameron, long-time senator and briefly Abraham Lincoln's Secretary of War, had retired just three years earlier, in 1877, leaving Don to inherit the family franchise—a seat in the U.S. Senate and near-dictatorial power over the Pennsylvania State Republican machine. Before that, the 47-year-old had already run a railroad—the Northern Central—and been Secretary of War in Ulysses Grant's cabinet.

Tonight, leading the Grant forces in the National Committee, Don Cameron felt very lonely. He looked down the long table under elegant mirrors and cut-glass chandeliers, cigar smoke clouding the air, and saw forty-six hard-faced men looking back, studying him like a bug under a magnifying glass. At best, he counted only sixteen allies. The other thirty, including all the Blaine, Sherman, and anti-Grant delegates, had met secretly that morning and decided to gang up against him, hopping mad over his own threats and strong-arms tactics. They had a clear voting majority here in the committee,* but had lost the benefit of surprise when word of their cabal was leaked all over town.

Cameron also had trouble at his rear, inside the "solid" Grant states. That afternoon, nineteen New York delegates had openly defied Roscoe Conkling by signing a public pledge to oppose Grant's nomination at all costs—a direct slap at Conkling's authority. Encouraged by the New Yorkers, seventeen Pennsylvania delegates—supposedly Cameron's own serfs—had launched a similar revolt. Without a unit rule, he confided, all fifty-eight Pennsylvania votes "would probably turn ... solid to Blaine."[2] And the twenty-two Illinois delegates whom John Logan had locked out from his State convention in Springfield now filed formal requests for credentials.

Cameron huddled that afternoon with Roscoe Conkling and John Logan, the "triumvirate," in their hotel suite at the Grand Pacific. Everything hinged on the unit rule, they agreed. With it, the Grant steamroller could not be stopped. It would silence the bolters and keep Logan's dissidents locked out. Without it, a sure-thing nomination could slip through their fingers.

Don Cameron, outnumbered and embattled, was still a formidable foe. He had been "threatened with removal" by the dissidents, he'd told Warner Bateman, and "would do nothing under threat."[3] Cameron too had a plan that played to his strengths: a thick skin, the power of the gavel, and no visible scruples.

Across the table from Cameron sat William Eaton Chandler, leader of the Blaine forces. Chandler, a slender, small-shouldered man, wore a dark beard that looked out of place on his boyish face with *pince-nez* glasses. But Chandler was no pushover. A 45-year-old Harvard-educated lawyer, Chandler had been secretary to the National Republican Committee from 1868 to 1876, from which he'd managed both of Ulysses Grant's winning presidential campaigns and conceived Rutherford Hayes' winning three-state electoral challenge in 1876. His loyalty to James Blaine grew from a fifteen year friendship.

Chandler, in fact, had organized the anti-Grant cabal that morning and

---

* Each of the 38 states and 8 territories had one vote in the National Committee, which magnified James G. Blaine's strength in the thinly-populated west.

held some strong cards. Counting noses at the table, Chandler had votes enough to carry the Committee on any fair roll call. His group insisted on forcing a decision barring the unit rule from the convention—here in the National Committee where they had the power. If Don Cameron tried to stop them, Chandler was ready to fight fire with fire and take away Cameron's gavel by removing him as chairman.

Most of the anti-Grant men, in fact, had wanted to unseat Cameron immediately, here and now. Even John Sherman, sitting at his Treasury Department desk in Washington, D.C., had become a hard-liner. "Every effort should be made… [to] allow each delegate to cast one vote and have it counted," he'd instructed Warner Bateman. "Any other rule is an outrage. Don't compromise this away—or yield it to threats or persuasion."[4]

Only Chandler's own calm voice had cooled the hotheads. A blow-up now in Chicago, a *coup d'etat* in the National Committee, he told them, could poison the party in November. The bitterness it produced could make its presidential nomination worthless to whomever won it.[5]

Don Cameron now rapped his gavel again and ordered the ushers to shut the doors. Seeing the committee members at their places, he wanted no visitors or newsmen watching this meeting, to see the deals that might be cut or the arms twisted. Dozens of delegates, dignitaries, politicos, and newsmen, senators and generals, packed the corridors, Philip Sheridan among them, digging for any scrap of news. They would simply have to wait.

This stark division between factions in the Palmer House matched polarized feelings all over town. On Chicago's streets, two competing demonstrations were being held on opposite sides of Michigan Avenue just as the National Committee was beginning its session. The roar of one crowd or the other occasionally floated in through an open window.

At the White Stockings* base-ball yards by the Chicago River, more than 15,000 anti-third-term delegates and friends crowded the field while hundreds of ladies and news men filled the grandstands. Speaker after speaker urged them to defy the phony Grant bandwagon. "The political trio of Bosses [has] regarded this [convention] as a rice plantation where the masters voted for the slaves," shouted Pennsylvanian Wayne MacVeigh, prompting loud cheers, hisses, and cat-calls at Conkling and Logan. "Lincoln never packed

---

* Later renamed the Cubs, playing in their fifth season in the recently-created National League. The current Chicago White Sox were founded in 1900 at the founding of the American League.

a convention,"* he told them. "[Senator Charles] Sumner never gagged his constituency."[6]

Public revulsion against the bosses had turned to ridicule. That week's *Chicago Tribune* ran a satire of Shakespeare's *MacBeth*, featuring Conkling, Cameron, and Logan as three wizards dancing around the stage reciting incantations. *Puck* magazine ran Joseph Keppler cartoons showing Don Cameron as a prison guard, leading delegates ball-and-chain into the Chicago convention penitentiary; or showing the Conking-led "triumvirate" praying to Grant, "The Golden Calf of Politicians."

Across the street in Dearborn Park,[7] over 5,000 Grant supporters heard harangues from Logan, George Boutwell, and even Frederick Douglass, the former slave and civil rights leader. "We have a majority of the convention and we are going to nominate him," Logan yelled. Ulysses Grant meant "peace and prosperity."[8] The crowd grew restless, though, when its featured attraction failed to show—their "moving impulse," the *Chicago Tribune* reported, was "a desire to see and hear Senator [Roscoe] Conkling."[9] Stewart Woodford had to shout over chants of "Conkling," "Conkling," to be heard.

Surprisingly, Woodford drew his loudest applause when he saluted their opponent, "the elegant gentleman from Maine," James G. Blaine. Men cheered, women waved handkerchiefs and hats, while others hissed and booed.

The rival crowds "overflowed into the streets all night, and the town, to the sleepless visitor, seemed to be in the hands of a mob." In hotel lobbies, betting "pools" offered $100 for the field against $40 for Grant.[10] Occasional fireworks lit the sky, silhouetting Chicago's famous limestone Water Tower, the only nearby structure to have survived the Great Fire in 1871. "Cheers and groans for the various candidates came from every street in the vicinity of the large hotels."[11]

Inside the Palmer House suite, Don Cameron now opened the national committee for business. The Palmer House, destroyed in the Great Fire, had been rebuilt as a magnificent showpiece, its eight-story rococo structure complete with granite columns, marble statuettes, furnishings which alone cost an unheard-of $300,000. It also boasted the "finest restaurant in the city" on the

---

* Not quite true. In 1860, Lincoln had packed the galleries at the Republican convention in Chicago with local supporters and his backers, imposed an Illinois unit rule to steamroll delegates. He defeated William Seward, the early leader, on the third ballot.

premises—its own. Now, the Palmer House's suite 27 would become the scene for a battle *royale*.

Within minutes of Cameron's opening gavel, Senator Jerome Chaffee demanded the floor. Chaffee, a Blaine delegate from Colorado, put two resolutions on the table. The first simply repeated the Convention's original "call" for two delegates from each congressional district and four per state. Nobody objected. But his second motion hit the raw nerve directly. Chaffee moved to recognize "the right of each delegate… freely to cast and have counted his individual vote… if he so decides, against any unit rule."

The issue had been joined. Knuckles whitened around the table; eyes narrowed. Members puffed their cigars and looked dead-on at the chairman.

Chaffee handed his hand-written motion down the table to Don Cameron, and Cameron read it carefully. Cameron recognized the script as probably boy-faced William Chandler's own; the conspiracy was obvious. Cameron had expected this. He knew that the anti-Granters, the "Half-Breeds," with their thirty votes, would instantly approve Chaffee's motion if he ever gave them the chance. This he could not do. As Cameron saw it, he had only one choice.

The motion was out of order, he said.

Chaffee looked at him cross-wise. Out of order?

Cameron explained. The national committee only had the power to appoint a temporary chairman for the Convention. The "unit rule" issue belonged to the Rules Committee or the Convention delegates themselves.

Chaffee gazed incredulously. He had never heard such a thing. "[A]rbitrary and infamous,"[12] he said with a huff.

But Don Cameron had come prepared. Not a good speaker himself, he had brought help in the form of George Gorham, a Stalwart delegate from California who for eighteen years had served as Secretary of the United States Senate. Gorham knew parliamentary procedure better than anyone. Sitting at Cameron's right hand, Gorham now spoke up. "If the Chairman entertains that resolution, which of course he will not do, I desire to offer an amendment."[13]

William Chandler, sitting across the table and sharing pained looks with Chaffee and the other Half-Breeds, quickly saw the game afoot. Don Cameron as chairman could make parliamentary rulings all day, he thought, but he, Chandler, had the votes to overturn them. Waving his arm, Chandler got recognition and immediately moved to appeal the chairman's ruling.

Out of order. Cameron banged the gavel again.

Out of order?

Cameron again looked to George Gorham at his side to supply a reason. "If there was any business before the committee to appeal from, an appeal would be in order," Gorham explained, but "as there is none, there is nothing to appeal from."[14]

So ruled, Cameron repeated.

Chandler was stunned. He fought to control his anger, then recited the history of the parliamentary right of appeal. Committee chairmen were not absolute tyrants; they could not arbitrarily veto whatever they pleased. Were there not any rights the committee had that the chairman was bound to respect, he asked.

Gorham provided the answer. Cameron could do "as he saw fit."

They tried it another way: This time, Richard McCormick, a Sherman delegate from Arizona, offered a resolution saying that, in calling the Convention to order, no unit rule could be imposed unilaterally before giving the delegates a chance to decide the issue.

Again, George Gorham chimed in. "If the Chairman entertains that resolution, which of course he will not do, I desire to offer an amendment."[15] On cue, Cameron gaveled it out of order. Again, Chandler appealed. He looked across the table at Cameron, almost pleadingly. The chairman was "a good man with a willing soul," Chandler said.[16] This caused a few laughs. Cameron shared whispers with Gorham. He banged the gavel again. Out of order.

They tried a third time. General Averill, another Blaine delegate, moved to create a special subcommittee to check the accuracy of delegate lists—a response to rumors that Don Cameron had ordered his flunkies to doctor the convention's official records, adding Grant supporters wherever they could.

Cameron gaveled this one into oblivion with special vigor. Averill appealed. Out of order.

Marshall Jewell, a Connecticut committee member normally friendly to Ulysses Grant,* spoke up. A few heads turned, confused at first at a Grant

---

* Jewell had served in Ulysses Grant's cabinet as Postmaster General. He came to Chicago in 1880 to attend the national committee meeting but refused to be a convention delegate because he opposed Grant's bid for a third term in the presidency and did not want to be forced to vote against his former chief.

supporter's questioning the chairman. These rulings, Jewell said, were simply unfair, no matter whom you supported, Grant, Blaine, or anyone else. The chairman should reconsider.

Don Cameron said nothing; according to one description, he "gazed at [Jewell] in sullen silence."[17]

By now, patience had run out. Tempers flared. Members began to shout. A few of them muttered threats. After a quick recess, Cameron recognized a motion from Chandler to elect as the convention's temporary chairman Senator George Frisbie Hoar of Massachusetts, a "neutral" who was equally objectionable among Grant, Blaine, and Sherman but probably wouldn't impose a unit rule. The committee split 29-17: Half-Breeds voted "yes," Stalwarts voted "no." Chandler had no illusions. The vote meant nothing. Don Cameron could simply overturn it whenever he pleased with a unit rule-driven roll call on the convention floor.[18]

Chandler now put his own cards on the table. He presented a final resolution saying that should Don Cameron, "through sickness or any other cause" fail to present Senator Hoar's name to the convention at its opening session, the committee would remove him as chairman and appoint Chandler in his place. They had put Cameron on notice; his days were numbered.

The committee adjourned at midnight, scheduled to reconvene the next morning. By then the news had spread like wildfire. Shock waves rocked Chicago; delegates bristled, both friend and foe. "The rulings of Don Cameron would have been a disgrace to the most despotic government of Europe or Asia, in this or any other age," an anonymous eastern delegate said.[19] It was the first attempt "to introduce the 'Boss' system into the management of the national committee" by which thirty members "were insulted and gagged all the evening," said another.[20]

By the next morning, newspaper readers from Boston to San Francisco talked about Don Cameron's "high-handed behavior in refusing even to entertain appeals."[21] Protests flooded the telegraph wires. "Down with the Grant Syndicate," read placards in the street.[22] Roscoe Conkling heard an earful about it from Connecticut delegates whom he visited to shore up support. Conkling saw the writing on the wall. Cameron's hard-line strategy had proven "suicidal."[23] The Grant managers needed to defuse this powder keg before they lost control of the Convention altogether. It would require diplomacy of the most delicate order.

Roscoe Conkling, supreme leader of the Grant forces in Chicago, turned to the one person in the world he trusted most in such situations—his friend and protégé, Chester Alan Arthur.

❋ ❋ ❋ ❋ ❋

Chester A. Arthur had never been to a National political convention nor ever held elective office. Still, he was surprisingly well known in 1880, though not in a good way. At home in New York, they called him "Gentleman Boss." This told a part-truth. "Gentleman," yes. "Chet" Arthur could pick a good Brooks Brothers suit or bottle of cabernet. Tall, handsome, he made a good drinking friend or dinner mate, or a hearty companion for hunting, fishing, or camping in the wild. He lived well in his Lexington Avenue mansion and put fresh flowers each day by a photograph of his wife, Ellen Herndon Arthur, who'd died the prior winter from pneumonia. Arthur had served as Quartermaster General for New York during the war, but resigned his commission in 1863, partly due to Ellen's southern family ties. As a young lawyer in the 1850s, Arthur had pushed his abolitionist views by winning the legal right for black citizens to ride in New York City street cars, and helping to free eight slaves improperly brought into New York State by a Virginia owner.[24]

"Boss," not really. Chet Arthur, rather, was a premiere political henchman. A skilled lawyer and manager, Arthur had dedicated his adult life to the New York Republican machine, capped by his six-year tenure as Collector of the Port of New York—the most visible patronage post in America. With 1,500 political employees, millions of dollars in tariffs to assess, and a whopping salary of over $20,000*, the New York Collectorship had made Chester Arthur a powerful figure in American government. Senators, Cabinet members, even Presidents knew to call him when in need of political jobs for a friend. His calm, smooth demeanor could defuse any tense situation.

At each step, Arthur had risen by the grace of his mentor, Roscoe Conkling.

Arthur's only national exposure had come with a black eye—when President Hayes and his Treasury Secretary [now presidential candidate] John Sherman had fired him, along with his deputy Alonzo Cornell, in 1878 for tolerating corruption. They never alleged fraud by Arthur himself, but that didn't save Arthur's reputation. Roscoe Conkling had fought tooth and nail to protect him and, with him, his control of the Custom House patronage.

---

* That would be equivalent to almost half-a-million by modern standards.

Ironically, Arthur had to juggle patronage demands from John Sherman for political friends right through to the end.* So much, Arthur thought, for "snivel service" reform.

After this indignity, Roscoe Conkling had installed Arthur as chairman of New York's own Republican Committee, while swearing vengeance against Hayes and vowing to recapture the Custom House. Already, he had made Alonzo Cornell New York's governor. Later that year, he planned to make Chet Arthur his junior colleague in the U.S. Senate. Then, with Ulysses Grant in the White House, he would take back the Custom House and become supremely powerful once again.

Now at the Chicago Convention, Arthur enjoyed the celebrity of being shoulder-to-shoulder with the majestic Conkling on the national stage. He focused his political skills quickly on the latest crisis. After talking with Conkling and Don Cameron late that Monday night, he saw it clearly. Arthur knew how to count votes: in the national committee, Don Cameron didn't have them.[25]

With Conkling's blessing, Arthur coolly took control. The next morning, he put his plan into action. He waited in the Palmer House as William Chandler and his platoon of anti-Grant, Half-Breed delegates stormed into the Hotel for the expected confrontation at the national committee. Chandler, his gang agitated after a morning caucus, carried under his arm a hand-written motion to unseat Don Cameron from the committee chair—with the strength of 30 votes to back it up. If Cameron ruled them out of order, then to hell with him. They'd vote him out anyway.

Reaching the committee's suite, though, Chandler found his path partly blocked. Waiting in the corridor, just outside the door, were Chester A. Arthur and Senator John P. Jones of Nevada. Arthur, large and imposing in a dapper new suit, crisp white shirt, and friendly tone, asked Chandler if he would step aside for a talk. A circle formed around the two men, Arthur and Chandler in the middle. The conversation grew animated—Arthur looking like a great bear next to the diminutive Chandler.

We'd like to compromise, Chet Arthur told the Blaine leader, and he laid out a proposition. Chandler listened closely. For all his faults, he knew, Chet Arthur spoke fully for Roscoe Conkling, the highest authority in Chicago on

* Though Sherman, to soften the blow, did offer Arthur the post of U.S. Consul to Paris, which Arthur refused. Sherman to Arthur, 10/15/1877. Arthur papers, LC.

the Grant side. An ugly committee showdown would split the convention and wreck the Party, Arthur explained. Nobody wanted that. Yesterday, the Grant men had rejected Senator Hoar as a compromise choice for temporary Convention chairman; today, maybe they would reconsider.

Chandler countered. What about guarantees against a floor fight? Or a back-door imposition of the unit rule? And what about the Illinois credentials protest?

Arthur was ready. He had considered each item in this maze of emotion-charged issues. What if they promised to let the delegates decide the unit rule in a free vote, he suggested. In return, though, Don Cameron would remain chairman of the national committee and the Illinois delegation must be allowed into the convention as is. They could vote on the credentials protest later. New York and Pennsylvania would guarantee the deal. He'd have their promise.

They haggled for many minutes. Soon, though, Arthur and Chandler had built the framework for a deal. Neither could promise anything on the spot. Chandler would have to sell the idea to his backers, some still mad as hell and in no mood to bargain.

Arthur too would take the deal back to the "triumvirate"—Conkling, Logan, and Cameron. But if Blaine and Sherman agreed, Arthur said, he "believed it would be agreed to by the Grant men."[26] When they had finished, Arthur and Chandler went together to ask that the committee delay its meeting so both sides could review the proposal. Then they shook hands.

William Chandler didn't say it, but he was thrilled. He too had received instructions that morning, telegraphed directly from James G. Blaine in Washington, D.C.: "It is every way desirable to avoid angry row and smash in the Nat'l Committee and if we can have Hoar for temporary chairman without contest or collision I could smother personal resentment for the general weal of the Party."*[27] Chandler had been at wits end trying to figure out how to avoid a blow-up. Now, he pulled together his cabal of 30 anti-Grant committee members behind closed doors and laid out Arthur's plan. He sent for James Garfield and brought him in to join the debate. Garfield, a hard-liner that morning, now quickly agreed that the proposition "must be accepted" in

---

* Blaine's "personal resentment" grew from 1876, when Hoar had led Massachusetts' delegation at the Cincinnati Republican Convention and opposed Blaine's bid for the presidency. Later, when Hoar backed Rutherford's Hayes' conciliation toward the South, Blaine blasted him in Senate floor debate as an appeaser who'd forgotten the party's obligations to freed slaves.

a "spirit of conciliation."[28] Seven of the delegates stormed out of the room rather than accept a bargain. The rest, down to twenty-three now but still enough to control the vote, returned to the Palmer House to seal the deal.

A few hours later, the National Committee re-convened in its suite behind closed doors with Don Cameron still sitting as chairman. This time, Cameron barely touched his gavel. Chester A. Arthur sat at his right hand, having taken over New York State's official seat. With William Chandler looking on from across the table, Arthur made a series of motions: Senator Hoar would be named temporary chairman, and Grant delegates from New York and Pennsylvania promised to stick behind him. No unit rule would apply until and unless the delegates had voted to accept it. Cameron called for a vote. There were no objections.

A few members shook hands after the meeting, but most just felt relieved. A *New York Tribune* reporter noted how the Stalwarts had been "saved from utter ruin by the excellent management of General Arthur and Senator Jones." "Chet" Arthur as his friends called him, Conkling's man, had made an impression. Not all the reviews were good. Don Cameron walked away sullen and angry despite having saved face. A note to John Sherman from a New York backer summed the outcome this way: "Unit rule dead. Grant dead. Blaine impossible. Rest in doubt."[29]

Whoever had gained an advantage, the unit rule compromise had been a victory for moderation, and the delegates approved. Now, strangely, that mantle was being worn, if only momentarily, by Roscoe Conkling's own genteel henchman, Chester Alan Arthur.

⊙ ⊙ ⊙ ⊙ ⊙

James Garfield had refused to speak at the mass anti-Grant rally on Monday night at the White Stockings baseball park. The organizers had asked him, hoping Garfield's presence would boost the crowd size. Already, gossip and newspaper clippings had painted Garfield as a dominant player in Chicago and a possible dark horse. But "[t]he fight of delegates should be in the convention," not in the streets, Garfield felt. "I never fight mock battles," he wrote that day.[30]

Besides, John Sherman, his own candidate for president, still hoped for an alliance with pro-Grant delegates on a fourth or fifth ballot after Grant had dropped from the race. Why make enemies now? Don Cameron knew this, and had tried to use it in his unit rule fight. "[T]he whole Grant vote of [the]

South would be turned solid for you," Cameron had signaled to Sherman before the national committee's Monday night meeting, if Sherman's friends would only back him on the unit rule.[31] "Reports also as to friendly expressions towards you from [Roscoe] Conkling," Warner Bateman had reported.[32] A few days earlier, the Grant camp had even expressed interest in placing Sherman as vice president on a Grant-led ticket, but Sherman declined. "Please prevent this from being acted upon," he instructed Bateman. "I do not desire that office and its duties would be irksome to me."[33]

Sherman actually seemed to believe the come-ons from Cameron, though he stuck to his guns on the unit rule. Garfield knew better. For one thing, in Washington circles, "Mr. Conkling's hatred of Sherman [was] well known,"[34] dating back to Sherman's shabby treatment of Chet Arthur. As for Cameron's promises of later ballot support should the tide turn Sherman's way, these came cheap from a politician who was fighting for his life.

To Garfield, the key goal in Chicago had to be blocking the juggernaut of a Grant third term. That done, other pieces would fall into place. He agreed with Wayne MacVeigh, the speaker at the anti-Grant rally on Monday night. A Grant nomination, MacVeigh had regaled the crowd, would burden the campaign with "the corruption of two of Grant's terms, and the trickery by which he might get the nomination for a third."[35] Garfield had seen that morning's editions of the *Cincinnati Commercial* that listed names of 2,000 Ohio Republicans who refused to vote for Grant in any circumstance.

Instead of mock battles, Garfield on Monday night had gone to the Palmer House to wait in the corridor outside the National Committee meeting. Though not a committee member, Garfield had joined fully in William Chandler's anti-Grant cabal. He attended every secret meeting, gave advice and encouragement, and urged the Blaine and Sherman factions to stick together. Garfield had known William Chandler for years and appreciated his feistiness—in fact, when Garfield in 1874 had faced charges of accepting $329 in tainted money in the Credit Mobilier scandal, he hired lawyer William Chandler to defend him before Congressional investigators. During the day, Garfield had even visited Roscoe Conkling—just a few steps down the hall at the Grant Pacific Hotel—looking for a compromise, but came away empty-handed. Conkling "did not appear willing to take much responsibility for his followers," Garfield reported, and he rejected a middle choice on a temporary chairman.[36]

When the unit rule deal did emerge, some newspapers mentioned Garfield's behind-the-scenes role.[37] To Garfield, the compromise had now changed everything. "I begin to feel quite confident that neither Grant nor Blaine can get the nomination," he wrote to Lucretia during a quiet moment that day.[38] A to-the-death stalemate between Grant and Blaine could open the door for John Sherman, he knew, or anyone else.

Meanwhile, his own rising celebrity only made Garfield's situation awkward. He increasingly heard his own name mentioned as a pawn to other peoples' private conspiracies. A Connecticut delegate, for instance, claimed to be working to raise Garfield's name for the presidency to torpedo John Sherman among the Ohioans, and thus clear the way for Blaine.[39] At the same time, Garfield's Ohio colleague William Dennison reported that the "opposition"—Conkling and Logan—were "busy circulat[ing] rumors that Blaine men and Grant men in New York and elsewhere [were] ready to fraternize in the nomination of Garfield. This is very annoying to Garfield who is doing all he can to stop it."[40]

The Blaine-Sherman alliance on the unit rule fight only fed the talk. "The cordial cooperation of the Sherman men ... has made the feeling between them and the Blaine men more cordial than it was before," reported Blaine's organ, the *New York Tribune*. Another report said that Ohio would shift to Blaine "after the first ballot" in exchange for Foster as vice president. "It is said that Garfield favors this plan."[41]

All these rumors reeked of disloyalty to John Sherman himself, and many Sherman friends in Chicago were starting to point fingers. "Garfield and Foster are the only weak points on our line," one of them wrote to Sherman in a private note. "Our friends say if [Garfield and Foster] are true, you will win. If they are not, I promise you that young Republicans will revenge their treachery."[42]

Garfield cringed at the bind in which he found himself. "You can hardly imagine the embarrassment I have been in from the moment of my arrival here by the number of delegates from all quarters who are openly expressing the wish that I was the Ohio candidate," he confessed to Lucretia in a letter. It was enough, he said, "to put me in constant danger of being suspected of ambitious designs."[43] Garfield sensed the whole tone of Chicago turning sour. The "bitterness already engendered ... will make it impossible for the Convention to restore harmony to the Party."[44] Yet, in a curious way, he himself was becoming its emblem.

Garfield, surrounded by friends, steeped in intrigue, his own ego stroked by the hour, was in his element here. "Swaim, Henry, Nichol, and a host of good fellows are here," he wrote Lucretia, listing just a few of the cronies he'd rubbed elbows with that day.[45] Politics is what James Garfield lived for, and in June 1880 there was no better place for it than Chicago.

◎ ◎ ◎ ◎ ◎

Roscoe Conkling stood at his full commanding six-foot three-inch height and loudly ordered quiet. As the drama was playing out in the national committee at the Palmer House a few blocks away, Conkling had called an emergency, closed-door caucus of his New York delegation. Now, standing at the front of a ballroom in the Grand Pacific hotel, he demanded attention. The meeting had a single purpose—to confront the traitorous New York "bolters."

Conkling seethed with anger at these dissidents. He had tried to smoke them out at a delegation meeting the day before by asking if there were any "disaffectants" in the group. If so, they "should let their grievances be known." None dared show themselves. "He was answered only by silence."[46] Then, the previous night, nineteen of these same silent men, New York delegates all, had thrown their bombshell—a signed "pledge" to "resist the nomination of Gen. U.S. Grant by all honorable means."[47] Within hours, they had printed up copies, with names attached, on little pink hand-bills, and scattered them around all the major hotels, restaurants, and saloons. Now, their infection had spread, prompting a similar revolt in the Pennsylvania delegation.

Unit rule or not, Roscoe Conkling would not tolerate this insolence in his delegation. "I cannot suppose any gentlemen have violated their obligations to the state convention or the courtesy due to the delegation,"[48] he snidely told reporters when asked about the outburst.

Conkling wanted to see them face-to-face. Now, all seventy New York delegates packed the room, along with most of the alternates. In the smoky light, Conkling looked every bit in fighting trim, despite signs of battle-scarred age. "[A] "silver-gray tint... overshadowed the reddish hue of his remaining hair and whiskers, the curled top-knot so dear to his caricaturists is no longer visible, and he stoops when he walks," noted one reporter, "[b]ut he has not lost a shade of his egotistic ambition."[49] This night, Conkling had entered "majestically, with a calm and conciliatory smile on his face," wrote another.[50]

Just last summer, newspapers had squawked over Conkling's romantic liaison with Kate Chase Sprague, the attractive wife of a former Rhode Island Senator. William Sprague, the husband, an incessant drunk, had driven Conkling off his property with a shotgun after finding the two together. The incident had set tongues wagging, but added to Conkling's legend.

The nineteen New York bolters too had arrived dramatically, as a group, for the emergency delegation meeting. They had marched across the street from the Palmer House, then commanded their way through the wide corridor filled with newspapermen, sympathetic delegates, and visitors. Leading the parade, looking stony-faced at entering the lion's den, were the bolters' two leaders: state senators William Woodin and William H. Robertson.

Robertson, 57 years old, a long-time judge, state senator, and one-term U.S. congressman from Westchester, had first announced his own personal decision to bolt in early May, about a month before the Chicago convention. His Westchester district supported Blaine for President, Robertson had told the *Albany Evening Journal,* and so too should he, on principle. Since then, he and Wooden—who'd announced his bolt the day after Robertson—had suffered a barrage of public insults from their Stalwart "friends": Robertson was a "knave or a fool," "without the saving pretence of shame," driven by patronage jealousy, a political "suicide," to name a few.[51] A few brave Conkling machine opponents applauded them. Long-time Albany wire-puller and *Journal* editor Thurlow Weed called Robertson's dissent "statesmanlike."[52]

Robertson also had selfish reasons to embarrass Roscoe Conkling in this most public setting. He had been on the outs with Conkling for years, ever since 1872 when his own bid to become New York governor had collapsed in a Conkling-run state convention. Robertson always blamed Conkling for secretly torpedoing him, though friends denied it.[53] In any event, should Blaine win the White House, he would be heavily indebted to the New York bolters. Whether Robertson now based his revolt on principle, vengeance, or ambition, it had hit its mark—directly rubbing Conkling's raw nerve over James G. Blaine.

Until yesterday, Robertson and Woodin had kept a low profile in Chicago. Now, prompted by William Chandler and the Blaine brain trust, they had begun to flaunt their rebellion. Beyond publishing their "pledge," they had hung a large placard in their Palmer House suite saying: "New York NOT solid for Grant," the "NOT" in huge red letters. Woodin chatted up visitors, offering to bet $2,000 that the Grant nomination would fail.[54]

Roscoe Conkling had dreaded this. Hearing of the "pledge" Monday

night, he "realized his danger and was completely broken up," said one observer.[55] He told friends the unit rule contest was "uncertain"[56] and tried to
think past it. Edwards Pierrepont, a Conkling ally, tried to put a good face on
the wound: "Grant can be nominated better without" the unit rule, he said.
"[A]nd [it would make] his election more easy."[57]

Conkling opened the meeting by calling on a friendly delegate to move
that, on the presidential roll call, Conkling himself as delegation chairman should cast all 70 New York votes as a block for Ulysses Grant. New
York would have its unit rule, regardless of what the rest of the Convention
did.

Woodin, speaking for the dissidents, immediately jumped up and moved
to amend. The chairman should announce a divided vote if the delegates disagreed, he said. No block, no unit. They debated back and forth. Chester
Arthur came in and out of the room with updates from the national committee and to lend Conkling his support. Finally Roscoe Conkling took the
floor himself. The rebels braced themselves. They knew they were about to
receive a tongue-lashing.

Conkling looked directly on the bolters as he paced across the ballroom,
his head cocked upright, eyes flared with their now-famous imperious glare.
He spoke loudly, his voice crystal clear in every far corner. How could "the
conscience of men ... allow them thus to disobey" their mandate, he roared,
looking the rebels directly in the eye. He decried their "betrayal," their "clan-
destine manner." These men deserved no "confidence," he said. He "would
never vote for nor favor men guilty of such conduct," he said. They were "dishonorable" and had violated "good faith."[58] He mentioned several by name:
Woodin, Sessions, Curtis. "Under what obligation are you?" he said, turning
to Woodin at one point, asking him a direct question. "You are bound both
by the State and district convention as well as by your speech in the Senate.
How do you explain your presence here in the delegation?"

Woodin mumbled an answer, but Conkling kept going. Robertson felt
the glare more than anyone. He knew he was Conkling's top target.

It was nearly an hour later when Conkling sat down. The motion came
to a vote. Not surprisingly, the delegation agreed to support its chairman. The
surprise, rather, was the narrow margin: 45 to 23. Twenty-three members had
voted "no" and might cross the line again. Holding them back, or enforcing
this state resolution without a strong-arm convention rule, would be nearly
impossible.

Still, Conkling had made his point. When the Chicago convention was over, his enemies could forget their political careers, starting with William Robertson. "We have burned our bridges," Woodin sheepishly told reporters.[59]

Robertson himself said nothing at the delegation meeting. Afterwards, he spoke with newspapermen in the hallway. He tried to wear a brave face. The meeting was simply a signal to other delegations that New York would "vote as a unit... despite the attitude of the nineteen independents," he said.[60] Otherwise, it meant nothing.

Later that night, Roscoe Conkling rubbed elbows with over 300 supporters whom he and the other Grant leaders had called together for a caucus in a Palmer House ballroom. He may have shared a brandy that night along with some laughs and stories, though generally he limited his alcohol. Roscoe Conkling, despite all the set-backs, had kept his focus. He saw himself still in command at the convention. He stood up on a podium and addressed the troops; they greeted him with cheers and applause. Do "not be frightened by a parcel of boys," he told them. Grant still dominated the candidates in Chicago. He would carry five Southern states, Conkling said, and he promised to carry New York by 40,000 votes.[61] They must stand firm. Conkling had hard facts to support this bravado. His latest delegate count, even after subtracting the "bolters," still gave Grant 322 votes. These votes, though shy of the 379 needed to win, were solid. They would be "cast for [Grant] ballot after ballot, until there is either a break in his favor or he receives scattering votes enough to secure his nomination."[62] Given time, they could not fail.

And after Grant won, he, Conkling, would collect his spoils. And should Grant falter, "In no event will the strength of Grant go to Blaine," they had decided. "The word had gone along the line that Blaine must be defeated."[63]

Many people admired Roscoe Conkling's determination, even his opponents. "It is the pluck of Conkling which is the back-bone of the Grant movement,"[64] commented Parker Chandler of Massachusetts. Others saw him as dangerous. "Conkling is about the only one who would rather have defeat with Grant than success with someone else," noted John Sherman.[65] And Warner Bateman, reporting from the scene, wrote: "We are satisfied that [the] Grant men intend the desperate game or surrender."[66]

James Blaine, who knew Conkling's dark side as well as anyone, called it by a different name: "Rule or ruin."

But in the pinch, Conkling had inspired confidence. After the caucus, his

Stalwart followers glowed with boldness. "We are perfectly sure of our position and shall nominate General Grant," John Logan told a reporter, "mark what I say."[67]

⊚ ⊚ ⊚ ⊚ ⊚

Far away in Washington, D.C., James G. Blaine smiled broadly that Tuesday as he walked out onto the brightly lit floor of the United States Senate. He waved at friends in the gallery; a few Senate colleagues came over to shake his hand and pat his shoulder. Blaine had mostly stayed away from Capitol Hill during the week of the Republican Convention. Congress did little legislating: many Senators were in Chicago as delegates, and those left behind spoke of nothing but politics—always asking about the latest telegrams or reports, or checking the bulletin boards with the latest news near the Senate floor. Rumors ran rampant that Don Cameron, one of their own, would be deposed from the national committee, then news spread of the unit rule "compromise." The outcome, most agreed, was a clear win for James G. Blaine. He seemed as likely as anyone now to become the next President of the United States.

Blaine had good reason for hope. His side too had held a caucus Tuesday night in the Palmer House. Theirs too drew about 300 delegates, as many as Grant's, loyal men who would stick together ballot after ballot. Blaine's hard-nosed lieutenant William Chandler had told him that Ohio, John Sherman's own state, might break for him on the second ballot. Nine Ohio delegates had already decided to bolt his way on the first. Now the New York and Pennsylvania revolts were succeeding as well.

To keep up momentum, Blaine, through Chandler, that morning had leaked a "short list" of possible vice presidents on a Blaine slate: "If Blaine should be nominated, the second place on the ticket would be given to Mr. Washburne, Governor Foster of Ohio, or the Honorable Benjamin Harrison of Indiana," reported Blaine's organ, the New York Tribune.[68] Blaine had earlier floated the vice presidency to Senator John Logan, one of Grant's own "triumvirate," but Logan was too loyal to Roscoe Conkling and Grant to accept.

Blaine knew this fight was far from over. He had come achingly close in presidential politics before and failed. The last time, four years earlier in 1876, he'd been undone by Roscoe Conkling—a full decade after their initial feud had started on the House of Representatives floor over the "turkey gobbler strut" incident in 1866. At the 1876 Republican convention in Cincinnati, Blaine had posted a huge lead on the first ballot: 285 votes for him, only 99 for Conkling, and the rest scattered among the field. Blaine had openly ridiculed Conkling's ambition that year: "He cannot carry his own state in the convention or at the election, and his candidacy is an absurdity," he'd told a reporter, knowing his comment would be published.[69] Six ballots later, Conkling had surprised everyone by switching his support to Rutherford Hayes, the ultimate nominee and winner—and destroying a year's worth of work by Blaine.

The pressures on Blaine in 1876 had been enormous, much worse than now. Just weeks before that year's convention, Blaine had faced accusations over fraudulent railroad stock dealings—revealed in the famous Mulligan letters.* Blaine literally had to steal the letters from Mulligan himself to plead his own defense on the House floor—reading aloud selected, edited portions with favorable evidence into the *Congressional Record* but hiding the rest; he never fully removed the tarnish of the charges. Days later, on the Sunday morning before balloting would begin in Cincinnati, Blaine had collapsed from exhaustion on the steps of the Washington Congregational Church and lay unconscious for two days, sending shock waves through his troops and possibly costing him the election. His enemies ridiculed the incident: "Blaine Feigns a Faint," the *New York Sun* had headlined.[70]

This time, Blaine paced himself. His chief manager Chandler, in fact, had complained all year that Blaine wasn't working hard enough for the prize. "[T]he anti-Grant, pro-Blaine men are fighting without a leader," Chandler had told Harriet Blaine as early as January. "They are very valiant but are flopping like a chicken with his head cut off."[71] And "I think the beloved [Harriet's nickname for her husband] don't like a fight as well as he used to."[72] As Chicago approached, Chandler had insisted on a bolder approach: "Mr. Blaine ... is for the second time a candidate for president. He must be nominated at Chicago in June, or else forever give up any idea of gaining the Chief Magistry of the nation.... I think he owes it to himself and to his friends all over the country who are ready to sacrifice everything for his success to do all that is in his power to win at Chicago."[73]

Chandler had suggested in late May that Blaine come to Chicago per-

---

* Named for James Mulligan, a former Blaine family clerk, the letters detailed Blaine's suspicious dealings with the Little Rock and Fort Smith Railroad, a scandal that would follow him for life.

sonally to manage the campaign and charm delegates with his "magnetic" presence, but Blaine had declined. The break from tradition, Blaine felt, would outweigh any gain.

In late May, Blaine had taken a long walk through Washington's Naval Observatory Grounds* with his friend James Garfield and confided his doubts about the campaign. Blaine "did not much expect the nomination at Chicago," Garfield noted in his journal, and "would not have become a candidate but for the belief that he could more effectively prevent the nomination of Gen. Grant than any one else."[74] Harriet Blaine reflected the same ambivalence in a letter to their daughter Maggie that week: "I am almost sure a combination will be made against your Father" in Chicago, she wrote.[75]

Reluctant candidate or not, Blaine had succeeded remarkably in 1880. Even running against a living legend like Ulysses Grant and weighed down by old scandals, Blaine had attracted enormous national support. He championed hard money (backed by gold), support for business enterprise, a strong tariff to protect American jobholders, Irish independence, and a stiff backbone against the old Confederacy—what some called "bloody shirt" politics, exploiting old Civil War passions long after Appomattox, but what Blaine considered loyalty to Republican values of Union and civil rights for freed blacks.

"Mr. Blaine always had a warm and ardent support by the younger Republicans," especially in the West and North, conceded even his opponent John Sherman. "His brilliant and dashing manner and oratory made him a favorite," Sherman wrote.[76] He was the brightest of the post-war generation of leaders, or, as Robert Ingersoll had called him in 1876, the "plumed knight."

"Rest assured we shall not fail if opportunity offers to show our gratitude in more tangible forms," Andrew Carnegie had written to Blaine in March on behalf of "the steel rail manufacture of the country"—one of his many backers in the financial world.[77] The opportunity now beckoned.

Blaine understood that Roscoe Conkling still hated him and would not shrink from undercutting him once more. He probably laughed at a line from that morning's *New York Tribune* describing William Chandler's response to concerns that Blaine could not carry New York State "on account of Senator Conkling's hostility to him." Conkling's "friends here say that he does not

---

* The Naval Observatory in 1880 was located in what is now Foggy Bottom, near the marshlands that would later hold the Lincoln Memorial.

speak harshly of Mr. Blaine," Chandler had said, presumably with a straight face.[78] Blaine had more trouble understanding the hostility of Don Cameron—an old friend and frequent guest at his dinner table.[79]

He also saw the ominous tone developing from the political stand-off, even in Washington. "The feeling between the champions of the rival candidates [in Washington] is so bitter," reported the *Washington Evening Star*, "that grave doubts are expressed by expert politicians of the success of either of them."[80]

This time, though, Blaine felt the country and the party behind him. His friends had dug in their heels, and he benefited from the growing unease toward a third term for Ulysses Grant. The Mulligan letters scandal was now four years in the past. Chandler had telegraphed from Chicago that week that as things are now he considered the chances of Blaine's nomination "as 4 to 1, but not to be counted on till it comes."[81] Blaine's Maine contingent alone filled six railroad coaches—200 boosters—all decorated with flags and portraits as they'd chugged across the Midwest toward Chicago, their banners beaming "James G. Blaine and No Second Choice" and "Burned our Bridges and Bound to have Blaine."[82]

Nominee or not, Blaine at least intended to use his power to dictate who would become the next President of the United States. Late that night, back in his home on Washington's Fifteenth Street, Blaine went into his library. After finishing with a long night of callers, telegrams, and letters, as his last thought of the day, he wired a note to his friend Chandler in Chicago. "WEC. Thanks and Congratulations. It was well and wisely done. It will prove much better for party harmony than harsher measures. Have sent your dispatch over to Mrs. Chandler. Now go to bed and get a good night's sleep. All quiet on the Potomac. JGB."[83]

He could not have known then that Chandler, by forcing a compromise with Chester Alan Arthur on the unit rule, had set the stage for one of the greatest political dead-locks in America since the Civil War.

• 4 •
FIRST VOLLEY

Saturday, June 5, 1880
Chicago.

AFTER FOUR DAYS OF DELAYS, haggling, side-shows, and back-biting, this night the Republican delegates would finally get down to the business of choosing a nominee for President of the United States.

The Great Fire had destroyed the old Crosby Opera House on Washington Street between State and Dearborn, which had housed the Republican's convention in Chicago in 1868. Tonight, almost 15,000 delegates, dignitaries, newsmen, clackers, and spectators packed the new Interstate Industrial Exposition Building, a marvel of iron and brick that locals called the "Glass Palace" for its huge windows and rounded glass ceilings. The structure had cost an eye-popping $250,000 to build. It stretched along Michigan Avenue from Monroe to Van Buren streets near the lakefront. Its great hall measured 400 feet long, 100 feet wide, and 80 feet high; its interior reminded some of New York City's Grand Central Railway Depot. Delegates entering the building past guards wearing red and gold badges marveled at the great vaulted ceilings. Flags and full-color portraits of Republican heroes lined the walls and hung from rafters; colorful state signs and banners dotted the floor, some featuring the party's new symbol taken from a Thomas Nast cartoon in *Harper's Weekly*—the strong, solid elephant.

Over 500 newsmen sat at wooden tables directly beneath the speaker's podium; telegraph wires ran from operator tables nearby. Words said here would flash instantly to bulletin boards posted in Washington, New York, Atlanta, and a dozen other cities. Men with megaphones stood through the hall to repeat messages so people in the far corners could hear over the clamor of voices and brass bands.

Royalty dotted the visitors' gallery tonight, including Prince Leopold of Belgium and a royal party from Canada. General Phil Sheridan looked sharp in his blue and gold- braided military formal dress. Susan B. Anthony, who had come to Chicago to lobby for a plank favoring women's suffrage in the platform, also moved among the delegates and celebrities.

Crowds had started gathering outside the hall that morning at 7 am. They found seat tickets selling from $2 to $10 apiece from delegates and, from street scalpers, for as high as $25.* Platoons of Chicago police and firemen set up ropes and barriers to control the surging human sea, predominantly men wearing buttons, banners, and badges for their candidates, with top-hats and frock coats against the weather. Ladies holding pink and green parasols dotted the crowd. They bought "Blaine lemonade" from sidewalk stands as "peddlers of all sorts of cheap trifles" blocked the streets with wagons and push-carts.[1] Pick-pockets also made a brisk business.

An estimated 50,000 people had come to Chicago for the Republican convention. Now in full force, they flooded the hall, the streets, the hotels, and the jails. Delegates stuffed themselves five and six into hotel rooms; those without rooms slept in hallways or saloons. Even Garfield shared his three-quarter-size bed in the Grant Pacific with a total stranger—the brother of another Ohio delegate. Chicago Mayor Harrison had ordered Michigan Avenue cleaned and repaired near the Exposition Building. Electric light displays graced the major hotels, along with glee clubs, floral bouquets, and posters and portraits. Hotels and shops hung new brightly colored awnings to attract the tourists and their bulging wallets.

In the Convention's opening days, the crowd in the Exposition Hall had already chosen favorites among the political performers. Roscoe Conkling had made his mark the first morning by leading his full New York delegation, all seventy, plus alternates, marching together down Clark and Adams Streets, greeting friends along the way, to enter the hall in unison—walking arm-in-arm with his friend Chester Alan Arthur. Once inside, Conkling and Arthur sat side-by-side at the front of the New York delegation, two large, crisply dressed New York sharpers. Since then, Conkling had entered the hall each morning about an hour late so he could receive cheers from the already-packed galleries.

---

* About $500 in modern dollars.

Getting down to business, the delegates already had voted to reject an official "unit rule" by 449 to 306, and had voted to admit the Illinois dissidents, 387 to 353—tests of strength that showed the Grant forces coming up short. Garfield chaired the convention's Rules Committee and presented the case against the unit rule. He too was quickly becoming a crowd favorite—always appearing, it seemed, as a nemesis to Roscoe Conkling.

They'd also adopted a platform with core Republican planks: protective tariff, strong federal powers, voting rights, limits on Chinese immigration, and lip service on civil service reform.*

As presidential balloting approached, behind-the-scenes scrounging for last-minute votes had reached a hot intensity. Money and liquor flowed freely. "Am advised of bribes offered and accepted," John Sherman wired from Washington.[2] William Chandler had to fend off visitors clawing for cash. "I am doing all I can to keep the Grant [southern] delegates from going over to Sherman or some 'dark horses'," wrote one anonymous operative, a Harry E. C___, "and it requires some little money to do it."[3] Chandler apparently never replied—worried perhaps that Henry C___ would keep the bribe money for himself.

Colonel Fred Grant visited delegation after delegation for his father, teasing them and boasting to reporters of their strength. He visited the Sherman headquarters at the Grand Pacific one day and told Governor Dennison "O, Father will be nominated on the first ballot." When a reporter asked Dennison whether Sherman would accept second place on a ticket with Grant and Dennison replied: "The Secretary will accept the Presidency or nothing," Colonel Fred said simply "Then he'll get nothing."[4] From the delegations of Ohio to Wisconsin and Georgia, Fred Grant kept up the chatter. He visited Blanche Bruce of Mississippi, the freed slave and now the sole black United States Senator and a serious candidate for Vice President.** Grant "talked to

---

* The civil service plank, added on the convention floor, did at least arouse one honest voice: a Mr. Flanagan from Texas, who objected: "There is one plank in the Democratic Party that I have ever admired and this is 'To the victors go the spoils' ... What are we up here for? I mean the members of the Republican Party are entitled to office, and if we are victorious we will have office." Most everyone agreed, but they still voted him down—perhaps an early case of "political correctness."

** Bruce was the second African American to reach the U.S. Senate (Hiram Revels of Mississippi was the first), the first to serve a full term (1875-1881), and the only black Senator during these years. Bruce had escaped slavery and gone north during the Civil War, taught school in Hannibal, Missouri, briefly attended Oberlin College, then returned south to make money as a planter. He rose in Reconstruction politics, becoming county registrar of voters, then sheriff and tax collector, then member of the Mississippi State levee board. As U.S. Senator, Bruce suffered stark

him and drank his whiskey," a reported observed, but Bruce had already promised his vote to John Sherman.[5]

Friday morning's session in the Glass Palace, though, had seen the sharpest clash yet between factions, putting Conkling and Garfield on a collision course.

Nobody had objected on that Friday morning when Conkling offered a resolution that pledged every delegate in the hall to support the party's nominee; "no man should hold his seat here who is not ready so to agree," Conkling had pronounced, standing tall on the convention floor, Chet Arthur seated at his side, to cheers and applause. A voice vote showed wide delegate support. But when a dozen or so voices answered "no," Conkling got his dander up. He insisted on unmasking them. "[Who] at a Republican convention," he bellowed, "would vote 'no' on such a resolution?" He demanded a roll call. As the clerk read each state, most of the dissenters shut their mouths rather than declare themselves in front of 10,000 spectators. But a tiny minority—three West Virginians—saw a principle. As they voted "no," hundreds of delegates and hangers-on in the galleries showered them with a "storm of hisses."[6] The motion carried by a whopping 716 to three.

Conkling, though, still wasn't finished. The three must be punished. Standing at his place, he now offered a motion to strip them of their votes and silence their voices at the convention. Suddenly, the crowd grew uneasy. They hadn't planned that morning on throwing Christians to any angry lions.

One of the three West Virginians, A.W. Campbell, had faced bullets and mobs in wartime Virginia, being an abolitionist in the heart of the Confederacy. Now he published a newspaper and nursed a strong stubborn streak. "I shall never go into any convention and agree beforehand that whatever may be done ... shall have my endorsement," he declared, climbing up to stand on his chair, raising his voice to be heard. "Sir, as a free man, whom God made free, I always intend to carry my sovereignty under my own hat." The delegates listened, struck by the human face of the supposed villain they'd wanted to expel a moment before. "If it has come to this that in the City of Chicago a delegate cannot have free expression of opinion, I for one am willing to withdraw from this convention," he said. Another West Virginia dissenter,

bigotry from colleagues with the notable exceptions of Roscoe Conkling—for whom Bruce would name his only child—and Mississippi Democrat Lucius Lamar. He gained a reputation for competence and energy, advocating federal support for freed slaves, internal improvements for Mississippi, and becoming the first black American to preside over the Senate floor.

named McCormick, angrily argued that in 1876 he had made over a hundred speeches for Rutherford Hayes while Roscoe Conkling had made only one. What gave the New York Boss such a claim on party loyalty?

James Garfield, sitting with the Ohio delegation on the convention floor, saw the crowd's unease and had no qualms about taking sides. Garfield had met A.W. Campbell, the West Virginian, over the years and knew his wartime record. He stood up from his seat and calmly approached the speaker's podium, causing a stir among the newsmen and delegates. "I fear this convention is about to make a great error," he stated matter-of-factly from the podium in a clear, loud voice, "and before they act, I beg leave to state the case."

Garfield, like Roscoe Conkling, had given thousands of speeches in his life, in churches, in small towns across Ohio, and in the U.S. Congress. Before this vast crowd in Chicago, he spoke in a mild, sensible tone, but forceful in logic and delivery. The West Virginians had every right to their opinions, Garfield now argued. "Are they to be disenfranchised because they thought it was not the time to make such an expression [about a candidate]?" he asked, extending his right arm toward the galleries, forming his words slowly so his voice would carry through the hall. "There never was a convention, there never can be a convention, of which I am a delegate, equal in rights to every other delegate, that shall bind my vote against my will on any question whatever."

Garfield then struck the emotional jugular, the Civil War. "One of [the West Virginians] I knew in the dark days of slavery, and for twenty long years, in the midst of slave-pens and slave-drivers, [he] has stood up for liberty with a clear-sighted courage and a brave heart," he said. "And if this convention expel him, then we must purge ourselves at the end of every vote" by forcing out the losers.

Few cheers went up, but Garfield could see by the faces, the nodding heads, and the quiet, private looks that he had won the crowd. When Roscoe Conkling now stood up at his seat on the Convention floor to reply, a new "storm of hisses" greeted him. A California delegate moved to table Conkling's resolution. But Conkling persisted. "Call the roll," he demanded, prompting another round of hoots and hollers. Senator George Frisbie Hoar, standing at the podium as convention chairman, banged his gavel for silence. Conkling, seeing that the tide had turned, finally withdrew his motion to scattered applause.

"Garfield's retort in [the West Virginia] matter was admirable," noted C.J. Moulton, an Ohio ally. It had "taken the convention and squelched Conkling."[7] All eleven West Virginia delegates thanked Garfield later that day for his "eloquent effort" for those "who dared assert the right of individual independence ... and refused to yield tamely to the tyranny of machine politicians." Their hint was clear. "We trust we may at no distant day have the pleasure of giving you more substantial evidence of our appreciation," they said.[8]

Conkling, of course, did not enjoy being squelched. As he watched Garfield's adroit performance on the podium, Conkling took a pencil from his pocket and scribbled a note on a small card, which he handed to Garfield as he stepped down from the dais. Garfield opened it when he reached his seat with the Ohioans. "New York requests that Ohio's real candidate and dark horse come forward," it said. "We want him in our sights while we prepare our ballots. R.C."[9]

All day long this factional clash had simmered, until well past midnight, when it degenerated into bedlam as a credentials fight erupted into an hourlong free-for-all.* Chicago lawyer Emery Storrs, having lost patience with heckling by some loud [and probably drunk] Blaine clackers in the gallery, had interrupted a legal argument from the podium to defy them: You "nominate him [Blaine] if [you] could," he shouted. The Blaine backers responded with a round of yells. Storrs, a Grant man with his own dander up, interrupted them: "when the gentlemen who are cheering in the gallery tonight are reposing under the soft summer sky, tired of politics and disgusted with its fatigues," he said, "you will find the followers of the grand old silent soldier awake by their camp-fires, and carrying the banner of the sluggard forward to triumph."

Storrs' remark set off a barrage of whoops, cheers, and shouts from both sides. Thousands of delegates and spectators, tired, frustrated, and impatient, needed to let off steam. "Blainiacs" tried to shout down the Grant men, and vice versa. In the melee, delegates danced and jumped, stamped their feet and banged the pine benches. Men waved flags, canes, hats, and umbrellas; women in the gallery waved bonnets and handkerchiefs. They broke into choruses of "John Brown's Body" and "Rally Round the Flag." Even Roscoe

---

* Over 50 credentials protests had been presented to the delegates that week, including seven that required floor debates and roll call votes.

Conkling stood on his chair and chanted. A Civil War veteran happily waved his crutch. One woman had to be forcibly removed after she tore off her bonnet and shawl (and perhaps more) and climbed onto the "Goddess of Liberty" statue on the stage to wave a flag.*[10]

The outburst was surreal in the late-night eerie glow of gas-lamps and calcium lights. Nothing quite like this had ever happened before at a national political convention.

Within minutes, word of the near-riot reached Washington, D.C., where the Blaines had already gone to sleep for the night. A telegraph messenger banged on their front door, waking up Harriet and James to news that "[t]he incidental mention of Blaine's name by a Californian roused gallery and convention to wild cheering for five minutes."[11] Prospects for his nomination looked bright.

To Garfield, standing with his Ohio cronies and joining the commotion, the scene "seemed [as if] it could not be in America, but in the Sections of Paris in the ecstasy of the Revolution."[12] It took until 2 am, a full hour later, before acting chairman General Raum could bang the official gavel, lead "three cheers for the victorious candidate," and end the demonstration.[13]

Now, the next night on Saturday, the delegates sat hoarse, red-eyed, and hung over as the real business of the Chicago conclave began.

The ritual of American political conventions, particularly the alphabetical roll call of states to present nominees, was already well entrenched by 1880. Then as now, a tingle of excitement ran through the hall as the clerk shouted "Alabama,"[14] then "Arkansas," then "California." Tonight, each of these early states passed; it was not until Michigan that a candidate emerged. James Blaine had chosen James F. Joy, the 70-year old president of the Michigan Central Railroad, to place his name in nomination. A dynamo in business, though, Joy fell flat as a speaker. Distracted by the rowdy crowd, he fumbled through a brief text, admitted his words would "benefit the candidate but little," and claimed to be rushing "because we are all now impatient for the voting." He ended by nominating for the White House the Senator from Maine, "James S. Blaine."

"G! G. Blaine, you fool," a dozen horrified voices shot back.[15]

After Michigan came Minnesota, whose Senator William Windom was

---

* Today, the thought of such a "spontaneous demonstration" at a national political convention is laughable. The demands of television coverage made them obsolete decades ago.

nominated as a favorite son. Then came Mississippi, Missouri, Montana, and half-a-dozen others until New York. Yes, New York had a candidate.

Anticipation around this moment had been building for months. A good nominating speech could dazzle a convention and determine the outcome. Robert Ingersoll's "plumed knight" performance had almost done it for Blaine in 1876. Now Conkling would have his chance to work magic for Ulysses Grant. Conkling had prepared thoroughly for this speech; he'd practiced his phrases, gestures, and intonations, and it showed in his bearing. He captured the crowd before saying a word. Reaching the convention hall's raised podium, Conkling dramatically climbed down from the dais onto one of the wooden tables used by the newspaper writers—placing himself closer to the delegates, almost a third of the way down the hall. He paused to accept the flood of cheers from the gallery, then waved them to silence with a flick of his hand. He threw back his chest, raised his head, and spoke in a strong, resonant voice that penetrated the vast Hall.[16]

"And when asked what State he hails from,
"Our sole reply shall be,
"He hails from Appomattox,
*"And its famous apple tree."**

The galleries erupted. Cheers, shouts, and demonstrations broke out. Conkling waited, then began to build the crowd's energy with a parade of cascading metaphors. "The election before us is to be the Austerlitz of American politics," he said, "it will decide for many years whether the country will be Republican or Cossack."** Quickly he turned to his candidate. "New York is for Ulysses S. Grant. Never defeated—never defeated in peace or in war, his name is the most illustrious borne by living man."

Cheers and more cheers. "Good for you," "That's it," "That's so," shouted voices in the crowd. Flags waved. Hats were flung in the air.

"He never betrayed a cause or a friend," Conkling went on. "And the people will never desert or betray him."

---

* The "famous" apple tree refers to the spot where General Robert E. Lee waited on the morning of April 9, 1865, to receive Grant's offer, hand-delivered by Union General Orville Babcock, to meet and finalize surrender terms in the living room of Wilmer McLean's farmhouse in the nearby small town of Appomattox Court House. It became a popular tourist attraction after the War.

** Austerlitz was one of Napoleon Bonaparte's greatest military victories, where his French armies defeated the combined forces of Russian Czar Alexander I and Austrian Emperor Francis II on December 2, 1805. Cossacks were fierce cavalry soldiers from central Russia who lay at the core of the czar's military strength.

Having built up his hero, Conkling now scolded his enemies. Grant had been "[v]ilified and reviled, truthlessly aspersed by unnumbered presses, not in other lands, but his own," he roared. Hisses and boos rolled down from the gallery. But "Calumny's ammunition has all been exploded… And the name of Grant will glitter bright … when those who have tried to tarnish that name have moldered in forgotten graves."

Conkling beamed, riding the exhilaration of 15,000 excited voices cheering him on. He now lined up his villains to knock them down. The third term issue? "Having tried Grant twice and found him faithful, we are told that we must not even, after an interval of years, trust him again. My countrymen! What stultification does such a policy involve?"

More cheers. "Hit 'em again." "That's right."

"Is this an electioneering juggle, or is it hypocrisy's masquerade?" General Grant had won his delegates "without patronage and without emissaries [laughter and applause], without committees, without bureaus, without telegraph wires running from his house to this convention or running from his house anywhere else."

Hoots and hisses now became intermixed with the applause. Blaine and Sherman backers bristled at Conkling's bald hypocrisy. "Syndicate," shouted one voice. "Machine," yelled another. As the delegates amused themselves with cat-calls, Conkling took a lemon from his pocket and "happily" sucked on it for a moment to soothe his voice, then launched back into the fray. The friends of Ulysses Grant "have never threatened to bolt unless the convention did as they say," he bellowed, unlike "the charlatans, jayhawkers, tramps, and guerrillas—the men who deploy between the lines, forage now on one side and then on the other." The eruption of noise now included cries of "Blaine" along with "Go on," or "That's it." The anti-Granters hollered and stamped their feet, but the Stalwarts knew that this was their moment. They jumped, clapped, cheered, and waved their hats.

When Roscoe Conkling finished a few minutes later, the hall exploded in a deafening clamor—opponents as well as supporters awed at the oratorical *tour de force*. It had brought forth "[t]he play of sarcasm, the saber-cuts of severity, and all the pageantry of eloquence," fawned one reporter.[17] Asked later how he made himself heard all through the hall that night, Conkling said: "By speaking very deliberately, and carefully pronouncing the vowels."[18] Had the presidential roll been called that moment, Ulysses Grant's candidacy would have stormed the hall.

But the night wasn't over yet. Barely had the delegates settled down from Roscoe Conkling's performance when the roll call continued. After New York came North Carolina, then Ohio. Ohio, too, had a candidate. All eyes now turned to the next speaker, James Abram Garfield.

Garfield had dreaded this moment for days. Amid all the convention hoopla, he had never actually written a speech. "I have not made the first step in preparation," he'd confided to Lucretia in a letter that week. "It was a frightful mistake not to write [the speech] before I came."[19] In fact, before leaving Washington, D.C., Garfield had visited John Sherman in his Treasury Department office and asked him directly what points about himself Sherman wanted Garfield to stress with the delegates. Sherman, according to Garfield's diary, "suggested that the chief characteristic of his life, from boyhood up, had been courageous persistence in any course he had adopted."[20]

But Garfield too was a practiced public speaker and found strength in the 15,000 faces looking back at him as he stood from his chair and stepped forward. He, like Conkling, recognized a dramatic moment. Conkling's address had been a firecracker. Garfield knew he could not stem the emotional tide; he needed, rather, to redirect it. "Conkling's extraordinary speech gave me the idea of carrying the mind of the convention in a different direction," Garfield later explained.[21] Loud cheering greeted him as he mounted the podium. But following Conkling's lead, Garfield too stepped briskly down from the raised platform and climbed onto the same wooden news table that Conkling had used a few moments earlier—as if trying to pick up the momentum exactly where Conkling had left it. He waited for quiet. "Mr. President, I have witnessed the extraordinary scenes of this Convention with deep solicitude," he began. "No emotion touches my heart more quickly than sentiments in honor of a great and noble character; but I have thought as I sat on these seats [that] you were the human ocean gathered in this circle." The metaphor of the ocean, the intimacy of "this circle," quickly set a quieter tone.[22]

"This assemblage seems to be a human ocean in tempest," he said, delegates in the far galleries craning their necks to hear him. "I have seen the sea lashed into fury and tossed into spray, and its grandeur moves the soul of the dullest man; but I remember that it is not the billows, but the calm level of the sea, from which all heights and depths are measured."

Conkling had thrilled the crowd with majestic phrases delivered grandly; Garfield now intrigued them with calm and measure. He had their attention, their minds, and spoke of many things: ending slavery, fighting the war, building industry, protecting the currency, and uniting the Party. "[B]y 4,000,000 Republican firesides, where 4,000,000 of voters with wives and children about them, with the calm thoughts of home," that's where the presidential election would be decided, Garfield said, "[n]ot in Chicago in the heat of July, but at the ballot-boxes in the Republic, in the quiet melancholy days of November." Laying out the issues, he asked the crowd "What shall we do?"

"Nominate Garfield," one voice yelled back, along with a few laughs.[23] Garfield ignored it. Not until near the end did he mention John Sherman, the candidate whose name he was placing in nomination for the presidency. Yes, John Sherman had played a central role in all of these great events, he said— though so too, of course, had many others.

"I shall always believe... that Garfield, while describing Sherman, was thinking of Blaine or himself," noted Robert Ingersoll, sitting in the hall that night with the Illinois delegation. "If any outsider is taken," he told a reporter as the crowd was breaking up, "I hope it will be Garfield. If Ohio wants a man, let Ohio ask for her best."[24]

Roscoe Conkling, asked about Garfield's speech later that night compared with his own, said simply that it had made him "sea-sick."[25]

The stage was set now. Monday morning, balloting would begin. Come what may, someone soon would win the prize.

※ ※ ※ ※ ※

In these days before public address systems run by electricity, many people inside the noisy Exposition Building never actually heard a word of either Garfield's nor Conkling's speeches above all the shouting and commotion, but their impact across America, outside the hall, was electric. Telegraph wires carried the speeches to newspaper offices in every major city. By early next morning, newspaper readers, millions of them, were sharing the words over breakfast or morning coffee. Those who couldn't read asked a friend or relative to read to them out loud, if not in English then German, Swedish, Gaelic, Yiddish, Polish, Chinese, or any of a dozen other languages—each that had its own daily press. The speeches became the talk of households, saloons, farms, street-corners, and factory workshops across the country.

Garfield's popularity soared with delegates, but his speech that Saturday night had also sparked a dark side—ugly finger-pointing within the Sherman camp. Telegrams started reaching John Sherman's Washington office. "The sickly manner in which Garfield presented your name has disgusted your friends here," one confidante secretly wrote to Sherman the next morning. "He has been of no service to you…. he was extremely lukewarm in your support. He is a Garfield man. If you should be nominated you need be under no obligation to him."[26] Another wrote to Sherman that "one quarter of the Ohio delegation supposed to be friendly to you [is] ding dong about Garfield," and "this seems precipitated by Foster…. These things are treason or foolishness among them."[27]

Governor Foster, Garfield's Ohio suitemate, his ego apparently tickled by the talk of him for the vice presidency, seemed to have lost all discretion. Foster's backroom scheming became the talk of the town, and the fact that he and Garfield shared adjoining hotel suites at the Grand Pacific fueled the accusations. "My information is that Foster is conspiring to bring Garfield out as candidate & transfer your forces to him," wrote another Sherman friend. "I think Garfield has full knowledge of the fact."[28] The rumors had even hit some newspapers, making them common knowledge. "There is a general belief that the Ohio delegation is getting ready to desert Sherman and go over to Blaine in a body," reported the *Albany Evening Journal* that week. "Mr. Foster desires to be nominated for Vice President on the ticket with Blaine, and that Gen. Garfield has been partly brought about to his view."[29]

Garfield cringed at these accusations and recognized the danger even of appearing to betray his candidate. He worried that the stain of dishonor would follow him for years. At the same time, after the Saturday night session, as he spent a quiet Sunday attending the small Disciple Church on Chicago's Indiana Avenue and then tending to his journal and letters, Garfield heard a tide of advice from friends and strangers alike. "In the event of a failure to nominate the candidates now in the field I hope you may be the one chosen," wrote his Ohio ally A.O. French in a private note. "Have talked with the Mississippi delegation who support you solid."[30] An anonymous letter Garfield received that week typified many: "sincerely hope the political lightnings of Chicago will single out JAG," and "if it cannot be this time I may live to four years from now and vote James A. Garfield for President of the US. Most respectfully. A Young Republican."[31]

But even from his closest friends, Garfield heard warnings against going too far, too fast. Lozenzo Coffin, who'd known James and Lucretia as young teachers in rural Ohio decades earlier, told Garfield to avoid this swamp. "I hear a great many rumors that … your… friends may try hard to induce you

to allow your name to come before the Convention," Coffin wrote. "Allow
me to voice the wish & earnest desire of your *real* & true friends that you will
under no amount of pressure consent. Your time is not yet."[32]

And another fear haunted Garfield: his week-long battles with Roscoe
Conkling, a man famous for grudges and hard feelings. Even if he won this
"contest," he wrote to Lucretia that week, "it will be likely to embitter him
and his followers against me"[33]—hurting him down the road in any campaign.

Lucretia, in turn, camped back at the Mentor, Ohio farmhouse surrounded by its domestic chaos of farm hands, workmen, and children, reading the daily reports about her husband through James' letters and from the
newspapers, had grown "half afraid the convention will give you the nomination," she wrote him. If so, "the place [Chicago] would be most unenvi-
able with so many disappointed candidates." She too sounded cool toward
the prospect. "I don't want you to have the nomination merely because no
one else can get it, I want you to have it when the whole country calls for you
as the State of Ohio did last fall. My ambition does not stop short of that."[34]

In the maelstrom of events, Garfield seemed adrift. "You can never know
how much I need you during these days of storm," he wrote to Lucretia that
week. "Every hour I want to go and state some case to your quick intuition."[35]

Late on Sunday night, hours before actual presidential balloting would
begin, Indiana Senator Benjamin Harrison came to Garfield's hotel room in
the Grand Pacific. One-on-one, behind the closed door, he asked Garfield
the direct question: In the event of a deadlock, under what conditions might
he accept the nomination? The question, both knew, was not academic. The
most likely outcome was for one of the front-runners, either Grant or Blaine,
to beat the other into inevitable submission. But if not, then who was left?
John Sherman? Elihu Washburne, the 64-year old former Illinois Congressman, Minister to France during the Franco-Prussian War, and Ulysses Grant's
mentor during his rise to Civil War fame? Not likely, given the recent personal bad blood between Washburne and Grant.* Senator Edmunds of Vermont or Windom of Minnesota? Each of these was a "favorite son" with little backing outside their region. Who did this leave?

---

* Grant found it unconscionable that Washburne, after years of loyalty, would jeopardize his
nomination by floating his own name as a candidate. The bad blood was worsened by Washburne's
public denials of his obviously-active bid. Garfield noted that the "perfidy of Washburne towards
[Grant] is working in Grant's favor." [Garfield diary, May 15, 1880.] The bad feelings ended a twenty-
year friendship.

But no, Garfield said. "My name must not be used," he told Harrison. He had come to Chicago to support John Sherman.[36]

Roscoe Conkling, too, took nothing for granted on the Sunday night before the balloting. He led a delegation that night, with him, Logan, Cameron, and Stephen Dorsey, walking through the downtown hotels to visit the delegations—particularly black delegates from southern states where Sherman or Blaine had threatened inroads. Conkling was "unusually affable" that night and shook hands with many of them, telling them to "stiffen... the spinal column." The mostly-southern black delegates in Chicago, though sentimentally inclined toward Grant, shared the same hard-headed split among Grant, Sherman and Blaine as the others. One black Grant backer, asked about convincing a stubborn Blaine backer to switch sides, said simply "It can't be done, boss; it can't be done."

Conkling spoke with this delegate for a few minutes. "Grant can't be defeated, and don't you forget it," he told the group as he moved on to the next hotel suite.[37]

◎ ◎ ◎ ◎

Delegates arrived early the next morning, Monday, April 7, at the convention hall. Senator Hoar at the chairman's podium gaveled the session open at 10 am. Eugene Hale of Maine moved to proceed at once to the balloting for the presidential nominee; Roscoe Conkling seconded. Senator Hoar appealed to the galleries for calm during the day. Then the clerk began to read the roll "amid a quiet that was almost oppressive."[38]

> *Alabama:* Alabama casts one vote for James G. Blaine,
> 3 votes for John Sherman, and 16 votes for Ulysses S. Grant.
>
> *Arkansas:* Arkansas casts twelve votes for Ulysses Grant.
>
> *California:* California casts twelve votes for James G. Blaine....

By Monday morning, the campaigns and newspapers had counted the delegates enough times to leave little room for surprise. First-ballot victories, other than for an incumbent president like Grant in 1872 or Lincoln in 1864, were not common and not expected.* Rutherford Hayes's nomination had

---

* By contrast, no Republican convention has gone more than one ballot since they needed three to nominate Thomas E. Dewey in Philadelphia in 1948; no Democratic convention has since 1952 when Adlai Stevenson was chosen in Chicago on the third. The last winning candidate chosen after a first ballot was Franklin D. Roosevelt, nominated by Democrats on the fourth in Chicago in 1932.

taken 7 ballots in 1876; Lincoln's had taken three in 1860. In 1852, Democrat Franklin Pierce, nominated on 49 ballots, beat Whig Winfield Scott who'd been nominated on 53 ballots. The real test would come later. Could the candidate hold his votes together in test after test, volley after volley, or would their backers scatter and break apart? How shrewdly could their managers bargain behind the scenes?

In later ballots, the delegates were expected to deliberate, to use their good judgment to resolve deadlocks and pick a candidate, and not be mere automatons "tied" or "committed" or "instructed" to a candidate.[39]

The biggest unknowns this morning on the first ballot in 1880 were the large states with internal revolts. Illinois broke early: of its 42 delegates, only 24 stuck with Grant—not at all "solid" as John Logan had advertised.

When the clerk called "New York," heads turned in anticipation. The ugly clash between Conkling and the New York bolters had become common knowledge—both Conkling's threat to impose a one-state unit rule and the bolters' plan to appeal it to the convention. Conkling answered the clerk's call for the state, but instead of either reciting New York's true vote breakdown or declaring a false "solid block" for Grant, he made an unusual request. Some of his delegates "prefer to vote for themselves," Conkling announced to the hall. The chairman should poll the delegation. No objection being voiced, the clerk began reading the names, starting with Conkling's own as chairman. He rose and announced himself for "U.S. Grant." So did three more New Yorkers until they reached John Birdsall, the first dissenter in alphabetical order. Birdsall, hearing his name from the podium, hesitated at first, stood, and then snapped out "J.G. Blaine" "as if the words burned his lips," as a reporter described it, then he "dropped into his seat as if he wished to get out of sight as quickly as possible, amid a roar of applause and hisses."[40] Each of the dissenters, James Husted, William Robertson, William Woodin (through Leander Fitts, his alternate)*, stood at their turn and voted for Blaine, bearing cat-calls from nearby seats mixed with applause from elsewhere in the room. Robertson alone seemed to find the courage to speak in a loud, confident voice despite Roscoe Conkling's glaring at him just a few

---

* Woodin actually was hiding behind a technicality to avoid violating the state convention's instruction. The instruction to support U.S. Grant applied only to himself as a delegate, Woodin argued, and not to his alternate Mr. Fitts. On the key vote, Woodin simply deferred to Fitts to circumvent the rule. William Robertson, on the other hand, felt no need for any procedural slight-of-hand and voted for Blaine himself.

feet away. The state's final tally was 51 for Grant, 2 for Sherman, 17 for Blaine. Nineteen had bolted.

The clerk finished polling the states and the total votes on the first ballot for the Republican nomination for President of the United States were: Grant, 304; Blaine, 284; Sherman, 93; Elihu Washburne, 30; Edmunds, 34; and Windom, 10—all well short of the 379 needed to win.

Add to Grant's 304 votes the sixty combined bolters from Illinois, New York, and Pennsylvania—the states once dictated "solid for Grant" and freed by the unit rule compromise—and his total would have reached 367, an insurmountable lead within a whisker of the magic number.

As it was, however, it was just the start of a very long day.

James Garfield sat with the Ohio delegation through the roll call. Ohio, too, was racked with dissension; nine bolters had publicly defected from John Sherman's column and voted for Blaine. That morning, Garfield had received a letter from Titas Coan, yet another Ohio friend urging him on in the race. "Your friends' thoughts are with you on this day of battle," Coan wrote. "Mine have followed your career now for many years, and let me say, now that the balloting begins, what I have heard said repeated in this club of late—That your name is the one that I would soonest see winning the 379 votes and the nomination. So may it be!"[41]

For now, to Garfield, that prospect seemed a far way off. By all outward appearance, the contest was still between the front-runners: Senator James Gillespie Blaine, John Sherman, and General Ulysses S. Grant.

First Ballot: Monday, June 7.

	Grant	Blaine	Sherman	Other
Ala.	16	1	3	–
Ariz.	–	2	–	–
Ark.	12	–	–	–
Calif.	–	12	–	–
Col.	6	–	–	–
Conn.	–	3	–	9
Del.	–	6	–	–
Fla.	8	–	–	–
Georgia	6	8	8	–
Idaho	–	2	–	–
Illinois	**24**	**10**	**–**	**8**

	Grant	Blaine	Sherman	Other
Ind.	1	26	2	1
Iowa	–	22	–	–
Kansas	4	6	–	–
Ky.	20	1	3	–
La.	8	2	6	–
Maine	–	14	–	–
Md.	7	7	2	–
Mass.	3	–	2	21
Mich.	1	21	–	–
Minn.	–	–	–	10
Miss.	6	4	6	–
Mo.	29	–	–	1
Mont.	–	2	–	–
Neb.	–	6	–	–
Nev.	–	6	–	–
N.H.	–	10	–	–
N. J.	–	16	–	2
N. Mex.	–	2	–	–
N. Y.	**51**	**17**	**2**	–
N. C.	6	–	14	–
Dak.	1	1	–	–
Ohio	–	**9**	**34**	**1**
Ore.	–	6	–	–
Penn.	**32**	**23**	**3**	–
R. I.	–	8	–	–
S. C.	13	–	1	–
Tenn.	16	6	1	1
Texas	11	2	2	1
Utah	1	1	–	–
Vt.	–	–	–	10
Virginia	18	3	1	–
Wash.	–	2	–	–
W. Va.	1	8	–	1
Wis.	1	7	3	9
Wyo.	1	1	–	–
D.C.	1	1	–	–
	304	284	93	75

Needed to win: 379 out of 756 total.

· 5 ·

THE BREAK

Monday, June 7, 1880
Washington, D.C.

SENATOR BLAINE RECEIVED the first ballot count from Chicago at his desk in the U.S. Senate. All around Washington, government work ground to a virtual halt that day. Clerks, deputies, officials, and lobbyists crowded bulletin boards at the offices and hotels. By afternoon, as news of the deadlock spread, some crowds grew to a hundred deep. They yelled as each vote was posted, cheering for their favorites.[1] Even Rutherford Hayes in the White House ordered a telegraph operator to bring him the latest dispatches.

Blaine's Senate colleagues barely focused on legislation. They sat about the chamber with tally sheets, pencils, and cigars, comparing rumors and telegrams each received from their friends at the convention. Many Republican chairs sat empty. Clerks milled about near the telegraph machines just outside the Senate chamber. Blaine himself sat slouched, showing the pressure of recent days; his chair "shoved back," and "resting his head wearily on his hand," wrote a reporter watching from the gallery, though he "roused up and engaged in animated conversation" as friends came by to talk.[2] When a Senate page handed him the first-ballot tally sheet, Blaine "scratched his head as if he didn't like the number of votes he got."[3]

In fact, he didn't like it at all. Blaine had been told to expect about 300 first-ballot votes; his actual count fell well short of that—one vote less, in fact, than he'd received on the first ballot four years earlier in 1876. Blaine "jumped up and darted about the chamber," wrote another reporter; he spoke nervously with "one Senator or another," received a few telegrams from a page, than "grabbed his hat and hurried on."[4]

With the voting now underway, Blaine decided to leave the Senate chamber and rode a private carriage down Pennsylvania Avenue to his home on Fifteenth Street. Here he could track events over his own private telegraph wire—a rarity at the time—along with his wife Harriet and his son Walker.[5] By the look of things, he might need to make painful decisions before the day was out.

A few blocks away, John Sherman had arrived at his office in the Treasury Department at 9 am and tried to conduct business as normally as possible. He met with clerks and assistants, keeping his door open to visitors and newsmen. "He was certainly cool today while the battle was going on,"[6] noted a reporter who was following him through the building. Sherman's eyes never strayed far from the telegraph machine, though. During the morning, his older brother William Tecumseh Sherman, General of the Army, came to show support. General Sherman, tall and starkly dignified in his blue military uniform with brass buttons and gold shoulder stars, seemed "very much more anxious" about the Chicago voting even than his brother John, the reporter noted,[7] his loyalties torn between family ties and his long-standing army bond to Ulysses Grant. General Sherman stayed all morning and much of the afternoon, elbowing his way to the telegraph along with the clerks as news of each new ballot arrived.*

Candidate Sherman himself seemed surprised by the first ballot numbers. He'd been told to expect about 110 votes, far fewer than Blaine or Grant. His chance would come later, he believed, when the Grant vote broke apart. "Since my last dispatch, report from Virginia delegation is that you will receive sixteen or seventeen votes as soon as Grant is out of the way," Sherman read in a dispatch from William Dennison in Chicago during the morning, "and from Tennessee... the seventeen Grant votes will go to you after Grant."[8] Still, "I had expected to have had twenty votes more," Sherman told the newsman, "they were to have come from Texas, Virginia, and North Carolina, but some of them were taken away from me before the ballot began."[9]

Sherman grew visibly angry only once that morning, when he heard

---

* It was in 1884, four years later, that General Sherman, urged to accept a possible presidential nomination himself, gave his "Shermanesque" response: "I will not accept if nominated and will not serve if elected."

about the nine Ohio bolters finally voting for Blaine instead of him and ruining his "solid" state delegation. Rumored for days, they had now shown
themselves in the open. Sherman blamed James Blaine for the defection more
than the defectors themselves. "Blaine has permitted, if not fostered" the
break "by falsehood, ridicule and treachery," he'd been told. How could he
now trust Blaine in a deal, or yield him the Ohio delegation on a later ballot? "If the nine will not go to the thirty five, it is hardly to be expected that
the thirty five will go to the nine."[10] "This was a fatal move for Blaine," Sherman would later claim. "The folly of a few men made cooperation impracti-
cable."[11] Bitterness between the two camps would grow during the day.

As the ballots wore on, Sherman grew restless. "Tell me what is going
on," he telegraphed to aid C.J. Moulton at one point. "We are all waiting and
will answer back if necessary."[12] Then, to Warner Bateman: "See Jack Wharton of Louisiana Delegation. Tell him that I appeal to him to stand fast as I
have assurances that if my friends will do so it will insure success."[13]

Around dinnertime, he had had enough. "I see that I have fallen off five
votes; I will be back in an hour," he announced. Maybe then, things would
look better.

Chicago:

Inside the convention hall, delegates and spectators settled into a tense routine after the opening salvo. Over the next four hours, they cast vote after
vote, eighteen ballots—each one consisting of a full roll call of each state
and territory with voting delegates—then broke for dinner. Then they came
back at night and cast ten more. As the hours dragged on, few people left
their seats, despite the heat, the tedium, and the hard pine benches. The
crowd studied each tally, state by state. The slightest change in delegate positions between ballots caused a stir. Telegraph operators broadcast the counts
in a flood of dots and dashes to offices across the country. Newsman at the
front tables sweated to keep pace with demands for multiple extra editions
being published in every major city. A dramatic break could come at any moment, and nobody wanted to miss it. But by day's end, after twenty-eight ballots, all the lines had held. Ulysses Grant's 304 votes had grown to a mere 307,
Blaine's 284 had shrunk to 279, and Sherman's 93 to 91.

"The forces were under a remarkable discipline," noted Charles Henry, "a
wave of the hand from Mr. Conkling or the other leaders being enough to
subdue anyone" from straying off course.[14]

Outside the Glass Palace on Michigan Avenue, dense crowds in top hats and frock coats gathered in the sunlight around a central bulletin board, cheering or booing each new result depending on which candidate they favored. Nearby, bookies took a steady stream of wagers.

On the second ballot, a Pennsylvania delegate, W.A. Grier of Hazelton, raised eyebrows by casting a lone vote for James A. Garfield. It sent the gallery into a "long and continuous whoop," though more to break the tedium than anything else.[15] Earlier, Grier had passed Garfield a note asking, "Are you in favor of the protective tariff?" Certainly Garfield was. "I desire a reply for my own information, and unless you object will show it to other Penn. delegates."[16] But after twenty-eight ballots, Grier's one vote had grown only to two—a curiosity but certainly no groundswell.

By mid-morning, after the first hour or so of balloting, the repetitive voting grew vaguely hypnotic to the people in the galleries: the clerk's voice, the endless state vote counts, the sunlight casting bizarre shadows across the room from ceiling skylights. The air grew hot and stale. To stay alert, men fanned themselves with hats, women with bonnets. On the third ballot, Roscoe Conkling decided to liven things up by announcing the New York vote with a sarcastic tone. "Two delegates are *said* to be for Sherman, seventeen are *said* to be for Blaine, and fifty-one *are* for Grant,"[17] he said, making a "wonderful sneer"[18] and prompting a few laughs from the delegates. A few minutes later, A.W. Campbell, the West Virginia dissenter whom Conkling had tried to expel a few days earlier, responded with a lampoon. When West Virginia's turn came on the seventh ballot, Campbell stood up and stomped around in a Conkling-like strut. Then, trying to capture Lord Roscoe's vocal intonations, he said: "Mr. Chairman, one of this important delegation is *believed* to be for Grant and eight of them *are known* to be for Blaine."[19] Conkling, seeing himself "in imitation and ridicule, ... flushed and fanned himself very hard," noted a nearby newsman.[20]

On the eighteenth ballot, Conkling took a break and let Chester Alan Arthur announce the New York vote. Arthur spoke in a notably straightforward, common sense fashion[21]—his first speech to such a national audience. The state's count was Grant, 50; Blaine, 18; Sherman, 2. They conducted a roll call to identify the new bolter—Dennis McCarthy of Syracuse—to "enthusiastic applause."[22]

Galena:

Ulysses and Julia Grant spent Monday tracking the convention balloting in Galena, their pretty town near the Mississippi River far from the noise and clamor in Chicago. During the morning, Grant strolled across the street to Colonel Rowley's house for up-to-minute telegraph reports. A newsman tagged along and watched his reaction to the stalemate. "[T]he silent soldier was smoking his cigar with all his usual serenity,"[23] he reported. As the voting stretched into afternoon, Grant kept a close eye on his pocket watch. Weeks earlier, he and Julia had arranged to leave Galena that Monday night and travel to Milwaukee, Wisconsin, for a reunion of the Grand Army of the Republic, stopping in Chicago early Tuesday morning on the way north. Certainly, they'd assumed, the Republican convention would be over by then. Perhaps, they hoped, the trip could be a victory march.

Now, on Monday, Julia kept mostly to herself. She said she'd seen this deadlock coming and yesterday had suggested a bold stroke. Why shouldn't Ulysses show up in Chicago early and surprise the delegates. "I entreated him to go on Sunday night and appear on the floor of the convention on Monday morning"[24] just as that day's balloting began, Julia later wrote. It would have roused the convention, rallied their voters, and perhaps tipped the balance in the General's favor.

The idea ran counter to everything Ulysses Grant believed about politics, though. He saw it smacking both of bad luck and bad manners. "[B]ut no! He said he would rather cut off his right hand," Julia wrote.

"Do you not desire success?" she'd asked him.

"Well yes, of course, since my name is up, but I will do nothing to further that end."

"Oh, Ulys," she'd sighed, "how unwise, what mistaken chivalry. For heaven's sake, go—and go tonight. I know they are already making their cabals against you. Go tonight, I beseech you."

Grant, though, was adamant. "Julia, I am amazed at you," he'd said.

So now, on Monday, as the ballots followed one another, Julia and Ulysses waited like everyone else. Grant did send a letter to Roscoe Conkling that day offering to meet him in Chicago, but "after the convention adjourns," as a gentleman should.[25] One newspaperman in Chicago on Monday reported hearing a "street rumor" that Grant had come to town on Sunday, but had ascertained there was "no truth in the absurd report."[26]

Chicago:

Late Monday night, after twelve long hours of balloting in the convention hall, Massachusetts delegate William Lovering moved to quit for the night. A few Grant delegates objected, as much from bravado as actual hope that they might gain any more ground by staying put. The tired delegates voted by 446 to 308 to adjourn. Beyond fatigue, the Blaine and Sherman leaders wanted to meet and talk. Most of the other delegates just wanted a chance to eat and drink or sleep.

By then, the hours of deadlock had made some things clear: No side could win unless another side broke, and none had shown signs of breaking. All the blocks seemed equally bull-headed and determined. Why not simply end the whole convention *sine die* tonight and call a new one, with new delegates, to break the dead-lock, suggested a few frustrated, liquored-up delegates.[27] From the Sherman camp's view, the hoped-for break-up of Grant votes had never come and perhaps never would. "The expectation that Grant would succeed or retire at the outset misled us all ... even up to the moment of balloting," Warner Bateman acknowledged.[28] Now, with Grant's forces holding solid, Blaine or Sherman could only win the nomination if one would transfer his strength to the other—an operation that was much easier to say than do. Otherwise, each group faced a break-up of its own ranks, or an uncontrolled rush by the delegates to a "dark horse."

William Chandler understood this, and he expected the Sherman troops to face reality, give up their fight, and fall in line behind Blaine. Late that night, as most delegates headed off to Chicago's saloons and brothels, or to receptions on the elegant North Side,[29] Chandler pulled together a small group in his hotel suite at the Palmer House. They closed the doors, locked them, lit cigars, and looked each other in the eye. Around the room sat Chandler, Maine Congressman Eugene Hale, and State Senator William Fry representing the Blaine side, and Bateman, Dennison, Garfield, and Foster for John Sherman. These tired, frustrated, impatient men all knew the bottom line. They had come to talk terms. Would Sherman throw his support to Blaine? Would Blaine throw his support to Sherman? Could either side control its own backers enough to avoid nominating Grant in the process?

The room filled with smoke, booze, and tough talk. This was politics.

Chandler, his eyes red and voice hoarse from the long day of haggling, ticked off the tallies state by state. Somebody kept notes.[30] Then Chandler laid down his terms: Blaine could not simply snap his fingers and nominate

John Sherman, he told the Sherman managers. "If Mr. Blaine permits his column to be broken," Chandler explained, then "Iowa, Nebraska, Kansas, Nevada, California, Oregon & twelve votes in the Territories will go to Grant," as would "Mr. Blaine's Southern votes … as also his vote in Delaware & that part of N.J. led by Gen. Small, & also part of Indiana."[31] In short, most of Blaine's delegates had no love for Sherman and actually considered Grant their second choice. In fact, Sherman couldn't even control his own state. Nine of his own Ohio delegates had refused to vote for him all day long.

Besides, Chandler argued, Blaine had 279 delegate votes to Sherman's 93. Why should the stronger surrender to the weaker? Sherman's managers had forced this entire day-long stand-off with no real chance of winning. Some Blaine backers were calling them "tools" of a Roscoe Conkling strategy to divide the anti-Grant forces and conquer them.[32] "[T]o attempt to transfer [Blaine's] strength to any candidate would nominate Grant at once," Chandler told the group. "If that result is reached" he said, "none of the responsibility shall lie at [our] door."[33]

They argued the points at length, but Chandler had been blunt and direct. Now how about the opposite? Could Ohio come to Blaine? Would it help if Governor Foster were named vice president?

We don't know exactly what the Ohioans said in response to the direct question. Certainly they told Chandler how John Sherman himself had fumed over Blaine's role in the Ohio bolt that morning, and that Sherman hadn't given them any authority to cut a deal. By the end of the parley, as clocks approached two or three in the morning, no decision had been reached, nor apparently had the Ohioans given a clear "yes" or "no."[34] When they broke up, a newsman was waiting in the hallway outside their suite. He confronted one of the participants, name unknown, and asked him flatly: "Do you think it is possible for the Blaine men to support Sherman?"

"No, Sir."

"Garfield?"

"Good evening."[35]

The Grant leaders too met late that Monday night in Roscoe Conkling's hotel room at the Grand Pacific—Chet Arthur, John Logan, Steven Dorsey, George Boutwell, and half a dozen others. They "freely discussed the situation," one of them told a reporter later on.[36] They too saw dangers. Chicago street betting now ran two-to-one against Grant[37] on expectations that the Grant vote would crumble after a few more volleys. Too many delegates opposed Grant on principle—resistance to a third term for anyone. Ultimately, Grant would lose. But then what? Blaine was unacceptable to them, as was Sherman. If only they had a good, sound Stalwart man to fill Grant's shoes. At this point, their eyes all turned to the obvious choice. The group was offering Roscoe Conkling the nomination to be President of the United States.

With Grant "out of the race," his friends argued, Conkling would face little resistance. Some delegates might dislike his tactics, but even many Blaine and Sherman supporters considered Roscoe Conkling strong, capable, sound on issues, and untouched by any real scandal.

Sitting in this closed-door, late-night, smoky-room meeting, Conkling refused. His friends credit him with a heroic speech. "I could not be nominated in any event, for if I were to receive every other vote in the Convention, my own would still be lacking, and that I would not give," he is quoted as saying. "I am here as the agent of New York to support General Grant to the end. Any man who would forsake him under such conditions does not deserve to be elected, and could not be elected."[38]

And, we know, the group felt that the nominee should be Grant or Blaine, and no dark horse.[39] "The only decision reached," one of them told a reporter, was "to stand by [Grant] and secure his nomination by waiting for the break-up of their opponents."[40]

Having turned down the Chief Justiceship of the Supreme Court when offered it by Grant in 1874, Conkling had now turned down the presidency the one time in his life when he actually might have won it.

For Tuesday morning's balloting, then, that left the Grant strategy not much different from Ulysses Grant's own approach at the siege of Petersburg, Virginia in 1864 when he was Lieutenant General of the Army facing Robert E. Lee near the climax of the Civil War: "Hold that line if it takes all summer."

◎ ◎ ◎ ◎ ◎

Tuesday, June 8, 1880
Chicago:

The delegates seemed determined on Tuesday morning as they reassembled at the convention hall for yet another run at choosing their presidential nominee. Today, somehow, they would cut the knot. All the candidates' camps had caucused, strategized, and planned their assaults. The morning's opening ballot, the twenty-ninth, saw two breaks: Massachusetts opened by switching twenty-one votes from Senator George Edmunds to John Sherman—hoping to spark a movement. Sherman's total jumped to 116, its highest yet. Spirits soared in the Sherman camp. "Mass. casts 21 votes for you on the first ballot this morning," telegraphed Massachusetts ally and delegate Parker Chandler to John Sherman in Washington. "We are on the road to success."[41]

On the same ballot, William Chandler convinced three Minnesota delegates to switch to Blaine from their Minnesota favorite son, Senator William Windom. This, in turn, was a strategic response to rumors that the Grant managers had organized a shift of half-a-dozen southern votes from Sherman to Windom—freeing them then to switch to U.S. Grant. Chandler's move had checked the plot.[42]

Still, Roscoe Conkling exuded confidence. "Members of the N.Y. Delegation assert that Grant will be nominated before one o'clock," announced a mid-morning Western Union bulletin.[43]

By the thirty-second ballot, the hoped-for Sherman stampede had stalled. Blaine too lost ground, dropping six votes, as Grant's total rose to 309. On the thirty-third, Wisconsin shifted nine votes to Elihu Washburne. This movement fizzled as well. Everyone knew that General Grant himself considered Washburne's candidacy a personal affront.* He could never be a second choice for the Stalwarts. William Chandler, watching his years of work for a Blaine presidency seem to slip away, sunk into apparent dejection; a reporter noticed him sitting quietly amid the clamor on the convention floor, his face "dark with disappointment" as he "bit his lips in vexation and stared into space."[44]

Then, on the 34th ballot, came another break. Far into the roll call, way down the list nearing the end of the alphabet, the clerk called Wisconsin— the same state that had launched the abortive Washburne movement two ballots back. This time, John B. Cassoday, chairman of the Wisconsin delegation, stood up on his chair and announced. "Wisconsin casts two votes for General Grant, two votes for James G. Blaine and," after a brief pause for effect, "SIXTEEN VOTES FOR JAMES A. GARFIELD."[45] This time, when the audience on the floor and in the galleries "cheered lustily,"[46] they meant it.

A century later, a rich harvest of conspiracy theories has grown up around what actually might have preceded the Wisconsin break. Clamoring by "friends" and "friends of friends" on all sides trying to break the deadlock had grown intense. By one account, several Wisconsin delegates had contacted

---

* See footnote, page 78.

the Ohio delegation that morning in a "state of excitement" and said "If you Ohio delegates will not bring out General Garfield, we shall," but were rebuffed.[47] By another, the Wisconsinites had been approached by Chandler, Governor Foster or other players from the prior night's Blaine-Sherman summit, hoping to use Garfield as a magnet to draw their combined voting strength. By yet another, Wisconsin had held a caucus that morning and decided to throw its weight to Garfield only by a slight majority over William Windom.[48]

Or it could be as the *Cincinnati Enquirer* had it: "It is probably true that there was no combination, and that Garfield won by mere pot-luck."[49]

Whatever the truth, this time James Garfield himself, sitting with the Ohio delegation, took the move seriously. He immediately jumped to his feet and sought recognition. "Mr. President!" he shouted, his voice barely audible at first above the commotion. Senator George Frisbie Hoar, standing solemnly at the chairman's podium, recognized him to speak.

"Mr. President, I rise to a question of order."[50]

"The gentleman from Ohio rises to a question of order," Hoar announced.

"I challenge the correctness of the announcement," Garfield said. "The announcement contains votes for me. No man has the right without the consent of the person voted for to announce that person's name and vote for him in this Convention."

Hoar banged his gavel a single time, cutting Garfield off almost in midsentence. "The gentleman from Ohio is not stating a question of order. He will resume his seat," Hoar announced. "No person having received a majority of the votes cast, another ballot will be taken. The Clerk will call the roll."[51]

Hoar would brag about this moment for the rest of his life. "I was terribly afraid that he [Garfield] would say something that would make his nomination impossible, or his acceptance impossible, if it were made," he later explained. Hoar had no intention of allowing the presidency to be undone over a "point of order."[52] Whether Garfield could have pressed the point harder, argued more strongly, once Hoar had shut him down, we will never know.* The Wisconsin vote stood. After 34 ballots, the vote totaled 312 for

---

* Two newspapers accused Garfield of only "acting" [*San Francisco Bulletin*] or "attitudinizing" [*New Orleans Times*] in raising his objection. A contemporary observer agreed, arguing that had Garfield "used his magnificent presence and stentorian voice" and "emphatically" declined, he would have prevailed. [James Ford Rhodes]. [See Clancy, 112-114.] Earlier that morning on the 29th ballot, Garfield had argued successfully that only a member of a state's delegation could challenge the correctness of that state's count, so he probably knew his own objection here would fail.

Grant; 275 for Blaine; 107 for Sherman; and 17 for James A. Garfield—the sixteen from Wisconsin plus the single vote from Pennsylvania that Garfield had been receiving steadily since the second ballot the day before.

The 35th ballot saw another shoe drop. When the clerk reached Indiana, Benjamin Harrison stood up and announced that his state was casting twenty-seven votes for Garfield, the bulk of them coming from the Blaine column. A few minutes later, four Maryland delegates cast their votes for Garfield. By the end of the roll call, Garfield's total had grown to 50.

Warner Batemen, sitting near Garfield in the Ohio delegation, seemed surprised by the turn of events. He scribbled a telegram to John Sherman back in Washington to ask instructions: "Wisconsin and Indiana have voted for Garfield with much enthusiasm. Our vote is restive—Garfield refuses to allow use of his name without effect," he wrote. "This is a new contingency. Give your views."[53]

In the growing chaos, someone handed Garfield a note marked "READ!" "You can make Blaine President- Don't stand longer," it said. Garfield must use his growing leverage immediately to throw the prize to Blaine. "If Grant is nominated You & Ohio will be responsible. Do yourself and the Rep[ublican] party an act of simple justice." It was signed by Stephens Elkins, a Blaine partisan from Maryland.[54] Whatever power Garfield may have had to work this miracle, though, was quickly slipping through his fingers.

Washington:

James G. Blaine remained closeted in the privacy of his own home in Washington, D.C. that Tuesday afternoon as he watched his second candidacy for the presidency of the United States unravel. By morning, he'd already seen his prospects dimming. He'd told a friend it was "scarcely necessary to have 'wasted a card upon a falling market,'" referring to his own chances."[55] Still, the thought of Ulysses Grant in a third term, or a Roscoe Conkling pawn in the White House, was unacceptable, and John Sherman, he felt, was no longer a viable choice. On the other hand, there was James Garfield. Garfield had been his friend and colleague for almost twenty years. James and Lucretia had been frequent houseguests of his and Harriet's.

If Blaine were going to be a vassal in someone else's administration, he could do far worse than Garfield—especially if he had placed Garfield in his debt by having won him the nomination with his votes. Blaine could work with Garfield, or maybe even control him.

Whether Blaine actually orchestrated the break to Garfield, or simply directed Chandler to give it a final push, such an outcome would suit him far better than most. Blaine took pen to paper and wrote a telegram to be delivered to Garfield, through Chandler, at the pivotal moment on the next ballot in Chicago: "Maine's vote this moment cast for you goes with my hearty concurrence. I hope it will aid in securing your nomination and assuring victory to the Republican party."[56]

For John Sherman, the stream of messages coming over his telegraph machine that day had been a roller-coaster: first the failure of the overnight summit with Blaine's managers in Chicago, then the switch to him of the Massachusetts delegates early that day. After that, the telegrams told him to hold steady. "You must see that your friends remain firm in all states. Personally direct this," wired one backer.[57] "Your friends here say: 'Hold the fort,'" wrote another.[58]

Now, suddenly, the picture had turned. He read the excited notes from Warner Bateman about the break to Garfield. From James Irwin he heard: "You cannot be nominated. Give your influence to Garfield and save the Republican Party."[59] Other messages carried a darker signal of betrayal. "If defeated, thank the ambition of Garfield, the defection of Foster, the cowardice of Bateman & the imbecility of the Ohio delegation."[60]

Sitting in his Treasury Department office, eyeing the White House itself next door through his office window, trying to follow events at a distance of a thousand miles, John Sherman understood that his future reputation could be colored by the dignity with which he bore his failure. He wrote a message to William Dennison and handed it to the telegraph operator to transmit to Chicago immediately: "Whenever the vote of Ohio will be likely to assure the nomination of Garfield, I appeal to every delegate to vote for him. Let Ohio be solid. Make the same appeal in my name to North Carolina, and every delegate who has voted for me."[61]

The newspaperman following Sherman through his day caught his reaction. As his hopes dimmed, the newsman noted, there "was possibly a slight disappointment visible upon Secretary Sherman's unyielding face."[62]

One report, widely repeated around Chicago, claimed that Sherman and Blaine actually had met face-to-face in Washington on Monday evening to resolve the Chicago deadlock. A reporter had seen Sherman leaving the Treasury Department, and his brother, General Tecumseh Sherman, lived in a house just a few doors up Fifteenth Street from Blaine's. The meeting, if it occurred at all, could not have gone well. Sherman had reportedly told people that "Blaine could have nominated him (Sherman) at any time he chose." And Blaine had reportedly been "incredulous" that Sherman, "who at the time had considerably less than 100 votes, should expect that Blaine with his 285 should surrender to him."[63] Afterward, having failed, the whole notion of a meeting between the two was flatly denied by all sides.[64]

Chicago:

As the clerk began calling the roll for the 36th ballot, Roscoe Conkling stood in the aisle, calmly telling his backers: "Keep steady, boys; Grant is going to win on this ballot."[65]

Within minutes, the logjam burst. Connecticut switched nine votes from Washburne to Garfield. A few minutes later, Benjamin Harrison, speaking in a "clear ringing voice,"[66] stood up on his chair and announced that Indiana had increased its tally for Garfield to 29 votes. Then Iowa moved all of its twenty-two votes to Garfield, from Blaine.

As the roll call continued and state after state flopped into his column, Garfield sought out Warner Bateman among the Ohio delegates. Garfield was "in much apparent emotion," Bateman recalled. He "protested in utmost earnestness that he had nothing to do with the movement," Bateman later reported. Garfield "said he would rather be shot to death by the inch than to have furnished any just ground for such suspicion and desired if I could that I should vindicate him against any charge of unfaithfulness…."[67]

By one account, John P. Jones, senator and delegate from Nevada, rushed up to Roscoe Conkling at about this point on the convention floor and urged him to stop the Garfield stampede. But how? Conkling had already directed allies in state after state—Maryland, Minnesota, Mississippi, South Carolina, Tennessee—to challenge their own state's tallies and demand name-by-name roll calls, just to slow things down. But it hadn't worked. Now Jones demanded a bolder stroke. Conkling must throw all of New York's seventy votes to James Blaine, his old rival. This would shock the convention, win Blaine the nomination, and prevent the presidency from going to a "dark horse." It would also put Blaine utterly in Conkling's debt. The idea must have made Conkling's skin crawl. He hesitated. He had no time to poll the delegation, he argued. "Cast the vote and poll the delegation afterward," Jones insisted. Conkling refused.[68]

In another moment, it was too late. The clerk called Maine, and Maine announced that all 14 of its votes had moved from Blaine to Garfield. Certainly, everyone in the convention hall knew, Maine would not have switched unless William Chandler had heard from Blaine himself that he supported the break. The magnetic man from Maine had thrown in the towel. The galleries interrupted the roll call by ten full minutes with yells, cheers, and songs.

Then, New York, at her turn, went fifty votes for Grant, twenty for Garfield.

As the balloting neared Ohio, the Ohio delegation seemed oddly surprised, caught off-guard, and unsure how to respond. They were seen standing huddled in "anxious, hurried consultation...."[69] Garfield still urged them to vote solid for John Sherman; others disagreed and were already cheering Garfield. Then, minutes before the clerk called their state, a messenger reached the Ohioans on the convention floor and handed Dennison the telegram from Sherman himself ceding his support to Garfield. Dennison read it out loud to the convention hall, prompting more rounds of shouts and applause.

Garfield continued to sit in his chair as delegates now crowded around him, shaking his hand, patting his shoulders. "Is there no place that I can go?" he asked a nearby friend. "My remaining here will interrupt business."[70] Meanwhile, the roll call reached Wisconsin. The clerk polled its delegates, and the state total—20 votes—put Garfield at 395, over the top for the nomination. Waves of wild applause flowed through the amphitheatre.

"They have nominated you," Nelson Sherwin, a fellow Ohio delegate, told Garfield. "Does it look so?" he answered. Garfield noticed a reporter from the Chicago Inter Ocean standing nearby and pulled him over. "I wish you would say [in your paper] that this is no act of mine," he told him. "I have done everything, and omitted nothing, to secure Secretary Sherman's nomination."[71] Garfield watched as delegates by the dozen now climbed over benches to surround him, be close to him, grab his hands, touch his shoulders, be nearby.

Warner Bateman scribbled out a new message to John Sherman at that moment: "The movement to Garfield swept with lightning rapidity through the Convention while I was writing the last telegram. It was the escape of a tired convention. He is nominated."[72]

A Kentucky delegate wearing a red Grant badge on his chest came up to Garfield and said: "General, we surrender; you have whipped us."

"You Grant men have made a splendid fight," Garfield told him.[73]

"Speech!" "Speech!" "Platform!" yelled voices from the crowd, waving him up toward the podium. Garfield waved them off. He sat "perfectly composed," according to James Henry. "No, no, gentlemen," he said, "this is no theatrical performance."[74]

"Different states have seized banners and gathered around Ohio where Garfield sits," reported a Western Union dispatch. "Cannons are being fired on the outside."[75] Said a reporter: "the entire convention centered around Garfield, and as each [cannon] salute was fired on the lake shore outside the roaring was taken up within. Garfield sat all this time immovable but pale and dazed."[76]

Surrounded by turmoil, Garfield sat as if in a stupor, apparently focusing enormous mental strength on trying to control an inchoate flood of emotions within. He looked "pale as death, and seemed to be half-unconsciously [sic] to receive the congratulations of his friends," noted the Inter Ocean reporter watching from close by.[77] Yet another newsman described his "rare modesty"[78] at the moment. Someone placed a few telegrams in his hand. "Sherwin," he said, looking for fellow Ohio delegate Nelson Sherwin, a long-time family friend, "won't you telegraph to my wife? She ought to know of this."[79]

"'Hurrah for Garfield' was cried by a thousand throats," reported another newsman. "The galleries took up the shout and later on the 10,000 people in the hall, led by the band, joined in singing the 'Battle Cry of Freedom.'"[80]

Roscoe Conkling sat bewildered at his seat in the New York delegation. He held his tongue as the celebration unfolded. Around him, as the convention hall resounded with cheers, his New York delegates sat conspicuously still, with "glum faces," and "making no effort to conceal their disappointment."[81] He heard Senator Hoar bang his gavel and announce: "James A. Garfield, of Ohio, is nominated for President of the United States." Still, Conkling had held all of his 306 votes for Ulysses Grant until the very end of the final ballot. His line had never broken.

It took Conkling several minutes to regain his composure. He stood and waved for recognition. Senator Hoar quieted the crowd enough to hear him. "I congratulate the Republican Party of the United States upon the good nature and the well-tempered rivalry which has distinguished this animated contest," Conkling announced.[82] He moved that Garfield's nomination be unanimous. But his voice, so strong just moments before, now betrayed him. Gone were the normal animation and flair. It sounded "funereal," noted one reporter, which "belied his nice words."[83] Some delegates called for Conkling to speak up; they couldn't hear him. "I would speak louder," Conkling insisted, "but, having for hours sat shivering under the cold wind of these open windows, I find myself unable to do so."[84] The cold, of course, hadn't bothered him up to this point. So too, the other Grant managers seemed to shrink away. One observer noted that: "Gen. [John] Logan was calm, but his dark face was darker than usual, and in Senator [Don] Cameron's gray eye the cold hard look was colder and harder."[85] Cameron, asked to give a speech, refused to answer to his name, pretending to be lost on the floor.

Conkling and his three hundred and six Grant delegates who had stuck together that day in Chicago through the final ballot would carry this fact as a badge of honor for the rest of their lives. They'd form a "Three Hundred and Six Guard" society, have annual dinners, and strike a commemorative gold coin, emblazoned "The Old Guard." For years to come, they'd reminisce (and bore their friends) over the glorious moment, repeating the details again and again with as much pride as any battle-line held during the bloodiest height of civil war. To have been one of the loyal "306" became an "insignia of the heroic," an ultimate bragging right among the Stalwart faction of the Republican party.[86]

Garfield, finally composed, ordered his own message to be sent to Lucretia back in Mentor, Ohio, on the farm: "Dear Wife. If the result meets your approval, I shall be content. Love to all the household. J.A. Garfield"[87]*

Washington:

On Capitol Hill in Washington, D.C., a large crowd gathered in the old Hall of Representatives in the Capitol Building as the latest Chicago bulletins streamed in over the telegraph. As the break for Garfield became certain, Republicans in the House of Representatives moved to adjourn the chamber for the day. Reaching the name of James A. Garfield in the roll call, they broke into a loud, sustained applause, matching cheers from the building corridors as news spread. They all cheered in public, though private feelings had split.

---

* The 36 ballots of 1880 stand as a record, the most ever cast to choose a Republican nominee for president, far more than the second and third-longest Republican face-offs: 10 ballots to choose Warren Harding in 1920 and 8 to nominate Benjamin Harrison in 1888. Five Democratic conventions have gone longer: 103 ballots to choose John Davis in 1924, 59 to nominate Stephen Douglas in 1860, 49 to pick Franklin Pierce in 1852, 46 to nominate Woodrow Wilson in 1912, and 44 to choose James Cox in 1920. Prior to 1936, Democratic conventions required a two-thirds majority to choose a nominee.

"The Grant men took the defeat of their candidate greatly to heart," noted a local news writer. "The Blaine and Sherman [forces] seemed almost as well satisfied as if their men had been chosen."[88]

Late that night, James Blaine, sitting in the library of his home on Fifteenth Street, sent a telegram to William Chandler in Chicago: "Thanks for everything that was done and so well done. I am more than satisfied. You have my sincere gratitude."[89]

At about the same time, John Sherman also sent a telegram to Chicago. "The nomination of Garfield is generally satisfactory," he told Warner Bateman.[90] Still, Sherman ached inside. Fifteen years later, writing his memoirs in 1895, Sherman would still harbor a grudge from this day. "It is probable that if I had received the united vote of the Ohio delegation I would have been nominated, as my relations with both General Grant and Mr. Blaine were of a friendly character, but it is hardly worthwhile to comment on what might have been."[91] For now, Sherman looked for a silver lining. To Bateman in Chicago he sent one more instruction: "Give us some first class man for Vice President."[92]

34th Ballot: Tuesday, June 8.

	Grant	Blaine	Sherman	Other
Ala.	16	4	–	–
Ariz.	–	2	–	–
Ark.	12	–	–	–
Calif.	–	12	–	–
Col.	6	–	–	–
Conn.	–	3	–	9
Del.	–	6	–	–
Fla.	8	–	–	–
Georgia	8	9	5	–
Idaho	–	2	–	–
Illinois	24	10	–	8
Ind.	2	20	2	6
Iowa	–	22	–	–
Kansas	4	6	–	–
Ky.	20	1	3	–
La.	8	4	4	–

Maine	–	14	–	–
Md.	7	2	7	–
Mass.	4	–	21	1
Mich.	1	21	–	–
Minn.	–	6	–	4
Miss.	8	4	3	1
Mo.	29	–	–	1
Mont.	–	2	–	–
Neb.	–	6	–	–
Nev.	–	6	–	–
N.H.	–	10	–	–
N. J.	–	14	2	2
N. Mex.	–	2	–	–
N. Y.	**50**	**18**	**2**	–
N. C.	6	–	14	–
Dak.	1	1	–	–
Ohio	–	**9**	**34**	**1**
Ore.	–	6	–	–
Penn.	**35**	**22**	–	**1** *
R. I.	–	8	–	–
S. C.	11	1	2	–
Tenn.	17	4	3	–
Tex.	13	1	1	1
Utah	1	1	–	–
Vt.	–	–	–	10
Va.	16	3	3	–
Wash.	–	2	–	–
W. Va.	1	8	1	–
Wis.	2	1	–	17*
Wyo.	1	1	–	–
D.C.	1	1	–	–
	312	275	107	62

Needed to win: 379 out of 756 total.

* For Garfield.

35th Ballot

	Grant	Blaine	Sherman	Garfield	Other
Ala.	16	–	–	–	–
Ariz.	–	2	–	–	–
Ark.	12	–	–	–	–
Calif.	–	12	–	–	–
Col.	6	–	–	–	–
Conn.	–	3	–	–	9
Del.	–	6	–	–	–
Fla.	8	–	–	–	–
Georgia	8	9	5	–	–
Idaho	–	2	–	–	–
Illinois	**24**	**10**	**–**	**–**	**8**
Ind.	1	2	–	27	–
Iowa	–	22	–	–	–
Kansas	4	6	–	–	–
Ky.	20	1	3	–	–
La.	8	4	4	–	–
Maine	–	14	–	–	–
Md.	7	3	2	4	–
Mass.	4	–	21	–	1
Mich.	1	21	–	–	–
Minn.	1	6	–	–	3
Miss.	8	4	3	1	–
Mo.	29	–	–	–	1
Mont.	–	2	–	–	–
Neb.	–	6	–	–	–
Nev.	–	6	–	–	–
N.H.	–	10	–	–	–
N. J.	–	14	2	–	2
N. Mex.	–	2	–	–	–
N. Y.	**50**	**18**	**2**	**–**	**–**
N. C.	6	–	13	1	–
Dak.	1	1	–	–	–
Ohio	**–**	**9**	**34**	**–**	**1**
Ore.	–	6	–	–	–

Penn.	36	20	–	1	1
R. I.	–	8	–	–	–
S. C.	11	1	2	–	–
Tenn.	17	4	3	–	
Tex.	13	1	1	–	1
Utah	1	1	–	–	
Vt.	–	–	–	–	10
Va.	16	3	3	–	–
Wash.	–	2	–	–	–
W. Va.	1	8	1	–	–
Wis.	2	2	–	16	–
Wyo.	1	1	–	–	–
D.C.	1	1	–	–	–
313	257	99	50	37	

Needed to win: 379 out of 756 total.

36th Ballot

	Grant	Blaine	Garfield	Other
Ala.	16	4	–	–
Ariz.	–	–	2	–
Ark.	12	–	–	–
Calif.	–	12	–	–
Col.	6	–	–	–
Conn.	–	1	11	–
Del.	–	6	–	–
Fla.	8	–	–	–
Georgia	8	10	1	3
Idaho	–	–	2	–
Illinois	24	6	7	5
Ind.	1	–	29	–
Iowa	–	–	22	–
Kansas	4	–	6	–
Ky.	20	1	3	–
La.	8	–	8	–
Maine	–	–	14	–
Md.	6	–	10	–

Mass.	4	–	22	–
Mich.	1	–	21	–
Minn.	2	–	8	–
Miss.	7	–	9	–
Mo.	29	–	1	–
Mont.	–	–	2	–
Neb.	–	–	6	–
Nev.	2	1	3	–
N.H.	–	–	10	–
N. J.	–	–	18	–
N. Mex.	–	–	2	–
N. Y.	**50**	–	20	–
N. C.	5	–	15	–
Dak.	–	–	2	–
Ohio	–	–	**43**	1
Ore.	–	–	6	–
Penn.	**37**	–	21	–
R. I.	–	–	8	–
S. C.	8	–	6	–
Tenn.	15	1	8	–
Tex.	13	–	3	–
Utah	–	–	2	–
Vt.	–	–	10	–
Va.	19	–	3	–
Wash.	–	–	2	–
W. Va.	1	–	9	–
Wis.	–	–	20	–
Wyo.	–	–	2	–
D.C.	–	–	2	–
	306	**42**	**399**	**9**

Needed to win: 379 out of 756 total.

Galena, Illinois:

General Grant heard the news of Garfield's nomination at Colonel Rowley's office over the telegraph. At the turn of events, according to a newsman with him, Grant "said it was all right; he was satisfied, and soon after he left for home."*

A few days later, *Puck* magazine would run a Joseph Keppler cartoon called "The Appomattox of the Third Termers." It would show a humbled Ulysses Grant handing his sword in surrender to an erect James Garfield standing before a "Fort Alliance" garrisoned by reformers, the Senate Bosses bowing prostrate on the ground. The *Puck* cartoon would ridicule the holiest moment of the Stalwart iconology: Ulysses Grant as national savior.

Grant himself would never comment on the satire. But his followers certainly took notice.

---

* After General Grant failed to win his third term, the custom of denial of service beyond two terms became even more deeply entrenched into American politics, and would not be breached until Franklin Delano Roosevelt sought and won a third term in 1940, then a fourth in 1944. The two-term limit would then be written into the Constitution by the 22nd amendment in 1951.

• 6 •

COMPROMISE

Tuesday, June 8, 1880
Chicago, Illinois

MINUTES AFTER IT HAD NOMINATED the surprise "dark horse" candidate James A. Garfield to be President of the United States, the clamor and celebrations ringing from 15,000 voices in the great hall, the convention recessed until later in the day.

Garfield, still in virtual shock, followed as his Ohio friends led him off the convention floor and out from the Exposition Building into the sunlight on Michigan Avenue. Here, a huge crowd gathered instantly on the nearby sidewalk, women and men pushing forward, trying to glimpse, touch, or shake hands with the sudden celebrity. Above the loud voices, Garfield could still hear cannon booming over Lake Michigan and sniff the acrid gunpowder floating in the air. Blue-coated Chicago police helped push him though the human sea toward a horse-drawn carriage waiting by the curb. He climbed up, turned and waved to the crowd. They cheered and waved hats and handkerchiefs in the air. Then he ducked inside, Governor Foster following. "Take off the horses," someone shouted, "we will pull the carriage." The carriage car shook as the mob surrounded it and men started to unhitch the harnesses. The driver, unaware at first whom he had inside, whipped the horses to escape, making the carriage lurch forward a few feet until the mob circled them again. Then the driver whipped his horses still harder; they whinnied, kicked their forelegs, and jolted away. Once free, he raced them forward, the carriage bumping along over the cobblestone streets of Chicago.[1]

Shaken from the ride, Garfield reached the Grand Pacific Hotel and here too faced a sea of faces. A glee club met him in the lobby with a serenade, joined in by an "immense throng" of well-wishers. Upstairs, his suite crawled with delegates, newsmen, and assorted hangers-on. He barely sat down before confronting a flood of telegrams—six hundred strong arriving within a few hours—from politicians, senators, heads-of-state, and lifelong friends. Rutherford Hayes in the White House, Blaine, Sherman, and Interior Secretary Carl Schurz, all sent regards. A reporter watched as Garfield "completely broke down" on reading a message from James and Harry, his two teenage sons away at boarding school in New Hampshire. "The nervous strain upon [Garfield] since yesterday has been terrible," the reporter noted.[2]

William Chandler and Eugene Hale from the Blaine camp arrived among the first to congratulate him, eagerly taking credit for delivering their votes on the convention floor to win Garfield his prize.

As telegraph wires flashed word across the country, celebrations erupted for the surprise nominee. Cannon fired into San Francisco Bay and a salute of 100 guns was fired at New York's City Hall Park. Shouts rang in streets of small Ohio towns and local Republican clubs fired volleys of rifle shots in the air. Artillery, bonfires, torch-light parades, and "jollifications"[3] continued into the night from Key West, Florida, to Michigan to California. Street hawkers on Michigan Avenue within an hour began selling bright-colored chest badges made of crimson ribbons with gold letters saying "For President, James A. Garfield, of Ohio." Delegates snapped them up by the hundreds. Newspaper offices demanded biographies, photographs, and artist sketches of the candidate for their next editions.

Garfield himself, at the center of the storm, had little time to absorb the shock. Suddenly as presidential candidate, he faced decisions. In barely three hours, the convention would reconvene to pick a vice president. Garfield had had no time to develop a plan. Not everyone in the convention hall had cheered his good fortune when lightning had struck for him that morning; plenty of Grant delegates had walked away angry. Of the Stalwart "triumvirate," only John Logan was willing to show outward support. He had mounted a large banner in his hotel suite saying: "Illinois 25,000 majority for Garfield."[4] Unless the Grant men could be won back, they could torpedo any hope Garfield had for November. Losing New York alone, with its 35 electoral votes, could wreck his campaign, and Garfield stood no chance against the New York Democrats' Tammany Hall machine without Roscoe Conkling's own organization behind him. Since the nomination that morning, grumbling from New Yorkers had grown loud. They "felt very ugly" over their defeat and "threaten[ed] all sorts of disasters" should the convention "pile insults" on them, a *New York Tribune* reporter wrote.[5]

With no organization, no hierarchy, no chief manager, Garfield's campaign invited confusion. Forced to pick a New York running mate, Garfield himself had a clear favorite: Levi P. Morton, respected financier, founder of Wall Street's Morton, Bliss, and Company,* a member of Congress since 1879, friendly both with Conkling and himself. In fact, Garfield had had the presence of mind to send Foster to grab Morton on the spot at the convention floor and make the offer then and there. But Levi Morton had already seen the hostile reactions of his New York neighbors, and may have also heard Roscoe Conkling telling people "I hope no sincere friend of mine will accept it."[6]

Morton would need to check first with his "associates" before giving Garfield an answer, he said.[7]

Meanwhile, old William Dennison had also taken matters into his own hands. Apparently without bothering to check first with the candidate, Dennison, as Ohio delegation chairman, had gone directly to Roscoe Conkling on the convention floor and offered the vice presidency to whomever New York picked. Ohio, he said, would support them. Conkling agreed to call his delegation together to consider the offer.

Word of these Ohio overtures to New York quickly reached the Blaine camp, and they were furious. Garfield, after all, had won the nomination with Blaine's votes—none of the 306 Grant men had backed him. By one account, Chandler and Eugene Hale were with Garfield in his suite at the Grand Pacific Hotel when Dennison blurted out that he'd offered the prize to Conkling. "The friends of Mr. Blaine, who furnished the bulk of the vote for Mr. Garfield, might desire to be considered," Hale supposedly had said in a huff, and they both left abruptly.[8] Congressman William Frye, whom Maine had considered putting up for the vice presidency, was heard exchanging "strong words" and accusing the Ohio delegates of "bad faith."[9]

Most angry of all were the New York bolters who had put their necks on the line to oppose Roscoe Conkling and make Garfield's nomination possible. "It was [William] Robertson who engineered the break for Garfield," John

---

* Morton, Bliss, & Company, a titan of its day, would later be merged into the J.P. Morgan empire.

Birdsall vented to a reporter. "We thought that Robertson ought to have been the man." On hearing about the New York offer, they immediately sent James Husted, one of the bolters, over to Garfield's hotel suite to demand terms.[10]

Levi Morton, meanwhile, had tracked down Roscoe Conkling, apparently still on the convention floor, and asked his advice on taking the vice presidency: "If you think the ticket will be elected; if you think you will be happy in the association, accept," Conkling reportedly told him.[11]

But Morton insisted on more than this lukewarm response. "I have more confidence in your judgment than in my own," he pressed.

"George Boutwell of Massachusetts is a great friend of yours," Conkling said. "Why don't you ask him?" Levi Morton recognized the cold shoulder for what it was and Boutwell gave him the same message. Word soon came back to Garfield that Levi Morton wanted no place on the ticket.

Having recovered from their initial celebrating, the full Ohio delegation now met formally in their Grand Pacific Hotel suite to consider how they might untangle the web. They decided to send their chairman, Dennison, officially to walk over to the New York delegation—soon to meet just down the hall in the Grand Pacific—and tell them that "Ohio would be glad to promise her cordial support to any nomination that might be submitted" by them.[12]

Word spread quickly through the New York delegation about the Ohio offer. Ears perked up; several were interested, including Chester Alan Arthur.

Whether Arthur came up with the idea first, or someone else whispered it in his ear, he seized on it quickly. He confided in some friends, including New York Police Commissioner Stephen French, and French mentioned it to Tom Murphy, an experienced, street-smart New York political fixer who had preceded Arthur at the New York Custom House in the early 1870s. "Murphy, we can get Arthur that nomination and he wants it," French told him. Murphy and French together jumped into a carriage and rushed to the Grand Pacific hotel to buttonhole New York delegates on Arthur's behalf.*[13]

Meanwhile, Arthur sought out his mentor, Roscoe Conkling.

Conkling, after the public convention session had ended, needed privacy. His head was still spinning over his stunning defeat. He had stormed off and

---

* Murphy described his own role in the affair to a reporter in August 1883, with Arthur in the White House, to explain why "I don't want to brag, but in my opinion Arthur would never have been President but for my exertions."

taken refuge in a back room of the Exposition Building, behind the podium, that newspapermen used for quiet talks. The room was deserted except for a few desks and chairs and a single reporter sitting in a corner. Conkling ignored the man, or perhaps didn't see him, though the reporter instantly recognized the New York Senator.* He held his tongue as Conkling, looking "perturbed," paced about the room, "gesticulating vigorously" and occasionally "muttering aloud," as he walked back and forth around the empty chairs. Then, after a few minutes, the door opened again and Chet Arthur entered— he too either ignoring or not seeing the newsman. "I have been hunting for you everywhere," Arthur said.[14] The two large men stood facing each other, just a few feet apart.

"Well, sir?" Conkling asked him.

"The Ohio men have offered me the Vice Presidency," Arthur said after a moment.

"Well, sir, you should drop it as you would a red hot shoe from the forge."

Arthur's face hardened. For any other person, Conkling's flip response would have ended the conversation. But Arthur stood his ground. "I sought you to consult, not—"

"What is there to consult about," Conkling said, raising his voice, cutting him off. "The trickster of Mentor will be defeated before the country."

"There is something else to be said," Arthur told him.

"What, sir, you thinking of accepting?"

Arthur hesitated, then, in a rare show of personal feelings, he put his cards on the table: "The office of the Vice President is a greater honor than I ever dreamed of attaining. A barren nomination would be a great honor. In a calmer moment you will look at this differently."

"If you wish for my favor and my respect you will contemptuously decline it," Conkling repeated.

Arthur looked the Boss directly in the eye. "Senator Conkling, I shall accept the nomination and I shall carry with me the majority of the delegates."

Roscoe Conkling stormed off, leaving the room through a far door. Arthur watched him for a moment, then walked off in the other direction.

---

* It is fortunate for posterity that Roscoe Conkling missed William Hudson, reporter for the *Brooklyn Daily Eagle*, who recorded the incident in the room that night and published his account thirty-one years later.

Conkling now rode a carriage over to the Grand Pacific Hotel, apparently unsure what to do. Reaching his suite a few moments before the New York delegation was to meet, he sent for Tom Murphy, who had already been working the room for Arthur. "Mr. Murphy, what is the meaning of this talk about General Arthur for Vice President?" he demanded. "Are you in favor of it?"[15] Murphy said he was. Now Conkling, according to Murphy's later account, confided his own split feelings on the matter. He had "a deep love for Arthur," but he'd wanted to make Arthur a senator, and feared that the whole arrangement was designed to weaken his machine. Still, "Arthur was Conkling's favorite to be his colleague and companion. He liked Arthur's company" better than anyone else's. By the time they'd finished talking, Conkling had softened.[16] Conkling would not support Arthur's bid for the vice presidency outright—he gave no nominating or seconding speech for Arthur at the convention—but he wouldn't raise a fuss over it either.

Fewer than fifty of the seventy New York delegates showed up for the caucus. Notably missing were the nineteen bolters—probably because no one had bothered to invite them. Conkling came and gaveled the meeting to order, but left after a few minutes. He wanted no fingerprints on this decision. Besides, by then, the fix was in for Chester Alan Arthur.

After a few minutes, someone led William Dennison and Governor Foster into the room, and they confirmed Ohio's offer of "substantial support" of New York's choice for second spot on the ticket under Garfield. Then they ushered the Ohioans out.[17] In the hallway, Dennison, embarrassed, explained to Roscoe Conkling that he couldn't guarantee every single Ohio vote in the deal as he'd promised earlier. "Sir, I am not surprised at anything from Ohio," Conkling snapped back.[18]

Once in private, Levi Morton told the New York delegates not to consider his own name for the vice presidency. One of them suggested Stewart Woodford, but to little interest. Lewis Payn then moved to select Chester A. Arthur, their fine state committee chairman and a fine man overall. Henry Pierson seconded the idea, Pierre Van Wyck called Arthur a "gentleman of integrity" and "unquestionable faithfulness," and Edwards Pierrepont added a glowing recommendation.[19] After half an hour, they didn't even bother to vote. Chet Arthur was their man.

Tom Murphy now led a delegation of New Yorkers back down the hall to Dennison and Foster to present their choice. As the Ohioans heard the news, their faces reddened. What about the Custom House scandals? and Arthur's removal? Newspapers would make a "rumpus"; they'd lose votes. "Gentlemen, if that is what you have to say, New York doesn't want the Vice Presidency," Tom Murphy told them.[20] Take it or leave it. Garfield's friends took it. No one had time to ask Garfield himself for his opinion on the matter; they'd simply tell him later.

When the convention reconvened in the Glass Palace at about five that afternoon, half the gallery seats were empty. A vocal quartet, the Lombard Group, serenaded the hall as delegates floated casually in and out. By now, the excitement over, many had already left their hotels, jammed the railway depots, and were streaming out of Chicago toward home. Workmen had decorated the podium with a huge floral ship resting on a sea of red, pink, and yellow flowers, its rigging made of green vines, and the name "Garfield" written in crimson blossoms—matching the crimson Garfield badges on the delegates' shirts and coats—but few took the time to notice.

The delegates needed only one ballot to seal the bargain for Arthur. Three other names were presented: Elihu Washburne of Illinois, Marshall Jewell of Connecticut, and Senator Blanche Bruce of Mississippi. Bruce, the freed black slave who'd made money as a Mississippi planter and risen through state politics under Reconstruction, had backing from the Negro National Republican Committee and would be the first black American to receive votes at a national political convention to be on a national ticket.

Those delegates who opposed Arthur's nomination as being a sop to Roscoe Conkling swallowed their pride. Fatigue had set in. They wanted the process done "in the greatest possible haste," reported the *New York Tribune*, and it would "take less time... by letting Mr. Conkling have his own way than by opposing him"[21]—ironic since Conkling himself actually had urged Arthur to reject the position. William Dennison eliminated any drama when he mounted the convention podium and seconded Arthur's nomination, pledging all the Ohio votes behind him. A.O. Campbell, the West Virginia dissident, stood almost isolated in even doubting the deed. "Let us not do a rash thing," he urged the delegates. He pointed to the party platform's plank on civil service reform, of which Chester Arthur's very history made a mockery. "Let us not stultify ourselves before the country," he argued.[22]

But nobody listened. The clerk called the roll and Arthur received 468 votes, next to 288 for all the rest combined, including eight for Blanche Bruce. All seventy New York votes went for Arthur—including the former bolters. Then, at 7:25 pm, Senator Hoar banged his gavel and declared the Republican National Convention, the longest ever, adjourned.*

⊚ ⊚ ⊚ ⊚ ⊚

James Garfield hardly knew Chester Arthur personally in June 1880. Now, at 11 o'clock on Tuesday night, Garfield and Arthur stood side by side in the Club Room of the Grand Pacific Hotel, two exhausted men, probably not yet appreciating the enormous political triumph each had achieved that day. Hours after the convention had ended, they stepped up onto an elevated plat-form and shook hands, their eyes wincing at the calcium lights. The roomful of newsmen, dignitaries, and delegates applauded. Senator George Hoar, tall and distinguished, joined them on the platform. As convention chairman, he had the honor to present Garfield and Arthur with formal ceremonial no-tification of the day's decisions. The convention had greeted their nomina-tions with a "unanimity of pleasure," Hoar told the candidates and support-ers; every state had offered its "cordial support" in the November election. Garfield, his voice raw from long days of talking, thanked Hoar for his "as-surances of confidence and esteem and unity." He accepted the nomination as a "grave responsibility" and great "gratification." Chester Arthur too prom-ised to "discharge my duties faithfully and conscientiously."[23]

The whole ceremony didn't last more than a few minutes. They heard more applause; the men lit cigars, drank their liquor, and shared a few last laughs with friends before heading off home. Garfield and Arthur, the can-didates, shook dozens and dozens of hands—so "heartily," Arthur said later, "that they dislocated one of my fingers."**[24] They probably didn't speak much with each other before collapsing in their rooms. By then, most of the dele-gates had left Chicago behind. A grateful city noted how "half the wild half-drunken mobs have left the hotels," noted a reporter, and the streets seemed "almost deserted."[25]

Beneath the fanfare, most people seemed to accept the political equa-tion: Whatever harm Garfield might suffer from hitching his star to Roscoe

---

* Nineteenth Century political conventions did not include a presidential nominee's acceptance speech to the delegates. Instead, candidates accepted their nominations by letter sent later and printed in all the newspapers—a much better way to transmit their views to the country in the days before television and radio. The convention itself was still considered a working session, not show biz.

** The finger, Arthur explained, was one on which he wore a ring, and the ring had to be cut off.

Conkling's wagon, he would be more than compensated for by New York's help in November. Even William Chandler finally agreed. "Arthur is able," he wrote to Warner Bateman a few weeks later "and the concession, if one was to be made… was the best one."[26]

As for the New York bolters, Garfield had come to terms with them too. They'd been horrified at first over Chet Arthur's place on the ticket. Sitting on the convention floor that afternoon, several had heard cat-calls from the Stalwarts: "Robertson and Woodin have got a good spanking," a few chuck-led."[27] But they knew who would have the last laugh. "We made our kick and pledges have been made," John Birdsall told the *Brooklyn Eagle*. After the election, William Robertson, their leader, would get "a big place in the Cabinet or something as good."[28]

What had Garfield promised, and to whom, if anyone? No comment for now.

Not everyone was happy. Garfield didn't have to wait long to hear from John Sherman. "The nomination of Arthur is a ridiculous burlesque, inspired by a desire to defeat the ticket," Sherman thundered from Washington in a letter to Warner Bateman. "He never held an office except the one he was re-moved from." Arthur brought "all the odiom of machine politics," and his selection was a "blunder," inexcusable "even in the heat and hurry of the clos-ing scenes." Still, Sherman said he would "keep quiet about it…"[29] [30]

Besides, it just didn't seem to matter. E.L. Godkin, writing in *The Nation*, even saw a bright side: "[T]here is no place in which the powers of mischief will be so small as in the vice presidency," he editorialized. As for the risk, "It is true General Garfield, if elected, may die during his term of office, but this is too unlikely a contingency to be worth making extraordinary provision for."

What Garfield, Arthur, and *The Nation* could not have known in June 1880 was that the choice of Arthur—the strange marriage of Garfield to Roscoe Conkling's Stalwart machine—would ultimately bring to bear on them the influence of an odd little man then living in Boston, Massachu-setts.

· 7 ·
CHANCE
OF A LIFETIME

Tuesday, June 8, 1880
Boston, Massachusetts

CHARLES GUITEAU[1] SAW THE HEADLINES in the afternoon extra editions of the *Boston Globe* and *Boston Post*. He heard the shouting in the street near the telegraph offices, heard the guns being fired by the Charles River. He, like everyone else in Boston and across America, had been swept up for days in the nomination drama from Chicago. Always interested in politics, Guiteau had not felt this excited over a presidential race in years. An early Grant supporter, he now shared the popular fervor for the surprise candidate James Garfield—a fresh face to many Americans outside the Midwest, but reassuring with his long Washington experience and sound Republican views.

Guiteau felt touched in a special way. This political contest, he decided, could change his life.

Guiteau, just three months shy of 39 years, slender, with an odd cat-like walk and confidential manner, had lived in Boston for three years. He sold insurance to make a few dollars, but not well. "I didn't have any success in doing business. Boston is a very stupid place for life insurance, I should say," he later explained.[2] Short of money, he wore old clothes and often looked shabby. Mostly, he indulged his religious bent. He gave an occasional speech, and sold religious tracts, including one he wrote and self-published called *The Truth, A Companion to the Bible*. Born in Freeport, Illinois, the fourth of six children of whom only three survived to adulthood, Guiteau had already lived in Chicago, Oneida, New York, and New York City, been married and divorced, become a preacher, lawyer, and debt collector, but never stuck with any job, and concocted business schemes that never came together. His father, Luther Guiteau, of Huguenot background, had raised Charles under strict religious tenets of good and evil. In the 1840s, Luther had adopted the theology of John Humphrey Noyes, founder of the utopian Oneida Community in upstate New York, known for "free love," shared labor, and mutual criticism. Luther had died earlier in 1880; Charles' mother had died in 1848 when he was just seven years old.

During the 1860s, Charles himself had gone to live in the Oneida commune, but fit in poorly. The girls shunned him, even in this haven of "free love"; he became moody and complained about doing menial work in the kitchen or factory. He left on bad terms and later even sued the Oneida group for back pay. He developed schemes to start at least two new newspapers, but never secured financial backers. His marriage to Annie Bunn, who had worked as a YMCA librarian in Chicago when he met her, lasted just five years. She grew tired of his short temper, constant lack of money, hiding from bill collectors, and fleeing apartments for lack of rent. He beat her, punched and kicked her, when she disagreed with him, and sometimes for no apparent reason at all. Finally, in 1874, Guiteau purposely slept with a prostitute in New York, where they'd moved after Chicago's Great Fire, to have legal grounds for a New York divorce.

To Charles Guiteau in June 1880, politics seemed much more interesting than selling insurance or religious tracts in Boston—a place where he had few friends and no roots. He'd already taken down notes for a political speech for Ulysses Grant; he could easily edit them to fit James Garfield. "As soon as General Garfield was nominated I decided I would go to New York and offer my services to the National [Republican] Committee and take an active part in his election," he explained later at his criminal trial for murder, "and I left [for] New York, I think, the 11th of June."[3]

Guiteau remembered the date well. June 11 was a Friday, just three days after Garfield's nomination. That night, Guiteau left from Boston on the overnight steamer *Stonington*[4] with about 300 other passengers. He couldn't sleep. Near midnight, far out over the water, he walked out on deck. The night was "black and dark as tar," he recalled. "You couldn't see an inch before your face."[5] Fog had blanketed Long Island Sound. The ship had just passed the Cornfield Lightship, moored about five miles south of the Connecticut shore. Guiteau heard whistles in the darkness; the *Stonington* was blowing its fog horn every half-minute as it groped blindly forward. Then another ship—the *Narragansett*—appeared directly in their path. After that, everything turned ugly.

The *Stonington* hit the *Narragansett* with such jarring force as to rip gaping holes in both ships. The impact threw passengers from their berths onto metal floors. Water flooded the *Narragansett's* hull, cabins, and passageways. It sank within minutes. Lights flickered out, plunging the *Narragansett* into fearful darkness and its 350 passengers into panic. Boilers exploded, sending plumes of hot steam whipping through the hulk. Then, as over a hundred screaming women and men climbed up onto its highest decks for safety, the *Narragansett* burst into flames. Many who threw themselves into the cold water died of hypothermia; others were burned alive. Meanwhile, on the *Stonington*, its own hull gashed above the waterline, passengers waited for hours, clinging to life preservers in case the crippled steamer capsized or sank. Finally, they were transferred to another vessel.

The awful disaster at sea that night pushed politics off the newspaper front pages for days. Almost 80 passengers were feared dead. For weeks, divers descended into the murky depths and recovered bloated, decomposing bodies.

Charles Guiteau survived the disaster, and marveled that his own life had been spared. "I saw and heard the wailing of the poor people who were in [the *Narragansett*]," he recalled, "but we were utterly powerless to do anything."[6] He reached New York City the next afternoon and found a room to board in. Then he began work on his political speech for James A. Garfield.

Eighteen months later, in December 1881, on trial for his life, pleading insanity, claiming in his defense that God had made him His instrument and directed his actions, Charles Guiteau would point back to his deliverance on the high seas that night of the great marine disaster of the *Stonington*. It was an early sign, he would say. God had important plans for him. He had saved his life for a purpose.

• PART II •

Candidate

● ● ● ● ●

*After Republicans had nominated Garfield and Arthur, Democrats
held their own national convention in Cincinnati, Ohio, and chose
a Union General, Winfield Scott Hancock, hero of Gettysburg,
to carry their White House banner in 1880. For vice president,
they chose William English, former congressman from Indiana.
Hancock could count on a united party, a solid South, and
New York's Tammany Hall to help lead him to victory.*

*By contrast, Republicans stood badly divided. Stalwarts who
had backed Ulysses Grant in Chicago nursed bruised egos and
distrusted Garfield, the nominee, despite the presence of Chester
Alan Arthur on the ticket. Garfield needed to heal this breach,
or he faced certain defeat. But by trying to appease Stalwarts,
he risked offending Half-Breed moderates, or being forced into
a humiliating bargain with the eastern Bosses.*

*A third party, the Greenback, advocating free coinage of
silver, an eight-hour work day, and more homesteads for farmers,
nominated Iowa Congressman James B. Weaver.*

THE BARGAIN

ULYSSES AND JULIA GRANT reached Chicago at 6:30 am on Wednesday morning, June 9, 1880, just hours after the Republican convention had adjourned. Their son, Colonel Fred Grant, met them at the depot and escorted them by private carriage to State Street. Here, he ushered them across the deserted sidewalk into the Palmer House through a side door. Grant walked past decorations—floral and bunting arrangements, bandstands, bright-colored portraits—set up to celebrate his own nomination for the presidency that had never come. An usher led Julia and Ulysses Grant into a private salon and closed the doors. Waiting to meet them here were John Logan, Don Cameron, Emory Storrs, and a dozen other die-hard supporters.

Despite every effort to keep the meeting secret, word soon leaked that Ulysses Grant had entered the hotel. A crowd of gawkers and well-wishers jammed the lobby. At Grant's insistence, the hotel staff moved his party into a more secluded room and locked the doors. After an hour or so, one newspaper man, from the Chicago *Inter Ocean*, managed to slip inside as waiters cleared away breakfast dishes. The newsman found Ulysses Grant standing in the center of "an admiring group," shaking hands, trading small talk, his Japanese valet at his side. Julia stood across the room amid a circle of wives including Mary Logan and Elizabeth Cameron, "smiling, unruffled, affable."[1]

Chicago had prospered during the two-week Republican convention. The Palmer House and Grand Pacific hotels each boasted at having housed over 2,000 guests. The Palmer House had set up 600 extra beds beyond its 800 rooms and had raked in $9,500, or about $1,050 each day just from bar tabs. That amounted to tens of thousands of whiskies and brandies—"a sad commentary upon the work of the political evangelists," remarked one observer. The hotel had employed 200 extra waiters during the affair; its restaurant had served over 3,000 people on the final Tuesday alone, feeding them 4,000 pounds of meat and 4,000 barrels of flour for pastry in a single day.[2]

Whatever disappointment Grant felt over losing his third presidential bid, he concealed that morning behind his "immobile features." As the circle of friends dwindled, he sat down with his handful of chief political managers and the conversation turned pointed. Logan and Cameron, voices hoarse from days of shouting, eyes red from lack of sleep, struggled to keep a positive tone facing Grant for the first time since their defeat. They'd been stung by public criticism—claims that they'd bungled Grant's nomination and "misled" him into "an unfortunate struggle" that "left by himself, he would never have entered."[3] Roscoe Conkling stayed away from the breakfast altogether, perhaps embarrassed to face the General so soon after their failure.

Cameron and Logan, squirming under Grant's steady gaze and Julia's pouting lips, launched into a diatribe against the Blaine and Sherman leaders they'd battled all week, blasting their underhanded tactics, the reporter noted, especially in "overriding state instructions" over the unit rule. The country had "sent a Convention here instructed to nominate [Grant]," they complained, but their opponents had ignored it. They made no effort to hide their tough talk from the *Inter Ocean* newsman, who scribbled notes before their eyes.

Grant listened to the griping but held his tongue, "careful not to express any opinion," the reporter wrote.[4] After a few more minutes, Colonel Fred Grant pulled his father away from the circle and toward the door. Grant had to catch a train to Wisconsin for a long-scheduled reunion of civil war veterans, he said. After a final round of handshakes, Grant left by another side door. Taking back hallways to avoid the crowds, he noticed a reporter from the *New York Times* chasing after them. He stopped to talk, reverting to his stoic persona. Grant was "not at all displeased" with the convention's choice, he told the newsman, and appreciated "the friendship of the 300 true men" who had stood by him on the final ballots.[5] Then the Grants hurried on to their carriage waiting outside in the street.

But Cameron and Logan weren't finished. Grant would be "nominated without question in 1884," they now told the *Inter Ocean* reporter as they lingered with him in the breakfast salon. "Garfield will be beaten" in 1880, they boasted; that was their "confident expectation." Grant "no more doubts his election to the presidency [in 1884] if he lives than he doubted his conquest of Richmond when his lines retreated in bloody confusion from Cold Harbor."*[6] It was nothing against their friend Chet Arthur, the vice presidential nominee. Arthur would still become a United States senator next year, they claimed.

From the Palmer House, Ulysses Grant headed his carriage directly back to the railway depot to catch his train to Wisconsin. Before leaving downtown Chicago, he made no effort to visit James Garfield, just three blocks away at the Grand Pacific. In fact, Grant never sent Garfield any congratulations at all: no telegram, no letter, no private message. Instead, the next day, speaking to a crowd of "old soldiers" at the Grand Army Reunion in Milwaukee under a sun-drenched sky, soaking in the adulation of his former troops, Grant would mention his recent White House candidacy only briefly. He was "grateful" to the friends who'd stood by him in Chicago, he'd tell them, and particularly Senator Roscoe Conkling, their leader, whom he'd say "should have been nominated" for the presidency in his place.[7] It was a nice gesture of friendship of Conkling, but an odd slap at the actual nominee, Garfield.

From Milwaukee, Grant traveled west. For the next two months, he tried to disappear from public sight. In Kansas, he hunted and rode horses on the wild frontier. Then he rode out to Manitou Springs, Colorado, to inspect mining properties. As weeks went by, people couldn't help but notice Grant's public silence on the presidential election, "so prolonged that many believed he intended to support [Democratic nominee Winfield Scott] Hancock," noted Adam Badeau.[8] Privately, alone with Julia and a few close friends, Grant apparently vented his real anger at the debacle in Chicago. One enterprising newsman tracked down Grant's Kansas host, army friend L.G. Entwright, and pumped him for some of the grumbling. Grant said he'd been "led to believe that his nomination was ... probable; in fact he rather expected it," Entwright told the newsman. His advisors had "greatly exaggerated" his chances, and Grant "could not conceal his disgust for Conkling, Logan , and others who had so recklessly miscalculated and overestimated his strength."[9]

"My friends have not been honest with me," a biographer quoted Grant

---

* Cold Harbor, the devastating Virginia bloodbath where Grant lost almost 10,000 troops in a fruitless 1864 assault, was probably not the best comparison to use. In his memoirs a few years later, Grant would admit "always regret[ing] the last assault on Cold Harbor" as "no advantage whatever was gained to compensate for the heavy loss we sustained."

as telling his private circle. "I can't afford to be defeated. They should not have placed me in nomination unless they felt sure of my success."[10] Toward Garfield, Grant's few off-hand remarks cut a fine wound. Garfield, Grant supposedly told Entwright, "had rather too many volumes of Congressional debates behind him to make a smooth and successful canvass on."[11] Garfield had talked too much over the years; his record gave too much ammunition to an opponent.

Grant would take many, many weeks to stew over his bad feelings from Chicago. From Milwaukee, he sent Roscoe Conkling a note thanking him for his effort. "Individually, I am much relieved at the result, having grown weary of constant abuse," he wrote, "always disagreeable, and doubly so when it comes from former professed friends."[12] Julia would take longer. Invited by James and Lucretia Garfield to visit their Mentor, Ohio farm months later, in September, after returning from their trip, Julia still refused. "The General went," she explained tersely. "But I would not go."[13]

❦ ❦ ❦ ❦ ❦

Awaking on Wednesday morning, June 9, James Garfield found himself in a new world. He was now the center of attention to a degree he'd never imagined. He was the name in every headline, the point of every comment, the topic of every conversation. He noticed peoples' eyes on him, their new solicitous attitude toward him. His hotel suite at the Grand Pacific bustled with callers, telegrams, messengers, and urgent requests. For the next five months, from now until November, he knew, enemies and friends would study his every word, every gesture, every idea or opinion. Total strangers would love him, hate him, and ridicule him. They would always be watching. Newspapers would follow his every step. Opponents would scour his past for secrets and pump his friends for any stories to make him look foolish.

Garfield had lived on the public stage before as a congressman, but this felt far different, like being a captive. And it was too late to complain. Congratulations, the callers all said. Garfield had awoken as the Republican Party's nominee for President of the United States.

As the shock wore off, Garfield had to appreciate the friendly tone of most reactions. "He is one of the ablest men in the country, and he represents the liberal and progressive wing of the party," crowed the Boston Herald.[14] And, "next to Senator Blaine, Garfield [is] the most popular man in Washington," a Congressional colleague said.[15] The Chicago Tribune called him "a balm for all the wounds received in the six days of strife," a man who "owe[d] his nomination to no intrigues or combinations, no partnership or affiliation with syndicates or bosses."[16] The *Cincinnati Commercial* hailed him "a happy solution" to the deadlocked convention.[17]

But he heard a negative drumbeat starting as well. Democratic newspapers wasted no time to attack him on two old scandals: Credit Mobilier* and DeGolyer pavement.** Ironically, the *Boston Globe* connected Garfield with "Grantism"—despite Garfield's having defeated General Grant for the nomination—and "the worst and most venal scandals of that scandalous regime."[18] Even some friends grumbled privately about Garfield's fitness for the White House. "Garfield [is] good, glorious, and yet—It is an escape," Massachusetts Senator Henry Dawes wrote to his wife from Washington. "Garfield is a grand, noble fellow, but fickle, unstable, [with] more brains, but no such will as Sherman, brilliant like Blaine, but timid and hesitating." Still, Dawes said, "It has saved us from the third term and its jackalls."[19]

From the moment Garfield left his room in the Grand Pacific Hotel that morning, friends, music, and celebration followed him everywhere. The convention over, Garfield today could begin his journey home, but not without first presenting himself in his new role as national curiosity and celebrity—enjoying the "penalties of greatness," as the *New York Tribune* put it.[20]

A huge crowd came to Chicago's Dearborn railway depot to see Garfield off, and crowds met his special train all along the route. They stopped at towns across Indiana and Ohio—Laporte, South Bend, Elkhart, Kendallville, and half-a-dozen others. Garfield would step out onto the train's decorated rear platform to be greeted by cheering, flag-waving townsfolk, booming cannons, bright brass bands, and local dignitaries giving rousing welcomes. Thousands of people waited in the hot sun to see his face, shake his hand, and hear his voice. Ladies handed him bouquets; he kissed babies and scribbled autographs. At Toledo, 100 guns saluted Garfield's train from atop a bluff on the Maumee River, and Governor Foster harangued over 2,000 people at the depot. "The great Senator [Conkling] a few days ago said that nothing but an

---

* Garfield had been accused in 1872 of accepting stock in the tainted company and profiting by $329, a relatively small sum but a bribe if true. An investigating committee took no action against him, but the stain of scandal remained.

** Garfield had accepted $5,000 in the early 1870s for helping to represent DeGolyer in winning street-paving contracts from the Washington, D.C., government at a time he also chaired the House Appropriations Committee. Congressmen were not barred then from private legal practice, but the case had a strong odor of influence peddling.

act of God would prevent the nomination of General Grant," he bellowed. "The act of God has come, and General Garfield has become your candidate."[21] People "wild with enthusiasm"[22] crowded Garfield. He shook their hands until his arm ached and the train literally dragged him away.

Between stops, Garfield could lounge in the parlor car while watching the green Ohio cornfields pass by outside. He lit cigars with his friends and told stories from Chicago. Garfield, if elected, would be the second-youngest United States president to that time at 48 years old,* the first elected directly from the House of Representatives,** and the first nominated while sitting as a national convention delegate. He would be the first left-handed president; the first who could write Greek and Latin and quote Shakespeare and Scripture with equal ease; and the fourth president from Ohio. The satirical *Puck* noted that Garfield also would be the fifth presidential James, the luckiest first name for White House candidates.***[23]

After a night in Cleveland with more dinners and celebrations, the next morning Garfield rode on to Hiram for the commencement ceremony at Hiram College, where he'd taught and been college president in the late 1850s. Here, current Hiram College President Burke Hinsdale introduced Garfield to the assembled alumni, students, teachers, and classmates as a friend "into whose face almost all of you have looked hundreds of times."[24] Finally, on Friday afternoon, Garfield came home to Mentor. He rode by carriage beneath a "glorious sun" over the dusty dirt roads of northeast Ohio, nearly every farmhouse along the way waving flags or banners in his honor. At the small towns of Bartoff and Chardon, neighbors fired guns and rang church bells at his approach; bands, parades, and ceremonies filled the town squares. Relatives and life-long friends lined the road; Garfield tried to stop and talk with each one. By the time he reached his own farmhouse, the clocks read nearly 11 p.m.

---

* Ulysses Grant had been 46 years old when elected president in 1868.

** No subsequent House member has jumped directly to the presidency, either.

*** They didn't know yet that Garfield also would be the last American president born in a log cabin. The other Ohio presidents were William Henry Harrison (born in Virginia, but living in North Bend, Ohio, when elected), Ulysses Grant (born in Point Pleasant, Ohio), and Rutherford Hayes. Four more Ohioans would follow Garfield to the White House: Benjamin Harrison (born in Ohio, though living in Indiana), William McKinley, William Howard Taft, and Warren G. Harding. By comparison, Virginia boasts eight presidents born on her soil (including Harrison, who is claimed by both states). The other presidential Jameses were James Madison, James Monroe, James Polk, and James Buchanan. Garfield would be the last James: even "Jimmy" Carter seemed to recognize the post-1880 taboo.

The next day, he and Lucretia stood for hours at the Mentor town rail-way depot to greet neighbors.

Lucretia Garfield must have shaken her head seeing her husband alone for the first time in two weeks, as candidate for President of the United States. Her own life, she knew, would now be thrown into as much turmoil as his. "The events of the past week grow to seem more and more unreal," she wrote. "But I suppose I shall grow accustomed to it all after a while."[25]

"Crete," as the family called her, slender, almost frail, with dark hair pulled back in a bun, wide eyes and delicate features, carried herself with a keen intelligence and calm. After twenty years of marriage to her soldier-politician husband, Lucretia had long suffered the role of political wife. Early in their marriage, he had left her alone in Ohio for months at a time to raise their young children while he traveled to Washington or went "on the stump" across Ohio. By late 1863, five years after their wedding, between the de-mands of politics and the war, she could complain that they'd actually lived together for only twenty weeks—despite her having already born him two children, their eldest son Harry and a daughter Eliza who'd died in childhood. That year, their marriage almost collapsed when Lucretia discovered James' one-time amorous affair with a Mrs. Calhoun in New York—a wound that took years to heal.[26]

Over time, though, they weathered the storms and their bond had strengthened. During the next decade, she bore him five more children (in-cluding another who died in early childhood) and, in 1869, Garfield brought her to live in Washington, D.C. in a new home that he'd had built. When separated, they wrote hundreds of letters to each other. By the late 1870s, when enemies attacked her husband, Lucretia felt the sting herself. She de-tested the "monstrous fictions" and slanders of political contests, and the peo-ple who didn't bother to "discriminate between truth and error" when mak-ing accusations.[27] Lucretia learned to gauge her words carefully and use discretion when she spoke. "She is one of the coolest and best-balanced women I ever saw," Garfield said of her. "She is unstampedable," and with the "intelligence and coolness of her character, she has never made the slight-est [public] mistake."[28]

Garfield increasingly turned to Lucretia for political advice, especially her judgments of people. When his friend James Blaine was making his first presidential run in 1876, Garfield told Lucretia about rumors he'd heard that Blaine, on meeting his wife-to-be Harriet Stanwood in Kentucky in the

1850s, had "anticipate[d] the nuptial ceremony," then rushed her home for their wedding, after which she gave birth to their first child six months later. "How does this story strike you," he asked in a letter. Would it affect his presidential bid?[29]

"I scarcely believe it," she'd answered quickly. "But if it is true, it ought not to affect the *voters* very much unless it would have been considered more *honorable* by the majority to have abandoned the woman—seduced," she said of this "queer piece of gossip." "My opinion of Mr. Blaine would be rather heightened than otherwise" by the story, she said, it showing him "not entirely selfish and heartless."[30]

Still, Lucretia sometimes bristled at the wifely role she had to play, "[t]he grinding misery of being a woman, between the upper and nether millstone of household cares and training children ," as she put it in the mid-1870s. "To be half civilized with some aspirations for enlightenment, and obliged to spend the largest part of the time the victim of young barbarians keeps one in perpetual ferment!"[31]

A presidential campaign raised the stakes. She and James had purchased the run-down 158-acre Mentor farm in late 1876, just four years earlier, partly as refuge for themselves and their five children, partly to "teach my boys to do farm work" as he put it, and partly to maintain his Ohio residency.[32] Since then, he had cleaned up the old pig pens and broken-down barns, raised a crop of oats, corn, and barley, while together they'd expanded the house from a small shack into a three-story home with white picket fence and shade trees. They kept most of their nicer furniture and serving plates in Washington, D.C., where they did more formal entertaining. But now the Mentor farm would have to serve for a national campaign. They could expect a flood of visitors that summer, and their household repairs stood far from finished. Workmen still had to seal roofs, paint walls, finish floors, and deliver fixtures. At the same time, Lucretia had to watch the youngest children—Abram and Irvin, seven and nine years old—though her sister-in-law Lide Rudolph had offered to help.

Still, Lucretia would do her part for the campaign, as she always had.

And what a campaign. Garfield had no organization, no managers, and no strategy. His two decades in Congress gave him some advantages—a long record on public issues, national credibility, and a wide network of contacts. Still, outside of his Ohio friends—Foster, Dennison, Charles Henry—and a few political allies like Whitelaw Reid, Blaine, and William Chandler, he had no real power. Even from Blaine, vacationing in White Sulphur Springs, Garfield heard only pessimism. "I should much prefer to see the party defeated with Garfield or some other candidate… to winning with Grant," Blaine told a reporter, saying "Garfield will be beaten" by a combination of hostility from Stalwarts and Sherman backers.[33]

For now, Garfield's friends all gave him the same advice: Do nothing. Say nothing. Whitelaw Reid, the *New York Tribune* publisher and a long-time Ohio confidante, sent a typical letter from New York, telling him urgently to "make no promises to anybody" and "don't make any journeys or any speeches."[34] Ohio politico George Baker told him he "[m]ust *not* make any statement to irritate the Democracy. Must not *do* any political talking."[35]

The fact is, even in its best light, Garfield's campaign faced a serious roadblock, and it ultimately took the form of Roscoe Conkling. Baker laid it out on a single piece of paper.[36]

The Electoral Outlook*

Solid South States (16):	Votes	Certain Republican (15):	Votes	Doubtful (7):	Votes
Alabama	10	Colorado	3	Calif.	6
Arkansas	6	Illinois	21	Conn.	6
Delaware	3	Iowa	11	Indiana	15
Florida	4	Kansas	5	N. J.	9
Georgia	11	Maine	7	N. Y.	35
Kentucky	12	Mass.	13	Oregon	3
Louisiana	8	Mich.	11	Nevada	3
Maryland	8	Minn.	5	Total:	77
Mississippi	8	Neb.	3		
Missouri	15	N. H.	5		
No. Carolina	10	Ohio	22		
So. Carolina	7	Pennsylvania	29		
Tennessee	12	R.I.	4		
Texas	8	Vermont	5		
Virginia	11	Wisconsin	10		
West Virginia	5	Total:	154		
Total :	138				

Electoral votes needed to win: 185.

*Based on George A. Baker analysis. Garfield papers. LC.

Outwardly, Republicans and Democrats seemed extremely well matched in the 1880s, running a uniquely close parade of national elections from 1876 to 1892. During this time, control of the U.S. House of Representatives flip-flopped five times between Democratic and Republican, the Senate had its first party tie, three presidential elections were decided by less than one percent of the popular vote, and, in two (1876 and 1888), the popular vote winner lost in the electoral college. Of five presidential contests in this period, Democrats won two and Republicans won three.

But this balance was an illusion created by fraud and violence. In any free, fair vote, Republicans should have dominated—winning many Southern states: Grant, after all, had carried eight former confederate states in 1872 and Hayes, in 1876, had carried three as a result of that year's electoral dispute. But after 1876, Democrats exercised a chokehold over the former confederate and border states, a block big enough to even the scales, through "bull-dozing"—crass bullying, and strong-arm tactics.

Once federal troops withdrew from Louisiana, South Carolina, and Georgia in 1876, ending Reconstruction, white Southerners dropped any pretense of protecting the "free vote" and "fair count" of freed black slaves or moderate whites. Democratic Party ranks swelled with former rebel soldiers and followers embittered by defeat and Yankee post-war occupation. The U.S. Constitution guaranteed racial fairness in federal voting,*[37] but prosecutors saw their witnesses murdered, juries stacked, and lawyers harassed whenever they tried to enforce the law. Districts with black majorities impossibly elected rabid white supremacists. Freed blacks wanting to vote faced threats of violence, arrest, or murder. Masked men stopped them at gunpoint; local officials denied ballots to many reaching the polls. During the 1878 contest, reported killings reached into the dozens in Louisiana and Mississippi alone. Typically, when federal prosecutors brought charges in Louisiana, a mob dragged their two key witnesses off a steamboat and lynched them. Elsewhere, whites used "tissue ballots"—single sheets of paper that would divide into dozens of thinner pages when an official physically shook the ballot box—to manufacture fake majorities.** In a rare case, a Florida jury convicted three certifying officials of falsifying returns outright.[38]

---

* "Jim Crow" or other legal pretexts to deny black citizens their votes would not exist for another two decades; Federal prosecutions of Southern voting denials, however futile, continued through the 1890s until the U.S. Supreme Court's 1896 decision in *Plessy v. Ferguson.*

** Each party printed its own ballots during this period, listing the party's own slate of candidates; generally, a voter simply would place his preferred party's ballot in the ballot box (scratching

Most northern Republicans in 1880 still believed their rhetoric about protecting the voting rights of freed black slaves, despite lacking the will to still back it with federal military troops. Garfield, as a loyal Ohioan, had been one of Rutherford Hayes' agents during the 1876 Electoral Dispute in meeting with Southern Democrats on ending military Reconstruction, and felt particularly bothered when Southerners failed to honor their pledges to black voters. Still, in 1880, he could expect no let-up on the abuses. Democrats saw a real chance to capture the White House with Winfield Scott Hancock and they'd fight hard for it. If Garfield complained, the South would point to its famous Union General and ridicule Garfield's complaints as mere "bloody shirt" tactics—emotional appeals to supposedly obsolete Civil War passions.

A united "solid South" alone would give Hancock 138 electoral votes—47 shy of the 185 needed to win. Against it, Garfield would need a "solid North," anchored in New York. New York, with its 35 electoral votes, would raise Hancock's total to 173, just a dozen shy of victory. After that, for Garfield to win, he would need virtually every single other state—almost impossible in a land as vast and diverse as America.[39] He could not afford to lose New York, yet New York normally went Democratic in presidential years, not Republican. Since the civil war, Tammany Hall—New York City's largest Democratic machine—had turned voting fraud into a fine art. Boss William M. Tweed, its "Grand Sachem" from 1863 until driven from power in 1871, just nine years earlier, had produced huge victories with tactics ranging from graft to ballot-box stuffing to fake voter-registration lists to bogus vote-counting.* Along the way, his "ring" had allegedly looted city coffers of an incredible $100 million.[40] Tweed's successor at Tammany Hall, "Honest John" Kelly, the new Democratic Boss, had settled his cross-town quarrel with Samuel Tilden and would push the limit in 1880.

To win New York, Garfield needed to beat Tammany Hall, and the only power in New York State strong enough to do it was Roscoe Conkling.

Conkling's New York Republican machine, rooted in upstate cities and driven by thousands of zealous federal patronage office-holders—postmasters, custom house workers, interior employees—had managed since the early

---

out any specific name he disagreed with), rather than having to check-mark a preferred candidate from a combined list.

* In 1868, for instance, Tweed's machine-controlled city judges had naturalized some 40,000 fresh-off-the-boat Irish immigrants in the weeks before Election Day to vote his ticket. That year the total New York City vote count exceeded the total number of actual eligible voters by 8 percent. Voting graveyards started in New York, not Chicago.

1870s to capture most statewide offices. Conkling's Republicans controlled the governor's mansion, both U.S. Senate seats, and majorities in the two chambers of the state legislature—fighting Tammany Hall jab-for-jab.

So far, though, by every indication, Conkling's New York troops showed no taste for a Garfield campaign. As Conkling led, so would follow Don Cameron in Pennsylvania, John Logan in Illinois, and a dozen others. "Conkling is not sincere in his support of Garfield, as I have had assurance since the nomination from friends of his," John Sherman warned from Washington.[41] "The 'triumvirate' talk very ugly privately. If they keep it up till Nov[ember] [Garfield] will surely be defeated," Senator Dawes had heard on Capitol Hill.[42] "The Radical machine in New York will not be worked to any great extent for Garfield," echoed a *Washington Post* newsman. "Conkling and his men will not care to aid a candidate whom they did not help make."[43] Conkling himself, asked if he would campaign for the ticket, had supposedly said: "But for the disgrace, I would rather spend the time required in [Utica's] Mohawk Street jail."[44]

Voters might like Garfield personally; President Hayes considered Garfield's "personal history as an ideal self-made man" as potentially "a most popular feature of the canvass."[45] But parties won elections in the 1880s, not candidates.

In mid-June, Garfield left Ohio for a quick, three-day trip to Washington, D.C., to collect papers from his congressional desk. "I shall make the trip as quietly and quickly as possible" and try to remain "untrammeled by pledges,"[46] he'd promised Whitelaw Reid. Lucretia gave him a long list of items from their Washington house to ship or carry back to Ohio: her "India shawl," the Limoges pitcher and square jardinière ("Have Daniel pack them carefully among your clothes," she said.), the glass fruit and berry dishes, the china dessert plates, the good coffee urn, and some larger items: the dining room table, a mahogany side table, and the Hungarian chairs and two ottomans from the sitting room—all things they'd need to entertain the crush of campaign visitors to Ohio.[47]

Quick and quiet, though, became impossible. Newspapers got word of Garfield's visit, and friends insisted on arranging gala events. The Washington, D.C. that greeted Garfield as a presidential candidate in 1880 had changed starkly from the swampy, wartime Capitol he'd known as a freshman congressman in 1863. The city's population had exploded from 75,080 souls in 1860 to over 177,000 now, including 40,000 freed slaves and almost

20,000 workers in the bulging federal departments and bureaus. Washington political Boss Alexander Shepherd had paved miles of streets, laid sewers, drained the City Canal and Tiber Creek, and planted 25,000 trees before fleeing to Mexico in 1874, leaving the city $20 million in debt. Blocks of showy new brick townhouses rose in new neighborhoods around Pacific (soon to be renamed Dupont) Circle, fringe areas of Capitol Hill, and to the north. Steel tracks for horse-drawn cars now lined most major avenues, and the city boasted two major railway stations along with the new Smithsonian Museum Building and new monuments to Generals Thomas, McPherson, and Scott.

Cows and sheep still grazed outside the White House under the shadow of the stump-like bottom half of the unfinished Washington Monument—on which work had stopped twenty-six years ago in 1854 and resumed only recently—but they stood now within blocks of elegant dinners, receptions, and mansions.

On Tuesday, June 15, Garfield dined with President Hayes and his wife at the White House and then met John Sherman at the Treasury Department. Sherman, by now reassured of Garfield's loyalty in Chicago, had swallowed any disappointment over his own failed bid long enough to give Garfield a hearty congratulations and pledge his support.[48] On Wednesday night, the National Veterans Club threw an outdoor serenade for Garfield, drawing over 10,000 people to the sidewalks around Fifteenth Street near Riggs House to hear songs and speeches under calcium lights and gas jets. Fireworks exploded in the summer sky as a band played "Hail to the Chief" and excerpts from H.M.S. Pinafore. On Thursday, the Army of the Cumberland Society feted Garfield with a lavish banquet. He enjoyed the night sitting beside General William Tecumseh Sherman swapping war stories and political talk.[49]

Beneath the fanfare, though, Senator Dawes smelled trouble. "Garfield comes here this morning," he wrote to his wife. "A pity. He had better stay away till Congress adjourns. But a big man does always like to show himself...."[50]

Early that week, on returning to the Riggs House after one of his meetings, Garfield found a note from Roscoe Conkling himself. Conkling had condescended to come calling for a visit. Garfield felt surprised; he hadn't planned to see the New York senator on this trip—trying to avoid any political deals—but perhaps, he thought, here was a chance to smooth waters. Garfield immediately sent a note back to Conkling's apartment at Wormley's

Hotel a few blocks away. He apologized for missing the call and asked Conkling to "name a time" to get together. "I wish to see you away from the crowd of callers," Garfield wrote[51]—certainly a courtesy, a chance to talk one-on-one and bury the hatchet.

Conkling had returned directly to Washington from Chicago for Senate sessions but still nursed a sore attitude after his defeat with General Grant. Before Garfield's response could even reach him, Conkling had found a new grievance over which to feel insulted. Garfield, during his day of rounds about the White House, at some point had shared a carriage on Pennsylvania Avenue with Interior Secretary Carl Schurz—one of Conkling's worst enemies from President Hayes' "reform" crowd. Conkling found out, and "the damning news drove Roscoe into the sulks!" an observer noted.[52] Garfield had snubbed him and consorted with his enemies, Conking apparently chose to believe. He "scornfully" declined to respond to Garfield's note, cringing "at the thought of holding commerce with a man who would be seen publicly with Schurz."[53] [54]

In fact, he never answered Garfield's message at all.

Garfield got wind of Conkling's tantrum and must have marveled at its pettiness. Whitelaw Reid called it a "trivial, beggarly thing," but the kind that "turned awry enterprises of great pith."[55] The two men would not meet face-to-face now for three more months—enough time for feelings to harden and attitudes to set.

◎ ◎ ◎ ◎ ◎

Stephen Dorsey, meanwhile, also recognized the need to bring James Garfield and Roscoe Conkling together face-to-face to save the Republican Party. But Dorsey, unlike Garfield, had the means to bring it about.

Stephen Dorsey's chance to dabble in president-making came on July 2 when the Republican National Committee met in New York City to pick new officers. Nobody, it seemed, wanted the top jobs. The committee had met briefly in Chicago after Garfield's nomination, but failed to choose a new permanent chairman or secretary when pro-Grant members had unexpectedly broached[56] the topic. Garfield had asked Don Cameron to stay on as chairman—another olive branch to the Stalwarts—but Cameron had absolutely refused.[57] As second choice, he'd suggested William Chandler, but Chandler too, exhausted from running Blaine's presidential campaign all year, reportedly had declined "in the most positive manner."[58]

But Dorsey, the former Arkansas Senator, Ohio carpetbagger, and rail-road swindler, had special ties with both Garfield and Conkling. With Garfield, Dorsey had shared the Civil War. Raised in Oberlin, Ohio, son of Irish immigrants, Stephen Dorsey had joined Ohio's militia in 1861 and served as one of Colonel James Garfield's young officers in the Sandy Valley and Shiloh campaigns. Later, Dorsey had moved east and marched into bat-tle with Ulysses Grant at the Wilderness and Cold Harbor. After the war, now a colonel, Dorsey discovered enterprise. Energetic and outgoing, with a handsome face, quick smile, dark hair and full beard, Dorsey had returned to Ohio, married a local beauty, cashed out his share of the Sandusky Tool Com-pany (which he'd helped found), took his money, and moved south. Here, as a rich Yankee in the impoverished post-war South at the height of radical re-construction, Dorsey had founded a railroad—the Arkansas Central (later bankrupted after he'd sold millions in bonds to British investors)—and, in 1872, had convinced (some say bribed) the Arkansas legislature to make him a Republican carpetbag United States Senator. In Washington, Dorsey had quickly fallen under the sway of his other mentor, becoming a trusted aide in Senator Roscoe Conkling's Stalwart faction.

Dorsey's Senate term had ended after Reconstruction, leaving him a ma-rooned Republican in the newly Democratic "solid south." Out of a job, he bought land in New Mexico and began investing in lucrative new postal schemes—the "Star Route" business*—all the while keeping close ties to pol-itics and waiting for opportunity to come knocking.

On July 2, the Republican National Committee met again, this time in New York City at the Fifth Avenue Hotel, to pick its leaders. This time, the factions came ready. Roscoe Conkling and John Logan, wearing matching "huge straw hats" and moving about the corridors "in a stately way," came together to push their Stalwart choice for party chairman, New York's Tom Platt.[59] Ohio Governor Charles Foster represented Garfield, carrying the party nominee's list of four moderates for the top post: William Chandler, Eugene Hale of Maine, Richard McCormick of Arizona, and Marshall Jewell of Con-necticut.

The committee, wanting to avoid another blow-up after their fight over the unit rule in Chicago, assigned the issue to a small group composed of

---

* "Star Routes," which would soon become the subject of disclosures of massive fraud, were postal delivery routes to remote areas [the "star" being an asterisk that appeared in printed postal schedules] for which the U.S. government paid special premiums for contract services.

Chandler (for the Blaine faction), Logan (for the Stalwarts), and John M. Forbes of Massachusetts (an independent). Forbes, wanting to keep peace, checked each of the names on Garfield's suggested list and found that only one, Marshall Jewell, had actually agreed to take the job. All the others had refused. Even Jewell, the committee's temporary chairman, showed little interest. "My whole duty... begins and ends with calling the committee to order to-morrow night," he told a reporter.[60]

Still, Jewell, a former Connecticut governor, Postmaster General, minister to Russia, and leather-tanning magnate, at least was "competent," explained Ohioan W.C. Cooper.[61]

When Forbes suggested Jewell for the job, though, John Logan balked. Jewell had been disloyal to Ulysses Grant in Chicago, Logan argued. He insisted on New York's Tom Platt. Forbes and Chandler refused, and Logan started shouting. He threatened to walk out. His Stalwart friends would have "nothing to do with the contest," he yelled, flailing his arms and raising his voice. The "Blaine men might run the campaign alone." John Forbes, apparently shaken by the bluster, offered a trade: If Logan would accept Jewell as chairman, then Logan could pick the committee's Secretary. Logan quickly agreed. He chose Dorsey.

Word of the deal got out, and some friends pulled Forbes aside in the hallway as the committee started voting. Dorsey had a bad reputation in Washington, they warned him. He was known to sell his vote, "often not for a very high price."[62] Forbes was appalled. He rushed back into the meeting. But before he could object, the committee had finished. Dorsey was in.[63]

Stephen Dorsey was thrilled. He threw himself into the job with energy, seizing the opportunity for his own future. "I have sense enough to know that if I want anything, ... the way to get it is to show myself entitled to it by the management of the canvass," he told friends.[64] He studied the political landscape. During July, he traveled out to Mentor, Ohio and spoke with Garfield, then rode up to the Thousand Islands in upstate New York where Conkling and Chet Arthur had gone fishing. Dorsey saw the problem clearly. Garfield and Conkling had to meet, face-to-face, and settle things. Garfield must come to New York City. Nothing else could get the campaign on track.

Dorsey sympathized fully with Roscoe Conkling's reluctance to back an Ohio candidate with no ties to his own faction—especially after the shabby treatment he and Arthur had received from Ohioan Rutherford Hayes. Garfield hesitated, but Dorsey insisted. He sent letters and telegrams. Garfield must guarantee the New York Stalwarts that, as president, he would "recognize" them, and not give in to "the 'Scratchers' and Independents and 'featherheads'" when it came time to give out patronage. "They intend to know it," Dorsey told the candidate, and "can only be satisfied by a personal conference with you."[65] It could be brief, just a thirty minute chat.[66] "Your presence," Dorsey wrote, "is a paramount duty that you owe to yourself and your party."[67]

⊚ ⊚ ⊚ ⊚ ⊚

Roscoe Conkling, his work done in Washington, D.C. with the Senate having gone into recess, could now start to enjoy his summer. He returned to Utica and his legal practice. Conkling and his wife Julia had grown estranged over the years because of Roscoe's escapades with other women; now, he often stayed in a hotel in Utica and avoided her. In July, Conkling came to New York City for the National Committee meeting at the Fifth Avenue Hotel. Having installed his friend Stephen Dorsey as secretary, Conkling could go on vacation. In early July, he and John Logan, still wearing their wide straw hats, swooped down on Coney Island, New York City's swank new resort. "It is the liveliest spot I have ever seen," Logan wrote home to his wife Mary in Illinois. "The hotels cover nearly a mile in length" along the ocean beach.[68] The two senators dazzled visitors at the Hotel Brighton, walking side-by-side through the piazza, Conkling's summer suit showing his "ruddy glow of good health."[69]

Conkling refused to talk to reporters that week; he'd rather let the world ponder his wounded feelings from Chicago. But through friends, he decided to start sending signals. At Coney Island, one "intimate personal friend"— probably Logan—pulled aside a *Brooklyn Eagle* reporter and denied the "loose talk" about Lord Roscoe's attitude. Conkling had gotten over his "disappointment and chagrin" since Chicago and now enjoyed "excellent health" and "excellent spirits," the friend said. "He is full of life" and "[h]is grip on the party machinery is supreme and absolute." As for campaigning, Conkling "likes Arthur as ardently as his nature will permit him to like any one," and he has a "disposition for work."[70]

From Coney Island, Conkling traveled to nearby Manhattan Beach for a dinner with William Chandler, still in town from the national committee meeting. Conkling held no grudge against Chandler; in fact, he seemed to like the feisty little politico despite his ties to Conkling's hated enemy Blaine. They spoke a common language of hard-knocks politics, and Conkling remembered Chandler's work managing Ulysses Grant's campaigns in 1868 and 1872. Chandler, for his part, understood perfectly Roscoe Conkling's complaints of bad treatment under Rutherford Hayes' presidency and agreed that Hayes' removal of Chester Arthur had been an outrage.

It was time well spent, Conkling believed. Chandler would send word back to all of his Half-Breed friends—Blaine, Reid, and Garfield—that Roscoe had a fair point.

In mid-July, Conkling joined his old protégé Chester Arthur, now the vice presidential nominee, on their annual fishing trip to the Thousand Islands on New York's St. Lawrence River at the Canadian border. Any personal friction between the two men quickly disappeared around campfires and fresh trout in the crisp country air. "Every day & everything was enjoyable," Conkling wrote to Levi Morton a few days afterward. "Gen[era]l Arthur's constant effort was to make every body else happy. No wonder we all like him."[71]

The fact is, wounded pride aside and looking past his sulky mood, Roscoe Conkling had reason to be large-minded these days. He understood the electoral map and Garfield's political dilemma as well as Garfield himself. This year could still bring good tidings, he knew, but only on his terms. Conkling recognized his own strength and felt ready to extract maximum concessions before lifting a finger for the campaign. Besides, what did he owe James Garfield? As all the newspapers said: Garfield "will be owned or controlled by no man or men"—including Conkling.[72] Who could trust such a man? And the people that Garfield associated with—Blaine, Rutherford Hayes, John Sherman, Carl Schurz—every one of them gave Conkling stomach pains. Certainly, Roscoe Conkling would campaign: for the ticket, for the Party, for New York's patronage and for himself, but not for James Garfield and not for free.

"There are some matters which must be attended to before I can enter the canvass," he told a reporter.[73]

Speaking through another friend, Senator Henry Blair of New Hampshire, Conkling made his terms remarkably frank. Conkling made a point to "converse" with Blair after his fishing trip, and Blair dutifully reported the talk to the *New York Times*. Conkling, he said, "probably" and "properly" would "demand" a few things before signing onto the Garfield ticket—specifically that the "Secretary of the Treasury shall not control the New-York Custom-house," and that "New York will be allowed to take care of herself."[74]

In short, Conkling's price for the election was full control of all New York patronage. The stakes were enormous—no less than control of key national government functions. The New York Custom House, that grand marble building on Wall Street with its granite columns, huge rotunda, and hundreds of narrow offices for hundreds of clerks and officials—all appointed by the Collector, its chief officer—held more power on its own than many cabinet departments. It collected over $110 million each year in customs duties, a whopping 75% of all federal customs receipts, and controlled a payroll of almost $2 million. Its Collector's fixed annual salary of $12,000 actually topped the $10,000 paid to the vice president and cabinet members or the $7,500 paid senators and congressmen. Add to this the nearly $50,000 in "moieties," fees, and kickbacks available, and total income through the mid-1870s normally surpassed the $50,000 paid the President.*[75]

Add to that the New York Sub-Treasury, plus literally thousands of postmasters and Interior employees, and the scale became huge. Garfield could accept Conkling's offer or he could go home to his Ohio farm after the election and grow corn. Democrats, at their convention in Cincinnati a few weeks after the Republicans' in Chicago, had reportedly made an explicit agreement about patronage: Hancock had promised specific slots to Samuel Tilden and other party chieftains in exchange for their support.[76] Should Conkling accept anything less?

After his fishing trip in the Thousand Islands, Conkling returned to Utica and bided his time. If nothing else, he could make a pile of money with his law practice. His retainers for that summer already amounted to tens of thousands of dollars. Meanwhile, his message was getting through. William Chandler, the most practical of political men, summed it up in a letter to Garfield in July. "The State of New York is important, probably vital," Chandler wrote, "and it is worth while to stoop a little to conquer much."[77]

● ● ● ● ●

---

* Congress in 1874 had abolished the "moiety" system—which allowed the Collector and top aides to divide certain "forfeited" property—after loud complaints of abuse.

As a modern comparison of Conkling's demand, imagine a U.S. Senator from Virginia arguing that, since the Pentagon sits on the Virginia side of the Potomac River, therefore he, not the president, should control the choice of Secretary of Defense (and all his appointees) as a matter of local patronage, or a New York senator insisting on controlling the Federal Reserve Board or the Securities and Exchange Commission since their major duties focused on the financial markets centered in New York.

Back in Ohio, Garfield had to wonder what he'd been thinking in Chicago when he'd agreed to this campaign. Over 200 callers had descended on Mentor during that first week after his return from Washington. He and Lucretia had served dinner to 28 people on Sunday night alone, their house "literally overrun with visitors and correspondence," a reporter noted.[78] Eight different book publishers had sent eight different biographers. Over 5,000 letters and telegrams sat piling up since the nomination, each awaiting an answer. Garfield had asked Hiram College president Burke Hinsdale to prepare an issues "textbook" for the campaign, and Hinsdale now demanded piles of documents for research. Garfield arranged for Joe Stanley Brown—the twenty-year-old clerk who'd helped in his congressional office—to move out to Ohio and handle campaign paperwork. All the while, Lucretia focused on finishing the household repairs, managing the guests and tending to their five children.

Bills for feeding and housing these multitudes began to mount up, soon reaching into thousands of dollars, and Garfield could only hope the Republican Party might help later with the expenses.

"Why before this is over you will be able to keep a hotel," Lucretia's sister-in-law Lide Rudolph wrote to her. "Is it not possible for the wife of a President to rebel? Try it, and do not kill yourself for a host of strangers.... The boys send a *bushel* of kisses to Aunt Crete."[79] The regular newsmen camped at the Mentor farm soon dubbed it "Lawnfield" for its wide grassy outdoor spaces; its wood-frame porch where Garfield enjoyed meeting visitors became a symbol of his "front-porch campaign."

With all the distractions, by July 1 Garfield had not even started on his formal letter accepting the Republican nomination—his only chance to address voters directly on the issues.

To make matters worse, Lucretia, usually steady under pressure, had already embarrassed herself with a rare political mistake. Speaking to a women's group in a nearby Ohio town, she'd taken a friendly question about Garfield's role in funding a local anti-drink crusade. "The general takes great interest in the affairs of our little village," she'd said, apparently not noticing the reporter from the *Detroit Evening News* in the room taking notes. But, she continued, "the general does not believe in total abstinence. Oh, no! he believes every man should have a mind of his own, but not drink to excess...." The newsman quietly telegraphed her remark back to his office, and it soon flashed across the Midwest, creating a bombshell among the zealous and highly organized Temperance movement.* Within days, a Midwest evangelist calling himself simply "A.P." led a charge of demands that she confirm her statement and explain "the views of your husband."[80]

"I have had to travel fast and think faster ever since I have known you, to keep even within seeing distance," she wrote her husband, now watching her words ever more closely.[81]

As a candidate, Garfield reluctantly agreed to follow tradition and not campaign directly. "It is against all precedent for a Presidential candidate to take the stump in person," Governor Foster told reporters, announcing the decision. "His friends will look out for him."**[82] Personally, Garfield would rather have looked out for himself. He enjoyed being on the road, meeting people, standing on his own feet and speaking his own words. "If it were the custom," he wrote in his journal, "it would insure better nominations."[83] Still, he chose to follow Whitelaw Reid's advice. "There is no place where you can do so much for your supporters and be so comfortable yourself from now until next November, as on your farm."[84]

The sitting made Garfield impatient. Some campaign work had been done. Committees had printed thousands of copies of Garfield's speeches on the Tariff Bill, homestead policy, and responses to attacks on his character. Supporters had created "Garfield and Arthur Clubs" all around the country, and Marshall Jewell had ordered the printing of 20,000 likenesses of him and Lucretia to distribute along with campaign biographies, songbooks, signs, and badges. But weeks went by, and the national committee seemed to float without direction, the New York Stalwarts sat in a huff, and Ulysses Grant, who had shown no enthusiasm for Garfield's candidacy, camped silently out on the Arizona frontier. And now Garfield had Stephen Dorsey pushing this preposterous idea of him going to New York City to meet Roscoe Conkling—the same man who'd snubbed him in Washington just weeks earlier.

Garfield still had his new seat in the United States Senate starting the

---

* The Women's Christian Temperance Movement, founded in Ohio in 1874, had become highly effective by 1880 under its strong president Frances E. Willard, forcing hundreds of saloons in 23 states to close. A Prohibition Party (giving women equal status as delegates and backing women's suffrage) fielded national presidential candidates from 1872 through 1916 and received 270,770 votes in 1892, its best year.

** The notable exception was Horace Greeley, who took "to the stump" against incumbent Ulysses Grant in 1872. Greeley not only suffered criticism, but lost the election badly and died a few weeks later. And, yes, the expression does go back to when early politicians stood on tree stumps to address rural crowds. The taboo against candidates "stumping" for themselves was not finally broken until William Jennings Bryan's well-received but losing effort in 1896.

next year if he were to lose the White House in 1880. He didn't have to sacrifice everything for this campaign—his dignity, his savings. Still, he'd invested his honor; he couldn't let himself even think of putting up less than
his best effort.

Garfield read Dorsey's urgent letters and telegrams and felt they "contained more anxiety than reasons."[85] He took his time about deciding how to
respond. He asked for advice—probably hoping that Blaine, Reid, Chandler
and other friends would confirm his own judgment against going. At first,
they did. "I don't believe in running after the malcontents. Let them run after
you," Whitelaw Reid wrote from his perch at the *New York Tribune*, where he
heard all the local talk in New York City. "They want promises about office.
They haven't any right to them. Nobody has,"—especially Conkling, "be-
having like a spoiled child."[86] In Washington, Carl Schurz echoed the feeling. "If Conkling himself sulks, his followers will go on without him and he
will lose [them]," he wrote.[87] George W. Curtis, the anti-Conkling "reform"
editor of *Harper's Weekly*, also wrote strongly to protest the meeting.[88] As
word of the idea spread, newspapers openly took sides. The *Springfield Republican* and *Boston Herald* both loudly warned Garfield against a surrender to
the Stalwarts.[89]

Garfield had reasons for concern. By running half-way across the country to curry favor with Lord Roscoe on his patronage demands, Garfield risked
not only alienating the anti-machine moderates who had backed him in
Chicago and now feared his surrendering to the New York machine.[90] He also
risked diminishing himself. He had nothing personal against Conkling, he
insisted. Garfield was "entirely willing, and indeed should be glad" to see him,
he confided to Chandler. He wouldn't expect Conkling to be "in the slightest degree dishonorable" or "unreasonable," he wrote. But why shouldn't Conkling come to Ohio instead? Garfield, after all, was the presidential candidate. Conkling could meet him at Mentor or some nearby place "without
embarrassment, and thus avoid all misconstruction." Otherwise, a closed-
door face-to-face session with the Stalwart Bosses could raise "all sorts of dis-
quieting rumors." The appearance, especially among independents voters,
could be damaging.[91]

But Stephen Dorsey did not easily give up. Instead, to sweeten the pot,
he devised an elaborate plan. Why not disguise the Conkling meeting behind a national party symposium? Garfield could come to New York as guest
of both the Republican National Committee and its Executive Committee,

which would jointly sponsor a major public event—say, a forum on the problem for Republicans in the post-war South. National figures from every state and faction would attend: Blaine, Logan, John Sherman, Chandler, southern blacks like Mississippi Senator Blanche Bruce, and others, Stalwarts and Half-Breeds alike. Then, at a convenient moment, Garfield could quietly slip away to a private room with Conkling for the real meeting. No one need lose face; no newspapers need even know.

Dorsey didn't wait for an answer. He started the wheels turning immediately. Time was short. He began sending invitations out for August 5 at New York's most prominent venue, the Fifth Avenue Hotel.

Garfield had to admit, the plan made good sense. Still, he balked and dragged his feet. He asked Marshall Jewell for advice, and Jewell met with Chandler in Boston to talk it over. Chandler liked the idea—Garfield needed an "eye to eye, face to face" with Conkling, he felt.[92] Blaine stood "decidedly against."[93]

Garfield also sent his longtime Ohio friend Charles Henry to New York to scout out the response, particularly among New York bolters like William Robertson. Hesitant at first, Henry too finally urged Garfield to come. "I cannot believe Conkling wants anything unreasonable," and the "anti-Conkling's" could be pacified by a visit, he wrote.[94] "The NY Senator pouts now. The independents may pout if they see him look pleased after your interview. You need God's help to keep both sides from pouting at the same time. They want taffy," Henry concluded.[95]

Whilelaw Reid too finally agreed to the trip, though mostly because "Dorsey's arrangements… [have] gone so far [that] more harm might be done by… refusing."[96]

Other letters piled in, from allies like Frank Hiscock, Anson McCook, and Thomas Nichol, all urging Garfield come and avoid "serious trouble" with Conkling and his crowd. The New Yorkers wanted "not a bargain, only 'a little fraternization,'" as Hiscock put it.[97] Dorsey finally laid down the law. "[A] failure to have matters put in better shape in this state by August 5 means our defeat in November," he wrote, adding that "I am going ahead in this matter" regardless.[98]

Garfield harbored doubts to the end. "I am very reluctant to go. It is an unreasonable demand that so much effort should be made to conciliate one man," he complained as late as July 28. But to snub the committee this late would be "ungracious."[99] As time grew close, he insisted that other key players make their appearances—especially Blaine. "Please meet me with Committee [on August] Fifth—without fail. Answer," he telegraphed from Ohio that week.[100] "You must not fail me. Chandler promised your presence and I rely on you."[101] Garfield also telegraphed John Logan in Chicago: "I earnestly desire you to join me at Geneva Ohio Tuesday noon next & go to New York with me. Answer."[102]

Garfield spent a last Friday afternoon with the workmen threshing wheat, barley, and rye. He took a long walk with Lucretia across their property, smelling the sweet July air that blew through the cornfields, passing farmhands who hauled in wagons of oats from the field under a mild summer sun. Weighing the harvest that night, Garfield's crops had produced nearly 33 bushels of pure grain for each acre, "the best [yield] yet reported in the vicinity," he bragged.[103] It was a good omen for Garfield, something he needed. Two days later, he left Ohio from the Mentor depot for what would become the Fifth Avenue summit, on which would rest his presidency and his life.

⊚ ⊚ ⊚ ⊚ ⊚

In the annals of political back-room deals, the Fifth Avenue Summit of August 1880 deserves its own special place. To this day, despite oceans of accusations, no one knows what deal actually was struck, let alone whether anyone later broke it. The choreography was spectacular—a huge event involving hundreds of prominent people, an entire conference, all staged as a "mere cover and a farce," according to Tom Platt,[104] an excuse for one brief side-meeting that one of the principals, Roscoe Conkling himself, refused to attend.

Garfield traveled from Ohio in a private railroad car named the "Northern Star" provided by the Lake Shore Railway Company. Ben Harrison and John Logan rode with him the entire way. At Geneva, Ohio, he dined with soldiers in the town hall and made a speech. Crossing into New York State at Buffalo, Garfield met his biggest crowd yet—a deafening throng of 50,000 cheering supporters. He entered the city at sunset and "passed through an almost continuing dense mass of 2 and ½ miles of people, from the Depot to the [Palace] Hotel and the buildings and its grounds packed with so many thousands," he recalled.[105] Friends told him it augured well for the coming political battle; "the more sanguine ones ... say that the [enemy] will be burned in the fire of this human prairie."[106]

He awoke at 5 am the next morning to begin a triumphal tour across upstate New York, stopping at Rochester, Batavia, Oneida, Rome, and Utica, each time to crowds, cannon, rifles, and music. Fifty guns roared at Schenectady, then twenty-one more guns at Albany, where Chester Arthur joined Garfield's entourage in his private car.* At Poughkeepsie, four thousand veterans met them, marching in Civil War uniforms behind brass bands, and the crowds grew larger as the caravan moved south down the Hudson River valley.

High drama surrounded every step of Garfield's arrival in New York City. Booming cannon announced his train's crossing of the Harlem River at 7 pm on Wednesday night, August 4, alerting the thousands jamming sidewalks around Grand Central Depot on 42nd street. As the train entered the station, its wheels triggered twenty-four "torpedoes"—loud explosive fireworks attached to the tracks—as a welcoming salvo. Bursting cheers filled the cavernous depot as Garfield stepped down onto the platform. Spectators mobbed him as Stephen Dorsey, Marshall Jewell, Tom Platt, Governor Cornell, and other dignitaries greeted him formally. Garfield took off his slouched felt hat and bowed to the crowd. Cheers followed him into the street as a line of carriages led him down Fifth Avenue toward Madison Square Park, where police escorted him across the sidewalk and through the elegant front lobby of the Fifth Avenue Hotel at 198 Fifth Avenue occupying the entire block between 23rd and 24th streets. When he reached his rooms on the second floor, people outside on 23rd Street spied his now famous profile through a window and began cheering again. Garfield stepped out onto his balcony into the cool night air to see hundreds of arms and handkerchiefs waving back at him. "Men took off their hats, threw them in the air and shouted until they were hoarse," a reporter noted.[107] Many in the crowd carried banners for local Garfield and Arthur Clubs. "The old 117th Volunteers will vote as they fought,"[108] read one.

Garfield received hundreds of visitors that night in his room and didn't get to sleep until well past midnight.

The actual conference, held the next morning in the Fifth Avenue Hotel's spectacular marble-columned ballroom, beneath huge crystal chandeliers and gilded moldings, drew over 200 party leaders of every stripe. The formal agenda asked whether Republicans should mount a strong campaign

---

* Four future presidents were now in the entourage: Garfield, Arthur, Benjamin Harrison, and William McKinley, then still a 37-year-old junior Ohio Congressman.

in the South, demanding a "free vote" and "fair count" for freed blacks and moderate whites. Speaker after speaker used the platform to plead for party unity. "Old discords have been outgrown and forgotten," a friendly reporter noted.[109] Blaine, Sherman, Logan, and Jewell all spoke eloquently of the party's duty to support equal rights and stand together. Only William Chandler ruffled feathers briefly by raising a realistic point about the South—perhaps they should check first with friendly southern whites and blacks on whether they wanted to "imperil their lives and deplete the pockets of their Northern friends" in challenging local bigotry.[110]

The morning's biggest surprise, though, came from an empty chair—Roscoe Conkling's. Conkling had grandly checked into the Fifth Avenue Hotel the night before, but his friends this morning looked everywhere for him in vain. Rumors began to swirl. Everyone knew that Conkling's demands had prompted this meeting; could he really be so arrogant as to snub it? Most theories centered on different people whom Conking had grudges with and might want to avoid. One version had George William Curtis as the target;[111] another pointed to his dislike of John Sherman.[112] And Blaine, of course, always made good grist for a Conkling enemies list. Even John Logan, his Stalwart friend, complained that Conkling, by his absence, would "place himself in a very bad light" and had been "squarely criticized."[113]

Garfield, meanwhile, held court all day in room 30, a large parlor overlooking 23rd street and Madison Square Park with bright windows and a large mahogany table holding a pillow of flowers, mostly roses, and purple immortelles spelling out the word "welcome" on a white panel. He greeted a steady flow of Republican leaders: John Sherman, Blaine, Logan, Thurlow Weed, Don Cameron, William Robertson, Curtis, among dozens. Even John Fremont, the old "Pathfinder" and Republican patriarch,* still frisky at 67 years old with long white hair and beard, came to slap shoulders and buck up the candidate. Chester Arthur came by to help greet the celebrities. Garfield did manage to pull aside Blaine during the melee for a "long and friendly talk." He found Blaine "the prince of good fellows" that day,[114] Garfield noted. Things apparently were going well, he felt.

All through the day, a reported "stream of messages" flowed "between

---

* Fremont, a California pioneer, had been the Republican Party's first presidential nominee in 1856, losing to Democrat James Buchanan. He served as General of the Army for the first months of the Civil War.

General Garfield's parlors and room 25," Roscoe Conkling's suite.[115] But the Senator had gone out; no one could find him. Conkling's "friends" finally decided they could wait no longer. The New Yorkers had made such a fuss over their private meeting where, as one source had already tipped the *New York World*, "Mr. Garfield is said to be ready to turn the patronage all over to Conkling if he will 'take hold'"[116] and support the campaign.

At a quiet moment late that afternoon, a handful of New Yorkers pulled Garfield away from his guests and led him down the hall to a private room in Levi Morton's suite. Here, Garfield found himself surrounded by about half-a-dozen senior state politicos. Looking around, he recognized wiry, sharp-eyed Tom Platt and stately Levi Morton, with wide side-whiskers, a clean-shaven chin, and a crisp black banker's suit. New York Congressmen Frank Hiscock and Richard Crowley, Joseph Warren, and probably a few henchmen rounded out the group. Garfield probably winced at noticing how Chester Arthur, his own running mate, sat far across the room with his New York friends. They closed the door; a few men lit cigars and drank whiskey. No one spoke at first; the New Yorkers seemed uncomfortable, as if still waiting for someone else. Garfield, getting impatient, finally broke the silence. He asked the obvious question: Where was Conkling? He, after all, had wanted this meeting. He "express[ed] his disappointment and indignation in strong terms," Platt recalled.[117] The New Yorkers seemed "embarrassed and somewhat indignant" at the absence, Garfield noted. He said it caused "unpleasant surmises as to his attitude."[118]

Tom Platt, a former small-town druggist, congressman, and now director of the United States Express Company and one of Conkling's rising stars, claims to have done most of the talking for the New Yorkers that day. He and Arthur fumbled at first to make excuses for their missing Boss, trying to reassure Garfield that Conkling had placed himself "in the hands of his friends."[119] Garfield could only shrug. Perhaps Conkling could agree to make "two or three speeches in Ohio," he suggested. Apparently, this settled, tensions eased and the group became more pleasant. They all pledged unity and support—despite all the earlier tough talk. "I think [Conkling's] friends are showing zeal and enthusiasm, and will work, whether he does or not," Garfield wrote that night in his journal. As for any direct promises on patronage, he noted: "There shall neither be nor appear to be, if I can prevent it, any mortgaging of my future freedom."[120] For their part, the New Yorkers too seemed satisfied. They and the candidates were "perfectly agreed," and

"no obstacle" now prevented a "zealous and vigorous contest," one told the
New York Times that night.[121]

Afterward, Garfield took Levi Morton aside and won his consent to head
a special committee to raise money for the campaign, calling on some of Morton's wealthy Wall Street friends. Morton, a once-poor Vermont farm-boy
and now the second most powerful banker in New York City after J.P. Morgan,[122] had refused such a role earlier, but this time Garfield offered Morton
a top post in his administration, either Treasury Secretary or head of a major
foreign mission, England or France.[123] Morton happily would accept either,
though his Stalwart friends recognized the enormous difference. Treasury held
the real power—it controlled the New York Custom House, the keys to the
kingdom.

The meetings over, Garfield congratulated himself. After all the weeks of
worry, he'd survived his encounter with the Stalwarts and the conference had
gone well if strangely, without Conkling. The next morning, he awoke early
and rode a carriage across town to Bogardus' gallery and to Sarony's to sit for
photographs. Whitelaw Reid served him a private lunch at his Madison Avenue mansion along with Jay Gould, the soft-spoken, widely-hated Wall
Street magnate and owner of the Western Union telegraph and Union Pacific
railroad. Garfield had once investigated Jay Gould for his famous 1869 corner of the New York gold market; now Gould wanted guarantees on upcoming Supreme Court decisions affecting his railroads in exchange for possibly
huge campaign donations—money for everything from printing campaign
leaflets to funding speakers to paying "walking around" money to political
hacks. Garfield hedged on the issue, but seemed to make progress on the
money. "I think he will help," he noted afterwards.[124]

That night, New York treated Garfield to his grandest reception yet, an
outdoor torchlight parade on 23rd Street drawing 50,000 people to Madison
Square Park. Garfield had to marvel at the visual display: Thousands of veterans marched in formation, each holding a lantern, banner, or oiled torch,
many on horseback, wearing full-color regimental uniforms. Choirs sang, fireworks lit the sky, and the Seventh Regiment Band played "Hail to the Chief."
Afterwards, Garfield, his face lit by brilliant calcium lights, addressed the
mesmerized crowd from his perch on the Fifth Avenue Hotel's front balcony.
He drew his topic from the party conference and spoke about protecting the
loyal freed black men in the South: "We have seen white men betray the flag
and fight to kill the union, but in all that long and dreary [civil] war you never

saw a traitor under a black skin," he shouted, his baritone voice carrying far across the hot summer night. People strained to hear him, hundreds standing in windows or on nearby rooftops. "In all that period of terror and distress, no union soldier was ever betrayed by any black man anywhere and so long as we live we'll stand by these black allies of ours."[125]

Marshall Jewell recognized a special eloquence in Garfield's presence that night, seeing a man who'd grown into his national role. Garfield spoke with "dignity and majesty" on "so high a plane of statesmanship," he wrote, reporting the dazzling scene to Lucretia waiting back home in Ohio. He was "perfectly superb," and his "effect upon his audience was electric," Jewell said. "[T]onight I am immensely proud of being, so to speak, his lieutenant," and "I believe he is going to be elected but if he is not, I am sure he deserves to be."[126]

It had been two glorious days. Garfield, by his presence, had united his party, sharpened his public message, and faced his demons without harm. Only one small irritation had marred the night: Near Garfield on the balcony sat an empty chair. Roscoe Conkling had once again failed to join him. Unfortunately for Garfield, though, the real business of his New York trip had only just begun.

Hours later, back at the Fifth Avenue Hotel, exhausted from a long day's schedule, Garfield found himself again being led by Chester Arthur and Tom Platt back to Levi Morton's hotel suite. They felt they'd left some things unsettled. This time, Garfield counted only five people in the room: Arthur, Platt, Richard Crowley, Morton, and himself. The New Yorkers had stacked the meeting four against one.

This time, they closed the door and locked it. One or two of them drank brandy, but not in a friendly way. They made no small talk. The distractions had gone on long enough. Now the real business would begin.

Today, over a century later, we don't really know who said what that night. Of only five who really knew—the attendees—each has been dead for eighty years or more. None of their surviving accounts can be trusted; each had reason to twist the truth and years of anger to warp his memory. Roscoe Conkling had taken special pains to remove himself and so be able to deny things later—apparently the real reason for his absence.[127] Garfield, stupidly, had brought no witness.

Tom Platt, by his own later account, quickly broached the heart of the matter. "Mr. Garfield, there seems to be some hesitation on the part of the other gentlemen present to speak; but I might as well say that we are here to speak frankly and talk business," he said, his long face looking extra pale beneath flickering gas lamps and blue cigar smoke. The question, he said, concerned how to divide the New York patronage. "[B]efore the work of this campaign commences," he said, they wanted it decided whom Garfield intended to "reward" or "recognize" in New York State: the regular party? or the rebels who'd bolted in Chicago? "We cannot afford to do all the work, and let others reap the reward,"[128] Platt said in his flat voice and direct, a matter-of-fact tone.

Garfield certainly felt the eyes of these plain-speaking, no-nonsense men on him as he struggled to choose words carefully. He replied "with great earnestness and at some length," Platt recounted. The "friends of Grant and Conkling" controlled the New York party, Garfield supposedly told them. He had no intention "to change the order of things, but desired us to take hold with zeal and energy and insure his election," Platt wrote. If that were done, then the Stalwarts' wishes would be "paramount" on "all questions of patronage." He would "consult with [Conkling's] friends and do only what was approved by them."

Tom Platt left no room for doubt in his version. "These assurances were oft repeated, and solemnly emphasized, and were accepted and agreed to by all those present," he said.[129] That done, he said, Garfield then "was given assurance that the canvass… would be pushed from that moment with the utmost energy and enthusiasm"[130]—a direct *quid pro quo*.

No other detailed account of the meeting exists. Two other briefer versions from non-participants claim that Platt went further and actually wrote up the agreement in "a formal document, frigid as a bill of sale."[131] No such paper, though, ever surfaced, even later at the height of controversy.

Could Garfield actually have made this promise, mortgaging his own future presidency to the Bosses, going against all his concerns and careful soundings of the prior month? In his own journal a few days later, he seemed to deny it: "no serious mistakes had been made" in New York, he wrote, with "[n]o trades, no shackles, and as well fitted for defeat or victory as ever."[132] Later, when faced with public charges of a campaign deal, he authorized a friend to deny them publicly as "full of misstatement and misrepresentations"—other than his offer of a top post to Levi Morton, which he conceded.[133] Still, the New Yorkers in Levi Morton's hotel room that night each had years of experience in politics. Garfield may have chosen careful, vague words, but Arthur and Platt should have understood any nod, wink, or handshake that went with them. The bare historical record gives no answer. Platt and Arthur may have misheard Garfield that night, their own judgment distorted by wishful thinking, or they may have lied outright. Garfield, too, under stress, may have tripped on his own words, deceiving himself later into thinking that he'd promised only to "consult" with the Stalwarts, his pride perhaps preventing him from admitting a mistake.

In his journal that night, after so grand a day in his life, Garfield wrote simply: "Did not sleep well. Had in the P.M. a long interview with Morton, Crowley, Arthur and Platt."[134]

When Roscoe Conkling finally surfaced a few days later—he had been hiding the whole time in the New York area at the home of his brother Frederick or at a hotel in Coney Island—Chet Arthur left him no doubt on the outcome. "Distinctly, clearly, such an agreement had been made," Conkling would later tell a newsman. "How willing Garfield then was," he explained, "when everything looked blue and certain defeat seemed to stare him in the face; how willing he was to concede anything and everything to the Stalwarts if they would only rush to the rescue and save the day!"[135] Even the *Nation* observed wryly that "Conkling's zeal in the campaign indicated that he had made a deal with the Republican candidate."[136]

Conkling at last appeared satisfied. He'd won his tribute. Now he could win the presidency for his party and his purchased candidate. "If you insist... I shall carry him through,"[137] Conkling told Arthur by one account after hearing the terms. A few days later, he wrote to Levi Morton that he'd cleared his desk and schedule "to read up and get ready for the campaign."[138] From that moment on, the campaign would sizzle and became brilliant.

Even Ulysses Grant, after months of seclusion out west, now finally broke his silence and declared himself ready for battle. "I will be going east the latter part of Sept[ember] and will gladly attend any meeting intended to further the success of the ticket headed by Garfield & Arthur," he wrote to John Logan from Manitou Springs, in Colorado, on August 12—coincidentally just days after the New York summit. "[I]t will not do to be beaten until every man ... can cast his vote just as he pleases, and can have it counted just as he cast it."[139]

Not surprisingly, Whitelaw Reid heard differently. "Everything I have seen since the conference convinces me that it turned all our way," he reported to Garfield a few days later, and "the only one in any way injured by it was Mr. Conkling himself."[140] *Harper's Weekly's* report said flatly: "All rumors of secret pledges are wholly baseless."[141] Garfield, after a week of snubs from the New York senator, now had his own view of the Boss: "If [Conkling] intends to take actively hold of the campaign, it is probably best that he does not call on me...."[142]

◉ ◉ ◉ ◉ ◉

Charles Guiteau, the odd little man with the uneven temperament, enjoyed the Fifth Avenue Summit as much as anyone. He attended every session he could. Far from shy, he seemed to flourish amid the throng of busy politicos. Guiteau walked about the grand hotel lobbies in his worn, shabby coat, hobnobbing among the elite. He stepped right up to the most famous leaders to introduce himself. In his arm, he carried freshly-printed copies of his campaign speech "Garfield versus Hancock," which he handed out to the dignitaries. Marshall Jewell, John Logan, Chet Arthur, all got copies. He tried to shake hands with Garfield directly, but had to settle for passing along to him too a copy of the speech. Guiteau never denied that he'd probably come across to most people as a nuisance, a nobody, a hanger-on. Still, he insisted, they treated him well: "Always very delightful and pleasant in every way," he later described the greetings he'd received.[143] When he'd mention his name, they'd recognize him, he said. "O, yes; I remember that; it was a very good speech," Guiteau claimed to recall hearing them say.[144]

Among the party leaders at the Fifth Avenue Hotel that day, he came across Emory Storrs, the Chicago lawyer who'd supported General Grant at the convention. Storrs had gotten to know Guiteau "by sight" over the years, he explained later. " I knew Guiteau ... as a young lawyer in Chicago," though "hardly ... an acquaintance." Guiteau "came up to me, and, patting me on the arm or shoulder, said that I was on the right track," Storrs later said, recalling Guiteau's mention of a speech he'd given in Vermont a few weeks earlier. He seemed in "apparently excellent spirits, rather exultant in his manner," Storrs remembered. Guiteau, of course, gave Storrs a copy of the speech. Storrs found it striking that it "seemed to have been printed under the auspices of the [Republican] National Committee"[145]—odd since Guiteau had no actual tie to the committee or the party.

Guiteau had arrived in New York weeks earlier in June after surviving the terrible *Stonington-Narragansett* steamship disaster and had spent the next several days polishing up his "Garfield vs. Hancock" paper. Now he seemed quite proud of it. The whole document ran just three pages, much of it reading like clichés of the era. Still, even a political connoisseur like George Gorham considered it "a pretty good condensed statement of the whole situation as viewed by a good many people. It is neither remarkable on the one hand nor ridiculous on the other."[146] The speech opened by recalling great past Republican leaders like Wendell Philips, Henry Clay, and writer Harriet Beecher Stowe, then went on to praise Ulysses Grant, "renowned in war and peace." It called Garfield a "clean-handed" and "high-toned, conscientious Christian gentleman." It culminated in stirring words, "Ye men whose sons perished in the war! What say you to this issue? Shall we have an other war? Shall our national treasury be controlled by ex-rebels and their Northern allies, to the end that millions of dollars of southern war claims be liquidated?" Then it concluded: "If you want prosperity and peace, make Garfield President, and the republic will develop till it becomes the greatest and wealthiest nation on the globe."[147]

In early July, Guiteau had left New York City and traveled upstate to Poughkeepsie and Saratoga. He'd tried to deliver the speech there, but couldn't find an audience. He'd posted signs, but something always went wrong—either it had rained or been too hot. Nobody came. It "didn't draw," he explained. Two weeks later, back in New York and eager for work, Guiteau had called at Chester A. Arthur's Lexington Avenue home to introduce himself. He knocked at the large front door but the doorman had sent him away, telling him that General Arthur had gone out. Guiteau had called on Arthur again at the Republican State Committee on Fifth Avenue. This time, he'd gotten through and enjoyed several minutes talking face to face with the vice presidential candidate. Guiteau told Arthur about his speech and asked for speaking assignments during the campaign—which generally were arranged through Arthur's office.

The Fifth Avenue conference in August gave Guiteau a great opportunity. He now got his speech printed and made a point to come and circulate in the lobby, introducing himself to the big shots and handing out copies. Apparently, party leaders actually gave him the chance to deliver the speech—perhaps as a trial run—during the Thursday night outdoor torchlight gala, standing on the platform along with the candidate. The next morning, he could read his own name in the *New York Times* along with the other speakers—Garfield, Arthur, Logan, Harrison, Congressmen Conger and Williams, Anon McCook … and "Charles Guiteau of Illinois," fine company for an obscure figure new to the city.[148] Throughout the day, Guiteau tried to act friendly and get his name out, even if his awkward style and appearance kept him from making friends.

Charles Guiteau recognized one reason he had trouble getting speaking assignments from the Republican committee, even after his Fifth Avenue debut. They "wanted men of reputation," he explained. Guiteau persisted, though. He began to spend time each day at the national committee's Fifth Avenue office, striking up conversations, reading the latest papers and circulars. He would stick with his plan, he decided. He didn't have much else to do that summer, and he saw a future here. After all, the Stalwarts had now cut a deal with the candidate Garfield on patronage. Everyone talked about it. If the Republicans won the election, there'd be plenty of political jobs to go around. Those who gave speeches or worked in the campaign, he knew, would get the best ones. Just ask anyone in politics: that's how the business worked.[149]

❋ ❋ ❋ ❋ ❋

Before he'd left Ohio for the New York summit in early August, Garfield had finally written and sent off his formal letter to the Republican Party accepting its nomination for president in 1880. The letter filled almost four single-spaced pages in the official proceedings. The party circulated it to all the newspapers, and most printed the full text. A few critics focused on its backtracking from Rutherford Hayes's bold advances on civil service reform. In making appointments, Garfield had written, a president should "seek and receive the... assistance of those whose knowledge of the communities in which the duties are to be performed best qualifies them to aid in making the wisest choice." These jumbled words sounded too much like old-style Senatorial Courtesy—giving government jobs to local political cronies regardless of merit. They looked like yet another sop to the Senate Bosses. Reformers blasted him for the apparent sell-out: Carl Schurz called himself "disgusted," and the Nation pronounced it "unworthy."[150][151]

Garfield, though, had a broader goal. Of the millions of Americans who'd read his letter, only a few really cared much about civil service reform. Garfield needed to reach a fuller body politic. What did the nation want in a president in 1880?

Garfield knew America as well as anyone; he'd traveled the country, met its people, and struggled with its legislation. From his porch in Mentor, Ohio, he saw a nation amid vast change, so dramatic that this single generation's parents and grandparents would barely recognize the new landscape. Political parties struggled to keep pace. The ante-bellum South and North both had been transformed. Just in the 1870s, three new inventions—the typewriter (1874), the telephone (1876), and the electric light (1879)—had begun to revolutionize daily life. Giant business entities—Jay Gould's telegraph and railroad empires, Andrew Carnegie's steel works, John D. Rockefeller's Standard Oil, among others—had changed how thousands of workmen made livings and channeled unparalleled wealth into a small circle.

The new economic engine had produced remarkable growth: pig iron production, for instance, had more than tripled since 1866, from 1.2 to 3.8 million tons a year, as working railroad track had exploded to over 93,000 miles. High-speed rail connections, improved telegraphs, and mass steam-driven presses had sparked a newspaper explosion making communications quicker and more diverse—building on the still-new technological marvels, the trans-Atlantic telegraph, completed in 1866, and the transcontinental railroad, completed in 1869. America's western frontier had given way to a vast quilt of farms, pushing production of wheat, corn, and barley to twice the levels they had reached in the late 1860s. The number of American towns, measured by operating post offices, had swelled from 28,492 to 42,989 in a decade. Some 60 percent of American workers still raised food, but millions now worked in huge mines or factories or for big corporations.[152]

As a result, unfamiliar new issues peppered public debate: strivings of labor organizations, the impact of world trade, the fragile prosperity, and the weight of poverty. Change brought fear, and anti-immigrant bigotry infected both coasts—in the East against Catholics, in the West against Chinese "coolies"—contract railroad workers paid pennies a day. Riots broke out in California against this so-called "yellow peril" to American jobs. The 120,000 Chinese who'd come to America from 1871 to 1880 made them the fifth largest immigrant group that decade behind Germans, Scandinavians, Irish, and English.

Voters still felt the emotions of the recent war: northern fears of southern resurgence, southern scorn at northern occupation, and the dimming promise of racial freedom. Civil War had forced Americans to recognize the stark impact of government decisions on their personal lives. As a result, voter turnout now routinely reached 80 percent in presidential years,* re-

---

* By contrast, current levels generally fall just above 40 percent.

flected already in huge crowds drawn by both Garfield and Hancock in their campaigns. Veterans, their families, and regiments had transferred their loyalties from the battlefields of war to politics. Republicans saw themselves as the party that had saved the Union and ended slavery; they saw Democrats as the ones who had torn it down.

Republicans had created prosperity, the party line went; Democrats would ruin it. "I belong to a party that believes in good crops; that is glad when a fellow finds a gold mine; that rejoices when there are forty bushels of wheat to the acre," boldly explained Robert Ingersoll, the Illinois lawyer and party activist. "The Democratic party is a party of famine; it is a good friend of an early frost; it believes in the Colorado beetle and the weevil."[153]

Nominating a Union General like Hancock, argued a partisan *St. Louis Globe Democrat*, "no more changes the character of Democracy than a figurehead of the Virgin on Kidd's pirate craft would change it into an honest ship."[154]

Garfield had evolved his own deeply-textured view of Washington after almost two decades in Congress. "The chief duty of government is to keep the peace and stand out of the sunshine of the people," he'd written in 1869.[155] For a political campaign, though, he had to address the immediate public issues while avoiding the quicksand controversies. His letter read like a checklist of good and bad:

- Opposition to the "pernicious doctrine of State supremacy" still mouthed in the defeated South;
- Support for the right of each citizen "free and without intimidation, to cast his lawful ballot ... and have it honestly counted";
- Support for popular education;
- Opposition to government aid of "sectarian schools," stressing the "separation of the Church and the State in everything relating to taxation." He gave this grudging nod to widespread anti-Catholic fears while resisting pressures to go further and make political hay over the fact that his opponent Winfield Hancock's wife was Catholic;*

---

* The virulently anti-Catholic *Cleveland Leader* (July 9, 1880) described how Hancock would run a "Romanish" church in the White House "fitted up... with the superstitious paraphernalia of Roman worship ... [that would] become the headquarters of priests, nuns, monks, and so on. The Pope of Rome would be influential in that house through Mrs. Hancock who would be the Romish power behind the throne!" John Sherman had faced similar bigotry because of his Catholic wife.

- Support for protective tariffs allowing American manufacturers to "compete fairly" with foreign producers—a bedrock Republican principle since the time of Henry Clay. The U.S. government in 1880 collected over $186 million in "tariffs," custom duties on imported goods, representing more than half of its total annual revenue (the rest coming mostly from excise taxes on alcohol and other goods). At the same time, it ran a budget surplus of over $50 million each year which it used to pay down Civil War-era debt. Democrats wanted to lower these tariff barriers, making imported goods cheaper. They demanded a tariff "for revenue only" with no extra duties to protect local American businesses—in other words, free international trade, a foolishly naïve concept to Republicans of the era.
- Opposition to "doubtful financial experiments" like free coinage of silver, an idea backed by Greenbackers to help debtors and poor people by enlarging the money supply but which Garfield, like most Republicans, thought would only corrode the currency and damage business;
- Improving the navigability of the Mississippi River;
- Controlling the inflow of Chinese workers on the Pacific coast—a nod to Californians' fears of cheap import labor and anti-immigrant xenophobia, though stopping short of hard-liner calls to expel foreigners or close America's doors to Asians; and
- Calling on Congress to "devise a method" to reform the civil service.[156]

Garfield made no mention of an eight-hour workday, the rights of labor unions, women's suffrage, government's response to the 1877 strikes, controlling railroads and other corporate giants, easing poverty, creating a graduated income tax, or confronting the remaining hostile American Indians on the frontier—all points that simmered just under the surface. Instead, he tried to ruffle no feathers and make no mistakes. He made his statesmanship implicit. "If elected, it will be my purpose to enforce strict obedience to the Constitution and the laws, and to promote, as best I may, the interest and honor of the whole country, relying for support upon the wisdom of Congress, the intelligence and patriotism of the people, and the favor of God," he wrote.

Now, in early August, Garfield had his platform. He had his party united, his friends energized, and his strategy in place. It was time to beat the Democrats and win the White House.

· 9 ·
THE NARROWEST MARGIN

CHESTER ALAN ARTHUR DELIGHTED AT finally getting down to work. From the large desk in his plush chairman's suite at the Fifth Avenue Hotel, where the New York State Republican Committee kept its offices, his window looking out over Madison Square Park and a grand vista of brick city neighborhoods beyond, Arthur set about doing what he did best— mobilizing the power of a vast, complex political machine to win an election—a job he pushed this year with extra zeal with himself as one of the candidates.

National parties set direction, but individual states took the lead in presidential campaigns in the 1880s. Arthur ran New York's push just as John Logan ran Illinois', Don Cameron ran Pennsylvania's, and James Blaine ran Maine's—each a king in his kingdom. Arthur liked it this way. He relished the hands-on political craft: from grand strategy to tiniest detail, from raising money, scheduling speakers, and organizing rallies, to getting out the vote and patrolling for frauds.

Starting immediately after the party's Fifth Avenue summit in early August, Arthur threw his full energy into the race. Rested and ready after his July fishing trip in Canada, he bounded around his office, speaking with hundreds of people, dictating dozens of letters, and clogging telegraph lines with orders to lieutenants all across the state. Each morning he scribbled out a detailed task list and checked each item as it got done. Backed by three secretaries, a clerk and a bookkeeper, his office noisy and cramped with visitors, Arthur took personal charge of party finances and approved every expense, big and small. He circulated blank forms to create "Garfield and Arthur Clubs" in every town and neighborhood, and he answered every request, be it from a small-time hack like W.T. Cogshill in western New York to "[s]end me one thousand more wrappers for newspapers and stamps,"[1] or from a big-shot like Levi Morton who'd arranged to print 25,000 copies of a Garfield immigration speech in German and now hinted that "I shall be glad to receive a check."[2]

After long days at headquarters, Arthur spent his nights sharing a beer or whiskey with local ward healers at a corner saloon or sipping brandy with New York's elite at the Union League Club or Delmonico's restaurant—equally at ease in each place. His commanding figure drew attention wherever he went—the possible next Vice President of the United States.

Behind the bravado, though, Chet Arthur also fought a constant sadness during these months, still tangled in grief from the death of his wife, Ellen Herndon Arthur, just eight months earlier after a twenty-year marriage. He sorrowed at being a widower at this grand moment in his life. One night that summer at his Lexington Avenue home, Arthur's little eight-year old daughter Nell had presented him a bouquet of flowers during a family dinner. Arthur had pulled her over to kiss her and thank her, a sister recalled, and then he "completely broke down." Little Nell reminded him of her late mother, his late wife; "there is nothing worth having now," he'd sobbed, then struggled to regain composure before friends arrived at the house.[3]

Work became Arthur's tonic. With the campaign in high pitch, he barely saw his home and two children now, spending the hours instead at headquarters or carousing with his fellow politicos. He happily declined dozens of speaking offers from around the country, preferring to stay in New York until the November voting. Arthur had never been a good public speaker, and the tradition against candidates going "on the stump" suited him fine. "Mr. Arthur directs me to say that the only active part he takes in the campaign is as ch[airman] of this Com[mittee]," his assistant wrote in refusing one invitation.[4] "My duties as Chrm. RSC confine me here constantly," he responded to another.[5]

Arthur's biggest headache these days, though, came from lining up speakers for all the rallies, parades, and demonstrations across the country to inspire voters and wage the public debate—and, in this process, to keep peace between the party's nominee Garfield and its favorite stump speaker Roscoe Conkling. Arthur kept his sharp eye on the main force driving this demand, the calendar.

Election day would fall on Tuesday, November 2, that year, the traditional first Tuesday after the first Monday in November.* All states would vote for president on that single day, and by 1880 most states had also consolidated their voting for state, local, and Congressional offices on this day as well. Three states, though, still preferred to keep separate dates for local elections.[6] Voters in these states would have to vote twice: after the separate local races, they'd then have to take a second trip to the polls in November to vote for president. Their early votes in the local elections became important barometers for party support and, by extension, the presidency—in fact, the only reliable measures of public support long before opinion polls. A strong showing for the party's local candidates in September and October could boost its presidential nominee and seal his victory; defeat could demoralize party workers and drive away financial backers—not unlike today's early election-year Iowa caucuses or New Hampshire primary for nomination contests.

Election calendar, 1880:

September 13: Maine; State, local, Congressional;

October 12:   Indiana and Ohio, State, local, Congressional;

November 2:   All states Presidential; and all others.

Maine traditionally came first, and had signaled November outcomes since the time of "Tippicanoe and Tyler Too" in 1840. This year, Arthur didn't waste time worrying about Maine. James Blaine, the State's own long-time chief, would manage its campaign and Blaine certainly wouldn't fail his friend Garfield. Blaine, in fact, had already thrown himself headlong into the battle; he'd sent out waves of telegrams from Augusta to arrange celebrity speakers for rallies and torchlight parades—Robert Ingersoll, John Sherman, and John Logan, among others. Logan had committed to three days there in August; William Frye had toured eight Maine cities, and even General Phil Sheridan had planned a visit in September.[7]

The October states, Ohio and Indiana, came next and posed a bigger danger. Ohio would support Garfield, its favorite son, but Arthur worried about Indiana. Indiana had grown fickle since the war, one of just four northern states to vote Democratic for president in 1876. This time, Democrats had targeted Indiana, putting Indianapolis banker and former Indiana Con-

---

* Congress set this formula in 1845. Early November came after farmers had mostly finished harvesting crops but before winter made roads impassable. A Tuesday avoided travel on the Christian Sabbath for voters traveling long distances to cast ballots and avoided interfering with merchants who generally settled their books on the first of the month.

gressman William English on the ticket for vice president solely to help capture the state again. Ugly rumors circulated that they planned to bring in armies of "floaters" and "vagabonds"—professionals who sold their votes to the highest bidder. If Republicans and Democrats had to match bribe for bribe, the cost could be huge.

Finally, come November, New York would cast more electoral votes than any other state. Chester Arthur considered New York a point of personal honor, his home state that he couldn't fail to deliver.

To wage this fight, Arthur and the Republicans needed money, and lots of it. While Levi Morton hit up Wall Street, Chester Arthur worked his traditional source: government workers, whom he gouged for a huge pot for New York with its estimated 20,000 state employees plus thousands of federal appointees.*[8] Before long, hundreds of thousands of dollars flowed into his coffers from this source alone.

For the public campaign, Arthur took personal charge of bookings for Ulysses Grant and Roscoe Conkling, the party's two biggest celebrities. Conkling, despite the August summit deal in New York, remained stubborn as ever. Beyond his usual *prima donna* attitude, he fought any effort to bring him face-to-face with Garfield, the candidate, or to drag him away from New York State. If anything, Conkling's tone toward Garfield had hardened over time. He had an insult or a sneer ready whenever Garfield's name came up. Garfield "would be humiliated in his own state," or "There's no sand in him," Conkling would tell friends.[9] All September and October, Arthur had to coax, scold, and pamper him into making a nationwide tour for the campaign, bickering over everything from railroad schedules and concert halls to getting proper stage platforms and acoustics.

For his own state, New York, Arthur took the cream of the crop. He booked Carl Schurz, Blaine, Logan, Emory Storrs, Henry Ward Beecher, Hamilton Fish, and Robert Ingersoll, to name a few. He even signed up Samuel Clemens, "Mark Twain," popular author of *The Adventures of Tom Sawyer*, *The Innocents Abroad*, and *The Gilded Age*, who claimed "no strength" as a "political speaker" but still told Arthur he'd like to do "one little bit of a

---

* Republicans in the 1880s generally demanded each government worker to pay the party three percent of their salary for their patronage job, plus special charges during elections. Today, the vast majority of Federal employees have civil service career status; for them, no contributions are required nor expected. Political solicitations on government property are banned, as are solicitations by supervisors.

15-minute speech at some big gathering in New York, merely to tranquilize the audience and hold them down whilst the real speakers of the evening are getting ready."[10]

To kick things off, Arthur wanted his strongest player. Local Republicans loved Roscoe Conkling's in-your-eye attitude and Arthur insisted that Conkling stage his campaign debut in mid-September in New York City where large, friendly local crowds would inspire a top-notch performance. Conkling balked at everything, even the date: "Seventeenth [of September] preferred to sixteenth. Should anything defer a little longer it will be agreeable," he telegraphed from Utica.[11]

"[W]e have finally determined to have the meeting on the seventeenth and have secured the Academy [of Music on Fourteenth street]," Arthur telegraphed back from his Fifth Avenue office, tactfully holding the line, to which Conkling complained again: "Latest day gives little time but will try. Please advise what kind of meeting together with any particulars you can."[12]

Arthur's concept worked perfectly. On a crisp September night, Conkling drew over 20,000 cheering boosters to a sold-out Academy of Music and delivered a stem-winder lasting three hours and forty minutes, much of it taken up with ovations from the crowd. He blasted southern democrats, hailed the Republican record, and even said a kind word about Garfield, though not until well into the fourth hour and buried in a few mumbled sentences. When a cat jumped out onto the calcium–lit stage, Conkling joked: "Don't hurt her. You may spoil a Democratic office-holder." The partisans loved it, sitting crammed twenty people into stage-side boxes designed to hold four. Conkling delivered his phrases "with more than the usual vehemence, precision and force" that night, a newsman on the scene wrote, "stirring the house deeply."[13] Chester Arthur sat in a front-row celebrity box, basking in cheers, cutting a dashing figure in black suit, top hat, and perfect whiskers, rubbing shoulders with friends, bowing at his introduction, but declining even to make a short public speech.

Arthur's next demand, he knew, would make Conkling chafe even more—going west to join Ulysses Grant in Ohio for a giant outdoor jamboree followed by a speaking tour in Indiana. Garfield had insisted on this Ohio visit.[14] He'd been snubbed twice already by Lord Roscoe and now expected him to perform. Grant had agreed at once, giving Arthur a virtual blank check on his arrangements. "I concluded to break other engagement that might conflict and go at any time you might fix," Grant wrote to Arthur from

Galena, Illinois—where he'd returned from his summer-long sojourn in Colorado. "But whatever may be done I will conform to."[15] That left Roscoe the odd man out.

"The suggestion is new & unexpected," Conkling telegraphed back from Utica on hearing the request, acting surprised, still trying to avoid any chance of direct contact with Garfield. "I should not begin by speaking outdoors. After New York I must return home for a brief space. Do you really wish me to go west?"[16] Then the next day: "I prefer staying indoors and will abide your arrangements giving me a reasonable interval to return home for a few days after the seventeenth."[17]

Certainly, Roscoe Conkling had every right to demand rest. Speaking for two to three hours before enormous crowds day after day, having to shout before the advent of microphones in the raw open air, could damage anyone's voice. But Arthur also wanted to make sure they won the election. Garfield had good reason to insist, he felt—the October states posed a real danger. As Garfield persisted and Conkling grew more averse, Arthur found himself the go-between; their telegrams crossed on his desk and demanded his highest diplomatic skill.

Garfield, isolated on his farm, seemed ready to move mountains to address Conkling's excuses. He quickly arranged indoor spaces to protect the Senator's precious tonsils. "We can give the Senator [Conkling] a hall in Cleveland that will hold four thousand if he will speak at a day meeting there or in Warren. We can give him and Grant an audience of twenty five thousand and he can speak from a covered platform blind on the sides. Answer," he telegrammed to Arthur.[18] Warren, a small town outside Cleveland, "offers to build a wigwam," a large enclosed tent, Garfield wired. "Can't the Senator make three speeches, [in] Warren, Cleveland and Cincinnati? Very important. Answer."[19] When Arthur didn't answer fast enough, Garfield wired again, his repeated telegrams reading more as from a frustrated clerk than from a prospective president: "What do you say Friday meeting [in] Warren, Twenty Eighth [of September], evening meeting Cleveland, Twenty Ninth & Cincinnati Thirtieth? Or would you prefer Cincinnati Oct[ober] first?"[20]

Arthur passed the demands along to Utica only to hear more complaints: "Three meetings in Ohio [are] enough. Consecutive days not wise," Conkling wired back.[21] It took four full days of back-and-forth telegrams, sometimes four and five rounds each day, to settle the plans. "Have announced Grant and Conkling [at] Warren twenty eighth afternoon and Conkling Cleveland twenty ninth and Cincinnati evening Oct[ober] first," Garfield finally wired in mid-September.[22] Conkling would follow these Ohio stops with three more speeches in Indiana, his appearances going right up to the very eve of the October voting.[23]

The schedule set, Chester Arthur should have felt relieved; he'd satisfied the candidate, mollified the Senator, and mounted a strong card for Ohio and Indiana. But Garfield hadn't finished yet. Arthur now probably shuddered as he delivered to Conkling the latest candidate request: "Please arrange that General Grant, Senator Conkling, and Yourself spend the night of September twenty seventh at my house."[24] Garfield had made his message very clear: He'd had enough of Roscoe Conkling's avoidances. Speeches in nearby towns were not enough. He wanted the New York Senator where all the world could see them together, standing side by side, shaking hands, smiling as friends, with no question of his support for the ticket. He wanted Conkling at his farmhouse in Mentor, Ohio.

◉ ◉ ◉ ◉ ◉

Garfield had left New York City early on the morning of August 7 after the weeklong party summit at the Fifth Avenue Hotel. Traveling home through New Jersey and western New York, his train had stopped for parades and speeches at town after town: Paterson, Port Jervis, Binghamton, Elmira, Corning, and Chautauqua, each with the hoopla of brass bands, cheering crowds, fireworks, and guns—fantastic events, though Garfield already now found them tedious and routine. He arrived back in Ohio "very tired," he wrote, with his "right hand badly swollen" from shaking so many hands.[25] He told friends about how well things had gone in New York: "I cannot now think of a single point in all the arrangements that could have been better," he wrote to Tom Platt in a thank you note.[26] But Mentor must have seemed a welcome refuge for him after so any days in the public spotlight, let alone his night of arm-twisting by the New York Bosses.

One particular piece of good news did cheer his homecoming. A letter from Ulysses Grant had arrived from Colorado while he'd been away, saying that Grant had now agreed to meet him publicly in Ohio in September on his return east. "I feel a very deep interest in the success of the Republican ticket … and have never failed to say a word in favor of the party, and its candidate, when I felt that I could do any good," Grant had written, breaking his curious silence. "I shall not fail in the future."[27]

Garfield, having chosen to stay home and not campaign, could now settle in for a long stay with Lucretia and the family at Mentor. Lucretia's ren-
ovations had transformed their old farmhouse into a comfortable three-story
wood-frame home surrounded by open porches, wide grassy lawns, picket
fences, and graceful shade trees, all just a mile from town. To handle campaign
work, Garfield turned his upstairs library into an office and made a small cabin
on the back lawn into his telegraph room with links to New York and Washington. He must have felt odd sitting idle in September and October, not "on
the stump" as he'd been for every fall election campaign since the 1850s. Still,
he soon developed a routine: On sunny afternoons, he played croquet with
the children. On good days, he dictated fifty to sixty letters, though never
keeping up with the incoming flood. Sometimes, he'd ride horseback over to
the Mentor post office and carry home the latest mail sack on his saddle;
other days, he rode across farm fields or down country roads with his clerk Joe
Stanley Brown or his sons just to clear his mind. He enjoyed family nights sitting at the fireplace or playing euchre with friends. Normally a voracious
reader, this year Garfield found time apparently only for a single romance
novel, *The Sisters* by George Ebers, and a history, Henry Lee's *Observations on
the Writings of Thomas Jefferson*. When artist John H. Witt came from New
York to paint his portrait for the Republican National Committee, Lucretia
read aloud to him as he sat impatiently for the artist.[28]

Occasionally, Garfield left the farm and visited nearby towns: to Cleveland for a serenade from the local Garfield and Arthur Glee Club, to Ashland
to greet visitors at a county fair, or to Canton for a military reunion with President Rutherford Hayes. Lucretia usually came along, often with their pretty
13 year-old daughter Mollie following at their sides. Most days at home, he
greeted delegations on his front porch or under a nearby elm or maple tree:
95 ladies and gentlemen from Indiana, Governors or Senators from nearby
states, friends and politicos from around the country. His younger boys,
Abram and Irvin, seven and ten years old, seemed untouched by the attention as they played in the fields, hiding behind trees, teasing the farm hands,
or swimming in a nearby creek. The older, teenage sons, Harry and James,
took turns helping around the farm until late August when they had to return
to boarding school in New Hampshire. They and Garfield's mother Eliza,
nearly 80 years old and spending her days in a rocking chair, became a pic-
turesque tableau. Visitors took ears of corn from Garfield's farm as souvenirs.
In September, he planted winter wheat and had workers install new flagstone

and plant fresh grass. By then, he'd even grown accustomed to the newspapermen always camped on the front lawn, recording every visitor, writing down his every message, and always asking questions.[29]

The campaign itself, though, made Garfield worry. He enjoyed much of the materials his backers had produced. A new *Campaign Songster*[30] contained over fifty musical selections to sing at rallies and parades. Along with "James Garfield Leads Us," it included tunes like "Soreheads on our Block"* with lyrics linking the Democrats to Tammany Hall, the "great unwashed" and Wall Street crooks, and the "Conspirators Song" which tied them to the Ku Klux Klan and Confederate Brigadiers. He also read some of the new campaign biographies about himself flooding bookstores around the country. They shamelessly glorified his rise from poverty, his birth in a log cabin, and his civil war battles. One summer as a teenager, Garfield had labored on an Ohio canal, and this became a popular theme. The popular novelist Horatio Alger later penned a book *From Canal Boy to President* about Garfield—nicely fitting his "rags to riches" motif.

Garfield actually had never seen his boyhood poverty as anything to brag about. "It was very bad for my life," he'd written to a friend years before, creating "chaos" and robbing him of "17 years in which a boy with a father and some wealth might have become fixed in some manly ways."[31]

At the same time, Garfield cringed at reading the Democratic newspapers. Day after day, they attacked him viciously, painting him as corrupt, money-grubbing, and weak. They pounded a litany of scandals: Credit Mobilier, DeGolyer Cement, the "Salary grab,"** and tried to link him with

---

* Sung to the tune of "Babies on our Block":
   "If you want some information, Next November come with us;
      And you will see the sickest 'braves' Let loose in Tammany!
   For routed bag and baggage Will the boasting crew be found
      And for the large majority They'll all be marching round;
   There'll be Kelly, there'll be Hendricks; and old Soapy Sammy too;
      And Hancock and bad English, All looking mighty blue;
   The fearful oaths they'll utter, All the startled air will shock;
      They all will sing this ditty Of the soreheads on our block.
   Oh! Little Soapy Sammy, Sitting on his bar'l
      Howling and raving, how he will snarl!
   Oh! Rise, Sammy rise, go and 'water' some more 'stock!'
      Will be sung by the soreheads that live on our block."
["Soapy Sam" referred to a then-common euphemism for campaign "walking around" money.]
** In 1873, when Garfield chaired the House Appropriations Committee, Congress enacted itself a pay raise that included several years' back pay at the higher rate. It was repealed the next year after a public outcry.

every crime from the Grant years. They accused Garfield of "bloody shirt" politics, treachery toward John Sherman in Chicago and General Rosecrans at Chickamauga,* intolerance toward Catholics,** and subservience to Wall Street villains like Jay Gould and John D. Rockefeller.

Sitting in Ohio, isolated from party leaders in New York and Washington except by telegraph or occasional visit, Garfield fretted. It felt odd, the two candidates pushed into semi-seclusion—he in Ohio and Winfield Scott Hancock at his military command on New York's Governors Island—as their "friends" carried the fight. His own "friends," Conkling and Chester Arthur, seemed far too preoccupied with New York State, Garfield felt. He worried instead about the October states in the Midwest, especially Indiana. "If we carry Indiana," he wrote them in early September, "the rest will be easy."[32]

But no one seemed to listen. Garfield had had to send telegram after telegram just to coax Roscoe Conkling to speak in the Midwest—and he still hadn't heard whether Conkling would condescend to visit him at his home. Garfield knew he needed Roscoe Conkling—his electric presence on the stump, his solid machine in New York—to win the election, but feared there'd be no end to the insults he'd have to tolerate from this one man. Garfield had also telegraphed John Logan in Chicago, asking him to pick "the places in Ohio you would prefer to speak, and ... I will see that the appointments are made for you in those places. Do not hesitate to do this." He added: "Why can't you make me a visit soon and bring Mrs. Logan. Mrs. Garfield and I would be greatly pleased to have you do so."[33]

Still, by early September, despite the frustrations, Garfield largely felt satisfied. His campaign was getting organized and on track. Certainly, he could count on his friend Blaine to deliver the first early-bird state, Maine, Blaine's own fiefdom, and a victory there would boost everyone's confidence. "I am led to expect about 5,000 majority [in Maine], but shall be content with 3,000," Garfield wrote on September 13 as voting there began.

Then, "[a]bout 9 o'clock in the evening the telegrams began to arrive," he wrote in his journal that night.[34] By 11 pm, the outcome had become clear.

---

* Rosecrans, running for Congress as a Democrat from California that year, complained about Garfield's alleged failure to defend him after Rosecrans' embarrassing 1863 retreat from the Chickamauga battlefield.
** Based on Garfield's opposition to government support of parochial schools, General William Tecumseh Sherman's Catholic wife wrote a public letter alleging his religious bias. Hancock at the time was defending himself from bigoted attacks, not limited to Republicans, based on his own wife's Catholicism.

Democrat Harris Plaisted had won Maine's governorship by 2,000 votes—
the first time in thirty years that Republicans had lost the statewide seat.
Maine had fallen. Unbelievably, Blaine had failed him. Garfield's well-or-
dered campaign now reached its first watershed crisis. "This will make the
contest close and bitter throughout the North," he confided.[35] In this era before public opinion polls, he could only guess what signal the voters in Maine
had been sending. Did the statewide loss there mean that they'd turned
against his national ticket?

Next came Indiana, the fickle October state. A defeat for local Republican candidates there, coming right after Maine's loss, could sink Garfield altogether in November. Indiana must be saved. What were his "friends" doing?

⦿ ⦿ ⦿ ⦿ ⦿

Marshall Jewell, chairman of the Republican national committee, gathered
around him the newspapermen jammed into the lobby of his Fifth Avenue
headquarters at nearly midnight on that night, September 13, to follow the
Maine returns. "[T]he result is a Republican reverse," he told them. "It is not
a Democratic victory." His face flushed, voice struggling, exhausted from a
long, frustrating vigil, Jewell explained patiently how the contest in Maine
had been unique, not a signpost for the presidency. Republicans had faced a
"fusion" candidate for governor there, Jewell told the newsmen. The Greenback Party had nominated Harris Plaisted, a popular union general, and Democrats had jumped on Plaisted's bandwagon only later. Plaisted had campaigned on the Greenback platform of easy money and freer homesteads. The
victory belonged to the Maine Greenbacks, not to the national Democrats or
Winfield Scott Hancock.

The Greenback victory should "[m]ake business men think more clearly
and earnestly of the possibilities of the future if the Democrats should come
into power," Jewell noted, warning his Republican backers of possible defeat
in November.[36]

A few days later, Roscoe Conkling tried to find humor in the crisis.
"These Democrats are going to visit every island, traverse every continent,
and vex every sea, whenever they think they can find a Greenbacker that
will 'fuse' with them," he told a New York audience. He relished, he said, the
chance to connect Winfield Hancock with a party "snake-bitten with the
idea of fiat money [paper not backed by gold] and inflation."[37]

But privately, Marshall Jewell heard panic among his lieutenants. He tried to put on a brave face.[38] Stalwarts pointed fingers at James Blaine for bungling his own state's campaign, but something else had gone badly wrong. The "set-back in Maine was a set-back,"[39] Jewell argued. They shouldn't deny it among themselves. Blaine, for his part, alleged fraud by the Democrats. He sent a telegram to Garfield—with copies to all the newspapers—pointing to "a large sum of money, $70,000 to $100,000* [that] was sent into Maine four days before the election and used by the Democrats as money was never used before"—vote-buying on a grand new scale.[40]

Blaine also saw a problem with the Republican's message. He admired the Greenbackers for effectively touting free coinage of silver—bad economics, he felt, but it showed concern for bread-and-butter problems of workers. Republicans had relied too much on the "bloody shirt"—emotional appeals to Civil War-era loyalties.

Blaine wasted no time brooding. He abruptly left Augusta just days after the defeat, rode an overnight train to New York City, and arrived unannounced at the national committee's office on Fifth Avenue. He burst in on Colonel C.J. Hooker, one of Marshall Jewell's deputies, startling some bystanders in the hallway, and launched into his argument. "Fold up the bloody shirt and lay it away. It's no use to us," Blaine announced, waving his arms, raising his voice. "You want to shift the main issue to protection. Those foolish five words of the Democratic platform, 'A tariff for revenue only,' give you the chance."[41] These words showed Democrats standing squarely for free world trade—a disastrously foolish notion to Nineteenth Century Republicans.

To compete, Blaine argued, Republicans had to push their own formula for prosperity: hard money and the protective tariff. They must hang the Democrats with their quirky "tariff for revenue only" language. Marshall Jewell agreed and quickly arranged for States to start pumping out posters, leaflets, and directions to "stump" speakers on the new theme. Still, even Blaine recognized that this wasn't enough. In Indiana, the next battleground, they faced a bigger problem—graft.

As with Maine, Indiana voters in October technically would elect only a Governor and local judges and congressmen—voters there would have to

---

* Since *none* of that amount would have gone for radio or television advertising, the largest line-item cost in modern campaigns, and only a tiny amount for newspapers, the bulk could go for "walking around" money to purchase a huge number of votes—10,000 to 20,000 easily at going rates of $2 to $4 per vote—even had Blaine exaggerated the amount to cover his failure.

return to the polls a second time in November to vote for president. The local Indiana party had already mounted a smart campaign.[42] Secret reports, though, painted a frightening picture of illegitimate action. "Our danger lies in the riff raff element, the purchaseable votes," William Birney reported to William Chandler after a scouting trip. He pointed to William English, the Democrat's vice presidential nominee and a leading Indiana banker, as chief spear-carrier for the pay-offs. " English is said to be receiving large amt's of money, and those who know him best say that he counts on buying all the votes in the market."[43] Garfield's friend Burke Hinsdale, after a round of speeches there, reported "30,000 merchantable votes in the State."[44] A *New York Times* reporter echoed the news: "Democrats are raising heaven and earth to carry the State at the October election, and are relying solely on the lavish use of money in the last two or three days before the election."[45]

Garfield too had heard these stories from friends in nearby Ohio towns. "[T]here has suddenly appeared in many parts of [Indiana] considerable sums of money among the Democrats," he warned Chester Arthur in late September. "I have now no doubt but that they are undertaking the Maine tactics in this state as well as in Indiana." The situation, the prospect that Democrats might be preparing to engage in massive vote-buying or bribery of voting officials, "is creating some anxiety if not alarm."[46] Panic indeed had set in among state leaders. "The Indiana delegation have been here in force—all clamorous for money," wrote Marshall Jewell's deputy R.C. McCormick from New York. Money, though, had to be used correctly. As is, he added, "I would not give a dollar."[47]

Addressing the crisis would take a special talent—someone prepared to work secretly behind the scenes and engage the enemy blow for blow, matching their tactics clean for clean and dirty for dirty. Arthur and Marshall Jewell had no intention to surrender Indiana, and had no scruples about doing what needed being done. Into the breach, they decided, would ride Stephen Dorsey.

Dorsey, the quick-tongued, handsome former Carpetbag Senator, already had made his mark at the Republican national committee since his surprise selection as secretary in July. In addition to pushing and staging the grand New York party summit, Dorsey had also backed James Blaine to the hilt during the contest in Maine. "You shall have what you ask & can depend on it," he'd telegraphed to Blaine from New York at one point.[48] Jewell might be the committee's chairman, but Dorsey provided its spark. In mid-August, Dorsey had slipped quietly out to Indiana to size up the problem. His report back echoed the conclusions of everyone else. To win, he said, he'd need solid planning, plenty of cash, and a free hand. His zealous style fit the need, and no one cared to ask questions.

"General, if I don't succeed, I shall never come back here again," Dorsey told Chet Arthur in New York City before heading off on his mission, plotting a retreat to his recently-acquired ranch in frontier New Mexico if he failed.

"Let me know if [you go back to the ranch] whether there would be room enough for me," Arthur responded with a laugh.[49]

Some old hands smelled trouble when word got out about Stephen Dorsey's new role. His reputation for swindling railroad bond-holders and selling his Senate vote had preceded him. "I tremble at the result," R. C. McCormick wrote to William Chandler in New Hampshire. "[S]ome of our worst men are in the lead, and God only knows what they will do. If they do not cover the party with disgrace I will be thankful."[50]

Doubters aside, Dorsey seemed to have the confidence of the one voice that mattered most, the candidate's. In late September, he traveled to Toledo and met with Garfield himself for two hours at the Boody House hotel. Here, Garfield confided his own fears that Democrats might use barrels of money to "ambush"[51] them in Indiana and even Ohio. A few days later, Garfield wrote to Dorsey from Mentor: "Don't relax any grip anywhere."[52] Levi Morton's secret Wall Street campaign fund by now had raised enormous piles of cash; news of the Greenback victory in Maine had sent shivers up the spines of corporate magnates. The Vanderbilts had given Garfield their pledge and John D. Rockefeller had responded to back-channel requests both for cash and use of his five hundred oil-selling agents in Indiana.[53] Wharton Baker in Pennsylvania had squeezed the local Union League clubs for $100,000 and Governor Foster had hit Ohio businessmen for another $50,000.[54] Later estimates of the total ranged as high as $350,000 to $400,000.[55]

In late September, the money began to flow: "a special messenger from New York" reached Indianapolis "with over four hundred thousand dollars, either in cash or in convertible paper," Dorsey later claimed, much of it in convenient $2 bills to scratch itchy palms.[56] For now, Dorsey kept his money operation secret, not even telling his party superiors. "Jewell has been kept in the dark about the Morton Committee," wrote R.C. McCormick from New York after learning the plan, fearing an explosion. "Jewell has been badly used, and is a model of patience to submit without making a row."[57] John New, the Indiana state chairman, had to apologize to John Logan for secretly taking money from an Illinois vault. "Mr. Spalding gave me a check for $4,500… raised by subscriptions expressly for Indiana," he wrote. "I know of no other money being used. If there was I know nothing about it."[58]

The Indiana battle had been joined behind the scenes. Now, for the one-two punch, the time had come to turn Ulysses Grant and Roscoe Conkling loose on the public to gain the advantage and ensure a Garfield and Arthur victory.

◎ ◎ ◎ ◎ ◎

Ulysses Grant invited the two men into the library and closed the door, the bright Illinois sun of a crisp September afternoon flooding the room through a window. Grant looked relaxed after almost three months on the Colorado-Arizona frontier and happy now to be back in his own house in Galena. He lit a cigar and offered one to his guests; his guests, both churchmen, certainly declined. "I have not seen you since we met at Chautauqua Sunday School Assembly," said the Reverend C.H. Fowler, D.D., looking prim in his crisp white collar and black suit, sitting down with tea. By his side sat Brother Cramb, the pastor at Grant's own Galena town church. Julia had left the men alone in the house. She and Ulysses had just returned home a few days earlier and already were planning to leave again—this time traveling east, first to Chicago to meet son Jesse and his new bride Elizabeth Chapman, then to Boston, Connecticut, and New York City, where they'd visit their son Buck (Ulysses, Jr.). Along the way, Grant would "stump" for Garfield and Arthur—the first former president ever to campaign publicly for his party's national ticket.[59]

"I suppose everybody tells you that he wanted to see you on the track [as candidate for president]," Fowler said.

"Yes, many, but not everybody." Grant must have hid a laugh behind his famous steady gaze and square jaw, sitting in a leather chair. "If everybody had wanted to see me on the track I would have been there."

"I am sorry for the country that you are not there," Fowler said, "not for your comfort or fame, but for the country."

"I am glad to be released from the care." Grant puffed his cigar and spoke easily, without shyness, about what a fine nominee he could have made. He cut the point short, though. Reverend Fowler, a leading figure in the

Methodist Episcopal church, took no written notes on their private talk that day, and Grant later would deny knowing that he'd planned to publish it in the newspapers. Still, Fowler didn't need to prompt Grant to turn his conversation to the real purpose: Winfield Scott Hancock—the Democratic nominee for President.

Ever since their national convention in Cincinnati that summer, Democrats had been trumpeting Hancock's civil war record, touting his heroics at Gettysburg and in the Wilderness campaign. Northern voters had nothing to fear from their party's southern roots, Democrats argued. Hancock, raised in Pennsylvania, educated at West Point, tall and distinguished-looking with broad shoulders and crisp mustache, carried himself proudly as one of the Union Army's true combat heroes. Hancock had commanded his Army of the Potomac corps through its every major encounter of the Civil War, from defeat at Fredericksburg in 1862 through ultimate victory at Appomattox, his record unmatched in bravery and success by any other northern General without a separate command.

After the War, Hancock had stayed with the Army as military governor in the south and west. As a result, fifteen years later, he could claim peacetime leadership experience but with no background in politics, business, or civil government and thus no known position on any public issue—a blank slate in a gallant frame. Great soldiers made great presidents, Democrats could crow, be it George Washington, Ulysses Grant, or now their own nominee.

Who better could knock Winfield Hancock down a few steps than the world-famous hero of Appomattox? What better service could Ulysses Grant provide for the Republican ticket? "I have known him for forty years," Grant said of Hancock without flinching. "He is a vain, weak man. He is the most selfish man I know."[60]

Grant and Winfield Hancock had been classmates at West Point in the 1840s and close friends during most of the Civil War. "It was on my nomination that [Hancock] was made a Brigadier General," Grant explained. In fact, he'd made that nomination in 1864 after Spotsylvania, one of Virginia's most harrowing bloodbaths where Hancock's boldness had barely saved the Union from disaster. Grant certainly remembered the scene that day, he whittling a stick of wood with a pocketknife as cannons boomed, rifles blasted, and terrified men dashed about. When a courier had brought news of Hancock's defeat, Grant had shouted: "I don't believe it." A few minutes later, another messenger had announced that Hancock had broken the rebel lines. "I have finished up Johnston and am now going into Early,"[61] his dispatch had said. "Hancock's a glorious soldier," Grant proclaimed. Hancock's corps had bled heavily for Grant in 1864, at Spotsylvania, Cold Harbor, and Petersburg, always taking the most dangerous spots on the line.

"Down to 1864," Ulysses Grant now told Reverend Fowler, sitting amiably in his Galena, Illinois home, their faces warmed by a gentle fire in the fireplace, Hancock "seemed like a man ambitious to do his duty as an officer; but in 1864 ... Hancock received one vote [for President] and that greatly excited and changed him." Grant's eyes doubtless twinkled behind his graying beard at the thought. "[Hancock] was so delighted that he smiled all over. It crazed him. Before that, we got on well; after that he would hardly speak to me." And after that, Grant said, Hancock had "'the bee' in his bonnet and shaped everything to gain Democratic and Southern favor." For fifteen years since the war, Hancock had "watched, and planned, and waited, till at last he has received the Democratic nomination."[62]

"General, do you think he is in sympathy with the South?" Fowler asked.

"He is crazy to be President. He is ambitious, vain, and weak. They will easily control him," Grant said flatly.

The real split between Grant and Hancock had come after the war, in 1867, at the height of President Andrew Johnson's fight with Congress over how to treat the defeated south (though before Johnson's impeachment by Congress). At one point during that period, Andrew Johnson removed General Phil Sheridan as military governor of Louisiana. New Orleans had become a hotbed of rebel dissent, and Sheridan's strong-arm post-war rule had polarized North and South. President Johnson had replaced Sheridan with Winfield Hancock, and Hancock's first action had been to issue his controversial Order No. 40,* read by many as a slap at Congress. Hancock had then used his power to remove several local officials whom Sheridan had installed just weeks earlier—the Louisiana governor and some state Commissioners—replacing them with former rebels sympathizers. Grant, loyal to Sheridan and to radicals in Congress, had used his authority as Lieutenant General of the

---

* Order 40, which Hancock had issued on arriving in New Orleans in November 1867, stated that when local "civil authorities are ready and willing to perform their duties, the military power should cease to lead and the civil administration resume its natural and rightful dominion"—widely read as abdicating a federal Reconstruction role coming so soon after the end of the war with local government still controlled by confederates. Almost a dozen years later, after Reconstruction, this impulse to limit the role of the military in local law enforcement led to enactment of the *Posse Comitatus* statute in 1878.

Army to intervene and overrule Hancock's decision. After a long stalemate, Hancock, deeply embarrassed, finally asked to be relieved from the command and Grant approved his request.[63]

On returning to Washington, Hancock showed his bitterness by snubbing his commanding officer at every chance. He'd reported to Grant's headquarters but refused a personal meeting with him. Passing Grant in the street the next day, Hancock saluted coldly and walked away. When Grant became president in 1868, he assigned Hancock to the desolate, far-off Dakota territory and then refused his requests for reassignment to California.

Now, in 1880, at the height of Winfield Hancock's Presidential campaign, Ulysses Grant freely dredged up these old episodes for his two houseguests as embarrassing blots on Hancock's record. He mentioned a meeting he'd had with Hancock in 1867 to warn him against Andrew Johnson's southern sympathies. "Well, I am opposed to nigger domination," he recalled Hancock's responding. "General, it is not a question of nigger domination. Four million of ex-slaves, without education or property, can hardly dominate 30,000,000 of whites with all the education and property," Grant recalled arguing back. "It is a question of doing our sworn duty." Hancock's Order No. 40 had "resulted in the loss of many lives," Grant recalled. More than that, Sheridan's original purpose in removing the controversial Louisiana officials in 1867, as Grant remembered it, had been to avoid a swindle involving $7 million in state levee bonds—a concern that Hancock and Johnson had allegedly both ignored despite Grant's warnings.

The more Grant talked, the more he warmed up to his topic. Before long, he had given Reverend Fowler more than enough material for his mission— to prepare the article he'd planned all along. A few days later, Fowler wrote up a summary of the "private talk" and shared it with Grant to check the quotations. Then Fowler sent it to the Cincinnati Gazette and the New York Times. Both ran the story on their front pages. "Ambitious, Vain, and Weak," read the Times' headline. It hit like a thunderclap. Newspapers across the country rushed to follow suit. Hancock was stung but made no public response.*[64]

---

* Grant and Hancock never spoke again. But Grant, writing in his memoir near death, still described Hancock as "the most conspicuous figure of all the general officers who did not exercise a separate command... never mentioned as having committed a blunder [with] personal courage [and] confidence of his troops." Hancock, not yet seeing the compliment, still returned it by marching at Grant's funeral.

The next week, Ulysses and Julia Grant packed their bags, closed up their Galena house again, and set off to Chicago. From there, it would be just a day's train ride to Warren, Ohio, for Grant to meet his old friend Roscoe Conkling and lead the giant Ohio rally for Garfield and Arthur.

Grant reached Cleveland in high spirits on Tuesday morning, September 28, along with John Logan, having taken the overnight train from Chicago. They breakfasted at Cleveland's Kennard House along with Simon Cameron who had come directly from Garfield's Mentor farm. All during the morning, Grant chatted away, dominating the conversation with stories of his recent travels in Japan and East Asia. Riding to Cleveland's railroad depot, he recalled how things had changed since he'd visited Ohio in the 1840s as a young man, back before the railroads. "I traveled from Cincinnati to Cleveland by stage-coach, from Cleveland to Buffalo by water, and from Buffalo to New York by the old 'strap' rail, occupying six days in making the journey," he said, this having been considered a "wonderful" transportation feat at the time.[65]

Large crowds cheered the Hero of Appomattox and former President all along the route of their special excursion train from Cleveland to Warren, just forty-five miles further east. On reaching Warren, Grant stepped from the train out into the sunshine and received a huge ovation. He removed his hat for the crowd. Near the platform, his eye caught the tall, dashing figure of Roscoe Conkling waiting to meet him. He and Conkling had not actually seen each other face to face in over three years, since before Grant's round-the-world trip. All their contact during the nomination fight had been indirect, by mail, messenger, or telegram. Now they shook hands and stopped to talk for a few minutes.

Roscoe Conkling had traveled to Warren directly from New York City, the first stop on his ten-day "stump" tour for the Republican ticket. Conkling, by one friendly account, had made a huge personal sacrifice for this trip: He'd had to return $18,000 in legal retainers that fall and absorb another $11,000 in expenses.[66] Conkling, when campaigning, followed a "strangely scrupulous" discipline about covering his own costs, according to friends. "He certainly paid every cent of his own expenses in the Garfield campaign, and would not allow anybody ... to settle a hotel bill or pay even hack fare on his account," wrote an Oswego, New York reporter who'd traveled with him. "But this was not a political distaste; he was very proud."[67]

The town of Warren had built a huge tent—the "wigwam"—for the day.

Over 12,000 people were seated, "packed together like herrings," by the time Grant and Conkling had arrived, a reporter noted, with tens of thousands more standing on nearby streets and fields. It was a remarkable throng of 40,000, unheard of in rural Ohio at the time. Once they'd settled down, Ulysses Grant took center stage, got the huge audience's attention, but spoke only briefly, barely for seven minutes "in a very low tone of voice, and was heard by only a few," a speaking style that hadn't changed in twenty years of public life.[68] Then he turned the platform over to Roscoe Conkling whose strutting theatrics, strong voice, and handsome curls quickly won over his audience of Ohioans. Conkling had learned his script well from his Academy of Music performance two weeks earlier; now he roused the townsfolk to deafening cheers and cascades of laughter in a two-hour talkathon. He mocked the South, praised the Republican protective tariff, and chided the Greenbackers. He seemed to leave only one thing out from his long-winded speech; neither he nor Grant all afternoon ever actually mentioned the name of the Republican candidate for president—James A. Garfield.

After speeches, songs, music and fireworks on a grand day for Warren, Ohio, the celebrities—Grant, Conkling, John Logan, Don and Simon Cameron—all rode carriages back to the railroad station and climbed together into a special train for Mentor, Ohio, just forty miles away. Even now, at the last minute, Roscoe Conkling balked at the upcoming high-profile visit to James Garfield's farm, complaining that he'd rather skip it and travel directly to Cleveland for his next speech. Grant and Simon Cameron insisted, though.[69] A heavy rain was falling as they reached Mentor. From the window of their parlor car, they saw two groups of horsemen waiting at the depot carrying torches—Garfield Guards, they called themselves, come to escort them to the candidate.

It wasn't until mid-day that day that Garfield got final word that General Grant and his entire entourage would actually visit his home. He sent his young clerk Joe Stanley Brown to the depot with his nicest carriage for the honored guests. A crowd of about 200 local townsfolk followed the delegation's caravan along the mile-and-a-half dirt road from the depot to Garfield's farm—most wanting the chance to shake hands with war hero Ulysses Grant. Joe Stanley Brown, squeezed tightly inside the lead carriage shoulder-to-shoulder with Grant, Conkling, and Logan, tried not to choke on the clouds of cigar smoke during what must have seemed like an interminable ride. He later recalled one snippet of the conversation, when Grant had looked across to Conkling at one point and said: "Well, I never like to give a man the benefit of the knowledge that I dislike him"—not saying whether he meant Garfield or someone else.

"I do," Conkling had shot back, eyes wide and lips askew. "I remember the case when the representative of a New York newspaper called to see me at the request of his chief. I said to him, 'Young man, please understand that what I shall say is not directed against you. You are merely fulfilling the duties of your office, but you return to your chief and say to him for me, that I will have nothing to do with the representative of a journal which has thriven on bribery and corruption and is edited by a thief." He and Grant both broke into loud laughing. All the while, as the old friends joked and shared memories, he recalled: "Cameron and Logan … sat in a subservient and characteristic silence."[70]

◎ ◎ ◎ ◎ ◎

James and Lucretia Garfield stood side-by-side on the front porch as the carriages finally pulled up to their Mentor farmhouse. The rain had paused and the road was lit by torches from the Garfield Guards. Garfield greeted each guest as they walked up the front steps. "How are you, Senator; How are you, General," he said, shaking their hands one by one. By one account, as soon as Garfield spotted Roscoe Conkling, he rushed up to him and took his hand with special feeling, saying: "Conkling, you have saved me. Whatever man can do for man that will I do for you!" By this version, Conkling on the spot extracted yet another pledge from Garfield over control of the New York patronage. By another account, Conkling simply said: "Senator, I am very glad indeed to meet you in your own home."[71]

In any event, once inside the house, Garfield introduced the celebrities to his wife Lucretia, then to his mother, then to the family. Lucretia served lunch in the dining room, though Conkling later claimed that he refused to eat. Afterwards, Garfield took some of the men to his upstairs library for cigars. By all accounts, though, "[t]he door remained open, and no political topics were discussed."[72]

Afterwards, the celebrities made brief remarks to the 200 townsfolk and newspapermen standing outside by the front porch. "Citizens of Mentor, I am glad to meet you tonight," Ulysses Grant announced in good cheer.[73] Conkling, too, spoke a few words, but only John Logan made a point to recognize their host—"our illustrious friend, Gen[eral] Garfield, whom we expect to make the President of the United States next November."[74] The rainstorm kept them indoors for a few more minutes. They left at 9:25 pm—the whole visit lasting barely one hour during which Garfield and Conkling never were alone together. "I had no private conversation with the party, but the call was a pleasant and cordial one all around," Garfield wrote in his journal.[75]

Newspaper writers captured the scene of unity, the candidate sharing his hospitality with his party's top leaders. Still, rumors of a "Treaty of Mentor," replete with new charges of patronage pledges, soon circulated in Stalwart circles—Garfield, it seemed, could not even shake Conkling's hand in front of a horde of witnesses without starting the conspiracy tongues wagging.[76] But at least, he had gotten the visit.

True to his word, Roscoe Conkling did continue his western tour after leaving Mentor. He parted ways with Grant and Logan at the Cleveland railway station, then stayed over in Cleveland and spoke for two hours the next night to a packed city armory. In Cincinnati the next day, he pulled 15,000 people to Highland House. Here, he spoke outdoors in the cold air, a "cruelty" according to one newsman. After half an hour, his voice grew "husky" as he "evidently suffered severely at his chest and throat"[77]—the constant days of long speeches taking a toll.[78] After a day's rest, Conkling made three stops in Indiana that each drew big enthusiastic crowds, including 30,000 people in Richmond and 25,000 in Terre Haute, where he spoke again for three hours.

At the same time, as Conkling traveled west, Ulysses Grant came east for his own remarkable reception in New York City: a six-mile-long parade down Broadway with 60,000 veterans and party activists marching and 300,000 spectators coming out for fireworks, music, torchlights, and speeches filling both Madison Square Park and Union Square Park. Today, no modern parallel exists for these huge Nineteenth Century spectacles staged by America's political parties for their presidential nominees. Only a World Series, a Super Bowl, or a NASCAR championship captures anything near the drama and excitement. By October of 1880, Americans of every stripe, rich, poor, urban, rural, robber barons and laborers, farmers, cowboys, seamstresses, and saloonkeepers, all had become fully caught up in the race of Garfield against Hancock. By the tens of thousands, they came out to hear the speeches; they cheered their favorites, argued and marched in parades, read the newspapers, books, and pamphlets, joined the clubs, volunteered for the parties, and sang the songs. And, of course, they had every plan to vote in the election—

turnout averaged 80 percent of eligible voters back then, twice the levels of today. Voting was a right, after all, for which Americans had recently fought a great war.

⊙ ⊙ ⊙ ⊙ ⊙

Close to 20,000 people jammed the streets around Washington, D.C.'s Willard Hotel and nearby newspaper bureaus as reports on Indiana's voting began hitting telegraph lines early Tuesday evening, October 12. Similar crowds filled neighborhoods around party headquarters in New York City; New York democrats had rented Cooper Union hall to post the returns.* "Dorsey telegraphs from Indiana," Marshall Jewell relayed news to Arthur and Garfield early in the night. "Our reports from all parts of the State are most encouraging… We have carried the state by a good majority—unless the Democrats have set up some scheme to count us out," he wrote, still fearing a trick to manipulate the returns. Stephen Dorsey, camped in Indianapolis, had anticipated this and sent detectives to watch every polling place. "We will get no accurate returns until about midnight."[79]

With the early vote counts came the first reports of fraud. Marshals had arrested three "repeaters" in Indianapolis—Dorsey's troops had tipped them off. One man, Prestley Guyman, had illegally voted in the Twelfth and Thirteenth wards "in neither of which he had a residence," the District Attorney announced. In another neighborhood, marshals had confiscated fraudulent ballots that listed Republican candidates under the Democratic column—designed to invalidate the votes. Dorsey's detectives had also alerted marshals to 800 Chicagoans, "Thugs of the East," who'd been given special one-day rail passes into Indiana before the election—the rumored "floaters."[80]

While the "hurrah-boys style" campaigning of Grant and Conkling had captured the headlines, Stephen Dorsey had taken quiet charge in Indiana and put together a corps of Republican activists—mostly government appointees and detectives. After taking a careful survey, he'd brought "the influences that could be brought to bear on each" voter, as he put it.[81] He'd trained poll watchers to catch frauds and provided guards for black citizens against strong-arm bull-dozing. He'd hired detectives to track vagabonds and repeaters. Where needed, he paid cash. He personally checked his paymasters

---

* Curiously, this same Cooper Union hall was where Abraham Licoln had made his famous speech twenty years earlier against the spread of slavery.

to "prevent, so far as possible, any of the money from sticking to the pockets of men who were trusted to distribute it," he explained.[82] How many bribes did they pay? How much money changed hands? Dorsey himself later claimed $400,000, certainly an exaggeration, though upwards of $70,000 is likely— plenty for greasing palms in a state with then only about 450,000 voters.[83] Newspapers at the time didn't say a word about it; within two years they'd treat the 1880 vote-buying in Indiana as common knowledge.

As the night wore on, good news filtered in. "The best indications are that we shall have twenty five thousand majority in the State [Ohio]," reported C.W. Moulton. "Both our Congressmen are elected."[84]

"Our Indianapolis man says forty-five precincts show one hundred & sixty nine Rep[ublican] gain," reported John Reed about the same time. "Election probably not decided tonight. Ohio seems to warrant acclaim of 15,000 majority with at least 14 of the 20 Congressmen" going Republican.[85]

Dorsey himself finally claimed victory at shortly after 3 am. "We have carried the State by majorities ranging from four to eight thousand," he wired. "Have elected eight of the thirteen Congressmen & probably nine. Think we have the legislature. It looks like a clean sweep."[86] As it turned out, the statewide victory margin had been less than 2,000 votes. At the going rate of $2 to $4 per vote, Dorsey's budget had covered it easily many times over.

Garfield followed the returns by the special telegraph line from his farm along with about a dozen neighbors. He stayed up until 3:30 am and then retired to a good night's sleep, he wrote, "with the news of certain and large Republican gains... [that we] have probably carried Indiana."[87]

⊛ ⊛ ⊛ ⊛ ⊛

The final weeks of the campaign through late October had all the chaos, energy, and suspense of any modern national contest. Chester Arthur raced about his office suite from one crisis to another. "Will you send me [a] check for $400 for printing electoral tickets [ballots, as each party printed its own at the time]? If you can give me any money please do it," begged party chairman Albert Doggett from Brooklyn. "The Democrats are 'slathering' out money at a fearful rate this morning, and I fear are making inroads on our voters. Anything you can give me will be well used."[88] From Buffalo, he read telegraphed news of "fifty boatmen here who would like to have transportation furnished them to go home to vote. Telegraph me at once if you can do it." Arthur responded within hours: "Send 50 boatmen home. We will reimburse you not to exceed $200."[89] He arranged New York City horse-car tickets to take voters to polls. He fielded legal questions—whether the election law "intends to make the technical distinction which printers make between plain white printing paper and book paper" in preparing ballots[90]—and more mundane demands: "Will State Committee make provision for [New York] Tribune bill? Important to know today," from Watertown.[91]

With victory in Indiana, rousing speeches being made across the country, and money flowing freely, prospects looked increasingly bright. "The battle is half over," Stephen Dorsey crowed from his Fifth Avenue office, flush from his Indiana triumph. "The Democrats are demoralized... we propose to keep up the fight and lose nothing by overconfidence. We will turn Democratic defeat into a rout," he boasted.[92]

By now, Blaine's idea of pushing the protective tariff as a national issue had hit home as well. By harping on the Democrats' awkward "tariff for revenue only" platform language, they had scared businessmen and workers across the country. Thousands of posters and pamphlets now warned against dangers of "Democratic free trade as dictated by the South." Winfield Hancock, utterly ignorant of economics, blundered badly when a newsman asked him about the attacks: "The tariff question is a local question," he'd said, which was nonsense since Congress imposed tariffs from Washington. "Manufacturers Aroused" read headlines; iron and textile leaders, dominant in Pennsylvania and New England, denounced the threat to their markets.[93] Thomas Nast drew a *Harpers Weekly* cartoon showing a bewildered Winfield Hancock in military uniform whispering "Who is 'tariff' and why is he for revenue only?"[94]

Tammany Hall's "Honest John" Kelly had thrown another wild card into the contest by securing the Democratic nomination for Mayor of New York City to William R. Grace, a Catholic. Neither party had a monopoly on religious bigotry at the time, but big city Democrats had built strong bases among Irish, German, and other largely Catholic immigrant groups that tried to nurture them with such high-profile appointments. Arthur's local Republicans had avoided attacking Grace directly, but nominated against him a Protestant former-Democrat named William Dowd and stood back as anti-Catholic newspapers then piled on, attacking Grace. The *New York Times* ran a headline calling "Public Schools in Peril," pointing to supposed past efforts by Roman Catholics "to secure hold of the schools" and dismissing Grace's and Kelly's reassurances with quotes that "neither would be a good

Catholic if he carried out the spirit of his promises."[95] With luck, to Arthur, the religious issue might cut the Democrat's normal victory margin in New York City and help the Republicans carry the state.*

To keep the pot stirring, Arthur orchestrated a final campaign swing for Grant and Conkling through upstate New York. Barely had Conkling caught his breath from his *tour de force* in Ohio and Indiana when Arthur sent new marching orders: "I am glad to know that you are at home again & hope you are well and satisfied at the evident result of your unparalleled campaign in the west," he'd telegraphed. "I understand from the military style of your telegram that you report for duty & so ask whether I shall now make some appointments for you in this state."[96] Within days, he had Conkling strutting across platforms with General Grant in Utica, Syracuse, and Rochester, then by himself in Albany, Oswego, Buffalo, Lockport, and Jamestown. Still, the public wanted more: "Urgent need for Conkling in Hornellsville. Secure him for twenty ninth if possible. Particulars by letter today."[97]

All across the country, the effort reached a crescendo. Ulysses Grant paraded before rallies in Boston, Connecticut, and New Jersey. In Illinois, John Logan stumped downstate until he nearly dropped from exhaustion. "We have had a great day, at least 30,000 people here, 8,000 torches tonight," he wrote from one stop to his wife.[98] "I have been constantly on the stump for three months. I have three more appointments to fill & fear I may fail in strength before I finish up on the 30th. I am not physically able to do any more," he told an Illinois colleague. "There is nothing that is in my power proper to be done that I would not do to aid in electing the whole Republican ticket, from President down to the least county offices.... *Work. Work. Work.* That is the basis of success."[99]

Arthur even recruited James G. Blaine, who'd been addressing parades and rallies in New Jersey, New England, and the west, to aid the New York cause in Norwich and Binghamton, and defended Blaine publicly when Blaine cancelled because his voice finally had given out. Arthur sent personal letters to every party leader demanding a strong finish. "We are daily receiving assurances that our forces in every county are united, zealous and confident. *By that very confidence we may be lured into a dangerous inactivity of which our alert and desperate foes will not be short to take advantage,*" he wrote. "*Push*

---

* Garfield himself was approached with stories that Pope Pius VII in Rome had sent $50 million in Papal funds to support Hancock's election, though even the anti-Catholic *Cleveland Leader* considered this too far-fetched to publish.

things!"[100] Arthur again contacted every government employee who hadn't yet contributed cash to the party. "As the matter seems to have been in part neglected," he threatened one, "and in order that there may be no misunderstanding, please let me know, by return mail, if we shall hear from you further and when."[101] Some officials chafed under multiple money demands from state, national, and local party committees, but got little sympathy. Someone had to pay for printing and distributing the 12 million documents that Republicans would circulate before the campaign was over.[102]

Days before the voting, Arthur made sure his top lieutenants had plenty of "walking around" money for last minute needs. Among others, he wrote disbursements of $2,000 to Thomas Smythe in Albany, $700 to Louis Payn in Columbia, $1,200 to Elihu Root, $200 to Tom Platt, and $7,500 to himself.[103]

Arthur felt confident. Just days before the voting, he gave his "not for publication" prediction that "we are certain to carry NY by a good majority, I should say not less than 20,000 and it may be nearer to 50,000."[104] He heard his own troops responding. "I will *do my utmost* to see that *every Republican vote in my district is polled and counted,* and look after *as zealously as possible any frauds or tricks of the enemy* (Dem)," reported party lieutenant Phil Balcom from Buffalo.[105]

Tom Platt also gave a confident prediction. "We ought to come to [the] Harlem River with 95,000 majority," he told the *New York Tribune* on October 30, confident of his upstate strength. And of the Democratic majority downstate in New York, Kings, Queens, Richmond, and Suffolk? "No more than 65,000 majority, I think," he said.[106]

Garfield, meanwhile, used the final weeks of his "front porch" campaign to greet a wave of visitors and present a calm face. He hosted several hundred Ohio German voters and addressed them in German—the first U.S. presidential candidate to campaign in a foreign tongue. He received 500 members of the Indianapolis Lincoln club all wearing three-cornered straw hats, then 900 ladies of Cleveland and nearby towns, and then 200 neighbors from nearby Portage county.[107] One afternoon in October, he received the Jubilee Singers of Fisk University, a group of black students, to an afternoon of coffee, fruit, and song. Garfield had been warned against publicly hosting a black group so close to election day, but he persisted. Joe Stanley Brown remembered their "vibrant and mournful spirituals" and Garfield telling them "I would rather be with you and defeated than against you and victorious."[108]

On one of these days, while Garfield was haranguing the latest pilgrims to his Mentor front porch, a high-pitched voice interrupted his speech with a yell: "Hurrah for Hancock." Heads turned to see the embarrassed face of Garfield's own seven-year old son Abram, who apparently thought it a cute prank before his mother whisked him away. Fortunately for Abram, his father could only laugh.[109]

During these late days in the campaign, Lucretia felt increasingly troubled by a changing tone in her own contacts with people. Gone, it seemed, were the warm sentiments of support from just after the nomination. Now, it seemed, everyone demanded something from her: every letter, each visitor, every man or woman she met in town: Help my husband get a job; pass this letter along to General Garfield; give me a domestic position in your home; send me a souvenir from your farm; tell me your opinion on this or that. "Thinking your husband will be elected President this fall, I take liberty to advise you and ask you to intercede with him on behalf of my husband in obtaining the position of Postmaster of this place," she read from a Mrs. Pierce, a total stranger from Watertown, Wisconsin. But "P.S. Please do not make this affair public as he has enough to contend with now in being a Garfield man and it might interfere with his business."[110]

Amid the selfish demands, though, Lucretia still every so often would hear kind thoughts, like those of another total stranger, Henry Bullard, who identified himself only as "Grandfather": "It now seems altogether *probable* that you will be the next mistress of the White House. God bless you there, you and your boys, & their father, and enable you to keep that fountain of social influence as fine, & sweet, & wholesome as it is now kept."[111]

◎ ◎ ◎ ◎ ◎

After months of being ridiculed, smeared, bullied and ignored—by friends and foes—privately and in the newspapers, Garfield still couldn't have imagined just how low would sink the final volley of the campaign. On Wednesday morning, October 20, less than two weeks before voting, he learned that a Democratic tabloid called the *New York Truth* had published what would become the original "October surprise"—the "Morey letter," a hand-written note supposedly written by Garfield the prior January 23, to an H.L. Morey of the "Employers Union" of Lynn, Massachusetts, labeled "Personal and Confidential."

The *Truth* printed its supposed text on the front page:

*"Yours in relation to the Chinese problem came duly to hand.
I take it that the question of employees is only a question of private
and corporate economy, and individuals or companys [sic] have
the right to buy labor where they can get it cheapest.*

*"We have a treaty with the Chinese government, which should be
religiously kept until its provisions are abrogated by the action of the
general Government, and I am not prepared to say that it should
be abrogated until our great manufacturing and corporate interests
are conversed in the matter of labor. JA Garfield"*[112]

On its face, the letter played right into the hands of anti-immigrant dem-
agogues. It showed Garfield being utterly dismissive of fears by California
workers of being undercut by imported "coolie" labor from China, let alone
of workers across the country suffering salary cuts by greedy employers. Unanswered, it could devastate Garfield's standing on the Pacific coast and lose
him support from laboring men in the east—throwing several states to the
Democrats and losing the election. Democratic Congressman Abram Hewitt
immediately pronounced the letter genuine, and Connecticut Senator
William Barnum, the Democrat's national chairman, ordered it distributed
nationwide, calling it "authentic. It is General Garfield's handwriting. Denial
is worse than useless."[113] The newspaper, of course, stood by its story.

Garfield began receiving telegrams early that day asking about a letter
"purporting to be written by me on the Chinese question," he recalled.[114] He
wired back saying that he'd written no such letter. He asked Marshall Jewell
to send him a copy as soon as possible and sent word for friends to search his
Washington, D.C. files in case a clerk had written it without his knowledge.
Garfield had never heard of H.L. Morey of Lynn, Massachusetts and the view
it expressed on Chinese immigration actually clashed with his own.

In fact, even a cursory glance at the letter would quickly confirm it a fraud.
The letter misspelled Garfield's own name, placing a dot over the "r" in
Garfield, connecting the "J.A.," and uncharacteristically misshaping the letters.
Quick investigation found no such thing as a Lynn, Massachusetts "Employers
Union," nor any person named "H.L. Morey" in that city. The letter had been
written on House of Representatives stationery at a time when Garfield was
in Ohio, and it contained simple spelling mistakes that Garfield never would
have made. "I can hardly believe that a rational and just-minded public will
be influenced by such a wicked device," Garfield noted in his journal.[115]

Still, with Garfield in Ohio, his files in Washington, and the newspaper offices in New York, it took three full days before Garfield could respond flatly in a hand-written note to Marshall Jewell. "[The letter] is the work of some clumsy villain, who cannot spell—nor write English nor imitate my hand-writing. Every honest and manly Democrat in America who is familiar with my hand-writing will denounce the forgery at sight. Put the case in the hands of able detectives and hunt the rascals down," Garfield said, instructing Jewell to "Publish my dispatch."[116]

Many newspapers ran copies of the two letters side-by-side—the Morey letter and Garfield's denial—so readers could compare the handwritings.[117] The Republican party offered a $5,000 reward for the forger's arrest; Garfield swore out a legal affidavit for prosecutors. Within days, New York detectives arrested Kenward Philp, a writer for the *Truth*, and a New York grand jury promptly indicted he and three other *Truth* employees, but a court never convicted them. The newspaper finally acknowledged that the letter had been a fake on January 4, 1881—two months after the election, and long after damage had been done. The *Truth* itself would cease publication in 1884, it reputation ruined by the affair.

Meanwhile, the slander circulated—designed, said Tom Platt, to "trick ... the tramp class of working men."[118] No one could predict its impact.

⬤ ⬤ ⬤ ⬤ ⬤

On the last Saturday before November 2, Garfield entertained 150 citizens of Youngstown, 500 from West Salem, 100 "iron men" from Cleveland, and 1,500 Garfield and Arthur Club members from around Ohio. The clubs paraded in cavalry and foot formations through the Mentor farm. Several from the Youngstown group wore badges reading "329"—meant to refer to Garfield's three years in the Army, two in the Ohio Senate, and nine terms in Congress, as opposed to the "329" badges worn at Democratic rallies for Garfield's alleged $329 take from Credit Mobilier.

By now, the continual stream of visitors to Mentor had decimated the farm. "And behold the pilgrims do walk through Garfield's fields and pluck his corn," Lucretia's niece Adelaide Rudolph had written to her from nearby Collinwood, Ohio. A neighbor, she wrote, said "your front lawn was trodden down until not a blade of grass remains, and [he] told how wearied Uncle James looked."[119] On the eve of the vote, Garfield spoke only to a handful of visitors, instead overseeing his farm hands in harvesting beets and replacing turf on the front lawn.[120] At this point, there was little else for him to do.

Election Day, November 2, Garfield spent dictating letters while arranging to plow and seed the garden. In the afternoon, he rode the mile-and-a-half into town and voted for the Republican slate at the Mentor town hall. Afterward, he recalled, he stopped at the cheese house and "settled dairy accounts." At one point in the day, to settle his nerves, Garfield busied his mind with an idle calculation: "During the hours in which the election has been in progress about 2,000 [ballots] have been dropped [into the ballot box] for every tick on the pendulum."[121]

That night, he and Crete followed the voting results by telegraph; he sitting in the small telegraph cabin on the back lawn with a dozen or so friends while she and a few neighbors sat around a raging fire in the livingroom. Abram, their seven-year-old son, ran back and forth between them carrying the latest dispatches—making "a splendid little Mercury," said family friend Martha Mays. Joe Stanley Brown, Garfield's young clerk, jokingly described the telegraph shack that night as being "filled with vile men smoking and spitting all over our nice floor," all feeling "uproariously enthusiastic, but decidedly stuffy."[122] Near midnight, Lucretia broke the tension by serving the men a late supper by candlelight: "canvasbacks—oysters—ham in champagne." By 11 o'clock, spirits soared as word came of victory in New York State. Then, a little later, they received a wire from Chester Arthur: "We have carried NY by 20 or 25,000 votes and are not likely to be counted out."[123] The neighbors stayed until well past midnight, the outcome still unknown. "At 3 A.M. we closed the office," Garfield wrote in his journal that night, "secure in all the northern states except N[ew] J[ersey] and the Pacific states, which are yet in doubt."[124]

Garfield wouldn't know until the next morning that he had actually won the election, and it would take many days before the razor-thin closeness of the victory became fully clear. More Americans had voted for president that election day in 1880 than any other yet in American history—over 9 million, or 78.4 percent of those eligible. Garfield won a popular majority of under 10,000 votes (by some counts less than 2,000), less than one-tenth of one percent of the total, the thinnest popular margin ever recorded.* Of the elec-

---

* Because (a) voting was decentralized, (b) states certified electoral votes, not popular votes, as "official," and (c) Democratic votes were divided among various splinter groups, there remains today a range of published "final results" for the 1880 presidential popular vote. See, for instance, Petersen (9,457 vote margin, Garfield over Hancock), Burnham (7,368 vote margin), and Rusk (1,898 vote margin).

toral votes, Garfield had won 214 to Hancock's 155. Had one single state, New York, with its 35 electoral votes, switched and gone Democratic, Hancock would have won the presidency by 190 to 179. And in New York, Garfield had won by barely 20,000 votes out of 1.1 million cast—555,544 for Garfield to 534,511 for Hancock and 12,373 for Greenback candidate Weaver.

On the other side, though, Garfield had lost California by less than 150 votes out of over 160,000 cast, clearly a product of the Morey letter fraud, and he heard widespread charges of fraud, violence, and intimidation in the South against blacks and white moderates, perhaps tilting two or three Southern states as well.[125] Other than this and his losing New Jersey, Garfield's "solid North" had held against Hancock's 14-state "solid South." Garfield, an "accidental nominee" with no national following just five months earlier, had kept his party united, made no serious mistakes, portrayed a positive, fresh image, and captured the country.[126] His Republican party had regained control of the U.S. House of Representatives for the first time in six years, and won a rare party tie in the U.S. Senate—37 Democrats, 37 Republicans, and 2 independents, with a Republican vice president to decide ties in their favor.*

James Weaver, the Greenback Party's candidate, received only 305,997 votes or just 3.3 percent of the total—up from his 75,973 four years earlier in 1876. By 1888, with growing national prosperity, the Greenbacks would have disappeared.

The day after the election, telegrams by the hundreds and letters by the thousands flooded into Garfield's Ohio farmhouse. Most contained simple congratulations; others began the clamor for jobs and favors that would crescendo with the coming new administration. Lucretia particularly enjoyed an encouraging note from Henry Ward Beecher, world-renowned preacher from Brooklyn, New York's Plymouth Church, which arrived that day and which she saved for many years: "That your husband is to assume the burdens of the Presidency of the United States, is a great joy to millions, & while not without its pleasure to him & must bring down an almost oppressive sense of responsibility," it read. "But you will be cheered and upheld by thousands of warm hearts praying for you, night and morning, and God will give his angels Charge of both of you."[127]

---

* The Senate would not have another elected party tie for 120 years, until 2001.

Puck, the satirical magazine, ran a cartoon the next week showing half-a-dozen European kings, counts, kaisers, czars, and princes gazing from far off across the ocean at small figures of James Garfield and Winfield Scott Hancock amiably shaking hands. "Astonished Europe!" read the caption. "Great Republican Victory! But where is the bloodshed?"[128] American democracy, for all its faults, had still set a standard for the world.

◎ ◎ ◎ ◎ ◎

All through August, Charles Guiteau had stuck with his plan. Almost every day, he'd walk up Fifth Avenue to either the Republican state committee or national committee offices just up the block and stay for a few hours. He'd made himself familiar to the clerks and staff. Chester Arthur remembered seeing Guiteau in his Fifth Avenue Hotel suite "at least ten and possibly as often as twenty times" during the campaign, and recalled having spoken with him "once or twice in answer to his requests to be employed in the campaign as a speaker" in addition to "return[ing] the ordinary salutations of the day."[129]

At first, Guiteau used every chance to insist on speaking roles in the campaign. He buttonholed top officials and finally took the initiative about a week after the August summit to send Arthur a letter on Republican national committee stationery. "I would like to stump New York for our ticket. I have practiced law in Chicago ten or twelve years & can make a good speech. It will take me an hour to work off the speech I handed you some time ago. I speak without notes. Please print my name on your list & notify Gov. Jewell. Yours sincerely. Charles Guiteau." Besides his own signature, Guiteau had also managed to corner Marshall Jewell, the national committee chairman, and get him to sign the letter as an endorsement. "I want to devote my time to our ticket till the election," Guiteau had scribbled at the bottom of the page, under his own and Jewell's signatures.[130]

A few days later, Arthur in fact had assigned Guiteau to speak to a rally of black New York voters on Twenty-fifth Street. The *New York Times* listed Guiteau as the lead-off orator for the event.[131] Guiteau gave copies of his speech to the newspapers, but apparently, once at the podium, he became uncomfortable and stopped after only a few paragraphs. "I didn't exactly like the crowd," he later explained. "It was a very hot, sultry night, and I didn't fancy speaking, with the torch-lights and the gas-lights and all that. They put me on the stand as the first speaker, and I spoke a few minutes. There were plenty other speakers there, so I retired."[132]

Still, he felt he'd done his part. For the rest of the campaign, Guiteau kept his vigil at Republican headquarters. "I met [Guiteau] on almost every occasion when I was in the city of New York, either at the room of the National Committee or at the rooms of the State Central Committee," Emory Storrs recalled, though "later on [he] seemed to have no special purpose nor employment. I don't know that I ever saw him doing anything except reading papers in both those places."[133]

Employment or not, Guiteau seemed drawn to the campaign offices, rubbing elbows with the famous men who seemed so friendly. His occasional hallway chats with Chester Arthur, the vice presidential nominee, may have meant nothing to Arthur, a simple brief courtesy to a well-meaning volunteer, treating him with good manners. To Guiteau, in his lonely life sparse of human contact, they meant the world. "I used to be on free-and-easy terms with them," Guiteau later recalled of the campaign chiefs during those weeks. "I used to go to General Arthur and talk just as freely with him as I would with anybody."[134]

In October, Guiteau had shared the tension in Arthur's Fifth Avenue Hotel suite over the early vote in Indiana. "It caused great anxiety," he remembered. "It was very uncertain how it would go. We believed that if it went against us Garfield was gone, but if [it went] for us he would probably be elected ..."[135] And so it went. As soon as victory in Indiana had made Garfield the likely next president of the United States, Charles Guiteau had jumped immediately to the next logical step. He had to get his place on line, before everyone else. "I wrote to General Garfield and sent him my speech, calling his attention to the fact that I possibly might marry a very wealthy lady there in New York sometime during the spring, and that we could represent the United States Government at the court of Vienna with dignity and grace. That was the way I put it."[136]

Charles Guiteau decided that he had played a vital role in the great Republican victory of 1880. Like every other loyal Stalwart, he now was prepared to accept his reward. Guiteau may have been quick to stake his claim and ambitious in his goal, but he was far from alone. This, after all, was what the whole campaign had been about. Just ask any of the Stalwarts in Chet Arthur's suite at the Fifth Avenue Hotel.

● ◎ ◎ ●

"I have heard some incredibly ridiculous things about [Roscoe] Conkling's demeanor," John Hay wrote from Washington, D.C. to Whitelaw Reid shortly after election day. "He really thinks he is the Savior of the Situation, and makes no bones about it."[137] Conkling, after all, had given twenty speeches to mass audiences during the campaign; now he and his backers loudly took credit for the victory. And Ulysses Grant, according to Chauncey Depew, had delivered the "whole of the old soldier vote" to Garfield and Arthur,[138] not to mention Chester Arthur's managing of the whole campaign from New York.

"The election of Garfield and Arthur was… made apparently impossible by the loss of Maine under Blaine's leadership in September," George Gorham wrote, summarizing the Stalwart case, and "made again possible by the work of General Grant and Senator Conkling in Ohio and Indiana in October, and made certain by their final efforts in New York."[139] In fact, the whole Grant "third term" faction, the "306ers," had swallowed their pride after the Chicago defeat, picked themselves up, and fought the hard fight for their party's ticket—Garfield at the lead. "If Mr. Garfield is indebted to Mr. Blaine for his *nomination*," many said, "he will have to thank Mr. Conkling for his *election*."[140]

Garfield, sitting out on his Ohio farm, heard this talk coming back from the east coast. He saw the cartoon in *Harpers Weekly* that week showing an over-sized Ulysses Grant, cigar in his mouth and smile on his face, carrying an under-sized James Garfield on his shoulders through the political hoopla, the caption asking: "Is the Garfield campaign simply an incident in the Grant campaign?"[141] Even as he sifted through hundreds of telegrams and letters wishing him luck and congratulations, Garfield shuddered at the prospect, once in office, of having to deal with a powerful, boastful, greedy Roscoe Conkling, roaring his demands down from Capitol Hill. "Conkling is a singular compound of a very brilliant man and an exceedingly petulant spoiled child," Garfield had written to a friend during the campaign. "It has become apparent that he, and some of the men who are working with him, are more concerned in running Grant in 1884 than they are for carrying the Republicans safely through the contest of 1880."[142]

Garfield couldn't help but remember how Roscoe Conkling had hounded Rutherford Hayes all during his presidency, attacking him constantly and ultimately pushing him into early retirement. He had no intention of letting the same thing happen to him.

To keep Conkling at bay, though, Garfield would need a counterweight, someone in his administration just as strong as Conkling, just as vigilant, to take the opposite side. He'd need someone whose loyalty he could trust without question. Garfield would have to lay this marker down quickly, as the first important decision he'd make as president-elect.

It took Garfield only three weeks to solve this riddle. On November 27, while visiting Washington, D.C. for a few days, Garfield paid a call on one of his closest friends in politics. He sent his card with a messenger to the Fifteenth Street home of James Gillespie Blaine. He and Blaine met alone over breakfast in Blaine's house that day, and they spoke for a long time. They talked about the future. "Blaine, I have not made a single final decision in reference to my cabinet, and shall not until February," Garfield told him. "But let us talk provisionally. If I should ask you to take a place in my cabinet, what would be your probable response, and before you answer, please tell me whether you are, or will be, a candidate for the presidency in 1884. I ask this because I do not propose for myself, nor to allow anyone else to use the next four years as the camping ground for fighting the next presidential battle."[143]

Blaine thought for a minute, then said that, no, he would not be a candidate for president in 1884, and he'd think about Garfield's proposition.[144]

By December 20, they'd settled the matter. Blaine had agreed to accept not just any cabinet position, but the top one, the premiership: Secretary of State.*[145] By this one action, Garfield had managed to shift the axis of power in American government. Instead of the New York Stalwarts who'd won him his election and demanded tribute, Garfield had now instead anchored his line to James G. Blaine, the "magnetic man" from Maine, who'd shown himself fully able and not the least bit hesitant to deal with Roscoe Conkling and his "turkey gobbler strut."

---

* Throughout the 1800s, presidents considered the Secretary of State their principal deputy, cabinet leader, and heir apparent—not the vice president. Newspapers called them the "Premier," as under European parliamentary systems. This approach changed only after assassinations of Garfield and McKinley dramatized the potential of unexpected vice presidential succession. Vice presidents remained marginal figures in administrations up through the 1950s.

• PART III •

President-Elect

• • • • •

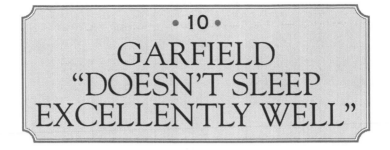

Can you believe that the long vigil, not tongueless, is over, and that we are all saved for four years, and I hope forty times four?" Harriet Blaine wrote to her daughter Maggie from their large, sunny house in Augusta, Maine, on Thursday afternoon, November 4. "Oh, how good it is to win and to be on the strong side!" The morning after Garfield's election, she and her husband James G. Blaine lingered in bed, laughing, talking, delighted. Blaine still felt exhausted from the campaign, suffering gout, a chest cold, harsh cough, and nervous fatigue. But they'd won. "Your Father and I have picked out Garfield's Cabinet for him," Harriet wrote, "and have devoted to him for two mornings our waking, but not risen, hours."[1]

The Blaines had known the Garfields ever since the two husbands had entered Congress together in 1863, eighteen years ago during the war. "Your father is much attached to General Garfield," Harriet had told their son Walker as early as 1872.[2] Over the years, the two wives, Harriet and Crete, had watched their husbands' speeches from the House ladies gallery and shared countless dinner parties, receptions, and Washington social seasons together. Their houses stood just four blocks apart—Blaine's on Fifteenth Street, Garfield's on I and Thirteenth. When Blaine became House Speaker in 1867, Garfield supported him; when he'd run for president in 1876, Garfield became his political confidante. After Blaine's defeat that year, it was Garfield who'd come to their home to cheer them. "I did ... give the General a kiss—which I meant as an ear of my feelings," Harriet had written to Lucretia back in Ohio that night, happy that theirs was "the faithful friendship of the good and strong."[3]

Now, in 1880, Harriet and James Blaine had sweated with every step of the election. If Blaine himself couldn't be the presidential nominee, then who could be better then their friend James Garfield? Harriet's congratulatory telegram had been among Garfield's first after his surprise nomination in June. Blaine had taken time in July to coach Garfield on his letter of acceptance, sharing political pointers on the Chinese question though declining to give actual "copy," recognizing Garfield's greater expertise on the tariff and financial issues.[4]

Since then, Blaine had thrown himself into the effort—and after his embarrassing loss managing Maine's September statewide contest for governor, he'd stumped doubly hard. He pushed the national committee to take up the tariff issue, spoke at major rallies in Newark and Philadelphia, and made the rounds of torchlight parades and state fairs throughout the West and Midwest—being sure to stop in Mentor for a night at the farmhouse with James and Crete.[5]

By late October, Blaine's voice had given way to chest colds and exhaustion and he had to cancel speeches in New York and Connecticut. Still, Harriet found him back in Augusta "full of enthusiasm," she wrote. In the final weeks, Blaine focused his remaining energy on the home vote in Maine, where voters would return to the polls in November to vote for president. He worked despite his multiple illnesses. "Your father is walking up and down the parlor," she wrote to her daughter Maggie days before the November vote, sharing his nervous tension till the final tally.[6]

Now, in November, Blaine had delivered Maine for Garfield's ticket by a 10,000 vote plurality—reversing the September defeat of Maine's statewide Republican ticket. After a few days' rest, he and Harriet hosted their friends William Chandler and Eugene Hale and their wives at their Augusta home for a long weekend to toast success, and then Blaine traveled south to Washington, D.C. for the final session of Congress, leaving Harriet alone through the Thanksgiving holiday: "I miss Mr. Blaine," Harriet complained to her friend Mary Dodge from her big empty house in Maine that month. "I miss the envelopes in the gravy, the bespattered table linen, the uncertainty of the meals ... I miss his unvarying attention, and his constant neglect."[7]

Once settled back in Washington, James Blaine's curiosity peaked when Garfield, in the hubbub of his first Washington trip as new president-elect, surrounded by swirls of callers, receptions, dinners, and gossip, had invited himself over for a private breakfast, one on one, at Blaine's townhouse—away from the crowds. Garfield's proposition for him that morning to join the new administration seemed to catch Blaine off guard. Do you really want me in your cabinet, he'd asked?

Of course, Garfield insisted. Blaine must have felt touched as his friend tried to win him over. It would be "better for his fame," Garfield argued, and better "for the health of his party in Maine" for Blaine to join him. He could pick either of the two top spots, State or Treasury. All through their careers, Blaine had always considered himself the more senior—Blaine the national figure, Garfield the loyal supporter. As early as 1863, Blaine had sized up his Ohio colleague as "a big good natured man that doesn't appear to be oppressed by genius."[8] Still, Garfield never failed him on any test of loyalty. Now the roles had reversed: Blaine's junior partner would be his senior, the president.

Garfield placed only one condition on a cabinet seat that morning. "[P]lease tell me whether you are, or will be, a candidate for the presidency in 1884," he'd asked.[9] To Blaine, exhausted from his own second futile bid for the presidency that year, the idea of a third in 1884 hardly appealed to him. Nor did his safe U.S. Senate seat from Maine hold much interest. Maybe Garfield had a point. Maybe he'd spent too many years already running Maine's political affairs and fresh blood would benefit them both. By contrast, Garfield's proposal offered a fresh beginning: a new presidency, a friendly White House, new fields of interest with radically different duties, and a chance to practice his political craft on the highest stage.

Garfield didn't expect an answer immediately that morning and Blaine didn't give him one—but they had a meeting of minds. And Blaine had plenty of advice to share. For one thing, just as Garfield had insisted on having no rival for the presidency from within his own government, Blaine too wanted no rival for preeminence in the Cabinet. John Sherman, the sitting Treasury Secretary and recent presidential candidate, must go. And Blaine also had ideas about foreign policy and America's role in the world.* They talked for over an hour. At the end, Garfield asked Blaine to keep the offer secret until he'd had time to fill in his other cabinet choices. Meanwhile, any more advice on political matters was welcome.

---

* Blaine's approach, a stronger America asserting itself in the Western Hemisphere, pushing a cross-Isthmus canal and standing firm against Europe, marked a bold departure that ironically would foreshadow that of Theodore Roosevelt twenty years later, though Roosevelt's own debut in national politics was to oppose Blaine's nomination for the presidency in 1884.

❀ ❀ ❀ ❀ ❀

Barely had Garfield finished his breakfast with James Blaine and returned to his room at the Riggs House that morning, when another visitor came and insisted on talking about cabinet seats. Levi P. Morton, his dapper banker friend, congressional colleague, Washington neighbor, and campaign financier, pulled him aside for a talk. The election over, Morton wanted to check with the new president-elect on his pledge to make him Secretary of the Treasury.

Since the election, Garfield had begun suffering insomnia and headaches. He rarely slept more than a few hours a night and seemed always preoccupied. He and Lucretia had come to Washington this late November week to pack books, furniture, and papers from their I Street home; job-hunters and politicos had mobbed them from the moment they'd gotten off the train. Most acted politely. Rutherford and Lucy Hayes had hosted them at the White House to share advice and meet the ushers, cooks, gardeners, and other personal staff there. Crete had a quiet talk with "Lemonade Lucy" about her policy of banning all alcohol from White House functions—whiskey, beer, and wine. Temperance activists already had started hounding Lucretia to keep the ban in place.[10] She and James did manage to enjoy private dinners with John Sherman and his wife and other long-time friends, but, back in public, the callers bore in on them with ardent purpose.

Levi Morton had shown his well-groomed face at many of the social events that week: Friday's lunch at General Schenck's house, Friday night's dinner party with Senator George Edmunds, and Saturday morning's lunch at Garfield's hotel. Now, on Saturday, after the other guests had left and Lucretia had gone off with the current cabinet wives, Morton had pulled Garfield aside and asked about his cabinet seat.

Garfield got "annoyed," he later admitted. No, he said. No, he'd never promised Morton the Treasury Department. Morton had a "misapprehension," a "misunderstanding." Giving the Treasury Department to Levi Morton, head of Morton, Bliss, and Company, one of Wall Street's most powerful investment banks, would create "a congestion of financial power—at [the New York] money center—and would create great jealousy in the west[ern states]," Garfield argued.[11] It was nothing against Morton personally, he assured him. In fact, Garfield liked Morton; he considered him his favorite of the Stalwart crowd and definitely wanted him in his cabinet. He'd even asked

Morton to be his vice president back in Chicago in June. But Treasury was "not my understanding and seems wholly inadmissible," he said.[12]

Levi Morton hadn't intended to offend his friend the president-elect. If anything, Garfield's response surprised him. What about the promises from last August, he asked? He, Morton, clearly had done his part: He'd raised oceans of money for the campaign, kept the New York Stalwarts in line, and even helped engineer Garfield's victory in Indiana. They'd had a deal.

Garfield kept his voice steady but clearly disliked the question's tone. Yes, he said, he'd promised Morton a top position in his administration— either the Treasury or Navy department or the ministry to France or England— but not specifically Treasury and at Garfield's choice, not Morton's.

Morton didn't remember it that way at all, nor did his New York friends.

They didn't talk for very long that day—Garfield had other appointments to keep and not much else to say. Levi Morton too needed time to collect his thoughts. But he made it clear. This issue was not over, not by any means.[13]

⚙ ⚙ ⚙ ⚙ ⚙

Barely had Garfield finished hashing through his "misunderstanding" with Levi Morton than he had to tell John Sherman that he'd have no place in a Garfield cabinet. That afternoon, as part of his round of courtesy calls on President Hayes' outgoing cabinet secretaries, Garfield stopped at Treasury where Sherman welcomed him warmly. Just two nights earlier, Sherman and his wife had hosted Garfield and Lucretia for a private social dinner where they'd spent hours talking about politics and old times over brandy and cigars. Now, closeted behind closed doors, seated face to face in Sherman's large office, Garfield got straight to the point: Would Sherman "feel wholly cordial if he were not retained."[14]

John Sherman didn't blink—he'd been through enough aggravation with his failed presidential bid that year to have a very thick skin. He "[r]esponded affirmatively, I think earnestly," Garfield recalled.[15] If fact, once Sherman thought about it, he recognized that Garfield actually was doing him a favor by breaking this news so early. Ohio would have a U.S. Senate seat coming open in January—the one that Garfield himself originally had been chosen to fill and promptly renounced upon winning the presidency. Sherman would now have plenty of time to signal his friends and make himself the top contender.[16]

Garfield kept the meeting short and must have appreciated Sherman's

polite tone. But John Sherman clearly recognized who had engineered his removal—James G. Blaine. And he made sure Garfield knew it: "Blaine
thought it would not be politic to continue me as Secretary of the Treasury,
as it would be regarded as an unfriendly discrimination by other members of
Hayes' cabinet," he later recalled Garfield's telling him. "I promptly replied
that I agreed with the opinion of Blaine."[17] That done, Sherman gave his
younger protégé a word of caution about his new closest friend, James Gillespie Blaine: "If you can only restrain [Blaine's] immense activity and keep
him from meddling with the other departments, you will have a brilliant
secretary."[18]

◎ ◎ ◎ ◎ ◎

Garfield didn't have to look far for causes of his headaches and insomnia in
November 1880. The U.S. Constitution then still gave new presidents four
leisurely months to pick their top advisors, from their election in early November to their inauguration in early March.* But Garfield enjoyed no
leisure. More than three months before his swearing in, he found himself already paralyzed by pressure over his cabinet. On paper, the puzzle looked simple: After all, the president's cabinet in 1880 had only seven seats: State, Justice, Treasury, War, Navy, Interior, and the Post Office.** Filling them,
though, demanded genius.

Cabinet seats carried pure political clout. The State Department had
prestige, but Treasury oozed with power—brimming with patronage from its
75 custom houses and dozens of revenue bureaus, subtreasuries, and financial
offices. Interior and Postmaster General also controlled thousands of appointees. Of the 100,000-plus total federal workforce in 1881, all appointed
by politicians, almost half worked in post offices. The Attorney General, War,
and Navy also each had the president's ear and their own legions to staff.

By picking a lightning rod like Blaine, Garfield knew he'd create jeal-

---

* It was not until 1933 when the Twentieth Amendment, adopted in response to the emergency
of the Great Depression, moved the president's inauguration forward from March 4th to January
20th.

** Compared with twenty-one positions of "cabinet rank" today, including the Vice President,
White House chief of staff, the Secretaries of the fifteen executive departments—including most recently the Department of Homeland Security - plus the directors of the Office of Management and
Budget, National Drug Control Policy, the administrator of the Environmental Protection Agency,
and the United States Trade Representative. While many positions have been added to the cabinet since 1880, only one has been removed: the Postmaster General.

ousies among Stalwarts and have to balance them with powerful seats of their own. He'd also need representatives from the West, from key states that had supported his election—Illinois, Indiana, and Pennsylvania, for instance—and possibly the South. Should Blaine decline his cabinet offer, Garfield would have to revise every calculation. Putting a New York Stalwart at Treasury would distort the whole picture with jealousies and back-biting.

Garfield the academic blanched at the raw politics. "I love to deal with doctrines and events," he wrote in his journal. "The contests of men about men I greatly dislike."[19]

⊙ ⊙ ⊙ ⊙ ⊙

James Blaine, meanwhile, sat and pondered what to do. Over the next few days circulating around Washington and traveling to New York City, he talked with friends and allies about the cabinet offer, blowing hot and cold. In early December, he confided to Whitelaw Reid, the *New York Tribune* publisher and mutual friend of both he and Garfield, that he "didn't relish the rumors flying around" and might just go off for a six-month junket in Europe until they cooled down.[20]

He also sought out Massachusetts Senator Henry Dawes. Dawes had already heard the Blaine cabinet talk through his well-rooted grapevine and "[t]his information produced a shiver," he recalled.[21] "The mere rumor was enough to kindle anew into fresh flame all the fire of the old hate." Dawes had served with Blaine in Congress since the 1860s and had personally witnessed the notorious Blaine-Conkling clashes on the House floor years before. He left Blaine no doubt about his feelings: "I warned Mr. Blaine that if he entered the cabinet with the intent or hope of circumventing his rival, it would be fatal to him and to the administration of Garfield" and, knowing Blaine's personality, that "it would be impossible for him to keep the peace if he took the office."[22]

Even as he cogitated, Blaine's creative juices stirred. In early December, sitting at the library desk in his Washington townhouse, he put pen to paper and described for Garfield his own vision of the political landscape. Garfield faced one basic problem, as Blaine saw it: treachery—from Roscoe Conkling, Ulysses Grant, Chester Arthur, and the entire Stalwart faction.[23] "You are to have a second term, or to be overthrown by the Grant crowd," Blaine warned. To avoid this fate, Garfield must create "an administration distinctly your own" and freeze the Stalwarts out from all power. Specifically, in choosing his cabinet, he must not give Treasury, Post Office, or Interior—the three Departments with the most patronage—to any supporter of Grant: "for God's sake fill [them] with *your* friends."

The "Grant Section," led by "rule or ruin leaders," contained "all the desperate bad men of the party, bent on boot and booty," he went on. Garfield must fight them, but he must do it shrewdly. "They must not be knocked down with bludgeons," he said. "They must have their throats cut with a feather."*[24]

The more James Blaine wrote and talked and schemed, the more he saw the potential in becoming Secretary of State, the closest advisor to a president who counted him an intimate. "The more I think of the State Department," he wrote to Whitelaw Reid in mid-December, "the more I am inclined to take it."[25]

⊛ ⊛ ⊛ ⊛ ⊛

Garfield had found his late-November Washington trip "very exhausting,"[26] and getting back to Mentor did not help. "The personal aspects of the presidency are far from pleasant," he wrote. After years of the back-slapping friendships of Capitol Hill, the army, and political clubhouses, Garfield recoiled at how people now treated him. "[A]lmost every one who comes to me wants something which he thinks I can and ought to give him, and this embitters the pleasure of friendship."[27] The job-seekers he found worst of all, flooding his mail, hounding his family, grabbing him on the street, stopping his carriage, surrounding him at railway stations, always shoving papers at him. One woman, a Disciple from his church, had spent five hours at the Mentor farmhouse one day, refusing to leave without a position at the Cincinnati post office.[28] Every morning they lined up at the door; every day he spent hours interviewing them, but more always came. " I shall be compelled to live in great social isolation," he lamented.[29]

December brought a quiet season to Ohio, with crisp air, cold nights, and

---

* The party, Blaine explained, was divided in three parts in 1880: (a) the "Blaine section," "the great body of the North" that had given Garfield the majority of his support in Chicago; (b) the "Grant Section;" and (c) the "Reformers by profession," those "upstarts, conceited, foolish, vain [men] without knowledge of measures, ignorant of men," and who made the "worst possible political advisors." Though "noisy," "ambitious" and "pharisaical," these reformers could be "easily dealt with," Blaine noted. "I can handle them myself without trouble." When Blaine did have his chance as Republican nominee in 1884, these "reformers by profession" would bolt to form the Mugwumps and help sink his bid.

bare trees dotting fallow farm fields. Garfield looked for calm during this time in Mentor. Joe Stanley Brown, his young clerk, remembered "many evenings [when] General Garfield, Mrs. Garfield and I sat around the woodfire and at such times the General freely discussed the problems which confronted him."[30] In the mornings, Garfield skimmed the vast piles of newspapers and letters streaming in from around the country and sitting stacked in his library. "They've got ahead of me," he told a reporter one day. He enjoyed riding about town on horseback, "graceful in the saddle as a trained cavalryman, but dressed like a plain farmer," a newsman wrote, "the broad brim slouch hat flapping in the wind."[31]

Try as he might, though, Garfield could not escape the growing pressure over his cabinet, hounding him even here in faraway Ohio.

On December 13, not two weeks after he'd returned to Ohio from his trip to Washington, D.C., Garfield found a New York delegation arriving at his doorstep: Governor Alonzo Cornell, Congressman Dick Crowley, and Louis Payn, all shepherded by Stephen Dorsey, his eager national committee secretary. Their carriage didn't reached Mentor until 7 pm that night, delayed by winter storms; Garfield offered them dinner and tea to warm up from the shivering cold. Roscoe Conkling had sent them, the men said. They had important business.

Levi Morton, after his blow-up with Garfield in Washington two weeks earlier, had gone running back to Conkling who had sent this delegation traveling across the December snowdrifts in Ohio to demand an explanation. After they'd warmed up around dinner and a rousing fire, Garfield took them upstairs to his library to talk over brandy and cigars. The New Yorkers had just one request, they told him: Garfield must keep his promise from the New York summit and pick Levi Morton for the Treasury. Nothing else would do.

Garfield listened politely as the politicos presented their grievance. Levi Morton, they said, had understood from Garfield last August that the Treasury Department "was one of several places he could elect to have."[32] Because Garfield now was backing away from his pledge, the New York Stalwarts felt misled and Morton himself had suffered personally; word of Garfield's offer had cost Morton any chance to compete for New York's open seat in the U.S. Senate coming up the next January.

Garfield heard them out but, having had his arm twisted by hordes of job-seekers all that month, he had little sympathy for their case. Not only hadn't he offered Levi Morton the post, he told them, but a federal conflict-of-interest statute barred Levi Morton specifically from taking the Treasury job.[33] And politically, placing a New York City financier over the Treasury would be "most unwise in a party sense," he argued, raising age-old fears around the country about powerful money-center banks in New York City.

They talked for almost three hours, until 10 pm, neither side conceding anything except the coldness of the Ohio winter. Garfield did make them one new promise, though. He would "not intervene" in the New York Senate contest coming up in January, he told them. If Levi Morton wanted to run, Garfield wouldn't stop him, and he'd put off making final cabinet choices until after the New York legislature had made its choice.

The New Yorkers headed back out into the cold Ohio night "evidently disappointed," Garfield recalled[34]—and with them went any hope he had of avoiding a new argument with Roscoe Conkling. About the same time, Garfield also received in the mail James Blaine's letter from Washington about the "rule or ruin" Stalwarts and the need to cut their throats "with a feather." Blaine's sometime penchant for "childishness and selfishness" worried Garfield.*[35] "On many accounts [Blaine] would be a brilliant Sec'y of State," he wrote in his journal, still hoping for intra-party peace. "Other adjustments might be more difficult."[36]

By then, for good or ill, his offer had been made and accepted. On December 23, another letter from Blaine arrived in Ohio, this one in an envelope addressed to Lucretia: "I send it under cover to you... because I wish no eye but yours and the general to see it." His acceptance of Garfield's cabinet offer rang clear as a bell. "I shall give all that I am and all that I can hope to be freely and joyfully in your service. You need no pledge of my loyalty both in heart and act... Your administration must be made brilliantly successful and strong in the confidence and pride of the people," he wrote. "I hail it as one of the happiest circumstances ... that in allying my political fortunes with yours, or rather merging mine with yours—my heart goes with my head."[37]

---

* As early as 1864, Garfield had clashed with Blaine on the House floor by proposing to end the practice of allowing wealthy men to avoid military conscription by paying $300 for a substitute. The House soundly defeated him, led by Blaine. Blaine and Garfield also bickering over committee chairmanships while Blaine was House Speaker—Blaine never giving Garfield the Ways and Means chairmanship that Garfield wanted. But, to Garfield, Blaine's positives clearly prevailed. When the Credit Mobilier scandal hit, Blaine as Speaker insisted on a House investigation of all members mentioned, including Garfield, but then blocked any formal censure of Garfield. When Blaine attacked Democrats in 1876 by refusing amnesty for Jefferson Davis because of his role in the Andersonville prison, Garfield happily fought at his side.

Only by late December did the tide of visitors to Mentor finally ebb as the snowdrifts piled up and winds blew fiercely cold off Lake Erie. Only the most determined office seekers braved the icy roads. When one Pennsylvania man came that month and presented Garfield a handmade hickory chair with an elaborate carving of a canal boat in its center, a reporter asked him: "You want an office, of course?"

"Mein Gott, no!" the man replied. "I shust vant to see Sheneral Garfield—*und advertise mein shairs!*"[38]

By year's end, Garfield badly missed his old life of relative anonymity. Normally in December, he and Lucretia would make the rounds of happy Washington dinner parties surrounded by friends, laughter, and music, followed by house visits and family reunions on New Year's Day. Now he'd grown fatalistic. "I close the year with a sad conviction that I am bidding good-bye to the freedom of private life, and to a long series of happy years, which I fear terminate with 1880."[39]

◎ ◎ ◎ ◎ ◎

In late December, Blaine saw his first chance to attack. Back in Ohio, Garfield may have promised his New York visitors not to interfere in their upcoming Special election for the U.S. Senate, but Blaine felt no hesitation about jumping right in.

While Garfield tried to steer clear of pushy office-seekers, Blaine traveled to New York City and conferred with his long-time friend, *New York Tribune* publisher Whitelaw Reid. At Blaine's urging, Reid hosted a New Year's Eve dinner at his Madison Avenue mansion for a small cabal of Half-Breeds: Blaine, William Robertson, and New York lawyer Chauncey Depew.

Whitelaw Reid made a perfect co-conspirator for Blaine. Utterly loyal to Garfield from their boyhoods in Ohio, Whitelaw Reid had made his fame during the Civil War with his pen. Starting out as correspondent for two Ohio newspapers, the *Cincinnati Gazette* and the *Xenia News*, his reporting on the 1862 Battle of Shiloh had portrayed Ulysses Grant as a shockingly bad general and the battlefield as a gruesome hell. The encounter had made Grant a life-long enemy of Reid's; his later work as civic reformer had soured him on Roscoe Conkling and his political machine as well. Horace Greeley, the *Tribune's* rumpled founder and long-time editor, had discovered Reid's talent and brought him to New York City in the late 1860s. When Greeley died in 1872 after losing his run for the presidency, Whitelaw Reid had seized the chance to purchase a controlling interest in the newspaper with backing from Wall Street bandit Jay Gould.

Since then, Reid had re-built the *Tribune* into a political dynamo, moving it into its palatial new Park Row headquarters building, the tallest tower in New York City after Trinity Church's steeple. Socially stiff, an introverted bachelor, slender with long hair, a long face, and a neatly-trimmed beard, Reid had recently discovered the joys of wealth and began courting Elizabeth Mills, the attractive young daughter of California banker Darius Ogden Mills, who'd made millions on the Comstock Lode silver strike.

Beginning with Garfield's surprise nomination for president in June, Whitelaw Reid had joined Blaine in tutoring their mutual friend on political hard knocks. Garfield needed more backbone, they felt. "I hope you will inoculate him with the gall which I fear he lacks," John Hay had advised them early in the campaign.[40] Blaine and Reid warned Garfield to be suspicious of Roscoe Conkling's crowd: "In a word, they mean to be your masters," Reid had told the president-elect, "they don't trust you; even their common mode of alluding to you ... 'this man Garfield.'"[41] Garfield must destroy Conkling before Conkling destroyed him.

And now the Stalwarts were griping over a new issue—Garfield's refusal to make Levi Morton the Treasury Secretary despite Garfield's supposed August pledges.

As Blaine, Depew and Robertson sat with Whitelaw Reid around Reid's sumptuous dinner table that New Year's Eve, Blaine quickly took over the conversation, his eyes alive with his latest scheme. In two weeks, he told them, the New York legislature would pick a successor to the State's retiring junior U.S. Senator, Democrat Frances Kernan. Three of Roscoe Conkling's crowd had thrown in their hats—Levi Morton, Richard Crowley, and Tom Platt—splitting the machine three ways, and Conkling himself had refused to pick a favorite. As a result, none had the votes to win on his own. Ultimately, they'd need a partner.

William Robertson, sitting across the table from Blaine, saw this new game at once—in fact, Robertson may have suggested it to Blaine in the first place. Sharp-eyed and crisp-spoken, looking younger than his 57 years except for his neat small gray beard, Robertson had already proven his political pluck that year by staring down Roscoe Conkling in Chicago as leader of the anti-Grant bolt. As Speaker of the New York senate, Robertson would preside over the vote for the new U.S. Senator and knew at least twenty anti-machine state senators who'd happily back any Half-Breed candidate—not enough to win but perhaps enough to pick the winner, giving them enormous power. If only the Half-Breeds had a candidate...

At this point, all their eyes turned to Chauncey Depew. What about it? Blaine asked. Would Depew run, not for himself of course, but "for ... securing the election of a Senator who would support the Administration?"[42]

Chauncey Depew, tall, handsome, with long dark side-whiskers, prominent forehead, and a Yale-educated, soft-spoken tongue, had no real interest in leaving New York City. As a lawyer, Depew represented the Vanderbilts, America's richest family, and their New York Central railroad. Still, with no small ego, a fixed income of $10,000 per year, and bushels of money stashed away, he could afford to dabble. Besides, he liked Blaine, wanted to help Garfield, and hated Roscoe Conkling as much as anyone. Before they'd slurped their last oyster, sipped their last brandy, and smoked their last cigar, Depew had bought the idea.

"I'm to go to Albany Sunday night, to tell our friends [in the legislature] that they'd be defended if they defy Conkling," Whitelaw Reid wrote to Garfield late that night after his New Year's champagne.[43] "At any rate, we shall show that Mr. Conkling doesn't own the state," he said.

For state legislatures, choosing a U.S. Senator was a key function in the 1800s. Chester Arthur hurried north to Albany to represent Conkling's machine in the affair. As Blaine had predicted, the legislature soon deadlocked among the three machine candidates—Levi Morton, Tom Platt, and Dick Crowley—and Chauncey Depew who controlled a united block of Half-Breeds. Telegrams flew between Depew in Albany and Reid in New York as the battle unfolded. Then William Robertson approached Dick Crowley with a deal: he'd deliver him all twenty Half-Breed votes in exchange for Crowley's pledge to support Garfield and the Half-Breeds. Chet Arthur "promptly and indignantly" rejected it on Crowley's behalf—seeing it correctly as a slap at Roscoe Conkling.[44]

Chauncey Depew then took the same offer to the next machine candidate, Tom Platt. Platt might be loyal, but he also had ambition—giving rise to suspicions that he wanted to "set up for himself."*[45] Chauncey Depew took

---

* If fact, he had already built a small empire: By one account, Platt had used campaign funds in 1880 to put at least thirty legislators "under implied obligation to him," had found jobs for some 75 people in the New York Custom House, Post Office or New York City government, had built support among state canal officials, had chosen the warden of Auburn prison, and maintained a loyal following.

Platt aside one cold night during the Albany deadlock and laid out his terms. "You can have my strength if as Senator you will support the President."

Tom Platt saw no problem in it. He agreed immediately. "I have done my best to elect a Republican president and as a senator I will support him," he said.[46]

Depew had his fish on the line. To reel him in, he arranged for Platt to meet face-to-face with some of the Half-Breed legislators in a hotel room at the Delavan House: Robertson, John Birdsall, and William Woodin, all veterans of the Chicago bolt and rabid Conkling-haters. Behind closed doors, when Platt repeated his pledge to support Garfield's nominees, Woodin interrupted him with a question: "Does that statement cover appointments?"

Certainly it did, Platt said.

"Even if Judge Robertson's name should be sent in?"[47]

Platt swallowed hard. His long, pale face blanched. Tom Platt knew full well the special bad blood that existed between Roscoe Conkling and William Robertson since the Chicago bolt. He'd been trapped; he may have felt stupid for it, but the deal still made sense to him. Would timid James Garfield ever actually make such an inflammatory appointment, especially after his August pledges at the Fifth Avenue Hotel? "[E]ven in so extreme a case as the possibility of its containing the name of Judge Robertson," Platt agreed, though he was careful to note that he was "much opposed" to the idea.[48]

They had their deal—signed and delivered. "We can trust Platt, and when he's elected senator we shall not need a step-ladder to reach his ear," Woodin announced, speaking for the Half-Breed group.[49] Now Chauncey Depew delivered his side of the bargain. "I saw him [Platt] last night and transferred the decisive strength," he reported in a telegram to Whitelaw Reid.[50] Tom Platt won the final roll call with 54 votes for him, 41 for everyone else. He'd been made a U.S. Senator, not by the grace of Boss Roscoe Conkling, but by the grace of Conkling's two worst enemies, William Robertson and James G. Blaine.

Blaine was delighted when word reached him in Washington, D.C. By then, he'd also engineered the elections of two other U.S. Senators in his own fiefdom of Maine—his trusted lieutenants Eugene Hale and William Frye, both elected by the Maine legislature in late December. To do this, Blaine had had to convince Garfield to let him leak word of his cabinet offer in order to create an extra Senate vacancy for the state. Now, with Platt, he'd have three new chess pieces in the upper chamber for any coming match.

Back in Washington, Harriet Blaine too had come to love her husband's new job. She quickly discovered the high social standing of being wife to the Secretary of State-designate. After a mammoth mid-January dinner party at their Washington townhouse with the Chief Justice, the ministers from France, England, and Germany, historian George Bancroft, several senators and cabinet members, and Levi P. Morton—still working his way into the Garfield crowd at every chance—she wrote to her son Walker: "All the world is paying court to the coming Secretary of State. Socially you know it is about the best position.... We intend to put up a very nice and expensive house."[51]

◎ ◎ ◎ ◎ ◎

In late January, Lucretia Garfield left James with their small children in snow-bound Ohio and traveled secretly to New York City to buy dresses and gowns for her coming role as First Lady. Whitelaw Reid hosted her in style at his Madison Avenue home. By day she haunted New York's finest shops as "Mrs. Greenfield" in an awkward attempt at anonymity, though the secret leaked out soon enough.[52] "The prices seem extravagant," she wrote home to her husband, but she'd developed an eye for bargains—like "slightly soiled" pants marked down to $10 from $18.

By night, she enjoyed Whitelaw Reid's elegant company with a few choice friends. Blaine even joined them for a dinner or two. She heard all their political talk: "Mr. Reid told me ... that [Levi] Morton had been very ugly in his talk about you, using that expression that seems so gratifying to the Conkling clique—'That Ohio man,'" she reported back home. Soon her let-ters sounded as vitriolic as anything Blaine or Reid themselves could have concocted: "You will never have anything from those men but their assured contempt until you fight them *dead*. You can put every one of them in his [sic] political graves ... and that is the only place where they can be kept peaceable."[53]

Lucretia enjoyed the getaway and she agreed with Blaine that her hus-band might grow "morbid" sitting around the snowbound Ohio farmhouse all these winter months. For her part, she missed her children and found New York a political snake pit.

◎ ◎ ◎ ◎ ◎

Chester Arthur came early to Delmonico's restaurant on Fifth Avenue one Friday night in early February for the social event of the season. A group of

New York's financial, social, and political elite had taken over Delmonico's magnificent grand ballroom for a gala dinner to honor their designated hero of the 1880 presidential election—Stephen W. Dorsey, national party secretary and secret architect of the October Indiana victory. Sponsors included John Jacob Astor, J. Pierpont Morgan, Jesse Seligman, and Jay Gould from Wall Street. Reverend Henry Ward Beecher of Brooklyn's Plymouth Church led the clergy contingent, and politicos covered the spectrum from Stalwarts George Gorham and Tom Platt to old-timer wire-puller Thurlow Weed and Illinois lawyer Robert Todd Lincoln, the martyred Abraham Lincoln's son. Arthur greeted them all; he even shook hands with William Robertson, archvillain to the Conkling crowd, who'd come to drink his share of whiskey.

Ulysses Grant, the nation's foremost icon, held court for a full hour before dinner, shaking hands and greeting guests, almost stealing the limelight from Dorsey. Garfield had declined an invitation; James Blaine, too, had sent his regrets by telegram and Roscoe Conkling was stuck in Washington on Senate business. Otherwise, the two hundred guests were a glittering array of Republican celebrities, including the new vice president-elect.

Chet Arthur, tall and debonair in tails and black tie, commanded almost as much attention as General Grant. Standing a full head taller than almost any other man there with his six-foot-two-inch frame, he enjoyed the back-slapping and small talk, basking in the attention and respect they gave him now. Arthur had spent much of that winter preparing for his move to Washington—mostly by upgrading his wardrobe. In the few months since November, he'd bought six new suits, a dress coat, and several pairs of pants, had two other coats altered and two others pressed at Clarence Brooks & Co. alone, running up a bill of $726.75 that he paid in cash.[54] Since vice presidents had no official residence in Washington, D.C., Arthur, as an unmarried widower, gladly accepted Roscoe Conkling's invitation to share his suite near Wormley's Hotel on Fifteenth Street near Lafayette Park.

After more than three hours of eating, drinking, and reveling, General Grant finally stood up at the ballroom's head table, his presence almost lost in the spectacular (and spectacularly expensive) floral arrangements dripping from the chandeliers, including a huge Indiana coat of arms complete with prairie, setting sun, buffalo, and pioneer made entirely of roses, vines, violets, and other flowers. Grant introduced Dorsey to the crowd, and Dorsey introduced Arthur. Neither spoke for more than a few minutes and all in good fun.

By the time Chet Arthur rose, the wine, talk, and cigars had loosened his tongue considerably. He beamed as they showered him with loud cheers. Like the others, he started out talking about the election and Stephen Dorsey's role in Indiana, but decided to tease his friends: "I don't think we had better go into the minute secrets of the campaign, so far as I know them, because I see the reporters present who are taking it all down," he told his liquored-up audience, pausing to let their laughs fill the room. "Indiana was really, I suppose, a Democratic state. It had always been put down in the box as a State that might be carried by close and careful and perfect organization and a good deal of...."

Again he paused, as if looking for the right word. The crowd guessed it; voice after voice shouted "soap!" "soap!" Then they laughed harder than ever. "I see the reporters here," Arthur went on in dead-pan, "and therefore I will simply say that everybody showed a great deal of interest and distributed tracts and political documents all through the country." More laughter. "If it were not for the reporters, I would tell you the truth because I know you are intimate and devoted friends."

Arthur, of course, had already just acknowledged it with his humor. Everyone knew the term "soap"—slang for vote-buying. Many people suspected as much about Stephen Dorsey's Indiana operation, but no one expected the vice president-elect to joke and brag about it in front of a public throng of party leaders including the New York newspaper writers.[55]

Tongues later clucked, but Arthur only shrugged at the criticism. Let the dilettantes talk.[56] His actions that night had been blessed by the Reverend Beecher, General Grant, and Jay Gould, as broad a moral spectrum as anyone could imagine in 1880s America. His Republican clique had now won the White House and he had helped put them there. Arthur knew exactly where his loyalties lay, and he looked no farther than his Stalwart friends in New York City.

◎ ◎ ◎ ◎ ◎

By February, Garfield felt himself being pulled from every side over his Cabinet choices—and instead of four months, he now had just a few weeks left before his swearing in. Each new visitor to Ohio prompted new rumors flashing across the country and new jealousies inflaming the factions. "If all the reports are true" of possible candidate choices, the *New York Times* reported, "Pres. Garfield's Cabinet will contain about one hundred twenty-five persons."[57]

Some positions fell into place easily. For Attorney General, Garfield had penciled in Wayne McVeigh, a Pennsylvania moderate who'd supported him in Chicago but also had Stalwart ties as Senator Don Cameron's brother-in-law. For the War Department, Garfield liked Robert Todd Lincoln, the late President's son who had strong support from John Logan and Ulysses Grant. Lincoln had no actual military background beyond having served on General Grant's staff for a few months late in the Civil War; since then, he'd been a Chicago lawyer and Illinois Central Railroad trustee, but his family name still opened plenty of doors.

He still hadn't decided whether to include a southerner, though he'd offered a seat to Stephen Dorsey from Arkansas, his energetic party secretary, who declined.[58] Indiana's Ben Harrison had declined as well, not wanting to suffer the financial hardship of leaving the U.S. Senate where he could continue his lucrative private law practice. The key missing links remained Treasury and the New York Stalwarts. As the days passed, Garfield seemed unable or unwilling to decide: He wanted a New Yorker in his cabinet for harmony but at anyplace other than Treasury; the New Yorkers wanted Treasury and nothing else.

Blaine watched Garfield's vacillation from far away in Washington, D.C. and barraged him with letters from his stable of party elders: William Chandler, Thurlow Weed, Joseph Medill, and William Robertson, all urging him to hold firm against the New York machine.[59] One the other side, Garfield received a broadside from none less than General Grant himself, now setting himself up in New York City as president of the newly-formed Mexican Southern Railroad, urging him to beware of Blaine. "I do not like the man [Blaine], have no confidence in his friendship nor in his reliability," Grant said of his recent rival for the presidency, though Garfield shouldn't "ignore him because I do not like him."[60] Still, if Blaine were going to be Secretary of State, Grant argued now, then Levi Morton or "someone friendly to Senator Conkling should take the Treasury."[61]

Looking to satisfy everyone, Garfield even considered putting Roscoe Conkling himself in the cabinet—hoping, surely, that he'd refuse. "What would you say," he asked Blaine, "to exchanging seats, you for the Treasury, he (Conkling) for State?" Blaine virtually choked at the idea: "His appointment would act like strychnine upon your Administration—first bring contortions, and then be followed by death."[62]

Caught betwixt and between, Garfield awoke one morning that winter in a cold sweat. He'd slept alone in a strange bed that night, visiting a friend in

Cleveland. He'd had a strange dream: In it, he, Arthur, and an aide had been riding on a canal boat during the night. A heavy rain had come and, in the dream, Garfield had jumped off onto dry land. He'd turned back to look and saw the boat sinking with "General Arthur lying on a couch very pale, apparently very ill." Garfield started to jump into the water to save Arthur, but the aide stopped him, saying "he cannot be saved, and you will perish if you attempt it." They were naked and alone in the wild storm in the night, and in a hostile country. To Garfield, the nakedness felt like a disguise. In the dream "for the first time in a dream, I knew I was the President-elect," he recalled. They'd journeyed, he'd found some cloth to cover himself, and then they'd entered a house where "an old negro woman took me into her arms and nursed me as though I were a sick child."[63]

Then Garfield awoke.

The long winter in Ohio had worn on his mind. A few weeks later, Garfield decided, he had to confront his demon.

◉ ◉ ◉ ◉ ◉

Roscoe Conkling had spent the winter months that year in Washington, D.C., as the Senate finished up its business. Every day, following reports from his friends and in the newspapers, he grew more suspicious of Garfield and his secret plotting. He saw James Blaine in the Senate chamber almost every day but they never spoke, and hadn't in years.

Conkling heard accounts of the shenanigans in Albany over the Senate election. He sent Tom Platt a telegram on his victory calling him "a Senator who never apologized for being a Stalwart."[64] How much he'd heard or suspected about Platt's backroom deals is unclear. Conkling also had heard from Stephen Dorsey, Platt, Cornell and the others who'd been out to see the president-elect in Ohio. They all carried the same news: that Garfield refused to appoint Levi Morton to the Treasury. So much for promises from "that Ohio man"—and after Conkling had stumped across Ohio and Indiana to save Garfield's failing election campaign. What ingratitude!

Former Senator George Boutwell at one point approached Conkling and told him he'd heard Blaine's statements in New York City that Garfield's crowd planned to treat the Stalwarts fairly. "Do you believe one word of that?" Conkling had asked.

"Yes, I believe Mr. Blaine," Boutwell had said, having known both for years.

"I don't," Conkling shot back.[65]

When in Washington, Roscoe Conkling lived in rooms adjoining Wormley's Hotel* at Fifteenth and H Street, just a short walk from the White
House, two block's from Don Cameron's home on Lafayette Square, and an
easy carriage ride down Pennsylvania Avenue from the Capitol. He often
took his meals either at Chamberlin's on New York Avenue or at John Wel-
cker's nearby restaurant, with prices almost as high as Delmonico's in New
York and a letter from Charles Dickens on the wall calling it among the
world's best eateries. Normally a loner, Conkling was glad Chester Arthur
had agreed to move into the same building with him: Conkling would occupy the entire first floor, Arthur the entire second. Despite his free spending on good food and sharp clothes, Conkling claimed to worry over money.
"You see these two rooms," he supposedly told one visitor, "they are all I can
afford, and by the utmost economy it is as much as I can do to make the strap
and buckle meet at the end of the year."[66]

These months after the election, Conkling showed a "fatalism" and
"weariness of the struggle," one biographer noted,[67] and may have confided
plans to resign his Senate seat altogether—despite still having four years left
on his term—fearing he'd have "no voice" in a Garfield administration. Besides, he wanted to make money from his law practice to pay off debts.[68] He
kept up his routine of exercise at the punching bag, rode horses through the
crisp Washington winter and occasionally still visited Kate Chase Sprague,
the sprightly daughter of late Chief Justice Salmon Chase, though he'd grown
more discreet since her husband had chased him away with a shotgun two
summers ago in a high-profile scandal.[69]

His own wife Julia, by now largely estranged, stayed home in Utica where
he saw her only rarely.

Conkling waxed hot and cold even on how to deal with the new president-elect during these months. At times he insisted on his deal from last August; at other times he stressed his own purity from deal making. "Not for a
moment during the canvass" had he been alone with Garfield, he proudly told
his disciples.[70] Conkling saw where he stood with the president-elect. "Conkling refused to consider [Garfield's] proposed appointment of Blaine as other
than a premeditated attempt to humiliate him," as Senator Dawes put it.[71]

---

* Wormley's was owned by black businessman James T. Wormley, and the irony was not lost
that a black-owned hotel had been the scene of the 1876 back-room deal where Rutherford Hayes
agreed to withdraw troops from the South, ending Reconstruction and any realistic hope of black
voting rights for the next eighty years, in exchange for southern acquiescence to his presidency.

In late January, Conkling was surprised to receive a confidential invitation from Garfield to visit him in Ohio to "consult you on several subjects relating to the next administration—and especially in reference to New York interests."[72] Had Garfield decided to offer him something? Perhaps a cabinet seat for Conkling himself? Or at least a chance to argue his case for the record? Ohio was a long trip from Washington, D.C., especially in winter. Certainly Garfield wouldn't ask him to travel through hundreds of miles of bad weather unless he had something important to say. "I felt it my duty to obey the invitation," he later told a reporter, "at whatever cost to my personal convenience."[73]

Conkling took ten full days before responding to Garfield's invitation, and he carefully loaded his response with warnings of his own: "I need hardly say that your administration cannot be more successful than I wish it to be," he wrote.[74]

After leaving Washington by train, it took him two days to reach Mentor, Ohio through the mid-February storms. He arrived finally at Garfield's farmhouse at 3 pm on Wednesday afternoon, February 16. For the next six hours, the two men spoke face-to-face and alone. Garfield described their exchange as surprisingly good, a "full conversation on the Cabinet and kindred subjects." He served Conkling dinner and marveled at his "knowledge of men" as being "fuller and more accurate than I had expected, and in the main his judgment was sound." He found Conkling himself "frank and friendly." When Conkling made his appeal for placing Levi Morton at the Treasury Department, Garfield told him "I thought the objections insuperable." When Garfield floated the name of New York's Chief Justice Charles Folger as an alternative, Conkling told him it would be "dangerous to the party in N.Y." to take him from the bench.[75]

In the end, as Garfield recalled it, "I told him I wanted his friendship, and believed we could work together with indepen[den]t and mutual respect, but I could not give Morton more than the War or Navy."[76] Otherwise, Garfield felt, the meeting had gone well. "I think much better of [Conkling] than I expected to," he wrote his friend Burke Hinsdale, "and I shall be somewhat surprised if he has not carried away the same impression."[77]

Unfortunately for Garfield, his wishful thinking about Roscoe Conkling's impression had been totally wrong. Conkling, in fact, found Garfield appalling and insufferable—or at least that's what he told people months later, though he kept mum about it at the time. Garfield's manner he found "trifling and undecided."[78] Instead of any new ideas, Garfield had simply repeated the "many reasons" why Morton could not be given the Treasury, and then they'd discussed Folger and a few other New Yorkers in a general way. After many hours, Conkling recalled having laid his marker down firmly: "Treasury is the only post that would satisfy New York," he told Garfield, and "our state would prefer to be passed altogether if it could not obtain the department to which its rank and service entitled it."[79] He underscored the point by insisting "at all events, that you will not give us the Navy when there is no Navy. That department would probably satisfy some other state," but not New York.[80]

To Conkling's amazement, Garfield, instead of responding to his flat statement, "evaded the question" and changed the subject. He invited Conkling to tea. "To tea! Tea! Tea!" Conkling recounted later with full theatrics.[81] It was then almost six o'clock at night and Conkling had hoped to catch an early train back east. He asked if they had any more business to discuss. "If it means hospitality, I must ask to be excused, for I have left important matters behind me," the Senator explained, but Garfield insisted that he stay. At that point, Garfield went for tea but his guest stayed behind in the library. When Garfield returned, the two men spoke for hours more—though what Garfield said "was of very little importance," Conkling claimed later.[82]

He didn't leave Garfield's house until 11 pm that night. He felt exasperated. "I have never been able to understand why this President so invited me," he said.[83]

According to Tom Platt, when Roscoe Conkling reached New York City on his way back home to Washington, he told him that Garfield, in their meeting, had "reiterated his pledges to make no New York appointments without consultation with the New York Senators."[84]

"Have you any faith in Garfield?" Platt asked.

"Not much, but we will try him out," Conkling replied.[85]

A few days later, Conkling learned that Judge Folger had in fact been summoned to Ohio where Garfield had offered him not the Treasury Department, but rather Justice, which Folger declined. Conkling seethed at the whole affair. "Was it only to find out what I would like and then do just the opposite, that this man Garfield called me to Mentor?" he said.[86]

⊚ ⊚ ⊚ ⊚ ⊚

Two days before leaving for Washington for his inauguration as president and ten days after Roscoe Conkling had laid down his Treasury-or-nothing gauntlet for New York State, Garfield sent Levi Morton a confidential letter offering him the cabinet post of Secretary of the Navy. Morton, still very much wanting a place in the new administration, responded by telegraph from New York two days later with the cipher code "your suggestion approved." Garfield then scribbled in his notebook his tentative list of cabinet choices:

1. For State: Senator James G. Blaine (Maine);
2. Treasury: William Windom (Minnesota);
3. Interior: Senator Samuel J. Kirkwood or William Allison (both Iowa);
4. War: Robert Todd Lincoln (Illinois);
5. Navy: Levi P. Morton (New York);
6. Attorney General: Wayne MacVeagh (Pennsylvania);
7. Post Office: William H. Hunt or Don Pardee (both Louisiana).[87]

The list had a leading New York Stalwart (Morton), a leading Half-Breed (Blaine), and nods to Pennsylvania (MacVeigh), Illinois (Lincoln), the South (Hunt) and the West (Windom and Allison)—perfect balance, a slate "which will not be much changed," he wrote hopefully in his journal.[88]

On February 28, Garfield loaded his family into a train and left Ohio for the long trip east to begin his new life. Three hundred neighbors saw them off at the station. "You know how much I leave behind me of friendship, and confidence, and home-like happiness," he told them, then said good-bye for the last time.[89]

They reached Washington, D.C., late on Tuesday morning, March 1, after a long, twenty-hour over-night train ride, looking "travel-tired and weary," a newsman wrote. "[Garfield] does not sleep excellently well," another reporter noted, but the "excitement keeps him well stimulated, having something of the effect of rich living."[90] Webb Hayes, the president's son, met them at the Baltimore and Potomac Railway station and escorted Garfield's mother Eliza and his youngest son, eight-year old Abram directly to the White House and their new rooms. Lucretia earlier had left the older sons, teenagers James and Harry, in Washington with a tutor named William Hawkes, a former Phillips Andover Academy instructor, to study their Latin and Greek grammar and Cicero orations for college examinations in July.

Riding up Pennsylvania Avenue that day, Lucretia saw a city decked out for celebration. She remembered "the sun shining a warm welcome, banners and flags fluttering out a 'Hail to the Chief' from every street corner and from every house top." They stopped briefly at the White House where Lucy and Rutherford Hayes made no secret of their eagerness to leave after four wrenching years: "the embarrassments, … the ever-present danger of scandals and crimes among those we are compelled to trust leave us no place for regret upon retiring from this conspicuous scene," Hayes had already told friends. "If there are any two men in the country whose opposition and hatred are a certificate of good character and sound statesmanship," he wrote at the time, "they are [Roscoe] Conkling and [Ben] Butler."*[91]

Reaching their rooms at the Riggs House, where they would stay until his swearing-in, the calls started immediately—"savage office-baiting," Joe Stanley Brown remembered, that "began then and there."[92] Within hours, Garfield's weeks of pain-staking cabinet building began to unravel. The first and biggest shoe to drop was Levi P. Morton, his erstwhile and eager Secretary of the Navy.

Levi Morton lived in a townhouse in Washington, D.C., at Fifteenth and H streets, just across the street from Roscoe Conkling's rooms at Wormley's Hotel. Morton, following Garfield's request for secrecy, had not told his Boss before accepting Garfield's offer to join the cabinet two days earlier. Late that Tuesday night, though, Conkling found out. He promptly telegraphed Tom Platt that "our unwise friend is making a great deal of trouble for us."[93] Conkling worked himself into a tantrum. He snapped his fingers and sent New York Congressman John H. Starin rushing across the street to fetch Morton immediately. Well past midnight, Starin crossed the deserted pavement to Levi Morton's house and knocked at the front door. A butler answered and tried to send him away. Mr. Morton was asleep in bed and "suffering from a chill," he said.

John Starin, though, refused to leave. He came inside, went to Morton's bedroom, shook him awake, and told him that Roscoe Conkling wanted to see him—*now*!

Levi Morton, dazed and surprised, dutifully got up and out of bed. He put on pants and a coat and drank a dose of quinine with brandy that Starin had

---

* Benjamin "Beast" Butler, longtime Congressman from Massachusetts and later Governor and unsuccessful candidate for the presidency on the Greenback ticket in 1884, had earned his reputation during the Civil War. As a Major General occupying New Orleans in 1862, he reacted to a wave of local women insulting his troops by issuing orders that any lady showing contempt for any Union soldier be arrested as a "woman of the town plying her trade"—a common prostitute. The incidents stopped, but Butler's order sparked protests across the South.

prepared for him. Then he followed Starin out into the cold night and across the street to "the morgue," as some Republican friends jokingly called Roscoe Conkling's apartment. Inside, Morton found two large, loud, wide-awake angry men staring back at him—Conkling and his new house-mate Chester A. Arthur, the vice president-elect, who had recently moved into Conkling's rooms. Together, as Morton sat and meekly listened, the two New York bosses gave him an earful—Conkling "orated" at him in a brash, sneering tone; Arthur "denounced" him as "ruinous to the Republican party of New York."[94] For hours they lectured him, not letting him leave, hide, or get back to sleep.

Finally Morton had had enough. As dawn broke over Washington the next morning, he had changed his mind. After coffee, he put on clean clothes and dragged himself over to Riggs House to tell Garfield that he no longer wanted to be Secretary of the Navy. "Morton broke down on my hands under the pressure of his N.Y. friends, who called him out of bed at four this morning," Garfield wrote in his journal.[95]

Iowa Senator William Alison came next, asking to withdraw his name from the Interior Department, claiming "family reasons"—an ailing wife - though Garfield suspected that Allison too had been muscled into refusing.[96] At the same time, other pieces started falling into place: Robert Todd Lincoln and Wayne MacVeigh both visited Garfield with good news: that they gladly accepted their selections for War and Attorney General. Senator Allison suggested fellow Iowa Senator Samuel J. Kirkwood for Interior, and Louisiana Judge William Hunt agreed to represent the South in the cabinet—though they wouldn't decide until later on exactly which seat he'd take.

With Levi Morton out of the picture, though, Garfield still wanted a New York Stalwart in his cabinet—even if Roscoe Conkling seemed determined to stop him. He sent for James Blaine and Whitelaw Reid and asked them to suggest another candidate. Blaine mentioned New York Postmaster Thomas James—a Conkling loyalist but generally considered honest and competent. He'd make a fine Postmaster General. Garfield didn't want any more mistakes. If it were going to be Tom James, he insisted, then they must keep the appointment secret and James must be prepared to promise his loyalty to Garfield, not the New York Senator.

That Wednesday night, Whitelaw Reid sent a telegram to New York City telling James to come to Washington, D.C. immediately by overnight train and not tell anyone about it. At 8 am the next morning, Reid awoke to a "tremendous knocking at the door," he recalled. James, clean-shaven with dark hair and a thick, dark mustache, bubbled with enthusiasm. He was delighted at the chance to join Garfield's cabinet, he told Reid. During the next few hours, Reid quietly escorted James to meet with Blaine and then Garfield. He waited until late that night before consulting with a New York Senator - not Roscoe Conkling but rather Tom Platt who'd recently committed himself to support Garfield's appointments. "I had to get Platt, and make him say that, while Conkling had nothing to do with this, and knew nothing of it," that he, Platt "fully approved," Reid recalled. Platt agreed, first in front of Reid, then in front of Garfield.

That done, Whitelaw Reid sent Thomas James far away to a secret location where Roscoe Conkling could not get his hands on him.

Conkling exploded in anger when Tom Platt delivered the news to him and Chester Arthur late that night at their apartment at Wormley's Hotel. Conkling wouldn't stand for it—one of his own New Yorkers being secretly lured into breaking ranks. A howling winter storm had hit Washington, D.C. that night, the eve of the president's swearing-in, but Conkling immediately stood up, grabbed his coat, and led Arthur and Platt back outside into the blizzard to march down the three cobblestone blocks to Riggs House. There, they barged into Garfield's bedroom and found the president-elect at a desk still struggling with his inaugural address. Before Garfield could say a word, Conkling launched into an angry oration. He'd been "cheated," he said, raising his voice. Garfield hadn't consulted him. He resented "interference" by "the tall young man from New York" (Whitelaw Reid) in the Cabinet appointments while he, Conkling, had been left in the dark. It was an insult.[97]

After a few minutes, Conkling's temper blew itself out. Garfield listened but he didn't argue with the New York Senator; he just let him speak his piece. He made no promises, no gestures, and no apologies. By now, his mind had moved on to other things. His Cabinet largely decided, he had to focus his mental energies on the duties of becoming President of the United States.

⦿ ⦿ ⦿ ⦿ ⦿

Garfield didn't finish writing his inaugural speech until 2:30 am, having stalled for weeks and thrown away earlier drafts. He worked through Roscoe Conkling's tirade, his own insomnia, and the storm outside.

Snow and sleet fell over Washington the morning of March 4, but by noon the sky had cleared. Lucretia awoke at 3 am that morning because of the storm. At 10:30 am, President Rutherford Hayes rode over to Garfield's room at Riggs House and they rode back to the White House together; Lucretia had come earlier to the White House for a morning reception with Lucy Hayes. Then the two families rode down Pennsylvania Avenue in an open barouche drawn by four horses; crowds lining both sides of the wide promenade cheered them; the First Cleveland Troop marched before them as an honor guard led by General William Tecumseh Sherman on horseback. By now the rain had stopped. "There! All is right now. I have no more anxiety," Lucy Hayes said as the sun finally broke through the clouds.[98]

At the Capitol Building, ushers led Lucretia, Lucy Hayes, and Garfield's mother Eliza to the diplomatic gallery overlooking the Senate chamber. Lucretia sat in the front row wearing one of her New York dresses. From here, she could see the glittering display as the Supreme Court justices in black robes, the diplomatic corps in court uniforms, Army and Navy officers in full dress blues, and cabinet members in morning suits all marched into the chamber to their assigned chairs among the Senators. She joined the burst of applause for James Blaine, still a Senator, who walked out onto the floor together with Winfield Scott Hancock in full Major-General uniform with gold braids and brass buttons. Then, with a "rustle of the galleries and the standing up of the whole body of people," she recalled, she saw the President, Rutherford Hayes, and her husband the President-elect, enter the chamber side by side. "[M]y heart grew stiller and stiller," she remembered, awed into silence.[99] The applause lasted long and loud.

Chester Arthur came last, presented to the chamber by outgoing vice president William Wheeler. Here, Arthur briskly repeated his oath of office at noon—though the Senate clock had to be turned back five minutes to make the time precise. Then the Senate session formally adjourned.

The distinguished group then marched in procession out into the March chill onto a wooden platform built facing the Capitol's East Portico. Wall-sized American flags draped the platform. From here, Garfield looked out at a sea of 50,000 faces. Streaks of sunlight broke through the clouds and reflected off the snow. Garfield sat in a raised chair used by George Washington at his first inaugural in 1789 ninety-two years earlier. Around him sat President Hayes, Vice President Wheeler, Arthur, Lucy Hayes, Lucretia, and his mother Eliza.

He stood up, took a breath, and began: "We stand today upon an eminence which overlooks a hundred years of national life, a century crowded with perils, but crowned with triumphs of liberty and love." He spoke slowly, forming his words carefully so that his rich baritone voice would carry over the crowd. His spoke for thirty-five minutes, pledging to end "bitter controversies" separating North from South and black from white, praising the freeing of black slaves as "the most important political change we have known since the adoption of the Constitution," asserting American authority over "any inter-oceanic canal across the Isthmus that connects North and South America," condemning the Mormon Church for "sanctioning polygamy" and pledging to preserve public credit, sound currency, and industry. His voice grew hoarse toward the end but finished strongly.

When he was done, he turned toward Chief Justice Morrison R. Waite* who stepped forward to administer the oath of office, his clerk holding the Bible. "Do you, James A. Garfield, solemnly swear that you will faithfully execute the Office of President of the United States, and will to the best of my Ability, preserve, protect, and defend the Constitution of the United States?" Whether Garfield simply said "I do" or followed the precedent of Abraham Lincoln and added "so help me God" is unclear from the accounts at the time. He shook hands with the Chief Justice and President Hayes, then took the hand of his mother and kissed her. Then he kissed his wife, shook hands with Lucy Hayes, and began shaking the hands of hundreds of others.

After the ceremony, Garfield, Hayes, and their families rode back up Pennsylvania Avenue in their carriage, receiving applause all along the way. Lucy Hayes hosted a brief lunch for them inside the White House. "I am glad to be a freed man," Rutherford Hayes said with a wink.[100] Then Garfield, as President of the United States, and Lucretia as his First Lady,** sat outside for two and a half hours reviewing the great parade—over 15,000 marchers and a gathering of spectators estimated as high as 100,000.[101]

Later, 6,000 celebrants jammed the new Smithsonian Museum Building for the formal inaugural reception. Lucretia wore a satin gown with lace trim, pansies, and no jewelry. At Garfield's request, the German Orchestra of Philadelphia interspersed dances with tunes from Gilbert and Sullivan.[102] Guests nibbled on 1,500 pounds of turkey, 100 gallons of oysters, fifty hams, and 15,000 cakes.[103] Outside, fireworks lit the sky and friends mingled at receptions in homes, restaurants, and clubs all across town. That night, their

---

* Waite had been appointed Chief Justice by Ulysses Grant in 1874 after the death of Salmon P. Chase, but only after Roscoe Conkling had been offered it twice and declined.
** Lucy Hayes was the first presidential spouse to call herself "first lady of the land." The tradition stuck.

first in the White House as President and First Lady, Lucretia "slept too soundly... to remember any dream," she recalled, "so our first night among the shadows of the last eighty years gave no forecast of our future."[104]

The next morning, after just five hours of sleep, Garfield faced a huge crowd of callers, primarily office seekers already barging in on him. He broke away during the morning to see Senator William Windom, coming to accept Garfield's offer to head the Treasury Department. At mid-day, Windom and Blaine came with news that Samuel Kirkwood had accepted Interior, the final piece of the puzzle. At 2:30 pm, Garfield signed and formally submitted to the United States Senate his final choices for his Cabinet: James G. Blaine at State, William Windom at Treasury, Robert T. Lincoln at War, William H. Hunt at Navy, Samuel J. Kirkwood at Interior, Wayne MacVeagh as Attorney-General, and Thomas L. James as Postmaster-General. At 6:05 pm, he received word back from Senate executive clerk Henry E. Peyton that the Senate, meeting in executive session, had unanimously confirmed the entire group.*

---

* This three-hour Senate turnaround on an entire cabinet slate is but a dream today. Absent then were the intensive background checks, financial disclosures, FBI investigations, political vetting, and televised hearings. By contrast, President George W. Bush announced his cabinet picks weeks ahead of his January 20, 2001 inauguration, and, even at top speed, his controversial choice of John Ashcroft as Attorney General was not approved until February 1, 2001.

JAMES A. GARFIELD, *with daughter Mollie holding a book. Garfield, father of five, lived every politician's dream—to win a surprise, unsought "dark horse" nomination for the presidency. But he found the reality to have a decidedly dark side.*

All illustrations are provided courtesy of the Library of Congress unless otherwise noted.

ULYSSES S. GRANT, *Civil War hero and retired two-term president, was at 58 years old the most celebrated American of his generation and the early leader to win the Republican Party's nomination in 1880 for an unprecedented third term in the White House.*

JAMES G. BLAINE *led the Republican Half-Breed faction in 1880. The "magnetic man" from Maine, a U.S. Senator and former House Speaker, Blaine was thought to be Grant's strongest challenger for the presidential nomination in 1880 with delegate support from across the north and west.*

(Top left) ROSCOE CONKLING, *the haughty New York Senator and Republican Boss, led the Stalwarts and was General Grant's chief manager at the 1880 convention.* (Top right) *Treasury Secretary* JOHN SHERMAN, *the "Ohio icicle," trailed Grant and Blaine for the Republican nomination in 1880 but counted on fellow-Ohioan Garfield to help manage his forces in Chicago.* (Above) *The Senate in the late 1870s, showing Roscoe Conkling (far left, standing, with hand raised) of New York addressing the chamber as James G. Blaine of Maine (far right) looks in the opposite direction. Courtesy of the U.S. Senate Historical Office.*

(Top) *Prior to the convention, Boss Conkling tries to decipher the presidential "puzzle" of 1880, with Blaine, Grant, and other hopefuls seen as mere pieces for his manipulation.* (Above) *A view inside Chicago's "Glass Palace" during the 1880 Republican National Convention. It drew 15,000 people and produced a 36-ballot stalemate, the longest ever for Republicans. Garfield (center, right) is on the podium waiting to speak.*

(Below) **LUCRETIA GARFIELD**, *normally reserved, struggled with the role of political wife; her role as First Lady changed drastically after her husband's shooting pushed her into the public spotlight.*

(Above) *"Gentleman Boss"* **CHESTER ALAN ARTHUR**, *outgoing and well dressed, was a skillful manager of New York's Republican machine. He always deferred to his mentor Roscoe Conkling until offered a chance for the vice presidency. (Below) In this cartoon, Puck compares Grant's loss of the nomination in 1880 to Robert E. Lee's 1865 military surrender to him ending the Civil War. Roscoe Conkling, John Logan, and Don Cameron are seen bowing behind Grant as John Sherman and James G. Blaine lower the flag of the Third Term movement.*

(Top) *Garfield's Mentor, Ohio farmhouse, dubbed "Lawnfield" by reporters, became the stage for Garfield's successful "front porch" presidential campaign.* (Above) *Garfield and family pose for a formal White House portrait. From left to right are: Abram (8 years old), James (15), Lucretia, Mollie (13), Garfield, Irvin (10), Harry (standing, 16), and Garfield's 80 year old mother Eliza.*

The forged Morey letter (on left) is shown side-by-side with Garfield's rebuttal. Note differences in the signatures. No "Employers Union" in Lynn, Massachusetts, nor a person there named H.L. Morey were ever found.

(Above) *Garfield hopes to tangle Conkling and Blaine into a "bond of friendship," but the feud between them makes friendship impossible.*

(Right) *Conkling's dramatic resignation from the U.S. Senate during the Robertson nomination fight is dismissed here as a "harmless explosion." Tom "Me Too" Platt makes a much smaller blast below.*

(Above) *President Garfield is shot by assassin Charles Guiteau at Washington, D.C.'s Baltimore and Potomac Rail Depot. Blaine is near the president. "I am a Stalwart and Arthur will be president," Guiteau said on being arrested.*

(Left) *The assassin Charles Guiteau told the prison photographer "If my picture is taken, it must be a good one." Guiteau chose an ivory-handled English Bulldog revolver to "remove" the president because he felt it would later look better in a museum.*

(Right) *Charles Guiteau portrayed in* Puck *as disappointed office seeker brandishing his gun while demanding political spoils.*

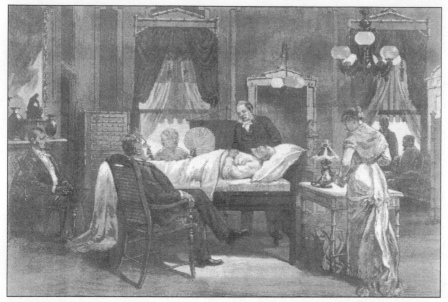

Garfield in his White House sickroom surrounded by doctors, including Willard Bliss (standing) who later demanded Congress pay him $25,000 ($500,000 in modern dollars) for his four months treating the president.

(Left) Garfield looks out at the Atlantic Ocean from his sickbed in Elberon, New Jersey, as Lucretia sits nearby. In sharing their private tragedy with the public, the Garfields made themselves the most human and accessible First Family up to that time.

Vice President Arthur takes the oath of office as president in his New York City townhouse just four hours after Garfield's death, assuming a job he neither wanted nor sought.

• PART IV •

President

• • • • •

The quick approval of Garfield's cabinet only delayed the inevitable confrontation. A deeper issue gnawed at the body politic, behind the pomp and ceremony of White House life: Who would control the new government? Would the Senators knock down Garfield as they had knocked down presidents from Rutherford Hayes and Andrew Johnson to even Ulysses Grant?

Despite initial shows of harmony, one crucial appointment would force the issue into blinding focus—more important than a cabinet seat or a vice presidency: the Collector of the Port of New York, the biggest patronage prize in America.

The battle would now shift to the grandest political stage of all—Roscoe Conkling wielding the power of the United States Senate and Garfield the power of the presidency. And one obscure man would wield the power of his own odd temperament.

· 11 ·
THE APPOINTMENT

C HARLES GUITEAU HAD JUST A FEW DOLLARS in his pants pocket when he boarded a train on March 5, 1881, the day after Garfield's inauguration, to leave New York City and travel south to Washington, D.C. The short, dark-haired man with rumpled clothes, black beard, and uneven eyes had high hopes. He told his story to anyone who'd listen: that he'd worked in the presidential canvass alongside Chester Arthur, Roscoe Conkling, U.S. Grant, and the other New York Stalwarts. He'd been at Republican headquarters and delivered his speech, "Garfield Against Hancock," that had turned the tide. Now he expected a major diplomatic post.

Reaching Washington, Guiteau walked across the newly-paved Pennsylvania Avenue and headed downtown, carpetbag in hand, with no winter coat and thin rubbers over his badly-scuffed shoes. He found lodging at Mrs. Lockwood's Boarding House, a modest home on Twelfth and G Streets just six blocks from the White House. Money would be no problem, he figured. By the time the first bill came for rent, he'd have his political appointment in the new administration and a fitting salary to match.

Like any good office-seeker, Guiteau had planned his hunt carefully. Before leaving New York, he'd checked names and backgrounds of all the current U.S. Ministers and Consuls in foreign cities and written to William Evarts, the outgoing Secretary of State, to ask whether they'd be resigning or staying in their posts.[1] Around January 1, he'd sent a second letter to President-Elect James Garfield in Ohio reminding him of his interest in the Austrian Ministry. Garfield had never answered but Guiteau hadn't expected a response. This time, Guiteau hadn't mentioned the "wealthy lady" in New York City whom he might marry to help finance his foreign mission; she'd simply been a lady whom he'd seen at church one Sunday morning and never been introduced to, though he was sure she'd marry him if he asked her.[2] He'd sent her letters, but the lady complained to police detectives who arrested him and sternly told him to stay away.[3]

Guiteau waited until Tuesday, March 8, before going to the White House to press his claim personally with the President. The White House in 1881 still opened its door to all comers and huge crowds thronged it in the first weeks of the new Garfield presidency. Guiteau joined more than a hundred others that morning, coming early for a good place on line. Garfield himself remembered that Wednesday as the busiest yet: "no day in 12 years has witnessed such a jam of callers…. Again and again we were compelled to shut the doors, with the files of people extending to the avenues."[4]

Job-seekers entered through a downstairs corridor and handed their cards to Mr. Loeffler, the chief doorkeeper. Another doorman led them to a parlor to wait; some of the hopefuls waited for hours, day after day. Leoffler would pass the cards forward to Joe Stanley Brown, the president's private secretary who had an office upstairs on the second floor. The doormen all had instructions to treat the office seekers "[r]espectfully and courteously," Joe Stanley Brown explained, "as all people are who visit the White House."[5]

Guiteau didn't get to see the president that first day; he waited a few hours and then left. "The room was very crowded," Stanley Brown recalled. Besides, Guiteau knew he had two legs up on all the other job-seekers: his speech "Garfield against Hancock," and his New York Stalwart friends. They wouldn't let him down.

After leaving the White House, Guiteau walked across the lawns and past the Treasury Department to the prestigious Riggs House on Fifteenth Street. Guiteau had discovered that he could arrange to receive his mail here at Riggs, sit in their library to read the daily newspapers and use their stationery for his letters. He greeted the clerks at the front door, found a seat at a desk, and proceeded to write a note to President Garfield stating his business: "I called to see you this A.M.," he told the president, "but you were engaged."[6]

Guiteau had changed his plans by the time he'd reached Washington, D.C. that March. Vienna looked out of reach. The current Consul there, a Mr. Kasson of Iowa, wished to stay and was a "good fellow. I should not wish to disturb him," he wrote Garfield.[7] Besides, James Blaine now had been appointed Secretary of State. Austria "would naturally go to a Blaine man," Guiteau figured. "I was not a Blaine man; I was a Grant man—a Stalwart."[8]

Instead, Guiteau now set his sights on Paris. The current consul there, a Mr. Walker of New York, had been appointed by Rutherford Hayes and expected to leave, creating a vacancy: "I think I prefer Paris to Vienna, and if agreeable to you, should be satisfied with the consulship to Paris."[9] It didn't matter to Guiteau that he'd never been abroad, spoke no foreign language, and had no experience in foreign affairs. He knew he had the most important qualification for the job. "I expected to get it on my personal standing" with men like Garfield, Blaine, Logan and Arthur, he explained later. These offices "are distributed more on account of personal relations with the President and Secretary of State."[10] Everyone knew that. That's why they worked on political campaigns in the first place.

"They all thought I was a good fellow," Guiteau recalled. " I used to go up and address them with the utmost freedom."[11]

A few days later, Guiteau tried again and this time had better luck. He came to the White House, passed his card to the doorman, and took his usual seat in the waiting room. After a short while, the usher called his name. Guiteau followed up a marble staircase to the second floor office of Joe Stanley Brown, Garfield's Private Secretary, a polite young man who seemed intent on everyone being well treated. Guiteau glanced for a moment out one of the two bay windows in Stanley Brown's office that overlooked the south lawn, the wide Potomac River, and the green Virginia hills beyond. The usher showed Guiteau to another parlor where he waited until Brown called his name and led him through his private door into the president's room.

Guiteau was startled for a moment on entering the private office. The famous figure of James Garfield, large, husky, and full-bearded, taller and more athletic than himself, stood before him, close enough to see the lines of weariness around the president's eyes, the gray patches in his beard, the heaviness in his step. Guiteau hesitated as Garfield waved him forward. The president was still occupied "in conversation with several politicians," Guiteau recalled. "I remember specifically Levi P. Morton… and General Tyner. I know both of these gentlemen. As soon as they saw me I was very cordially received by them…. Mr. Morton especially asked about my health and how I was getting along, and so forth."[12]

Guiteau stood quietly at first, keeping a discreet distance and waiting for Garfield to finish with the other men. Then he stepped forward, introduced himself, and handed the president a copy of his speech: "Garfield against Hancock"—the nice printed version listing his address as the National Re-

publican Committee in New York. "[Garfield] recognized me at once," Guiteau remembered. Guiteau had taken a pen and marked his name and the
words "Paris consulship" on the front cover of the speech, "connecting it with
my name," he explained. "I told him that I was an applicant for the Paris consulship, and he looked at it."[13]

Guiteau sat quietly as the president now took his seat across the desk
from him, held the printed speech in his large hand, and began to read, apparently absorbed in the text, his eyes following it line by line. Guiteau sat
back and watched. He decided not to press himself; it was good enough, he
thought, that the president actually seemed interested in his writing. Being
perfectly proper and polite, he stood up and left the room, apparently without another word—or even telling the president he was leaving. "I left him
reading the speech and retired," he explained.[14] The president now would remember him in connection with the speech

Guiteau came back again to the White House a few days later, but this
time he got only as far as the front parlor. Joe Stanley Brown, the private secretary, greeted him "very cordially," he recalled. Stanley Brown often circulated among the men and women waiting in the parlors to ask their business.
This morning, he saw Guiteau and recognized him at once. Guiteau's papers
had been sent forward to the "proper channel," he told him.[15] "His application was for a consular appointment, a matter which came entirely under the
State Department," Stanley Brown later explained. "It is customary in the
White House to refer such matters to the bureau officers. It would be impossible for the President to see every office-seeker, and it is customary to inform
such gentlemen to make application" to the proper Department.[16]

Guiteau seemed pleased with the news and started making plans promptly
to visit Secretary Blaine at the State Department. Meanwhile, he carried
himself about Washington, apparently at ease in his role as prominent diplo-
mat in waiting.

◎ ◎ ◎ ◎ ◎

Ulysses Grant too had stayed in New York City during President Garfield's
swearing-in ceremony, busy setting up his new Mexican railroad on Wall
Street. Besides, he still felt no mood for celebrating after his own recent political defeat in Chicago. "I do not wish to be in Washington at the time of
the Inauguration," he wrote to John Logan that week. "I should very much
like to meet Garfield & his wife, but I have no fancy for hobnobbing with

John Sherman or [Carl] Schurz"—two of Rutherford Hayes' crowd. He and Julia hadn't set foot in the White House since 1877, having grown to despise Hayes and his self-anointed "reformers." "But I respect the latter [Schurz] the most. I have not heard of his punishing innocent people because of their friendship for me," he wrote, still smarting over John Sherman's alleged patronage tactics in the campaign.[17]

At first, Ulysses Grant had planned to stay away altogether from the White House; "his mortification was extreme" at first hearing Garfield's plan to appoint James Blaine as Secretary of State, Adam Badeau noted.[18] "If Garfield puts Blaine in his cabinet, I'll never speak to Garfield again," Grant had been overheard saying.[19] Seeing Garfield's final cabinet choices in the newspapers only irritated Grant more: Blaine's name at the top, Levi P. Morton's name missing from the Treasury, none of his own close friends in top spots, his advice to Garfield apparently ignored. "I must confess disappointment," he wrote to Roscoe Conkling. "I shall try however to say but little about it for the present."[20]

By the time Grant reached Washington, though, he had reconsidered. Maybe Garfield still could be friendly, especially since Grant had worked so hard to get him elected. On Wednesday morning, March 10, he and Julia arrived together at the White House for breakfast with the new President and First Lady. The old-time staff greeted them warmly, including Mr. Loeffler, the chief doorkeeper whom Grant himself had hired in 1869. Not much had changed in the building since they'd left. For the past four years, Democrats in Congress had denied "His Fraudulency" President Hayes any money for White House decoration or repairs—their petty revenge for the 1876 election dispute. As a result, all the new carpets, paintings, and decorations that Julia had installed years ago still remained where she'd left them, though much worse for wear.

James and Lucretia Garfield hosted the Grants to an informal breakfast along with a few other houseguests: General Sheldon and his wife, a Miss Mason from Cleveland, and Ohio Governor Charles Foster, who'd dropped by that morning. Grant couldn't help but notice the chaos around them and the strain in Garfield's face—far different from how Garfield had looked as a candidate in October, six months earlier.

After breakfast, Lucretia took Julia Grant for a walk through their old home, leaving their husbands to talk privately over coffee and boiled eggs. Grant lit a cigar, hardly his first of the day. He and Garfield hadn't spoken one-on-one in years. Grant had known Garfield for almost two decades, since the war, but they'd never been close—there'd been "no approach to intimacy" as Adam Badeau put it.[21] Garfield, eight years younger, had served only a few months under Grant's command during the war and had reached Congress before Grant became supreme military leader in 1864. In Washington, Garfield had been loyal to Grant as president, but not zealously like Roscoe Conkling. If anything, Garfield had always privately doubted Grant's fitness for office. In 1876, for instance, when then-Congressman Garfield had heard of President Grant's remarkably calm reaction to the scandal-driven resignation of his Secretary of War, William Belknap, he'd confided: "[Grant's] imperturbability is amazing. I am in doubt whether to call it greatness or stupidity."[22]

Now, sitting across the breakfast table, talking as one president to another, Garfield assured Grant of his "gratitude" for Grant's stumping during the election campaign and promised to keep the older man's advice in mind. Certainly he planned to "regard [his] wishes so far as possible in … policy and appointments," Garfield told him. Grant seemed pleased with the olive branch and held his tongue about Garfield's cabinet choices thus far. He did, by the way, though, have one special favor to ask—a position for a friend, Adam Badeau. Badeau, Grant's wartime aide, post-war biographer, and constant advisor, had held the post of consul-general in London, England, since 1870. Grant had put Badeau in that job himself and now wanted to keep him there while Badeau finished writing his latest Grant chronicle. A few days later, Grant sent Garfield a personal letter repeating his request for Badeau's "retention [in London] unless he could receive the post of Naval Officer" in New York City."[23] He also wrote Badeau a letter of introduction to use in visiting the White House a few weeks later.

Garfield had known Adam Badeau over the years and found him capable and likeable. Grant didn't press the point over breakfast that morning. He knew better; that would be impolite. But Garfield understood perfectly. Here was one more job seeker backed by one more powerful politico who couldn't be ignored.

❧ ❧ ❧ ❧ ❧

One morning about that time, Charles Guiteau knocked at the door of one of the other residents at Mrs. Lockwood's Boarding House. Illinois Senator John Logan rented a suite of rooms on an upper floor there, and Guiteau had noticed him in the dining room at breakfast. Guiteau and Logan met briefly in New York City during the campaign; perhaps the politician would remember him.

Hearing no answer, Guiteau opened the unlocked door and stepped inside. He found a reception room and sat down in a chair by the door. Logan, still getting dressed at 8 am, heard the noise and came to see who had knocked. Guiteau stood up and greeted him. Logan, surprised at first that this stranger seemed to know him by name, nevertheless gave him a polite greeting and they started talking. Guiteau pulled from his pocket a copy of his printed speech, handed it to Logan, and asked if he would read it. Logan opened it and saw the title—"Garfield against Hancock"—and laid it on his desk. "I will read it when I have the time," he said pleasantly.[24]

"That speech," Guiteau said, "elected the President of the United States Mr. Garfield." Speaking without any shyness to the half-dressed Senator, he explained how he had delivered it during the campaign in New York City and mentioned that he'd been given a "promise of an appointment of consul-general to France." He'd been to the White House and seen the President about it and was going to see Secretary Blaine, but needed a recommendation.

Logan couldn't help but notice the man's odd clothing. Instead of shoes or boots, Guiteau wore "sandals of India rubber" and "I do not think he had on any stockings." He had no coat and he wore "a very light pair of pants"—strange for a mid-March day with snow on the ground. "I do not know you, sir; I have no knowledge of who you are, and I cannot recommend you," Logan recalled saying.

Guiteau persisted, though. He explained to Logan that he came from Chicago, making him a constituent of the Senator. Logan asked where in Chicago Guiteau lived; Guiteau said in a round-about way that he actually lived in Freeport but had an address in Chicago on State Street. He gave no number. He'd been to New York to work at the national committee, he said, and had seen the president there. He asked again for a recommendation. As John Logan looked on, Guiteau took from his pocket a sheet of "foolscap" paper on which he'd already written a brief recommendation. Would Logan sign it?

John Logan, a larger man than Guiteau with dark mustache, burly arms, and lanky dark hair, took the paper, read it, and shook his head. "I treated him as kindly and as politely as I could," Logan recalled "but I was very desirous of getting rid of him."[25] Guiteau remembered his saying something like "I haven't got any pen and ink here, but come upstairs and I will sign it for you." In any event, Guiteau finally left after about fifteen minutes and went about his day.

The next morning, though, Guiteau tried again. He came back to John Logan's room and managed a few more minutes alone with the Senator. Again he asked Logan to sign the recommendation. "He claimed that I was his Senator and that it was my duty," Logan recalled. Logan again refused.[26] As Guiteau remembered it, Logan "seemed to have changed his mind after thinking it over." It was "the kind of way these politicians have. They say they will do a great many things in an off-hand sort of way, and when you come to press them they say, 'I guess I won't do that now; come and see me in a week or two.'"[27]

Wanting to be rid of the intruder and end the meeting, Logan recalled telling Guiteau simply this: "The first time that I see the Secretary of State I will mention your case to him."

That was good enough for Guiteau. "I consider General Logan one of my friends," he said later.[28] After all, Logan had been polite and proper. He'd been helpful, like all the other Stalwarts. He could use Logan's name now when he went to the State Department to see Secretary Blaine.

After Guiteau had left his room, though, John Logan finished getting dressed and then made a point to go downstairs and find Mrs. Lockwood, the owner of the boarding house. He took her to the dining room and pointed out Guiteau, who was quietly having breakfast by himself. "I do not think he is a proper person to have in your boarding-house," Logan told her.

Why not? Mrs. Lockwood asked.

Logan told her about the pushy office seeker's bothering him in his room that morning. "I think he is a little off in the head," Logan remembered telling her.[29]

A few days later, Mrs. Lockwood presented Charles Guiteau a bill for his first two weeks' rent. The next day, she found his room empty. Guiteau had disappeared, leaving her only a note saying that he would pay her the rent as soon as he'd received the well-paying political job in the administration that he'd been promised.[30]

⊚ ⊚ ⊚ ⊚ ⊚

Garfield's first days as president gave him little time to think; the crush of appointments, events, and office-seekers sapped his attention. Callers the first morning formed a line stretching from the White House up the driveway past horses and carriages through the gate and out onto Pennsylvania Avenue; thousands of out-of-town guests wanted to shake the new president's hand before heading home from the Inauguration. James and Lucretia stood side-by-side in the Red Room for hours that morning greeting, smiling and making small talk with an endless stream of faces. Crowds surged into the East Room and doormen had to push them out to make room for yet another reception. At 11 am, aides pulled Garfield away to his private study on the second floor—the same room Abraham Lincoln had used during the war with large windows overlooking the south lawn, the stump-like bottom of the unfinished Washington Monument, and the Potomac tidewaters. Here he met privately with callers—Whitelaw Reid, Phil Sheridan, Robert Ingersoll, Benjamin Harrison, members of his new cabinet, senators, and friends.

All day he rushed through the building from appointment to appointment. At 2 pm, he met with Rutherford Hayes' outgoing cabinet and asked each Secretary to remain until their successors had been installed. In the afternoon, he received salutes on the portico from two military regiments—the Ninth New York and Sixth New Jersey. Then he received the Boston Fusiliers and the National Rifles in the East Room, and after dinner he and Lucretia heard serenades from the Columbus, Ohio Garfield and Arthur Club, an Iowa band, and the Army of the Cumberland veterans. Then came still more callers—delegations from Ohio and Connecticut, the Cleveland Grays, a few straggling members of Congress, and others stretching well into the night.

Garfield enjoyed much about the White House, by far bigger than any home he or Lucretia had ever dreamed of living in—the sense of history, the bright vistas and rooms filled with sunlight and outgoing people. But he and Lucretia found the building itself old and threadbare. The rooms smelled of mold and hadn't been restored since the early 1870s when Julia Grant had replaced wall paper, installed new hallway carpets, redone the Blue Room in blue satin upholstery, and restyled the East Room in "New Grecian" style with massive Corinthian columns, gilded trim, and Greek-themed ceiling frescoes. Now, a decade later, the drapes hung in tatters and furniture had to be placed over bare spots in the rugs.

Rats plagued the White House basement; Garfield could hear them scurrying in the night around decayed eighty-year-old plumbing and fouled septic pipes.

Rutherford Hayes had installed a new-fangled telephone machine on the second floor—largely useless since so few people had telephones in Washington, D.C., in 1881—but Grant, more practical, had built a billiards room next to the conservatory that Garfield immediately seized on as an escape from the crowds. He played billiards almost daily with his friend Colonel Rockwell whom he'd installed as Commissioner of Public Buildings. Garfield's two younger sons, Abram and Irvin, eight and ten years old, quickly discovered the large East Room as a great place to race bicycles and soon gouged tracks in the smooth carpet. Irvin, the more adventurous, liked to careen his high-wheeled velocipede down the marble stairways on rainy days to terrorize the servants and callers. The two older sons, Harry and James, studied with their tutor, Professor Hawkes, for college entrance examinations the next summer. Garfield hoped they both might soon enter Williams College, his own *alma mater*, if their grades held up. Mollie, their fourteen-year-old sister, practiced on the grand piano and spent her days at Madam Burr's school nearby.

The boys even adopted a little yellow stray dog that had befriended Garfield when he was a Congressman.

Garfield kept a tight regimen as president: up at 7 am, breakfast with the family at 8 am after perusing the morning newspapers, then to his office to dictate letters for an hour before facing the callers. He tried to limit his appointments to Congressmen and invited guests until noon and then saw office-seekers until 2 pm when he had lunch with Lucretia and the children. In the afternoons, he read the New York City daily papers and met with his cabinet. Blaine called on him more than anyone else; he and Garfield found time almost every afternoon to talk about politics. On Sundays they took carriage drives together. For cabinet meetings, Blaine almost always arrived early and closeted himself with Garfield before the others came.[31]

Garfield didn't mind being pulled to the East Room five and six times a day to greet different delegations; these were pleasant people, not like "the Spartan band of disciplined office hunters who drew paper on me as highway men draw pistols," he wrote.[32] The job seekers drove him to distraction. He had little problem personally with the concept of political spoils. Garfield happily found government jobs for his own friends. Many, perhaps most Americans in 1881 still equated spoils with good government: keeping the workers accountable to the voters.

But now there were so many of them, and they acted so rudely—each "pursues his prey with the grip of death," he despaired.[33] Politicians—Garfield and his cabinet—picked almost every one of the over-100,000 job-holders in the federal bureaus and departments; only a handful were chosen based on "merit" competitive examinations.* The sheer volume created a frenzy. Senators pushing jobs for friends could be just as forward as any local hack. One southern Republican that week confronted Garfield and "demanded" he be a true Stalwart and not give patronage to Democrats as Rutherford Hayes had done. "I told him I declined to be lectured at or to have my Republicanism questioned," Garfield recalled, causing the man to storm off.[34]

To protect himself, Garfield limited himself to picking only senior postmasters, department heads, and important foreign ministers, and referred most of the other appointments to his cabinet secretaries. Still, the job-seekers came. No wonder his insomnia continued in the White House. Days went by when Garfield couldn't sleep more than a few hours and remained housebound, breaking the demands of meetings only with an occasional game of billiards, a few minutes with his wife, or by slipping sometimes out of the building to ride horseback along the Potomac River.

To handle the crushing White House workload, Garfield relied on seven clerks working under Joe Stanley Brown, his young aide whom he'd offered the job of Private Secretary, though only after he'd first floated an offer to John Hay.** Hay, who'd held the post under Abraham Lincoln during the war, had declined.[35] "Well, my boy. I may have to give it to you," Garfield had told Stanley Brown back in Ohio before coming to Washington.

"Well, that is complimentary, to say the least, when all these other fellows have been first considered," Stanley Brown had shot back, chagrined at being third choice after all the work he'd done for the president-elect. Fortunately for him, he recalled, Garfield laughed.[36]

Now, Stanley Brown and his clerks struggled against a tidal wave of incoming mail, callers, and government business. Using the obsolete White House systems, they sorted, logged, summarized, and filed all the daily mail, nine-tenths of it being applications for jobs, and selected those pieces that the

---

* Today, of some two million federal civilian employees, political appointees are limited to a relative handful: the 2000 "Plum Book" (Policy and Supporting Positions" published every four years by the Senate Committee on Government Affairs, the modern job-seeker's bible) listed 6,722 non-competitive federal positions, including 1,203 requiring Senate confirmation.

** By contrast, the modern White House employs a staff of about 75 in the West Wing, 95 in White House service positions, and another 5,700 in White House-related offices.

president needed to see personally. Two of them skimmed the nearly three hundred newspapers that arrived at the White House and clipped leading articles for scrapbooks to keep the President posted on events around the country.[37] Other clerks kept detailed schedules and logs of every caller and every appointment.

In addition to the clerks, Garfield's White House employed a staff of fifty household servants: a steward, five doorkeepers, five messengers (two on horseback), a telegraph operator, a watchman, laundresses, ten gardeners, maids, a barber, and a fireman. Many of the servants had long memories of earlier presidents they'd served under—the head doorkeeper Mr. Loeffler appointed by General Grant, the disbursing clerk Mr. Crook by Abraham Lincoln, and the fireman Mr. Herbert by Millard Fillmore.[38]

The White House budget did not, however, cover cooks, waiters, coachmen, stables, or any entertainment. Garfield had to pay for these himself from his $50,000 salary. With a single White House reception costing thousands of dollars, the life could bankrupt a man like Garfield who had no private fortune to finance his public life—though Garfield did convince Rutherford Hayes to lend him his $1,150 carriage and a lame old horse.

Garfield had rejected the idea of posting uniformed guards at the White House. A president in democratic America should not have to worry about assassins like a European monarch, he felt. Abraham Lincoln's murder had been a fluke of the Civil War, which was long over. "Assassination can no more be guarded against than death by lightning; and it is not best to worry about either," he'd written to John Sherman.*[39]

Lucretia, normally shy in public, had to push herself into the social lioness role demanded of a First Lady. She faced four public receptions during the first week, grueling affairs that required her to stand rigidly in place for hours while greeting hundreds of strangers under the glare of society critics and strict protocol rules. She leaned on the cabinet wives for support, and especially Harriet Blaine, an experienced Washington *grande dame*.** On Tues-

---

* The Treasury Department's Secret Service would not begin protecting presidents for almost another two decades until two agents were quietly assigned to guard President Grover Cleveland in 1894 after operatives in Colorado had heard threats against the president. The agency's legal authority to do so would not become permanent until 1951. See generally Melanson, *The Secret Service: The Hidden History of an Enigmatic Agency.*

** Harriet Blaine also weighed in on protocol among cabinet wives. When Lucretia asked who should initiate calls, she said "I do not think there need be any rule as to the interchange of visits between cabinet wives," since they should be on "cordial terms," but was "perfectly willing to make

day, March 8, she greeted the old and new cabinets, then two days later the diplomatic corps. For the Army and Navy officers the next night she brought the Marine Band to the Blue Room and dazzled them with a "magnificent dress of white brocaded satin," the *Washington Evening Star* reported.[40] Afterwards, she and James led the cabinet members and wives for a promenade through the Mansion. "The House was beautifully decorated with flowers and plants from the Conservatory," she noted, and was "really brilliant in spite of all its shabbiness."[41]

On Saturday, she and the President hosted their first open public reception in the Blue Room. Lucy Hayes had started the tradition of regular Saturday afternoon affairs for "all men on equal footing," with "the ladies generally appearing in street costume and always retaining their bonnets."[42] Now Lucretia stood side-by-side with Harriet Blaine in the stuffy room for two full hours shaking hands with guest after guest. She wore a gown of Lyons velvet in a rich shade of garnet and lace trim that was "exceedingly becoming, and her manner was quietly self-possessed, leaving a favorable impression upon strangers," a reporter noted.[43] "Before the first hour was over I was aching in every joint, and thought how can I ever last through the next long sixty minutes," she wrote that night in the journal she'd begun keeping since moving into the White House. "But the crowd soon made me forget myself, and though nearly paralyzed, the last hour passed more quickly than the first."[44]

Harriet Blaine wore a cinnamon-brown silk and satin gown that day making herself a "cynosure of interest" with "stately figure and commanding presence," wrote a society reporter.[45] She seemed positively to enjoy the experience. "I stood up with Mrs. Garfield, while all the American people, who wanted to, came to pay their respects to her and the President," she wrote to her daughter. "It is not any of it so bad as I expected, and much of it is really amusing."[46]

The receptions seemed to bring good tidings. That morning, even Roscoe Conkling had come by with a group of Senators. It was Conkling's first visit to the White House in years—he, like Grant, had stayed away so long as Rutherford Hayes had lived there. "It is noticed that many Republican and Democratic Senators who were not seen at the White House before the 4th of the month are now frequent callers," noted the *Washington Evening Star*.[47]

---

the first call on the other ladies of the Cabinet... I called on Mrs. Kirkwood without a thought yesterday. I returned Mrs. Windom's visit today, am going to Mrs. MacVeigh's & Mrs. James." She also arranged meetings for Lucretia with Mrs. Evarts and diplomatic corps wives.

Lucretia's good feeling came across even in her messages home to the family. "We received your letter and were all glad you are so much more pleasantly situated than you expected," her sister-in-law Lide Rudolph wrote back from Ohio, though they marveled at the ponderous receptions. "I imagine you must be rather tired receiving so many strangers," Lide wrote.[48]

The National Temperance Society had deluged her with telegrams urging her to retain Lucy Hayes' ban against wines or alcoholic drinks at White House functions and to oppose "the social drinking usage of our times, by which many in our highest circles are unsuspectingly led into habits of excess, ending in degradation and ruin."[49] A few days after the inauguration, temperance leader Frances Willard had led a group of fifty ladies to the East Room for a ceremony to dedicate a new full-length portrait of Lucy Hayes and used the occasion to lecture Garfield on their demands.[50] Garfield had kept his calm, though. When his turn came to speak, he'd praised Lucy Hayes for her "freedom of individual judgment" and declared himself a temperance supporter "not in so narrow a sense as some, but in a very definite and practical sense."[51]

⊙ ⊙ ⊙ ⊙ ⊙

"How do you do, Mrs. Garfield?" Charles Guiteau leaned in close to her ear so that she could hear his quiet voice above the music and other guests. Lucretia Garfield looked back unblinkingly at a small man with dark hair, old suit, and confidential manner. She gave him a friendly smile and extended her hand. Guiteau noticed how the president's wife had a slender, frail build—not unlike his own. He gave her his card and introduced himself. He pronounced his name Get`-o, he said.

Charles Guiteau made a point to attend the White House reception that Saturday[52] to keep his name in front of the officials there. Any good office-seeker would do the same. Guiteau had made himself ubiquitous about Washington since arriving the week before. He spent his time mostly in the libraries and parlors of public buildings: Riggs House, the Treasury, the State Department. He'd also found himself a second, cheaper boarding house on Fourteenth Street to move to after having left Mrs. Lockwood's. He had no qualms about not paying her usurious rent; Guiteau had left landlords unpaid in cities from Boston to Chicago to Dubuque, Iowa. In Milwaukee, he'd contracted in 1878 with the *Evening Wisconsin* to print copies of his book *The Truth* for $75, then stole a handful and left without paying.[53] He knew how to stay a step ahead of bill collectors.

For the White House reception, Guiteau came early, walked in past the ushers who now recognized his familiar face,[54] and stood on line with dozens of others to meet Mrs. Garfield. While waiting, his eyes darted about the Blue Room with its rich treasures of artwork, knots of socialites, and brilliant chandeliers. He kept mostly to himself until he finally reached the First Lady.

He was from Chicago, he told her, though he hadn't lived there for two or three years, and he'd been active in the political canvass in New York. "I was one of the men that made Mr. Garfield President," he told her, and "she was quite pleased with that of course—quite chatty and companionable," he remembered.[55]

They spoke for just a few minutes. She told him she remembered the name, Guiteau, and that she was very glad to see him. Then he moved on, and she stayed in her place greeting the next of the many, many visitors.

The next day, a Sunday, after a morning at church and making social visits, President Garfield returned to the White House and found waiting for him a telegraph message from overseas. The Czar of Russia, Emperor Alexander II, had been murdered, assassinated by a "nihilist" as the Europeans called them. Alexander had survived a first bomb thrown under his carriage in St. Petersburg that day; a second bomb exploded under his feet in front of the Winter Palace a few hours later and killed him. Garfield ordered his Secretary of State Blaine to send a condolence note to the Russian foreign minister, but they decided to send no special ambassador to the Czar's funeral. Instead, Washington held its own special Requiem Mass for the Czar in which Harriet Blaine and her husband both assisted. "I had never anticipated going into black for any of the European sovereigns," Harriet quipped in a letter to her daughter, but she'd "pinned my old black lace cape on to my old black chip, so that I went *en regle*."[56]

ⓖ ⓖ ⓖ ⓖ ⓖ

"Mr. President, I call up the unfinished business," Senator George Pendleton of Ohio, leader of the Senate Democratic caucus, announced. The clerk began reading Pendleton's resolution in a nasal monotone.

"I move that this resolution be indefinitely postponed," Republican Senator Henry Anthony of Rhode Island answered.

"On that motion I ask for the yeas and nays," Pendleton responded.

"The yeas and nays have been ordered on the motion to indefinitely postpone the resolution," Vice President Chester Alan Arthur declared, his loud, stentorian voice easily heard throughout the Senate Chamber. He sounded his gavel and the Senate clerk began calling the roll. The contest for power had now begun.

Chester Arthur looked the picture of dignity in his black tailored suit that Friday morning, sitting at the raised president's* desk, gavel in hand, presiding over the United States Senate. He looked down over concentric circles of Senators milling around their antique oak desks piled high with papers. Some smoked cigars or chewed tobacco; others mingled with friends, sharing jokes or stories or working on their correspondence.

Famous faces dotted the chamber: This generation of Senators counted John Sherman, Benjamin Hill of Georgia, Pendleton, John Logan, George F. Hoar and Henry Dawes of Massachusetts, and Wade Hampton of South Carolina among its luminaries, along with future president Benjamin Harrison— let alone New York's Roscoe Conkling. While others wore black or gray suits, Conkling enjoyed playing to the galleries by wearing lavender, green or even red coats, pants, and cravats on the Senate floor. For the first time since the height of Reconstruction in the mid-1870s, all of the Senators' faces were white; black Senator Blanche Bruce of Mississippi had ended his term on March 4.**

Arthur still marveled at the Senate's arcane procedures, its host of strong-willed, loud-voiced members, and his own sudden visibility as its presiding officer.

Spectators—society ladies, diplomats, and hordes of newspapermen— had packed the galleries that morning since 10:30 am, two hours early. Underneath his polished demeanor that morning, Arthur felt his own stomach tied in knots. Just two weeks into his new post, he now found himself presiding over the thorniest parliamentary tangle to confront the Senate since the Civil War. Senator Pendleton's motion, now being voted on, would organize the chamber under firm Democratic rule, with Democrats chairing all the committees and choosing all the Senate officers.

Republicans had vowed to block him. They counted on Chet Arthur, as Vice President, to deliver the decisive blow.

State legislatures in 1880 had produced a new United States Senate with 37 Republicans and 37 Democrats, a tie, plus two Independents. One of these

---

* As Vice President of the United States, Arthur served as President of the Senate.
** Bruce would be the last black member of the U.S. Senate until Massachusetts voters elected Edward Brooke in 1967.

independents, David Davis of Illinois, had been elected by a Democratic-led State legislature and felt duty-bound to organize with the Democrats. The other, William Mahone of Virginia, had kept his plans secret. Mahone, a pugnacious, scrawny (weighing less than 100 pounds) former Confederate brigadier whose iron-gray beard dominated a sharp-edged, leathery face, had waged an insurgency against Virginia's "Bourbon" Democrats and been elected as a "Readjustor."* From the start, Republicans had milled about him, courted him, and offered him "taffy."

To complicate things, three Republican Senators had resigned in early March to join President Garfield's new cabinet—Blaine, Windom, and Kirkwood, the new Secretaries of State, Treasury, and Interior. A fourth, Matthew Carpenter of Wisconsin, had died. It would take the State legislatures a full week to fill these vacancies, leaving Republicans short-handed in the meantime.

Democrats had seized the moment and moved to take control—hoping to snatch not only control over legislation but also the Senate's patronage: the forty-two committee clerks, Sergeant-at-Arms, Senate Secretary, Chaplain, and dozens of messengers, doorkeepers, stenographers, postmasters, and watchmen on the Senate payroll, all appointed by the ruling politicos. For days the two sides had wrangled. On March 14, Democrat Benjamin Hill of Georgia succeeded in shaming Mahone, the Readjuster, into declaring his loyalties in public. Standing on the Senate floor, he'd looked directly at Mahone and virtually accused him of treason: "if any gentleman who was chosen to this body as a democrat has concluded not to vote with the democrats," he'd said, then "[m]anhood, bravery, courage, fidelity, morality, [and] respect for the opinions of mankind requires that ... he should return the commission and tell his constituents." Otherwise, he "disgraces the commission he holds."[57]

Mahone, enraged and embarrassed, had stood up finally to respond: "I came here, sir, as a Virginian to represent my people, not to represent that democracy for which you stand, ... I do not intend to be run by your caucus. I am in every sense a free man here." As for his party? "I was elected as a readjuster."

Mahone demanded a steep price from Republicans for his conversion to

---

* Readjustors favored walking away from some of, or "readjusting" downward, the State's onerous Civil War-era debt.

their side: the chairmanship of the Senate Agriculture Committee for himself, patronage spots for his friends, control of all federal patronage in Virginia, and pledges of support from the local party. He'd forced the Republicans to go against their every principle and embrace a confederate general and a debt repudiator. But in return, he'd offered them power and they'd grabbed it.

"I would rather have Mahone's chance of today than my [own] work," Garfield had written wistfully in his journal that day.[58] He'd sent Mahone a bouquet of flowers to his desk in the Senate chamber.

Now, on Friday, March 18, Republicans again had their full strength. All 37 Republican members sat in their seats plus Mahone. They intended to set things straight. As the clerk called the roll and members cast their votes on Senator Anthony's motion to kill Senator Pendleton's resolution, a newsman noted the "grim row of clerks" crowded in the chamber's rear corners—the Democratic appointees—showing "solemn interest" in "the proceeding which would deprive them of snug positions."[59]

When the clerk finished the roll call, Chester Arthur checked his tally sheet: it showed 37 yeas, 37 nays, and two absent—a tie. Looking around the chamber, its packed galleries and corners, every Senator in his seat, the newsmen each with pen in hand, Arthur saw all the eyes on himself. He suddenly found his hands shaking and his voice knotted. How easy it would be to trip over the complex Senate rules, he thought, and how embarrassing it would be, with so much at stake. He handed the tally sheet to the clerk who double-checked the names. The clerk handed it back. He swallowed. "The Senate being equally divided, the Chair votes 'yea,'" he announced.

Before he could say another word, a voice interrupted him—Democrat Eli Saulsbury of Delaware: "Mr. President, I do not rise to interpose any objection to the vote but I rise to express my opinion...."

Republicans smelled a rat. George Hoar of Massachusetts stood up and shouted: "I submit that nothing is in order until the vote is declared."

"Announce the vote," Roscoe Conkling too yelled from his seat.

Arthur banged his gavel. He needed to regain control. "The clerk will declare the vote."

"The yeas are 38, and the nays are 37," the clerk said, reading from his tally.

Then, with hands trembling so hard that newsmen in the galleries could see them, Arthur declared that "the resolution of the Senator from Rhode Island is agreed to." The clerk immediately jumped up and whispered into

Arthur's ear. No, he'd gotten it wrong. "Excuse me," Arthur said. I mean the *motion* of the Senator is agreed to; the *resolution* of the Senator from Ohio is indefinitely postponed."

Now, Senator Saulsbury could bellyache all he wanted. He launched into a long speech arguing that the Vice President "is not clothed by the Constitution" to decide "the organization of the Senate and the organization of its Committees,"[60] but it didn't matter. Arthur's vote had counted; the Democrats couldn't change it.

John Logan now jumped in as well and dredged up precedents going back to John Calhoun and Henry Clay demonstrating the vice president's perennial power to break a tie. A few minutes later, Henry Anthony stood up and presented a Republican slate of committees with Republican chairmen and demanded a vote. The roll call again came to 37 yeas and 37 nays; again Arthur broke the tie for the Republicans.

He banged his gavel; the resolution was approved.

Afterwards, Roscoe Conkling cornered his friend and roommate the Vice President in the Senate cloakroom and congratulated him on his show of nerve. Arthur, still sweating in the stuffy chamber, must have appreciated it, relieved at the victory. Conkling had news of his own, he told him. He'd been invited to the White House to meet with Garfield again to discuss the New York patronage. Maybe things over all were turning in the Stalwart's way.

❈ ❈ ❈ ❈ ❈

"I must resist a very strong tendency to be dejected and unhappy at the prospect which is offered by the work before me," Garfield wrote in his journal just ten days into his presidency.[61] He continued to sleep badly in the White House. The building had a sour smell; sewage odors wafting in from the sometimes-malarial swamps beyond the south lawn* and from the basement often gave him and Lucretia headaches or nausea. Carriage rides with her or James Blaine, billiard games with Colonel Rockwell, or playing with the children offered some relief; sometimes his older sons or Joe Stanley Brown would join him on afternoon horseback rides along the Potomac River or up Rock Creek Park. But the pressures drained him. One night the prior week he had

---

* In 1881, the area south of Constitution Avenue and west of Fifteenth Street was mostly submerged under the Potomac and its tidal swamps; the half-finished Washington monument stood on a peninsula. The White House south lawn, including the current "Ellipse" area, stretched right down to the water line.

lain tossing in bed until 2 am, unable to sleep from his "sense of annoyance and worry," he wrote, feeling "[v]exed with more thought that I am wholly unfit for this sort of work."[62]

Every day brought the same parade of callers and job seekers, the same wrenching choices of this or that man for this position or another. Joe Stanley Brown cringed at the "outrageous demands" of some of the callers. "An Associate Justice of the Supreme Court was infuriated [once] because he was not permitted to break in on the President when engaged in a most important conference," he recalled, while "on the same day, the weeping and hysterical post-mistress of Fort Worth, Texas, had to be soothed, seated in a chair before an open window, so that … she could view the charming landscape and gradually regain her composure."[63]

Garfield enjoyed many of the White House receptions. Irish Societies had marched through the East Room on St. Patrick's Day that week, followed by greetings from the Supreme Court and leading Senators in the Blue Room. But at night he'd go to bed and rise an hour later to walk the halls. "This must be changed," he wrote after several nights, "[I]f I know any way to change it."[64] "I do not take kindly to this sort of life."[65]

Lucretia, if she worried about him, tried not to show it. Instead, she tried to enjoy the beautiful season in Washington, D.C.—the yellow crocuses popping up in the White House gardens "beginning to show their color" as winter snows melted away and the "breath of Spring" rose in the air. She felt happy that March that "we were not among the lingering snow banks of our Mentor home."[66] After the fatigue of her four back-to-back receptions, Lucretia now organized her public life to take callers only on Tuesdays and Fridays, leaving herself privacy the other nights for family and close friends.

James Blaine too fell sick in mid-March, probably as much from exhaustion as from any flu bug, and limited himself to his bed at home. Garfield envied him the escape.

Now, increasingly, another old headache had reemerged—the New York patronage. For weeks since his swearing-in visitors had chewed his ear over it: The two Massachusetts Senators, Henry Dawes and George Hoar, had come to the White House and raised it over breakfast; a few days later Congressmen McCook, Miller, and Hiscock had pressed him on it at lunch, as did Edwards Pierrepont after that. Blaine and Whitelaw Reid always brought it up when they saw him, and Tom James, Garfield's New York Postmaster General, had kept close ties with Roscoe Conkling.

Garfield knew he'd left things unsettled with Conkling on that last night before his swearing in—he could still hear the Senator's irritated outbursts ringing in his ears. He wished he could find a way quickly to make peace with the New York Boss and not let things fester. He sent Tom James and his Attorney General Wayne MacVeigh over to Conkling's rooms at Wormley's hotel for a talk; the talk lasted all afternoon and night and into the following day. Finally, by mid-March, James felt it time for Garfield and Conkling to meet face to face and perhaps bury the hatchet. Tom Platt, New York's new junior Senator, had been pulled away to New York City for a few days but Conkling insisted he had his colleague's proxy.[67] They should go forward.

Following James' advice, Garfield invited Roscoe Conkling to the White House on Sunday afternoon, March 20, and the two men spoke together for almost three hours—their friendliest meeting in over a year, since before Garfield's surprise dark horse nomination for president in Chicago. James and Chet Arthur also sat in but Conkling did the talking for the New Yorkers. He seemed expansive after his and Arthur's victory over the Senate Democrats that week. Garfield laid out his dilemma for them clearly: Certainly he wanted Roscoe Conkling's support and planned to "recognize" his share of local patronage, but "I must recognize some of the men who supported me at Chicago" he insisted. He knew that Conkling had no love for William Robertson and the other bolters, but these men had backed him in Chicago and made his nomination possible, Garfield argued. He couldn't abandon them.

Conkling listened and didn't disagree outright—no bombast, no hysterics, just calm talk. They considered several names—mostly Conkling's friends at first. The Senator rejected some ideas and supported others. "I adopted many of his suggestions," Garfield acknowledged later.

When it came to the bolters, though, they found little common ground. Conkling suggested giving them foreign posts. Sending William Robertson to Shanghai or Rangoon or some other spot halfway around the world would suit him fine, but Garfield wouldn't have it. These men didn't deserve "exile," he argued, but a place in their own state.[68] Perhaps Robertson might make a good district attorney for New York, he suggested, an idea that Conkling didn't discourage. "Well, Mr. President, I suppose I can go out into the lobby and hold my nose while the Senate is voting on the nomination," he remarked.[69]

Conkling was struck by "the President's evident liking" for Robertson.[70] "Mr. Conkling, I am extremely anxious that you and your friends should agree upon some *projet* by which I can get in the independents," Garfield now told the New York Senator.[71] Conkling should talk with Arthur, Tom Platt, and New York Governor Alonzo Cornell and "draw up some plan" to find suitable jobs for them. The president was "most anxious to have the question disposed of satisfactory to all parties," Conkling recalled. The Senator agreed. He'd come up with a plan, though of course he'd take his good long time about doing it.

As the hour grew late and the New Yorkers prepared to leave, Roscoe Conkling asked Garfield one more question, as if an afterthought: "Mr. President, what do you propose about the collectorship of New York?"

All the heads turned to listen, and Garfield didn't hesitate with an answer. "We will leave that for another time," he said.[72] It didn't surprise Conkling, even if this was the single most important political post in New York State. Edwin Merritt, the current New York Collector, was no friend of Conkling's—Rutherford Hayes had appointed him after his notorious removal of Chet Arthur from the job. But Merritt still had two years left on his term and had been relatively neutral in New York politics. Conkling could live with the delay. They'd consult on it further.

Conkling, Arthur, and James all left the White House "in very good humor" that day.[73] Perhaps the Senator and the President could work together after all; maybe "that Ohio man" would still deliver on his August pledges. The next day, Conkling even received a follow-up note from Garfield saying: "it will not be necessary for me to delay the NY appointments on account of Senator Platt's absence," but "I would be glad to know what can be done for the Jacobins—If you have found anything in that direction, please drop me a note."[74] Evidently, Roscoe Conkling had found nothing to suggest for the bolters. They could wait till hell froze over, as far as he cared.

On Tuesday morning, March 22, Garfield delivered on his end of the bargain. He sent five nominations up to the U.S. Senate for confirmation, all friends of Roscoe Conkling[75]—plus two Conkling friends for local postmasters. In addition, Garfield that week had nominated Levi P. Morton as Minister to France, fulfilling his August pledge to the New York banker, and he'd already made Tom James his Postmaster General. All this, and he had his friend Chet Arthur ensconced as the vice president. Roscoe Conkling had to feel satisfied.

Word soon began to filter out across the country, though. The president had come to terms with the New York Boss. Newspapers headlined the Stalwart nominations as a landmark Conkling victory. The Boss finally had wrestled control of New York patronage away from the president. Within hours, Half-Breeds and moderate journals in New York, Boston, and Philadelphia began a drumbeat of dismay. It was "weakness," "surrender," and "ingratitude."[76] There'd been pressure, and weak-willed Garfield, the accidental president with no mind of his own, had crumbled.

Someone had to protest.

◎ ◎ ◎ ◎ ◎

That night, as Garfield hosted a small dinner party at the White House, an usher interrupted him with a card: James G. Blaine was waiting in the hallway and needed to see him immediately. It would just take a moment. Garfield knew that Blaine had been bed-ridden that entire week with a fever. What could be so important as to raise him up on a cold March night? He rose from the table, made his apologies, and left Lucretia to entertain their guests.

Out in the hallway, he found Blaine looking horrible: pale, fatigued, and sneezing. He led Blaine to a private room and closed the door. Blaine, so agitated he could barely sit, got straight to the point. He "expressed great distress at the N.Y. appointments," Garfield recalled.[77] In fact, Blaine launched into a tirade. How could Garfield have made such a mistake? Why hadn't he checked with Blaine first? Blaine felt humiliated, he said; all day long he'd been hearing from his Half-Breed friends and they were horrified; Blaine himself might have to resign from the cabinet. Robertson especially felt betrayed, after all the work he'd done and all the risks he'd taken. Whose advice did Garfield plan on following in this administration, Blaine's or Roscoe Conkling's?[78]

Garfield didn't return to his dinner until two or three courses later. When he did, he looked "very pale, but composed," Lucretia recalled. "A hush fell on all at the table and no one had quite the courage to ask why," nor did Garfield volunteer a reason. Only later, alone, did Garfield tell his wife: "I have broken Blaine's heart with the nominations" of the New York Stalwarts. "He regards me as having surrendered to Conkling. I have not but I don't know but that I have acted too hastily. Perhaps I should have consulted Blaine before sending in some of those New York appointments."[79]

An hour later, after the dinner guests had left and Lucretia had gone to bed, Blaine shuffled his sick body back again over to the White House and he and Garfield spoke privately, one on one in a White House parlor together in front of a warm fire, until almost midnight. Afterward, Garfield couldn't sleep—he tossed and turned in bed. He'd made a decision. Whatever larger strategy he might have had for balancing the New York patronage among Stalwarts and Half-Breeds, it now took back seat to Blaine's urgency: "on account of [Mr. Blaine's] anxiety," he told Lucretia later, he'd chosen "to send in another batch of appointments tomorrow which will very thoroughly antidote the first."

Garfield had planned to send them up later in any event, he told her, but Blaine had convinced him that "*now* is the time."[80]

● ● ● ● ●

Chester Arthur had grown increasingly comfortable in the President's chair of the Senate chamber, especially having now passed his first trial by fire. All the best people came here to the Senate gallery to watch the debates, and Arthur enjoyed his place at the center of things. His mind quickly grasped the parliamentary minutiae—no more difficult than managing the New York political machine or the complicated New York Custom House once he got used to it. Arthur even enjoyed the prickly Senate personalities and the corridors buzzing with gossip.

Ever since he'd cast the deciding vote to block the Democrat's power grab and create Republican-led committees, the Democrats had been devising counter-attacks. All through March, day after day, they refused to allow Republicans to appoint Senate officers—especially friends of that Virginia turncoat William Mahone. As a result, everything had frozen. Senate business had settled into a tense stalemate: Most mornings, a Republican would start by moving to appoint the Sergeant at Arms or Senate Secretary, Democrats would object, they'd trade insults and then they'd vote. Then a Democrat would move to go into closed executive session, Republicans would balk, and they'd vote again. Sometimes, one side or the other would move simply to adjourn, and they'd vote on that. The Senators took roll call after pointless roll call, neither side able to prevail even with Arthur there to break a tie.

No one knew how long the filibuster* would last—days, weeks, or

---

* "Filibusters" had been an accepted Senate practice since at least 1841 when John Calhoun launched one against Senator Henry Clay's bill to re-charter the Bank of the United States. The Senate refused to adopt a formal "cloture" rule to shut off debates (Rule 22) until 1917 when it was needed to pass enabling legislation for entering World War I. Invoking cloture today requires 60 affirmative votes.

months. Meanwhile, nothing moved; not the president's nominations, not the new treaty on Chinese immigration, not legislation to refinance expiring government bonds, not anything except pointless debate and gratuitous insults.

As that Wednesday afternoon's session drifted on, a handful of Senators engaged in dialogue before a half-empty gallery. Their colleagues sat glumly at their desks doing paperwork, writing letters to their wives or smoking cigars in the dim light. Arthur knew that time and the votes ultimately backed the Republicans, but that it would take patience.

At one point during the routine, a clerk interrupted Arthur at his chair on the President's platform and handed him a formal message from the White House. Arthur opened it and looked at its form: a list of new presidential appointments. Garfield hadn't told Arthur anything about it, but that hardly surprised him. Vice president or not, everyone recognized that Chet Arthur still answered to Roscoe Conkling, not "that Ohio man" in the White House—even after their cozy Sunday afternoon chat. Arthur started to read carefully through the list of names. When he got about halfway down the list, his heart jumped into his throat. His eyes stopped at one name that jumped off the page. He looked across the chamber and saw Conkling sitting quietly at his Senate floor desk rummaging through routine papers. Calmly, Arthur took the paper and folded it so that the one name stood out. Then he handed it back to the clerk, pointed to Conkling, and asked him to please walk it over to the New York Senator. The clerk stepped down from the rostrum, quietly stepped over to Conkling, and handed him the sheet.

Conkling, looking up from his paperwork, took the paper and read it quickly. He noticed the name instantly. He didn't say a word but his face suddenly froze and turned crimson.

A few Senators sitting nearby noticed the incident and stepped over to read the paper on Conkling's desk. They started whispering. The name itself didn't surprise them: William H. Robertson of New York. Garfield had told Conkling on Sunday that he wanted to find a position for the obnoxious bolter, though he'd promised first to consult and wait for Conkling to submit his plan—another broken pledge on top of all the others.

What made Conkling shudder, though, was the position for which Robertson had been nominated: Collector of the Port of New York. Just two days earlier, Garfield had told Conkling to his face that he had no plan to change that officer—the single most important appointment in New York

State controlling hundreds of jobs and millions in revenues. Either Garfield had lied to his face or someone had forced his hand.

Reading down the page, Conkling saw things getting even worse. To make room for Robertson at the Custom House, the current Collector, Edwin Merritt, had to be removed. To do this, Garfield had set in motion a game of diplomatic musical chairs: He'd nominated Merritt to be Consul-General to London, England.[81] To make room in London, the current Consul-General there, Adam Badeau, General Grant's friend, had to be removed as well. For this, Garfield had nominated Badeau as consul to Copenhagen. And to make room in Copenhagen, Michael Cramer, the current minister there and Ulysses Grant's brother-in-law, was moved to Switzerland.

In making these changes, Garfield had consulted none of the New York Stalwarts: not Conkling, not Tom Platt, not his Postmaster General Tom James nor his Vice President Chester Arthur, not even Robertson or the other nominees. In fact, Garfield had spoken to no one at all about the appointments; he'd kept them secret.[82] In doing so, he'd managed to cross not only Conkling but also the most popular figure in America: the Hero of Appomattox, Ulysses S. Grant himself.

Sitting on the Senate floor in full flush of anger, barely listening to the growing chorus of whispers around him, Roscoe Conkling had little doubt whose footprints really matched those at this crime scene. They all looked too familiar. Garfield had given Conkling's worst enemy a political hatchet. As an unnamed ally described it to the New York Herald, it was "an attempt by the President to give control of New York politics to the small faction which is bitterly opposed to Roscoe Conkling."[83] Garfield might be untrustworthy, but was he really clever enough to have thought of this? Conkling shook his head. No, this had all the markings of someone else. Robertson was a Blaine man, not a Garfield man. And Blaine as Secretary of State would have had to approve all the consular appointments.

Garfield didn't have the backbone for this, Conkling decided. James Gillespie Blaine had twisted him around his fingers.

As icing on the cake, Conkling noticed yet another Blaine footprint further down the same list—William E. Chandler, Blaine's campaign manager from Chicago, being nominated as Solicitor General.

Garfield's appointments, March 23, 1881:

- **William H. Robertson**: to be *Collector of the Port of New York;*

- **Edwin Merritt** (current Collector): to be *Consul-General, London;*

- **Adam Badeau** (current Consul-General, London): to be *Charge D'Affairs, Denmark;*

- **Michael J. Cramer** (current Charge D'Affairs, Denmark, and Grant's brother-in-law): to be *Charge D'Affairs, Switzerland;*

- **Nicholas Fish** (current Charge D'Affairs, Switzerland, and son of Hamilton Fish, Grant's Secretary of State): *no position;*

- **William E. Chandler**: to be *Solicitor General.*

Tom Platt, standing near Conkling on the Senate floor as the news broke, could only hang his head in silence. He had hoped to avoid this collision by insisting on Garfield's promise to consult. Now Conkling would have to find out, if he hadn't already, about the embarrassing deal Platt had made in Albany the prior January to support William Robertson's appointment to the Custom House in exchange for the Half-Breed's support for his Senate seat.[84]

But Conkling could care less about Tom Platt at that moment. He steadied himself. This was far from over. Presidents had the power to nominate, but the United States Senate had to give its advice and consent. He would not make this easy for Garfield and Blaine. For Robertson to become New York's Collector, his name must first come here, to the United States Senate, and Roscoe Conkling of New York would be ready to meet it. And certainly his Senate colleagues would back him; they'd recognize the larger issue here. If a president like Garfield could impose this insult on Conkling, then he could do the same or worse to any other one of them. The sacred principle of Senatorial Courtesy—that a Senator be allowed to veto any obnoxious appointment by a president of his own party in his own state—must be upheld.

Blaine himself said nothing that day to the newspapers as word of the appointments electrified the City, but Harriet Blaine had been around her husband long enough to recognize the real fingerprints in the affair. "Did you notice the nominations sent in yesterday?" she wrote the next day in a letter to her daughter. "They mean business and strength."[85]

❊ ❊ ❊ ❊ ❊

Charles Guiteau waited until late March to visit the State Department to press his application for the Paris consulship with the Secretary of State, James G. Blaine. "I spoke to the General [Garfield] about it, and he said your endorsement would help it, as it was in your department," Guiteau had written to Blaine on Riggs House stationery as early as March 11—just after seeing the president in the White House. He enclosed a copy of his speech "Garfield Against Hancock"—his calling card, in case Blaine hadn't seen it yet.[86] He followed up with another note a few days later: "The pressure has been so enormous on you for office that I have studiously kept away from you, believing you would do the fair thing by me."[87] Then he sent another a few days later: "I think the President feels well disposed towards me about the Austrian mission, and with your help I can get it." This time he added some flattery: "I am very glad, personally, that the President selected you for his premier. It might have been some one else. You are the man above all others for the place."[88]

Guiteau knew that all the Stalwarts distrusted Blaine—especially after Garfield's surprise nomination of Half-Breed William Robertson to the New York Custom House and his reshuffling of a half-dozen foreign postings. Guiteau himself had written a letter to Blaine the prior summer asking to be a stump speaker in the Maine presidential contest, but Blaine had never answered—so different from General Arthur in New York City who'd always given him the time of day. Still, Blaine was President Garfield's Secretary of State and Guiteau would have to make the best of it.

Meanwhile, he used his time in Washington to build support. He visited Colonel C.J. Hooker at the Republican National Committee, and then one day he happened to spy Indiana Senator Benjamin Harrison sitting in the Riggs House library reading newspapers. Guiteau had introduced himself to Harrison in New York City in August during the campaign; maybe he'd remember. He sent over his card and then walked up and introduced himself. Harrison tried to be friendly and in fact remembered having "several private conversations" with the New York stranger who soon became an acquaintance. Guiteau, of course, gave Harrison "several" copies of his "Garfield Against Hancock" speech and mentioned his application for the Paris diplomatic post. "He appealed to me for some assistance," Harrison recalled, "and I responded that I was already overloaded with applications of that kind from my own State."

Throughout the spring they'd talk now and then, sitting together on elegant lounge chairs in the Riggs House lobby—about the deadlock in the Senate, or Guiteau's job hunt, or the general state of politics. The Indiana Senator always treated Guiteau politely. If Guiteau dressed oddly or spoke in a vague, self-conscious way, Harrison found nothing peculiar in it; as a politician, he'd dealt with a wide range of human characters. Guiteau recalled him as a "real good fellow,"[89] and Harrison never saw anything in Guiteau's behavior to make him seem "less than sane."[90]

As with the White House, an usher met Guiteau at the door as he entered the massive new building at Pennsylvania Avenue near 17th Street that housed the State, War, and Navy Departments.* The waiting parlor held about forty people on most mornings that month. Guiteau decided to try a more direct approach at first. Spying out the territory, he noticed that Blaine himself normally entered the State Department each morning through a private entrance near an elevator to his upstairs office. Guiteau posted himself there and waited in the hallway. Finally, one morning, "I came in one way and he came in his private way, having just left his carriage," Guiteau explained. Before Blaine could slip by and enter the elevator, Guiteau had cornered him and started a conversation.[91]

Blaine, of course, was "exceedingly cordial" to Guiteau. When Guiteau mentioned his "Garfield against Hancock" speech Blaine said "O, yes," appearing to remember it. Beyond that, Blaine said little and soon wriggled away. After that, Guiteau became a regular at Blaine's public audiences. Blaine made a practice to receive visitors at the State Department every day at noon. "[T]he doors [were] thrown open and everybody can come in;" Blaine would then enter the room, walk around, and "whisper to each man confidentially as to his business," as Guiteau recalled the process.[92]

Blaine too remembered seeing the small dark-haired man beginning in March, and his coming "repeatedly" after that. Blaine saw nothing unusual about Guiteau; to Blaine, all the office-seekers were "alike in desire, and pretty nearly all alike in disappointment," he'd say later. "Probably if I had never seen but one office seeker I should have thought [Guiteau] was very persistent, but I had seen so many of the same kind that I was not surprised."[93] Like Benjamin Harrison, John Logan, Arthur, and Joe Stanley Brown, Blaine saw no reason to act harshly toward a well-meaning if misguided fellow like Guiteau. He spoke with him, always said good day, and tried to be polite,

---

* Known today as the Dwight David Eisenhower Old Executive Office Building.

even if he never had news about the Paris consulship. "We have not got to that yet; we are waiting for a break on the deadlock in the Senate," became his standard answer.[94]

Besides, Blaine knew that his own crush of job-seekers at the State Department paled in comparison with what his friend Garfield was facing every day in the White House. "I could be Secretary of State easily enough," Blaine quipped, as opposed to being president, "because I am not genial and magnetic, and have no friends, God be thanked."[95]

12

THE SENATE

THE WAR OF THE ROSES has now begun in good earnest," trumpeted the *Boston Daily Advertiser* on the morning after Garfield had nominated William Robertson to head the New York Customhouse. "Blaine's star is in the ascendant. And the proud New York Senator, after being flattered with taffy, is now remanded to the rear."[1] Garfield's newspaper clippings bulged with excited headlines from the affair. Wherever he looked, he saw Roscoe Conkling's "friends" shouting defiance. In the *Philadelphia Press* they declared "open rupture" now between "the President and the Grant element."[2] In the *St. Louis Republican* they proclaimed "Conkling will fight the Robertson nomination. And 90 percent of the Republican party will back him," and "[n]o stalwart worthy of the name will desert Conkling while he is under the fire from Jim Blaine's masked batteries."[3]

Garfield tried to follow a normal routine that day. Winter had gripped Washington again in late March and snow covered the ground. He closed the door early on White House public callers and, in the afternoon, he and Lucretia drove a carriage to the Soldiers Home on the city's northern fringe to inspect the cottage where presidents spent the summer months. Then, returning home, he played billiards for an hour with David Swaim. After dinner, he listened to his teenage son Hal play *Fra Diavalo* on the piano. But he couldn't escape the storm he'd unleashed—his "very lively bombshell," according to the *New York Herald*.[4] It dominated all his talks with cabinet members and Senators who did reach his office that day, each more frantic than the next.

Personally, Garfield had known William Robertson only slightly over the years—mostly during Robertson's one term in Washington as a Congressmen in the late 1860s. He'd seen Robertson lead the New York Half-Breed revolt at last summer's Chicago nominating convention and had marveled at how the sharp-eyed, wiry man had stared down Roscoe Conkling in front of 10,000 people. Even Robertson's own friends recognized that his nomination would cause an explosion. William Chandler considered him "an extreme man on our side."[5] When Garfield, in a fit of anger back in February, had said he was tempted at one point to appoint Robertson as Postmaster General or Interior Secretary, even zealous Whitelaw Reid urged him to back off.[6]

The size of the eruption, though, caught Garfield off-guard. Stalwarts called it simply a "catastrophe."[7] "The change of [Adam] Badeau from London to Copenhagen will not be pleasing to General Grant," Garfield had written coyly in his journal,[8] but that wasn't half of it. All that winter, he'd designed his New York appointments trying to achieve pure Euclidean balance: to the Stalwarts, the larger group, he'd given a half-dozen New York plum jobs, a Postmaster General, and the Ministry to France; to the Half-Breeds, he'd now matched the score in one bold stroke.

This way, to Garfield's mind, he'd rewarded *both* sides with "taffy." Neither could complain; he'd been utterly fair and reasonable. "I think the Senate will approve," he assured himself, despite the sensation.[9]

All this careful balancing, though, meant nothing to Roscoe Conkling and his followers. They wanted dominance, not fairness. William Robertson should be punished, not rewarded. Besides, presidents should mind their own business and not meddle in state politics. And Garfield had made pledges during his campaign to consult with the "regular" Stalwart leaders, promises he'd made in exchange for their help. Had he no honor? Had he never planned to stand behind them?

Oddly, even the self-styled "reformers" who'd battled Conkling's machine for years now mostly gave Garfield a cold shoulder. "It is said in some quarters that Mr. Robertson's appointment means 'war' on Conkling," high-minded E.L. Godkin wrote in *The Nation*. "Now we are in favor of 'war' on Conkling, but we do not think it ought to be carried on at the expense of public business, or with Conkling's own weapons."[10] *Harper's Weekly* editor George William Curtis dismissed the Robertson nomination simply as a "political change" in a "political office"—hardly worth all the hubbub.[11]

Not all the reactions were negative.[12] But the cat-calls clearly drowned out the applause in those first few days, and triggered Garfield's own instinct in a pinch to compromise. Already in his mind, he was scouting the lines of retreat.

❀ ❀ ❀ ❀ ❀

William Henry Robertson, in the eye of the storm, kept a low profile the day the news broke in Washington. Word of his nomination didn't reach Albany, New York, where he'd spent the day presiding over the State Senate, until late afternoon. That night, when he appeared at the Kenmore Hotel dining room for dinner with his wife, friends rushed up with handshakes, back slaps, and congratulations. One colleague, a Senator Wagner, threw his silk hat at the ceiling, crashing it into the delicate crystal chandeliers. Waiters piled telegrams onto Robertson's table.

"This is a complete surprise," Robertson told them all. He called the nomination "especially gratifying because it comes to me unsought," insisting with a wink "I assume that I shall have the support of both Senators from New York"[13]—as though he didn't expect screams of protest from the Stalwart camps.

Robertson's Half-Breed allies, having suffered for years under the boot-heel of Roscoe Conkling's Stalwart machine, celebrated openly. "This evens things up," Dennis McCarthy crowed to reporters.[14] They rushed into the State Senate chamber the next morning and produced a resolution backing the nomination and sent it off to Washington, D.C. They'd already heard talk of a bruising confirmation fight and wanted to stiffen the president's spine. Thirty New York Senators voted in favor.[15]

Robertson himself, now almost 58 years old with thirty years as lawyer, state judge, one-term Congressman, and State legislator behind him, had long set his eye on the New York governor's mansion in Albany. He'd failed twice to win it, first in 1872 and again in 1879. This year, he'd hoped to get a top federal job in a Blaine or Garfield administration, but the New York Custom House was better than anything he could have realistically expected. Beyond the power and salary for himself, Robertson happily contemplated using it to destroy Roscoe Conkling's base once and for all—cutting off Conkling's friends from patronage while rewarding his enemies. It easily could tip the political balance in the State, and tipping New York could tip the entire country.

Obviously, he assumed, this was why Blaine and Whitelaw Reid had pushed him for this position, why Roscoe Conkling opposed him so strongly, and why Garfield would fight for him.

That weekend, Robertson took a train down to New York City and met

Reid for a strategy session over breakfast: "I have had the new Collector of the Port and Chauncey Depew here all morning," Reid wrote to his fiancé that day.[16] Robertson put his cards on the table. "Under no circumstances... will I ask President Garfield to withdraw my nomination," he wrote in a letter that he signed and handed to Reid, "nor will I consent to its withdrawal." It's withdrawal, he insisted, "would make [Garfield] Conkling's abject slave for the residue of his term."[17]

Others might want harmony in the party; William Robertson wanted power almost as much as Conkling himself, and he certainly knew what to do with it when he got it. Roscoe Conkling had good reason to fear him.

◙ ◙ ◙ ◙ ◙

Garfield must have expected the worst when two of his cabinet members, Postmaster General Tom James and Attorney General Wayne MacVeigh, stormed into his White House office together and asked for a "confidential talk."[18] The two men were so agitated that Garfield had to calm them down, make them sit in chairs and steady their nerves, before they could even speak. Tom James, as Garfield's cabinet go-between with the New York Stalwarts, had helped to arrange the meeting just three days earlier where the president had flatly denied to Conkling, Platt, and Arthur having any plan to change personnel at the New York Custom House. Now, James said, he felt embarrassed and betrayed. He had no choice, he said, but "regretfully" to resign his cabinet seat to show his New York friends that he'd had no part in the decision.[19]

Wayne MacVeigh, as Attorney General, also felt betrayed by Garfield, in his case by Garfield's nomination of William Chandler to be Solicitor General. MacVeigh had strongly opposed Chandler's appointment—primarily over Chandler's hard-line attitudes toward the South. Yet Garfield had kept MacVeigh totally in the dark on this, a key post in MacVeigh's own department. Now, his advice ignored, MacVeigh too felt "compelled" to resign.

Garfield must have shaken his large head in frustration. Could anything else go wrong for him this week? He knew he couldn't afford to lose two top cabinet members right now, just three weeks into his term and at the start of a major political fight. The Senate, the newspapers, and the public all would see the resignations as proof of double-dealing. He'd never recover politically. "I gave them both to understand that I had meant no discourtesy," Garfield noted in his journal.[20] In fact, he groveled, pleading with them to stay, at least for now. If that meant cutting loose Robertson and Chandler, then he'd just have to swallow hard. If Garfield were considering retreat before, this now settled the issue. Saving his cabinet had to come first; salvaging his honor could wait.

Garfield put his arm around Tom James. Couldn't they find a compromise? Maybe a good job for Robertson, but someplace other than in the Custom House? Perhaps James could talk with Roscoe Conkling and broker a deal.[21] James doubted it at first, having heard the New York Boss's ranting and raving over the past few hours, but he agreed at least to try. Garfield gave him a pat on the back, firm marching orders, and sent him off hoping for the best.

With Wayne MacVeigh, too, the President tried to cut his losses. "The appointment of Chandler may prove to have been a mistake," he conceded later to friends.[22] Chandler, the sharp politico, had made far too many enemies in his long career. Southern Democrats and Republican Stalwarts would stand in line to block his appointment, even had MacVeigh supported him—something Garfield kicked himself for not having thought of earlier. Now, though, Garfield looked MacVeigh in the eye and pleaded for time. He wanted to back out, but gracefully. MacVeigh agreed reluctantly. He wouldn't resign on the spot, but he made himself clear: If Chandler ultimately won confirmation and became Solicitor General of the United States, he fully intended to quit the cabinet.[23]

Garfield had always liked William Chandler, but sentiment couldn't get in the way now. To keep his Attorney General, he needed to let the hardnosed lawyer down, gently but firmly. James Blaine, his zealous Secretary of State whose late-night tantrum had pushed him into these bombshell decisions, would have to help.

The next day, with James's and MacVeigh's resignation threats still ringing in his ears, Garfield left the White House and rode a carriage the three blocks through snow-crusted avenues over to Blaine's house on Fifteenth Street. Here he found his Secretary of State still confined to home with "inflammatory rheumatism." All that week, Garfield had seethed at charges that he'd let Blaine railroad him into the Robertson nomination. He had to wonder if Blaine himself were spreading these rumors for his own glory, but didn't want to believe it.[24] Already, newspapers had gotten wind of Blaine's late night visit to the White House on the eve of the announcements. "Some servant has leaked about the callers here, for Mr. Conkling is reported to have

said that Mr. Blaine called at the White House at 10 PM," Garfield complained to the staff, furious at the breach. "The next leaker leaves."[25]

Even more frustrating, when Garfield insisted that he, not Blaine, had
made the decision, people refused to believe him. Blaine had known nothing
about it, he told Marshall Jewell directly that week, and, when Blaine had
learned of it, he "came in very pale and much astonished."[26] Garfield also insisted to Tom Nichol that "[t]he attempt to shift the fight to Blaine's shoulders is as weak as it is untrue. The fact is, no member of the Cabinet behaves
with more careful respect for the rights of his brother men than Blaine."[27]

Still, other people heard other stories, and local gossips feasted on the
clashing rumors. Edwin Merritt, for one, heard that Blaine had insisted on
Robertson's appointment at the late-night *rendezvous*.[28] Besides, what else
could Blaine and Garfield have been talking about during all those hours in
the White House the night before? Critics painted the picture of a president
utterly subservient to his stronger-willed Secretary of State, a pawn in Blaine's
machinations to settle old political scores.

"Your work of today... creates a splendid impression," Blaine now told
Garfield, sporadically coughing into a handkerchief, having gotten up
from his sick bed to sit in the library with the president by a blazing wood
fire. Garfield shouldn't worry about protests from the Stalwarts, he said; they
only proved that his enemies were being utterly unreasonable and it disclosed
their design "that would have used *your* adm[inistration] to crush *your*
friends."[29]

Garfield managed to ignore Blaine's flattery that morning and get to the
point. Blaine had to help him avoid catastrophe.[30] He had to ask his friend
Chandler to decline the Solicitor General post—even though Chandler had-
n't ever actually asked for it.

Blaine coughed and shrugged. He didn't quite understand. Are you sure,
Mr. President? he asked. Hadn't Garfield taken a stand on this, drawn a line,
prepared to fight? Hadn't they talked about it all before? Why retreat before
the first volley had even been fired?

When Garfield explained about the threatened cabinet resignations,
Blaine protested even more. Certainly, the president shouldn't back down
over a threat from Wayne MacVeigh. He had to "enforce discipline" in his
Cabinet and not take orders from mere ministers.[31] Besides, Blaine insisted,
William Chandler would make a far better Attorney General than MacVeigh
and, anyway, Chandler would never agree to withdraw.

Blaine threw his usual huff, but Garfield stood his ground; he'd made up his mind to cut Chandler loose—no matter how weak it would make him look in the short term—and Blaine had to help him do it. If pulling Chandler's nomination outright was too abrupt, then Chandler at least could stick it out and have his Senate vote. After that, though, once the Senate had confirmed him, Chandler had to step aside so that Wayne MacVeigh could remain in the cabinet as Attorney General.

James Blaine, feeling a little sicker now, agreed to follow orders.

◉ ◉ ◉ ◉ ◉

Postmaster General Tom James left the White House directly after his meeting with Garfield and walked immediately the few blocks down Pennsylvania Avenue to Roscoe Conkling's apartment at Wormley's hotel. He found the Senator at home and surprisingly cheerful; Conkling apparently had tired himself out after twenty-four hours of non-stop ranting since first hearing of the Robertson nomination on the Senate floor the day before, and perhaps he'd enjoyed an extra-long workout at the punching bag that morning. In any event, Conkling now sat back and listened carefully as Tom James described his situation with the president. His lips must have eased into a wide smile at the end. Conkling recognized surrender when he saw it. If James was telling the truth, then Garfield was offering him a way to keep his enemy William Robertson ever from becoming New York's Custom House Collector—not to mention giving the president himself a public slapping down—all without even mounting a fight. Certainly, Roscoe said in his friendliest way, he'd be happy to accommodate.

With Conkling's help, James now pulled together the New York leaders for a quick strategy talk—Conkling, Tom Platt, and Chet Arthur coming downstairs from his own room in Conkling's building. Behind closed doors, they quickly hammered out the framework for a deal. They kept the musical chairs to a minimum: Stewart Woodford (one of Conkling's friends appointed earlier) would withdraw his nomination as New York City's District Attorney—they'd give him a mission to Italy, Portugal, or some other warm European locale in exchange for his role—and then Garfield would name William Robertson to replace him. This done, everything else could stay the same: Edwin Merritt could remain New York's Custom House Collector, and General Grant's friends Adam Badeau and Michael Cramer could keep their cushy consular posts in London and Copenhagen.

Conkling balked one last time before giving his final blessing, wondering if Garfield was leading him down another dead-end road. But finally he pronounced himself "sick of a perpetual row" over office seekers and accepted the deal.[32]

When Garfield heard the terms, he too agreed. Blaine and Robertson would complain, but ultimately they'd have to accept realities and come around. Eager to settle things before anyone changed their minds, Tom James arranged for all the New Yorkers—Conkling, Platt, Arthur, and himself—to meet with the President at the White House that very afternoon.

With the time and place arranged, Tom James now hurried back over to Roscoe Conkling's apartment to escort him to the President's office, and Wayne MacVeigh joined him. They found Conkling happily flitting about the room dressing himself for the outing. "How are the envoys extraordinary tonight?" he asked.[33]

The envoys were in "happy spirits," MacVeigh answered.

"Tis well, gentlemen," Conkling said, brushing his hair and trimming his golden bread to perfect proportions. By the time Conkling finally got to putting on his coat and buttoning his gloves, though, a messenger had come to the door with an envelope marked Urgent. Conkling gave him a few pennies, then took the letter and opened it. It was written in cipher code. He took his codebook down from a shelf and began to translate. Then the playful mood vanished. A shadow crossed the Senator's face and he started stomping around the room, grumbling under his breath. He said nothing at first. "Gentlemen, I won't go," he announced finally. "I am no place-hunter, and I won't go."

The others stopped laughing. Why? they asked, but Conkling refused to explain. What was the message? He wouldn't tell them that either, but one of them slipped a look at it and found out. The letter had come from New York Governor Alonzo Cornell in Albany—a normally reliable Conkling underling but with an erratic independent streak. Governor Cornell had decided on his own that Conkling should to drop his fight against Robertson for the sake of party unity.

"I am no place-hunter and I won't go! I am no place-hunter and I won't go!" Conkling repeated, hitting the table again and again, his voice growing louder and angrier.

"If you will put that in writing, Senator Conkling, I will agree to make you President of the United States," Wayne MacVeigh said, trying to lighten the mood, but nobody laughed. For over an hour, he, James, Platt, and Arthur all appealed to the Senator to finish getting dressed and meet the president, but Conkling wouldn't change his mind. Tom James finally gave up. He'd tried his best, but Conkling clearly had dug in his heels. There'd be no deals today. He left the Boss behind in his lair with Chet Arthur and Tom Platt and returned to the White House alone.

Garfield by then had been waiting in his office for almost two hours for James and Roscoe Conkling. The longer he'd waited, the more he'd paced the room, shuffled papers, stared out the window, and wondered what was wrong. When Tom James finally came in and told him that Roscoe Conkling had thrown yet another tantrum and wasn't coming, Garfield fought to control his temper. How many times was this that Conkling had made a fool of him? How many more times would there be? "I must remember that I am president of the United States. I owe something to the dignity of my office and to my own self-respect." He glared at Tom James standing sheepishly in front of him, giving no excuses; he glared at other clerks around the room who looked away in embarrassment. He brimmed with anger one moment, then in the next he seemed to reach a resolution. Then he spoke again, very slowly: "you may say to this senator that now, rather than withdraw Robertson's nomination, I will suffer myself to be dragged by wild horses."[34]

In fact, at that moment, standing in his White House office, the same room from which Abraham Lincoln had led the nation in war, seeing through his window the graves of Arlington Cemetery to the south, embarrassed, indignant, frustrated, but oddly calm, James Garfield seemed to cross a psychological bridge. He'd made a discovery about his new position: As president of a great country, once he'd made a decision, even a close, dubious one, he had to stick with it. People respected backbone, and without their respect his authority meant nothing. Garfield could no longer live with Roscoe Conkling's petulant demands hanging over his presidency. Conkling would not be dealt with nor tolerated. If that meant political war, then he had no choice but to fight it.

No, he told Tom James, there'd be no compromises on William Robertson.

The next day, James, still acting as loyal go-between to the Stalwarts, delivered to Garfield's office a formal protest letter signed by himself, Conkling, Platt, and Arthur, asking the President to withdraw Robertson's name. "We had only two days before this been informed from you [that a new Collector was] not contemplated," the letter argued, suggesting that Garfield somehow had cheated them.[35] Within hours, Roscoe Conkling's newspaper friends joined the chorus, blasting Garfield for "duplicity," "grave discourtesy," and "deception."[36]

Garfield read the criticism and simply put it aside. For the first time in months, he felt himself on solid ground. And Tom James, his Postmaster General, saw no further reason to resign from the cabinet. He'd done his duty for his New York friends.

Later that day, John Hay came to Garfield's office carrying a private note from *New York Tribune* publisher Whitelaw Reid that he asked to read aloud: "I wish to say to the President that in my judgment this is the turning point of his whole administration—the crisis of his fate. If he surrenders now, Conkling is President for the rest of the term and Garfield becomes a laughing stock. On the other hand, he has only to stand firm to succeed." Garfield listened politely, perhaps finding it ironic that he and Reid had reached the same conclusion within hours of each other. "In one word, there is no safe or honorable way out now but to go straight on. Robertson should be held firm. Boldness and tenacity now insure victory not merely for this year but for the whole term. The least wavering would be fatal."[37]

When Hay had finished, Garfield told him simply: "Robertson may be carried out of the Senate head first or feet first... I shall never withdraw him."[38]

"Whether Garfield meant it or not," one biographer later said of the president's transformation, the Robertson nomination had become, "in a sense, his declaration of independence."[39]

◎ ◎ ◎ ◎ ◎

"I suppose you don't attend this Senatorial fight," Lucretia's sister-in-law Lide Rudolph wrote to her from Ohio that week. "If I remember rightly your tussles do not run into warfare."[40] But like it or not, girlhood reputation aside, the First Lady could no more avoid the contest than her husband could.

Initially, in fact, Lucretia seemed to enjoy it. She found the political drama fascinating: "the two New York factions stood looking into each others' eyes astonished and enraged, but feeling themselves thoroughly fettered and outwitted," she wrote in her journal at the outset.[41] Her husband seemed "much less disturbed" now, she noted.[42] Her only real worry, it seemed, was that the clash might ruin some of the new friendships she'd been forming in the White House. Lucretia had grown attached to the cabinet wives, particularly Mrs. James MacVeigh, and felt relieved when the Attorney General had backed down from his early threat to resign. "I am coming [to Washington from Philadelphia] on Monday next to take possession of the house we have rented," Mrs. MacVeigh wrote to her in a letter that week, "and am going to *stay*."[43]

Lucretia even felt a certain fondness for the debonair vice president, despite his Stalwart leanings. "I am sorry that" the Senate fight "will probably alienate Vice President Arthur altogether," she wrote.[44]

Toward Roscoe Conkling, though, she felt nothing but scorn. For months she'd found Conkling's attitude toward her husband "contemptible." Now, she almost celebrated at no longer having to "pretend politeness" to him. Conkling's treatment of women particularly put her off. "I have despised him ever since I have known of his relations with Mrs. [Kate Chase] Sprague," she told friends, especially the way Conkling had shunned his paramour after their secret affair had exploded in the newspapers two summers ago, "selfishly compromising [her] reputation." At the same time, Conkling had been "cruelly neglectful of his own wife," Julia, who lived quietly in Utica as her husband cavorted blatantly around Washington and New York—something that didn't miss the eye of Lucretia Garfield.[45]

Harriet Blaine saw the pressure that Lucretia struggled under each day and it made her wonder why she'd ever encouraged her own husband to pursue the presidency. "They hate the situation, but this is not to be spoken of," she wrote to her daughter after she and Blaine had hosted James and Lucretia at their home one Saturday in March. "I never want to be nearer the White House than I am now."[46]

⊛ ⊛ ⊛ ⊛ ⊛

Garfield himself now began to organize his campaign to win Senate confirmation for William Robertson to the New York Custom House. He expected a terrible fight, facing not only loud, zealous opposition from Conkling, but he'd also be challenging the tradition of Senatorial Courtesy. Garfield had allies in the Senate, but far fewer than his New York enemies did. He took a long carriage ride with John Sherman that week, who'd now returned to Washington as Ohio's new junior Senator, and asked him to "take charge" of the Robertson fight on Capital Hill. Sherman hesitated at first out of friendship with the current New York Collector, Edwin Merritt, but finally agreed.[47] Garfield also met with Iowa's junior Senator William Allison, who'd recently been pulled aside by Conkling and heard his angry outbursts against the president. Allison repeated Conkling's basic line of attack: that Garfield "did not consult him."[48]

Garfield saw it as a weak dodge. After all, he argued: Suppose Conkling had been consulted? What then? Would he then have voted for Robertson? Obviously not. "If yes, on what ground of reason can he now vote no?"[49]

In fact, Garfield increasingly saw a principle in Robertson's nomination: protecting the powers of the national government. "[S]hall the principal port of entry," New York City, "in which more than 90% of our customs duties are collected be under the direct control of the Administration or under the local control of a factional Senator," he wrote, bouncing the idea off Burke Hinsdale at Hiram College. "I think I win in this contest."[50] Or as he put it to Whitelaw Reid: "It better be known ... whether the President is the head of the Government, or the registering clerk of the Senate."[51]

If logic was his ally, though, then the Senate's parliamentary rules were his enemy. Garfield could win this battle only if the Senate would vote—cleanly, directly, and publicly—on the appointment. But the United States Senate was a strange place that gave opponents endless chances to delay and obstruct. And Roscoe Conkling, the consummate Senator, with a bit of skill, nerve, and bombast, could easily delay this nomination into oblivion.

❦ ❦ ❦ ❦ ❦

Ulysses Grant felt disgusted reading in the New York City newspapers about Garfield's appointments. He followed the unfolding Washington drama even as he prepared to leave New York on a long journey to Mexico for his new railroad venture. Mexico fascinated Grant, but as former president he couldn't keep his mind away from local politics. And this new president Garfield irritated him badly—the man just couldn't be trusted. Besides the insult to his friend Adam Badeau and his brother-in-law Michael Cramer, Grant bristled at Garfield's showy reward to William Robertson, the pugnacious traitor who'd back-stabbed Grant's own presidential bid in Chicago last summer.[52] Grant assumed the appointments were "intended to be offensive" to him, he told Badeau. And Garfield had told Grant nothing about them—he hadn't consulted at all, even after their friendly White House breakfast just a few days earlier when Garfield had promised his "friendship and deference."[53]

Within hours of leaning about Garfield's odious appointments, Grant had flashed off a telegram to Badeau telling him to hold fast: "See the President at once with my letter. Tell him to withdraw your nomination [to Copen-hagen], and if he cannot leave you in London, ask him to give you either Italy or the Naval Office in [New York]. Show him this dispatch as my en-dorsement of you for either place."[54]

Adam Badeau himself, Grant's long-time aide and biographer, had ar-rived in Washington, D.C. in late March from London to press his own case for keeping his comfortable European post. He only then learned that his name had become tangled in this newest political firestorm. Taking along Grant's telegram, he went to the White House where the president agreed to see him immediately. Badeau and Garfield had known each other over the years and had always been friendly. Now, they had a good talk. Garfield as-sured Badeau that he'd had no intention of "disapproving my services or dis-pleasing General Grant" in his latest appointments, Badeau recalled. In fact, Garfield even encouraged Badeau to see it in a good light. He actually might enjoy Copenhagen, a "pleasant and easy diplomatic post." Through it all, though, the president showed no sign of changing his mind.[55]

Adam Badeau dutifully reported back to Grant on his talk with the pres-ident, but Grant sent him back another telegram within the same day with the same message: "I advise you to decline Copenhagen and stick to London unless you can get Naval Office, Italy, or some equally good place. Advise with Conkling and Platt. It would be better to come here without govern-ment appointment than to take Copenhagen."[56]

Grant left New York City for Mexico a few days later. He traveled with his Mexican business partner Matias Romero; Julia stayed behind. All during his weeklong trip over train, steamship, and stagecoach, mile after dusty mile, he stewed over the affair. Along the way, smoking his cigars and watching the scenery go by, he took pen to paper and wrote Garfield a long formal let-ter venting his anger. Garfield's appointments were an "undeserved slight" to the New York Senators, he told the new president in a scolding tone. "I do claim that I ought not to be humiliated by seeing my personal friends pun-ished for no other offense than their friendship and support." And Robertson "did not support the nominee of the Republican party in 1872"—Grant him-self—and deserved no reward from any friend of Grant.[57] To make certain Garfield didn't ignore him again this time, Grant mailed the letter from Mex-ico in late April not to the White House but to his trusted friend Senator John Percival Jones of Nevada with instructions for Jones personally to place it in the president's hands.

Arriving in Mexico City on May 7, Ulysses Grant still hadn't gotten the bad taste from his mouth. He wrote yet another letter, this one to Adam Badeau who'd since gone back to London to await the outcome of the Senate contest: "I am completely disgusted with Garfield's course.... I will never again lend my aid to the support of a Presidential candidate who had not strength enough to appear before a convention as a candidate," he said. As for the president personally: "Garfield has shown that he is not possessed of the backbone of an angle-worm."[58]

It wouldn't take long for all these letters to find their way to the newspapers. Ulysses Grant's sentiments toward the new president became no secret to anyone who cared to know.

◉ ◉ ◉ ◉ ◉

Charles Guiteau walked the six blocks from his rooming house to the State Department almost every day in April to press his claim for the Paris consulship. He had no job in Washington that Spring and little else to do beside pass his days in public libraries or on a bench in Lafayette Park near the White House. He got to see Secretary Blaine several times, and Blaine came to know Guiteau by sight. Each time, the Secretary told him they "have not got to" the Paris appointment yet. They'd decide it "after the break in the Senate."

On days when he didn't visit Blaine, Guiteau sat at his regular table at the Riggs House reading room and scribbled letters to him in pencil. "I have got the President and Gen. Logan worked up" about his Paris appointment, he wrote to Blaine on April 2. "I press my application on personal and political grounds.... I know of no one who had a better claim on it that I do."[59] Then he wrote again a few days later: "I understand from Colonel Hooker [of the Republican national committee] that I am to have a consulship. I hope it is the consulship at Paris, as that is the only one I care for."[60]

Guiteau seemed optimistic, and he even wrote a letter about it to the President: "I think Mr. Blaine intends to give me the Paris consulship with your and Gen. Logan's approbation, and I am waiting for the break in the Senate."[61] He now started going to the White House too almost every day to press his case—the White House being just an easy walk next door from the State Department on Pennsylvania Avenue. The White House doormen all recognized Guiteau and knew his name. Most days, they took his card at the door, sent him to wait in the parlor, then came back an hour or so later with the same news: "Mr. Guiteau, the President says it would be impossible for him to see you to-day." Guiteau read this as favorable. The words "to-day," he believed, meant that Garfield was still "entertaining the proposition."[62]

One day that month, Guiteau even got close enough to the president to shout at him from across the room. Garfield, hearing the noise, gave him back only a puzzled look, though, before walking away.[63]

As the weeks passed by, Charles Guiteau spent hours alone by himself or waiting in parlors with strangers. Occasionally he watched debates from the Senate gallery and became a regular at the Navy Department library. Sometimes he'd page through a book there: Lang's *American Battles*, a manual for the consular service, or John Russell Young's *Tour of General Grant*.[64] Having no job, no friends, and no other way to pass his time, Guiteau began expanding on himself in his letters to the president. He gave Garfield pointers on politics, on the Senate, and on running his office. "Would it not be well to withdraw" the Robertson nomination, he suggested in late April, "on the ground that Mr. Conkling has worked himself into a white heat of opposition? I am on friendly terms with Senator Conkling and the rest of our Senators, but I write this on my own account and in the spirit of a peacemaker."[65] A few days later he assured the President: "I stand by you" in the conflict since "Mr. Conkling ought to have been satisfied" with his earlier patronage.[66]

Guiteau even gave the president advice on his re-election prospects: "Run the presidency on your account.... The American people like pluck; and in '84 we will put you in again." He added: "P.S.—I will see you about the Paris consulship to-morrow unless you happen to send my name in today."[67]

Chicago lawyer Emory Storrs, who'd seen Guiteau on and off in New York City during the campaign, came to Washington for a few weeks that April and came across Guiteau at the Riggs House one day. He found the strange dark-haired little man in "excellent spirits" and almost "exultant" in his manner. Guiteau eagerly told Storrs that he was going to have either the Austrian mission or the Paris consulship, and that he was "solid" with Blaine. Storrs saw where the conversation was headed, though, and before Guiteau could ask him for help, he warned that his own political "hostility" toward Blaine in Chicago would make any support from him useless for the Paris consulship.

Charles Guiteau kept a poker-player's face but saw through the dodge. He didn't ask Storrs for any favors that month. During the rest of his stay in Washington, Storrs saw Guiteau "repeatedly about the hotel" but they never spoke again. Storrs' refusal to help Guiteau "seemed to be rather discouraging" to the job seeker.[68]

By now, Charles Guiteau hadn't bought new clothes or shoes in months; his coat and shirts looked threadbare, with missing buttons and rips that never got mended. He moved from one rooming house to another, disappearing in the night to avoid paying rent, but kept up his daily visits to the White House and State Department. The Paris consulship, when it came though, would solve all these many problems.

By now, of course, the news had grown discouraging for all the Stalwarts.

@ @ @ @ @

Chester A. Arthur, Vice President of the United States, saw no irony in his convening a meeting to plan the defeat his own president's most important political decision to date. On Saturday night, April 2, he brought together himself, Tom Platt, Governor Cornell, and a cadre of experienced wire-pullers at his Lexington Avenue home in New York City for a long political talk on just that subject—how to kill the nomination of William H. Robertson as Collector of the Port of New York.

By early April, Arthur recognized that his Stalwarts had a real fight on their hands. The Robertson nomination to the New York Custom House had exploded into a national sensation, a battle-cry against political Bossism, and Garfield's strong stand had attracted wide support. Newspapers had rallied to his side, reflecting their readers. Even in New York State, only seven papers (led by the New York Times) supported Roscoe Conkling, their own senior senator, while sixty-six backed Garfield. Outside New York, the odds looked even worse: thirty-five for the president versus only two for the Senator.[69]

Public opinion aside, though, Arthur knew that the real battle would be fought on more friendly ground—in the United States Senate, behind closed doors, where he presided as Vice President and where his friend Roscoe Conkling ruled the roost.

No one understood the Senate better than Conkling. In his dozen years there, he'd emerged as its leading member, chairman of the Commerce Committee, titan in floor debates, and keen backroom tactician. Conkling had long ago mastered the web of rules and customs that shaped Senate decisions while mystifying outsiders. He recognized that the seventy-eight individual United States Senators constituted a unique human cauldron, a group personality with moods and temperaments to discern and shape. Conkling almost single-handedly had used the Senate to block Rutherford Hayes's assault on the New York Custom House for almost two years during the late 1870s. This time, fighting for survival, he'd spare no quarter.

His arrogance and sarcasm may have won Conkling plenty of enemies among his colleagues; he'd even come within hot-talking range of actual gunplay with two headstrong Southerners and frequently traded insults with Senators from all regions*—not to mention his old bitter encounter with James G. Blaine. In a pinch, though, he knew his colleagues; they'd always close ranks around one of their own.

The U.S. Senate in 1881 still operated largely in secret, despite its reputation for grand oratory built by giants like Daniel Webster, Henry Clay, and Charles Sumner—particularly in considering nominees for office. Senate rules placed nominees on the "executive" calendar: Their names never appeared in the Congressional Record, and all debate occurred behind closed doors, in secret "executive sessions"—a practice lasting until 1929. Senate committees rarely held hearings on nominees, either public or private. The Senators didn't need the publicity; State legislatures elected them, not voters.

In addition, Senators reached most of their important decisions in separate Republican and Democratic party caucuses—also held behind closed doors—and party discipline demanded that each Senator follow the line. Violating a caucus decision could cost members dearly; they'd lose friends along with committee assignments and be branded as disloyal. The Senate's laborious rules looked to most outsiders as stalling, but Senators proudly saw them as guaranteeing full deliberation on important issues, giving all sides the chance to speak their piece and work things out.

In this case, Roscoe Conkling held a special trump card. No member relished having to take sides in a direct clash between a leading senator and a new president, but they all had reason join in Conkling's defense of the power they so elegantly described as Senatorial Courtesy.

The U.S. Constitution, in one of its delicate compromises, had originally

---

* His only recorded fist-fight with another Senator was with mild-mannered Matt Carpenter of Wisconsin who had visited Conkling's apartment and noticed the home gymnasium Conkling kept there. When Conkling asked if Carpenter would like to spar a few rounds, Carpenter agreed, and Conkling punched him solid several times, knocking him to the floor. On the next visit, though, Carpenter bought along a professional pugilist, Jem Mace, introduced him as a constituent, and encouraged the two to box. Mace promptly knocked Conkling down. The threatened duels were with John B. Gordon of Georgia and Lucius Lamar of Mississippi.

divided the power for filling top federal positions between the president, who chose nominees, and the Senate, which gave its advise and consent. But a century later, arguments still flared: In 1868, President Andrew Johnson had been impeached over violation of the Tenure in Office Act, a statute that prohibited a president from *removing* any of his own cabinet members without first obtaining the Senate's approval. This statute, repealed in 1887, would not be ruled unconstitutional for another forty-five years, until 1926.[70]

Politicians commonly traded federal patronage in the 1880s. Congressmen offered jobs to supporters to win nominations and elections, and presidents routinely let Congressmen control this "local" patronage—the jobs falling inside their home States or districts. Even Garfield as a Congressman had objected when Rutherford Hayes had blocked him from picking a postmaster in his Ohio district in 1877.

Senatorial courtesy—deferring to Senators of the president's party on local positions—helped the party in power to build a national base. Cracking the system apart would threaten everyone.

Beginning in early April, Conkling started making the case to his Republican colleagues in their closed-door caucus meetings. Here, he was surrounded by familiar faces, friends he'd served with for decades. Meeting in their cozy Capitol Building hideaway suite, smoking cigars or chewing tobacco, they could speak freely with no newspapermen or outside critics to interfere. Conkling could look senators in the eye, pamper their egos, tickle their funny bones with snide humor, or bully them with his fierce intellect. "Conkling seems to have a magic influence over them," John Hay wrote after one of these closed-door sessions. The senators "talk as bold as lions to me, or anybody else—and then they go into caucus, or the Senate, and if [Conkling] looks at them they are like Little Billee in the ballad."[71]

Conkling had told some of his close friends that he'd "made up his mind" to leave politics at the end of his Senate term in 1884 to earn some money and that he'd abandoned all idea of the presidency, preferring to "spend the next four years simply in wreaking his revenges."[72] Now was his perfect chance. If his speeches sounded bitter, his colleagues would understand; he'd been injured by a deceitful, arrogant president. They all had a stake in righting this wrong.

Even Eugene Hale and William Frye, James Blaine's own junior protégés from Maine whom Blaine had made senators just the prior January, fell under Lord Roscoe's sway. The two visited Garfield at the White House after one of the caucuses and told him directly that Robertson must be withdrawn. "Conkling makes a very strong case," they argued.[73]

All through April, the Senate itself remained stalled, paralyzed by its multiple filibusters. Each day in public session, they followed the same pointless routine: Democrats refused to let Republicans elect officers and Republicans refused to let Democrats go into executive session or adjourn. Meanwhile, the country's business stagnated. Garfield had sent over three hundred nominations to the Senate by late April and none except his original seven cabinet choices had been approved. Offices by the dozen sat vacant—all frozen, along with the popular new treaty on Chinese immigration. After a few weeks, Senators felt the embarrassment. Winter had changed to spring in the nation's capitol, and Senators knew they'd have to make decisions soon. Otherwise, they'd never finish their work, and no sane person wanted to swelter through one of Washington, D.C.'s hazy, hot, malarial summers.

On April 27, the Republican Senators finally took matters in hand. By then, over twenty of them had met personally with Garfield in the White House to hear his side of the quarrel, and they'd all heard Roscoe Conkling's outbursts in their private meetings. Conkling threatened an ugly scene on the Senate floor if the Robertson nomination ever moved forward and Garfield was telling members that he viewed the Robertson vote as "a test of friendship or hostility" to his administration.[74]

Senators cringed at the prospect: An open clash could rip the party apart. No Senator wanted to back the wrong horse, or have to live with a sore loser for four years. A handful like George Hoar saw a deeper issue at stake, a "principle ... as serious in result as has ever taken place since the beginning of the Government," he told his son in a letter.[75] But most Senators had trouble seeing past the personal quarrel that had no business cluttering their agenda. Surely, responsible men could work this out.

But the president had to understand; he simply must not challenge the United States Senate.

With Garfield and Conkling at loggerheads, the Senators decided to appoint a "Committee of Conciliation" to mediate between them—talk with Conkling and the president both and devise a plan to secure harmony. It included backers of both sides with Henry Dawes as chairman.[76] Dawes, a Yale-educated lawyer and twenty-four year veteran of Congress (eighteen in the House, six in the Senate), had long known both Garfield and Conkling and had a well-known disdain for each: "The one wants to be watched like a child, the other like an assassin," he wrote to his wife that week.[77] He would be as fair as anyone.

However, Dawes had little enthusiasm for the assignment. That month, he had his own quarrel with the White House over patronage: his wife Ela back in Pittsfield was pushing him to find a suitable job for their 26-year-old lawyer son. Assistant Attorney General would be fine, but the Attorney General wasn't cooperating.* Still, Dawes went to work with his usual diligence.

The Committee met first with Conkling. They invited him to appear in a private Capitol Building nest in late April and closed the doors. Once Dawes gave him the floor, they sat back as the senior New York Senator dazzled them with oratory. Roscoe Conkling "raged and roared like a bull" for three hours, Dawes recalled, strutting the floor, waving his arms, fixing them with sharp asides. Conkling accused the president of every possible deceit and deception in a soliloquy crafted finely enough to make Shakespeare jealous. He called Garfield's nominations worse than anything Rutherford Hayes had ever done—this from a supreme Hayes hater. Conkling "surpassed himself" in "flights of oratorical power—genuine eloquence, bitter denunciation, ridicule of the despised faction in New York, and contempt for its leader," as Dawes recalled;[78] and he decried "the man at the other end of the avenue," as Conkling now called the president.[79]

Toward the end of this epic harangue, with his audience enthralled in his web of words, winks, and allegories, Roscoe Conkling surprised even Dawes himself by resorting to a naked blackmail that fit perfectly his context of wounded defiance: "I have in my pocket an autograph letter of this President ... which I pray God I may never be compelled in self-defense to make public," Conkling exclaimed, pausing for dramatic effect, "but if that time shall ever come, I declare to you, he will bite the dust."[80]

With that, Conkling wiped his brow with a handkerchief, rested his case, and took his seat. The Committee members in the room sat awestruck. One or two asked a soft question, which Lord Roscoe handled easily. And then

---

* "I want you to see something done before you come away from Washington," she wrote to him from Pittsfield on April 25, 1881. "Did you say anything to [Attorney General] MacVeigh about that? Something worth *more* than $1,200 a year *ought* to be found for your son—and if I were in your place I would make sure he should have it—You might as well *insist*, as other people. If Logan wants a new Dist. Atty., why can't Chester have *that*? A man twenty six years old is capable of doing his best, or working into it— man doesn't usually get *more* than he *asks* for. Yes, I *know* I am a woman! But, you know, even women have *rights*." Dawes papers. LC.

they let him leave. Conkling had made his impression. The Senators couldn't possibly oppose this giant among them. They'd keep their minds open, of course, until after meeting with the president and hearing his side of the story, but most had already decided which horse to back in this race. Their own.

◉ ◉ ◉ ◉ ◉

Garfield tried to live a normal life in the White House that April as the controversy swirled around him. He and Lucretia hosted the new annual Easter egg roll for local children on the south lawn—a tradition that Lucy Hayes had imported after Congress had stopped the annual rite on Capitol Hill in 1878. They threw a White House dinner party for Williams College president Mark Hopkins and visited the Washington Navy Yard to see a new-fangled petroleum-driven "air engine" that took only fifteen seconds to reach full power.[81] Congress had appropriated $30,000 for Garfield to redecorate the White House and, before starting, he and Lucretia visited the Librarian of Congress to research the mansion's history. Lucretia even planned to ask several New York decorators for ideas.

By now, Spring had finally burst upon the city; on some mornings, Garfield rode horseback for a full hour up F Street and along the Potomac River. He made a point to find time for reading books, his passion since a teenager, even if he couldn't attend the regular Smithsonian Institution Literary Society meetings that he'd always enjoyed as a mere Ohio Congressman. He read the novel *Ben Hur*, which inspired him to appoint its author, Lew Wallace, as minister to Constantinople to spark his literary imagination, then the new romance *Louisiana* by Frances Burnett. For heavier fare, he took up the *Critical and Miscellaneous Essays* and *Reminiscences* of Scottish historian Thomas Carlyle.

Visitors noticed how the White House now seemed filled with books: "Everywhere- in every nook and corner," a reporter wrote. "A case in the parlor contains editions of Waverly and Dickens," along with "French history in the original, old English poets and dramatists richly bound in black and gold" in the hallways and dining room.[82]

Stopping his carriage one day on the cobblestone street outside his now-vacant townhouse at Thirteenth and I Streets, Garfield still felt "homesick" for the life he'd left behind since coming to the presidency. Visiting Capitol Hill a few days later gave him "more regret… at being separated from my old associations" in Congress.[83] His headaches returned, but less often. One April morning he awoke "feeling as if I had been struck a light blow with a hammer" and the pain lasted all week.[84]

Newspapers lampooned Garfield for his bookishness, picturing him wearing Prince Albert coats and quoting poetry from Browning and Shelley. "I have been thinking of suggesting Greek as the language of the cabinet," the *New York Herald* had him telling James Blaine, his hard-nosed henchman, in one broadside, as Blaine shoots back: "What I'm after now is the Oshkosh Post Office, and I'll afraid you'll forget it."[85] Over time, Garfield grew resigned to this media limelight: "The number of coats he wears, the size of his hat, the purchase of a new pair of gloves, the dresses of his wife, a walk or drive, attendance at church," all became grist for newspaper writers, taking in print "the most exaggerated and distorted form."[86]

The passing of time gave Garfield no let-up from the crush of office seekers, who still besieged the White House day after day: "These people would take my very brain, flesh and blood if they could," he erupted after one long day with them. It occurred to him that in his first two months as president, he'd done virtually nothing except bicker over jobs and patronage—no policy, no goals, no substance. "My God! What is there in this place that a man should ever want to get into it," he exclaimed.[87] His friend Whitelaw Reid commiserated: "I hope the mob infesting all the approaches to the White House is gradually being fought off a little. When I last heard from any of my friends there you were having a terrible time of it."[88]

The New York controversy, though, never seemed far away. Senators called on him constantly to hash it over. Roscoe Conkling had stopped visiting the White House, but Tom Platt and Chester Arthur came repeatedly. Garfield knew that his vice president was actively supporting his enemies. Arthur had told people directly that he'd resign the vice presidency if it would help Roscoe Conkling,[89] and Garfield had heard all about Arthur's living arrangement in Conkling's house. The Constitution never said that Presidents and Vice Presidents had to be allies, let alone friends, but it seemed to Garfield that some rule of political decency was being badly abused here. Garfield often wouldn't even let Arthur into his office without consulting first with Blaine. "You spoke of calling this evening," he wrote to Blaine one night during April. "Please come early, for I learn that the Vice President is to call at 9½ and I want to see you before that hour."[90]

In fact, after hearing Arthur repeat the same old tired arguments at one face-to-face meeting in his office that month, Garfield only hardened his resolve. When Arthur had claimed that Robertson's confirmation would "inevitably defeat the party in New York," Garfield had snapped back: "Yes, if the leaders determine it shall." Afterwards, he described the meeting to Whitelaw Reid and said: "Of course I deprecate war, but if it is brought to my door the bringer will find me at home."[91] Garfield and his vice president wouldn't meet again for three more weeks.

By the time Henry Dawes and his Committee on Conciliation came to the White House, Garfield had heard all about their deliberations and secret closed-door meetings. Dawes himself came early to get a few minutes alone with the president to ask him about Roscoe Conkling's blackmail threat.

Garfield had heard all about the threat, and Dawes, sitting across the president's large mahogany desk, was struck at how "lightly" he treated it. "Oh, you allude to a letter Conkling is saying that he has of mine, which he represents to be a pretty bad one," Garfield said quickly. "I know what it is, and have a copy of it."[92] He lifted it from his desktop and handed it to Dawes. The letter, dated August 22, 1880—at the height of the president's election campaign—was to a Washington, D.C., party official named Jay Hubbell and concerned fund-raising: "Please say to [Assistant Postmaster General Thomas A.] Brady that I hope he will give us all the assistance he can," and "Please tell me how the [Federal] Dep[artmen]ts are doing."[93]

Dawes studied it carefully but could only shrug. He saw no scandal here. Collecting political money from federal bureaucrats was no crime in 1880. The letter's only embarrassment was in connecting Garfield to Thomas Brady, the Assistant Postmaster who'd recently resigned in disgrace in the growing Star Route postal scandal*[94] that had broken that month in the *New York Times*.

Why not simply publish it in the newspapers and neutralize the mystery, Dawes suggested. He volunteered to take it to the Associated Press himself that very night. Garfield didn't disagree, but he'd already asked Blaine his

---

* Garfield had first learned about the scandal in early April when Postmaster General Tom James had come to his office, along with a postal special agent, to tell him about huge fraud they'd uncovered—potentially the worst since the Whiskey Ring. At its heart were the postal "Star Routes"–marked by a star on the printed postal schedules—special mail delivery routes to remote outposts on the frontier. Contractors charged special rates to serve them, and a handful had raked in millions of dollars in crooked profits. Two names topped the list of suspects: Stephen Dorsey, the former Arkansas Senator, current Republican national committee secretary, and Garfield campaign advisor, and Thomas Brady, Second Assistant Postmaster General, co-owner of the powerful *National Republican* newspaper, and Garfield campaign fund-raiser.

opinion and Blaine had argued the opposite—that Garfield should just ignore it.

By then, the other Senators had arrived and taken chairs around the president's desk. They lit cigars and shook hands in a friendly way, their faces illuminated by gas lamps, the sounds of the muggy Washington night floating in through an open window, but they finished the small talk quickly. Then, as they'd done with Roscoe Conkling, Henry Dawes started by giving the president a chance to present his case. Garfield launched in, using the opportunity to press the Senators to approve his nominees—*all* of them. The Senate deadlock, he argued, was being driven only by members afraid to confront Conkling and it wasn't fair to him as president. He laid the blame for the quarrel squarely with the New York Senator. By one account, Garfield "arose in his chair, walked about the room, became very earnest, gave emphasis to his speech by striking the table."

The Senators then began peppering Garfield with ideas for compromise—certainly the president didn't expect to force them to vote: He should withdraw all the New York nominations—Robertson included—for the sake of party harmony, several suggested. No, Garfield answered quickly. He would not. For him to abandon the moderates would be "base ingratitude and the worst of politics."[95] Dawes then raised another idea: Why not have Robertson and William Chandler trade appointments—Chandler to become New York Collector and Robertson to become Solicitor General. Garfield balked again. He wasn't interested in compromise, and besides, it wouldn't work. Chandler and Robertson each had his own enemies in the Senate to block him for either spot. And any proposal that allowed Roscoe Conkling to move his own friends through the Senate first but then delay on Robertson "would not be just."[96]

Garfield made little attempt to hide his irritation at the pestering questions. "The shortness and sharpness of [Garfield's] replies indicated to the committee that he was vexed," one member told the *Albany Times* afterward.[97] "The president is intoxicated by his power," another complained. "That man at the white house has thrown off his palavering, goody-goody disguise and stands revealed."[98] The Senators had expected Garfield to grab gratefully at any compromise they offered; now they found his refusals "obstinate" and "sullen."[99]

They spoke for two hours that night, until 10 pm, bickering, haggling, trading verbal jabs, but resolved nothing. Garfield saw the Senators themselves as the problem: "The Committee had been bull-dozed by Senator Conkling," he wrote in his journal.[100] Alone with Dawes afterwards, he warned there could be "no peace by evading the NY contest."[101] Dawes came back again two nights later with another Senator, Joe Hawley of Connecticut, and they spent another two hours talking with the president. Hearing them repeat Roscoe Conkling's latest bombast from their secret Senate caucus meetings, Garfield squirmed and bristled. He gave the Senators his own message to take back to Capitol Hill: "I do not propose to be dictated to," he told them. "Senators who dare to oppose the Executive will henceforth require letters of introduction to the White House."[102]

Over the next few days, Garfield kept his temper hot, openly threatening Senators who opposed him in this fight to cut off their patronage, invitations to White House dinners, and other favors.[103] Stalwarts accused him of "trading and dickering with Senators for their votes" and punishing his opponents—as if it were somehow immoral. In fact, presidents had rarely ever dirtied their hands over this type of contest before, grubbing for votes in so undignified a way on an issue always assumed to fall in the province of the Senate. But Garfield didn't deny it; he seemed to enjoy it. For his taste, the Senate's province had gotten far too big.[104]

◉ ◉ ◉ ◉ ◉

On Thursday morning, May 3, the Republican Senators met again in their back hideaway of the Capitol Building for a closed-door caucus and listened closely as Henry Dawes stood before them to present the grand conclusions of his Committee on Conciliation. By now, Dawes had spoken with almost every one of the Senators privately and knew exactly where they stood. The underlying issue didn't concern them, but they'd found Garfield's behavior shocking. The president had a duty, they felt, to take them off the hook by bending to their demands for "harmony." They'd heard Roscoe Conkling's threats to "arraign the President" on the Senate floor and shuddered at the thought of an ugly clash in front of newspaper writers and gawking spectators in the gallery.

Even Henry Dawes voiced impatience with the president. Garfield, "of whose great brainpower political sagacity formed no part, could not be made to see in the opposition anything but an attempt by dictation to trench upon his constitutional prerogatives," he wrote, and "all 'Blaine men' agreed with him."[105] A reporter standing in the hallway found the Senators in a giving mood: whatever it took to make Conkling "satisfied," he wrote, "it is proba-ble the Republicans will accommodate him."[106]

As the Senators listened, Dawes' now spelled out his formula—an escape. The Senate should stop its deadlock and begin secret executive sessions to vote on treaties and nominations. The president needed his vacancies filled, and the Senate had a duty to act. But… and here was the rub … local nom-inations should come in a certain order: first, those with no opposition, fol-lowed by those with one of the state's Senators opposed. Only last, if ever, would come those nominees opposed by both senators of their home state.

Roscoe Conkling, sitting shoulder-to-shoulder with his colleagues, must have let out a hoot. He understood Dawes' formula exactly. Of all President Garfield's 300-plus nominations sent to the Senate, only one fell into the definition of Dawes's last category—William H. Robertson. The senators were buckling to him, but they'd camouflaged it in procedural mish-mash so they could later wash their hands of it. Conkling easily could use this rule to shep-herd his own cronies' confirmations through right away, and then simply ad-journ the Senate before Robertson's name ever came up.* "So binding are the influences of the Senatorial position," a reporter for *The American* mag-azine noted, "that even Senators supporting Garfield supported the plan in caucus."[107] A few of them grumbled anonymously about bullying tactics, but not a single member stood up to protest.

The next day, backed by the full weight of party discipline, Henry Dawes rose on the Senate floor with Chester Alan Arthur in the president's chair and broke the six-week deadlock on a unanimous, 53-0 vote to go into ex-ecutive session. The next morning the Senate, meeting secretly, confirmed the first of the "uncontested" New York appointments.

Garfield, following the situation from the White House, saw his game slipping away. The Senators were robbing him of his vote.

Only one thing could be worse for him than losing on the Robertson nom-ination to a crowing, loud-mouthed Roscoe Conkling after he'd thrown the full weight of his office and personal reputation into the battle: On May 8, at the contest's height, he sent an urgent telegram out from the White House to Doctor S.A. Boynton in Cleveland, Ohio: "Crete is severely ill. Please come by first train. Do not mention this. Answer immediately. J.A. Garfield."[108]

---

* This delay would open the door to a "recess appointment" for Robertson, but that would be only temporary, lasting until the end of the next Congressional session, followed by sure defeat.

Lucretia had first fallen sick in early May after having just returned from a four-day shopping trip to New York City. On May 3, after a round of receptions and then a day-long dedication of the new statue to Admiral Farragut in muggy Washington, she'd held a long public audience in the White House Red Room and afterwards had felt chills. Odors from nearby sewers and stenches floating in from the Potomac River swamps across the south lawn had touched off a malignant fever—typhoid, they thought. Over the next few days, her headaches worsened. She confined herself to bed and her husband moved to a guestroom.

During the weekend, her condition deteriorated. She twisted painfully through the nights in sweat-soaked sheets. A doctor, a Miss Edson, moved into the house as her fever climbed to 104 degrees; in the morning, she found her pillow covered with clumps of hair that had fallen from her head. Garfield sat for hours with her, terrified of the mysterious disease. He read to her when she wasn't sleeping. As Senators came calling on him to confer over the confirmation battle, Garfield struggled to pay attention, concerned whether his wife might survive another night. "My anxiety for her dominated all my thoughts, and makes me feel that I am fit for nothing," he wrote.[109]

Still, he had to focus on the battle at hand. Fortunately for Garfield, news of his worsening position on Capitol Hill hadn't caught him fully by surprise. He'd heard through the grapevine about Henry Dawes' one-sided voting plan and had time to think it through. Garfield felt confident of the public's support, but, without a vote, he would have no voice. Robertson would be smothered without a whimper. He brought Blaine into his office and they talked it over. If Blaine were such a Machiavellian as the newspapers painted him, then Garfield certainly needed his cunning now. Between them, Blaine and Garfield knew a thing or two about the Senate's rules. The Constitution provided no direct check and balance against a Senate caucus hell-bent on protecting it own perquisites, and presidents normally weren't invited to interfere with Congress' internal workings, but these weren't normal times. Garfield found himself in a corner. It didn't take them long to devise a plan.

The next day on Capitol Hill, as Conkling, Dawes, and the other Senators sat at their desks in the Senate chamber, doors shut and galleries emptied for secret executive session, ready to pass the next batch of "uncontested" nominees, a messenger interrupted them with an urgent dispatch from the

White House. Chester A. Arthur, standing at the president's desk, handed it to the clerk to read aloud. Some Senators didn't quite understand it at first; they crowded around Roscoe Conkling's desk, who recognized the impact at once. In precise, formal language, it said that Garfield hereby was withdrawing all pending nominations of all New Yorkers for positions in the federal government. He was wiping the slate clean—all, that is, except for one: William H. Robertson, to be Collector of the Port of New York. Robertson's nomination alone still stood.

Conkling explained it to them quietly. Obviously, he said, he and Tom Platt were being cut off. All patronage now had been made contingent on the Senate's approval of one single item—Robertson. The president had drawn a line: Robertson or nothing. As a reporter put it, the president had told them: "Gentlemen, if you do not want to control a single nomination during my four years' administration, stand by Conkling, and that will settle it."[110] No longer could the Senate avoid voting on Robertson by hiding behind other business; the other business had been scrapped.

"This will bring the Robertson nomination to an issue," Garfield explained in his journal that day. "It may end in his defeat; but it will protect me from being finessed out of a test."[111] Blaine positively glowed at his own shrewdness in concocting the idea: "I *know* by inspiration that it will work like a charm," he said.[112]

This time, in fact, public reaction was electric. Newspapers coast-to-coast erupted in headlines. "[S]tick and let the Senate squirm. Compromise impossible, victory certain," telegrammed *Cincinnati Commercial* publisher Murat Halstead from Ohio.[113] Letters poured into the White House: "Thank the Lord for the news this morning that you propose to stand firm.... We elected you president—and when we want Mr. Conkling to take your place we will notify him in due time," wrote Charles D. Mott of Washington, D.C. "It is gratifying & refreshing to know that the country has at its head a man with a backbone," said D.H. Dyer of St. Louis.

Support came even from New York City, Conkling's own base. "I trust that you will not withdraw the nomination of Judge Robertson under any circumstances whatever," John Dingman of Scribners & Sons insisted, or else "a thousand of us will feel personally humiliated and despondent."[114] The *Trenton Times* pictured Garfield as the "foot" of the Republican Party, and "all of its energy and enthusiasm was in the wholesome kick he administered to Bossism on Thursday."[115]

The few complaints he heard sounded like back-handed compliments: Garfield had wielded "the tomahawk and scalping knife" griped an Ohio Stalwart.[116]

The burden had now shifted. As Roscoe Conkling now looked around the chamber at his Senate colleagues, cozy friends who had supported him firmly during the past few weeks, he noticed several now keeping a safe distance away from him and avoiding looking him in the eye.

❀ ❀ ❀ ❀ ❀

Lucretia's condition worsened all that week. Telegrams had gone out to Dr. Boynton, her long-time personal physician in Cleveland, but it took two full days to find him. "Dr. Boynton is in Kansas, probably at Wichita," the Western Union Telegraph Company had reported back on May 9. "Doctor is in Kansas. Your message was forwarded at a venture it may not reach him," the Doctor's wife had telegrammed. Meanwhile, the White House called in another local doctor, a Doctor Baxter, who diagnosed Lucretia as suffering from "malaria and overwork" with a "danger of cerebrospinal meningitis."[117] A third physician, a Doctor Pope, came and insisted on moving Lucretia to a room on the White House's north side to escape the putrid air blowing in from the Potomac. That night, Garfield stayed up with her until 4:15 am and slept only four hours. After breakfast, he took a bath and returned to bed only to toss and turn some more. The next night he sat up with her until 4 am again.

As Lucretia's fever topped 104 degrees, Doctor Pope furiously applied "fever powders" and bathed her with alcohol and ice water. Afterward, her fever fell only slightly, to 103½ degrees, though she felt strong enough to eat a few strawberries with enjoyment. That night, Doctor Boynton finally arrived from Kansas; seeing the First Lady's fever still hovering near 104 degrees and her pulse at 100, Boynton immediately changed course and began administering "heroic doses" of medicine. "This will burn her out if not arrested," the doctor told Garfield, who could barely concentrate on the Senate fight anymore. It was "[h]ard to think of business with any shadow of doubt hanging over the life of my life," he lamented after one of the long late-night vigils, "but forced myself to think of other things."[118]

❀ ❀ ❀ ❀ ❀

In early May, Roscoe Conkling decided that he too needed to turn up the public pressure. His weak-kneed Senate colleagues had appalled him, the way they lost their nerve after Garfield's latest parliamentary trick. And he wondered if public sympathy for the president's ailing wife also would hurt his case. He had to hit back hard and do it quickly.

At Conkling's command, his loyal helper, Vice President Arthur, sent a telegram to New York City addressed to T.C. Connery, editor of the *New York Herald* and confidante of *Herald* publisher James Gordon Bennett, Jr. Within the day, Connery came to Washington, D.C. and knocked on the door of Conkling's apartment. Arthur opened it for him—the Senator, Arthur said, was still out having breakfast. "I am so glad you decided to come here," he told the *Herald* editor and sat him down in a comfortable chair. "Conkling was very anxious for it."[119]

"What is all the mystery about?" Connery asked, glad to have some time alone first with Arthur whom he considered more likely to give him straight answers. The telegram had been vague.

Arthur told him: They wanted to lay out their case against the president. Connery gave him an odd look. "Garfield has not been square, nor honorable, nor truthful with Conkling," Arthur explained in a calm, unflinching tone. "It is a hard thing to say of a president of the United States" –especially coming from a vice president, Connery must have thought—"but it is, unfortunately, only the truth. Garfield—spurred by Blaine, by whom he is too easily led—has broken every pledge made to us; not only that, but he seems to have wished to do it in a most offensive way."

Connery had never quite trusted Roscoe Conkling, but he'd always respected Chet Arthur as an honest dealer. These revelations were astounding, he thought—certainly, they'd sell plenty of two-penny newspapers. And perhaps they had more behind them than sour grapes. "How so?" he asked.[120]

Arthur, now sitting down himself with the *Herald* editor, began to elaborate. "Long ago we heard that Garfield said he intended to 'break' Senator Conkling." Just then, the door opened and the great New York Senator himself entered the room, "looking quite serene and unconcerned," Connery recalled. Roscoe Conkling joined them, pulling up a chair so they could all sit together in a circle. They lit their cigars and settled in for a talk. The attention seemed naturally to shift from the self-effacing Arthur to his animated housemate. Conkling, with little prompting, launched head-long into a full-throated exposition of his whole train of secret dealings with James Garfield over the past year, filled with hyperbole and bombast. He was giving this story to the *New York Herald*, the nation's most widely-read newspaper, as a "special," he said, because they wanted James Gordon Bennett's personal backing in any political war against the president.

Connery took careful notes. He knew that publisher Bennett had a long history with Conkling and would eagerly join the crusade. Sure enough, on Wednesday morning, May 11, just as Senate Republicans were making their final decisions on the Robertson affair in their closed-door caucus meetings in Washington, D.C., the *New York Herald* unleashed a dramatic expose—dictated by Conkling, penned by George Gorham, and attributed to an anonymous "Occasional Correspondent"—containing a long, tongue-in-cheek indictment of James Garfield's double-dealing against the New York Stalwarts, from last summer's Fifth Avenue Summit through all the alleged pledges and broken promises, all under the headline "The Wriggler." It painted the president as a weak-willed liar bent on destroying his own Party's best members for no reason other than his domination by the spidery megalomaniac James G. Blaine.[121]

By Roscoe Conkling's calculation, the story would shock the Senators and stop them in their tracks. Robertson's nomination would be doomed, along with the president who'd made it.

While he was at it, Conkling also gave Connery a copy of the embarrassing fund-raising letter tying Garfield to Tom Brady, the infamous Star Route fraud villain—his promised blackmail. He supplied rumors, which the *Herald* happily printed, that the U.S. Senate soon would hand him Garfield's head on a platter—either "the absolute rejection of Robertson," "a speedy adjournment without a consideration of his name," or some other "Conkling victory."[122] The *Herald*'s editorial page joined the fray, mocking Garfield as an "Angry Boy!" being led by the nose by Blaine, "a man without convictions, without friendships, without shame—a dominant intellectual force" next to whom the president was "secondary."[123]

The *Herald* printed all of it and the Senators read every word.

* * * * *

On Monday May 9, with the Senate deadlock broken and the field of New York nominees narrowed down to one, the Republican caucus had no excuse left but finally to consider the nomination of William Robertson to be Collector of the Port of New York. They asked Roscoe Conkling to wait outside in the hallway at first; the bickering began before he re-entered the room. Ambrose Burnside of Delaware* moved to scrap Henry Dawes' recent rule against "contested" nominees that had put Robertson's vote on permanent hold. John Logan opposed him and their debate grew "pointed and personal," according to press accounts.

Conkling, finally given his turn, joined the caucus and addressed his colleagues for over two hours. They listened politely as he repeated his now-well-practiced diatribe, sounding the "danger of permitting the executive to influence the Senate" and recounting all his grievances against Garfield and Blaine and how they'd treated him in such "bad faith."[124] Robertson, he claimed, had been so traitorous to the Party in Chicago as actually to oppose Chet Arthur's inclusion on the ticket as Vice President. And it all got worse from there.

By now, though, the Senators had heard it all before. They'd tested the winds and found them blowing for the White House these days. Americans backed Garfield; he'd struck a chord with the country. People respected his pluck, his obstinacy, his willingness to fight even the Senate itself. The high-profile stalemate made all the Senators look bad, not just the New Yorkers. They'd grown tired of Conkling's filibuster just as they'd grown tired of Garfield's petulance the week before. They wanted this argument just to vanish. And besides, winning with Garfield would keep their local patronage far safer than losing with Conkling, even if it gave their principle of Senatorial Courtesy a black eye.[125]

After failing to reach a decision, they met again on Wednesday, May 11—the same day as the *New York Herald* covered its front page with its vituperative Conkling-inspired smear on the president. They all read the *Herald* expose; Conkling had arranged for copies to be carried down by train from New York City during the morning. But the Senators found nothing new in it. They'd heard far worse from the Senator's own silver-tongued mouth and by now considered it a jumble of half-truths and belly-aching. They felt far more troubled by the growing public anger against the Senate itself. "Feudalism dies hard," the *Chicago Tribune* scoffed at them. "The Senatorial Barons insist upon what they call their constitutional prerogative. Senatorial courtesy is to them a Magna Carta."[126]

---

* Burnside, who had led the Union Army to disaster at Fredricksburg and had a bad case of the "slows" at Antietam in 1862 still was able to use his wartime celebrity to be elected Senator in 1874 and 1880.

Henry Dawes' own wife had written to him from Pittsfield that week complaining: "I don't know for my part why so much attention should be paid to 'Conkling's wishes.' In everything … Let New York go—and Conkling with her."[127] Dawes even felt compelled to deny stories in his own New England newspapers that he'd urged Garfield to withdraw Robertson's name. "Fabricators of facts," he called its sources[128]—never mind that his own "harmonious" compromise had amounted to the same thing. When fragments of Roscoe Conkling's own caucus speech from Monday leaked to the newspapers, Albany partisans sent telegrams denying that William Robertson ever had opposed Chester Arthur's nomination in Chicago. In fact, they confirmed, Robertson had *supported* Arthur, arguing that he'd strengthen Garfield's chances in November. A Senator couldn't even twist the truth in a private conversation anymore. What had things come to?

Now, behind closed doors again, the Senators inched toward a decision. White-bearded George Edmunds of Vermont, a Conkling backer, proposed that they act only on pending nominations to fill existing vacancies, a subtle trap that would block Robertson's name since it hadn't yet been reported from a Committee. But the caucus voted him down by a lopsided margin. Joe Hawley of Connecticut wrote to Garfield that "every Republican Senator desires peace in the family" but "no resolution to gain peace by asking you to withdraw Robertson could pass the Republican caucus." Suddenly, Hawley told Garfield, he'd become "master of the situation if you will it."[129]

Outside in the hallway, Conkling heard Henry Dawes tell newsmen that Conkling could expect only about one-fourth of the Republican Senators to support him.[130] He bristled at the news. But again the Senators failed to reached a decision that day, and they put off a final meeting for another two days—perhaps to see if the *New York Herald* expose would change any minds.

As Senators streamed into the White House that week to hear the president's latest advice on the contest, they sat waiting, sometimes for hours, as Garfield ignored them to sit at his wife's bedside. He watched Lucretia float in and out of consciousness, her skin hot with fever, her arms and shoulders looking frail and withered, her face a contortion of pain and fatigue. He had nothing to tell the Senators at this point; he'd long ago rejected any compromise. "Garfield is all worn out and fairly broken down when talking with me," Henry Dawes confided to his wife[131]—though Garfield pointed happily to a newspaper clip quoting Andrew Jackson's response to John Calhoun during the nullification crisis in 1828: "I will not compromise with traitors."[132]

On Friday, May 13, the Republicans Senators caucused again. By now, they'd lost any delusion that they could avoid an open clash on the Robertson issue. "If the President would only see the danger we are in and fix the matter up harmoniously," one nameless Republican lamented.[133] Even old gray-bearded Henry Anthony, a die-hard Conkling backer with 22 years of Senate seniority, shuddered at rumblings from his home state of Rhode Island about his own upcoming re-election because state legislators there now considered him too close to Roscoe Conkling.[134]

After two hours, they opened the doors and emerged. One Senator told the *New York Tribune*: "No committee will attempt to smother any nomination." Said another "I can see only one possible danger now. This hot weather may drive enough Senators away to break our quorum." The caucus had spoken; Senators could vote as they chose. The "contested nominations" rule had been scrapped. Robertson would have his day.

Roscoe Conkling promised the caucus that, come next Monday, he would not prevent the nomination from moving forward—though what he would do when it reached the Senate floor was another matter. Then Conkling stormed out of the room. He'd used a back doorway to avoid reporters in the hall, but the newsmen had no trouble hearing his screams through the heavy wooden closed doors. His friends had deserted him, and Conkling had blasted them over it.[135] "Those laugh best who laugh last," he'd told them. Those who'd abandoned him would "have occasion to remember it to their sorrow."[136]

Garfield's friends knew not to celebrate quite yet. The New York Boss still had one last chance to win a victory: on the Senate floor, a forum whose tricks he knew better than anyone else. "This is Conkling's Bull Run—only his first battle in which he is worsted," a friendly colleague told reporters, "and a mere skirmish to what will follow."[137] But the signs were propitious for the president. Joe Hawley reported the "good news" that Democrats now would oppose any move to adjourn the Senate until after Robertson had gotten his vote. "Nothing but a failure on Robertson's part to appreciate his own importance in the country can prevent an invaluable administration success," he wrote.[138]

"I think several things are working out right—ie. As you and I think right—which is right enough for all practical purposes," Whitelaw Reid told the president.[139]

On Saturday, Lucretia's fever fell to 101 degrees, down from 104 just twenty-four hours earlier. On Sunday, it fell further to 100½ degrees. That night, nearly all the cabinet members and their wives called at the White House to visit and ask about her. The next day, she relapsed into weakness and fatigue, but her fever held moderate. Garfield barely left the building, afraid to stray too far from her bedside.

◎ ◎ ◎ ◎ ◎

Charles Guiteau made his usual daily walk to the State Department on Saturday, May 14,[140] to pursue his application for the Paris consulship. As usual, he saw Secretary Blaine at his public audience and got close enough to mention his case. The Senate deadlock had broken now; certainly there'd be news. Blaine, though, seemed distracted, and Guiterau didn't notice why. When he made his usual pitch, Blaine looked him directly in the face: "Never speak to me again on the subject of the Paris consulship," he snapped in a loud voice, causing embarrassed heads to turn in the parlor. Guiteau stopped cold and Blaine instantly seemed embarrassed by his own bad manners. "I did not do it with any special harshness," Blaine recalled later, remembering the incident, "but merely to conclude a matter which was of no value to me and was interrupting" him in his work.[141]

James Blaine stood easily a full head taller than Charles Guiteau, but that didn't stop the persistent little dark-haired man from standing his ground. "I am going to see the President about this," he said firmly back to the Secretary of State, "and I think I can get the President to remove Mr. Walker, and then I can get the appointment."

Blaine looked at Guiteau in a "compassionate way," Guiteau recalled, and said: "Well, if he will." To Guiteau, it was as if he'd said "If the President wants to remove Walker [from the Paris consulship to make way for Guiteau] I won't interfere with him."[142]

Blaine, of course, hadn't meant it that way at all, and Guiteau clearly misunderstood it. "I should have had very decided objections" to Guiteau's appointment to Paris, Blaine explained later. "The Paris consulship is a very important office" that should be filled with a "well-known public man" of "conspicuous rank for intelligence and public service" and "I did not think that Mr. Guiteau belonged to that rank."[143]

Guiteau had felt the sting of Blaine's verbal slap. It had "hurt my feelings," he later confessed.[144] He left the State Department and walked all though the streets of Washington. He ended up finally at the Riggs House. Here, he took paper and sat at his usual table to write a letter to the president. Guiteau had written President Garfield letters almost every day that week: "I hope Mrs. Garfield is better. Monday I sent you a note about the Paris consulship; Tuesday one about '84," he wrote as introduction to yet another letter on Friday about the 1884 election. The president, through these letters, seemed almost the only person in Washington that Guiteau had to talk to. He had ended Friday's by asking: "May I tell Mr. Blaine to prepare the order for my appointment to the Paris consulship, vice Geo. Walker, recalled?"[145]

Now, Guiteau told the president all about his painful run-in with the Secretary of State: "Until Saturday I supposed that Mr. Blaine was my friend in the matter of the Paris consulship," he scribbled in pencil. Beware of Blaine: "he is trying to run the State Department in the interest of the Blaine element in '84"—not Garfield's. Guiteau reminded Garfield of his own roster of prominent backers. "I am in with Mr. Morton and Gen. Arthur, and I will get them to go on my bond," and "Gen'l Logan and Senator Harrison and the rest of my friends will see that it is promptly confirmed." He ended on a personal note: "I am sorry Mrs. Garfield is sick, and hope she will recover soon."[146]

Even as he wrote, though, the lonely man with the rumpled clothes and guarded manner wondered about the president himself and whether he could trust him. He'd read the New York Herald's shocking revelations of Garfield's shameful deceits toward his New York friends Conkling and Arthur. What kind of man is this who won't keep promises—promises like the New York Custom House for them, and the Paris consulship for a loyal Stalwart like himself? One Sunday a few weeks earlier, Guiteau had visited the small wood-frame Disciple Church where Garfield worshipped with his family—he'd gotten the address from the newspapers—just "out of curiosity," he later explained, "to see what kind of church he attended."[147] Now, Guiteau had doubts if even the president's strong religion faith could counter-balance his political duplicity.

But by then, if Charles Guiteau had tried to see the president and ask him for help, he would have found his way blocked. In mid-May, Joe Stanley Brown, the president's private secretary, had spoken to the White House doormen about the overly-persistent little man always wasting their time with his unrealistic job demands. Stanley Brown had told them to keep him out—to "see that Mr. Guiteau no longer troubled the office."[148]

⊚ ⊚ ⊚ ⊚ ⊚

That Saturday night, May 14, Roscoe Conkling rode alone in his carriage through the streets of Washington, D.C., sullenly quiet in his dark mood, his rage at Garfield matched only by his anger toward his spineless Senate colleagues. At one point, he looked out and happened to see Henry Dawes on the sidewalk walking in the hot night air along Pennsylvania Avenue. Conkling asked the driver to stop. He climbed down from the carriage car and caught up with his Senator friend. They started walking together and, before it was over, ended up talking for nearly an hour, oblivious to passers-by on the street.[149]

Dawes listened patiently as his friend of almost eighteen years recounted yet again all his frustrations, his never-ending gripes and injuries, amusing in the telling but painful to the ear. Henry Dawes tried his best to sympathize, but even he had grown tired of Conkling's constant whining. It had brought him to the verge of defeat. Maybe a friend needed to tell him the hard truth. And if anyone could make Roscoe Conkling listen to anyone but himself, it was probably Henry Dawes.

"Suppose all you say is true." Dawes interrupted Conkling almost in mid-sentence after a while, turning to face him as they stood near a street lamp on the sidewalk, trying to spark a new thought: "nevertheless this is your opportunity, by a stroke of magnanimity, to win a victory.... Go into the Senate on Monday morning, and present your indictment, if you choose—as strong a case as facts will permit," but conclude it with "a declaration ... to the Senate and the country that there is something higher in the mission of the Republican party than the redress of personal grievances... and then call on all friends and foes alike to put the past behind them, and close up the ranks with their faces to the future."

Conkling should concede, Dawes suggested, but gracefully. He could win by losing; he could vote for William Robertson in a show of party unity that would shame his opponents. He'd gain so much by humility. His Senate colleagues would rally around him, grateful for saving them from the awful choice. His power in the Caucus would never be higher. And the New York Custom House? It was nothing, Henry Dawes told his friend. Roscoe Conkling could live without it. Let smaller men squabble over patronage. Conkling was a giant. He shouldn't bother himself with trivia.

"Your medicine, Dawes, is much easier to prescribe than to take," Conkling said, barely taking a minute to think it through. Even now, with victory so easily in reach just with a subtle change of strategy, Roscoe Conkling could not find it in himself to bend. "Why, you have no idea of the bitterness of the feeling in New York in condemnation of these men…. I… should be burned in effigy from Buffalo to Montauk Point," he said. Did he really believe it? Years ago, Conkling had turned down the Chief Justiceship of the United States Supreme Court when offered it by President Grant and more recently he'd turned down a presidential nomination in Chicago, all out of pride. Now he'd turned down perhaps his last chance for a clear moral victory and survival on the national stage.

Henry Dawes had nothing more to suggest. He, like everyone else, would have to wait until Monday to see what his brilliant and brilliantly flawed friend had decided. And so they parted ways in the night.

⬤ ⬤ ⬤ ⬤ ⬤

For Tom Platt, New York's junior Senator, the situation had turned hopeless: If Robertson's name came up for a vote in the Senate on Monday, he'd be doomed. He could never betray Roscoe Conkling by supporting Robertson; but, at the same time, he'd made binding pledges back in Albany in January to do just that. If he broke his word, Whitelaw Reid and the Albany Half-Breeds would expose him to the world as a liar. They'd ruin him in politics and in business.

Tom Platt had visited Garfield in the White House repeatedly for months trying to avoid this awful dilemma.[150] He'd floated compromises, but the president had refused to listen.[151] On May 5, just the prior week, he and Chet Arthur had gone to see Garfield together to renew their plea, but Garfield "did not take kindly"[152] to their ideas and, later that day, he'd withdrawn all the Stalwart nominations. Platt, dragging his tail between his legs, could only tell friends his "self-respect" would "hardly allow him or the vice president to visit the president again very soon."[153]

Platt had visited Whitelaw Reid in New York City too to beg for help, but Reid had only repeated his threats to expose him if he violated his pledges.[154]

Now, Tom Platt saw only one way out. If William Robertson's name came to a Senate floor vote, he had no choices: to vote "yes" would break faith with Conkling; to vote "no" or even avoid voting at all would break his Albany pledges. Over the weekend, he walked over to Roscoe Conkling's apartment at Wormley's hotel and the two Senators spoke long into the night about their options. Platt told Conkling his idea; it was one that Conkling had rejected before, but now he too saw no other way.

They agreed to act together. They told no one outside a small handful of friends. The others would find out soon enough on Monday.

◎ ◎ ◎ ◎ ◎

Chester A. Arthur entered the Senate chamber a few minutes late on Monday morning, May 16, and took his place on the raised podium behind the presiding officer's desk. The few newspapermen who noticed Arthur's flushed face and nervous hands thought nothing of it, attributing it to simple nerves. Throngs of gentlemen and society ladies packed the galleries that day. All official Washington by now had heard that, today, William Robertson's name could come up for debate. It could be Roscoe Conkling's finest moment on the public stage, or his worst. Certainly, it couldn't help but be dramatic.

Barely had the Chaplain, Reverend J.J. Bullock, finished reciting his prayer when Arthur banged his gavel, called the Senate to order, stood up, and made a routine announcement with no explanation: "I am directed to lay before the Senate the communication which the clerk will now read." His loud voice could barely be heard above the buzz of small talk in the room. He handed the clerk a plain-looking paper to read and continued to stand.[155]

"Sir: Will you please announce to the Senate that my resignation as Senator of the United States from the State of New York has been forwarded to the governor of that State?" the clerk announced in his usual nasal monotone. "I have the honor to be, with great respect, your obedient servant. Roscoe Conkling."[156]

Members looked up from their desks. Most hadn't been paying attention. Heads turned in the galleries. A few members asked that the clerk read it again. As he did, Republican Senators looked over to gaze at Roscoe Conkling's desk and noticed it conspicuously empty. A few sharp-eyed Democrats looked over from across the aisle at the Republicans and made a quick count. Some of them cracked smiles or laughed under their breath; with Conkling gone, the Democrats suddenly had regained a voting majority in the Senate. Power had shifted in the blink of an eye.

Then Arthur, still standing at the president's podium, handed the clerk a second message to read: "Sir: I have forwarded to the governor of the State of New York my resignation as Senator for the State of New York. Will you be pleased to announce the fact to the Senate? With great respect, your obedient servant, T[homas] C[ollier] Platt."[157]

Ambrose Burnside, apparently oblivious to what had just occurred, stood stiffly at his desk and now moved to read a report from the Committee on Foreign Relations on an unrelated subject. Henry Dawes sharply interrupted him; the Senate must go immediately into closed Executive Session.

Democrats, though, had other ideas. Maybe this would be a good time to elect Senate officers, Democrat Ben Hill suggested with a smirk. After all, hadn't the Republicans been complaining all month that "the government would be subverted" without them?

"But the Senator would never be convinced until he had an accidental majority," Henry Dawes shot back, having now counted the noses for himself. "An accident is an eye-opener to my friend from Georgia."

"We will be liberal." Hill backed off. He'd had his fun.

In secret session, the Senators now heard all the details from Chet Arthur and other Conkling confidantes. Conkling and Tom Platt, in fact, seeing no good outcome in the Senate, unwilling to face the embarrassment of losing a public vote, had resigned their seats. They planned to take their case to the New York State legislature in Albany, which they expected immediately to re-elect them and send them back to Washington. That would settle the issue between themselves and the president and return them to the Senate with a fresh strong mandate to fight their cause in favor of local control of patronage.

Blunt-spoken Missourian George Vest shook his head. "Conkling has made a fool of himself," he muttered.[158] Other Senators couldn't believe their ears. "Senator Conkling acts like a boy," Philetus Sawyer of Wisconsin said. "It's bad enough without discussing it, and I don't care to say anything," grumbled Sam McMillan of Minnesota.[159i]

Henry Dawes, having waged Conkling's fight in the caucus for weeks, couldn't believe that his colleague had abandoned him in the moment of truth: "A great big baby boohooing because he can't have all the cake and refusing to play any longer runs home to his mother," he wrote to his wife from the Senate chamber that morning. "That is all there is too it."[160] His Massachusetts colleague George Hoar quoted from a letter: "the people will endure ill nature even to ugliness but not stupidity."[161]

Garfield, hearing the news in the White House, couldn't believe his good fortune. "[A] very weak attempt at the heroic," he called it. "If I am not mistaken, it will be received with guffaws of laughter." Still, his attention remained focused on Lucretia, lying in bed each day wracked with pain and grogginess. "We were depressed by a worse day for *her*," he noted in his journal that morning, through at least her fever was stabilizing at just above 100 degrees. Perhaps she had now survived the worst, they hoped.[162]

Outside the Senate chamber, crowds formed around bulletin boards by the Capitol Building, the hotels and newspaper offices, and the government offices as word electrified the City. In the excitement, all but Roscoe Conkling's most die-hard friends seemed to abandon him. "Sometime, somehow I *knew* the end would come and that the trouble would be over," long-time Stalwart Edwards Pierrepont wrote to Garfield from New York. "I heartily rejoice."[163] The shock was felt as far away as London, England, where the daily *Times* called Conkling's resignation the "great sensation" from America.[164]

But Roscoe Conkling and Tom Platt heard none of these cat-calls. They had already left Washington, D.C., and headed north by train for Albany, New York, the first step in what they hoped would be a brief, temporary exile, though they really didn't know how long it would be before they would return.

◎ ◎ ◎ ◎ ◎

"I was in bed. I think I retired about eight o'clock. I felt depressed and perplexed on account of the political situation," Charles Guiteau recalled.[165] He lay awake in his rooming house, friendless, money-less, and alone in Washington, D.C. He couldn't sleep. It was late on Wednesday night, two days after Roscoe Conkling and Tom Platt had resigned their seats in the U.S. Senate. Guiteau's mind churned over betrayals—not just his own rude rebuff from Secretary Blaine on the Paris consulship. He worried even more for those he imagined his friends, the Stalwarts, whom Blaine and Garfield likewise had betrayed and routed.

Guiteau read the newspaper reports, the sneering comments about Conkling and "Me Too" Tom Platt, and they made his skin crawl; "senatorial suicide," one of the papers called it.[166] He reread the long, blistering *New York Herald* attack on the president, soaking in its every detail as it confirmed all the dark suspicions he'd held against Blaine and Garfield—their deceits, their conspiracies, their prejudice against the Stalwarts. He lay awake in the hot, humid night with no one to talk to and thought about all these things.

Then he had an epiphany: "the idea flashed through my brain," he remembered. "[I]f the President was out of the way everything would go better."[167]

The idea startled him, its terrible simplicity, its compelling logic. With Garfield "removed," then Chet Arthur, who'd treated him so politely and respectfully in New York City during the election campaign and given him the chance to deliver his speech "Garfield against Hancock".... Chet Arthur would become president. Arthur would set things right—for Guiteau, for his friends, for the country.

He slept fitfully that night. When he awoke the next morning, "the same impression came upon me with renewed force," he recalled.[168] Guiteau began studying the newspapers from his new focal point, and saw everything looking much clearer. His idea still horrified him, but it "kept growing on me, pressing me, goading me," he explained later.[169] For two weeks it "kept bearing and bearing and bearing down upon me that the only way to unite the two factions of the republican party and save the Republic from going into the hands of the rebels and democrats was to quietly remove the President."[170]

After two weeks, his mind became "thoroughly fixed," not just on the idea itself but also on its origin. Guiteau conceded that he alone hadn't the capacity to originate such a powerful notion. "I never had the slightest doubt as to the divinity of the inspiration," he explained. God had chosen him, he reasoned, because "I had the brains and the nerve to do the work" as well as "to advertise my theological book—'The Truth.'"[171] It was an "inspiration" in the purest sense, "where a man's mind is taken possession of by a superior power, and he acts outside of his own nature—outside of himself."[172]

After all, Guiteau had been a theologian among his many careers. He'd written books and lectures about God and Christ and Divinity. He prayed over his new revelation. He asked God that "if it was not the Lord's will that I should remove" the president then He should "intercede."

Events in his own life now suddenly made sense to Guiteau, such as his survival that night on the *Stonington* steamship disaster on Long Island Sound, or at another time when he'd been forced to jump from a moving railroad train in New Jersey. And he also now saw a deeper logic in politics. Garfield had made a bargain in Chicago, the presidency for himself and the vice presidency for the Stalwarts. The Stalwarts had won the second spot on the ticket. To redeem the bargain's value, one simply had to remove the holder of the first spot.

Guiteau had met James Garfield and Mrs. Garfield face to face and had liked them both. But his plan was nothing personal; it was a political necessity—like removing hostile Indians from the Plains to make way for settlers and railroads or removing the confederates from their lines during the war. And it had nothing to do with his failure over the Paris consulship—he knew

now that he'd lost that job only because he'd been a Stalwart. He'd been victimized by Garfield and Blaine right along with Conkling, Arthur, and Grant.
"[M]y getting an office or not getting an office... had nothing to do with my
attempt to remove the President," he insisted later. "That was purely a political necessity, under divine pressure, and I acted under an inspiration of the
Diety."[173]

He, Charles Guiteau, wanted only to save the Republican party, prevent
another civil war, and respond to the dictates of God. Once the shock wore
off, people would applaud him. Arthur, as president, surely would give him a
presidential pardon to save him from the hangman. He'd be grateful, after
all, since Guiteau would have made him president in the first place. Guiteau
saw it all clearly. "Had Jefferson Davis and a dozen or two of his co-traitors
been shot dead in January 1861, no doubt our late rebellion would never have
been," he explained. "I am a patriot."[174]

After he conceived of the idea "I did not go near Mr. Blaine or near the
President to press my application," Guiteau explained.[175] He bided his time
and started to prepare in his usual practical way.

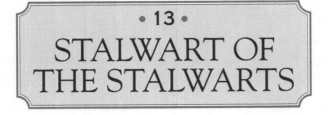

13

STALWART OF
THE STALWARTS

NOT FORTY-EIGHT HOURS after Roscoe Conkling and Tom Platt had announced their surprise resignations from the United States Senate, their former colleagues acted as if they'd never existed and confirmed William H. Robertson's nomination as Collector of the Port of New York by unanimous voice vote; any hope they might have had that the Senate would wait for their re-election before addressing the issue vanished. Celebrations erupted across upstate New York. Despite heavy rains that day, local politicos fired 100-gun salutes into the skies over towns from Cold Spring to Rochester to Hudson and Utica. In Albany, the state capitol, fireworks and roman candles lit sidewalks in front of the Kenmore Hotel on North Pearl Street* as a brass band played music to over 8,000 people on the street. They cheered as Robertson waved from his window and came down for a speech. The state legislature itself, meeting in Albany's baroque new Capitol Building atop State Street hill, interrupted its session to give Robertson three hearty cheers, followed by three cheers for President Garfield. Only a handful of Stalwart members sat glumly in their seats. Where was their leader, they wondered.[1]

Robertson stirred his friends by vowing to delay leaving Albany for his new post until after his Half-Breeds had beaten Conkling and Platt in the legislature. And he set about leading the job himself.

Long-time Conkling haters recognized this chance-of-a-lifetime to rid themselves of the Boss forever and allies across the country egged them on. "It is no time for timidity or palliations," trumpeted Murat Halstead from

---

* The Kenmore lasted well into the twentieth century; gangster Legs Diamond was shot to death there by a rival gang on December 18, 1931.

Ohio in the *Cincinnati Commercial*. "The practical duty of New York seems plain ... Mr. Conkling has issued his challenge, Caesar or nothing!"[2] Should Conkling and Platt win their game and be returned to Washington, John Sherman warned: "the President would [be] powerless to appoint anyone in New York without consulting [them], practically transferring to them his constitutional power."[3]

Even timid reformers like E.L. Godkin now rolled up their sleeves for a fight. "Persons of [Conkling's] temper are not fit for public life," he crowed mockingly in *The Nation*. "The proper sphere for him is the monastery, or some solitary pursuit like metaphysics or shepherding."[4]

Robertson's backers had already won a tactical skirmish, blocking any chance of Conkling's re-election being railroaded through the legislature. By law, a Senate vacancy had to sit over from one Tuesday to the next before the legislators could vote on filling it. The formal notice of Conkling's and Platt's resignations had reached Albany that week on a Monday afternoon, May 16. By simply notifying the legislature that day, Governor Cornell could have guaranteed a vote on sending them back to Washington on the next Tuesday, May 24. Instead, he'd vacillated. "What does this mean, marshal?" he'd asked Louis Payn after getting the news at the governor's mansion. "Well, marshal, what is to be done?"[5]

"Send for [Assembly] Speaker Sharpe and our other friends and consult as to the best line of getting even with this—ingrate in the White House," Payn had roared back, but the Governor still didn't see the urgency.

Instead of rushing, Governor Cornell had sent a single lone messenger to the two legislative chambers—the Senate and the Assembly—at opposite ends of the Capitol. Robertson, seeing the delay, had pounced. He'd arranged for State Senator Loren Sessions, sitting in the Senate chair, promptly to recognize a motion to adjourn and slam it through on a voice vote (despite several Stalwarts clamoring with objections). As a result, the governor's messenger had arrived ten minutes later to an empty house—delaying the formal notice by a day and pushing the vote off a week.

This gave time for reporters and politicos now to come pouring into Albany from all around the country. They filled the Kenmore and Delavan Hotels and began running up tabs at the nearby brothels and saloons. The siege of Albany, America's premier political contest of summer 1881, had begun.

◉ ◉ ◉ ◉ ◉

Roscoe Conkling reached Albany by train on May 24. With Chet Arthur having come to join him at his side, Conkling signed the register book at the Delavan House Hotel on Broadway by the Hudson River* and started shaking every hand in sight. He asked politely for their votes to re-elect him as United States Senator from New York State. Conkling sported his friendliest face and brightest demeanor: "no statesman ever wore a more winning smile," a shocked reporter noted.[6]

At first Conkling had not wanted to come to Albany at all, stewing over the avalanche of criticism at his dramatic resignation from the U.S. Senate in Washington the week before. He agreed only after a stormy meeting at Chet Arthur's townhouse on Lexington Avenue in New York City a few days earlier. At first, he and fellow former-senator Tom Platt weren't sure they even wanted to stand for re-election anyhow. Certainly Lord Roscoe couldn't imagine lowering himself to ask mere state legislators for support. Let them come and beg for him, not the other way around. He was, after all, the Boss, and he was, after all, right. He'd based his fight on valid grievances and civil service principles (nobody, of course, missed the irony of this, coming from the mouth of Conkling, the long-time enemy of what he himself called "snivel service" reform).

Tom Platt especially resented being painted as Conkling's weak sister in the affair. "I have been portrayed as a 'Me, too,' and 'Echo' and 'Dromio' of Conkling," he complained, yet he'd been the one who'd originated the resignation idea. It wasn't fair. Newspaper cartoons showed Platt as a little boy sticking out of Conkling's back pocket holding a sign saying "Me, too."[7]

They were sick of public life, the ex-senators had huffed over tea, brandy, and finger food served on Chet Arthur's finest china. Some of the loyal aides in the room tried to paint a rosier picture. They pointed to George Gorham's *National Republican* that had reported a "general impression" among party insiders that "Senators Conkling and Platt would be returned to the Senate within ten days by an overwhelming vote."[8] "We shall win this battle without any trouble," Assembly Speaker George Sharpe had told the group.

But hardheaded realists had spoken up too. "Huh, but you will be the first to desert us,"[9] Louis Payn had shot back. Payn, one of the five Conkling loyalists whose own re-nomination had been withdrawn by Garfield the week

---

* Destroyed by fire in 1895, it became the site of Union Station, Albany's main railroad station since 1900.

before, had been up in Albany watching the jockeying and found it alarming. The state legislature's two chambers—the Senate and Assembly—met in joint session to choose U.S. Senators, their 160 combined members voting together as one body. Even at best, Payn could count only 69 votes for Conkling and Platt—far short of the 81 needed to win and slipping by the hour. Only one thing could stop it, Payn argued: Roscoe Conkling must come to Albany and work the legislators personally.

Conkling had stood up and paced. He didn't like it. He wanted "vindication" from Albany, not a degrading campaign where he'd have to beg for votes. Personally, he'd prefer to make his plea to a mass public audience in New York City—like one of his thrilling campaign stump speeches—but the others overruled him. Worst of all for him would be to lose his seat outright and give his enemies reason to gloat. Finally, he agreed. To Albany he came.

But Conkling's charm offensive in the State Capitol quickly wore thin. After over a decade as supreme party Boss, Roscoe Conkling expected people to jump when he snapped his fingers. Now, they shrugged. He'd trained his followers well: they keenly recognized power, and just as keenly recognized its absence. Many of his long-time backers found themselves in a bind: Loyalty went far, but nobody wanted to burn bridges to their own party's president in the White House at the start of a four-year term. Conkling was asking them, in effect, to equip him as a "political privateer, armed with letters of marque and reprisal, to seize and destroy all that belonged to a Republican administration." To any Albany legislator who wanted a future, it simply made no sense.[10]

When Conkling tried to organize the 106 Republican legislators in a caucus to muscle through a "unit rule" on the vote, he failed; forty Half-Breeds had signed counter-petitions refusing to meet. During the week, an anti-Conkling rally drew 57 Republicans versus only 30 at a reception for the Boss. Had Conkling expected a spontaneous movement to send him back to Washington, none was developing. John Hay marveled at the miscalculation: "a freak of insanity on the part of a man who has lost sight of his true relations with the rest of the world."[11]

The legislators met in joint session in the State Capitol at noon on May 31 to take their first roll calls and Conkling and Platt saw the bad news plainly: For Conkling's seat, the vote was Conkling 35; Democratic Senate leader John C. Jacobs 53, former Vice President William Wheeler 16; Governor Cornell 9, and 42 scattered on other names.[12] Tom Platt fared even

worse. On the ballot for his seat, former Senator Kernan took all 54 Democratic votes to Platt's 29—six fewer than Conkling had received—with
Chauncey Depew closing in on him at 24.

From here on, the law required the legislators to meet every day, six days
a week, to cast ballot after ballot until someone prevailed. It would be a long
hot summer in Albany.

⊙ ⊙ ⊙ ⊙ ⊙

Lucretia gained strength, but slowly. Her fever hovered at 102 through late
May before dropping; her exhaustion lingered. Anna Boynton, the Doctor's
wife, came east from Ohio and moved into the White House to help care for
her. Garfield tried lifting her out of bed into a lounge chair one day, but it
tired her. "Her weakness is most pitiful," he wrote in his journal.[13] By May 31,
Doctor Boynton pronounced the disease over, but her stamina had been almost totally destroyed. That day she ate beef for the first time in a month.

Garfield began to sleep well for the first time in the White House. Despite
busy days, he considered himself lucky; he'd now passed his first real test as
president. He enjoyed the sunny late-May mornings with long rides on horseback out along the wide Potomac riverbanks, up the C&O canal, or through
the wilds of Rock Creek Park. He favored the White House's newest stallion
named "Denmark," cantering and galloping ten to twelve miles at a stretch
with Joe Stanley Brown or his older sons James or Harry at his side. On some
days, he stopped to marvel at the Washington monument—which had sat
just across the south lawn as an unfinished marble stump for twenty years.
With work now resumed, stonemasons had added thirty feet just since spring
began. The shaft now stood two hundred feet tall, the highest structure in
the City. Ultimately, it would rise to 550 feet, making it the tallest manmade
tower in the world—built not in Europe but here in America.

The Senate adjourned *sine die* in late May—"a great relief" to Garfield[14]
who noted proudly that, of all his nominees, they'd rejected just one, William
Chandler to be Solicitor General. Senators streamed into Garfield's White
House office before heading home; soon they'd make Washington a ghost
town for the summer. Garfield's days became less frantic. He began to consider
the future while nourishing his mind with books like Edward Freeman's *Historical Geography of Europe*, the newest Atlas of the old world (perhaps picking places he'd like to visit) and Albert Riddle's latest collection *House of
Ross, and other Tales*. He worked with Treasury Secretary Windom on a suc-

cessful refinancing of expiring government bonds and gave out diplomas at Washington, D.C.'s Howard University.

The president followed the unfolding political drama in Albany but tried to avoid getting involved: Roscoe Conkling's enemies seemed eager enough to finish him off without needing help from the White House. Arthur Hickman, a Half-Breed assemblyman in Albany, had assured Garfield that "Conkling and Platt cannot be reelected by the legislature," though he also warned: "Do not make the mistake of stopping now."[15] When Blaine traveled to New York City days before the Albany balloting, Garfield complained but did nothing to stop him. Blaine had told friends openly that "everything possible or impossible must be done to beat those fellows at Albany," and the president didn't disagree.[16] Doubtless he knew Blaine's plan to convince Chauncey Depew, the Republican Half-Breed moderate, to enter the race. Depew had now finally warmed to the idea actually of becoming a United States Senator, and Garfield didn't seem to mind Blaine's egging him on.[17]

As summer blossomed, Garfield got himself out on the water. He took the younger children on a steamer from the Washington Navy Yard down to Mount Vernon one day, then the next week they rode another Navy ship, the *Dispatch*, all the way to Fortress Monroe at the mouth of the Chesapeake Bay where it meets the Atlantic Ocean. Garfield had loved the water ever since working canal boats as a teenager. When he and Lucretia had visited Europe in the late 1860s, the long steamer passages on the high seas had thrilled him. Now, as president at Fortress Monroe, three war-ships, including the German ship *Nymphe*, saluted him with manned yard-arms and twenty-one blazing guns.[18]

On June 11, John Phillip Sousa led the Marine Band in its first concert of the summer on the White House lawn. That day, Garfield and his oldest son Harry together carried Lucretia downstairs to the dining room—the first time she'd eaten there in 36 days. The next day, she braved the muggy Washington air to ride outside in a carriage, and each day she rode a bit longer, enjoying the sun and the open city streets. Soon she'd be able to travel.

Garfield still disliked the bickering over patronage that dominated his days. "My services ought to be worth more to the government than to be thus spent....[19] My day is frittered away by the personal seeking of people, when it ought to be given to the great problems which concern the whole country."[20] His first three months as president had been marked with pain, sickness, and strife. He and Lucretia itched to get out of Washington—she to recuperate, he to unwind. And for people who enjoyed the ocean, no other resort in America held more appeal in the 1880s than Long Branch, New Jersey.

* * * * *

Charles Guiteau didn't own a gun. "I am no expert on firearms at all, and never had a pistol before in my life," he explained, even growing up in rural Illinois.[21] But he figured he'd need one to remove the president.

He talked a relative into lending him $15 and went to John O'Meara's gun shop on the corner of 15th and F Streets in Washington. Two pistols in the display counter caught his eye: One, a snub-nose five-shooter with an ivory handle, cost $10; a similar model with a wood handle cost only $9. He couldn't decide, so he left. Two days later, he came back, this time leaning toward the more expensive model. After all, he thought, this gun might end up in a museum at the Patent Office or the Smithsonian—the fancier handle was well worth it. When Guiteau hesitated, the storeowner offered him the pistol for $9. Guiteau agreed; he bought it along with a little penknife for fifty cents and several boxes of cartridges, the total bill coming to $10. The gun was a .44 caliber 5-shooter English Bulldog. "I looked at it as if it was going to bite me," he later said. The storeowner showed Guiteau how to load the cartridges into the pistol and suggested he go outside Washington city limits to try shooting.

That evening at dusk, Guiteau walked down Seventeenth Street to where it ended at the muddy banks of the Potomac. Finding an isolated spot, he loaded the pistol and fired off two loads of cartridges, first one, then the other, ten bullets altogether. He aimed at a sapling tree or just the water—"just to get used to the outward act of handling the weapon."[22] He became comfortable with it: the gun's jolt, its warm feel after shooting, the acrid smell of gunpowder. It fit easily in his coat pocket. A few nights later he came back to the same spot by the river and shot off two more loads of cartridges. Soon, he started carrying the pistol often on his vigils.

Having already visited the White House dozens of times during his job hunt, Guiteau now studied it. He tracked the president's movements—through newspapers and from his bench in Lafayette Park across the north lawn that gave him a clear view of the front and side White House doors. He could see the people and carriages coming and going. He decided against trying to remove Garfield in the White House building itself; there'd be too many employees around and someone might stop him. Instead, he found a better idea.

One June Sunday morning, he followed Garfield to the small wood-frame Disciple Church where Garfield worshipped. He'd been there before to watch the president; this time, he walked in and stood at the rear door, his revolver in his pocket, and noted in his mind the exact spot where the president sat—in a pew near an open window with his family at his side. He listened impatiently to the pastor's sermon, at one point shouting "What think Ye of Christ?" He surprised even himself by his loud outburst; heads turned in the room, even the president's. (Garfield, in his diary that day, mentioned him as "a dull young man, with a loud voice, trying to pound some noise into the question."[23])

Guiteau seemed pleased with his choice; the church would be perfect. What better place to "remove" a man than "at his devotions?" he figured.[24] In fact, Guiteau saw the hand of God in all parts of his mission: "The President's nomination was an act of God; his election was an act of God; his removal is an act of God. These three specific acts of the Diety may give the clergy a text."[25] He spent several days editing a copy of his manuscript *The Truth, A Companion to the Bible*—knowing it would be a top seller after he'd removed the president.

After the church service had ended and the congregation had dispersed, Guiteau walked around to the side of the building to inspect the window by the president's pew. "I thought to myself, 'That would be a good chance to get him.' I intended to shoot him through the back of the head and let the ball pass through the ceiling, in order that no one else should be injured.... I made up my mind that the next Sunday I would certainly shoot him if he was in church."[26]

For several days, Guiteau felt satisfied with his plan. "I never mentioned the conception to a living soul," he said, but he continued going to Riggs House or the nearby Arlington House each day to check the newspapers.[27] Here, luckily, he discovered a change. Garfield would not be attending church the next Sunday, after all. Instead, he and his wife—still recuperating from her illness—planned to leave the City on a trip to Long Branch, New Jersey, by the ocean.

Guiteau quickly modified his own plan. On Saturday morning, when the president was scheduled to leave town, Guiteau waited for him at Washington's Baltimore and Potomac railroad station on Sixth Street. "I went to the depot all prepared to remove him and had the revolver with me. I had all my papers nicely prepared." He arrived early, at 9 am, and sat in a quiet corner. At 9:25 am, he watched Garfield and Lucretia climb down from the White House carriage onto the sidewalk and followed them through the waiting rooms to the train platform. But then he softened. "Mrs. Garfield got out and they walked through the ladies' room, and the presence of Mrs. Garfield deterred me from firing on him," he said later. She "looked so thin and she clung so tenderly to the President's arm that I did not have the heart to fire upon him."[28]

Guiteau waited a few minutes, then he left. He walked back to Lafayette Park and sat there on his bench for an hour or two. Then he walked across the street to the Treasury Department library to read the day's newspapers.

His lingering humanity, his hesitation, had kept him from doing God's work. After all he'd seen and been through, he still seemed to lack a final spark, a final confirmation. Soon, the newspapers themselves would remove any doubt.

◉ ◉ ◉ ◉ ◉

It took Ulysses Grant two months to win Mexican government permission to build his new Mexican Southern Railroad, intended to link Oaxaca province in the south to the United States in the north across the Rio Grande River. Traveling the country, Grant enjoyed the usual banquets and fiestas, though the "butcher" of Cold Harbor surprised his hosts by refusing to witness the gory Mexican bullfights.[29] But all those weeks in Mexico couldn't pull Grant's mind away from his irritation over politics back home in America. Telegrams, letters, and newspapers fed him daily reports. Roscoe Conkling's surprise resignation from the U.S. Senate had made headlines from Tokyo to Berlin to Buenos Aires, and reached Mexico City, too. Seeing his long-time friend Conkling humbled only heightened Grant's pique toward James Garfield's White House. The Old Soldier had no qualms about plunging into the Senate contest in Albany to help his friend.

Before even leaving Mexico City in late May, Grant started sending telegrams to Albany: "I hope that the Legislature will sustain our Senators," he told friends.[30] Reaching New Orleans on his journey home, he eagerly buttonholed a news reporter to declare that Conkling "has been shamefully treated, Sir, and for no cause whatsoever that I can discover."[31] Along the way, he received Garfield's response to his own earlier critical letters, and its preachy tone only irritated him more: "while I am incapable of discriminating against any Republican because he supported you," Garfield had written him, "I am sure you will agree with me that I ought not to permit any one to be proscribed because he did not support you." The letter had then laid out in detail the many friends of Grant whom Garfield had picked for top jobs: Robert Todd Lincoln for the cabinet and "ten other important positions to your friends in N.Y."[32]

Grant took the message plainly enough; Garfield would do as he pleased, despite Grant's advice. After eight years as president, five as General of the Army, and more as national icon, Ulysses Grant didn't take kindly to people treating his words as mere suggestions that could be lightly ignored.

Reaching New York City, Grant checked into the Fifth Avenue Hotel where he and Julia lived on "very liberal terms made for us by the proprietor," as Julia put it. A retired president with no pension had to worry about money, and, to Julia's mind, "General Grant was poor" in 1881, living on barely $6,000 a year from investments. The start-up Mexican railroad paid him a salary and gave him a Wall Street office, and that spring Philadelphians Anthony Drexel and George V. Childs happily had raised money from local tycoons to buy the Grants a new house in New York City. Even more promising was the new Wall Street investment firm that their son Buck had co-founded with a bright young financier named Ferdinand Ward.[33]

Within days of coming home, Grant summoned his New York political friends—Conkling, Arthur, and Platt—to join him in New York over dinner and cigars. They had a long talk and Conkling gladly filled him in on the political drama, solidly confirming all of Grant's worst suspicions about the White House. Grant told the roomful of friends (who dutifully told the newspaper writers in the hallway) that he felt "very bitter on the administration" and that it "would be a disgrace to the state if Conkling and Platt were not re-elected" in Albany.[34]

That done, he'd said his piece. With summer now in full blast, the Hero of Appomattox and Julia decided to rest. They left New York City and rode the steamboat across the harbor to Long Branch, New Jersey, where they'd spent every summer since the late 1860s. Over the years, the Grants had grown to love this pretty little seashore town, with its quaint oceanfront houses, quiet sand dunes, and long wooden pier where steamboats from New York docked every day. Just an hour's boat-ride from lower Manhattan, Long Branch had long been popular with New York's rich and famous who built huge waterfront mansions to throw lavish parties and dinners. The Grants too had purchased a "cottage" there—a three-story beach house with plenty of room for guests and grandchildren. Grant relaxed immediately at the ocean. He enjoyed the long summer days with walks in the surf and carriage rides through the dunes. A reporter who followed him there described how he "smokes and reads and receives his friends" while "attracting little attention." Seeing cartoons of himself in the illustrated newspapers, Grant "laughs at them in the utmost good nature."[35]

This year, though, something had gone terribly wrong. Since their own cottage needed repairs, he and Julia had chosen to stay instead in the cottage of their son Fred a few miles south in Elberon. Once they'd settled in, Grant learned to his surprise that the hotel across the street, the Hotel Elberon, was hosting a famous couple for the next two weeks, here to enjoy the crisp ocean air. The whole town talked about it, looking forward to meeting them: the new president and his wife, the Garfields.

Grant was mortified. What could he possibly say to the president? He and Julia had heard rumblings through friends. "[I]n private conversation, [Garfield] spoke of Grant very contemptuously, and said he would not speak to him under any circumstances," they told him.[36] If so, Grant certainly was not going to speak first. He had his honor.

⊚ ⊚ ⊚ ⊚ ⊚

Lucretia and James had left the White House together in mid-June for the ocean as soon as she'd felt strong enough to travel, happy as birds to be free and away from hot, muggy Washington. Doctor Boynton had insisted that the "bracing and invigorating salt air" would do wonders for her recovery.[37] Lucretia had clung to Garfield's arm the whole trip; the younger children— Mollie, Irvin, and Abram—had followed with Colonel Rockwell. Doctor Boynton and his wife Anna had come too to keep an eye on Lucretia, as had half the cabinet: Secretaries Windom, Hunt, and James and their wives.

Once settled in at the Hotel Elberon—a large complex of bungalows, dining rooms, and reception halls by the ocean—they quickly adapted to the slow-paced beach resort. By day the children splashed in the surf while the president and Lucretia enjoyed long carriage rides through the pleasant town of luxury cottages and hotels. He read aloud to her from books including Edmondo de Amicis' *Holland and its People*. By night, they dined with the cabinet families and played card games by the fire. One day during the week, the

New York Seventh Regiment held a formal military review and banquet for the president.

It came as a surprise at dinner Wednesday, then, when whispers spread through the Hotel dining room. General Grant had come to town and moved into a nearby house, they said; he'd come to the Hotel that very night while the Garfields were dining. Grant had seen them from a distance across the room, but he hadn't come over to talk nor even left a card. People noticed; the snub caused a stir. Newsmen though it worth noting: "As yet, they have not met," the *New York Times* reported.[38]

Garfield too had heard gossip about General Grant's bad feelings toward him, and his cabinet members now raised it directly. None of them—especially Garfield—should call on General Grant until Grant had called first on Garfield, they insisted. Garfield, after all, was the president. "It is now evident (what I had not supposed) that Grant had his heart fully set on the nomination in Chicago, and was deeply hurt at its failure," Garfield wrote in his journal that night. "He is talking wildly and very unjustly."[39] In fact, Grant's rudeness had bothered the president ever since he'd gotten Grant's letter on the Robertson appointment back in mid-May. The General "seems to have forgotten that he is only one citizen—and hence is unconsciously insolent," Garfield had written; he'd found the letter "remarkable."[40]

Soon, the icy standoff became the talk of the small ocean-side town. People speculated "what kind of scowl Grant would give Garfield and what kind of face Garfield would make at Grant." For three days, newsmen had a field day, mocking the two beach cottages on opposite sides of the road. They portrayed Grant as "spen[ding] the better part of his daylight time behind the window shutters of his house trying to see what President Garfield was up to across the way." When Garfield went for a carriage ride on Friday and happened to pass Grant on a narrow path through the sand dunes, Grant simply raised his hat and said nothing. Garfield rode on and Grant walked home as dozens of beachcombers looked on in amazement.[41] "This is his only courtesy to me since he came four days ago," Garfield grumbled. "It is evident that the third term passion had entered very deeply into his heart, and that he does not bear himself as becomes a citizen."[42]

On Saturday afternoon, the Elberon Hotel threw an informal reception for its famous guest, a chance for people to meet the president. Word got out and soon vacationers from all around Long Branch came to pay their respects; Garfield and Lucretia stood for over an hour shaking hands. Toward the very end, a "buzz of excitement" filled the parlor as the door opened and General Grant entered the room, hat in hand, cigar in mouth. He'd come alone; Julia waited outside in a carriage. A *New York Times* reporter described the scene: Grant "approached Mr. Garfield and extended his hand, which was heartily shaken by the President. A moment of whispered conversation ensued between them, when Gen. Grant stepped back and, walking out to the platform, entered his carriage" and left.[43]

Garfield later called it a "tardy recognition of the respect due to the office he once held."[44] Grant hadn't stayed more than two or three minutes and hadn't said a word beyond basic pleasantries; he'd performed the absolute minimum social obligation. No one could help but notice the insult.

◎ ◎ ◎ ◎ ◎

By late June, a full month after Roscoe Conkling and Tom Platt had resigned their U.S. Senate seats in Washington, the stalemate in Albany over their reelection had degenerated into bedlam. "Argument is displaced by billingsgate," a reporter lamented by late June.[45] All that month, day after day, the Albany legislators had marched up State Street to the State Capitol and cast one ballot for each of the two vacant U.S. Senate seats. Chauncey Depew had taken the lead from Platt among Republicans for Platt's old seat and Conkling had fallen behind William Wheeler, the former vice president under Rutherford Hayes, in balloting for the other.

By night, politicos in the Albany saloons dreamt up schemes to break the log-jam: one whispered deal had Stalwarts and Half-Breeds agreeing to split the pie, putting Chauncey Depew in one of the empty seats in exchange for Conkling in the other—leaving Tom Platt to the wolves. Another had the Half-Breeds teaming up with Democrats to elect Depew along with Democrat John Jacobs to the two seats. But nothing came of either idea.

Big-city newsmen soon got bored with small-town Albany and openly mocked its pretentious new $25 million State Capitol, decorated in "most gorgeous colors of the Oriental and Egyptian types" with gilded lamps and red Russian leather "costlier and handsomer than the national capitol" in Washington, D.C., designed, one said, "to daze the eye of a constituent and to disgust any admirer of art."[46]

Name-calling came next—"Senatorial criminals" on one side versus "corrupt gangs" on the other[47]—followed by charges of bribery. One State Senator, John H. Strahan, accused the White House of offering to make him a federal marshal in exchange for "turning against" Roscoe Conkling. Money allegedly changed hands, just like the old days of Boss Tweed. The members acted "shocked" and "astonished." A special committee opened an investigation and the district attorney convened a grand jury. Nothing came of any of the accusations.

Roscoe Conkling found himself increasingly the butt of jokes and insults. One night, he crossed paths with Half-Breed State Senator Ed Madden in a Delavan Hotel hallway. "I will not shake hands with you," Conkling scolded him. "If you were not a Senator I might say something more to you." Madden just laughed; he walked away and happily repeated the story to late-night cheers in the hotel bar.[48] The *New York Tribune* smugly suggested that Conkling should leave the Republicans and start a new party by himself: "He would hardly leave behind ... a single person with whom he is on speaking terms."[49] Conkling in turn began calling New York Governor Cornell "the lizard on the hill" for his weak-kneed support.[50]

As if his latest embarrassment weren't enough, one of Conkling's older scandals chose that moment to rise and haunt him. His old paramour Kate Chase Sprague had filed for divorce that summer from her drunken husband, sparking new rounds of gossip about their famous tryst. When Conkling's long-suffering wife Julia grumbled about it to friends in Utica, Conkling threw a fit. "Do you not think it better to abstain with acquaintances from discussing family affairs of a private nature?" he complained in a letter from Albany, warning her to hold her tongue.[51]

Julia couldn't believe her husband's nerve—of all people to complain about public griping! And over *his* affair! "I confess I feel dismayed that years of well tested loyalty fail to outweigh the stories of talebearers or mischief makers," she wrote back. "These 'family difficulties'—a phrase I copy from the newspapers, have not been of my making."[52]

Even Chet Arthur no longer felt safe from critics. Tongues wagged all over town about his role as Roscoe Conkling's lackey in Albany, covering bar tabs and arranging carriages as the Boss cut his deals[53]—"the Vice President of the United States, lobbying like any political henchman," as *Brooklyn Eagle* reporter William Hudson described it, the irony finally striking a public chord.[54] "If General Arthur does not desire four years of public contempt," the *New York Tribune* observed, he should stop before his "inexcusable indiscretion becomes a national scandal."[55]

Thomas Nast, the *Harpers' Weekly* cartoonist whose pictures had sunk

Boss Tweed himself a decade earlier, now turned his "Nast-y" pen on Chet Arthur. In a front-page cartoon for his widely-read journal, he drew Arthur dressed in a woman's apron, standing in a hallway outside Roscoe Conkling's hotel room, shining Conkling's shoes, as a woman figure representing New York tells him : "I did not engage you, Vice-President Arthur, to do this kind of work." "Out-'Shining' Everybody in Humiliation in Albany," the caption read.[56] Everyone saw it. It made even Arthur blanch.

● ● ● ● ●

Back in Washington, D.C., Charles Guiteau tracked Garfield's movements carefully while Garfield was away at the New Jersey seashore. He studied the newspaper articles and began cutting out the ones that struck his eye. He saved them in a neat package in his room. He started with the *New York Herald*'s mid-May expose "The Wriggler" on Garfield's deceits and broken promises during the election campaign. To this, he now added stories on the Albany election stalemate, particularly the vote-buying charge by State Senator John Strahan "which justifies [Garfield's] removal in disgrace from office," he underlined.[57] He clipped almost a dozen articles on this topic alone, including one with the headline: "How Long Will The Republican Party Last?[58]

Guiteau found even more shocking the reports from Long Branch about Garfield's icy standoff with General Grant. What gall, he thought. Where would an upstart like Garfield be without a giant like Grant? Where would the country be? Such ingratitude! "The President and Gen. Grant have not yet met, more than to give a passing salute in the road," one of the articles said. Another described the reception at the president's hotel where Grant, "trifled with by General Garfield and made the victim of his insincerity," had satisfied the "claims of etiquette ... and nothing more." Said another: "General Grant would not walk across the street to see President Garfield unless he were invited, and I doubt very much whether he would go then."[59] Guiteau saved all these stories. They settled any question in his mind.

On Thursday, Guiteau decided that he needed to have a more direct explanation of his reasons for removing the president—something to give the newspapers afterward. Sitting in his boardinghouse room, he took pencil in hand and scribbled the title "Address to the American People" on a sheet of paper. "I had no ill-will against the President," he began: "the President's removal was a political necessity, because he proved a traitor to the men who made him, and thereby imperiled the life of the Republic.... Ingratitude is the basest of crimes." The phrases came easily; he'd been practicing them in his mind and soon would repeat them over and again in letters and interviews. "It is not murder.... It will make my friend Arthur President, and save the Republic.... I leave my justification to God and the American people."[60]

On the Saturday before Garfield's return to Washington, Charles Guiteau took a very long walk: past the Capitol Building, past the surrounding Capitol Hill streets, all the way to the banks of the Anacostia River to the east. Here on the edge of town sat the District of Columbia Jail near the Congressional Cemetery and the District Poorhouse (just across Independence Avenue from the site of today's RFK stadium). Guiteau had seen jails before; he'd spent a month in New York City's infamous "Tombs" in 1874 and been locked up in Chicago as well. Now he walked up to the front door of Washington's "Bastille" and waved to a Deputy Warden. He wanted to look around, he said. Could he come inside? "I wanted to see what sort of quarters I would have to occupy," he'd explain later.[61]

The Deputy Warden gave an odd look to the small, dark-haired man with the cat-like walk and uneven eyes. Go away, he said. Come back on Monday. Charles Guiteau didn't bother. He'd seen enough. Just looking in through the doors and lobbies, he decided that, as jails went, this one was "excellent."[62]

⊙ ⊙ ⊙ ⊙ ⊙

Garfield left Lucretia and daughter Mollie in Long Branch on Monday, June 27, and headed back home to Washington, but already he'd set his mind on leaving again. Long Branch had given him and Lucretia a chance to heal. The next week, beginning July 2, they'd leave on their first official trip into the country as President and First Lady. Barring an emergency, they'd be gone for most of the summer.

Garfield had planned this trip for months. He, his older sons Harry and James, and three of his cabinet ministers and their wives all would leave together from Washington; Lucretia and Mollie would travel east from Long Branch and join them in Philadelphia. The younger boys, Irvin and Abram, meanwhile, would spend the month in Ohio with Lucretia's brother and sister-in-law, Joe and Lide Rudolph, at their farm. From Philadelphia, Garfield and his friends would ride up to New York City, then cruise up the Hudson River in Cyrus Field's steam yacht past the tree-covered Palisades to spend the night at Field's waterside mansion at Irvington-on-Hudson. Then they'd continue north to Massachusetts for the commencement ceremony at Williams College; Garfield especially looked forward to showing his sons his *alma mater* where he hoped they'd soon qualify to enter. Then they'd all whistle stop through New England, culminating with a weekend at James and Harriet Blaine's home in Augusta, Maine.

After returning to Washington, they'd be off again, this time to Ohio to spend August at the Mentor farm—far from the hot, steamy, putrid air of Washington, D.C.'s summer.

"I had a splendid sleep last night, more natural than any since my illness and was more sleepy at eight this morning than when I was in bed, and am feeling very well this morning," Lucretia wrote to him from Long Branch on Thursday, two weeks in fresh ocean air having returned some color to her cheeks and some bounce to her step. "For two nights I have taken a glass of port wine, and conclude that is one reason I have slept better."[63]

Garfield telegraphed back that day to finalize the travel plans: "Is there anything you wish [David] Swaim to bring except the children's clothes? Tell me specifically how you are."[64] He sent another telegram the next day: "How are you this morning? I hope there is no doubt that you will be well enough for the New England trip... Answer."[65]

All that week, Garfield plowed through work, trying to clean off his desk for the trip. He dictated piles of letters, decided dozens of appointments, conferred on the Star Route frauds, and closed out the government's fiscal year (which ended on June 30 until 1976 when it was changed to September 30). He spent hours closeted with his cabinet, and especially Blaine. With Blaine, he hashed over the political contest in Albany and Roscoe Conkling's apparent self-demise: "And this is the 'vindication' he appealed for," Garfield noted. "Suicide is the chief mode of political death after all."[66]

Blaine also bent the president's ear on world affairs. Blaine had just finished coming to terms with British Foreign Minister Sir E. Thornton in Philadelphia that month on settling the Fortune Bay fishery dispute, with Britain agreeing to pay Gloucester, Massachusetts fishermen $75,000 to compensate for Canadians trespassing on American waters. Blaine had also laid groundwork that month for his favorite pet project, a Pan American conference bringing all the Latin-American leaders together with the United States in a joint movement.

By then, Blaine had contracted yet another summer fever. "You cannot imagine how uncomfortable I am with the closed rooms," his wife Harriet had complained all that week. "Your Father has a fire, all the windows closed, and of course I nearly suffocate," she wrote her daughter.[67]

Mostly, though, with Blaine, Garfield spoke about the future. In the fall, he hoped to launch a new start to his presidency. He'd accepted an invitation to address the centennial celebration of the Battle of Yorktown, and he wanted to use the occasion to lay out his ideas on civil rights and the South[68]—stressing education and enforcement to guarantee freed blacks a real free vote and fair count while healing the wounds of war. He'd already appointed a handful of former slaves to prominent federal posts: Frederick Douglas as Washington, D.C. Recorder of Deeds, former-Senator Blanche Bruce as Registrar of the Treasury, and John M. Langston as Minister to Haiti.[69] Finally he'd be addressing real issues facing the country—not just petty wars over patronage.

Blaine fed the vision, talking of a "united America, reciprocity, arbitration, trade, glory, and the rest."[70] Now, having become president in truth as well as in name, having united his party, assembled a cabinet, established his strength in Congress, made his appointments, and having won the country's trust—now Garfield could begin actually to lead.

The chance to leave the moldy White House with its bad memories for a few weeks excited him, but not near as much as the prospect of coming back and serving as president. It had taken him a long time to reach this point.

⊚ ⊚ ⊚ ⊚ ⊚

If Roscoe Conkling thought that things couldn't get any worse for him in Albany, he learned otherwise on Thursday night, June 30. Around dinnertime that night, a Mrs. Baldwin walked into the Delavan House hotel, ambled past the politicos in the lobby and the bar, and checked herself in. The clerk gave her a room for the night: room 113. None of the regulars had seen her before: she was a stranger, notable only as a single woman traveling alone. About an hour later, though, a young boy working at the Hotel happened to notice long-faced, long-whiskered, former-senator Tom Platt—known by now simply as "Me, too"—walking down the same hallway. Platt quietly entered the same room as the strange lady, closed the door, and locked it.

The young boy dashed immediately over to Albert Daggett, a Brooklyn state legislator in the anti-Conkling crowd, and told him what he'd seen. Daggett gave the boy a few coins and rushed over to tell his Half-Breed friends. Within minutes, half a dozen of them had congregated in the hallway outside room 113. They waited, and when no one came out after a long while, someone got the idea to pull over a stepladder. One by one, each of the men quietly tiptoed up the ladder to peek through a small window over the door. It gave them a clear view of the bed. "It will suffice to say that the couple were scantily attired and were caught in *flagrante delictu*," one of them later told reporters.[71] Another called it simply a "compromising" sight.[72]

Word spread. Half-Breed legislators woke up their friends and pulled them out of bed to come running over, some still in nightshirts. Each waited his turn to climb the stepladder and see for himself. Over twenty witnesses had come before it was over.

Finally, the light in room 113 went out and the Half-Breed voyeurs decided to show themselves. One of them rapped loudly on the door. A woman's voice asked what they wanted and someone slid a note under the door, addressed to Platt: "We will give you ten minutes to get out of that room. Yours, etc., The Half-Breeds."

After a few minutes, the door opened a crack. Tom Platt stuck his head out into the darkened hallway and looked both ways. Seeing nobody, thinking the coast was clear (it was, after all, almost 2 am by now), he tiptoed out in his rumpled clothes and started walking quickly, keeping his eyes straight ahead. At the first doorway, though, he found a handful of Half-Breed legislators waiting, staring at him with smirks and leers. "How are you, Thomas," one said. Platt didn't stop; he kept walking. At each doorway along the hall, he found several more Half-Breeds, each giving him the eye. A few of them whistled and laughed.

Platt finally disappeared down the hall. Soon, lights went on in Roscoe Conkling's room, then in Chet Arthur's. Eavesdroppers in the hall outside could hear the screaming.

Tom Platt denied everything; had he seen anyone "peeping into his room over a transom he would have blown his head off," he told reporters the next morning.[73] But by then the story had swept through Albany and local newspapers had re-written their front pages. "A Disgusting Scandal," headlined the *Springfield Republican*; "The Shame of Albany" echoed the *New York Sun*. Platt's own backers called it "a blunder and an outrage."[74] "Sickening," "nauseating," were the more proper reactions. "Platt evidently and unfortunately is a very weak man," one said.[75] One source claimed to have seen "Mrs. Baldwin" leaving the Delavan House the next morning, describing her as a severe-looking woman with gold-rimmed spectacles—a "married woman" whose husband was "on his way here with a shotgun."[76]

By the time the legislature met that day in the State Capitol for its daily roll call, Tom Platt had become a national joke. When his name came up in the balloting, legislators greeted it with "shouts of laughter" and cries of "Oh, Oh."[77] On the vote itself, Chauncey Depew out-polled him 51 to 28; a few minutes later, William Wheeler out-polled Roscoe Conkling 43 to 32. Tom Platt had had it; he sent word asking the legislature to withdraw his name from the race.

Roscoe Conkling could not have been more angry with Platt, both for his stupidity in getting caught in bed with a strange women and for his cowardice in backing out of the contest. "For goodness sake, don't do it!" allies complained; Louis Payn refused at first even to deliver Platt's withdrawal message to the State senate chamber. Platt would later insist that he backed out only to help his more-senior colleague. "I became satisfied on the night of June 30 that by remaining in the field I was very much injuring Conkling's chances for re-election."[78]

That night, Friday, July 1, Roscoe Conkling and Chet Arthur had had their fill of Albany. They decided to take the overnight steamboat back down to New York City—avoiding the newspapermen and gawkers on the train. In the late-night hours out over the Hudson River, chugging their way south, hearing the sounds of the paddle-wheels splashing cool river water, sharing a whiskey and a good cigar, the two old friends could commiserate over the shambles that had become of them. A year ago, they'd stood together in Chicago at a pinnacle of success, on the verge of electing General Grant to a third term as president, Conkling supreme in the Senate and Arthur getting ready to join him as junior Senate colleague. They were the toast of the town, the power of the Party, and the center of attention.

Now, a year later, they'd lost it all, it seemed. Their enemies had stolen it. Conkling found himself begging for survival, grubbing for votes among hayseed upstate legislators who two months ago wouldn't be worth his time of day. His friends, probably even Arthur, urged him to save his dignity by dropping the Albany fight, but Conkling's stubborn streak had taken over as it usually did. And as long as Roscoe Conkling led, no matter how hopeless the cause, Chet Arthur would follow.

In those late night hours, Conkling and his friend the Vice President must have given vent to all their thoughts, and especially Conkling this night

his disgust with all the people who'd failed him: Tom Platt, the state legislators, the turn-coat U.S. Senate, the manipulative Blaine, and that no-good
liar in the White House James Abram Garfield.

⊚ ⊚ ⊚ ⊚ ⊚

On Friday, July 1, his last full day in the White House before his long summer trip, Garfield tried to clean off his desk, tying up as many loose ends and
as much unfinished business as he could. He appointed nearly 25 foreign ministers and consuls that day, removed a railroad commissioner and a register of
wills, and appointed Blaine's son Walker as 3rd Assistant Secretary of State.
He dictated letters and took his usual time for callers while finishing packing
and nailing down travel plans.

By late afternoon, he'd gotten through most of the work, but still had
several points to discuss with his Secretary of State. At about 7 pm, Garfield
got up from his desk and walked downstairs from his second-floor office. He
went past the doorman and headed alone outside through the White House's
front entrance. He felt the hot summer air against his face. Long shadows of
dusk had settled over Washington's streets by now as the president crossed the
north lawn and then ducked between the few horses and carriages darting
along Pennsylvania Avenue at that hour. He took his time to cover the familiar blocks around Lafayette Park, glancing over at the statue of grandiose
Andrew Jackson on his horse and at Saint John's Church at the corner. He'd
come this way dozens of times before, with friends and by himself, and knew
every landmark by heart. He didn't think twice about it, walking alone
through the park, as president of a free country in his own city. He didn't for
a minute think to look back over his shoulder and see if he were being followed.

⊚ ⊚ ⊚ ⊚ ⊚

Charles Guiteau, sitting on his bench in Lafayette Park with the best view of
the White House, watched the president as he left the building that night. He
followed Garfield's movements across the White House grounds toward the
Park. Guiteau had been watching Garfield all week. On Monday, he'd gone
to the railroad station when Garfield's train had brought him back from Long
Branch, New Jersey; he'd watched as the president, his young sons Abram
and Irvin, his cabinet Secretaries James and Hunt and their wives had all
passed through the lobby. He'd brought his pistol with him, but decided that

that "terrible hot sultry day"[79] wasn't the right time. The next morning, Guiteau had woken himself at half-past five, thinking to catch the president on his morning horse-ride, but Garfield hadn't gone out that day. On Thursday, sitting in Lafayette Park, he'd seen Garfield and his teenage son James enter a carriage and drive off toward Vermont Avenue. He'd followed on foot, then waited almost an hour to catch them coming back in the opposite direction, but they'd taken a different route.

By then, Guiteau had read the accounts in the newspapers about Garfield's planned trip to New England that weekend. He knew he'd have to act soon or perhaps lose any chance of removing him that summer. To make sure he didn't fail, Guiteau sharpened his own plans. Since mid-May, Guiteau had been staying at a boarding house on Fourteenth Street run by a Mrs. Grant, hiding behind a string of excuses to avoid paying rent. On Thursday that week, he'd snuck away without a word and had taken a room at the Riggs House—far more expensive than Mrs. Grant's, but he knew the bill wouldn't come for a few days at least, until after he'd removed the president.

Now, on Friday evening, he watched Garfield make his way to the far corner of Lafayette Park and cross onto H Street opposite Wormley's Hotel. Guiteau got up from his bench and followed. "I was several yards behind him," he recalled; it was a "splendid chance," he remembered, the president being alone. "I walked along on the opposite side of the street from him.... The pistol was in my hand and in my pocket."[80]

Reaching Fifteenth Street, though, he saw Garfield now enter a large brick townhouse with a woman sitting in the front bay window—Blaine's house. Guiteau stepped back into a shadow. He found a nearby alley, took out his revolver, wiped it, and put it back in his pocket. Then he went back to the street, walked up the sidewalk to the stoop by Wormley's Hotel, and sat down. Then he waited.

❋ ❋ ❋ ❋ ❋

Harriet Blaine remembered sitting in the bay window of her house on Fifteenth Street that night trying to catch the cool evening breeze and seeing the president approaching on the sidewalk, dressed sharply in a gray summer suit with a pink flower in his coat. What a "very handsome & happy looking man" he was that night, she remembered thinking. She got up and opened the door for him: "a President ought never to be kept waiting," she later explained. Garfield sat down with her for a few minutes and they talked about

travel plans. Harriet recalled his face "beaming with anticipation of the enjoyment of freedom away from the White House."[81] She asked him to stay
for dinner but Garfield declined; he'd promised one of the children to attend
a "little French play" that they were appearing in that night.

A minute later, Blaine himself came bounding down the staircase, bub-
bling with energy, grabbing the president's arm to tell him the latest gossip.
Harriet remembered watching through the bay window as the two men in
matching gray summer suits walked together back out onto Fifteenth Street,
the "shades of evening" separating puddles of light from gas lamps along the
sidewalk. Weeks later, as the truth came out, she'd feel chills leanring that a
strange man in an invisible perch across the street was watching her at that
very moment, watching the window where she sat, his hand cradling a pistol
as the president and her husband walked into his sights.

⊚ ⊚ ⊚ ⊚ ⊚

Charles Guiteau, having waited nearly half an hour, now watched Garfield
leave the brick townhouse side-by-side with James G. Blaine—two very familiar faces to him. Guiteau followed them both, walking on the opposite
sidewalk so they wouldn't notice him. He took his time to study the two men,
noticing how Blaine seemed to lead the president, walking on his left side, his
arm hooked around Garfield's. They talked "in the most delightful and cozy
fellowship possible," Guiteau recalled, "just as hilarious as two young school-
girls; and they had their heads together just like that ... and Blaine was striking his hand just like that ... and Garfield listening very intently... laughing
and joking." The easy friendship seemed foreign to the dark-haired little man
with the pistol; to Guiteau it only confirmed what he'd read in the newspapers, "that Mr. Garfield had sold himself body and soul to Blaine, and that
Blaine was using Garfield to destroy the Stalwart element of this nation."
This was his "eye confirmation" of the damning truth, that "Blaine is a bold,
wicked, vindictive man."[82]

Back along H Street, around Lafayette Park, and across Pennsylvania Avenue, he followed as Blaine and the president walked together. Guiteau never
came closer. He stayed hidden in the shadows until the two men had crossed
the north lawn and disappeared back within the large front door of the White
House.

Guiteau then knew he'd have only one more chance.

After sitting on his bench for another hour or so, he left the park and walked upstairs to his room at Riggs House, the most spacious he'd had since coming to Washington. He thought about final preparations he'd need for the next morning. Sitting alone in the night in his silent room, he took pen to paper and wrote another explanation of his reasons for removing the president, another paper to give the newspapers. This time, his words seemed to flow with unusual grace—like a man trying to convince himself of a final truth:

"To the White House:

"The President's tragic death was a sad necessity, but it will unite the Republican Party and save the Republic. Life is a fleeting dream, and it matters little where one goes. A human life is of small value. During the war thousands of brave boys went down without a tear. I presume the President is a Christian, and that he will be happier in Paradise than here.

"It will be no worse for Mrs. Garfield, dear soul, to part with her husband this way than by natural death. He is liable to go at any time anyway.

"I had no ill will towards the President. His death was a political necessity. I am a lawyer, a theologian, a politician. I am a Stalwart of the Stalwarts. I was with General Grant and the rest of our men in New York during the canvass. I have some papers for the press, which I shall leave with Byron Andrews [Washington correspondence of the Chicago Inter-Ocean] and his co-journalists at 1440 N.Y. Ave., where all the reporters can see them.

"I am going to jail. CHARLES GUITEAU"[83]

He finished the letter, sealed it in an envelope, and placed it in his suit pocket where the police could find it easily.

Then it occurred to Guiteau that perhaps not everyone would accept his reasons, especially in the instant panic right after he'd taken his action. An ugly mob might gather, or the police might not understand him. Guiteau wrote another letter that night, this one addressed to General William Tecumseh Sherman, General of the Army:

"To Gen. Sherman:

"I have just shot the President. I shot him several times as I wished him to go as easily as possible. His death was a political necessity. I am a lawyer,

a theologian, and a politician. I was with Gen. Grant and the rest of our men in New York during the canvass. I am going to jail. Please order out your troops and take possession of the jail at once.

"*Very respectfully, CHARLES GUITEAU.*"[84]

This letter too he placed in an envelope, and put the envelope in his coat. Then he washed himself with a towel and went to bed.

❂ ❂ ❂ ❂ ❂

Garfield woke up early the Saturday morning of his New England trip. Getting out of bed, he went to the children's room where he found his young sons Abram and Irvin already up and making a ruckus, jumping on their beds. "These boys think they can do great things," Garfield said laughing. Then he took a breath, balanced himself, and did his own handstand on the floor—amazing a servant with his agility at 210 pounds. Then Garfield started tossing the boys in the air while singing one of his favorites songs from Gilbert and Sullivan's *Pinafore*: "I mixed these babies up."[85]

When they all got done giggling and playing, Garfield went to get dressed. He'd asked Blaine to take him to the train station that morning so they'd have one more chance to talk, and Blaine had come to the White House with the State Department's small, two-seat carriage at a few minutes past 9 am—giving Garfield plenty of time to catch the 9:30 am train. ("Don't have breakfast till I get back," Blaine had told his wife Harriet before heading out.[86]) He came inside as Garfield was making his final good-byes before leaving the building.

The White House clerks and servants hoped to enjoy their own vacations that week while the president was away; many came by to shake his hand and wish him well. Garfield made a point to stop in on Joe Stanley Brown, his personal secretary who'd just returned from London, England, on his first trip overseas. "Both [Garfield and Blaine] were at their very best, with new gray spring suits" that morning, Stanley Brown remembered. They looked "particularly debonair." Garfield placed his hand on his young aide's shoulder: "Good-bye, my boy, you have had your outing and now I am going to have mine. Keep watch on things and use the telegraph as freely as you deem necessary."[87]

The Baltimore and Potomac Depot, one of two railroad stations serving

Washington, D.C., stood on 6th and B Streets,* about half-way between the White House and Capitol Hill, its tracks cutting across the wooded Washington mall on their way out of town. Garfield and Blaine chattered all along the way as Blaine drove the small carriage for the brief ride. They probably had a good laugh about Tom Platt's latest indignity in Albany; maybe they saw the headline in that morning's *Philadelphia Inquirer*: "Little 'Me Too' Drops Out, Unable to Wag Any Longer."[88] Otherwise, the newspapers that morning bespoke a peaceful summer Saturday—Yale beating Harvard at the rowing regatta off New London, social notes from the ocean resorts, a railroad accident here and there.

The Baltimore and Potomac Depot, just built in 1873, already had a decrepit look from its belching steam engines and dingy redbrick walls. Blaine parked his carriage on the B Street side. Before getting up from their seats, he and the president spoke for a few minutes more, Garfield's hand on his shoulder. "I will escort you to the car,"[89] Blaine finally said as Garfield turned to leave. The president's young sons Abram and Irvin had already reached the station in an earlier carriage with Colonel Rockwell for their separate train trip to Ohio; his cabinet members and older sons, who'd be joining Garfield and Lucretia for the trip north, already were waiting for him at the platform. Garfield turned to a policeman and asked: "How much time have we, officer?"

The officer, Patrick Kearney, said: "About 10 minutes, Sir."[90]

◎ ◎ ◎ ◎ ◎

Charles Guiteau had awoken at 4 am that morning, his mind "perfectly clear," he recalled.[91] He'd taken an early breakfast at the Riggs House dining room and charged the meal to his room. "I ate well and felt well in body and mind." Afterward, he stepped outside and sat in Lafayette Park, then walked down Seventeenth Street to his familiar spot along the Potomac River. He practiced firing a round of cartridges from his pistol, then walked over to the railroad station.

Still early with plenty of time before the president's train was scheduled to leave, Guiteau got his boots blacked, then found a hack driver whom he promised to pay an extra $2 (which he didn't have) to wait and take him to the Congressional Cemetery. He walked over to a newsstand and asked the

---

* The site of the current National Museum of Art on the Washington Mall, "B Street" being the 19th Century name for today's Constitution Avenue. It was replaced by today's Union Station in 1907.

proprietor to hold a package for him for a few minutes—a thick envelope addressed to a local reporter with the *New York Herald*. It also included a separate letter addressed to *Chicago Inter Ocean* newsman Byron Andrews.

These things done, Guiteau spent a few private minutes in the men's
washroom, and then found himself a quiet corner in the ladies waiting room
near the B Street entrance.

◉ ◉ ◉ ◉

Garfield finally climbed down from the carriage and stopped to greet a few
well wishers on the sidewalk. Then he and Blaine entered the red brick railroad station together walking side-by-side—not arm-in-arm as Blaine normally preferred. Once inside, they walked briskly between rows of chairs. The
depot didn't seem terribly busy this Saturday morning, though the nearby
ticket office overflowed with people. Garfield turned at one point as if seeing
a familiar face, but Blaine didn't notice. They were just a few steps from the
doorway to the main waiting room and the train platforms beyond.

Then Garfield heard a loud, sharp clap. Some witnesses later described it
as sounding like a firecracker, but Garfield's military ear recognized it instantly
as gunfire. He didn't see it, the small man standing just six feet behind him,
but he felt a sting in his right side. He turned, flinching. He "straightened up
and threw his head back and seemed to be perfectly bewildered," a witness remembered.[92]

"'My God! What is this?"[93] Garfield said.

Then he heard another shot. He felt it hitting him square in the back on
the right side, flattening his lungs, jolting him forward. He reeled sharply to
the right and fell over, hitting the floor hard. According to a witness:[94] "His
lower limbs gave away, broke from under him. He didn't fall lengthwise."

Blaine, standing at his side, likewise heard "a very loud report of a pistol
discharge, followed in a very brief interval by a second shot." Blaine at first
thought the gunfire had come from someplace else. "I touched the President
as though to hurry him on" in case there might be "stray bullets flying
around."[95] Then he turned and saw the president sinking at his side. He heard
screams, sounds of people running. An instant later, he saw a man holding a
pistol, a small man with dark hair and a distinctive walk. He was running
away.

Blaine followed a few steps. He recognized the man—the odd little job-
seeker from the State Department. For an instant, he started to chase him, but

then saw the president, his friend Garfield, lying on the floor, bleeding, vomiting, barely conscious. He turned to protect him.

⊚ ⊚ ⊚ ⊚ ⊚

As soon as Guiteau had shot the president twice with his pistol and watched him fall, he concentrated on walking the few steps from the ladies waiting room through the main hall of the railroad station toward the exit on Sixth Street. The pistol still hung in his hand at his side. He heard the screams and shouts, the voices of men following him. "There he goes!" "There he goes!" He quickened his step. He reached the doorway and stepped out onto the sidewalk, the daylight blinding him for an instant. But then he couldn't move any farther. A large man, a police officer in a blue uniform, blocked his path. The officer had been coming toward the door. Then Guiteau heard voices from behind him: "Stop him." "He shot the president." Guiteau felt the officer grab his arm and start pulling him back into the station.

Guiteau saw the angry, agitated faces crowding around them. "I have sent a letter to General Sherman," he told the officer. "Keep quiet, my friend. I want to go to jail."[96] The officer didn't seem to care. He led Guiteau back into the station, through the main hall, to the ladies waiting room where the president lay bleeding on the floor. Another officer joined them; together, they led Guiteau back outside. By now, the street crowd had grown. "Lynch," "lynch," came the shouts. The officers, big burly men, paid no attention to the crowd. One man grabbed Guiteau's wrist; another knocked his hat off. The officers quickly led him outside onto the sidewalk and away from the crowd toward Pennsylvania Avenue, gripping his arms tightly. As they guided him to the corner, Guiteau wanted to make sure there'd be no mistake. He turned to one of the officers and said: "I did it. I will go to jail for it. I am a Stalwart and Arthur will be President."[97]

⊚ ⊚ ⊚ ⊚ ⊚

Back inside the depot, Garfield lay on the floor in a pool of blood and vomit. Sarah White, a ladies room attendant who'd seen the shooting, had rushed over and now cradled his head in her lap, tears running down her face, blood staining her dress. Blaine stood over the president, shielding him from the crowd. Garfield's teenage sons Harry and James had heard the commotion and run over and now knelt at his side, James in tears; the president leaned over and whispered something in his son's ear. Robert Todd Lincoln, who like Blaine had come to see the president off this morning, stood off to the side, his mind racing back sixteen years to the awful night outside Ford's Theatre when he'd watched his own father die from an assassin's bullet.*

A doctor appeared; he knelt down on the floor next to Garfield and noted the president's cold, clammy skin, his shallow breathing, his weak, rapid pulse. The doctor immediately administered brandy and ammonia aromatic scents, placing a handkerchief under the president's nose. Garfield snapped to alertness and the Doctor asked where he felt the most pain. In his right leg and foot, the president answered. Two more doctors appeared and they decided to move Garfield to a more private place. They rounded up some men to pull a mattress from a Pullman railroad car and bring it over, then they lifted the president onto it and carried him upstairs. Here, in a private room, one of the doctors examined the wound; he stuck his finger far up into the hole in Garfield's back and probed it with his fingertip. Pain wrenched his body, but the president didn't howl or whimper, clenching his teeth instead.

He hadn't found the bullet in his back and didn't think the wound was serious, the doctor told him. He'd recover. "I thank you doctor," Garfield said, fighting to control his voice, "but I am a dead man."[98]

Other doctors appeared and examined him, but they couldn't do much other than watch and wait. Garfield asked someone to send a telegram to his wife Lucretia in Long Branch telling her what had happened and asking her to come. Then, after almost an hour, still conscious, he asked to be taken back to the White House.

---

* Robert Todd Lincoln would also happen to be with President William McKinley in 1901 on the day that he too was shot and killed by an assassin in Buffalo, New York. At a cabinet meeting that week, Garfield had happened to ask Lincoln to relate his father's dream the night before his 1865 shooting.

• PART V •

Calamity

* * * * *

*News that an assassin had shot President Garfield electrified
the nation. Telegraph wires flashed word across the country
and around the world. Within hours, newspaper Extra Editions
appeared on city street corners and at small-town railroad stops
from New York to Chicago and on to California; crowds gathered
at public buildings that posted the latest bulletins while riders on
horseback carried word from farm to farm across the plains.*

*People prayed for the president and his wife, hanging on every
medical report from Washington. They also saw the assassin's
statement: "I am a Stalwart and Arthur will be President." Shock
and curiosity gave way to anger: the strange man Guiteau may
have pulled the trigger—and he'd damn well hang for it—but few
doubted that politicians had put the idea in Guiteau's feeble mind.*

· 14 ·
BULLETINS

THE PRESIDENT'S BEEN SHOT! The President's been shot!

Morning fog rolling off the East River made it nearly impossible to see the South Street piers of New York City just a hundred yards away. Chester Alan Arthur, standing on the steamboat deck, strained to hear the man shouting from the end of the dock, his voice barely audible above sounds of sea birds, lapping waves, and harbor traffic. Arthur, like everyone else, barely understood a word. Garfield? Shot? Could that be right?

Arthur had stayed up late with Roscoe Conkling the night before on their overnight trip from Albany; now the two men kept to themselves. It took another hour until the fog lifted enough for their boat to reach shore. All the while, rumors swept the deck and staterooms. On the pier, someone handed Arthur a telegram that confirmed the shooting but contained little new information; he heard men talk wildly but few could answer even basic questions: Was the president alive? Had anyone been arrested? Was Arthur in danger?

Arthur and Conkling commandeered a carriage and told the driver to whip his horses hard through the teeming alleyways of lower Manhattan. Speeding through bumpy, narrow streets, they saw men and women gathered at corner shops and around newspapers and bulletin boards, their faces frozen in awed expressions, looking dumbfounded. An odd quiet hung over them. Boys hawking Extra Editions of the *Sun*, *Herald*, and *Tribune* did a brisk business. Should Garfield die that day, he would be President of the United States! As the reality sunk in, Arthur must have felt a pang of fear. This was something he'd never bargained for. Vice President was one thing—any fool could do that job. But president! He'd never pretended either to want the office or to be qualified for it. And this man Garfield: Hours ago, he'd hated him, vilified him. Now that someone had shot him, how was he supposed to act?

By the time they reached the Fifth Avenue Hotel at Madison Square Park, hundreds had gathered there to read the latest bulletins and share their dismay. The building became a magnet for newsmen, politicos, and New York's elite in times of crisis. By then, they'd heard more news. Telegraph bulletins from Washington now carried word of an assassin. Police had captured an odd-looking dark-haired man leaving the train station after firing at the president. He'd carried a gun, and they'd found letters in his pockets admitting the crime. They'd also reported words he'd said on being arrested: "I am a Stalwart and Arthur will be president."

Arthur noticed people staring at him with cold, hard faces. He'd always attracted looks from people before because of his six-foot, two-inch height and smartly tailored clothes; now the looks must have given him shivers. He followed Conkling into the lobby; the two tall, distinguished-looking men couldn't help but draw eyes from around the room. As they elbowed their way to the reception desk, they heard more talk: On Wall Street, share prices had tumbled that morning in chaotic trading. Then a hotel clerk pulled them both aside for a private word. There'd been "warnings" that "should Garfield die, Arthur, Conkling and [Tom Platt] should pay the penalty."[1]

Conkling, still freshly angry from the embarrassments in Albany that week, refused to talk with anyone. As soon as he signed the hotel register, he stormed out of the lobby and bounded up the stairs, ignoring reporters who tried to chase him. Arthur didn't follow, though. He felt compelled to stay behind. Didn't he have a responsibility as Vice President to say something? If he hid behind closed doors now, what wild rumors might people actually start to believe? Standing squarely in the hotel lobby, he allowed a handful of newspapermen to gather around him.

"What is the latest report?" he asked them. One reporter noted Arthur's trembling voice, how he was "evidently laboring under excitement, though endeavoring to maintain a cool demeanor," as he put it.[2]

"The latest dispatch says that [the doctor] does not think the wound will prove fatal," someone replied.

"I certainly trust so. It is a most shocking event." Arthur chose his words carefully, sensing that his reputation for years to come could hinge on an awkward phrase at this moment. He was "horrified" at the crime, he told them, and felt "extremely sorry" for Garfield. "Express to the President and those about him my great grief and sympathy, in which the whole American people will join."[3] The reporters scribbled it all down; the words would be wired across the country within the hour.

He'd said enough. Arthur then excused himself and now walked upstairs to join Roscoe Conkling in his private suite. There, over the next few hours, a stream of visitors came to see them—Tom Platt, Hamilton Fish, Senator John P. Jones of Nevada, and dozens of local politicos. They'd all heard the news. What should he do? Arthur asked them. Should he rush back to Washington in the crisis, or might that only fuel suspicions by making him look too eager to take over the White House? By now, several of them noted the ugly mood outside in the streets. To Tom Platt, who'd also reached New York City that morning, it reminded him of the angry hours before the 1863 draft riots.[4] Peoples' horror at the crime had turned to suspicion toward them—the Stalwarts. When Roscoe Conkling stepped out into the hallway at one point during the morning, a newsman cornered him and asked if he had any regrets about how he'd treated the president in recent months; Conkling "promptly shook his head in a decidedly negative manner and without uttering a word walked away," the reporter wrote.[5] News of Conkling's gesture and his silence were also telegraphed instantly across the country.

"Men go around with clenched teeth and white lips," a reporter wrote, describing the mood on the streets that morning, "if any Stalwart in New York should be seen rejoicing he would be immediately lynched."[6]

Arthur's friends urged caution. More assassins might be lurking. After all, he could be in danger. Arthur knew these men well enough to see through their polite veneers. Already he'd heard the wisecracks. "Chet Arthur President of the United States! Good God!"—that was the reaction even among Arthur's own circle of friends.[7] What had he gotten himself into?

After a few hours, Arthur finally left Conkling's hotel room, navigated a private exit from the building, and rode a carriage across town to his own brownstone on Lexington Avenue. He found piles of telegrams waiting for him there; his eye quickly caught the one from Washington, D.C., delivered hours ago, from James G. Blaine. Arthur had barely spoken a civil word with Blaine since the Robertson nomination had been announced months ago. He read it quickly: "The President of the United States was shot this morning by an assassin named Charles Guiteau." Charles who? Guiteau? Arthur met so many people in his work that it was hard to remember all the names.

"The surgeons in consultation regard his wounds as very serious though not necessarily fatal…. He had not lost consciousness for a minute."[8] Charles Guiteau. Arthur searched his memory. Later that day, he'd tell Senator Jones he'd never heard of the man, and Jones would repeat it to the newspapers.[9]

Arthur immediately sent a wire back to Blaine: "Your telegram with its deplorable narrative did not reach me promptly, owing to my absence. I am profoundly shocked at the dreadful news."[10] By then, he could hear voices of boys in the street selling newspaper Extra Editions, all carrying the quote from the man Guiteau for all his neighbors to see: "I am a Stalwart and Arthur will be President."

* * * * *

Lucretia Garfield had just finished packing and gotten daughter Mollie ready to leave the pretty ocean-side resort of Elberon, New Jersey, that morning when she heard the first reports. She saw people all around the Hotel running back and forth, talking in excited voices, repeating snippets of news or rumor. The president's been shot, they said. It couldn't be true. She was supposed to meet him in Philadelphia in a few hours. She tried to ignore it, but then a messenger came to her cabin door with a telegram from Washington, D.C. signed by their friend Colonel Rockwell: "The President wishes me to say to you from him that he has been seriously hurt—how seriously he cannot say. He is himself and hopes you will come to him soon. He sends his love to you."[11] It *was* true. She read the message, then read it again. "Seriously hurt." What did that mean? Was he suffering? Was he dying? Was he dead already?

Doctor Boynton, who'd spent the week with her in Elberon and now planned to travel back to Washington that day, came to Lucretia's room after hearing the news and found her in a panic, "almost frantic," he'd later say.[12] Lucretia had only just recently survived her own near-death illness leaving her still terribly frail and weak. How much shock could she absorb, he wondered. Boynton waited in the cabin with her, reading the telegrams that arrived every few minutes; he held back the most alarming stories—after all, half of them might not even be true.

Then a knock came at the door. Lucretia felt puzzled at first as she opened it and saw Ulysses Grant standing in front of her. He asked to come in; he'd come over from his cottage across the street, the first time in two weeks he'd taken the initiative. She showed him inside and he sat down with her. Whatever qualms Lucretia felt after all the weeks of tension between Grant and her husband and their political estrangement seemed to vanish in an instant; Grant's remarkably steady gaze and mild eyes made the old quarrels moot. He'd come at the first word of trouble; he wanted to show Lucretia a telegram he'd received from one of his own friends in Washington that morning: "The President's wounds are not mortal; shot in arm and hip."[13] Grant thought it would give her hope, he said. These kinds of wounds can heal. He'd seen it during the war.

Years later, Lucretia would remember Grant's "quiet firm words"[14] that day and their effect on her. She quickly understood how a generation of soldiers had trusted this man with their lives and followed him at moments of greatest peril. He stayed just a few minutes but seemed to give her strength he his simple presence; afterward, she picked herself up and made ready to leave.

Lucretia left Elberon on the local train at 12:40 pm with her daughter Mollie at her side. At Monmouth Junction, they transferred to a special train that the Pennsylvania Railroad had arranged to rush her home to Washington—an engine and a single Pullman car. They'd ordered the track cleared for her, and the engineer pushed the locomotive to full throttle, speeding it along at over 60 miles per hour as it belched clouds of black smoke into the skies over New Jersey and Maryland. Near Bowie, Maryland, about twenty miles south of Baltimore, though, the engineer suddenly felt a jolt and heard a sickening loud crack. The locomotive's wheels had been turning at 250 revolutions per minute; now, looking out his window, he saw that a steel engine rod had busted; a six-foot spike of jagged metal stuck outwards and had begun swinging out of control, tearing up track ties and crashing against the engine's own wheels. It made the train itself veer wildly side to side, its wheels barely holding the steel track. He yanked hard on the air brakes, jolting Lucretia and the others from their seats, throwing them forward. The train took two full miles to reach a stop; a derailment would have killed them.[15]

If the near-accident affected her at all, Lucretia didn't show it—only her impatience at now being stranded on an immobile train in rural Maryland, perhaps for hours, as her husband might lay dying another twenty miles up ahead in Washington, D.C.

❦ ❦ ❦ ❦ ❦

Harriet Blaine had just started breakfast that morning when the interruptions began. It was bad enough that her husband, who'd told her to wait until he'd gotten back from taking the president to the train station, was late. Then a loud knocking on the front door startled them. Her son Walker went to get it, and she could hear shouting from the street as he opened the door. Before he'd come back, the telephone machine—that useless object that almost never rang since virtually nobody else in Washington owned one—made a rare clanging sound. A maid answered it: "They have telephoned over to you [from the White House], Mrs. Blaine, that the President is assassinated."[16] Assassinated? Harried jumped up. Her son Emmon flew out the door. What about her husband? Hadn't he been with the president? Had he been assassinated too?

Harriet went to the front door; looking outside, she saw "everybody on the street, and wild." She grabbed her bonnet and walked down the Fifteenth Street sidewalk until she found Mrs. Sherman, the General's wife, who'd gotten a carriage; together they rode toward the White House. Word of the shooting had sent thousands of people streaming into the street under a cloudless blue sky and glaring sun; the crowd grew most dense around the hotels and newspapers offices at Fourteenth and F Streets. Turning onto Pennsylvania Avenue, Harriet and Mrs. Sherman saw the wedge of horse-mounted police officers clearing a path through traffic for a black horse-drawn ambulance. Inside, people said, it carried the president; the crowd gave way with a respectful, almost eerie silence. Harriet and Mrs. Sherman followed the ambulance up to the White House's south door. Here, Harriet learned that her own husband was safe; they climbed down and watched as a dozen men carried Garfield carefully from the ambulance into the Mansion and up the stairs. Harriet followed them inside.

The men reached the second floor and laid Garfield in a bed in a far corner room. Harriet followed and there she saw the president noticing her and waving her forward. She walked up and sat beside him; she saw Garfield lying there before her, crippled, bloody, and breathless. She felt the president's hand on her shoulder; he pulled her down and kissed her on the cheek. "Whatever happens I want you to promise to look out for Crete," the president told her in a parched voice, looking directly at her face. Harriet nodded. "Don't leave me until Crete comes."[17]

Then the doctors pushed her away. Harriet stepped back out into the hallway, took off her bonnet, and sat down in a chair, steeling herself for whatever might happen in that room the rest of the day.

⊙ ⊙ ⊙ ⊙ ⊙

Joe Stanley Brown hadn't moved from his second floor White House office that morning since he'd seen the president and Mr. Blaine leave for the train station an hour earlier, busying himself with paperwork. Now one of the White House doormen came bursting into his room. "Mr. Secretary, the President's has been shot."

"Nonsense," he said: "it's a silly rumor."

Then, a few minutes later, a messenger rushed in waving a telegram. "My God, Mr. Secretary, it is true."[18]

Stanley Brown got up from his desk and walked over to look out his window onto the south lawn; he saw crowds gathering around the building. Down the hall, he heard loud, frantic voices of cabinet members and wives beginning to arrive. The president had been shot and the doctors were bringing him back here, they told him. He needed to get a room ready for them.

Stanley Brown's mind whirled. What was happening? With Garfield and Blaine both gone, his own 23-year-old shoulders carried prime responsibility for the White House itself. As personal secretary to the president, he had to make arrangements—just as he'd organized the president's office work and guarded him from pushy callers. But arrangements for what? He quickly gathered the head doormen and clerks into his office and gave them instructions. They must close the White House grounds, close the gates and keep any strangers out, at least until police officers or soldiers came. He sent messengers to summon any of the cabinet members who hadn't already heard the news. Then he telegraphed the War Department and learned that General William Tecumseh Sherman, commander of the Army, had already taken matters in hand. Sherman had gone to the train station immediately on hearing the news, conferred there with Blaine and War Secretary Robert Todd Lincoln, and ordered troops marching toward the White House, one company each of cavalry and infantry to surround the building in case the shooting had been part of a conspiracy or coordinated attack. Sherman had also sent infantry troops marching toward the D.C. Jail where police would take the assassin; they'd guard against either an escape or a lynching. He'd asked the District of Columbia militia too to go on ready alert.

Robert Todd Lincoln, for his part, had sent wires to a dozen leading Washington physicians telling them to come immediately to the White House to attend the president.

Stanley Brown then left his office and went down to the south door. A few minutes later, he recalled, "an express wagon slowly drove up to the rear door of the mansion." Inside, it carried the crippled president, "the splendid man, abounding with health and the joy of living who had only that morning, in spite of his two hundred pounds, turned a handspring in competition with his sons."[19]

◎ ◎ ◎ ◎ ◎

Garfield remained awake and aware the entire time as men carried him outside from the railroad station to the ambulance and during the long bumpy ride up Pennsylvania Avenue to the White House. Doctors had given him a half-ounce of brandy to steady his nerves for the trip, along with small sips of water. He still felt pain in his feet and legs, apparently from the bullet wound in his back.

On reaching the White House, Garfield lay still on a mattress as a dozen large men now lifted him again and carried him inside; he wondered if he'd ever leave this dreary building again. On the second floor, he saw the hallway and nearby offices overflowing with people; doctors had taken over a bedroom in the southeast corner as a makeshift ward. Seeing his son James looking upset, he leaned over to reassure him with a nautical image: "the upper story was unhurt; it was the hull" that was damaged.[20] Garfield seemed to recognize that the eyes of the world were on him at that moment. Whatever trials awaited him, however much pain and fear he'd have to swallow, he was determined to maintain his public dignity: not yell, nor whimper, nor complain. He was President of the United States, symbol of the nation. He couldn't afford to show any weakness, especially now.

They set Garfield down on a bed, laying him on his wounded side. After moving everyone else outside, the doctors closed the door and posted an armed guard there. Garfield found himself surrounded by almost a dozen doctors; surgeon Willard Bliss, a boyhood friend from Ohio—his family's farm had been just two miles up the road from Garfield's—was the only long-time familiar face. The doctors noticed Garfield's twitching feet and legs, signs of pain, his feeble pulse and shallow breath. They gave him stimulants again; when he perked up, they each began probing the wound, sticking either a finger or a metal rod as deeply as possible into his back and manipulating it to find a channel. None of the doctors had washed their hands first.* The

---

* "Anti-septic" medicine—washing hands and using sterilized tools—had recently been developed by Louis Pasteur in France and gained limited but growing acceptance in Europe and America, but was still a relatively new idea.

poking and twisting made the wound hemorrhage; blood poured out and covered the bed sheets. Garfield writhed in pain and they gave him morphine through a hypodermic injection. He vomited, and then vomited over and over, almost every half hour. They gave him limewater and milk for the nausea, but it wouldn't stop.

Where was Lucretia, he asked? Hadn't they sent for her? Hadn't she sent word? He felt desperately thirsty and asked for more water, but the doctors said that drinking too fast could injure him. Garfield had watched men die on Civil War battlefields and apparently thought his own time was at hand. He asked Willard Bliss to tell him frankly his condition. "Mr. President, your injury is formidable," Bliss told him, and gave his hopes for recovery at "one chance in a hundred."

"Well, Doctor, we'll take that chance."[21]

After the examination, Blaine came in at one point to relieve the nurses. When Garfield looked up and saw him, he pulled him close, wondering perhaps if he'd ever see him again. "You know how well I love you," he told Blaine, even though "[p]eople … have sought to prejudice me against you."[22] Blaine listened silently, holding back his emotions. Then he asked Blaine who was the man who'd shot him at the train station. Blaine told him—Charles Guiteau, the office seeker. Garfield looked puzzled. "Why did that man shoot me? I have done him no wrong. What could he have wanted to shoot me for?"[23] Blaine told Garfield he assumed Guiteau had been disappointed over not getting an office. Garfield said nothing; he never raised the issue again.[24]

❋ ❋ ❋ ❋ ❋

After the shooting, Blaine had stayed with Garfield as doctors examined the president at the railroad depot, then he'd ridden back separately, stopping along the way at his own house long enough to send two telegrams: one to the Vice President in New York City, the other to James Russell Lowell, the American Minister in London, to alert world capitals of the disaster: "The surgeons, on consultation, regard his wounds as very serious, though not necessarily fatal," he wrote. "His vigorous health gives strong hopes of his recovery. He has not lost consciousness for a moment. Inform our ministers in Europe."[25]

By the time he reached the White House and got past the guards and soldiers, the doctors had placed strict orders—no one could see the president except themselves, his nurses, and his wife, and there must be absolute silence around his room. For Blaine to see Garfield, he had to take a turn at nursing. Now, after visiting with his friend for a few minutes, he felt devastated. "My God, it is terrible," he told a handful of reporters who surrounded him in the hallway—Joe Stanley Brown had issued passes to a handful of familiar newsmen to make sure accurate information reached the public. Asked if Guiteau were a "tool of any conspirators," Blaine just shook his head. He didn't think so, he said.[26]

Afterward, Blaine walked down the hall to the telegraph room and sent a second wire to Chester Arthur in New York—never mind that Arthur still hadn't responded to the first. Blaine may have disliked the Vice President and shuddered at the thought of Arthur's ever taking Garfield's place, but he said nothing of it; the Vice President had a right to know and he, Blaine, had a duty to keep him informed. "At this hour (1 p.m.) the President's symptoms are not regarded as unfavorable, but no definite assurance can be given … There are strong grounds for hope and at the same the gravest anxiety as to the final result."[27] Then Blaine met with the Cabinet; most of the secretaries had come to the White House to follow the news and waited in an upstairs room. As Premier, Blaine now had the duty to oversee these meetings. Somehow the government must function until Garfield recovered; fortunately, not very much happened in Washington during the summer.

By mid-afternoon, Blaine saw the doctors' reports turning markedly negative. At 2:45 pm, they issued their third official bulletin in three hours: "Internal hemorrhage is taking place, and the gravest fears are felt as to the result."[28] Robert Todd Lincoln sent a mid-afternoon wire to Senator John Logan in Chicago with the same message: "The president's condition is alarming. There is internal hemorrhage undoubtedly. The surgeons are evidently anxious and guarded in their expressions."[29]

❀ ❀ ❀ ❀ ❀

Word went quickly out around the country and people gasped at the news. Telegraph wires followed railroad tracks across America, to every frontier stop all the way to California. News offices in New York and Washington connected, directly or indirectly, with machines in large hotels, government offices, newspaper bureaus, railroad depots, and businesses in every major city and town. Newspapers used vast steam presses to crank out Extra Editions within the hour, delivered by scores of young boys for a penny or two. Neighbors told neighbors, shouted the news in saloons, in factories, and on street-corners, and carried it by horseback to remote farms. The president had been shot! An assassin had been caught—a Stalwart who wanted to make Arthur president.

In cites from Boston to Baltimore to New York and Chicago, crowds mobbed the downtown streets; police stood guard, fearing anger might boil over into riots. Church bells rang and flags flew at half-staff. Emotions rose, fell, and rose again with each new medical report from Washington. People made obvious comparisons to Abraham Lincoln's murder just sixteen years ago—a fresh memory to most—but in some ways this was worse: Lincoln had been murdered in wartime, martyred over great issues of ending slavery and saving the Union; Garfield had been shot in a petty squabble over political patronage. What had become of our nation? "It is a sad state of affairs when the President of this country can be shot down like a dog in the street," someone said.[30]

In Ohio, Garfield's home state, feelings ran especially bitter. Businesses closed in Cincinnati sending hundreds of workmen into the streets: "Vice-president Arthur and his master, the Primate [Conkling, are] objects of deep suspicion," an Ohio newsman reported. "Scores of men were heard to say that they would willingly, if called upon, shoulder their muskets and go to Washington to prevent the inauguration of Arthur" and only "loyalty of our form of government" caused them to assume the shooting the work of a madman and not deliberate murder.[31] In Albany, where the political fight over Roscoe Conkling's Senate seat still raged, Half-Breed politicians at first called the news a trick to manipulate balloting. William Robertson, asked if he though perhaps a "nihilist" had done it, said simply: "I have my own opinion as to where this originated"—having already heard the assassin's "Arthur will be president" line.[32]

Rutherford Hayes, just four months out of the White House himself, could hardly believe the dreadful news: "Arthur for President! Conkling the power behind the throne, superior to the throne!" It was a "national calamity whose consequences we cannot now confidently conjecture," he wrote that day.[33] "This is the result of placating bosses," others were heard saying. "If Conkling had not been placated at Chicago [by placing Arthur on the ticket], Garfield would not now be lying on his deathbed."[34]

"Send C.O.D. that s___b that shot Garfield," came a telegram from Bridgeport, California. "The citizens [here] will make short work of him."[35]

German Americans were "indignant" at early reports in one newspaper that Guiteau had German roots. In fact, Guiteau's family had been Huguenots, but Germans demanded a public apology nonetheless.[36] A few business leaders shrugged off the shooting; railroad baron Henry Villard told reporters that the president's death "can't stop our railway building. Can't stop our mills." Life, the economy, would go on.[37] But most Americans saw it as one of the most important events in their lives, an assault on their country, their community, and a public figure they'd come to embrace.

In Ohio, Garfield's two sisters Mary Larabee and Mehetable Trowbridge kept the news from their 90-year-old mother Eliza, who'd come to visit for a relative's funeral. They'd first heard it when a passing train had thrown newspaper Extra Editions onto the platform at their small town of Solon, Ohio; they immediately took their mother to the Trowbridge farm, cut off from communications, and agreed to wait for better news before telling her. "Mother is so wrapped up in James that this will certainly kill her," they explained. Garfield's eldest son Harry sent his grandmother a telegram from the White House: "Don't be alarmed by sensational rumors: doctors think it will not be fatal. Don't think of coming until you hear further."[38]

At the same time, Lucretia's sister Lide Rudolph had tried to keep the news from Garfield's two young sons Irvin and Abram who'd traveled by train from Washington the morning of the shooting and now were staying at her Ohio farm. All along the way, the railroad conductors had protected the two boys from hearing any inkling of the shooting; once in Ohio, though, ten-year old Irvin figured it out from all the people calling at the farm. When Lide finally leveled with him about "their Papa's accident," as she called it, the boys worried first about their mother. Then they questioned her about all the particulars; Irvin "has been my shadow, wanting to talk it over," Lide wrote to Lucretia in a letter. "Both he and Abram seem perfectly contented. So, banish all care of them."[39]

⚙ ⚙ ⚙ ⚙ ⚙

Charles Guiteau kept very quiet right after the shooting as police officers dragged him from the train station down Pennsylvania Avenue to the nearby police headquarters at Fourth Street. Here, they brought him inside and searched him. They took his gun—it still had three live cartridges loaded into it—and two silver coins from his pants pocket. In his suit jacket they found the letters he'd written the night before; they'd reach the newspapers within hours of his arrest, just as Guiteau had planned. "They... examined me and took all my personal effects away from me and put me in a cell," Guiteau recalled.[40]

"Have you got anything to say?" an officer asked.

"I have nothing to say. The papers speak for themselves," he answered. They asked his name. "Charles Guiteau, a theologian and lawyer," he pronounced.[41]

After a few minutes in his cell a detective came. "I want to go to jail," Guiteau told him.[42] They put him in handcuffs and led him back outside onto Pennsylvania Avenue to a police wagon waiting at the curb. Told they were headed to the District of Columbia Jail on the outskirts of town, Guiteau finally began to relax inside the cramped space. As they rode along the bumpy street, the detective started asking him questions and Guiteau found his tongue. Where was he from? "I am a native-born American. Born in Chicago, and am a lawyer and a theologian." Why had he done it? "To save the Republican party.... I am a Stalwart, among the Stalwarts. With Garfield out of the way we can carry all the northern states." As he warmed to his subject, it occurred to Guiteau that the detective actually might want to help him; it was the first time he'd spoken of his plan out loud to another human being. "You stick with me and have me put in the third story, front, at the jail," he told the detective, who took careful notes. "General Sherman is coming to take charge. Arthur and all those men are my friends, and I'll have you made chief of police."[43] Guiteau explained all about the bundles of papers for the newspapers he'd left at the railroad station. Had he mentioned the plan to anyone else? the detective asked. "Not a living soul," Guiteau answered.

By the time they reached the jail, Guiteau had even gained a sense of humor. In the warden's office, a Deputy Warden recognized him and Guiteau explained "rather flippantly" about his visit to the jail the prior Saturday. The detective then searched him again. They took his shoes and Guiteau demanded them back. "I will catch cold on this stone pavement," he insisted.[44]

They locked him up and began the long process of interrogation. Charles Guiteau held back nothing. A weight seemed lifted from his shoulders. "I had not been so happy for weeks until the 2d day of July when it was all over and I was in my cell. Then I said to myself, 'Thank God, it is all over.'"[45]

☉ ☉ ☉ ☉ ☉

Arthur could not stand being alone that day. After barely an hour at home, he got in his carriage and rode back across town to the Fifth Avenue Hotel to rejoin Roscoe Conkling in his private suite. New York City Police Commissioner Stephen French now joined them—they'd heard more warnings about possible revenge attacks against the vice president. Two uniformed patrolmen had taken positions at the hotel's main door along with a detective in the lobby; other plainclothes detectives mingled in the hallway near Roscoe Conkling's room. In the afternoon, a telegram reached the hotel saying that the president had died at 3:05 pm; when someone told Conkling about it, he'd said nothing and gone out for a carriage ride. Within an hour, the report had been refuted as incorrect.[46]

After a few more hours closeted with Conkling and friends, Arthur left again and this time stopped for another handful of newspapermen on the way out, telling them he was "overcome with grief" at the shooting.[47] He returned home to Lexington Avenue and found another telegram from Blaine: "At the hour Six O'clock the condition of the President is very alarming. He is losing his strength and the worst may be apprehended."[48] At 7 pm Arthur returned to Conkling's hotel room and they had a long talk about whether he should go to Washington that night. Arthur now was convinced that going too soon might look indecent; he'd rather wait until he'd actually been invited.

Before leaving for home once again that night, Arthur learned from the hotel front desk that they'd received yet another anonymous hand-scrawled card during the day: "Gens: We will hang Conkling and Co. at nine P.M. sharpe. [sic.] The Committee."[49]

❀ ❀ ❀ ❀ ❀

Lucretia and Mollie finally reached Washington, D.C., at about 6 pm that evening after a second locomotive had gone out to rescue their disabled train in rural Maryland and pull it the rest of the way. From the Baltimore and Potomac Depot, they rode a carriage through streets clogged with bewildered crowds—it took a full half hour to reach the White House just a dozen blocks away and get past the closed gates and the soldiers camped on the north lawn. Attorney General Wayne MacVeigh met Lucretia at the north door and lifted her down from the carriage; her son James helped her inside. Her husband was still alive, they told her; she started immediately up the stairs to see him. Harriet Blaine greeted her and remembered how Lucretia looked at that moment: "frail, fatigued, desperate, but firm and quiet and full of purpose."[50]

When Lucretia reached the president's makeshift ward upstairs, the doctors could hold her barely long enough to brief her on the president's worsening condition. It had been ten hours since the shooting; his fifth rib had been fractured and he'd vomited constantly all afternoon; his stomach couldn't hold anything. He'd lost large amounts of blood and they still hadn't found the bullet despite repeated probes. Then they left her alone.

Lucretia didn't know what to expect on seeing her husband for the first time after the shooting, but she'd prepared herself for the worst. One newspaper artist drew her throwing her arms around her bed-ridden husband in a deep embrace. Just as he had helped keep her own spirits up during her recent sickness, Lucretia decided she must try to help bolster his. She wouldn't let him think about anything but survival. She tried to be cheerful; when Garfield lapsed into moping about how she might need to raise the children alone, she interrupted impatiently: "Well, my dear, you are not going to die as I am here to nurse you back to life; so please to not speak again of death."[51] After a few minutes, her presence seemed to relax him.

By the time the doctors came back, they'd held a conference in a nearby room on the president's condition. It hadn't taken them long to agree on their medical outlook. They'd seen severe bleeding and signs of "profound collapse."[52] The bullet must have penetrated the abdomen and damaged important organs, they decided. Willard Bliss spoke for the group to reporters: "There is no hope for him," he said, "he will not probably live three hours, and may die in half an hour. The bullet has pierced the liver, and it is a fatal wound."[53] In fact, they had no idea where the bullet was, but felt compelled to make their best guess.

Lucretia sat with her husband in his sickroom until late that night. As the hours passed, she saw him seeming to defy the doctors' dire outlook. "Within the last two hours the President's condition has had a marked improvement & we are very much encouraged," Robert Todd Lincoln reported to John Logan in Chicago during the evening.[54] Lucretia took time to look at some of the piles of telegrams pouring in to her from around the country that day, many from total strangers: "I love my father. Am sorry for you and your children," wrote a Jewette Scheibenzuber of Dayton, Ohio. "A Southern sympathizer would have you know that from the family altar of many a home a prayer is being offered for the restoration of the President," wrote H.E.W. from Charleston, South Carolina. "God preserve the President and bless you and the country," Governor Eli Murray of Utah said.[55] World leaders too sent telegrams, Queen Victoria's from London being among the first. She was "most anxious" to hear the president's condition, she wrote. "Please wire latest news."[56] Lucretia, like her husband, recognized the eyes of the world on her. As First Lady, her dignity and composure could bring courage to the country—her lack of it could bring despair. People needed her strength; she only hoped that she'd be able to provide it and not crumble under the weight.

Late that night, Garfield, still alert, saw the fatigue and strain in her face. "Go, now, and rest," he told her. "I shall want you near me when the crisis comes."[57] Reluctantly, Lucretia left him to the other nurses and went off to get some sleep for herself. If the worst happened, they'd call her.

@ @ @ @ @

At about 9:30 pm, Arthur received another telegram from Blaine: "It is the judgment of the Cabinet that you should come to Washington to-night by the midnight train."[58] The vice president got another wire about the same time from Postmaster General Tom James: "The President is no better, and we fear, sinking."[59] The decision had been made for Arthur; he must leave New York for Washington immediately.

An hour or so later, Arthur took the last ferry boat from the Desbosses Street pier across the Hudson River to the Jersey City railroad station. Roscoe Conkling came along, carrying Arthur's bags. Arthur had asked Senator John P. Jones to travel with him and Jones had agreed to let Arthur stay at his large townhouse in Washington during the next few days rather than at the apartment Arthur shared with Conkling at Wormley's Hotel—better to avoid bad appearances from the recent political quarrels. They all walked together from the ferry to a carriage that took them to the nearby station and then onto the platform. Arthur led; Conkling and the others followed a few steps behind. A Detective Cosgrove from the New York police department hung at Arthur's side carrying a pistol in his coat; Cosgrove planned to accompany Arthur to Washington as protection against any threats of violence. A reporter for the *New York Sun* also followed close behind. Their small group tried to look as inconspicuous as possible in the night.

At the platform, as Arthur prepared to climb onto the train, Roscoe Conkling took his hand and shook it. "Good-bye, Arthur, and God bless you. Will see you Thursday. After all, it is perhaps best that you should go to Washington tonight." Then in a whisper he added: "You have nothing to fear."[60]

The overnight "owl" train, leaving Jersey City at nearly midnight, would not reach Washington until the next morning. Once on board, Arthur and Senator Jones took seats in a back row and spoke quietly, most people in the car not even noticing their presence. After about an hour, Arthur ordered a berth made up for him to get some sleep. He climbed in, but only tossed and turned in the darkness, keeping awake the *New York Sun* reporter lying nearby. He didn't finally doze off to sleep until some point after Elizabeth, New Jersey. He slept fitfully past Philadelphia, Wilmington, and Baltimore, and woke with barely time enough to get dressed before they reached Washington, D.C. itself.

Whatever thoughts and emotions haunted his sleep that night, Chester A. Arthur awoke the next morning with one firm resolution in his mind: he must see the president as soon as possible that day, face-to-face, and speak with him. He had to set things straight if he could.

◎ ◎ ◎ ◎ ◎

All that night in the White House, they'd kept watch: the doctors, old army friends Colonel Rockwell and David Swaim, the cabinet members and their wives. They took turns in the president's room as nurses. Garfield woke up every half hour to vomit. Doctors gave him morphine twice for the pain and fed him milk and limewater for the nausea. His pulse rarely fell below 120. Still, he managed to sleep; by Sunday morning, he seemed refreshed and the pain in his feet had lessened.

Starting at dawn, crowds formed outside the White House gates and soldiers worked to keep them quiet. Benjamin Harrison, one of the callers, found the doorways "thronged with people awaiting the issuing of bulletins on the President's condition."[61] All that day the medical reports flip-flopped, first hopeful, then despondent, then back again. The doctors issued six different official bulletins just during the morning; the newspapers ran them in multiple Extra Editions—even on a Sunday—and telegraphed them instantly across the country. "The President has just awakened, greatly refreshed, and has not vomited since 1 A.M.," they reported at 4 am. "The patient is decidedly more cheerful, and has amused himself and watchers by telling a laughable incident from his early career." At 7:50 am, the doctors announced their decision that "no effort will be made at present to extract the ball [bullet], as its presence in the location determined does not necessarily interfere with the ultimate recovery of the President." At 11 am, they said: "The President's condition is greatly improved."[62]

By afternoon, though, the outlook had reversed: The President was "suffering from pain in both feet and ankles" they announced at 2 pm; by 10:30 pm they reported his condition as "less favorable," his pulse gyrating between 100 and 120, the pain returning to his feet and legs.

During the morning, Willard Bliss called together all the doctors— enough to fill a small room—and told them that he'd had a private talk with the president and Mrs. Garfield and they'd made a decision. The president had complained that there were too many physicians treating him and he'd suffered through too many painful examinations. Bliss alone would be in charge now. Only a handful of the other doctors could stay, he told them; the rest would have to leave.

They were shocked; several objected, raising their voices. What gave Bliss the right to assert himself this way? They quarreled, right there in the hallway near Garfield's sickroom where the newspapermen could hear them. One doctor accused Bliss of angling to win himself an appointment as Surgeon General: haggling over patronage even now![63] Another claimed that Bliss wasn't a good enough doctor. Bliss, a surgeon in the war, had resigned from the army and carried on a quiet private practice in Washington since 1865— hardly the credentials for such a major case, they argued. "I am afraid Bliss will probe the wound and if he does inflammation will set in and the President will die," one of them anonymously told the newspapers. Bliss wanted power, pure and simple, he said.*

Willard Bliss stood his ground and claimed he had the president's authority. Besides, he said: "If I can't save him, no one can."[64] He decided to bring in two new prominent consultants: Doctors D. Hayes Agnew from Philadelphia and Frank H. Hamilton from New York. The incident stuck in the public mind, though. Did the doctors have motives of their own? Did they really know what they were doing?

❀ ❀ ❀ ❀ ❀

No one came to meet Vice President Arthur and Senator Jones when they arrived at the Washington, D.C. railroad station at 7 am Sunday morning; they

---

* Doctor Silas Boynton, who stayed on as a nurse under Bliss's direction, later produced a written statement claiming that Bliss had no authority at all for taking charge. According to Boynton, Garfield had told him on about August 8, 1881, that he'd had "no knowledge of ever having placed himself under the professional care of D.W. Bliss and he did not believe that Dr. Bliss had ever spoken one word to him upon the subject." Nor had Lucretia been consulted on the matter either, Boynton claimed. Bliss, however, insisted on his story in sworn testimony.

took a curbside cab directly to Senator Jones's large townhouse at 3 Independence Avenue, just across the street from the Capitol Building.[65] Arthur immediately sent word by messenger that he wanted to see the president. Word came back quickly that he could not; the doctors wouldn't allow it. Maybe things would change later in the day.

Arthur took a light breakfast, then a nap. Then he waited. By mid day, he couldn't stand waiting any longer. He and Senator Jones rode a carriage over to Attorney General Wayne MacVeigh's office to ask his help. "I was so nervous and depressed last night... I was so late receiving the news of his injuries and feared the President might misinterpret my silence," Arthur told MacVeigh. "It is my earnest desire to see the President. Is there no possibility of seeing him?"[66]

At Arthur's insistence, MacVeigh and Senator Jones went to the White House to plead his case again, but the doctors refused to listen. None of the cabinet members had been allowed to see Garfield since they'd issued their orders, and they'd make no exceptions now. Arthur rode back to Jones's house to wait for more news. Meanwhile, he read the newspapers and must have felt devastated at the comments he saw about himself. Even the normally-friendly *New York Times* attacked him that morning as unqualified and unworthy: "Gen. Arthur has been untrue to his better self as clearly as he had been faithless to the demands of the aggregate of political intelligence and conscience," it argued in a featured editorial. "Grossly slanderous as it would be to impute any suggestion of homicidal intent," it said, Arthur's role in the "disgraceful squabble" in Albany made even his friends "recoil from the prospect of his ever being anything more than Vice President.... The man to whom the criminal act of Guiteau ought to bring the gravest reflections is the man who has apparently most to gain from its fatal issue."[67]

What must people think reading this? Arthur had to wonder. How could he possibly become president under these conditions? Garfield's friends would crucify him and the public would hate him; he'd never win their trust. But he was the Vice President of the United States; if Garfield died, what choice did he have? He couldn't walk away from the presidency if it fell to him now.

Late that afternoon, two horse-drawn carriages pulled up to the curb outside Senator Jones's house and Arthur stepped outside finally to some good news. The entire cabinet, all seven secretaries, had come to pay him a visit. Arthur was thrilled; he bounded down the stoop and virtually hugged them, greeting each man with a handshake as newspaper writers recorded the scene.

James Blaine came first, and Arthur gave him the fondest welcome of all. They "grasped each other warmly by the hand," a reported wrote. Arthur stood with Blaine on the sidewalk as the others went into the house. Had Blaine gotten his telegrams from New York? Arthur asked. Had he understood why he'd been delayed in responding, that he hadn't received Blaine's message until late in the day?[68]

Inside the house, Arthur hosted Blaine and the others to tea and lunch. The cabinet members kept their conversation away from politics and stayed only a short time, but by coming and appearing with Arthur for the reporters, they'd sent a purposeful message. Bitterness from the recent factional wars aside, America had a stable government and decent people running it. Its leaders would act in a dignified way and give Arthur the respect his Constitutional office demanded.

Arthur looked "less depressed," a reporter noted, after they'd left.[69]

That night, Arthur and Senator Jones rode their carriage back down Pennsylvania Avenue to try again to see the president. Benjamin Harrison saw Arthur at the White House that night, looking "all anxiety."*[70] The doctors again refused to let Arthur into Garfield's room, but Lucretia agreed to talk with him for a few minutes. Despite all the political quarreling, Arthur had always been friendly with Lucretia, at least outwardly; now he sat opposite her in a small room on the second floor and saw her face wrought with strain, her shoulders and hands sagging with fatigue. He told Lucretia how grief-stricken he felt over the shooting and how he hoped for Garfield's recovery; his words "greatly affected" her, she said. Arthur could only imagine how deeply this woman, the president's wife, must have resented him at that moment, her husband lying down the hallway with a bullet in his back, his life hanging by a thread. But she treated him with perfect respect and "did not give way to her emotions," according to a reporter.[71]

Afterward, Arthur stepped down the hall to where the cabinet members had gone to wait for news. "I pray to God that the President will recover," he told them. "God knows I do not want the place I was never elected to."[72]

After returning to Senator Jones's house late that night, Arthur saw the sharpest rebuke yet. Henry Watterson, publisher of the *Louisville Courier Jour-*

---

* Harrison, who found the suggestions of Arthur's or Conkling's involvement in the shooting "cruel and unjustifiable," recalled how many old Whigs still believed that his own grandfather, President William Henry Harrison, had been poisoned when he died in office of pneumonia after delivering a two-hour inaugural address during a winter storm in 1841.

nal, had now said in print what others had only whispered behind his back: "Mrs. [Mary] Surratt [of the Lincoln murder conspiracy] was hanged on less circumstantial evidence than occurs to the mind as to Roscoe Conkling and Chester A. Arthur. The vile nature of the contest at Albany, the despicable rancor of the combatants and the base methods accepted by both parties render murder as likely a weapon as any other, and wilst we should be loath to accuse anybody, and pray that the man Guiteau is not the instrument of a conspiracy, we should not be eager to assume the innocence of a body of political wretches.... who may have planned this assassination as their last redout."[73]

There it was: He'd been publicly accused of murder.

⊙ ⊙ ⊙ ⊙ ⊙

Charles Guiteau seemed to enjoy the new life he'd found in the D.C. Jail; the attention, the free food and cell, the deference he enjoyed as the prison's foremost inmate. Sunday morning he ate his breakfast heartily: salt herring, boiled potatoes, and wheat bread with coffee. They took him to be photographed; he wore a dark suit, standing collar and black cravat, and treated the event as an honor. "I don't want to appear strained and awkward," Guiteau told the photographer. "If my picture is taken at all it must be a good one." They took frontals, sides, three-quarters, and full-face portraits. "Did you get me good that time?" he interrupted once. "I want to look natural."[74] The District Attorney questioned Guiteau for four hours that day as police chased down rumors of accomplices and conspiracies, but discounted them quickly. Guiteau was their man, they decided, and he'd acted alone.

During his free time, Guiteau read the newspapers and didn't seem at all bothered that most of his celebrity politician "friends" now were denying him publicly. Benjamin Harrison, for one, admitted meeting Guiteau in Washington but dismissed him as a "nuisance."[75] Ulysses Grant told of seeing Guiteau during the campaign, but insisted that he'd brushed him off. "He wanted me to sign a paper recommending him as a proper person to appoint as Minister to Austria," Grant told reporters. "I refused to sign his papers. I told my servant not to allow him to enter my parlors. He subsequently forced himself in one day, but I refused to talk with him and dismissed him speedily."[76] Chicago newsmen tracked down Emory Storrs who too described Guiteau as a crank: "He hung around Washington last winter, during the coldest weather, in the thinnest clothes, with no stockings on and with his toes out of his boots. Wild-looking as he was, everybody thought him to be harmless and simply 'off his nut.' For that reason only he was tolerated. In fact, people pitied him…. Such a man ought to have been placed in an asylum years ago."[77]

Guiteau read the interviews and just shrugged his shoulders. He understood their dilemma; once the shock wore off, they'd change their minds and recognize him as a hero.

A growing chorus of voices by now was insisting that Guiteau be dismissed as a madman or a lunatic. Guiteau's "I am a Stalwart" statement had sent chills through Stalwart politicians who feared a public backlash; if Guiteau were sane, then the stigma of the crime (if not actual guilt) might fall on them. They called Guiteau's words "simply the bravado of an insane man" and insisted the crime had no "political significance." "The anti-Administration Republicans love their country and its institutions, all of which the President represents," George Gorham explained in the *National Republican*.[78]

Even the president's anti-Stalwart friends found themselves on a delicate tightrope over Guiteau. Americans in the 1880s saw political assassinations as part of the corrupt Old World. Europe had its "anarchists" and "nihilists," South America its scheming generals and revolutionaries, but not free, democratic America. In fact, the Old World and South America had suffered a plague of political killings recently: Just since 1860, assassins had murdered Prince Michael of Serbia (1868), President Balta of Peru (1872), President Maena of Ecuador (1875), Sultan Abdul Aziz of Ottoman Turkey (1876), President Gill of Paraguay (1877), and Czar Alexander of Russia (1880), and had made attempts on the Emperor of Germany, the Kings of Spain and Italy, the Queen of Greece, the King of Prussia, Napoleon III of France, Prince Bismarck of Prussia, and Russia's royal family. Even Queen Victoria in England had been attacked in 1850, though the British had seemed to find an effective deterrent in publicly flogging the attacker.[79]

Most Americans thought their country immune to political murder, the murder of Lincoln brushed off as a fluke byproduct of Civil War. This second assassination of a president within sixteen years, though, with a fully home-grown assassin (a "Stalwart," not an "anarchist"), made them cringe. If Guiteau were sane, then had murder become a normal feature of American political practice? Had we become like Russia?

Finding Guiteau insane, though, had its own downside; it would save him from the hanging that most Americans felt he richly deserved. Guiteau had clearly known what he was doing in shooting Garfield. He might have a "crazed mind, seeking infamous notoriety, and madly believing he would find someone to glorify him," Joseph Medill's *Chicago Tribune* argued, but this didn't absolve him of guilt and didn't absolve the Stalwarts from judgment for pushing him over the edge.[80] To *Harpers Weekly* George W. Curtis, Guiteau's act "may have shown madness, but it was certainly madness with a method."[81] Guiteau's "insanity," to many observers, "differed only in degree" from the attitude of certain Senators and politicos.[82]

The law put "insanity" in a small box in the 1880s—having little to do with the prisoner's actual mental health. By far, most states, including the District of Columbia, followed the M'Naghten Rule which presumed every defendant sane if he knew what he was doing and that it was wrong.[83] Hostility toward the whole concept of "insanity" rippled among jurists. When New York State had considered the so-called "irresistible impulse" test as an alternative, a judge had said: "If a man has an irresistible impulse to commit murder, the law should have an irresistible impulse to hang him."[84] Police detectives themselves saw no basis for insanity in Guiteau's case. "All the facts point to a deliberately formed plan of assassination," Colonel Cook explained, "accompanied by the preparation of a means of escape and simulated defense based upon pretended insanity."[85]

Reformers found it much easier to attack the spoils system, the rabid greed for political office, as the villain. A reformed civil service based on merit would avoid the patronage squabbling that had spun out of control with Guiteau, they argued. For the first time, most Americans now agreed that somehow the system must be fixed.

◉ ◉ ◉ ◉ ◉

The nation celebrated a muted Fourth of July that year. A few brass bands played music in cities like Chicago and New York; children set off fireworks and base-ball teams played their regular games. But most towns cancelled their celebrations in favor of prayer meetings. The biggest crowds still remained those huddled around the bulletin boards and newspaper offices hanging on the latest medical reports from Washington.

Some element of national honor had been damaged in the shooting, and it cast a pall over the festive holiday. Many speeches that Fourth of July quoted the hopeful words of Garfield himself as a young Congressman in 1865 facing an angry crowd the night that Abraham Lincoln had been shot by John Wilkes Booth: "Fellow citizens! God reigns, and the government in Washington still lives!"[86]

◎ ◎ ◎ ◎ ◎

Ulysses Grant stayed on at the New Jersey seashore after Garfield's shooting. He followed the news closely, walking across the sand dunes almost every hour to scan the telegrams posted at the Hotel Elberon. Newsmen sought him out, crowded around him, looking for any pearls of wisdom he chose to share; Grant enjoyed the attention and always tried to oblige with a quote. He told a *New York World* reporter how Garfield's gunshot wound reminded him of wounds he'd seen back during the Mexican War and told the story of a General Walker who'd been shot back then, considered near death, and ended up traveling all the way home to Tory, New York and living long enough to be shot again and killed in the Civil War fifteen years later. Then he told of another soldier shot off his horse who walked away from the incident, seemed perfectly healthy, made a cheerful joke, then died suddenly a few hours later. You just couldn't tell. "If the President should live two or three days longer, with his strong constitution and absolutely correct habits, I should expect he would eventually recover."[87]

Another newsman confronted Grant that Sunday about why he'd sent only one message to Washington asking about the president health. Several journals by then had expressed "Great surprise" at the absence of sympathy calls from Conkling, Grant, "nor any of the leading Stalwarts"[88]—as if their political warring had made them indifferent to whether the president lived or died. Grant brushed it aside; he'd called on Mrs. Garfield directly after the crime and sent his sympathies, he said. "More than this is not necessary, unless the President dies, when I will proceed to Washington."[89]

Instead, Grant relished repeating how he'd thrown the assassin Guiteau out of his hotel room back during the spring. He also voiced a fear common among public figures even then—that some quiet, inconspicuous person might choose "to redeem some fancied public wrong by sacrificing a life. They are thought to be brainless until they startle the community with some such terrible crime as this."[90] What had happened to Garfield could have happened to any of them, Grant suggested.

◎ ◎ ◎ ◎ ◎

Lucretia spent the Fourth of July closeted in the White House, trying to keep up a brave face for the newspapermen: "outwardly, she holds herself with much composure," one of them wrote; with her husband she "whispers to him words of cheer."[91] She'd managed to sleep soundly the night before. "If the President passes through to-day without losing strength, it will be exceedingly encouraging," Doctor Bliss announced that day.[92] When Blaine had left the White House at 2am that night and passed reporters, he'd said only: "We are hopeful, but there is great anxiety. We hope."[93]

Telegrams to Lucretia from across the country had grown to a torrent. President's wives rarely occupied the public spotlight in the 1800s, but Lucretia quickly came to fill a vacuum left by her husband's incapacity and the public's thirst for news during the crisis. Her quiet dignity seemed to strike a chord. "You are so calm and brave yourself," her niece Adelaide wrote to her from Ohio that week, "that we all, I think, do as we did in childhood, look at Mama's or Aunt Crete's face, and, seeing hope and confidence there, believed all will be well, and go to our play with a light heart."[94] Now Lucretia had to be brave "Aunt Crete" for the entire nation.

Many of the messages reflected the peoples' deep religious bent in time of need. "Dear Lady. May the God of all grace sustain you in this most trying hour," a Captain E.C. Northrop wired from Tower City, Pennsylvania. "A humble American wife and mother prays earnestly to God that your good husband may be spared," wrote Mrs. Louis Aldrich of Boston. Even military men felt compelled to bare their grief. One wrote: "Dear Mrs. Garfield. Weeping may endure for a night. But joy cometh in the morning. 30 Psalm of David. From a weeping friend & one arm soldier."[95]

Medical experts contacted her as well, telling her to keep a particularly sharp eye on the president's doctors: "Do not allow probing the wound," a physician named E.L. Patee wired from Manhattan, Kansas. "Saturate every thing with carbolic acid, one part to 20 parts water about. Use quite freely of this about the wound. Probing generally does more harm than the balls...."[96] Letters came from the new Czar of Russia, from the surviving family of the Marquis de Lafayette, and from other heads of state. Benjamin Harrison, visiting the White House that week, marveled at her presence of mind. "I do not believe there is another woman in the country who could have acquitted herself more magnificently." He called her "the most heroic woman I ever knew."[97]

⚜ ⚜ ⚜ ⚜ ⚜

Roscoe Conkling avoided leaving his suite at the Fifth Avenue Hotel. On the Sunday after the shooting he came out only once; he walked down to the hotel office wearing a black cashmere suit and black hat, stepped nervously to the clerk's office, mailed a letter, shook a few familiar hands, then hurried back to avoid the people milling about the lobby reading the latest telegraph reports. Police officials met privately Sunday night and agreed to beef up the guards around him. "Gen. Arthur had received about fifty letters warning him to take care of his personal safety," Commissioner French announced; he didn't say how many threats had come against Conkling, but it was enough to justify sending over two additional squads of detectives.[98]

Privately, Roscoe Conkling raged against his accusers. Why should he be blamed for a madman's bullet? He had no blood on his hands! But how could he argue against the public emotion? He told visitors that Garfield's shooting was "one of the most terrible incidents in the history of the country" and how he had "grave doubts" whether the president would recover. But certainly nobody would believe that Stalwarts who'd been involved in the political "contest" had anything to do with it, he insisted.[99] He rejected advice from friends to drop his Senate bid in Albany. Why should he? Conkling argued. He hadn't done anything wrong.

Still, the attacks came—and with a special viciousness. An Indiana newspaper quoted Conkling as saying that week: "The President has forced me to commit suicide or murder. I prefer murder." Conkling took two full weeks before even bothering to deny it. "All I know is that some scoundrel set afloat this particular falsehood," he wrote back finally.[100] His critics had "seized a dark and dangerous hour " for their "'devilish machinations,'" he wrote an ally, "but in the end reason will prevail."[101]

Conkling settled into a siege. He refused to leave New York City while the president was in danger, he announced, and never went far without police protection. When people came to visit, he often refused to see them. He left letters unanswered and stayed behind his closed doors, keeping a few loyalists in the hallway outside smoking cigars and swinging their canes. He wrote a letter to Attorney General Wayne MacVeigh that week mentioning his "abhorrence" at the attack but dealing mostly with an intellectual question: whether the attempted murder of a president should carry a special penalty. It ended: "Please also give to Mrs. Garfield my most respectful condolence."[102] Conkling seemed unable to bring himself to contact Lucretia Garfield directly to offer a simple consolation, blocked by some combination of pride and anger. Only on July 7—five full days after the shooting and after Garfield's medical condition started to improve—did he finally send a note through Arthur: "Please say to Mrs. Garfield for me that today's reports are most welcome and rejoice me for the happiness they give to her," he wrote.[103]

When confronted, he tried to minimize the affair. "There is no occasion for public apprehension or excitement," he told one reporter who did manage to snag him in a Hotel hallway, "the Constitution points out just what should be done…. The Vice-President on the death of the President instantly succeeds, and the government goes on as if no change had occurred."[104] This dismissive attitude, though, only rankled his critics more.

The trickle of visitors Conkling did allow into his room—long-time allies like Tom Platt, Stephen Dorsey, and John Smythe of Albany—he used to defend himself in the newspapers. The bitterness of his "faction fight" had "led this deluded assassin to believe that he could make a hero of himself by killing Mr. Garfield," a "well-known" New York judge in the hallway told newsmen.[105] Conkling had his friends attack the opposition newspapers as well for pumping up the bad feeling against him: "his enemies might try to manufacture such a sentiment," they told reporters.[106]

This last insult was the last straw to many; Conkling had picked a bad time to start a new public fight and Whitelaw Reid's anti-machine *New York Tribune* was happy to slap him back. The *Tribune* thundered back with a prompt and direct personal challenge: "That Mr. Roscoe Conkling and his friends, who have made a savage factional warfare upon the President, and have done everything in their power to break down respect for him and to inflame the bad passions of their followers to the utmost, caused a state of things of which assassination was a not unnatural result."[107] The police had to heighten once again their vigilance around Conkling's hotel suite.

The *Philadelphia Inquirer* spoke for many when it wrote that Roscoe Conkling should just "Keep Quiet" and "withdraw at once from public life and public notice."[108] Conkling had become a symbol for an entire approach to politics that had gone out of control and become unacceptable in these sober days after the shooting; growing sympathy for Garfield had been matched by growing contempt for a villain, and Conkling made himself the prime choice.

◎ ◎ ◎ ◎ ◎

Arthur barely slept, sitting day after day in Senator Jones's house, hanging on each new medical report, constantly afraid at any moment of being sum-

moned to the White House to take the oath as president; a horse-drawn hack
waited constantly on the street outside for the emergency. Cabinet members
came each day to update him on the latest news, but their upbeat support
paled against the barrage of attacks. Arthur saw decades of hatred against
Conkling now being directed toward him: George William Curtis crowed
publicly that under an Arthur presidency, Conkling "would be the controlling influence" and that Arthur had been "trained in a very bad school."[109]
Others blasted his "utter insufficiency" for the White House.[110]

Even moderates like Thurlow Weed described Arthur as too weak to
stand up to his old Boss: "With Garfield dead, Arthur would be President
and Conkling would be supreme. Of course, there would be great repug-
nance, even opposition to it."[111] E.L. Godkin of *The Nation*, recounting
the history of Conkling's machine, concluded: "It is out of this mess of filth
that Mr. Arthur will go to the Presidential chair in case of the President's
death."[112]

Arthur, an outgoing, friendly man, felt profoundly hurt on learning how
badly so many people thought of him. Rather than rage against it like Conkling, though, he wondered if perhaps they might be right. No vice president
ever had been as openly disloyal to his president as he had. Even if he hadn't
pulled the trigger, purchased Guiteau's gun, or ordered him to fire, his and
Conkling's partisan wars had pushed Guiteau to the brink. Arthur peered in
the mirror and saw his own face looking back at him accusingly.

In fact, thinking about it, he did finally remember meeting the assassin
Guiteau "two or three times" in the streets of Washington during the spring,
in addition to the many times in New York City during the campaign. He'd
never given the odd little man a second thought. Asked later if Guiteau had
done service in the campaign giving him reason to expect "political prefer-
ence," Arthur said "None that I know of."[113]

Those who saw Arthur that week found him "not in good health;" he
"suffered severely" and sat "in a kind of stupor." A reporter visiting the Jones
house described Arthur alone on a sofa in a darkened room, "his head bowed
and looking vacantly through the low open window."[114] Said another reporter:
"Tears stood in [Arthur's] eyes, and the orbs themselves were bloodshot. On
his face were the traces of recent weeping. He would trust himself to speak but
little, and was evidently afraid of being overcome by his emotions."[115] Arthur
tried to defend himself from the worst accusations. "No one deplores the
calamity more than Senator Conkling and myself," he told one reporter. "I am

an American, among millions of Americans, grieving for their wounded chief."[116]

Postmaster General Tom James came by the house one night that week to bring the latest news about Garfield's medical condition and felt compelled to raise the issue directly. James told the Vice President: "I wish to inform you, Mr. Arthur, that I and the entire Cabinet scout the idea that any responsibility for this calamity rests upon you, and, should you desire it, the members of the Cabinet will make a formal and public statement of their belief."[117] If Arthur found it reassuring, he didn't show it. After James left, he was seen pacing the hallway, hands clasped behind his back, his face toward the floor. The fact that a cabinet member had found it necessary to assure him he didn't consider him an accessory to murder gave little comfort.

On Tuesday, July 5, Arthur visited the White House once again. As before, the doctors forbade him from seeing the president. After returning to Senator Jones's house, he rode a carriage out into the Washington suburbs for almost ten miles to clear his mind and enjoy some fresh air. While he was away, Senator Jones entertained a few newspapermen who'd stopped by to ask questions. Certainly Arthur felt badly about Guiteau's statements, Jones told them, but "what can he do about it?" Arthur didn't want the presidency but, as vice president, "he cannot shrink from its requirement." As for the actual threats of violence against him: "General Arthur has told me that life is not worth living if one has to be in constant dread of losing it."[118]

* * * * *

After the Fourth of July, the signs became unmistakable; Garfield had started to mend. On Tuesday that week, he'd rejected a milk diet and chicken broth as well. "He is now, six o'clock, still comfortable, and has asked for beefsteak," Harriet Blaine wrote to her daughter after returning home from a turn at nursing. "They will not, of course, let him have it, but if they would, it ought not to come from the White House kitchens. Such tough leather as they had there for breakfast the other morning, is a disgrace to the cattle on a thousand hills."[119]

The turning point came on July 5. "The President had a natural movement with which surgeons are much pleased," Robert Todd Lincoln reported to John Logan in Chicago that day.[120] A "natural movement"—moving his bowels and urinating with no trace of blood—meant that Garfield's main internal organs near the bullet wound, his intestines, stomach, and kidneys had not been damaged, and his liver still functioned enough for digestion—perhaps allowing him to get enough nourishment to heal.

With optimistic bulletins now coming from the doctors, fewer people crowded around the White House gates. "The President passed a very comfortable night, and for the first time since he was wounded his pulse this morning is below 100," Blaine wrote to the Minister at London the next morning.[121] Robert Todd Lincoln wired John Logan in Chicago: "The conditions reported by the surgeons give great encouragement in which the surgeons share with less reserve than on any other day."[122]

The doctors that day gave their most detailed diagnosis yet. The bullet, they said, had hit Garfield's twelfth rib about 2-and-a-half inches to the right of the spine, plunged down and forward, penetrating the peritoneal cavity, hitting the liver, and lodging in the abdomen.[123] But, having never found the bullet, they couldn't be sure; they'd based their conclusion about the damaged liver primarily on the yellowish color of Garfield's skin. The mystery soon became an obsession among medical men around the country—doctors in New York City actually tried firing pistols at cadavers at Guiteau's angle to see what direction the bullet would take after hitting the body.[124] In fact, as they'd learn much later, Guiteau's actual bullet had hit Garfield's spine, traveled forward, and become lodged near the pancreas, almost a foot away from where Garfield's doctors now thought it was.

By mid-July, the immediate crisis seemed to have lapsed. "His physical strength keeps up wonderfully, and his mind is entirely clear and active, without showing excitement," Blaine wired to the London ministry on July 11, nine days after the shooting.[125] The doctors stopped giving Garfield nightly doses of morphine. "Arthur can go back to New York and we soon to Augusta, and all of the pain and woe and anticipated peril will not be lost on the country," Harriet Blaine wrote to her daughter that week, making her own plans finally to leave town: "I am rapidly getting unpacked and fast getting all my washable dresses ready for the laundry."[126] Two days later, though, she had to change her plans again, this time because of her husband: "The President is doing very nicely. There is no need, so far as he is concerned, of my staying here, but your father must, and he cannot be left [alone]."[127]

⊙ ⊙ ⊙ ⊙ ⊙

The doctors wouldn't allow Blaine to see the president again until July 21, almost three weeks after the shooting; even then, they gave him only six minutes. By late July, Blaine's face showed the weeks of constant strain. "His hair is white, and his florid color has changed to a marked pallor," a reporter noted after seeing him.[128] Both he and his wife Harriet spent hours each day at the White House, she taking turns at nursing, he managing the cabinet and the public crisis. William E. Chandler worried about them: "I want you and Mr. Blaine not to forget yourselves. It is fearfully hot in Washington" and they faced a "long, anxious period of suffering," he wrote to her from his home in New Hampshire.[129]

Garfield too had changed during his weeks of convalescence after the shooting; he'd grown lonely for friends and moody in his isolation. The doctors had put screens around his bed so he couldn't see out. Day after day, he lay immobile on his back, unable to lift his head and barely able to lift his arms. The doctors shifted his position frequently to prevent bedsores, a painful process that inflamed the wounds. They'd only allowed him to see his three younger children once, and only one at a time. Garfield tried to act cheerful, always thanking his doctors and shaking their hands after each examination, but he grew to detest his bland diet of oatmeal, milk, and limewater. As the Washington summer lingered hot and humid, his White House room developed a foul stench.

Doctor Bliss became increasingly worried over his failure to find the bullet inside Garfield's body. At one point he brought in Alexander Graham Bell, already famous for his invention of the telephone, who had developed a new contraption called an "induction balance," a rudimentary metal detector whose electrically-charged needle supposedly could locate a hidden metallic object inside a patient's body. Bell came and tried it on Garfield but never found the bullet, partly because Bliss himself told him to look for it in the wrong place, near the liver. Also, the heavy metal springs in Garfield's bed apparently threw off the mechanism. More successful were the Navy engineers who devised a way to fight the humid 90-degree Washington heat. The doctors had tried placing huge blocks of ice in Garfield's room or in air vents, but the ice only made the air damp and worsened the humidity. Instead, the Navy engineers tried pumping ice-cooled air through cotton filters before pumping it through a vent into Garfield's room—the first working air-conditioner. Beginning late July, it kept the room at a steady, dry 77 degrees.

Political allies, hearing reports of Garfield's apparently improving condition, began to see a great opportunity. Garfield's popularity in the country had soared. "Garfield will now have a hold on the hearts of the people like that of Washington and Lincoln. He can do any righteous and necessary work," Rutherford Hayes wrote to John Hay in mid-July, thinking now how he might use it to tackle his own pet project of civil service reform.[130] Garfield had won peoples' respect for facing down not only Roscoe Conkling's filibuster but now death itself: "I like him," an unnamed New York Stalwart said simply. "When things are going against him he don't up and resign."[131] William E. Chandler, writing from New Hampshire, saw it as well: "The whole country has been agonized about the President and is almost deifying him already. This wasting will make him all-powerful if he lives."[132]

When the New York Chamber of Commerce announced plans that summer to raise a special subscription fund for Lucretia and the children, Blaine seized on the opportunity to build a political dynasty: "one thing is necessary now to clinch his popularity & double the people's love for him—and that is, that he should in a *manly* way decline to *accept presents*," he advised Lucretia. "In this matter lies an opportunity—a golden opportunity... Guiteau's bullet has killed Conkling and his gang—and it has made Gen'l Garfield the most popular and best *loved* man today in the country."[133]

Garfield himself puzzled at the predicament. Seeing the hour-by-hour medical bulletins going to the newspapers from his doctors and embarrassed by their intimate detail of his bodily functions, he joked: "I should think the people would be tired of having me dished up to them in this way."[134] As president, he saw how he'd become a national symbol. One day in mid-July while Colonel Rockwell was watching him, Garfield asked for a pencil to write something. Rockwell held paper by his hand as the president scrawled out the words: "Strangulatus pro Republica"—strangled for the Republic.[135] He found it easy to be generous these days. Garfield learned in late July that the New York legislature in Albany finally had ended Roscoe Conkling's re-election drama. After 56 ballots, it had compromised on two little-known upstaters to fill the unfinished Conkling and Platt terms: State Senators Elbridge G. Laplan (a Stalwart) and Warner Miller (a Half-Breed). "I am glad it is over. I am sorry for Conkling," Garfield told Rockwell that day. "He has made a great mistake, in my judgment. I will offer him any favor he may ask, or any appointment he may desire."[136]

Conkling had visited the White House one last time on July 14 while Garfield was convalescing, but had left only his card. He didn't want to disturb Mrs. Garfield, he told the doorman, and had no wish to see the president.

He asked the doorman simply to pass along his "profound sympathy," and then he left.[137]

In late July, though, Garfield's medical signs took an ominous turn. He began to suffer "rigors"—convulsive chills, signs of infection and blood poisoning. His fever rose to 101, then 104 degrees with new waves of vomiting; his pulse reached 125. Doctors discovered an ugly sac of pus near the wound in his back, a sign of rapid infection. Doctor Bliss and his cohorts decided to operate; Bliss described the painful procedure to the president, and Garfield felt little choice but to agree. "Very well; whatever you say is necessary must be done," he told Bliss.[138] With no anesthetic, they used a knife to cut an incision into his side two inches long and an inch-and-a-half deep, then inserted a tube to drain the sack. Garfield had to fight every instinct against crying out or jerking his muscles until they'd finished—an enormous feat of stoic concentration. Afterward, he slept soundly.

A few days later, a doctor probed his finger an inch deeper into the wound in his back and found pieces of bone coming loose. Beginning mid-summer, the doctors had begun focusing on a channel inside Garfield's lower back; they assumed it led to the bullet. They washed and drained it daily but it never healed. It too, actually, was a long sack of pus created by internal infections; each new probe only aggravated it more. Garfield's body by now actually had healed from the original gunshot wound; the bullet, resting near the pancreas, had become encased in a cyst. Instead, the president now was starting to die slowly from a combination of infection, blood poisoning, and starvation.

The president seemed to improve somewhat after the operation; he was able to sit with a prop supporting his head and back, but his body continued to rebel. His stomach rejected any solid food, limiting him to a liquid diet. They fed him fresh milk from a cow kept on the south lawn. His body weight began falling rapidly. Once he asked if he could smoke a cigar for the simple pleasure of it but the doctors refused him.

On August 8, the doctors operated again, this time using ether. After that, his digestive system seemed to break down totally, rejecting even his daily milk. The doctors tried using emergency forced feeding—"nutrient enemas," they called them, essentially forcing nourishment up his rectum. Then the parotid gland behind his right ear began to swell; infection and blood poisoning paralyzed the right side of his face. Doctors lanced the gland to relieve the pressure, which cleared his mind and eased the pain for a few days.

He even ate some solid food, but the new wound itself never healed and continued to ooze pus day after day.

Blaine, watching his friend's deteriorating condition, began to worry
about its impact on the country. Even if Garfield survived, he'd probably be
bed-ridden and disabled for months, maybe years. "[Y]our Father says an administration with a sick bed for its center is not a pleasant thought," Harriet
Blaine wrote to her daughter after he'd confided in her.[139] What would happen when Congress came back into session and real decisions had to be made?
What if a national emergency arose in the meantime? How long could the
country go without a functioning president?

Blaine raised the issue at a cabinet meeting. Perhaps Arthur should become president immediately, he suggested. The Constitution did provide that
the Vice President could assume presidential powers in cases of the President's "Death, Resignation, and Inability to Discharge" his office, but who
would be impertinent enough to declare a president "inable," especially if
that president might later disagree?* Blaine read a proposal to the cabinet, but
most of them objected—some considered it almost treasonous and grumbled
that Blaine was trying to "trim his sails for places in Arthur's cabinet" should
the president die.[140] They sent Tom James to New York City to get Arthur's
own opinion on the idea, but Arthur refused it. He refused even to travel
back to Washington to discuss it.

Fortunately, through the quiet summer, government departments could
run with little direction; everyone waited to see what would happen.

◉ ◉ ◉ ◉ ◉

Arthur returned to New York City in July after the president's medical signs
had improved and secluded himself in his Lexington Avenue townhouse. He
rarely went outside and kept a careful distance from his old political friends.
Even as Roscoe Conkling continued to push his Senate re-election contest in
Albany, Arthur stayed away; when Conkling finally lost, Arthur conspicuously declined to visit him or even send him a wire. In mid-August Arthur invited Conkling, Ulysses Grant, and a few old cronies to come to his house and
talk politics one day, but this itself sparked rounds of newspaper speculation

---

* Article III, Section 1. The Twenty-Fifth amendment, adopted in 1967 after the assassination
of President John F. Kennedy, creates a procedure for the vice president and a majority of the cabinet to declare a president "unable to discharge" his duties allowing the vice president to step in, but
it has never been invoked, even after President Reagan was shot by John Hinkley in 1981.

over who really would hold power in a future Arthur presidency. "The less Arthur has to do with Conkling the better for his Administration, if he is called to form one," Rutherford Hayes fumed in August. But even Hayes sympathized with Arthur's dilemma. "He will come in, if at all, under embarrassing and difficult circumstances. We must give him a fair trial—a fair hearing." He recognized a difference between "Guiteau Stalwarts" and "Arthur Stalwarts."[141]

Over time, Arthur saw fewer mentions of himself in the daily press. Late that month, he received a letter from a stranger that touched a nerve: "The hours of Garfield's life are numbered—before this meets your eye, you may be President. The people are bowed in grief; but—do you realize it?—not so much because he is dying, as because *you* are his successor." Arthur looked at the signature; it had come from a woman named Julia Sand. He read on: "What president ever entered the office under circumstances so sad! The day he was shot, the thought rose in a thousand minds that you might be the instigator of the foul act. Is that not humiliation which cuts deeper than any bullet can pierce?" Oddly, though, this Julia Sand was no critic. Instead, she seemed to offer a direction, a way out of the maze: "If there is any spark of nobility in you now is the time to let it shine…. It is for you to choose whether your record shall be written in black or in gold."[142]

Arthur checked the return address; it was listed as the home of banker Theodore V. Sand, a man he'd never met. He saved the letter; he would look at it often over the next few months as he struggled in his mind over what to do.

* * * * *

By late August, James Garfield's body had shriveled to 130 pounds, little more than half its normal weight; he literally was starving to death. Beneath his bedcovers, he'd become a virtual skeleton, ribs protruding through his chest, legs reduced to matchsticks. Multiple infections sent streams of pus and mucous pouring into his mouth, nose, and ears, making him gag and choke. Chunks of dead bone and cartilage had started to rot inside his body. Queen Victoria, hearing private reports, sent an urgent message through her Minister: "I am most deeply grieved at the sad news of the last few days, and would wish my deep sympathy to be conveyed to Mrs. Garfield," she wired from Balmoral.[143] Blaine often sat quietly with Lucretia in the White House these days reading letters and telegrams from well-wishers around the country. Lucretia strived to put on a bold face for the country. She let the newspaper writers see her taking an occasional carriage ride or sitting at dinner, always composed and hopeful—especially around her husband.

Garfield recognized the strain on her and worried about her own fragile health. "Yes, go and ride; I want you to," he'd tell her after she'd been sitting with him for hours at a time. "You must go to bed now" or "Go down to the table; you must preside there."[144] He tried to make light of his troubles. Told that Sitting Bull, the Sioux Indian chief being held prisoner after his role in the Little Bighorn battle, was starving in an army jail in the Dakota Territory, he snapped "Let him starve," then "Oh, no, send him my oatmeal."[145] Of all things, he wanted to play cards with his friend Colonel Rockwell— the kind of social pleasure he so sorely missed. But this too the doctors refused him.

Garfield performed just one single act of state in August: signing an extradition paper prepared by the State Department. Rockwell put the pen in his hand and held the paper under it. A few days later, Garfield found energy to write a letter to his mother, Rockwell again holding papers under the pencil in his hand.[146] "Dear Mother—Don't be disturbed by conflicting reports about my condition. It is true I am still weak and on my back, but I am gaining every day and need only time and patience to bring me through. Give my love to all the relatives & friends & especially to sisters Holly and Mary. Your loving son—James A. Garfield."[147]

The city of Washington grew increasingly unbearable in August, the Potomac River issuing terrible smells, the drinking water turning foul, waves of fever, dysentery, and malaria spreading through nearby neighborhoods; "the heat is so great, and every particle of moisture seems to be dried out of earth, air, and sky. I am not sleepy, but neither am I hungry," Harriet Blaine complained. She felt even worse for Garfield whom she took turns nursing during the summer—"how wretched it is! Wounded and sore and hurt to the death ... I send into his unseen room sympathy enough to float his bed, but he never knows it."[148]

Garfield hated the isolation; it sapped his morale, making him feel like a prisoner in his sickroom. "Doctor, how soon do you think we can take our wives and go to Mentor?" he asked.[149] They all wanted to leave town— Garfield, the doctors, the cabinet members. The doctors began seeing the risk of keeping Garfield in Washington as greater than that of moving him. Frank Hamilton of New York, one of Bliss's consulting surgeons, recoiled on getting his first whiff of the Potomac River "flats"—the swamps then surrounding the base of the Washington Monument—in late summer. "We must get the President out of this," he insisted. "It's enough to kill a well man in a week."[150] With their patient sinking, the doctors tried to put a good public face on the situation. "I think the president is doing very well today," Boynton, back working as a nurse under Doctor Bliss, told the Associated Press in early September, "he is better than he had been for a week past."[151]

After rounds of internal debate, they decided the fresh sea air of Elberon, New Jersey, near Long Branch, the President's favorite ocean side resort, would do him a world of good—either help him recuperate or at least better enjoy his final days alive. They told the newspapers it would speed his recovery: "I think [the President] will be immediately benefited by the change," Boynton informed reporters.[152] Enormous care went into the trip. By now, Americans had formed a unique bond with their crippled president; they'd accepted Garfield and Lucretia as virtual family members; they cried, prayed, and worried for them while admiring their courage. Churches held special prayer meetings for the president's safe passage. The Pennsylvania Railroad designed a special car to carry Garfield with cushioned bed and loads of ice. The train itself had three cars: one for Garfield, a second for Lucretia, and a third to carry a special detachment of twenty soldiers to carry Garfield's special stretcher. Two thousand volunteers worked through the night of September 5 to lay 3,200 feet of rail track from the Elberon train station to the door of Garfield's seaside cabin. No newsmen would be allowed on board the train and none complained of it.

Before leaving, Lucretia, by now leaning heavily on the cabinet wives as her circle of support, wrote a note to Harriet Blaine: "I hope you are coming to Elberon. It will do the President good to know you are there, and I do hope he may soon be able to see you. Until the Rubicon is passed. Lovingly goodbye."[153]

Garfield waved farewell—struggling to lift his hand—to White House aides as the soldiers carried him outside to an ambulance waiting by the south lawn that day. Thousands lined the railroad tracks north from Washington, D.C. through Maryland, Delaware, and New Jersey; rather than cheering as the president went by, they showed their respect by their ghostly silence, hats in hand. Woman waved their bonnets. When his car reached Elberon after dark that night and started along the newly-laid special track, it got stuck on a final hill near the cabin; two hundred railroad workers immediately rushed forward, rolled up their sleeves and together pushed it with their bare hands the last few hundred yards.

The cottage, owned by New York financier Charles G. Francklyn, was located near the Elberon Hotel; Garfield could see the surf and smell the ocean air from his bed. "This is delightful," he said on reaching the cabin. Dozens of newsmen set up camp at the nearby West End Hotel along with cabinet members and their wives; a few of them took time to play in the ocean surf and escape the somber mood. They all seemed to recognize it as a death-watch. For two weeks, Garfield lingered there; the world followed every fluc-tuation of his pulse, temperature, diet, and mood through the newspaper and telegraph reports. "To this day I cannot hear the sound of the low slow roll of the Atlantic on the shore, the sound which filled my ears as I walked from my cottage to his bedside, without recalling again the details of that ghastly tragedy," Joe Stanley Brown would write of those days forty years later.[154]

Things went well the first few days, but then the familiar symptoms re-turned—fever, chills, vomiting, and a sharp cough from a new complication, pneumonia. Garfield's fever rose well above 100 degrees and stayed there. On Monday morning, September 19, Garfield's doctors saw new "rigors" and a "respiratory murmur" and delayed changing the dressing on his wounds until the chills had passed. During the day Garfield tried to pick up a glass but could barely raise it a few inches. "I can't understand how it is, feeling and looking so well as I do, that I am so weak," he complained.[155] They bathed him and issued the usual bulletins on his pulse—bouncing between 143 and 126—and temperature. Late that night, after the reporters had gone back to their hotel to file their daily stories, Doctor Bliss asked Garfield if he felt un-comfortable. "Not at all," the president said, then fell asleep. Bliss went to his own room, as did Lucretia, and Colonel Rockwell came in to watch the pres-ident. At one point alone with Rockwell, Garfield awoke and made a motion with his right hand as if dealing cards—asking Rockwell to play. By now, though, he couldn't; Garfield no longer had the strength to hold them.

At about 10:15 pm that night, Garfield woke up and put his hand to his chest. A rupture had occurred in a large aneurysm near his heart causing mas-sive internal bleeding. David Swaim had come to take a turn watching the president, and Garfield shouted out to him: "Oh, Swaim. I am in terrible pain here.... Swaim, can't you do something for me? O' Swaim."[156] Swaim sent for Doctor Bliss who came into the room a moment later and found Garfield un-conscious. Bliss searched for a pulse in the president's wrist, then checked his neck, then placed his ear over Garfield's heart. He barely heard anything. He took a hypodermic needle from his case and administered a dose of stimulants; he sent for mustard powder. The pulse fluttered faintly then faded again.

He sent for Lucretia and another doctor. "Mrs. Garfield, the President is dying," he told her.

She watched, standing with daughter Mollie at her side, as her husband lay motionless on the bed, barely breathing, a slight tremor in his hands and feet, then leaned over and kissed his forehead. "Oh! Why am I made to suffer this cruel wrong?" she moaned.[157] Members of the household came into the room as word spread through the hotel. They stood around the bed, though Garfield's eyes stayed fixed on Lucretia, following her movements. She kept one hand on his forehead, the other on his chest, as Doctor Boynton fanned the president's face. For twenty minutes they stood in silence as the president's rasping breaths became farther apart. Then the breathing stopped altogether.

"It is over," Bliss said.[158]

Lucretia turned abruptly and walked away. She left the room, then came back a few minutes later and sat down in a chair "shaking convulsively," a doctor said, tears on her face, making no sound. Mollie threw her arms around her dead father. After the others had left, Lucretia sat alone in the darkness with the body of her dead husband for a long time until Doctor Boynton and Colonel Rockwell both insisted she get some sleep. She agreed and went to her room, but Bliss, from his own room next door, could hear the sounds of her pacing the floor for much of the night.

Church bells began ringing throughout Long Branch, New Jersey, then across the country, then around the world. Garfield had lived seventy-nine days after being shot by Charles Guiteau at the Washington, D.C. train station; just 49 years old, he'd died on the eighteenth anniversary of the Battle of Chickamauga in which he'd served so long ago.

❀ ❀ ❀ ❀ ❀

A messenger boy knocked at the front door of Chester Alan Arthur's brownstone at 123 Lexington Avenue in New York City at about 11:30 pm that night. Arthur had been sitting in the second floor study with a few friends: lawyers Elihu Root and Daniel Rollins and Police Commissioner Stephen French. "I hope—my God, I do hope it is a mistake," he said on hearing the news, but other telegrams soon arrived to confirm it.[159] At the same time, he heard church bells starting to sound through the streets of Manhattan. Newspaper writers congregated on the sidewalk but Aleck Powell, his butler, refused to allow them into the house. "He is sitting alone in his room sobbing like a child, with his head on his desk and his face buried in his hands," Powell told one of the reporters when asked how Arthur had received the news. "I dare not disturb him."[160]

Arthur had heard warnings for weeks about the president's deteriorating condition: Wayne MacVeigh had wired him in early September that Garfield was "grave and critical."[161] Arthur had told Chauncey Depew days earlier how deeply he feared Garfield's death. "The most frightful responsibility... would be the casting of the Presidency upon me under the conditions which you and all my friends so well understand."[162] Around midnight, Arthur's oldest son Alan arrived in a carriage from Columbia University where he was a student. At 12:25 am, formal notice came in a telegram from Elberon signed by all the cabinet members there. "It becomes our painful duty to inform you of the death of President Garfield and to advise you to take the oath of office as President of the United States without delay. If it concur with your judgment we will be very glad if you will come on the earliest train tomorrow morning."[163] A few minutes later, two New York City police detectives stationed themselves as guards in front of his house.

Arthur immediately sent a wire back: "I have your telegram, and the intelligence fills me with profound sorrow. Express to Mrs. Garfield my profound sympathy. C.A. Arthur."[164]

Arthur originally had wanted to take the oath of office in Washington, D.C.; now, though, he conferred with his friends and decided to proceed that night. He sent Root, Rollins, and French out into the street searching for a judge. Just before 2 am, Root returned with Judge John R. Brady of the New York Supreme Court; twenty minutes later Commissioner French appeared with Judge Donohue, also of the State Supreme Court, both Democrats. (Two Republicans, including Chief Judge Davis, were still away for the summer.)

They held the ceremony in the front parlor of Arthur's home at 2:15 am, Arthur standing apart from the others. Judge Brady, the first judge to have arrived, administered the oath. Arthur, 51 years old, raised his right hand and put his left hand on a bible that Brady held for him. "I, Chester Alan Arthur, do solemnly swear, that I will faithfully execute the Office of President of the United States, and will to the best of my Ability, preserve, protect and defend the Constitution of the United States. So help me God." Then Arthur shook hands with the men in the room.

The transition from President Garfield to President Arthur had taken less than four hours. Other than half-a-dozen carriages and a knot of reporters on the street, neighbors on Lexington Avenue had little idea that such a momentous event had occurred in their neighborhood. Arthur couldn't sleep that night. He wrote a proclamation summoning the United States Senate to a special session to choose a *President Pro Tempore* and mailed it to himself at the White House to assure a line of succession in case he himself were murdered before reaching Washington.[165] Then he sat up for two more hours that night, smoking and chatting with James Reed, his private secretary. Newspapermen on the sidewalk noticed that the gas lamp in his bedroom window didn't turn off until 5 am. It would also be an early morning for the new president.

· 15 ·
ARTHUR

THE MORNING AFTER Garfield's death, President Arthur rode a special train from New York City south to Elberon, New Jersey, and accompanied Garfield's body back to the Capitol. He traveled with the former President's widow and cabinet members. In Washington, he took the oath of office again, this time from Chief Justice Morrison R. Waite who administered it in front of a roomful of dignitaries that included former Presidents Rutherford Hayes and Ulysses Grant as well as several senators. Arthur's first days in office were consumed leading the national outpouring of grief over the death of James A. Garfield. Arthur led an estimated 100,000 mourners in filing past Garfield's body as it lay in state in the Capitol Building Rotunda for two days. His first public act as president was to proclaim Monday, September 26, the day Garfield was buried in Cleveland, Ohio, after some 150,000 people there had walked past his funeral bier, a national day of mourning.

A surprising level of sympathy greeted Arthur's elevation to the presidency. Even his harshest critics agreed to give him the benefit of the doubt. Arthur had won their respect by his dignified conduct during Garfield's convalescence and by his apparently genuine remorse over Guiteau's crime. "No man ever assumed the Presidency of the United States under more trying circumstances; no President has needed more the generous appreciation, the indulgent forbearance of his fellow citizens," the New York Times argued. "He is a much better and broader man than the majority of those with whom his recent political career has been identified."[1] Even Joseph Medill's staunchly anti-Stalwart Chicago Tribune acknowledged the "extremely embarrassing" circumstances Arthur had confronted and how he'd acted as "a gentleman of the finest sensibility." Arthur's demeanor had served to "soften, if not to remove, whatever unpleasant anticipations" people had for his presidency.[2]

Before 1881, only three American vice presidents had assumed the White House because of a president's death, and their experience gave little cause for comfort. Andrew Johnson had come within an inch of being removed from office for his policies as president after Abraham Lincoln's assasination. John Tyler and Millard Fillmore, elevated after the deaths of William Henry Harrison and Zachary Taylor, respectively, both broke with their party (both were Whigs), became hated by former friends, and saw their party defeated in the next election.

American Vice-Presidential Presidents:

- **John Tyler** (1841-1845): Whig, upon death of William Henry Harrison. Failed to win re-nomination; replaced by Democrat James Polk in 1845.

- **Millard Fillmore** (1850-1853): Whig, upon death of Zachary Taylor. Failed to win re-nomination; replaced by Democrat Franklin Pierce in 1853.

- **Andrew Johnson** (1865-1869): Republican, upon assassination of Abraham Lincoln. Survived impeachment by single Senate vote; failed to win re-nomination in 1868 and replaced by Ulysses S. Grant.

- **Chester A. Arthur** (1881-1885): Republican, upon assassination of James Garfield. Failed to win re-nomination; replaced by Democrat Grover Cleveland in 1885.

- **Theodore Roosevelt** (1901-1909): Republican, upon assassination of William McKinley. Elected in 1904, declined to run in 1908, and defeated running as a Progressive in 1912.

- **Calvin Coolidge** (1923-1929): Republican, upon death of Warren Harding. Elected in 1924.

- **Harry Truman** (1945-1953): Upon death of Franklin D. Roosevelt. Elected in 1948.

- **Lyndon B. Johnson** (1963-1969): Democrat, upon assassination of John F. Kennedy. Elected in 1964 but declined to seek re-nomination in 1968 due to controversy over the Vietnam War.

- **Gerald R. Ford** (1974-77): Republican, upon resignation of Richard M. Nixon. Nominated but defeated for election in 1976 by Democrat Jimmy Carter.

Arthur, as president, offered a conciliatory hand. He asked all seven of Garfield's secretaries to stay in place at least for a few months, until December 1881, to give the country continuity. Recognizing that Arthur would want to pick his own cabinet members loyal to him, Blaine submitted his own resignation in October but Arthur refused to accept it. Since Arthur had no vice president, he called a special session of the Senate to meet quickly and elect a *President Pro Tempore* to assure a successor should he himself die in office. Arthur chose not to move into the White House itself during the first few months, returning instead to the Capitol Hill townhouse of Senator John P. Jones where he'd stayed after the shooting. There he set up living quarters and an office; clerks shuttled back and forth with official papers all day long. Arthur decided to use this transition time to undertake a major renovation of the White House building, replacing the worn carpets, tattered drapes and old furniture dating back to Ulysses Grant's time as well as the rotting decades-old plumbing in the basement; he commissioned New York decorator Louis Tiffany to lead designers in giving the dreary old building a new elegance. As a widower, he asked his younger sister Mary Arthur McElroy to join him in Washington four months a year as "Mistress of the White House," filling the social role of First Lady.

Arthur won praise these early days for diligence, humility, and hints of independence. He impressed critics with his friendly openness; they began to trust him, at least grudgingly. So it came with some trepidation to Arthur in early October, just two weeks after Garfield's death and with his own reputation still tenuous, when he learned that Roscoe Conkling had come to Washington and wanted to see him. Arthur hadn't seen Conkling since the summer, before becoming president; he had to assume his old mentor wanted something. But Conkling was also Arthur's best and most loyal friend; his door could never be closed to him.

Roscoe Conkling in late 1881 still had hints of golden curls in his hair, the old haughty, imperious glare in his eye, and a garish collection of suits and cravats. He still stood tall and erect and drew glances from ladies passing in the street. But stress and age had taken a toll on him this past year. He walked a bit more slowly now, his hair and beard almost fully gray; his lips often hardened into a sneer. Conkling had fought till the bitter end to regain his United States Senate seat that summer; when the Albany legislature had finally rejected him, he'd announced an end to his public life. "I am done with politics now and forever," he'd told friends.[3] Exhausted, emotionally drained, and financially broke, Conkling had retreated to far-off Utica, to the house on tree-lined Rutger Park where his wife Julia lived. He spent his time staring at the Mohawk River, trying to make peace with his family, and considering his future.

Friends kept his name alive in local politics, but public revulsion against his wars with Garfield that year made any quick revival impossible; Conkling failed in September even to win a seat to the next Republican state convention—conventions he once ruled with an iron hand. Conkling already had his eye on launching a private legal practice in New York City and, with his protégé Arthur in power in Washington, his time for a position of true eminence in national affairs seemed at hand. As speculation about Arthur's new cabinet began to peak in early October, Roscoe Conkling's name always bubbled to the top, a likely pick either to a top slot himself or as behind-the-scenes voice dictating Arthur's choices. Conkling certainly expected Chet Arthur to repay the years of loyalty, perhaps by offering to name him Secretary of State—even knowing that Conkling probably wouldn't accept it. Conkling may have relished the thought of yanking the State Department portfolio away from his old enemy James G. Blaine.[4]

The talk of a resurrected Conkling wielding dominant power in an Arthur presidency appalled most Washington moderates and quickly sparked ugly warnings. "The topic is exciting and... will tend to stir up the old quarrels and dissentions," Thurlow Weed opined from his perch in Albany, even suggesting the possibility of violence: "there is danger we may have more Guiteaus around."[5] But Roscoe Conkling dismissed the old man's notion as silliness. Power was power, and his friend Arthur could use it as he saw fit.

Conkling came to Senator Jones's house on Capitol Hill late on Saturday morning, October 8; a reporter described him arriving that day "dressed with usual care and looking in the best of health."[6] Senators had returned to Washington that week for their emergency session but both the Republican and Democratic members were holding caucus meetings that day; this left Arthur and Conkling to meet in relative privacy.

Arthur showed Conkling into his private upstairs room he used as his presidential office and closed the door; the two men spoke for hours, sitting together until late afternoon. No actual record of the meeting exists and there were no immediate leaks about its content. Rumors swirled around the Capitol that night that Arthur had agreed to appoint his old master as the next Secretary of the Treasury—perhaps letting Conkling choose his own Custom

House Collector, or had sought Conkling's blessing for an entire cabinet slate. When a reporter approached Conkling that evening at his hotel, Conkling playfully put him off: "I came to see the President. He and I have long been friends. I have not seen him since he became President until to-day. We had a conversation on various subjects. I do not know when I shall see him again," he told the newsman: "but it seems that the gentlemen of the press are exercised over it. I assure you that you have no reason to be, and I wish you a very good evening."[7]

Privately, though, troubling word soon began to circulate among close friends: the meeting had not been friendly at all. Instead of a happy reunion of master and pupil, Arthur and Conkling had had a terrible fight. Conkling, seeing his long-time protégé Arthur finally in power, apparently had confronted him behind closed doors that afternoon with one single direct demand: William H. Robertson, the new Collector of the New York Custom House recently rammed down Conkling's throat by that man Garfield in the White House, must be fired. Garfield was dead now, Arthur was president, and the insult must be undone. As one insider told Brooklyn Eagle reporter William Hudson: "you put it down for a fact that 'Conk' wanted 'Chet' to remove Robertson and appoint one of our fellows collector."[8] Nothing else mattered to Conkling that day; the rest of the meeting amounted to mere chit-chat.

Arthur recognized exactly what this demand meant. After all his weeks of soul-searching and careful cultivating of public support, Conkling was asking him to throw it all away—as if he'd learned nothing from Garfield's assassination at the hands of Charles Guiteau. Firing Robertson would re-ignite the Stalwart and Half-Breed wars with a vengeance, and cast Arthur as dismantling the most visible symbol of the martyred Garfield's term. It would divide the country and sabotage his own fragile reputation in one stroke— all just to settle Roscoe Conkling's old grudge. Arthur refused to do it; the demand was "outrageous," he told Conkling to his face. He felt "morally bound to continue the policy of the former President."[9]

They quarreled; they raised their voices and pounded their fists on tables. Arthur was "bound neither morally nor politically nor in any other way," Conkling bellowed back at him, according to friends. Garfield's policy had been utterly hostile to his New York party. Where were his loyalties? Conkling demanded.[10] But Arthur refused to be bullied. He'd gone through too much the past few months to back down now. He wouldn't change his mind.

Conkling ran into a brick wall. He stormed out of the room finally, swearing "all our friends have turned traitor."[11]

Conkling didn't have many friends left in Washington, D.C. to confide in at this point. Many old colleagues from the Senate had now turned against him after his resignation in May; others he couldn't trust with a secret. Instead, after leaving Arthur's office at Senator Jones's house that October afternoon, Conkling rode his carriage across town to visit Kate Chase Sprague, his old romantic liaison whom he still saw now and again. Kate Sprague, still attractive at 41 years old, if worn-looking after seventeen years of abusive marriage to the drunken Rhode Island former governor William Sprague, had been pressing formal divorce proceedings since that summer and gossips said that Conkling was giving her legal tips on the process; unlike earlier years, they now kept their friendship well hidden—and at this point, it may have been just that, a friendship. Kate Sprague was one of very few people to whom Roscoe Conkling would reveal weakness and despair. "When I saw him *afterwards* & saw *how he was suffering*, I urged his quitting Washington without delay," she reported to Arthur in a private note after her visit from Conkling that afternoon. "Friends who have seen him within a day or two, report him as very ill."[12] She urged Arthur to reconsider; perhaps he could still make amends by naming Conkling his Secretary of the Treasury; Conkling could be a "tower of strength" in his cabinet, she insisted.[13]

By the time Roscoe Conkling left Washington, D.C. for home in New York two days later, a reporter described him as "suffering from his old malarial troubles, and looking what he really was, a sick man." Still, the aura of his vast political power remained, even if it was only a chimera: "It is the general impression, at least, that [Arthur's] Cabinet was arranged during [Conkling's] lengthy conversation with the President," the newsman reported.[14]

Chester Arthur, for his part, remained very bitter over Roscoe Conkling's demand that day; he "doesn't like to talk about it," a friend confided.[15] Its sheer selfishness rubbed against Arthur's own good nature. A handful of his New York political friends recognized the principle he'd defended. "The President is right," local party leader John O'Brien confided. "He isn't 'Chet' Arthur anymore; he's the President" and must demonstrate that he's "nobody's servant."[16] Still, when word got out, most of Arthur's old cronies sided against him; Arthur had betrayed them, they felt. He was a coward, afraid of his enemies, and couldn't be trusted anymore.

Despite all the pressure from long-time friends, Arthur stood his ground.

As president, he would not take any orders from the New York machine and would not reopen the wounds between Stalwarts and Half-Breeds. He had become his own man. "For the Vice-Presidency I was indebted to Mr. Conkling," he told one ally, "but for the Presidency of the United States my debt is to the Almighty."[17] A year earlier, in June 1880 at the great Republican nominating convention in Chicago, Chester Alan Arthur had not even wanted to be President of the United States; he'd considered the vice presidency as "a greater honor than I ever dreamed of attaining" and had defied Roscoe Conkling to accept it even then. Now, the presidency itself, that office whose terrible duties had send James Garfield to an early grave, had also cost Arthur the dearest friendship in his life. But he had determined not to tarnish the honor that fate had thrust into his hands.

⊛ ⊛ ⊛ ⊛ ⊛

Chester Alan Arthur lasted only one term as president. Republicans refused to nominate him for a run on his own in 1884. He tried to mend fences with Roscoe Conkling soon after their stormy falling-out, naming Conkling to a seat on the United States Supreme Court that came open in January 1882, but Conkling turned it down even after the Senate had confirmed him by a 39 to 12 majority.[18] The estrangement between Arthur and Conkling lasted the rest of their lives.

As president, Arthur followed a moderate course and developed a reputation for competence. He named a broad-based cabinet that included even William E. Chandler, Blaine's old campaign manager, as Secretary of the Navy; Chandler became Arthur's closest political advisor and took charge of building a new generation of ironclad warships that would prove their worth later in the Spanish-American War. Reformers applauded Arthur when he signed the landmark Pendleton Civil Service Act in 1883 and pressed the prosecution of the Star Route postal frauds, even when they turned against his old friend Stephen Dorsey as the principal defendant. They recognized his term as being among the most scandal-free in recent memory.

Politically, though, Arthur became isolated. The New York Stalwarts abandoned him in droves: "the organization was not disposed to forgive Arthur for refusing to get rid of Collector Robertson," explained Tom Platt, their emerging new leader.[19] Arthur's "career would have been more agreeable to himself" had he just gone along with Roscoe Conkling's demand that day in October 1881, George Boutwell later observed.[20] On the other side, when

James Blaine got the presidential bug again in 1884, he took most of the "Garfield Republicans" with him. Arthur got little public credit for his show of backbone against Conkling's demands.

Arthur's presidential style came as an eye-opener to some White House veterans: he was the first president with his own valet, a man who could try on 20 pairs of pants before picking the right one and always ended up looking fine and distinguished. He guarded his privacy jealously; when a temperance lady hectored him once about keeping Lucy Hayes' ban against alcohol at White House functions, he complained: "Madam, I may be President of the United States, but my private life is nobody's damn business."[21] He continued to put fresh flowers at the picture of his dead wife Ellen Herndon Arthur each day in the White House.

Arthur made a credible run for re-nomination in 1884—after all, who knew better how to organize an election campaign then he did. Republicans convened that year at the same Glass Palace in Chicago where they'd nominated Garfield four years earlier. But the votes were against Arthur from the start and not even William Chandler's shrewdness could help: Blaine outpolled Arthur 334½ to 278 on the first ballot [the half vote reflecting an argument in the Kentucky delegation] and won the nomination outright on the fourth. By then, Arthur faced a bigger worry. Secretly, he'd learned from doctors that he was suffering from Bright's disease—a breakdown of the kidneys that often proved fatal. His presidency lasted just long enough for him to dedicate the completed Washington Monument—all 550 feet of it—in December 1884; his last official act was to sign an Act placing Ulysses S. Grant, himself then dying of cancer and recently bankrupted, on the army retired list with full pay.

Beginning in early 1885, Arthur's medical condition deteriorated, his kidney disease spreading to his heart and prompting colds and infection. Cheerful to the end, he pulled himself from bed to attend President Grant's funeral in late July but finally succumbed after a long illness in November 1886, dying just twenty months after leaving the White House. Among the thousands of celebrities who attended his funeral service in New York City, Arthur would have appreciated the lone figure of Roscoe Conkling, keeping to himself in a side pew, quietly grieving for his old friend with whom he hadn't spoken in years. Arthur was buried alongside his wife at the Rural Cemetery in Albany, New York.

Willard Bliss and the president's doctors: Doctor D. Haynes Agnew performed the autopsy on President Garfield's body the morning after Garfield's death in Elberon, New Jersey; he quickly confirmed how wrong he and the others had been from the start. He "passed his little finger gently down the spine until it slipped entirely through the wounded vertibra," recalled Joe Stanley Brown, who attended the autopsy as a witness. "Gentlemen, there is the wound," Agnew said sadly, "we were mistaken in our diagnosis." Then he turned and abruptly walked out.[22]

Had it happened today, modern medicine certainly would have saved James Garfield's life after his shooting by Charles Guiteau; with some physical therapy, Garfield probably would have walked again and enjoyed a wave of popularity not unlike President Ronald Reagan a century later after Reagan's March 1981 shooting by John Hinckley. Even in 1881 a competent physician probably could have saved Garfield. Many contemporary doctors cringed in embarrassment at the bungled treatment: "It is indeed humiliating to the historian to record such a mass of irretrievable blunders," one has written.[23] Had the doctors done nothing but ease Garfield's pain, fed him, and let his body alone, he probably would have avoided the deadly infections and survived, though doubtless as an invalid.

The bickering among Garfield's doctors sparked a harsh public response. Willard Bliss became a particular target for criticism: the Chicago Medical Review blasted him as early as August 1881 for continuing to treat Garfield after having contracted blood poisoning through a cut in his own finger, violating "the most ordinary precautions of medical surgery" even by 1881 standards.[24]

Incompetence was bad enough, but the doctors' demands for government-paid fees after Garfield's death became a national scandal. For their four months' work treating the president, Bliss and Frank Hamilton each demanded $25,000 payment from Congress (about $500,000 each in modern dollars). Agnew asked for a more modest $14,700. By contrast, Silas Boynton, who'd worked just as hard as the others and treated Lucretia for many additional weeks during her own illness, requested a mere $4,500 and had refused to accept a $1,000 check from Garfield himself. Congress, reflecting public impatience with the whole lot of them, limited the doctors to $35,000 (out of a total of over $100,000 requested) and left them to fight among themselves over it before a special audit committee; they wouldn't see a dime from Washington until well over a year after Garfield's death.[25]

Joe Stanley Brown: Just 23 years old at the time of Garfield's assassination, Stanley Brown turned down President Arthur's offer to stay on as White House private secretary and instead followed Lucretia Garfield out west to Ohio to organize Garfield's dozens of boxes of presidential papers. Later, he studied at Yale then married Mollie Garfield, the president's daughter, when she turned 21 years old in 1888. Stanley-Brown (he added a hyphen to his name at Lucretia's urging when he married Mollie) went on to become an investment banker and editor at the National Geographic Society. He lived until 1941.

William E. Chandler: After serving as Arthur's Secretary of the Navy, Chandler enjoyed a long career as United States Senator from New Hampshire until returning to his law practice in Concord in 1901. After Arthur's abortive 1884 renomination effort against his old friend Blaine, Chandler never again managed a national political campaign.

Chauncey Depew finally did become a United States Senator, elected from New York in 1899 and serving two full terms until 1911. Before that, in 1885, he'd gotten his full reward from the Vanderbilts and been appointed president and later chairman of the New York Central and Hudson River Railroad Company, one of the premier corporate leadership positions in America.

Stephen Dorsey's trial for the Star Route postal frauds ended in his acquittal on charges of stealing some $412,000 through various schemes, though he never cleared his name. Afterwards Dorsey publicly blasted Arthur and Garfield both for treachery in the affair; he settled finally at his large ranch near Springer, New Mexico—today called Dorsey Mansion—which has since become a major tourist attraction there.

Lucretia Garfield outlived her husband by thirty-seven years and during that time became a popular figure in America. She moved back to Ohio after the assassination, living on the Mentor farm and also in a townhouse she purchased in Cleveland. Friends visiting a year later found Lucretia looking healthy and cheerful but aged: "There is a better color in her face and she is more fleshy. She looks older and is more careworn, and numerous wrinkles have appeared in her face since I last saw her," one wrote, but her "frank and outspoken" attitude remained.[26]

Congress granted Lucretia the franking privilege plus a $50,000 pension while the New York subscription fund gave her a nest-egg of nearly $300,000; she'd never have to worry about money again. Over the next twenty years, she devoted herself primarily to her children, but remained a good draw for political events. She returned to Washington, D.C. briefly in 1887 and stood with President Grover Cleveland at the unveiling of the grand new statue of President Garfield at the base of Capitol Hill on Maryland Avenue. (If you live in Washington, D.C., you've likely driven past it hundreds of times without even noticing.)[27] Politically, she backed Theodore Roosevelt's brand of Republican reformers and proudly held a Founders Certificate for the 1912 Progressive Party. With Joe Stanley Brown's help, she organized the first modern presidential library, arranging her husband's voluminous books and papers in a fireproof room at Mentor—now a National Historic Site.

Meanwhile, her children gave her the pleasure of their own successes. Lucretia threw a double wedding at the Mentor home in 1888 when two of them married on the same day: Mollie to Joe Stanley Brown (now "Stanley-Brown") and her eldest son Harry to Belle Mason of Cleveland. She lived to see her son James, the second oldest, serve with Theodore Roosevelt in Washington on the U.S. Civil Service Commission and then join Roosevelt's presidential cabinet as Secretary of the Interior; she saw her son Harry, the oldest, become president of Williams College, Irvin a Boston lawyer, and Abram a leading Cleveland architect.

Lucretia never entirely healed from the shock and despair of her husband's death, nor did she ever lose her bitterness at the politicians behind it. After James Blaine's defeat to Grover Cleveland for the presidency in 1884, she wrote to his wife Harriet: "For you personally, my dear friend, I cannot be sorry. The treacherous foe did not lurk in camp to help elect Mr. Blaine, and with his diabolic hatred then arm the assassin. Your husband is spared to you."[28] Lucretia died in southern California in 1918, where she'd begun spending winters in later years, and was placed aside her husband in Cleveland.

Ulysses Grant badgered President Arthur on nominees, making dozens of suggestions for cabinet members, ministers, and other appointments, and groused when Arthur ignored him just as Garfield had. Grant concentrated instead in the early 1880s on his business ventures in New York City; sadly, none went well. As his Mexican Railroad foundered, Grant invested deeply

in his son's Wall Street brokerage firm, relying almost blindly on their brilliant young financial partner Ferdinand Ward. Ward, unfortunately, turned
out to be a thief who embezzled millions of dollars exploiting Grant's good
name. The firm collapsed in 1884, throwing Grant into an embarrassing public bankruptcy. That summer, doctors diagnosed a pain in Grant's throat as
cancer from his lifetime of cigar smoking.

Despite ample problems of his own, Ulysses Grant managed one more
magnanimous act during that summer of 1884; he reconciled with James G.
Blaine, his political rival from 1880 now running for president in his own
right. Grant called on Blaine at a New York City reception where reporters
could see them together; the two men spoke for about an hour.[29] Grant told
Adam Badeau he thought Blaine would make an "excellent president."[30]
Grant never campaigned for Blaine publicly beyond the one incident, but he
and Blaine no longer saw themselves as enemies.

As cancer consumed him over the next year, Ulysses Grant produced
what is today considered perhaps the finest memoir written by a former president (though not covering his presidency), an account of his life and times
through the Civil War. At his death in 1885, Ulysses Grant was widely considered the greatest American of the Nineteenth Century next to whom
Abraham Lincoln was a shooting star. Since then, history has more than reversed those judgments and Grant has suffered more than his share of harping from historians with political agendas for belittling his enormous role.
Today, Grant is experiencing a well-earned re-evaluation among scholars,
with his reputation being considerably upgraded.

Charles Guiteau's trial for the murder of President Garfield became one of
the great courtroom dramas of the Nineteenth Century. Beginning on November 14, 1881—just two months after the president's death—it lasted fifty
four days, playing out before a packed courtroom near the District of Columbia jail. Telegraphed daily across the country and printed in the newspapers, the drama mesmerized the nation for three months. Guiteau pled innocence and defended himself with the help of two lawyers including his
brother-in-law George Scoville. Before the trial, he courted the press and savored his celebrity status: he dictated a lengthy biography from his jail cell to
the *New York Herald* and, the day after Garfield's death, wrote a letter to incoming President Arthur taking credit for Arthur's elevation and recommending cabinet appointments for his new administration, including Roscoe

Conkling for State, Levi Morton for Treasury, and Emory Storrs for Attorney General.[31]

At the trial itself, Guiteau's defense raised two principal issues—insanity and causation. Guiteau blamed medical malpractice for killing Garfield: "The doctors did that. I simply shot at him."[32] As for insanity, both sides produced batteries of experts and the argument was hard fought even by 1881 standards. The prosecution called over ninety direct and rebuttal witnesses, the defense another fifty. Together with legal arguments, their testimony filled a transcript running over 2,600 pages. Guiteau himself took the stand to answer questions for four full days. The proceeding often became a grotesque theatre; Guiteau's constant outbursts and interruptions often reduced the courtroom to a circus.[33]

Harriet Blaine attended many of the trial sessions and at first found it "the most interesting place, by all odds, in Washington."[34] But she too soon grew disgusted with Guiteau's outbursts in "that vile room." Like most Americans, she wanted to see Guiteau "out of the way. I want it impossible for that hoarse, cracked voice, ever to raise itself again."[35]

A jury convicted Guiteau on January 25, 1882, and he had to survive two murder attempts just to reach his hanging in the D.C. Jail on June 30, 1882.* His execution drew a large crowd of newspaper writers and curiosity seekers to the D.C. Jail courtyard; standing on the gallows, hands bound in front of him, Guiteau read first from a Bible that a minister held for him. Then he read aloud a few verses of poetry he'd written himself that morning for the occasion, intended to portray "a child babbling to his mama and his papa" as he described it. He held the page in front of him in his bound hands. "If set to music they may be rendered very effective," he explained, and then proceeded in a high-pitched childlike voice:

> *I am going to the Lordy; I am so glad,*
> *I am going to the Lordy, I am so glad,*
> > *I am going to the Lordy,*
> *Glory hallelujah! Glory hallelujah!*
> > *I am going to the Lordy!*

---

* On September 11 a jail guard fired a shot at Guiteau through the window of his cell, then on November 16 a rider on horseback shot into the police carriage carrying him from the courthouse back to jail during the trial. Both shots missed their target, and neither assailant was ever tried for his attack.

I love the Lordy with all my soul,
     Glory Hallelujah!
And that is the reason I am going to the Lord,
Glory hallelujah! Glory hallelujah!
     I am going to the Lord.

I saved my party and my land,
     Glory hallelujah!
But they have murdered me for it,
And that is the reason I am going to the Lordy,
Glory hallelujah! Glory hallelujah!
     I am going to the Lordy!

I wonder what I will see when I get to the Lordy,
I expect to see most glorious things,
Beyond all earthly conception,
When I am with the Lordy!
Glory hallelujah! Glory hallelujah!
     I am with the Lord.[36]

When Guiteau had finished, the hangman placed a black hood over his face and Guiteau let the paper with the poem fall him his hand. Then the trap door promptly dropped under his feet, the rope snapping his neck and killing him. Police never returned Guiteau's body to his family. Instead, after an autopsy that discovered nothing more abnormal than an enlarged spleen, they preserved his skeleton, spleen, and brain and placed them in storage at the National Museum of Health and Medicine in Washington, D.C., where they are listed as remaining to this day.

Of the four assassins of American presidents, John Wilkes Booth (Lincoln, 1865), Leon Czolgosz (McKinley, 1901), Lee Harvey Oswald (Kennedy, 1963), and Guiteau, history usually gives Guiteau the least regard, dismissing him as a madman and "disappointed office seeker"—much as the 1881 Stalwarts would have liked. In some ways, though, insane or not, Guiteau was the most successful. Unlike the others, he not only killed a president but deliberately installed a perceived friend, Arthur, in his place. And by his crime he brought about one of the most important reforms of the era: the 1883 Civil Service Act which, in little over a decade, had placed some 86,000 federal positions under a merit system administered by an independent new Civil Service Commission. Today, the vast majority of federal employees have professional civil service status rather than owing their jobs to politicians, a bedrock concept of modern governments around the world.

Levi P. Morton returned home to his New York bank in 1885 after four years as Minister to France, and then failed two more times to become a United States Senator. His chance for high political office came in 1888 when Benjamin Harrison, nominated for president that year, asked Morton to join his ticket as vice president. Harrison defeated Grover Cleveland in the election and Morton spent the next four years presiding over the "millionaires club" Senate of the late 1880s. By 1892, though, political winds had changed and Harrison decided to drop Morton from his re-election ticket in favor of Whitelaw Reid. Disappointed, Morton returned to New York and enjoyed a term as governor before retiring permanently to enjoy his wealth.

Tom Platt, after his embarrassing demise in Albany in 1881, managed to climb back and emerge by the mid-1880s as undisputed leader of the New York Republican machine, a role he played through the early 1900s. He never settled his differences with Roscoe Conkling after the Albany debacle, though. One day in the late 1880s, Platt saw Conkling arguing with Jay Gould on the sidewalk outside his office at the U.S. Express Company and rushed downstairs to offer them a private place to talk. When Conkling responded with a typical angry tirade, Platt said simply. "If you would like to come upstairs to my office, Mr. Gould, you will be welcome. But as for you, sir (turning to Conking), you may go to the devil!"[37]

Platt, as party boss, is remembered today mainly for nominating the young New York Governor Theodore Roosevelt as William McKinley's vice presidential running-mate in 1900—mostly trying to get the eager reformer out of his hair in New York State*—and setting the stage for Roosevelt's ascension to the presidency on McKinley's assassination in 1901. Platt returned to the United States Senate for two more terms from 1897 through 1909.

Whitelaw Reid had married Elizabeth Mills in April 1881 and was on a European honeymoon when he heard of Garfield's assassination. He returned to

---

* Among other things, Roosevelt had removed Louis Payn, Platt's long-time henchman and key supporter during 1881, from his position as N.Y. State Superintendent of Insurance in 1900 over Platt's objections.

New York but soon sailed again to Europe again as President Benjamin Harrison's Minister to Paris in 1889. Harrison liked Reid enough to make him his vice presidential running mate in 1892 but they lost the election to Grover Cleveland, making Cleveland the only American president with two divided terms (and the only Democrat elected president during the fifty-two years from 1860 to 1911). By then, Reid had turned over active management of his *New York Tribune* to his son Ogden. Theodore Roosevelt sent Reid abroad again as Minister to the Court of Saint James in 1901. In 1924, Elizabeth Mills and Ogden Reid would purchase the *New York Herald* and merge the two venerable journals into the *Herald-Tribune*, which would remain a New York journalistic landmark until the 1960s.

William H. Robertson waited until August 1, 1881, after Roscoe Conkling and Tom Platt both had been soundly defeated for re-election to their United States Senate seats, to begin his new job as Collector of the Port of New York, where he served honorably for four years. Robertson never conducted any massive purge of the Conkling-Stalwart Custom House crowd and Arthur consistently resisted pressure to remove him. After Grover Cleveland replaced him in 1885, Robertson resumed his seat in the New York legislature in Albany.

John Sherman served in the United States Senate for another sixteen years after Garfield's assassination until President William McKinley appointed him to a brief term as Secretary of State in 1897. Sherman is remembered today principally for authoring the Sherman Anti-Trust Act under which John D. Rockefeller's Standard Oil, Bill Gates' Microsoft, and labor leader Eugene Debs all were prosecuted for anti-competitive practices.

The Feud: The great feud between Roscoe Conkling and James Gillespie Blaine, already having spanned fifteen years, still had one more major episode to run after the Garfield assassination. Blaine left President Arthur's cabinet in December 1881 a tired man: "The death of Garfield is a fresh grief to me. My enjoyment of public life seems gone," he wrote a friend just after the funeral.[38] Blaine was "never quite the same" afterwards, a biographer noted. "The flow of animal spirits was not quite so free."[39] He busied himself during the next few years with some enjoyable private projects: writing a massive two-volume political history of the Civil War and post-war eras—*Twenty*

Years of Congress: From Lincoln to Garfield, 1861 to 1881—and building a large new home in Washington, D.C., in the still-unspoiled wilds near Dupont Circle.

When the presidency dangled itself again in 1884, Blaine rediscovered his focus. He launched a well-organized campaign; ironically, his strongest allies that year included New York Stalwarts who'd soured on Arthur and lacked Roscoe Conkling as leader—demonstrating just how little substance had been behind their feud in the first place. Tom Platt himself seconded Blaine's nomination in Chicago and helped him defeat Arthur in the balloting; to cement his alliance with the Stalwarts, Blaine chose as his vice presidential running mate Illinois Senator John Logan—a pillar of General Grant's original "triumvirate" from 1880. In the general election, Blaine faced reformist New York Governor Grover Cleveland—the first time two non-soldiers had opposed each other for the presidency since the Civil War. Their race became close and dirty: Disclosures that Cleveland had fathered a child out of wedlock ("Hey. Ma. Where's Pa? Gone to the White House. Ha ha.") were matched by claims that Blaine's 1851 marriage to his wife Harriet Stanwood had been invalid and that they had conceived their eldest son Stanwood out of wedlock. Blaine benefited from lingering good will from his Garfield days, but reformers that year chose to launch a full-scale bolt; they formed the "Mugwumps"* and cast their lot with Cleveland, citing Blaine's history of scandal and machine politics.

Like James Garfield in 1880, James Blaine too now looked at a map and recognized that, to win, he'd need to carry New York State with its 36 electoral votes, and doing so would be far easier with the support of its humbled but still-powerful former Senator, Roscoe Conkling.

Conkling, after spurning Chester Arthur—he now regularly referred to his old friend as "His Accidency" or "the stalled ox of the White House"[40]— had built by then a quite successful legal practice in New York City, working from rooms on West 29th Street. Conkling eschewed public speeches and instead enjoyed playing *prima donna* to juries and judges for large fees and without the headaches of politics. His clients included Wall Street tycoon Jay Gould, inventor Thomas Alva Edison, California railroad magnate Collis P. Huntington and the *New York World*. Conkling mostly stayed away from pol-

---

* "Mugwump" came from an Algonquin Indian word meaning "great man" or "chief," though critics used it to deride their wishy-washy politics, with their "mugs" on one side and their "wumps" on the other.

itics; still, when Tom Platt told him in 1884 that the New York Stalwarts were supporting Blaine for president that year, he was "struck speechless," Platt recalled. They were making an "egregious blunder," Conkling warned.[41]

Blaine hoped that Roscoe Conkling actually might bury the hatchet and support him in 1884 for the good of the party, perhaps even making a speech or two on his behalf. "Can Conkling be induced to speak for us? It would be an immense thing for us. How can he be induced to do it?" he asked ally Stephen Elkins early in the campaign.[42] Conkling never gave them a direct answer and, in fact, never lifted a finger for Blaine. "I am out of politics," he told anyone who asked.[43]

When a group of Republican leaders privately approached him about working for Blaine, Conkling famously responded: "No, thank you, I don't engage in criminal practice."[44]

Behind the scenes, though, Conkling took off the gloves and actively focused on sabotaging his old enemy. He wrote several virulent ant-Blaine columns for the *New York World* signed simply "Stalwart Republican" and put out word through his upstate network for Stalwarts to support Grover Cleveland. Perhaps most pointedly, Conkling secretly advised Cleveland's camp on Blaine's weaknesses and helped uncover a second batch of "Mulligan letters"—re-igniting the old scandal over Blaine's railroad stock dealings from the 1870s. Blaine's off-hand remark at the close of one of these letters, written to railroad financier Warren Fisher in 1876, produced one of the Democrats' more memorable chants of the campaign: "Burn, burn, burn this letter! Kind regards to Mrs. Fisher!" Democrats recited it at rallies and parades along with: "Blaine, Blaine, James G. Blaine! Continental liar from the State of Maine!"

Even after this blow, Blaine still enjoyed a narrow lead, but luck turned against him in the final days when a speaker in Blaine's presence described the Democrats as the party of "Rum, Romanism, and Rebellion." Democrats pilloried Blaine over the remark, portraying it as an ugly slur against Catholics, Southerners, and anti-temperance voters. Blaine lost the race by a whisker—out of over 9.6 million votes cast, Cleveland's popular majority was a tiny 26,000. Cleveland won 219 electoral votes to Blaine's 182.

How large a role had Roscoe Conkling played in his defeat? Oneida County, Conkling's home, which Garfield had carried by 1,946 votes in 1880, this time went for Cleveland by a margin of 100—itself alone more than enough to have tipped New York State's 36 electoral votes to Cleveland who carried the state by less than 1,100 votes. After the election, Conkling openly represented the New York Democratic Party in pressing charges of election fraud against Blaine.

All through the 1880s, Roscoe Conkling thrived in his private legal practice and apparently became friends again with his wife Julia. When he traveled west to Yellowstone Park in 1883, Julia came along with him. To the end, though, Conkling could never step out into any public role. He remained haunted by the ghost of James A. Garfield, never able to refute suspicions that his confrontational tactics had driven the weak-minded Charles Guiteau to murder. "How can I speak into a grave? How can I do battle with a shroud? Silence is a duty and a doom," he complained.[45]

It took a force of nature finally to kill him. When a hack driver refused to carry him across town after a court date during a March snowstorm for less than $50, Conkling refused to pay and set out on a two-mile walk through what turned out to be the Great Blizzard of 1888 that brought 75 mile-per-hour wind gusts, zero-degree temperatures and over 20 inches of snow to New York City. After hours of fighting through chest-high snowdrifts, he fell unconscious on the street. A few days later, he took ill with fever and delirium. Doctors operated on him to relieve pressure in his brain. "Don't you think I'm better? I think I am," he asked Julia a few days later, but he never recovered. He fought on for almost another week before he died at 58 years old.[46]

James Blaine took an extended trip to Europe with his wife Harriet and their younger children after losing the presidency a third time in 1884, leisurely touring England and the continent as the Cleveland administration unfolded in Washington, D.C. When friends tried to lure Blaine back into the next presidential contest in 1888, he demurred. From Florence, Italy, Blaine wrote to supporters: "having had my chance and lost I do not wish to appear as a claimant with the demand 'Try me again.'"[47] When Benjamin Harrison captured the White House that year, he asked Blaine to come home and serve as his Secretary of State. Blaine accepted, but the two men were never close and drifted apart over time.

Blaine saw three of his older children die of sudden illnesses during this period: son Walker and daughter Alice in early 1890 and then son Emmon in 1892. These deaths took much of the wind from his sails. When Harrison's popularity began to fall and friends pushed Blaine to run yet again in 1892, the once-Magnetic Man felt too old and battle worn: "When the American people choose a President they require him to remain awake four years," he told his biographer Edward Stanwood. "I have come to a time of life when I need my sleep."[48] He made only one brief campaign speech—for his friend Whitelaw Reid running for vice president—and resigned from Harrison's cabinet outright late that year. He died a few months later at his home in Augusta, Maine, in January 1893.

◎ ◎ ◎ ◎ ◎

After 1884, the feud had run its course. Conkling and Blaine themselves became increasingly irrelevant figures in American politics; after a few more years, Slatwarts and Half-Breeds themselves became extinct, forgotten armies of forgotten empires. By the next century, their entire generation of politicos had been largely dismissed as a parade of misanthropes, spoilsmen, and mediocrities. Thomas Wolfe called them "lost Americans" whose "gravely vacant and bewhiskered faces mixed, melted, swam together."[49] Henry Adams minimized Garfield's brief term as "a sort of *delirium tremens* vision with Blaine as the big and active snake" and Arthur's as "a nasty *chopping-sea* in politics."[50] Woodrow Wilson pigeon-holed Arthur simply as "A non-entity with side whiskers."[51]

Their era, the Gilded Age, became remembered not for them, its politicians, but instead for the dynamic people they led—cowboys, robber barons, inventors, immigrants, frontier settlers, laborers, social activists, and others building a modern country during a pivotal time of change.

Today, from a distance, the Garfield assassination drama, capstone of the long feud between Stalwarts and Half-Breeds, seems like a repressed childhood trauma trapped in the American subconscious—not just forgotten but deliberately distorted for more than a century, buried, lost, and rarely thought about. History largely has reduced it to its lowest denominator—a president killed by a disappointed office seeker, resulting in a reform of civil service laws, as if the Stalwarts and Half-Breeds and their political wars had never existed. The busy Twentieth Century has made Garfield's era seem remote and irrelevant, its leaders ridiculed for their very obscurity.

To the generation of Americans then alive, though, their dramas, humanity, and dignity were a compelling part of daily life. For twenty years after the Civil War, America was led by a group of larger-than-life figures with clay feet who fought and raged and plied their craft with nerve and ambition while following a code of honor riddled with blind spots and inconsistencies; during that time, public involvement in politics reached levels far higher than

today. Garfield held a special place: one of the most promising of his generation, shot down in his prime, martyred for taking a principled stand. People
who knew him understood his contribution perfectly well. "I am a poor hater,"
Garfield confided once in his daily journal while still a Congressman.[52] Even
in his own day and age, he showed that one didn't need to be a "good hater"
to be a good politician and president, had time and fortune only given him
the chance.

SOURCES AND NOTES

Few books about James Garfield and his era have appeared in recent years, but several among them have been excellent works of scholarship and enjoyable guides to me in developing this manuscript. Biographies of principal players were particularly useful, and I owe their authors my thanks: Allan Peskin's *Garfield*, (1978, 1999), Thomas C. Reeves' *Gentleman Boss: The Life and Times of Chester Alan Arthur* (1975), David M. Jordan's *Roscoe Conkling of New York: Voice in the Senate* (1971), and Charles Rosenberg's *The Trial of the Assassin Guiteau* (1968). Among the more-numerous works on Ulysses Grant, McFeely's *Grant: A Biography* (1981) and Jean Edward Smith's *Grant* (2001) were especially helpful. (Missing in this regard is a recent full biography of James G. Blaine, and my compliments to whomever takes up the challenge. Edward Crapol's recent exploration of Blaine's diplomatic career, *Architect of Empire* (2000), is a good start.) Recent works on Gilded Age elections such as *Rum, Romanism & Rebellion: The Making of a President 1884* by Mark W. Summers (2000), and publications of period memoirs and correspondence such as *Crete and James: Personal Letters of Lucretia and James Garfield*, edited by John Shaw (1994), *Politics and Patronage in the Gilded Age: The Correspondence of James A. Garfield and Charles E. Henry*, edited by James D. Norris and Arthur Shaffer (1970), and *The Personal Memoirs of Julia Dent Grant*, edited by John Simon (1975), also open important windows on the era. Finally, the well-annotated four-volume edition of Garfield's daily journal, *The Diary of James A. Garfield* edited by Harry J. Brown and Frederick Williams (1967), is indispensable to any exploration of this period.

The research of this book owes heavily to the Library of Congress in Washington, D.C., whose vast collections of newspapers, periodicals, manuscripts, pamphlets, and other primary and secondary sources provided the backbone to this effort. Personally, I am an unabashed newspaper lover and, to my good fortune, the events in *Dark Horse* were intensively covered by the most talented newsmen of their generation, creating a public record rich in detail and insight that was a pleasure to rediscover. Some key players, notably Garfield himself and John Sherman, had enough sense of history to leave extensive paper collections—letters, telegrams, notes, scrapbooks, hotel and liquor tabs, train tickets, song books, posters, scribbles, and the rest—that capture the drama and nuance of these events. Others, regrettably, notably Blaine and Roscoe Conking, combed their papers and destroyed many secrets, not only robbing historians of good source materials but also diminishing their own future voices in our collective memory.

Finally, a growing and formidable array of information is today just a click away through easily accessible and well-designed Internet web pages: including full editions of the *Congressional Record* and *Globe*, period journals, extensive biographical listings, background on locales, and oceans of demographic and political data. The convenience was enormous and much appreciated.

A bibliography and line-by-line reference notes follow.

BIBLIOGRAPHY

Manuscripts Collections

- Chester Alan Arthur papers, Library of Congress (LC)
- Warner Bateman papers, WRHS
- Joseph Stanley-Brown papers, LC.
- William E. Chandler papers, LC, NH.
- Roscoe Conkling papers, LC
- Henry Dawes papers, LC.
- James A. Garfield papers, LC.
- Lucretia Garfield papers, LC.
- Ulysses Grant papers, LC.
- Charles Guiteau papers, Georgetown University.
- Hinsdale-Garfield letters.
- Rutherford Hayes papers. Hayes Presidential Center.
- John Logan papers, LC.
- Whitelaw Reid papers, LC.
- Carl Schurz papers, LC.
- John Sherman papers, LC.
- Files on individual Senators, United States Senate Historical Office.

Newspapers and Publications

- Albany Evening Journal
- The American
- Atlantic Monthly
- Boston Daily Advertiser
- Boston Globe
- Boston Post
- Brooklyn Eagle
- Buffalo Express
- Century Magazine
- Chicago Inter Ocean
- Chicago Medical Journal
- Chicago Times

- Chicago Tribune
- Cleveland Herald
- Cleveland Leader
- Cleveland Press
- Cincinnati Commercial
- Cincinnati Enquirer
- Cincinnati Gazette
- Congressional Globe
- Congressional Record
- The Cosmopolitan
- The Daily Graphic
- Detroit Evening News
- Frank Leslie's Illustrated Weekly
- Harpers New Monthly Magazine
- Harpers Weekly
- The Independent
- Indianapolis Journal
- London, The Times
- Louisville Courier
- National Republican
- The Nation
- New York Herald
- New York Sun
- New York Times
- New York Tribune
- New York World
- North American Review
- Philadelphia Inquirer
- Puck
- St. Louis Globe Democrat
- St. Louis Republican
- Springfield Republican
- Toronto Globe
- Utica (NY) Herald
- Washington Evening Star
- Washington Post

Selected Internet Sites

- Abraham Lincoln Historical Digitization Project: *Lincoln.lib.niu.edu;*
- Atlas of US Elections (historical election results): *www.USElectionAtlas.org;*
- Bartleby's quotations: *www.Bartleby.com*
- Biographical Directory of the United States Congress (with bibliographies and research collections): *bioguide.congress.gov;*
- Chicago Public Library: *cpl.lib.uic.edu/cpl.html;*
- Cornell University, Making of America collection (click "Browse" to access online editions of the *Atlantic Monthly, The Century, North American Review*, Putnam's Magazine, and several others)— *cdl.library.cornell.edu/moa;*
- Dorsey Mansion Ranch: *www.DorseyMansion.com;*
- Garfield National Historical Site: *www.nps.gov/jaga;*
- Graphic Witness, visual arts and social commentary (including *Puck* online): *www.GraphicWitness.com;*
- *Harpers Weekly* online: *www.HarpWeek.com;*
- History Central: *www.multied.com;*
- History House: *www.HistoryHouse.com;*
- Library of Congress, American Memory project: *memory.LoC.gov;*
- New Jersey History's Mysteries, Death of a President: *www.NJHM.com;*
- Ohio Historical Society: *www.OhioHistory.org;*
- The Political Graveyard: *www.politicalgraveyard.com;*
- Prints Old and Rare: *www.printsoldandrare.com;*
- United States House of Representatives, Office of the Clerk: *clerkweb.house.gov;*
- United States Senate: *www.senate.gov;*
- U.S. presidential election maps: *fisher.lib.Virginia.edu/elections/maps;*
- Virtual American Biographies: *www.FamousAmericans.Net*
- White House Historical Association: *www.WhiteHouseHistory.org;*
- White House, History and Tours: *www.WhiteHouse.gov.*

Books and Cited References

- Alexander, DeAlva Stanwood Alexander. *A Political History of the State of New York: 1861-1882*. New York: Henry Holt & Company. 1909.

- Badeau, Adam. *Grant in Peace: From Appomattox to Mount McGregor*. Freeport, N.Y.: Books for Libraries Press,1971.

- Baker, Richard Allan. *The Senate of the United States: A Bicentennial History*. Malabar, Florida: Robert E. Krieger Publishing Company. 1988.

- *Biographical Directory of the United States Congress*. Washington, D.C.: United States Senate Historical Office.

- Blaine, Harriet S. *Letters of Mrs. James G. Blaine*. Edited by Harriet S. Blaine Beale. New York: Duffield and Company, 1908. 2 vol.

- Blaine, Harriet S. *"July 2, 1880—A Narrative of the Day."* Unpublished Manuscript in the Blaine papers. LC. 1881.

- Blaine, James G. *Twenty Years of Congress: from Lincoln to Garfield*. Vols. I & II. The Henry Bill Publishing Company, 1884. 2 vols.

- Bliss, Dr. Willard. "The Story of President Garfield's Illness." *Century Magazine* (Vol. 23, Issue 2), December 1881.

- Boller, Paul F., Jr. *Presidential Inaugurations: From Washington's Election to George W. Bush's Gala*. New York: Harcourt, Inc. 2001.

- Bonadio, Felice A. *North of Reconstruction: Ohio Politics, 1865-1870*. New York: New York University Press, 1970.

- Boutwell, George S. *Reminiscences of Sixty Years in Public Affairs*. New York: Greenwood Press, Publishers, 1968. 2 vol.

- Burnham, Walter Dean. *Presidential Ballots 1836-1892*. Baltimore: The Johns Hopkins Press.

- Byrd, Max. *Grant, A Novel*. New York: Bantam Books. 2000.

- Byrd, Senator Robert C. *The Senate, 1789-1989*. Washington, D.C.: Government Printing Office. 1988-1994.

- Caldwell, Robert Granville. *James A. Garfield: Party Chieftain*. New York: Dodd, Mead & Company, 1931.

- Calhoun, Charles W., editor. *The Gilded Age: Essays on the Origins of Modern America*. Wilmington, Delaware: SR Books. 1996.

- Caperton, Thomas J. *Rogue: An Account of the Life and High Times Stephen W. Dorsey*. Santa Fe, New Mexico: The University of New Mexico Press, 1978.

- Cater, Harold D. *Henry Adams and His Friends: A Collection of His Unpublished Letters*. Boston: Houghton Mifflin Company. 1947.

- Clancy, Herbert J. *The Presidential Election of 1880*. Chicago: Loyola University Press, 1958.

- Clews, Henry. *Fifty Years in Wall Street*. New York: Irving Publishing Company. 1908.

- *Congressional Directory: Forty-Seventh Congress*. Washington, D.C.: Government Printing Office. 1881.

- Conkling, Alfred R. *The Life and Letters of Roscoe Conkling: Orator, Statesman, Advocate*. New York: Charles L. Webster & Company, 1889.

- Connery, T.B. "Secret History of the Garfield-Conkling Tragedy." *The Cosmopolitan* (Vol. 23, No. 2), June 1897.

- Cortissoz, Royal. *The Life of Whitelaw Reid*. New York: Charles Scribner's Sons, 1921.

- Crapol, Edard. *James G. Blaine: Architect of Empire*. Wilmington, Delaware: SR Books, 2000.

- Curran, Michael P. *Life of Patrick A. Collins*. Norwood, Massachusetts: The Norwood Press, 1906.

- Dawes, Henry L. "Garfield and Conkling." *Century Magazine* (Vol. 47, Issue 3), January 1894.

- Doenecke, Justus D. *The Presidencies of James A. Garfield & Chester A. Arthur*. Lawrence: University Press of Kansas, 1981.

- Dole, Senator Robert. *Great Presidential Wit (...I Wish I Was in the Book)*. New York: Touchstone Books. 2001.

- Eaton, Dorman B. *The "Spoils" System and Civil Service Reform in the Custom House and Post-Office at New York*. G.P. Putnam's Sons, New York. 1881.

- Edmunds, George F. "The Conduct of the Guiteau Trial." *North American Review (Vol. CCCIV, No. 304)*, March 1882.

- Evelyn, Douglas E. and Dickson, Paul. *On this Spot: Pinpointing the Past in Washington, D.C. Washington, D.C.* National Geographic. 1992, 1999.

- Fellman, Michael. *Citizen Sherman: A Life of William Tecumseh Sherman*. New York: Random House. 1995.

- Foner, Eric. *Reconstruction: America's Unfinished Revolution, 1863-1877*. New York: Harper & Row. 1988.

- *Garfield and Arthur Campaign Songster*. New York: New York Popular Publishing Company. 1880. [Copy in C.A. Arthur papers, Library of Congress.]

- Garfield, James A. *The Diary of James A. Garfield*. Edited by Harry J. Brown and Frederick D. Brown. Michigan State University State, 1981.

- Goldman, Robert M. *"A Free Ballot and a Fair Count": The Department of Justice and the Enforcement of Voting Rights in the South, 1877-1893*. Fordham University Press, New York. 2001.

- Gosnell, Harold F. *Boss Platt and his New York Machine*. Chicago: University of Chicago Press, 1924.

- Grant, Julia Dent. *The Personal Memoirs of Julia Dent Grant (Mrs. Ulysses S. Grant*. Edited by John Y. Simon. Carbondale: Southern Illinois University Press, 1975.

- Geary, Rick. *The Fatal Bullet: A True Account of the Assassination of President James A. Garfield*. New York: ComicsLit.

- Haynie, James Henry. "Socialistic and Other Assassinations." *Atlantic Monthly*. October 1880.

- Hesseltine, William B. *Ulysses S. Grant: Politician*. New York: Frederick Ungar Publishing Co., 1957.

- Hinsdale, B.A. *The Republican Text-Book for the Campaign of 1880*. New York: D. Appleton & Co., 1880.

- Hinsdale, Mary L. ed. *Garfield-Hinsdale Letters: Correspondence Between James Abram Garfield and Burke Aaron Hinsdale*. Ann Arbor: University of Michigan Press, 1949.

- Hoar, George F. *Autobiography of Seventy Years*. New York: Charles Scribner's Sons, 1903.

- Hoogenboom, Ari. *Outlawing the Spoils: A History of the Civil Service Reform Movement, 1865-1883*. Urbana: University of Illinois Press, 1968.

- Howe, George F. *Chester A. Arthur: A Quarter-Century of Machine Politics*. New York. 1935.

- Hudson, William C. *Random Recollections of an Old Political Reporter*. New York: Cupples & Leon Company, 1911.

- Jordan, David M. *Roscoe Conkling of New York: Voice in the Senate*. Ithaca, New York. 1971.

- Jordan, David M. *Winfield Scott Hancock: A Soldier's Life*. Indiana University Press. 1988, 1996.

- Josephson, Matthew. *The Politicos: 1865-1896*. New York: Harcourt, Brace & World, Inc. 1938, 1966.

- Josephson, Matthew. *The Robber Barons: The Great American Capitalists 1861-1901*. New York: Harcourt, Brace and Company. 1934.

- Kaplan, Justin. *Mr. Clemens and Mark Twain.*
  New York: Simon and Schuster. 1966.

- Kingsbury, Robert. *The Assassination of James A. Garfield.*
  New York: The Rosen Publishing Group, Inc. 2002.

- Kluger, Richard. *The Paper: The Life and Death of the New York Herald Tribune.* New York: Vintage Books. 1986.

- Logan, Mary. *Reminiscences of the Civil War and Reconstruction.*
  Carbondale, Illinois: Southern Illinois University Press,
  Feffer & Sons, Inc. 1970.

- Marszalek, John F. *Sherman: A Soldier's Passion for Order.*
  New York: The Free Press. 1993.

- McClure, Alexander K. *Our Presidents and How We Make Them.*
  Freeport, New York: Books for Libraries Press, 1970.

- McFeely, William S. *Grant: A Biography.* New York:
  W.E. Norton & Company. 1982.

- McNulty, Elizabeth. *Chicago: Then and Now.*
  San Diego, California: Thunder Bay Press. 2000.

- Melanson, Philip H. with Stevens, Peter F. *The Secret Service;
  The Hidden History of an Enigmatic Agency.* New York:
  Carroll & Graf Publishers. 2002.

- Merritt, Edwin A. *Recollections, 1828-1911.*
  Albany: J.B. Lyon Company, Printers. 1911.

- Mitchell, Alexander D., IV. *Washington, D.C.: Then and Now.*
  San Diego, California: Thunder Bay Press. 2000.

- Morris, Edmund. *The Rise of Theodore Roosevelt.*
  New York; The Modern Library. 1979, 2001.

- Muzzey, David S. *James G. Blaine: A Political Idol of Other Days.*
  New York: Dodd, Mead & Company. 1934.

- *National Party Conventions, 1831-1996.* Washington, D.C.:
  Congressional Quarterly, Inc. 1997.

- Nevins, Allan. *Hamilton Fish: The Inner History of the Grant
  Administration.* New York: Dodd, Mead & Company. 1936.

- "The New York Custom-House." *Harpers New Monthly Magazine*
  (No. CCCCIV, Vol. LXIX), June 1884.

- Norris, James D. and Shaffer, Arthur H., editors. *Politics
  and Patronage in the Gilded Age: The Correspondence of
  James A. Garfield and Charles E. Henry.* State Historical
  Society of Wisconsin. Madison, Wisconsin, 1970.

- *Official Proceedings of the Republican National Convention Held at Chicago, Illinois.* Chicago. 1990.

- Parton, James. "The Power of Public Plunder." *North American Review* (Vol. 133, Issue 296), July 1881.

- Penczer, Peter R. *Washington, D.C.: Past and Present.* Arlington, Virginia: Oneonta Press. 1998.

- Peskin, Allan. *Garfield.* The Kent Sate University Press. 1978.

- Petersen, Svend. *A Statistical History of the American Presidential Elections.* Westport, Connecticut: Greenwood Press. 1981.

- Platt, Thomas C. *The Autobiography of Thomas Collier Platt.* New York: Arno Press, B.W. Dodge & Company, 1910.

- Reeves, Thomas C. *Gentleman Boss: The Life and Times of Chester Alan Arthur.* Newtown, Connecticut: American Political biography Press, 1975.

- Reid, Whitelaw. *Ohio in the War: Her Statesmen, Generals, and Soldiers.* Columbus, Ohio: Eclectic Publishing Company, 1893.

- *"Report of the House Select Committee to Investigate the statements and charges made by Hon. Roscoe Conkling, in his place, against Provost Marshall General Fry...."* Congressional Globe, p. 3935 et. seq. July 19, 1866.

- "Republican Candidates for the Presidency." *Atlantic Monthly.* April 1880.

- Richardson, Leon Burr. *William E. Chandler, Republican.* New York: Dodd, Mead & Company, 1940.

- Ridpath, John Clark. *The Life and Trial of Guiteau the Assassin and the Sentence of Death.* Jones Brothers & Company, 1882.

- Ridpath, John Clark. *The Life and Work of James A. Garfield and the Tragic Story of his Death.* Jones Brothers & Company, 1882.

- Rockwell, Colonel Almon. "From Mentor to Elberon." *Century Magazine* (Vo. 23, Issue 3), June 1882.

- Rosenberg, Charles E. *The Trial of the Assassin Guiteau: Psychiatry and the Law in the Gilded Age.* The University of Chicago Press. 1968.

- Ross, Ishbel. *Proud Kate: Portrait of an Ambitious Woman.* New York: Harper Brothers Publishers, 1953.

- Rupp, Robert O. *James A. Garfield: A Bibliography.* Westport, Connecticut: Greenwood Press. 1997.

- Rusk, Jerrold G. *A Statistical History of the American Electorate.* Washington, D.C. CQ Press. 2001.

- Sautter, R. Craig and Burke, Edward M. *Inside the Wigwam: Chicago Presidential Conventions 1860-1996.* Chicago: Wild Onion Books. 1996.

- Scaturro, Frank J. *President Grant Reconsidered.* Lanham, Maryland: Madison Books, 1999.

- Shaw, John, editor. *Crete and James: Personal Letters of Lucretia and James Garfield.* East Lansing, Michigan, 1994.

- Sherman, John. *Recollections of Forty Years in the House, Senate, and Cabinet. An Autobiography.* The Werner Company. 1895. 2 vol.

- Sievers, Harry J. *Benjamin Harrison, Hoosier Statesman: From the Civil War to the White House, 1865-1888.* New York: University Publishers Incorporated, 1959.

- Simpson, Brooks. *The Reconstruction Presidents.* Lawrence: University Press of Kansas, 1998.

- Smith, Gene. *Lee and Grant; A Dual Biography.* New York: McGraw-Hill Book Company. 1984.

- Smith, Jean Edward. *Grant.* New York: Simon & Schuster, 2001.

- Smith, Theodore Clarke. *The Life and Letters of James Abram Garfield.* New Haven: Yale University Press. 1925.

- Stanley-Brown, Joseph. "Memorandum Concerning Joseph Stanley-Brown's Relations with General Garfield." Stanley-Brown papers, Library of Congress. June 24, 1924.

- Stanwood, Edward. *James Gillespie Blaine.* New York: Houghton, Mifflin Company, 1905.

- Staff of the *Chicago Tribune.* Stevenson Swanson, editor. *Chicago Days: 150 Defining Moments in the Life of a Great City.* Chicago: Cantigny First Division Foundation, 1997.

- Stampp, Kenneth M. *The Era of Reconstruction, 1865-1877.* New York: Vintage Books. 1965.

- Stoddard, Henry L. *As I Knew Them: Presidents and Politics from Grant to Coolidge.* New York: Harper and Brothers. 1927.

- Summers, Mark Wahlgren. *Rum, Romanism & Rebellion: The Making of a President 1884.* Chapel Hill: The University of North Carolina Press, 2000.

- *The United States vs. Charles J. Guiteau.* In the Supreme Court of the District of Columbia, Criminal Case No. 14056. June Term, 1881.

- Trefousse, Hans L. *Rutherford B. Hayes*. New York: Times Books , Henry Holt and Company. 2002.

- Walling, George W. *Recollections of a New York Chief of Police*. Montclair, New Jersey: Patterson Smith. 1887, 1972.

- Weisman, Steven. *The Great Tax Wars*. New York: Simon & Schuster. 2002.

- Welch, Richard E. Jr. *George Frisbie Hoar and the Half-Breed Republicans*. Cambridge, Massachusetts: Harvard University Press, 1971.

- Werner, M.R. *Tammany Hall*. New York: Doubleday, Doran & Company, Inc. 1928.

- Whitcomb, John and Whitcomb, Claire. *Real Life at the White House: 200 Years of Daily Life at America's Most Famous Residence*. New York: Routledge. 2002.

- Wilson, Woodrow. *Division and Reunion, 1829-1889*. London: Longmans, Green, and Company. 1908.

- Woodward, C. Vann. Reunion and Reaction: *The Compromise of 1877 and the End of Reconstruction*. Garden City, New York: Doubleday Anchor Books. 1951, 1956.

- Woodward, W. E. *Meet General Grant*. New York: Liveright Publishing Corporation. 1946, 1965.

REFERENCE NOTES

The Feud (pages 1–16)

1. "I move to strike out section twenty": Dialogue from House floor debates comes from the *Congressional Globe*, the official reporter of debates at the time. *Congressional Globe*, April 24, 1866. Pg. 2151.

2. "Roscoe Conkling of New York, is strong, positive, and critical": *The Independent*. April 12, 1866.

3. "the House, partaking of the magnetic manner ...": Stanwood, 64.

4. "Though the gentleman from New York has had some differences ": *Congressional Globe*, April 24, 1866. Pg. 2152.

5. "long and acrimonious"..., "very spicy debate"..., "desultory discussion" ...: *New York Times, Chicago Tribune, Washington Evening Star*, April 24, 25, 1866.

6. Blaine noticed the change and attacked Conkling: *Congressional Globe*, April 25, 1866. Pg. 2180.

7. "Mr. Speaker, I hold in my hand a letter ...: *Congressional Globe*, April 30, 1866. Pg. 2287 *et seq.*

8. The House investigating committee cleared Conkling...: See "*Report of the House Select Committee to Investigate the statements and charges made by Hon. Roscoe Conkling, in his place, against Provost Marshall General Fry...,*" *Congressional Globe*, July 19, 1866, Pg. 3935 et seq.

9. "That attack was made without any provocation ...: Boutwell, 264.

10. "the man-milliners, the dilettanti ... When Dr. Johnson ...": *New York Times*, September 27, 1877.

1. Chicago (pages 19–32)

1. "General Garfield?": Garfield's interview with the *Chicago Tribune* appears on May 30, 1880.

2. "I have just arrived. Please don't ask me ...": *Chicago Tribune*, May 30, 1880.

3. Garfield had just reached Chicago that morning : Movements from Garfield diary, May 26-29, 1880.

4. "a place composed of old men": Garfield to Hinsdale, Jan. 28, 1880. Hinsdale, 437.

5. Garfield had heard the talk about himself as a "dark horse": A few weeks earlier, Wharton Barker of Philadelphia had come to Garfield's house and told him directly that he and other Pennsylvania delegates were plotting to make Garfield the nominee once Blaine and Grant had been blocked. Garfield hoped he'd fail: "There is too much possible work in me to set so near an end to it all, as that would do," he wrote in his diary on April 24, 1880.

6. "Few men in our history have ever obtained the Presidency ..." Garfield diary, February 4, 1879.

7. "I go with much reluctance,": Garfield diary, May 28, 1880.

8. "the wonderful ruin, ... the exhibition of marvelous energy..." : Garfield diary, August 1, 1872.

9. "I arrived here at 8 o'clock,...": Garfield to Lucretia Garfield, May 29, 1880. Shaw, 368.

10. "How do you stand on the unit rule?": *Chicago Tribune*, May 30, 1880.

11. "Outlook is very encouraging, ... All talk is favorable to you." : Bateman to Sherman, May 27; Arthur Bateman to Sherman, May 29. Sherman papers. LC.

12. Kentucky's Sandy Valley weeks before ... Grant's first success... : Grant won his victories at Fort Henry and Fort Donelson on February 9 and February 26, 1862; Garfield's Sandy Valley victory came on January 9 of that year.

13. "the most able and prominent ..." Reid, 739.

14. "reserved, self-contained, affable when approached, ...": *Albany Evening Journal*, May 29, 1880.

15. "[M]en are scattered over the country...": Henry to Garfield, February 20, 1880. Norris, 274.

16. "nowhere greeted with any cheering": *New York Times*, April 3, 1880.

17. "[I]n my District the popular feeling is for Blaine": Some of Sherman's friends, in fact, already were trying to soften the blow. "Your days of usefulness will not be over if you do not succeed," wrote Nelson Miles from Cleveland. "I hope you will not be greatly disappointed if you are not successful but your friends will do everything in theirs for your interests." Miles to Sherman, May 28, 1880. Sherman papers. LC. Sherman himself seemed to recognize his diminishing prospects. "Indeed I'm becoming very indifferent to the nomination," he told a New York supporter shortly before the convention. "I see it is going to be a very dangerous and doubtful struggle [for the presidency] in which I will have to take great risk and incur great cost. If selected I will do so. If not, I want to be in a condition to support heartily the nominee." Sherman to Albert Doggett, May 15, 1880. Sherman papers. LC.

18. ... lining up Sherman delegates, using ... patronage to lure allies: In fact, he was still at it that morning: "Your friends here from Wis[consin] are very anxious to have John ___ appointed Collector of Milwaukee," he'd telegraphed to Sherman, fishing for yet one more delegate vote. "I hope their wishes may not be disappointed."

19. "Our people here are as bitter ...": John Kentworthy to Chandler, May 24. Chandler papers. LC.

20. "Stand by your gun ...": Letter from "Stalwart." May 24. Chandler papers. LC.

21. "result in a separation ... into two rival conventions": Chandler to Farwell, May 13. Chandler papers. LC.

22. "I was invited by Logan to go see C[ameron] yesterday": Bateman to Sherman, May 30. Sherman papers. LC.

23. "Much anxiety displayed by Grant men": Bateman to Sherman, May 28. Sherman papers. LC. Chandler had recently given Bateman a proposition that only heightened this fear. "[T]he Blaine men [propose]that a Sherman man should act as temporary chairman [at the convention], and under his lead we should make the fight.... This brings upon us all the odium and bitterness of the contest and correspondingly affects the relations which you as a candidate will have towards the friends of Grant." It would "place our forces in an antago-

nistic position to the third-termers." Bateman to Sherman, May 29, 1880. Sherman papers. LC.

24. "I... urged them to take a bold and aggressive stand": Garfield diary, May 29, 1880. Bateman to Sherman, May 29. Sherman papers. LC.

25. "I do not... want to lose sight of the fact ...": Bateman to Sherman, May 29. Sherman papers. LC.

26. "It is strange that the two leading papers ...": Sherman to Dennison, March 26, 1880. Sherman papers. LC.

27. "Say to parties that we cannot waive ...": Telegram from Sherman to Bateman, May 31. Sherman papers, LC.

28. "You know that my heart is with you ...": Garfield to Lucretia Garfield, May 29, 1880. Shaw, 368.

29. "I have time only for a word": Lucretia Garfield to Garfield, May 29, 1880. Shaw, 369.

2. The Hero (pages 33–44)

1. "The atmosphere [in Galena] ...": Julia Grant, 83.
2. The parlor conversation that day ...: *Albany Evening Journal*, June 1, 1880.
3. "extremely anxious to receive the nomination": Badeau, 319.
4. Grant "manifested as much anxiety ...": Badeau, 320.
5. "He is as calm as a summer morning": *Washington Post*, June 1, 1880.
6. "telegraph to New York that Mrs. Grant ...": Julia Grant, 242; McFeely, ch. 26.
7. "I do not want to be here [in the White House]": Julia Grant, 186.
8. "third-rate non-entity, whose only recommendation ...": Quoted in Richardson, 177.
9. "to abandon the remnant ... No act of President Hayes Stanwood, 193-4; Hesseltine, 425.
10. "as near to slavery as possible,": Foner, 199.
11. a "man of iron" to replace the "man of straw": Hesseltine, 432.
12. "You cannot realize ... how deep the Grant sentiment ...": *id.*
13. "Most every letter I get ... asks me to remain abroad": Badeau, 316.
14. "I assure you that there was no intentional neglect ": Grant to Logan, May 25. Logan papers. LC.
15. "I bravely stood looking out": Julia Grant, 196-7. Grant had refused to show her his resignation letter before sending it to the Senate. Otherwise, he told her, it "would never have gone," suggesting she would have blocked it.
16. "Nothing but an act of God ...": *Cleveland Herald*, May 31 [spoken May 30], 1880.
17. "I did not feel that General Grant would be nominated": Julia Grant, 321.
18. "I don't think he ought to be nominated"... "under no circumstances would he join in advising...": *Chicago Tribune*. May 24, 1880.
19. "Gen. Grant's name has never gone before the public ...": *id.*
20. "could be the means of ending ...": Julia Grant, 331n.
21. "Mr. Young was unwise enough ... tell Senator Cameron *not* to use the letter":

Julia Grant, 321. It is not clear whether Julia issued her instruction before the convention, or the following week once balloting had begun.

22. "Young returned [from Galena] today": Boutwell, 270.

23. "the report in circulation that he has a letter ...": Western Union Bulletin. June 5, 1880. Sherman papers. LC.

24. "influenced by this phase of irresolution": Badeau, 322. Boutwell, 267-270.

25. "[T]he report that he had gone that far ...": *Albany Evening Journal*, June 2, 1880.

3. Bosses *(pages 45–65)*

1. the Republican National Committee: The meeting of the National Committee and surrounding events are detailed in the *Chicago Tribune, New York World, New York Times, New York Tribune, Albany Evening Journal*, and other papers from June 1 and 2, 1880. Direct quotations are footnoted below.

2. "would probably turn ... solid to Blaine": Bateman to Sherman, May 31, 1880. Sherman papers, LC.

3. "would do nothing under threat ": *id.*

4. "Every effort should be made": Sherman to Bateman, May 31, 1880. Sherman papers. LC.

5. Chandler's own calm voice had cooled the hotheads: Chandler had protested Don Cameron's election to the National Committee chair from the beginning. "Cameron is the Grant candidate," he had reported to Harriet Blaine, "a most unnatural, and almost provocative" choice. "If we had defeated him, ... we should have very nearly captured the Penn.[sylvania] delegation...." Chandler to Harriet Blaine, December 13, 1879. Blaine papers. LC.

6. "The political trio of Bosses": *Washington Post*, June 1, 1880.

7. Dearborn Park: Southwest corner of Michigan and Randolph. Today the site of the Chicago Public Library.

8. "We have a majority of the convention": *Washington Post*, June 1, 1880.

9. their "moving impulse ... a desire to see ... Conkling.": *Chicago Tribune*, June 1, 1880.

10. "overflowed into the streets all night": *Albany Evening Journal*, June 3, 1880.

11. "Cheers and groans for the various candidates": *Washington Evening Star*, June 1, 1880.

12. "[A]rbitrary and infamous": *Washington Post*, June 1, 1880.

13. "If the Chairman entertains that resolution": *New York World*, June 2, 1880.

14. "If there was any business": *id.*

15. "If the Chairman entertains that resolution": *id.*

16. "a good man with a willing soul": *Chicago Tribune*, June 1, 1880.

17. "gazed at [Jewell] in sullen silence.": *Id.*

18. The vote meant nothing. Don Cameron could simply overturn it : To underscore the point, Senator Jones of Nevada, a Grant partisan, told the group that he reserved the right to vote for anybody else who might be nominated, and George Gorham demanded assurances from Cameron that he could nominate someone else from the Convention floor.

19. "The rulings of Don Cameron": *Chicago Tribune*, June 1, 1880.
20. "to introduce the 'Boss' system": *New York Tribune*, June 2, 1880.
21. "high-handed behavior in refusing": *id*
22. "Down with the Grant Syndicate": *New York World*, June 2, 1880.
23. strategy had proven "suicidal": *New York Tribune*, June 2, 1880.
24. Chester A. Arthur … As a young lawyer: See Reeves, 14-16; Alexander, 445.
25. votes: in the national committee, Don Cameron didn't have them: Arthur also checked with Colonel William Strong, the Sergeant at Arms, on whether he might recognize Cameron to open the convention even had the national committee deposed him. Strong asked his lawyers and confirmed that, no, he must respect the committee's vote, closing this back door to Arthur as well. See Clancy, 85-86.
26. "believed it would be agreed to by the Grant men": *New York Tribune* June 2, 1880.
27. "It is every way desirable to avoid angry row": Blaine to Chandler, June 1, 1880. Chandler papers. LC. See also Welch, 81; Cong. Record, Jan. 22, 1878, pg. 458-9.
28. "must be accepted" in a "spirit of conciliation": *New York Tribune*, June 2, 1880.
29. "Unit rule dead….": Anonymous to Merritt, June 1, 1880. Sherman papers, LC.
30. "[t]he fight of delegates should be in the convention": Garfield diary, May 31, 1880.
31. "[T]he whole Grant vote of [the] South …Reports also as to friendly expressions": Bateman to Sherman, May 31, 1880. Sherman papers. LC.
32. Cameron had signaled: This gushing up from Cameron to Sherman took many forms. That week, Don Cameron's wife Elizabeth, the attractive niece of Sherman's older brother William Tecumseh, had invited Sherman for dinner in her Washington, D.C., home. Invitation in Sherman papers, Library of Congress.
33. "Please prevent this from being acted upon …. I do not desire that office": Sherman to Bateman, May 24. Sherman papers, LC.
34. "Mr. Conkling's hatred of Sherman": *Washington Evening Star*, June 1, 1880.
35. "the corruption of two of Grant's terms": *Washington Post*, June 1, 1880.
36. Conkling "did not appear willing": Garfield diary. June 1, 1880.
37. newspapers mentioned Garfield's behind-the-scenes role: See e.g. *Washington Post*, June 1, 1880.
38. "I begin to feel quite confident": Garfield to Lucretia, May 31, 1880.
39. A Connecticut delegate … claimed to be working to raise Garfield's name: *New York World*, June 2, 1880.
40. the "opposition" … were "busy circulat[ing] rumors": Dennison to Sherman, June 2, 1880. Sherman papers, LC.
41. "The cordial cooperation of the Sherman men": *Washington Post*, June 1, 1880.
42. "Garfield and Foster are the only weak points": Fearing to Sherman, June 3, 1880. Sherman papers, LC.
43. "You can hardly imagine the embarrassment": Garfield to Lucretia, May 31, 1880.

44. "bitterness already engendered": *id.*

45. "Swaim, Henry, Nichol, and a host of good fellows": Garfield to Lucretia, June 1, 1880.

46. "disaffectants ... should let their grievances be known": *New York World*, June 1, 1880.

47. "pledge" to "resist the nomination": *Chicago Tribune*, June 1, 1880.

48. "I cannot suppose any gentlemen have violated": *Washington Post*, June 1, 1880.

49. "[A] "silver-gray tint... overshadowed the reddish hue": *Chicago Tribune*, May 20, 1880.

50. "majestically, with a calm and conciliatory smile": *New York Times*, June 1, 1880.

51. "knave or a fool," "without the saving pretence of shame": *New York Times*, May 10, 1880.

52. "statesmanlike": *Albany Evening Journal*, May 10, 1880.

53. friends denied it: Clews, 297-312.

54. "New York NOT solid for Grant,"... Woodin chatted up visitors: *New York World*, June 1, 1880.

55. Conkling ... "realized his danger": *Chicago Tribune*, June 1, 1880.

56. unit rule contest was "uncertain": *New York World*, June 1, 1880.

57. "Grant can be nominated better without": *Washington Post*, June 1, 1880.

58. "the conscience of men ... would never vote for nor favor men guilty": *Washington Post*, June 2, 1880.

59. "We have burned our bridges": *New York Times*, June 2, 1880.

60. "vote as a unit... despite the attitude": *New York Tribune*, June 2, 1880.

61. "not be frightened by a parcel of boys": *Albany Evening Journal*, NY World, June 2, 1880.

62. "cast for [Grant] ballot after ballot": *New York Times*: vote estimate, June 2, 1880; quote June 1, 1880.

63. "In no event will the strength of Grant": *Washington Evening Star*, June 2, 1880. "G.W.A."

64. "It is the pluck of Conkling": Sherman to Halstead, March 9, 1880; P. Chandler to Sherman, May 31, 1880. Bateman to Sherman, May 31, 1880. Sherman papers. LC.

65. "Conkling is about the only one": Sherman to Halstead, March 9, 1880. Sherman papers. LC.

66. "We are satisfied that [the] Grant men intend": Bateman to Sherman, May 31, 1881. Sherman papers. LC.

67. "We are perfectly sure of our position": *Washington Post*, June 2, 1880.

68. "If Blaine should be nominated": *New York Tribune*, June 2, 1880.

69. "He cannot carry his own state": Reeves, 94.

70. "Blaine Feigns a Faint": Muzzey, 100.

71. "[T]he anti-Grant, pro-Blaine men are fighting": Chandler to Ms. Blaine, January 17, 1880. Blaine papers. LC.

72. "I think the beloved": Chandler to Ms. Blaine, Dec. 13, 1979. Blaine papers. LC.
73. "Mr. Blaine ... is for the second time a candidate": Chandler to Ms. Blaine, May 22, 1880. Blaine papers. LC.
74. Blaine "did not much expect the nomination": Garfield diary. May 23, 1880.
75. "I am almost sure a combination": Harriet Blaine, 170.
76. "Mr. Blaine always had a warm": Sherman, 767.
77. "Rest assured we shall not fail": Carnegie to Blaine, March 3, 1880. Blaine papers. LC.
78. "on account of Senator Conkling's hostility": *New York Tribune*, June 2, 1880.
79. Don Cameron—an old friend: Senator and Mrs. Chandler appear frequently in Blaine's Library of Congress records from the 1870s as guests for Blaine's dinner parties, or visits by the Blaines to the Camerons' country home.
80. "The feeling between the champions": *Washington Evening Star*, June 1, 1880.
81. "as 4 to 1, but not to be counted": Harriet Blaine, 171.
82. "James G. Blaine and No Second Choice": Boutelle to Chandler, May 28, 1880. Chandler papers. LC.
83. "WEC. Thanks and Congratulations": Blaine to Chandler, June 1, 1880. Chandler papers. LC.

4. First Volley *(pages 66–82)*

1. "peddlers of all sorts of cheap trifles": *New York Times*. June 3, 1880.
2. "Am advised of bribes offered and accepted": Sherman to Bateman, May 31, 1880.
3. "I am doing all I can to keep": Curly to Chandler, Chandler papers, LC.
4. "Father will be nominated on the first ballot": *Chicago Tribune*, May 27, 1880.
5. Grant "talked to him and drank his whiskey": *Chicago Tribune*, June 1, 1880.
6. "no man should hold his seat here ... [Who] ... would vote 'no' on such a resolution?": *Washington Evening Star*, June 4, 1880.
7. "Garfield's retort in [the West Virginia] matter": Moulton to Sherman, June 4, 1880. Sherman papers. LC.
8. thanked Garfield later that day for his "eloquent effort": Hogans et al to Garfield, June 4, 1880. Garfield papers. LC.
9. "New York requests that Ohio's real candidate": Conkling to Garfield, June 4, 1880. [The copy in the Garfield papers is marked in different places June 2, June 5, and July, all apparently after the fact.] Garfield papers. LC.
10. One woman ... climbed onto the "Goddess of Liberty": *Washington Evening Star*, June 5, 1880.
11. "[t]he incidental mention of Blaine's name": Harriet Blaine, 170-171 More details of the demonstration arrived on Blaine's private telegraph from Chicago minutes later in a message from Maine delegate Eugene Hale: "The Grant men made a point of seeing who could howl loudest and longest, and cheered and hurrahed and waved flags for fifteen minutes—Conkling himself condescending to wave." Hale to Blaine, June 5, 1880. Blaine papers. LC.
12. "seemed [as if] it could not be in America": Garfield to Lucretia Garfield, Shaw, 376. June 6.

13. "three cheers for the victorious candidate": *Washington Evening Star*, June 5, 1880.

14. "Alabama": Arizona, next in alphabetical order with two voting votes at the convention (both for Blaine), was still a territory in 1881 and thus its name did not come up until the end of the roll call with the other territories.

15. "benefit the candidate but little... James S. Blaine": *Official Proceedings*. Muzzey, 169. Sautter and Burke, 41. Famousamericans.net.

16. *"And when asked what State he hails from"*: For Conkling's speech and crowd reactions, see *Official Proceedings*, *Chicago Tribune* and other newspapers, June 6, 1880.

17. "[t]he play of sarcasm, the saber-cuts of severity": *Chicago Inter Ocean*, in Platt 111.

18. "By speaking very deliberately": AR Conkling, 601.

19. "I have not made the first step": Garfield to Lucretia Garfield, June 2, 1880. Shaw, 373.

20. Sherman ..."suggested that the chief characteristic": Garfield diary, May 25, 1880.

21. "Conkling's extraordinary speech gave me the idea": Garfield to Lucretia Garfield, June 6, 1880. Shaw, 376.

22. "Mr. President, I have witnessed the extraordinary scenes": On Garfield's speech, note wording differences between accounts in newspapers versus the official convention proceedings, not surprising as there was no prepared text and notes were inexact. The *Chicago Tribune* version is used primarily here.

23. "Nominate Garfield": The official proceeding account has the audience outburst as "We want Garfield."

24. "I shall always believe... that Garfield": *Washington Evening Star*, June 6, 1880.

25. it had made him "sea-sick": Jordan, 337.

26. "The sickly manner in which Garfield": J.H. Geiger to Sherman, June 6, 1880. Sherman papers. LC.

27. "one quarter of the Ohio delegation": M. Halstead to Sherman, June 6, 1880. Sherman papers. LC.

28. "My information is that Foster is conspiring": W.P. Nixon to Sherman. Sherman papers. LC.

29. "There is a general belief that the Ohio delegation": *Albany Evening Journal*, June 4, 1880.

30. "In the event of a failure to nominate": French to Garfield, June 6, 1880. Garfield papers. LC.

31. "sincerely hope the political lightnings of Chicago": "A Young Republican" to Garfield, June 2, 1880. Garfield papers. LC.

32. "I hear a great many rumors": Coffin to Garfield, June 7, 1880. Garfield papers. LC.

33. "it will be likely to embitter him": Garfield to Lucretia Garfield, June 3, 1880. Shaw, 374.

34. "half afraid the convention": Lucretia Garfield to Garfield, June 4, 1880. Shaw, 375.

35. "You can never know how much I need you": Garfield to Lucretia Garfield, June 3, 1880. Shaw, 374.
36. "My name must not be used": Sautter and Burke, 42.
37. "Grant can't be defeated": *Chicago Tribune*, June 7, 1880.
38. "amid a quiet that was almost oppressive": *New York Times*, June 8, 1880.
39. delegates were expected to deliberate: To Crosby Noyes's *Washington Evening Star*, the Chicago dead-lock demonstrated "folly and danger of the instruction system and the favorite son business in politics" which "invariably put the man above the cause" and "takes away from the [delegate]the quality of a free agent with discretion ... being at liberty to select the best and strongest candidate." A national convention, "stands in precisely the same relation to its party that Congress does to the whole country. It could therefore be no more foolish or hurtful... to direct representatives which laws to pass and which not to pass when assembled together." June 9, 1880.
40. delegates "prefer to vote for themselves": *New York Times*, June 8, 1880.
41. "Your friends' thoughts are with you": Coan to Garfield, June 7, 1880. Garfield papers. LC.

5. The Break *(pages 83–104)*

1. All around Washington: *Washington Evening Star*. June 7, 1880.
2. chair "shoved back," and "resting his head": *Washington Post*, June 8, 1880.
3. "scratched his head as if he didn't like the number": *Washington Evening Star*, June 7, 1880.
4. Blaine "jumped up and darted about the chamber": *Washington Post*, June 8, 1880.
5. Blaine ... rode a private carriage ... to his home... Here he could track events: *New York Times*, June 8, 1880; Washington Evening Star, June 7, 1880.
6. "He was certainly cool today": *Chicago Tribune*, June 9, 1880.
7. General Sherman ... seemed "very much more anxious": *id.*
8. "Since my last dispatch": Dennison to Sherman, June 2, 1880, Sherman papers. LC.
9. "I had expected to have had twenty votes more": *Chicago Tribune*, June 9, 1880.
10. Dyer to Sherman, June 6, 1880. Sherman papers. LC.
11. "Blaine has permitted, if not fostered ... If the nine will not go": Sherman. 774-5.
12. "Tell me what is going on": Sherman to Moulton, June 7, 1880. Sherman papers. LC.
13. "See Jack Wharton of Louisiana Delegation": Sherman to Bateman, June 7, 1880. Sherman papers. LC.
14. "The forces were under a remarkable discipline": *Cleveland Herald*, June 12, 1880.
15. a "long and continuous whoop": *New York World*, June 8, 1880.
16. "Are you in favor of the protective tariff?": Grier to Garfield. June 7, 1880. Garfield papers. LC.
17. "Two delegates are *said* to be for Sherman": *Official Proceedings*; *Id.*

18. "wonderful sneer": Jordan, 339.

19. "Mr. Chairman, one of this important delegation": *Albany Evening Journal*, June 8, 1880.

20. Conkling ... "in imitation and ridicule": *New York World*, June 8, 1880.

21. Arthur spoke: *id.*

22. "enthusiastic applause": *Albany Evening Journal*, June 8, 1880.

23. "[T]he silent soldier was smoking": *Washington Post*, June 8, 1880.

24. "I entreated him to go on Sunday": For this incident, the principal source is Julia Grant, 321-322.

25. "after the convention adjourns": Grant to Fred Grant, June 8, 1880. Conkling papers. LC.

26. "no truth in the absurd report": *Chicago Tribune*, June 9, 1880.

27. end the whole convention *sine die* tonight: *New York World*, June 7, 1880.

28. "The expectation that Grant would succeed": Bateman to Sherman, June 12, 1880. Sherman papers. LC.

29. receptions on the elegant North Side: One of the nicest receptions apparently was thrown on Sunday night by Potter Palmer at his new mansion on North Lake Shore Drive in honor of Senator Don Cameron's wife Elizabeth, who had now come to Chicago for the convention.

30. Somebody kept notes: An unsigned memorandum laying out the dilemma from the Blaine side, titled "Message from Blaine's Friends," was sent to Sherman the next morning—obviously not for public consumption but it survives in the Sherman papers at the Library of Congress. Quotes ascribed here to Chandler are from that document, assuming Chandler the likely author.

31. "If Mr. Blaine permits his column to be broken": "Message from Blaine's friends," received June 8, 1880. Sherman papers. LC.

32. "tools" of a Roscoe Conkling strategy: *Chicago Inter Ocean*, June 8, 1880.

33. "[T]o attempt to transfer [Blaine's] strength": "Message from Blaine's friends," received June 8, 1880. Sherman papers. LC.

34. nor apparently had the Ohioans given a clear "yes" or "no": Two days later, after the convention was over, Foster acknowledged that "we were making arrangements to transfer our strength, in Ohio at least, to Blaine, and this would certainly have been done within a few ballots." [Unidentified newspaper, Garfield papers, LC.] If so, then his failure to close the deal on time probably cost him the vice presidency.

35. "Do you think it is possible for the Blaine men": *Chicago Tribune*, June 9, 1880.

36. They "freely discussed the situation": *New York Times*, June 8, 1880.

37. betting now ran two-to-one against Grant: *New York World*, June 8, 1880.

38. "I could not be nominated in any event": A.R. Conkling, 605; Boutwell, 269; Platt, 113. Conkling's biographer and nephew, Alfred R. Conkling, writing in 1889, is the main source for this incident and quote and presumably had spoken with participants. By then, the story had likely been embellished. Boutwell, also writing long after the fact, cites "the suggestion" to substitute Conkling for Grant being "made, but without authority [by] those charged with the management" of Grant's campaign, and Conkling's "sturdy refusal."

Platt, writing in 1910, said "delegates from various states" had been making the Conkling suggestion "during the day."

39. no dark horse: AR Conkling, 607.
40. "The only decision reached": *New York Times*, June 8, 1880.
41. "Mass. casts 21 votes for you": Parker Chandler, June 8, 1880. Sherman papers. LC.
42. Chandler's move had checked the plot: *Chicago Tribune*, June 9, 1880. See also Richardson, 256.
43. "Members of the N.Y. Delegation": Western Union Bulletin, June 8, 1880. Sherman papers. LC.
44. "dark with disappointment": *New York Times*, June 9, 1880.
45. "Wisconsin casts two votes": Peskin, 474.
46. the galleries "cheered lustily": *New York Times*, June 9, 1880.
47. "If you Ohio delegates": *Cleveland Herald*, June 12, 1880. Garfield's friend Charles Henry, the source, claimed that a variety of anti-Grant delegates had been approaching Ohio all week asking, "Why don't you Ohio men take up Garfield" instead up Sherman and "We will vote for him," but the only answer they received was "We have come [to Chicago] to urge the claim of John Sherman." According to this theory, Wisconsin, in an experimental mood, finally took the bull by the horns.
48. Wisconsin had ... decided ... only by a slight majority: Jordan, 340; McClure, 273.
49. "It is probably true that": *Cincinnati Enquirer*, June 9, 1880. Benjamin Harrison of Indiana, as close as anyone to the event, told a reporter that "all these stories about this or that candidate having originated the break are pure inventions. The break was spontaneous, originating itself, so to speak." *Washington Evening Star*, June 14, 1880.
50. "Mr. President, I rise to a question of order": *Official Proceedings*; newspaper accounts.
51. "The gentleman from Ohio is not stating a question of order": *Official Proceedings*; Clancy 112-113. Welch, 96.
52. "I was terribly afraid that he [Garfield]": Welch, 96; Hoar, 396-7.
53. "Wisconsin and Indiana have voted": Bateman to Sherman, June 8, 1880. Sherman papers. LC.
54. "You can make Blaine President": Elkins to Garfield, June 8, 1880. Garfield papers. LC.
55. "scarcely necessary to have 'wasted a card": *Chicago Tribune*, June 9, 1880.
56. "Maine's vote this moment cast for you": *id.*
57. "You must see that your friends": Kumler to Sherman, June 8, 1880. Sherman papers. LC.
58. "Your friends here say": Lynch to Sherman, June 8, 1880. Sherman papers. LC.
59. "You cannot be nominated": Irwin to Sherman, June 8, 1880. Sherman papers. LC.
60. "If defeated, thank the ambition of Garfield": George Filch, June 8, 1880. Sherman papers. LC.

61. "Whenever the vote of Ohio will be likely": Sherman to Dennison, June 8, 1880. Sherman papers. LC.

62. "was possibly a slight disappointment": *Chicago Tribune*, June 9, 1880.

63. "Blaine could have nominated him (Sherman)": *id.* The *New York Times* (June 9) also reported this meeting, based on "unquestioned authority," stating: "The managers suggested that Gen. Garfield alone, in their opinion, could obtain the desired undivided vote. Blaine and Sherman assented, and their respective managers were directed to take up Garfield at the proper time."

64. flatly denied by all sides: Chicago *Inter Ocean*, June 9, 1880.

65. "Keep steady, boys": Jordan, 340.

66. "clear ringing voice": *Cleveland Herald*, June 12, 1880.

67. Garfield was "in much apparent emotion": Bateman to Sherman, June 12, 1880. Sherman papers. LC.

68. "Cast the vote and poll the delegation afterward": Stanwood, 230.

69. "anxious, hurried consultation": Unidentified newspaper, Garfield papers. LC.

70. "Is there no place that I can go?": Chicago *Inter Ocean*, June 9, 1880.

71. "They have nominated you." ... "I wish you would say [in your paper]": *id.*

72. "The movement to Garfield swept": Bateman to Sherman, June 8, 1880. Sherman papers. LC.

73. "General, we surrender; you have whipped us": Chicago *Inter Ocean*, June 9, 1880.

74. "No, no, gentlemen,... no theatrical performance": *Cleveland Herald*, June 12, 1880.

75. "Different states have seized banners": Western Union Bulletin, June 8, 1880. Sherman papers. LC.

76. "the entire convention centered around Garfield": *Washington Evening Star*, June 9, 1880.

77. "pale as death": *Chicago Inter Ocean*, June 9, 1880.

78. "rare modesty": *New York World*, June9, 1880.

79. "Sherwin ... won't you telegraph to my wife": *Chicago Inter Ocean*, June 9, 1880.

80. "'Hurrah for Garfield' was cried": *New York Times*, June 9, 1880.

81. "glum faces, ... making no effort to conceal": *New York Tribune*, June 9, 1880.

82. "I congratulate the Republican Party": AR Conkling, 607.

83. "funereal,... belied his nice words": *New York World*, June 9, 1880.

84. "I would speak louder, ... but": *Official Proceedings*, 276-77. "Mr. Conkling had a bad cold and could hardly be heard," echoed the *Washington Evening Star* that day.

85. "Gen. [John] Logan was calm, but": *New York Times*, June 9, 1880.

86. "Three Hundred and Six Guard" society: See Platt 118-123; Alexander 441.

87. "Dear Wife. If the result meets": Garfield to Lucretia Garfield, June 8, 1880. Shaw, 377.

88. "The Grant men took the defeat": *Washington Evening Star*, June 8, 1880.

89. "Thanks for everything that was done": Blaine to Chandler, June 8, 1880. Blaine papers. LC.

90. "The nomination of Garfield is generally satisfactory": Sherman to Bateman, June 8, 1880. Sherman papers. LC

91. "It is probable that if": Sherman, 775.

92. "Give us some first class man": Sherman to Bateman, June 8, 1880. Sherman papers. LC

6. Compromise (*pages 105–113*)

1. "Take off the horses,... we will pull the carriage": Charles Henry related this incident to the *Cleveland Herald*, June 12, 1880.

2. Garfield "completely broke down... The nervous strain upon [Garfield]": *Washington Evening Star*, June 9, 1880.

3. "jollifications": *id.*

4. "Illinois 25,000 majority for Garfield": *New York Times*, June 9, 1880.

5. "felt very ugly" ... and "threaten[ed] ... disasters": *New York Tribune*, June 9, 1880.

6. "I hope no sincere friend of mine": Jordan, 341. According to Stewart Woodford's memory twenty-eight years later in an interview with DeAlva S. Alexander, Conkling immediately considered the Garfield ticket a loser and told him "The Convention has nominated a candidate but not a president," and, regarding the vice presidency, "whom shall we place on the altar as a vicarious sacrifice." Alexander, 443.

7. Morton ... check first with his "associates": Alexander, 444.

8. "The friends of Mr. Blaine, who furnished the bulk": Reeves, 180

9. Frye ...was heard exchanging "strong words": *New York World*, June 9, 1880.

10. "It was [William] Robertson who engineered the break": Hudson, 105.

11. "If you think the ticket will be elected": Jordan, 341; Alexander, 444, citing a letter to him from Morton dated September 14, 1908, twenty-eight years after the fact.

12. "Ohio would be glad to promise": *New York Times*, June 9, 1880.

13. "Murphy, we can get Arthur that nomination": *Cincinnati Enquirer*, August 14, 1883.

14. "I have been hunting for you everywhere": The ensuing dialogue is from Hudson, 97-98; see also Jordan 342, fn. 20.

15. "Mr. Murphy, what is the meaning of this talk": Murphy told his story to the *Cincinnati Enquirer* three years later, August 14, 1883.

16. Conkling had softened: Stephen Dorsey also claims to have buttonholed Conkling in his hotel suite on Arthur's behalf at this point in the day, but to no avail. "You cannot be serious about this," Conkling supposedly told him, and threatened to throw Dorsey out of the room when he pushed the point. Dorsey disclosed his story in late 1882, however, after he had been indicted by Arthur's administration in the Star Route postal frauds, making it highly suspect. See *Cincinnati Enquirer*, September 27, 1882.

17. Then they ushered the Ohioans out: At this point, Dennison reported to John Sherman: "The Ohio delegation have instructed me to give their vote for the Vice Presidency as New York and the friends of General Grant may direct,

which I have just communicated to the New York delegation"—apparently Sherman's first indication of the coming deal. Sherman papers. LC.

18. "Sir, I am not surprised at anything from Ohio": Reeves, 181, and sources at fn. 39, ch. 9.

19. "gentleman of integrity" and "unquestionable faithfulness": *New York Times*, June 9, 1880.

20. "Gentlemen, if that is what you have to say": *Cincinnati Enquirer*, August 14, 1883.

21. "in the greatest possible haste": *New York Tribune*, June 9, 1880.

22. "Let us not do a rash thing": *Official Proceedings*; *New York Tribune*, June 9, 1880.

23. "unanimity of pleasure," … "assurances of confidence and esteem and unity." … "discharge my duties faithfully." Proceedings, 297-298.

24. so "heartily … that they dislocated one of my fingers": *New York Tribune*, June 12, 1880.

25. "half the wild half-drunken mobs": *Official Proceedings*, 297-8; Boston Globe, June 9, 1880.

26. "Arthur is able": Peskin, 481; Chandler to Bateman, June 22, 1880.

27. "Robertson and Woodin have got a good spanking": *New York World*, June 9, 1880.

28. "We made our kick and pledges": Hudson, 105.

29. "The nomination of Arthur is a ridiculous burlesque": Sherman to Bateman, June 9, 1880. Sherman papers. LC.

30. even Sherman agreed to "keep quiet": Rutherford Hayes, sitting in the White House with even less love for Conkling or Arthur, was more sanguine: "The sop thrown to Conkling in the nomination of Arthur only serves to emphasize the completeness of his defeat," he wrote in his diary that week. "[Conkling] was so crushed that it was from sheer sympathy that the bone was thrown to him." Hayes diary. June 11, 1880.

7. Chance of a Lifetime *(pages 114–116)*

1. Charles Guiteau: The best recent work on Guiteau is Rosenberg's *The Trial of the Assassin Guiteau*. Rick Geary's *The Fatal Bullet* relates the assassination story in a very accessible comic-book format. The most revealing window on this odd character, however, is Guiteau's own words in the trial testimony (United States v. Charles Guiteau) and various press interviews from prison, cited herein.

2. "I didn't have any success": Guiteau testimony: United States v. Charles Guiteau, 583.

3. "As soon as General Garfield was nominated": Guiteau testimony: United States v. Charles Guiteau, 583.

4. the overnight steamer *Stonington*: For accounts of the *Stonington- Narragansett* disaster, see *New York Times* and *Boston Post*, June 12, 1880 and subsequent days.

5. "black and dark as tar,… You couldn't see an inch": Guiteau testimony: United States v. Charles Guiteau, 583.

6. "I saw and heard the wailing": Guiteau testimony: United States v. Charles Guiteau, 584.

8. The Bargain (pages 119–156)

1. "an admiring group," ... "smiling, unruffled, affable": *Chicago Inter Ocean*, June 10, 1880.
2. "a sad commentary upon the work of the political evangelists": Unidentified newspaper, Garfield papers. LC.
3. "misled" him into "an unfortunate struggle": *Chicago Tribune*, June 9, 1880.
4. "careful not to express any opinion": *Chicago Inter Ocean*, June 10, 1880.
5. "not at all displeased": *New York Times*, June 10, 1880.
6. "Garfield will be beaten": *id.*, quoting the *Chicago Times*, June 9, 1880.
7. Conkling ..."should have been nominated": *The Nation*, June 17, 1880.
8. "so prolonged that many believed": Badeau, 324.
9. "led to believe that his nomination was ... probable": *Cincinnati Commercial*, July 12, 1880. Garfield papers. LC.
10. "My friends have not been honest": Woodward, 475.
11. "had rather too many volumes of Congressional debates": *Cincinnati Commercial*, July 12, 1880. Garfield papers. LC.
12. "Individually, I am much relieved": A.R. Conkling, 608-609.
13. "The General went, ... I would not go": Julia Grant, 322.
14. "He is one of the ablest men in the country": *Boston Herald*, in the *Chicago Tribune*, June 8, 1880.
15. "next to Senator Blaine, Garfield [is] the most popular": *Albany Evening Journal*, June 9, 1880.
16. "a balm for all the wounds": *Chicago Tribune*, June 9, 1880.
17. "a happy solution": *Cincinnati Commercial*, June 9, 1880.
18. "the worst and most venal scandals": *Boston Globe*, June 9, 1880.
19. "Garfield [is] good, glorious, and yet—It is an escape": Dawes to Ela Dawes, June 9, 1880. Dawes papers. LC.
20. "penalties of greatness": *New York Tribune*, June 10, 1880.
21. "The great Senator [Conkling] a few days ago said": *New York Times*, June 10, 1880.
22. "wild with enthusiasm": *New York Tribune*, June 10, 1880.
23. *Puck* ... the fifth presidential James: *Puck*, August 18, 1880.
24. "into whose face almost all of you have looked": *New York Times*, June 11, 1880.
25. "The events of the past week": Lucretia to Garfield, June 15, 1880.
26. James' ... affair with a Mrs. Calhoun: Peskin, 160-1.
27. "monstrous fictions" ... "discriminate between truth and error": Lucretia Garfield to Hinsdale, February 19, 1880. Mary Hinsdale, 445.
28. "She is one of the coolest and best-balanced women": *Cincinnati Enquirer*, April 17, 1880.
29. Blaine ... had "anticipate[d] the nuptial ceremony": Garfield to Lucretia Garfield, April 21, 1875. Shaw, 305.

30. "I scarcely believe it": Lucretia Garfield to Garfield, April 25, 1875. Shaw, 306-7. This story would erupt during Blaine's 1884 presidential campaign, circulated by backers of Democrat Grover Cleveland to deflect attention after revelations that Cleveland had fathered a child out of wedlock, prompting the chant that year "Hey, Ma! Where's Pa? Gone to the White House. Ha! Ha!"

31. "[t]he grinding misery of being a woman": Lucretia Garfield to Garfield, undated, in Shaw, x.

32. "teach my boys to do farm work": Garfield diary, Sept 26, Oct 31, 1876; Peskin, 431.

33. "I should much prefer to see the party defeated with Garfield": Muzzey, 172; Curran, 82-83.

34. "make no promises to anybody ... don't make any journeys": Reid to Garfield, June 12, 1880. Reid papers. LC. Cortissoz, 35.

35. "must *not* make any statement": G.A. Baker memorandum [undated]. Garfield papers. LC. Emphasis in original.

36. Baker laid it out on a single piece of paper: *id*.

37. The U.S. Constitution guaranteed racial fairness: The Fifteenth amendment, adopted in 1870, provided that "the right of citizens ...to vote shall not be denied or abridged... by any State on account of race, color, or previous condition of servitude." Also, the Fourteenth amendment, adopted in 1868, provided that "when the right to vote" in any Federal election "is denied... except for participation in rebellion or other crime," then the state's basis for representation in Congress "shall be reduced in proportion...." This enforcement tool, pushed by James Blaine as a Congressman, was never implemented even during the worst days of Jim Crow abuse.

38. Freed blacks wanting to vote faced threats of violence, arrest, or murder: On Southern voting frauds and violence generally, see Goldman. See also, e.g. Letter from Paul Strobach to Chandler, November 8, 1880. Chandler papers. LC.

39. for Garfield to win, he would need virtually every single other state: Hayes had won in 1876 despite losing New York and Indiana only because he was able to wrestle away three Southern states in his electoral dispute under Reconstruction—an option not open to Garfield.

40. Tweed ... driven from power in 1871,: New Yorker Samuel Tilden's role in prosecuting Tweed in the early 1870s became a key factor in launching his presidential bid in 1876, making him an ideal "reform" candidate against the party of "Grantism." Tilden won the popular vote against Rutherford Hayes in 1876 but lost the presidency in the electoral dispute.

41. "Conkling is not sincere in his support": Sherman to Dennison, June 9, 1880. Sherman papers. LC.

42. The 'triumvirate' talk very ugly": Dawes to Ela Dawes. Dawes papers. LC.

43. "Conkling and his men will not care": *Washington Post*, June 9, 1880.

44. "But for the disgrace, I would rather": Peskin, 485, citing AR Conkling.

45. Garfield's "personal history as an ideal": Hayes diary, June 15, 1880. Hayes papers.

46. "I shall make the trip as quietly": Cortissoz, 35.

47. Lucretia ... long list of items to ship ... back to Ohio: Lucretia Garfield to Garfield, June 15, 1880. Shaw, 378.

48. Garfield dined with President Hayes ...met John Sherman: *Washington Evening Star*, June 15, 1880. See also Bateman to Sherman, June 12, 1880, and Moulton to Sherman, June 11, 1880. Sherman papers. LC.

49. outdoor serenade.... Army of the Cumberland Society ...banquet : Generally see coverage in *Washington Evening Star* and *Washington Post*, June 15-18, 1880.

50. "Garfield comes here this morning": Dawes to Ela Dawes. Dawes papers. LC.

51. "I wish to see you away from": Garfield to Conkling, June 15, 1880. Conkling papers. LC.

52. "the damning news drove Roscoe into the sulks!": Cortissoz, 36.

53. Jordan. 347.

54. cringing "at the thought of holding commerce": Years later, after the falling out, Conkling's biographer A.R. Conkling would ascribe a more sinister motive: that Conkling was "unwilling to trust to Mr. Garfield's imperfect memory of a private conversation, however unimportant" and was "not willing to be a party to any agreement with the candidate that required secrecy."

55. a "trivial, beggarly thing,": Cortissoz, 36.

56. Republican National Committee met in New York City: *New York Tribune*, July 1, 1880.

57. Garfield had asked Don Cameron to stay: *Washington Evening Star*, June 10, 1880; *Cincinnati Enquirer*, June 10, 1880.

58. Chandler ... had declined "in the most positive manner": WC Cooper to Garfield, June 9, 1880. Garfield papers. LC.

59. "huge straw hats" ... "in a stately way": *New York Tribune*, July 3, 1880.

60. "My whole duty... begins and ends": *New York Tribune*, July 1, 1880.

61. Jewell ... at least was "competent": WC Cooper to Garfield, June 9, 1880. Garfield papers. LC.

62. sell his vote, "often not for a very high price": Peskin 486.

63. the committee had finished. Dorsey was in: Generally on the National Committee meeting, see newspapers, Peskin 485-486 and Richardson258.

64. "I have sense enough to know": Peskin 487.

65. "the 'Scratchers' and Independents and 'featherheads'"... "They intend to know it": Dorsey to Garfield, July 26, 1880. Garfield papers. LC.; Jordan, 350.

66. "They intended to know it":Dorsey to Garfield, July 26, 1880. Garfield papers. LC.; Clancy 187-188.

67. "Your presence ... is a paramount duty": Dorsey to Garfield, July 28, 1880. Garfield papers. LC.

68. "It is the liveliest spot I have ever seen": Logan to Mary Logan. July 26, 1880. Logan papers. LC.

69. Conkling's ... "ruddy glow of good health": *Brooklyn Eagle*, in *Chicago Tribune*, July 8, 1880. Garfield papers. LC.

70. "He is full of life ... "[h]is grip on the party machinery": *id.*

71. "Every day & everything was enjoyable": Conkling to Morton, August 1, 1880, in Reeves, 191.

72. Garfield "will be owned or controlled": *Washington Evening Star*, June 14, 1880.

73. "There are some matters which must be attended": A.R. Conkling. 613.

74. Conkling … "probably" and "properly" would "demand": *New York Times*, July 17, 1880.

75. The New York Custom House: Generally on the New York Custom House during this era, see "The New York Custom-House," *Harpers New Monthly Magazine*, June 1884.

76. Hancock had promised specific slots: *Washington Evening Star*, August 5, 1880.

77. "The State of New York is important, probably vital": Richardson, 261, citing Chandler to Garfield, July 24, 1880.

78. "literally overrun with visitors": *Cleveland Press*, in *Washington Post*, July 2, 1880.

79. "Why before this is over": Lide Rudolph to Lucretia Garfield, July 7, 1880. Lucretia Garfield papers. LC.

80. "The general takes great interest in the affairs": A.P. of Plainwell Michigan to Lucretia Garfield, June 14, 1880. Lucretia Garfield papers. LC.

81. "I have had to travel fast": Lucretia Garfield to Garfield, June 15. Shaw, 377-8.

82. "It is against all precedent for a Presidential candidate": *Washington Post*, July 2, 1880.

83. "If it were the custom": Garfield diary, August 10, 1880.

84. "There is no place where you can do so much": Reid to Garfield, June 12, 1880. Reid papers. LC.; Clancy, 181.

85. "contained more anxiety than reasons": Garfield diary. July 27, 1880.

86. "I don't believe in running after the malcontents": Cortissoz, 37.

87. "If Conkling himself sulks": Schurz papers, IV,3; Jordan, 349.

88. Curtis … also wrote strongly to protest the meeting: Clancy, 189.

89. The *Springfield Republican* and *Boston Herald* both loudly warned: *Washington Evening Star*, August 5, 1880.

90. Garfield risked not only alienating the anti-machine moderates: Garfield diary, July 27, 1880.

91. Garfield was "entirely willing, and indeed should be glad": Garfield to Chandler, July 26, 1880. Garfield papers. LC. Clancy186; Garfield diary, July 27, 1880.

92. Garfield needed an "eye to eye, face to face": Chandler to Garfield, July 24, 1880, Garfield papers. LC; Clancy, 184.

93. Blaine …"decidedly against": Jewell to Garfield, July 28, 1880; in Garfield diary, July 28, 1880, fn. 200.

94. "I cannot believe Conkling wants anything unreasonable": Henry to Garfield, July 26, 1880. Norris and Shaffer, 283.

95. "The NY Senator pouts now.": Henry to Garfield, July 27, 1880. Norris and Shaffer, 286.

96. Dorsey's arrangements… [have] gone so far": Reid to Blaine, July 30, 1880. Blaine papers. LC.

97. "not a bargain, only 'a little fraternization": Garfield diary, July 28, 1880, and fn. 109.

98. "[A] failure to have matters put in better shape": Dorsey to Garfield, July 25. Garfield papers. LC.; Garfield diary, July 27, 1880, fn. 197. Peskin, 488.

99. "I am very reluctant to go": Garfield diary, July 28, 1880.

100. "Please meet me with Committee": Garfield to Blaine, July 30, 1880. Blaine papers. LC.

101. "You must not fail me.": Garfield to Blaine, July 30, 1880. Garfield papers. LC.

102. "I earnestly desire you to join me at Geneva": Garfield to Logan. August 1, 1880. Logan papers. LC.

103. "the best [yield] yet reported in the vicinity": Garfield diary. July 30, 1880.

104. a "mere cover and a farce": Platt, 127.

105. "passed through an almost continuing dense mass": Garfield to Lucretia Garfield, August 4, 1880. Shaw, 379.

106. "the more sanguine ones ... say": id.

107. "Men took off their hats": New York Tribune, August 5, 1880.

108. "The old 117th Volunteers will vote": id.

109. "Old discords have been outgrown and forgotten": New York Tribune, June 6, 1880.

110. "imperil their lives and deplete the pockets": New York World, August 6, 1880.

111. One version had George William Curtis as the target: Cortissoz, 37.

112. his dislike of John Sherman: New York World, August 6, 1880.

113. Conkling ... would "place himself in a very bad light": Logan to Mary Logan. August 5, 1880. Logan papers. LC. The best pro-Conkling "spin" came from the New York Times, which attributed Conking's absence to "his sincere desire for party harmony." Recognizing Conkling's "talent for making enemies," he had graciously tried to "avoid any occasion to reopen wounds.... This scrupulous regard for the feelings of others augurs well for the tact and self-sacrificing effort" of Conkling. "Mr. Garfield will doubtless leave New York thoroughly impressed with the magnanimity and disinterestedness of our senior Senator." New York Times, August 6, 1880.

114. Blaine "the prince of good fellows": Garfield diary. August 5, 1880.

115. "stream of messages" flowed "between General Garfield's parlors": New York World, August 6, 1880.

116. "Mr. Garfield is said to be ready": New York World, August 6, 1880.

117. He "express[ed] his disappointment and indignation": Platt, 129.

118. New Yorkers seemed "embarrassed and somewhat indignant": Garfield diary, August 5, 1880.

119. Conkling ... "in the hands of his friends": Reid to Garfield, August 15, 1880, in Cortissoz, 38; Platt 127.

120. "I think [Conkling's] friends are showing zeal": Garfield diary, August 5, 1880.

121. "no obstacle" now prevented a "zealous and vigorous contest": New York Times, August 6, 1880.

122. Levi Morton: Description of Morton is from Josephson, 290.

123. Garfield offered Morton a top post: *Chicago Tribune*, May 13, 1880. Garfield spoke through Thomas Nichol.

124. "I think he will help": Garfield diary, August 6, 1880.

125. "We have seen white men betray the flag": Garfield speech from *New York Times*, August 7, 1880.

126. Garfield spoke with "dignity and majesty" on "so high a plane": Jewell to Lucretia Garfield. Lucretia Garfield papers. LV.

127. Conkling ... the real reason for his absence: Tom Platt claims Conkling's "private reason" was that "he knew Garfield so well that he would not keep any promise or regard any obligations made and taken under such circumstances" and wanted to avoid charges of deal-making. Conkling's nephew A.R. Conkling makes the remarkable claim that "He desired no pledges concerning the control of patronage in New York. In fact, he detested pledges in politics."

128. "Mr. Garfield, there seems to be some hesitation": Platt 130. Platt's account, written almost thirty years later, appears to merge the two meetings with Garfield, but he is specific on who was in the room for the direct pledges, and his list matches Garfield's August 6 journal entry name for name. Reeves (p.463, fn. 24) argues that only one meeting occurred, on August 5, citing an August 6 *New York Times* article ("Leaders in Conference") and a "misleading entry in Garfield's diary." The *New York Times* article, though, lists a larger group of attendees than Platt's and Garfield's accounts. Admittedly the record is unclear, but taking Garfield's journal as accurate on dates and names argues for two meetings rather than one.

129. "These assurances were oft repeated": Platt, 131.

130. Garfield then "was given assurance": *id.*

131. "a formal document, frigid as a bill of sale": *New York Sun*, July 16, 1883. The later versions come from (a) Stephen Dorsey in July 1883 after he had been indicted in the Star Route mail fraud cases and was extremely vitriolic against Garfield and Arthur and (b) a Conkling-inspired slam against Garfield published in the *New York Herald* (May 11, 1881, "The Wriggler") at the height of their subsequent blow-up and likewise highly combative.

132. "no serious mistakes had been made": Garfield diary, August 9, 1880.

133. "full of misstatement and misrepresentations": *Chicago Tribune*, May 13, 1881. Garfield apparently passed up more timely opportunities to deny rumors of "deals" in the weeks after the New York summit, including a friendly request from the *Cleveland Leader*, fueling suspicions. See Clancy, 192. Whether Garfield would lie to his own diary on something so sensitive, recognizing that his diary might one day become a public historical document, is unclear.

134. "Did not sleep well. Had in the P.M. a long interview": Garfield diary, August 6, 1880. Smith, reviewing the situation, finds it "inconceivable" that Garfield would have compromised himself by making the claimed promise that night. (Smith II 1016.) It may be less "inconceivable" that Arthur and Platt might have shaded the truth rather than having to face Roscoe Conkling with news of anything less than total success. The strict historical record, however, is inconclusive. See also Clancy, 192, fn. 79.

135. "Distinctly, clearly, such an agreement had been made": Connery, 150.

136. "Conkling's zeal in the campaign indicated": *The Nation*, October 21, 1880; Clancy, 191.

137. "If you insist... I shall carry him through": Peskin, 490.

138. "to read up and get ready for the campaign": Conkling to Morton, August 29, 1880, in Clancy, 192.

139. "I will be going east the latter part of Sept[ember]": Grant to Logan, August 12, 1880. Logan papers. LC.

140. "Everything I have seen since the conference": Reid to Garfield, August 15, 1880, in Cortissoz, 38.

141. "All rumors of secret pledges are wholly baseless": *Harpers Weekly*, August 28, 1880.

142. "If [Conkling] intends to take actively hold": Garfield diary, August 5, 1880.

143. "Always very delightful and pleasant": Guiteau testimony: United States v. Charles Guiteau, 585.

144. "O, yes; I remember that": Guiteau testimony: United States v. Charles Guiteau, 585-586.

145. "I knew Guiteau ... as a young lawyer": Storrs testimony: United States v. Charles Guiteau, Guiteau, 718-719.

146. "a pretty good condensed statement of the whole situation": Gorham testimony: United States v. Charles Guiteau, Guiteau, 789.

147. The speech opened by recalling: "Garfield against Hancock." For full text, see United States v. Charles Guiteau, 124-6; Guiteau papers.

148. "Charles Guiteau of Illinois": *New York Times*, August 7, 1880 ("The Candidates Honored... Addresses by Other Speakers"); Garfield diary: fn. 223 to entry for August 6. No other newspaper account mentions Guiteau by name, though the *New York Tribune* suggests that several lesser-known speakers, perhaps including Guiteau, gave presentations after Garfield had left the stage.

149. Those who gave speeches ... would get the best ones: See, for instance, Guiteau testimony: United States v. Charles Guiteau, 602, where he explains how offices "are distributed more on account of personal relations with the President and Secretary of State."

150. Formal letter to the Republican Party accepting its nomination: Garfield to Hoar, July 10, 1880. The full text of the letter is contained in *Official Proceedings*, 298, and newspapers.

151. "disgusted,"... "unworthy": Peskin, 484.

152. economic engine had produced remarkable growth: Data on American economic growth are from Appendices to Blaine, Volume I.

153. "I belong to a party that believes in good crops": *New York Tribune*, October 29, 1880; in Josephson, 289.

154. "no more changes the character of Democracy": *St Louis Globe Democrat*, June 25, 1880, in Clancy, 175.

155. "The chief duty of government": Garfield to Eldridge, December 14, 1869. Garfield papers. LC.; Peskin, 262; Bartleby.com.

156. "devise a method" to reform the civil service: Garfield to Hoar, July 10, 1880.

9. The Narrowest Margin *(pages 157–192)*

1. "[s]end me one thousand more wrappers": Cogswell to Arthur, October 13, 1880. Arthur papers. LC.
2. "I shall be glad to receive a check": Morton to Arthur, September 25, 1880. Arthur papers. LC.
3. "there is nothing worth having now": Reeves, 198-190.
4. "Mr. Arthur directs me to say": VR to Pavey, October 14, 1880. Arthur papers. LC.
5. "My duties as Chrm. RSC confine me": Arthur to Harmon, October 22, 1880. Arthur papers. LC.
6. "separate dates for local elections": For the presidency, article II, section 1, authorized "The Congress [to] determine the Time of choosing the Electors, and the day on which they shall give their votes; which day shall be the same throughout the United States." For Congress, article I, section 4, however, allowed each state, by its legislature, to choose "The Times, Places and Manner of holding Elections for Senators and Representatives," subject to regulation by Congress.
7. Blaine … had sent out waves of telegrams: Only Ohio governor Charles Foster begged to stay away: "Maine & Indiana have so effectually cleaned us out of speakers for Ohio as to make it impossible for me to come," he wired.
8. Arthur worked his traditional source: government workers: Arthur that year sent letters to every federal office in New York State demanding names and salaries of all employees with urgent calls for cash. He carefully tracked payments, and sent collectors to the desk of government clerks who dragged their feet to browbeat them into giving "voluntary" contributions, as President Rutherford Hayes' civil services reforms had already barred direct taxing of federal workers by politicians. At the same time, Assistant Postmaster General Tom Brady covered all the Washington, D.C. federal offices for contributions.
9. "humiliated in his own state," or "There's no sand in him": A.R. Conkling, 614.
10. "one little bit of a 15-minute speech": Clemens to Arthur, September 15, 1880. Arthur papers. LC.
11. "Seventeenth [of September] preferred to sixteenth": Conkling to Arthur, September 7, 1880. Arthur papers, LC.
12. "[W]e have finally determined" … "Latest day gives little time": Arthur to Conkling, September 10, 1880; Conkling to Arthur, September 12, 1880. Arthur papers, LC.
13. "Don't hurt her. You may spoil"… "with more than the usual vehemence": *New York Times*, September 18, 1880.
14. Garfield had insisted on this Ohio visit: Garfield to Morton, September 10, 1880. Arthur papers. LC. See also discussion of Fifth avenue summit, part II(a) above.
15. "I concluded to break other engagement that might conflict": Grant to Arthur, September 13, 1880. Arthur papers. LC. Earlier, he had written: "Leave Chicago for east September thirtieth…. I might go a day or two earlier … and leave my family to meet me at place named. Do not make the meeting earlier than twenty eighth." Grant to Arthur, September 10. Arthur papers. LC.

16. "The suggestion is new & unexpected ... I should not begin": Conkling to Arthur, September 11, 1880. Arthur papers. LC.

17. "I prefer staying indoors": Conkling to Arthur, September 12, 1880. Arthur papers. LC.

18. "We can give the Senator [Conkling] a hall": Garfield to Arthur, September 13, 1880. Arthur papers. LC.

19. Warren ... "offers to build a wigwam": Garfield to Arthur, September 14, 1880. Arthur papers. LC.

20. "What do you say Friday meeting [in] Warren": *id*. See also, e.g., Garfield to Arthur, September 13, 1880. Arthur papers. LC.

21. "Three meetings in Ohio [are] enough": Conkling to Arthur, September 20, 1880. Arthur papers. LC.

22. "Have announced Grant and Conkling": Garfield to Arthur, September 14, 1880. Arthur papers. LC.

23. three more speeches in Indiana: Arthur to Conkling, September 22, 1880. Arthur papers. LC.

24. "Please arrange that General Grant, Senator Conkling, and Yourself": Garfield to Arthur, September 15, 1880. Arthur papers. LC.

25. "very tired ... right hand badly swollen": Garfield diary, August 10, 1880.

26. "I cannot now think of a single point": Garfield to Platt, August 17, 1880. Platt, 134.

27. "I feel a very deep interest in the success": Grant to Garfield, August 5, 1880. Garfield papers. LC.; Garfield diary, August 9, 1880, fn. 232.

28. Garfield ... soon developed a routine: Garfield diary. Entries from August through November, 1880. See also Stanley-Brown, 6-7.

29. Occasionally, Garfield left the farm and visited nearby towns ... Most days at home: Garfield diary. Various entries, summer, 1880.

30. *Campaign Songster*: *Garfield and Arthur Campaign Songster*. Arthur papers. LC.

31. "It was very bad for my life": Garfield to J.A. Rhodes, November 19, 1862. Garfield papers. LC.; Peskin, 13.

32. "If we carry Indiana,... the rest will be easy": Garfield diary, September 2, 1880.

33. pick "the places in Ohio you would prefer to speak": Garfield to Logan, July 23, 1880. Logan papers. LC.

34. "[a]bout 9 o'clock in the evening the telegrams began": Garfield diary. September 13, 1880.

35. "This will make the contest close": Garfield diary. September 14, 1880.

36. "[m]ake business men think more clearly": *New York Tribune*, September 15, 1880.

37. "These Democrats are going to visit every island": *New York Times*, September 18, 1880.

38. Jewell ... tried to put on a brave face: *New York Tribune*, September 15, 1880.

39. The "set-back in Maine": Jewell to Garfield, September 14, 1880. Garfield papers, LC.

40. "a large sum of money, $70,000 to $100,000": Garfield diary. September 14, 1880.

41. "Fold up the bloody shirt and lay it away": Hudson, 112.

42. Indiana ... had already mounted a smart campaign: Their best strategy was at-tacking English himself. In August, friendly local newspapers published a "star-tling" two-page, single-space list of "judgments and foreclosures" by English's bank against local voters under the sarcastic headline: "The 'Poor Man's Friend' in Indiana." Republicans also could appeal to 22,000 Indiana mem-bers of the Disciples of Christ, Garfield's church, and Indiana Senator Ben-jamin Harrison drew good crowds on the stump.

43. "Our danger lies in the riff raff element": Birney to Chandler, September 16, 1880. Chandler papers, LC.

44. "30,000 merchantable votes in the State": Hinsdale to Garfield, October 5, 1880. Mary Hinsdale, 459-60.

45. "Democrats are raising heaven and earth": *New York Times*, September 28, 1880.

46. "[T]here has suddenly appeared in many parts of [Indiana]": Garfield to Arthur, September 25, 1880. Arthur papers. LC.

47. "The Indiana delegation have been here in force": McCormick to Chandler, October 5, 1880. Chandler papers. LC.

48. "You shall have what you ask & can depend on it": Dorsey to Blaine, August 18, 1880. Blaine papers. LC.

49. "General, if I don't succeed, I shall never come back": *New York Times*, Feb-ruary 12, 1881. Arthur mentioned this exchange in his speech to the Febru-ary 1881 Dorsey testimonial dinner at Delmonico's restaurant.

50. "I tremble at the result": McCormick to Chandler, October 5, 1880. Chandler papers. LC.

51. Dorsey ... traveled to Toledo and met with Garfield: Garfield's description from his diary, September 18, 1880.

52. "Don't relax any grip anywhere": Garfield diary, September 27, 1880. Reeves, 202.

53. Vanderbilts ...and John D. Rockefeller had responded: Josephson, 291.

54. Wharton Baker in Pennsylvania ...and Governor Foster had hit Ohio busi-nessmen: Peskin, 498.

55. estimates of the total ranged as high as $350,000 to $400,000: In Reeves, 201.

56. "a special messenger from New York": *New York Sun*, July 16, 1883.

57. "Jewell has been kept in the dark": McCormick to Chandler, October 5, 1880. Chandler papers. LC.

58. "Mr. Spalding gave me a check for $4,500": New to Logan. October 3, 1880. Logan papers. LC.

59. "I have not seen you since we met at Chautauqua": Dialogue between Grant and Rev. Fowler is from the *Cincinnati Gazette* and the *New York Times*, Octo-ber 5, 1880.

60. "I have known him for forty years.... He is a vain, weak man": *id.*.

61. "I have finished up Johnston and am now going into Early": Grant, 478; Badeau, 369.

62. In 1864 ... Hancock received one vote [for President]": *id.* Adam Badeau,

Grant's aide during the war, remembered the particular incident in 1864 when Grant, Hancock, and General George Meade had dismounted to rest as their troops marched across the Chickahominy River in Virginia, talking "in complete personal accord," and Meade referred to a Pennsylvania state democratic convention's nominating Hancock for the Presidency. "Both Grant and Mead poked fun at Hancock for this, and [Hancock] good-naturedly received it all. Indeed it rather tickled him," Badeau wrote. Badeau, 372.

63. Johnson removed ... Sheridan as military governor of Louisiana .. replaced Sheridan with Winfield Hancock: For a fuller version of these events, see Jordan (*Hancock*), 200-212.

64. Hancock was stung but made no public response: Asked the next day to disavow the story, Grant backtracked only slightly. He corrected a few factual details and claimed that the conversation had been private. *New York Times*, October 6, 1880. He'd never meant to insult Hancock publicly, Adam Badeau later wrote on his behalf; the article had consisted simply of "caustic criticisms to an indiscreet visitor." Badeau 371. Still, Marshall Jewell in New York called Grant's broadside attack "the most valuable contribution which has been made to the campaign," as only Grant could "do Hancock justice." Jewell to Garfield, October 7, 1880; cited in Jordan [Hancock], 290.

65. "I traveled from Cincinnati to Cleveland by stage-coach": *New York Times*, September 29, 1880.

66. Conkling ... had to return $18,000 in legal retainers: A.R. Conkling, 614.

67. "He certainly paid every cent of his own expenses" *Buffalo Express*, undated, quoted in AR Conkling, 621.

68. "packed together like herrings": *New York Times*, September 29, 1880.

69. Even now ... Roscoe Conkling balked: A.R Conkling, 620.

70. "Well, I never like to give a man the benefit of the knowledge that I dislike him" ..."I do": Stanley-Brown, 6-7.

71. "How are you, Senator"..."Conkling, you have saved me": The "you have saved me" version is from A.R. Conkling, 623, and Platt, 135; the other version is from the *New York Tribune*, November 21, 1880. Both accounts, written much later, reflected narrow agendas: the first by those arguing that Conkling in fact had secured the pledges, the second by those arguing that Conkling had been too much of a gentleman to ask.

72. "[t]he door remained open, and no political topics": AR Conkling, 624. Again, for contrast, see account in *New York Tribune*, November 21, 1880. Here too, Conkling, though his nephew and biographer A.R. Conkling, adds a conspiratorial spin, claiming that Conkling so distrusted Garfield that he asked Uriah Painter to stay at his side every moment inside Garfield's house so that he and Garfield would never be alone together. By this version, when Garfield asked Conkling at one point to "Come upstairs to my study," Painter followed. Garfield, seeing the uninvited third guest, asked "What are *you* doing here?" but Painter stayed put. After a few minutes, others wandered it, thus avoiding any private "conference." A.R. Conkling, 624.

73. "Citizens of Mentor, I am glad" *New York Times*, September 29, 1880.

74. "our illustrious friend, Gen[eral] Garfield": *id.*

75. "I had no private conversation" Garfield diary, September 28, 1880.

76. rumors of a "Treaty of Mentor": See Hesseltine, 441; *New York Tribune*, November 21, 1880.

77. "evidently suffered severely at his chest and throat": *New York Times*, October 2, 1880.

78. constant days of long speeches taking a toll: Bad health didn't stop Conkling in that speech from regaling the crowd not to desert the party over "personal objections" to the candidate, noting he himself had been "disappointed in the nominations"—a strange tribute to the candidate in Garfield's own state. *New York Times*, October 2, 1880.

79. "Dorsey telegraphs from Indiana": Jewell to Arthur, October 12, 1880; 9pm. Arthur papers. LC.

80. "in neither of which he had a residence" ... "Thugs of the East": *New York World*, October 13, 1880.

81. "the influences that could be brought": *New York Sun*, July 16, 1883.

82. "prevent, so far as possible, any of the money": *id.*

83. $70,000 is likely: Peskin, 504.

84. "The best indications are": Moulton to Arthur. October 12, 1880. Arthur papers. LC.

85. "Our Indianapolis man says forty-five precincts": Reed to Arthur. October 12, 1880. Arthur papers. LC.

86. "We have carried the State": Dorsey to Arthur. October 13, 1880. 3:20 am. Arthur papers. LC.

87. "with the news of certain and large Republican gains": Garfield diary, October 12.

88. "Will you send me [a] check for $400": Doggett to Arthur November 1, 1880. Arthur papers. LC.

89. "fifty boatmen here who would like":WB Simett to Arthur, October 31, 1880; Arthur to Simett, October 31, 1880. Arthur papers. LC.

90. "intends to make the technical distinction": Richard Stewart to Arthur, October 30, 1880. Arthur papers. LC.

91. "Will State Committee make provision": Skinner to Arthur, November 1, 1880. Arthur papers. LC.

92. "The battle is half over": *New York Tribune*, October 17, 1880.

93. "Manufacturers Aroused": See e.g. *New York Times*, October 23, 1880.

94. "Who is 'tariff' and why is he for revenue only?": Reeves, 196; Clancy, 210.

95. "Public Schools in Peril," ... "neither would be a good Catholic" *New York Times*, October 30, 1880.

96. "I am glad to know that you are at home": Arthur to Conkling, October 16, 1880. Arthur papers. LC.

97. "Urgent need for Conkling in Hornellsville": Davenport to Arthur, October 27, 1880. Arthur papers. LC.

98. "We have had a great day, at least 30,000 people": Logan to Mary Logan: October 20, 1880. Logan papers. LC.

99. "I have been constantly on the stump": Logan to Raleigh, October 25, 1880. Logan papers. LC.

100. "We are daily receiving assurances": Arthur to unnamed party leaders, October 23, 1880. Arthur papers. LC.

101. "As the matter seems to have been in part neglected": Theo. Scanlin, Eqs. U.S. Surveyors Office, from Johnson, New York State Committee Secretary. October 23, 1880. Arthur papers. LC.

102. 12 million documents that Republicans would circulate: Peskin, 495.

103. Arthur … wrote disbursements: Financial records are from Arthur papers. LC.

104. "we are certain to carry NY": Arthur to unknown. October 28, 1880. Arthur papers. LC.

105. "I will *do my utmost"*: Balcom to Arthur, October 29, 1880. Arthur papers. LC.

106. "We ought to come to [the] Harlem River": *New York Tribune*, October 30, 1880.

107. Garfield … final weeks of his "front porch": Garfield diary. Entries throughout October 1880, including October 18, 19, 27, and 28.

108. "I would rather be with you and defeated": Joe Stanley-Brown memoir, in Garfield diary, August 30, 1880, fn. 287.

109. "Hurrah for Hancock." … Garfield's …son Abram: *Cleveland Leader*, April 6, 1904.

110. "Thinking your husband will be elected President": Mrs. Pierce to Lucretia Garfield, September 2, 1880. Lucretia Garfield papers. LC.

111. "It now seems altogether *probable"*: H. Bullard to Lucretia Garfield, October 14, 1880. Lucretia Garfield papers. LC.

112. *"Yours in relation to the Chinese problem"*: Purportedly Garfield to Morey, July 23, 1880, in Peskin, Rippath, period newspapers, and elsewhere.

113. "authentic. It is General Garfield's handwriting": Jordan [Hancock], 303.

114. "purporting to be written by me on the Chinese question": Garfield diary, October 20, 1880.

115. "I can hardly believe that a rational and just-minded public": Garfield diary. October 21, 1880.

116. "[The letter] is the work of some clumsy villain": Garfield to Jewell, October 23, 1880, in Peskin, Rippath, period newspapers, and elsewhere.

117. newspapers ran copies of the two letters side-by-side: In fact, newspapers clamored for copies of the plates. See, for instance, Binghamton, New York Republican, to Arthur, October 27, 1880. Arthur papers. LC. Or "Can you send us stereotyped plates of forged Garfield letter & of genuine letter to Committee. Ans[wer] immediately."

118. "trick … the tramp class of working men": *New York Tribune*, October 30, 1880.

119. "And behold the pilgrims do walk through Garfield's fields": Adelaide Rudolph to Lucretia Garfield. Lucretia Garfield papers. LC.

120. harvesting beets and replacing turf: Garfield diary, entries from throughout October 1880.

121. "During the hours in which the election": Ridpath, 477.

122. "a splendid little Mercury,"... "filled with vile men smoking and spitting":
     Descriptions and JS Brown quote from Garfield diary, November 2, 1880, fn.
     321.

123. "We have carried NY by 20 or 25,000 votes": Arthur telegram, [recipient un-
     stated, but apparently to multiple addressees, including Garfield]. November
     3, 1880. Arthur papers. LC.

124. "At 3 A.M. we closed the office": Garfield diary, November 2, 1880.

125. intimidation in the South against blacks and white moderates: For instance,
     Paul Stroback reported from one Alabama county that week: "I can prove the
     loss of over 2,000 votes by failure to open the polls, by men coming armed to
     the voting places and by threats of arrest driving the voters from the polls if
     they would dare to open the polls by themselves (as provided by law, in case
     'inspectors' refuse to serve)... [and] proof in this and other counties that
     white Republican precincts were thrown out" and supervisors were "pre-
     vented *by force* from witnessing the count." Stroback to William Chandler,
     November 8, 1880. Chandler papers. LC. See also Goldman generally on
     this history of abvuses and efforts to address it.

126. Garfield ... had ... captured the country: At that moment, Garfield found
     himself with three jobs at once: member of the U.S. House of Representatives
     in the 46th Congress; Senator-elect for the 47th Congress starting in 1881;
     and President-elect of the United States. He resigned his House seat on No-
     vember 10, 1880, and renounced his Senate seat a few days later, making him
     jobless for four month until his March 1881 inauguration as President.

127. "That your husband is to assume the burdens": Beecher to Lucretia Garfield.
     Lucretia Garfield papers. LC.

128. "Astonished Europe! ... But where is the bloodshed?": *Puck*, November 17,
     1880.

129. "at least ten and possibly as often as twenty times": Arthur's responses to writ-
     ten questions: United States v. Charles Guiteau, 896.

130. "I would like to stump New York for our ticket": Guiteau to Arthur, August
     19, 1880. Arthur papers. LC.

131. Guiteau as the lead-off orator: New York Times, August 22, 1880.

132. "I didn't exactly like the crowd": Guiteau testimony: United States v. Charles
     Guiteau, 585.

133. "I met [Guiteau] on almost every occasion": Storrs testimony: United States
     v. Charles Guiteau Guiteau, 719.

134. "I used to be on free-and-easy terms with them": Guiteau testimony: United
     States v. Charles Guiteau Guiteau, 585.

135. "It caused great anxiety": Guiteau testimony: United States v. Charles Gui-
     teau Guiteau, 586.

136. "I wrote to General Garfield and sent him my speech": *id.*

137. "I have heard some incredibly ridiculous things": Hay to Reid, undated, in
     Cortissoz, II. 38.

138. "whole of the old soldier vote": Hesseltine, 442.

139. "The election of Garfield and Arthur was... made apparently impossible":

AR Conkling, 617. Gorham wrote this description in June 1888, reflecting attitudes from 1880.

140. "If Mr. Garfield is indebted to Mr. Blaine": AR Conkling, 614.

141. "Is the Garfield campaign simply an incident": *Harpers Weekly*, November 6, 1880.

142. "Conkling is a singular compound of a very brilliant man": Smith, II, 1032; Reeves, 197-198.

143. "Blaine, I have not made a single final decision": Garfield diary, November 27, 1880.

144. Blaine ... said that, no, he would not be a candidate: *id*. After Garfield's assassination the next year, Blaine would consider this pledge moot and proceed to win the Republican nomination for president in 1884.

145. Blaine had agreed ... Secretary of State: Muzzey, 178.

10. Garfield "Doesn't Sleep Excellently Well" (pages 195–224)

1. "Can you believe that the long vigil, not tongueless": Harriet Blaine to M, November 4, 1880. Harriet Blaine, 179.

2. "Your father is much attached to General Garfield": Harriet Blaine to Walker, May 15, 1872. Harriet Blaine, 126.

3. "I did ... give the General a kiss": Harriet Blaine to Lucretia Garfield, June 6, 1876. Lucretia Garfield papers. LC.

4. Blaine ... to coach Garfield on his letter of acceptance: Muzzey, 174.

5. Blaine ... spoke at major rallies in Newark and Philadelphia: See e.g. *New York Times*, September 24, 1880, on his rally in Newark.

6. "Your father is walking up and down the parlor": Harriet Blaine to M. October 27, 1880. Harriet Blaine, 179.

7. "I miss Mr. Blaine": Harriet Blaine to Dodge, December 3, 1880. Harriet Blaine, 185.

8. "a big good natured man": Blaine to Israel Washburn, December 21, 1863, in Peskin, 246.

9. "[P]lease tell me whether you are, or will be": Muzzey, 178.

10. Temperance activists already had started hounding Lucretia: See, for instance, letter to Lucretia Garfield from J.B. Hughes, February 12, 1881: citing Lucy Hayes' rule as a "high moral innovation.... How forbidding the venture that would tear it down;" and Mrs. George Mackey, Secretary, WCTU of Bangor Pennsylvania, February 24, 1881: "Should intoxicating beverages be again introduced in the White House the entire Liquor interest would be greatly encouraged and rejoice," but should "Temperance prevail there, you will have the love and prayers and sympathy of the Christian Temperance Woman through the land." Lucretia Garfield papers. LC.

11. "a congestion of financial power—at [the New York] money center": Garfield diary. November 26, 1880.

12. "not my understanding and seems wholly inadmissible": Garfield diary. November 27, 1880.

13. Morton ... This issue was not over: The next morning, he and Morton went

at it again, this time over breakfast at the home of D.C. Chief Justice David Cartter where they repeated their argument for the judge. After talking it through, Garfield again stood his ground: "I will not tolerate, nor act upon any understanding that anything has been pledged to any party, state or person," he told them, hoping to settle the issue.

14. "feel wholly cordial if he were not retained": Garfield dairy. November 27, 1880.

15. He "[r]esponded affirmatively, I think earnestly": *Id.*

16. Ohio would have a U.S. Senate seat coming open: In seeking this seat, Sherman would have the added satisfaction of blocking the Senate hopes of Ohio Governor Charles Foster, whom Sherman still begrudged for loyalty to him at the Chicago convention.

17. "Blaine thought it would not be politic": Sherman, 802.

18. "If you can only restrain [Blaine's] immense activity": Sherman to Garfield, January 21, 1880, in T.C. Smith, II. 1148 and Muzzey, 187.

19. "I love to deal with doctrines and events": Garfield diary. March 14, 1881.

20. "didn't relish the rumors flying around" Cortissoz, 44.

21. "[t]his information produced a shiver": Dawes, 341.

22. "I warned Mr. Blaine that if he entered the cabinet": Dawes, 342. Blaine disagreed. Once in the cabinet, he assured Dawes, he planned to "ignore all past difficulties" and work to "force reconciliation." He shouldn't be "debarred from the great opportunity" of managing foreign policy over old bad blood. But Dawes rejected rejected this argument: "I foresaw the rocks all too plainly, and advised him to remain in the Senate." Dawes later wrote to his wife: "Blaine's vanity to be always in the newspapers will defeat the scheme ... The 'better element' getting wind of it will frighten Garfield out of it. I would not have anything to do with a man who leaks everything into the newspapers." Dawes to Mrs. Dawes, December 13, 1880. Dawes papers. LC.

23. one basic problem, as Blaine saw it: treachery: As early as October, Blaine had warned Garfield that Roscoe Conkling and Ulysses Grant had bad motives behind their high-profile stump campaign. "Grant and his associates are specially busy in running the campaign [for Grant] of 1884," he told him. But Garfield was still dismissing the idea at this point, seeing 1884 as "rather too far in advance to lay plans." Garfield diary, October 4, 1880.

24. "You are to have a second term.... "They must not be knocked down": Blaine to Garfield, December 10, 1880. Garfield papers. LC.

25. "The more I think of the State Department": Blaine to Reid, December 10, 1880, in Garfield diary, November 27, 1880, fn. 356.

26. "very exhausting": Garfield diary. November 29, 1880.

27. "The personal aspects of the presidency are far from pleasant": Garfield diary. December 11, 1880.

28. One woman ... had spent five hours: Garfield to Lucretia Garfield, January 21, 1881. Shaw, 380.

29. " I shall be compelled to live in great social isolation": Garfield diary. December 11, 1880.

30. "many evenings [when] General Garfield, Mrs. Garfield and I sat around the woodfire": Stanley-Brown, 7.

31. "They've got ahead of me" ... "graceful in the saddle": *New York Tribune*, December 20, 1881.

32. Garfield listened politely as the politicos presented: Garfield diary. December 13, 1880.

33. a federal conflict-of-interest statute barred Levi Morton: Section 8 of the 1789 Act creating the Treasury Department barred any person "carrying on the business or trade of commerce or... concerned in the purchase or disposal or any public securities" from holding the post. This provision had been used to block Ulysses Grant's nomination of Alexander T. Stewart, the famed Manhattan retail magnate, to the position in 1869.

34. "evidently disappointed": Garfield diary. December 13, 1880.

35. Blaine's sometime penchant for "childishness and selfishness": Peskin, 435.

36. "On many accounts [Blaine] would be a brilliant Sec'y": Garfield diary. December 12, 1880.

37. "I send it under cover to you... because": Blaine to Garfield, December 20, 1880. Cited in Garfield diary, November 27, 1880, footnote 356; and Stanwood, 235-6. Garfield noted in his diary that day: "Important letter from Blaine today—may have marked influence on his future and mine."

38. "You want an office, of course?": *New York Tribune*, December 20, 1880.

39. "I close the year with a sad conviction": Garfield diary. December 31, 1880. Adding to his bad mood, Garfield at a New Year's reception saw his older brother Thomas as "greatly failed in health and is a stooped old man," he told Burke Hinsdale. On January 3, he'd taken laughing gas as a dentist withdrew a tooth, "since when I have had a dull pain in the face and head which is not conducive to effective work." His year, Garfield wrote, "brought more sadness than joy.... I have never had... the Presidential fever... I am not elated with the election to that office... I feel keenly the loss of liberty [and feel it will] stop my growth." Garfield to Hinsdale, January 5, 1881. Mary Hinsdale, 474-475.

40. "I hope you will inoculate him with the gall": Cortissoz, 34.

41. "In a word, they mean to be your masters": Reid to Garfield, 1 am, January 1, 1881. Garfield papers. LC.; Cortissoz, 47.

42. "for ... securing the election of a Senator": D.S. Alexander, III, 466; Muzzey, 181.

43. "I'm to go to Albany Sunday night": Reid to W.W.P. December 31, 1880, in Cortissoz, 44-45. To bolster Depew's chances and support the Albany Half-Breeds, Blaine then wrote an article for Reid's *New York Tribune*, claiming to be "fully authorized" by the Garfield Administration, saying that the administration would "see to it that the men from New York or from the other States, who had the courage at Chicago to obey the wishes of their districts in the balloting for the President and who thus finally voted for Garfield"—that is, the pro-Blaine bolters like Robertson—would not "lose by it."

44. Arthur "promptly and indignantly" rejected it: Jordan, 367.

45. Platt ... wanted to "set up for himself": Cortissoz, 49. Gosnell, 26.

46. "You can have my strength if as Senator you will support the President": Gosnell, 26.

47. "Even if Judge Robertson's name should be sent in": *id*. On this, see also D.S. Alexander. III, 335.

48. Platt agreed: Cortissoz, 49. Platt also agreed not to oppose any Garfield appointments in the Senate, to help in confirming Garfield's cabinet, and to use his best efforts "to keep Conkling reasonable."

49. "We can trust Platt": D.S. Alexander. III, 335, fn. 5.

50. "I saw him [Platt] last night and transferred the decisive strength": Cortissoz, 49.

51. "All the world is paying court": Harriet Blaine to Walker, January 16, 1881. Harriet Blaine, 191.

52. the secret leaked out soon enough: Roscoe Conkling had sent two more delegations out through the Ohio blizzards that winter to remind Garfield of his promise to name Levi Morton to the Treasury: Edwards Pierrepont on January 24 and Governor Alonzo Cornell and Tom Platt five days later. "I wrestled with them as best I could," Garfield wrote to Lucretia in New York City. On the second trip, Platt and Cornell had asked if Mrs. Garfield weren't at home to see them. When Garfield dodged, one of them mentioned hearing that she was in New York at a "private house," and "I knew then that Mr. Conkling knew you were the guest of his enemy and I cursed the dressmakers that they had ... betrayed your whereabouts." Garfield to Lucretia Garfield, January 31, 1881. Shaw, 382-3.

53. "Mr. Reid told me ... that [Levi] Morton": Lucretia Garfield to Garfield. January 21, 1881. Shaw, 380-1.

54. Clarence Brooks & Co. ...bill of $726.75: Bill from Clarence Brooks & Co., February 25, 1881. Arthur papers. LC.

55. "I don't think we had better go into the minute secrets": *New York Times*, February 12, 1881.

56. Let the dilettantes talk: William Chandler, for instance, who himself had made 21 speeches during the campaign, found Dorsey's "self-adjulation" at the dinner obnoxious and cringed at the "gross want of sense, propriety, and taste" in public "glorification of the use of money to carry elections," especially a "noisy parade and almost public proclamation that it was used to buy votes." Chandler to Garfield, February 17, 1881, in Richardson, 266-267. "The Dorsey dinner was a curious affair whose whole significance I do not yet understand," Garfield noted in his journal. Garfield diary, February 17, 1881.

57. "If all the reports are true": *New York Times*, January 18, 1881.

58. he'd offered a seat to Stephen Dorsey ... who declined: Dorsey himself is the source for this (see *Cincinnati Enquirer*, September 27, 1882), though Garfield is very complimentary of him in his journal during this period, calling Dorsey "a man of great ability, and with strong and decisive views on the merits of men" (Garfield diary, December 14, 1881), making Dorsey's claim credible.

59. Blaine ...barraged him with letters from his stable of party elders: Chandler to Garfield, February 19, 1880. Chandler papers. LC. "The machine in New York cannot be disestablished with the Treasury Department in its favor," insisted

Chandler, and "no New York Secretary not now at absolute war with it would wield Treasury power against it." He went on: "It would be a great mistake to give them [the Stalwarts] any ground for dissatisfaction…. Nevertheless there should be no excessive delivery of power into the hands of the Third Term men. From them alone three years from now is disturbance liable to come. Any weak or under concession would not conciliate so much as it would embolden them, and mischief in the future will result."

Chicago Tribune publisher Joseph Medill saw the issue as a more personal matter for Blaine: "With Conkling 'bossing the Treasury… [h]ow long will he let you alone …?" he asked. " How much haggling and undermining and thwarting would you stand before tendering your resignation?" He hoped "rumors" of Garfield's "surrender" were wrong. Medill to Blaine, February 22, 1881. Blaine papers. LC.

William Robertson in Albany insisted that a Conkling-controlled Treasury Secretary, added to New York's two stalwart Senators and stalwart Vice President, would "effectively put our Independent delegates to the Chicago Convention in a political metallic casket, hermetically sealed." Robertson to Reid, January 25, 1881.

60. "I do not like the man [Blaine]": Grant to Garfield, January 26, 1880, in Garfield's diary, January 29, 1881, fn. 41; McFeely, 485. Grant had never seemed to dislike Blaine before their 1880 collision, according to Adam Badeau; Badeau wrote that they'd always been "amicable" during Blaine's long years as Speaker of the House while Grant was serving as president in the 1870s.

61. "someone friendly to Senator Conkling should take the Treasury": Grant to Garfield, January 26, 1881, in Garfield's diary, January 29, 1881, fn. 41.

62. "What would you say … to exchanging seats": Smith, II, 1078; Muzzey, 182. Garfield even raised the idea with Tom Platt and Alonzo Cornell in mid-January on one of their Ohio treks, but no, they said, Conkling "could not be spared from the Senate," Garfield diary, January 29, 1881

63. He'd had a strange dream…. "General Arthur lying on a couch very pale": Garfield diary, January 20, 1881, fn. 30.

64. "a Senator who never apologized for being a Stalwart": Jordan, 367.

65. "Do you believe one word of that?" … "Yes, I believe Mr. Blaine Boutwell, 273.

66. "You see these two rooms … they are all I can afford": A.R. Conkling, 636.

67. "fatalism" and "weariness of the struggle": Jordan, 367.

68. he wanted to make money from his law practice: A.R. Conkling, 632.

60. visited Kate Chase Sprague: See e.g. Sprague to Arthur, January 18, 1881. Arthur papers. LC; Reeves, 213.

70. "Not for a moment during the canvass": A.R. Conkling, 613.

71. "Conkling refused to consider [Garfield's] proposed appointment of Blaine": Dawes, 342.

72. "consult you on several subjects": Garfield to Conkling, January 31, 1881. Conkling papers. LC. The invitation from Garfield itself sparked waves of rumors among "Conkling stalwarts" in Albany who were heard before the meeting

"telling everybody that General Garfield by a recent letter has placed at Senator Conkling's disposal any position in the Cabinet except that of Secretary of State. They are greatly delighted over the news, and have begun already to figure out the distribution of the Custom-House loaves and fishes." *New York World*, February 16, 1881.

73. "I felt it my duty to obey the invitation": Connery, 151.

74. "I need hardly say that your administration cannot": Jordan 372.

75. "full conversation on the Cabinet and kindred subjects": Garfield diary. February 16, 1881.

76. "I told him I wanted his friendship": *id.*

77. "I think much better of [Conkling] than I expected to": Garfield to Burke Hinsdale. February 18, 1881. Mary Hinsdale, 480-1.

78. "trifling and undecided": Connery, 151.

79. "Treasury is the only post that would satisfy New York": *id.*

80. "at all events, that you will not give us the Navy": *New York Herald*, May 11, 1881.

81. "To tea! Tea! Tea!": Connery, 152.

82. "If it means hospitality, I must ask to be excused": *New York Herald*, May 11, 1881.

83. "I have never been able to understand": Connery, 151.

84. "reiterated his pledges to make no New York appointments": Platt, 145.

85. "Have you any faith in Garfield?": Platt, 135. Platt, in his memoirs published thirty years later, remembers this exchange as occurring in October after Conkling's visit to Garfield's farm during his stump speaking tour with General Grant during the campaign. Conkling himself, though, insists that he and Garfield made no arrangements that day—the exchange more likely belongs here.

86. "Was it only to find out what I would like and then do just the opposite": Connery, 152.

87. Garfield ... his tentative list of cabinet choices: Garfield diary, February 27, 1881, fn. 78.

88. a slate "which will not be much changed": *id.*

89. "You know how much I leave behind me of friendship": Ridpath, 483. Lucretia may have bolstered herself by re-reading some of the kinder letters she'd received since the election. Reverend Henry Ward Beecher had written: "For yourself, the change will be great... But you will be cheered and upheld by thousands of warm hearts praying for you, night and morning, and God will give his angels Charge of both of you." Harriet Hawley, wife of the Connecticut Governor, had written: "I am glad that you are to be in the White House because of the fine and noble influence you will exert there" rather than some "woman of small and petty ambitions."

90. "[Garfield] does not sleep excellently well," ..."excitement keeps him well stimulated": Ridpath, 485.

91. "If there are any two men in the country whose opposition and hatred are a certificate": Hayes diary, January 16, 1880.

92. "savage office-baiting ... began then and there": Stanley-Brown, 8.

93. "our unwise friend is making a great deal of trouble": Connery, 152.

94. "ruinous to the Republican party of New York": Connery, 153.

95. "Morton broke down on my hands": Garfield diary, March 2, 1881.

96. Garfield suspected that Allison too had been muscled: Garfield diary, March 4, 1881.

97. "I had to get Platt" ... "the tall young man from New York": Garfield diary, March 3, 1881; Cortissoz, 57.

98. "There! All is right now. I have no more anxiety": Lucretia Garfield diary, March 4, 1881.

99. "[M]y heart grew stiller and stiller": id.

100. "I am glad to be a freed man": Dole, 170.

101. the great parade: Garfield's was the second post-inaugural parade, the first being staged for Ulysses Grant's second inaugural in 1872; Rutherford Hayes skipped his in 1876 because of the electoral dispute. After Garfield's spectacle, the parade became standard fare.

102. the formal inaugural reception: Boller, 202.

103. 1,500 pounds of turkey, 100 gallons of oysters: Reeves, 221.

104. "slept too soundly... to remember any dream": Lucretia Garfield diary. March 5, 1881.

11. The Appointment *(pages 235–264)*

1. Guiteau had ... written to William Evarts: Guiteau to Evarts, November 11, 1880, in United States v. Charles Guiteau, 124; Rosenberg, 36.

2. the "wealthy lady" ... simply been a lady whom he'd seen at church: Rosenberg, 36.

3. police detectives ... arrested him: Walling, 502-505.

4. "no day in 12 years has witnessed such a jam": Garfield diary, March 8, 1881.

5. "[r]espectfully and courteously": Stanley-Brown testimony: United States v. Charles Guiteau, 213.

6. "I called to see you this A.M.": Guiteau to Garfield, March 8, 1881. Garfield papers. LC.

7. "good fellow. I should not wish to disturb him": Guiteau to Garfield, March 8, 1881. Garfield papers. LC.

8. "I was not a Blaine man; I was a Grant man": Guiteau testimony: United States v. Charles Guiteau, 586.

9. "I think I prefer Paris to Vienna": Guiteau to Garfield, March 8, 1881. Garfield papers. LC

10. "I expected to get it on my personal standing": Guiteau testimony: United States v. Charles Guiteau, 602.

11. "They all thought I was a good fellow": id.

12. "in conversation with several politicians ... I remember specifically Levi P. Morton": Guiteau testimony: United States v. Charles Guiteau, 586.

13. "[Garfield] recognized me at once": id.

14. "I left him reading the speech and retired": id.

15. Joe Stanley Brown ... greeted him "very cordially": Guiteau testimony: United States v. Charles Guiteau, 587.

16. "It is customary in the White House": Stanley-Brown testimony: United States v. Charles Guiteau, 208.

17. "I do not wish to be in Washington at the time": Grant to John Logan. February 28, 1880. Logan papers. LC.

18. "his mortification was extreme": Badeau 327.

19. "If Garfield puts Blaine in his cabinet, I'll never speak to Garfield again": *Washington Evening Star*, March 10, 1881. Garfield papers. LC.

20. "I must confess disappointment": Grant to Conkling, March 5, 1881. Conkling papers. LC.

21. there'd been "no approach to intimacy": Badeau, 324.

22. "[Grant's] imperturbability is amazing": Garfield diary. December 3, 1876.

23. Badeau's "retention [in London] unless he could receive": Grant to Garfield, March 11, 1881. Garfield papers. LC.

24. "I will read it when I have the time": Logan testimony: United States v. Charles Guiteau Guiteau, 445.

25. "I treated him as kindly and as politely": Logan testimony: United States v. Charles Guiteau Guiteau, 445-446.

26. "He claimed that I was his Senator": Logan testimony: United States v. Charles Guiteau Guiteau, 446.

27. "the kind of way these politicians have" Guiteau testimony: United States v. Charles Guiteau Guiteau, 614-615.

28. "I consider General Logan one of my friends": Guiteau testimony: United States v. Charles Guiteau, 615.

29. "I do not think he is a proper person": Logan testimony: United States v. Charles Guiteau, 447.

30. Mrs. Lockwood presented Charles Guiteau a bill: Rosenberg, 38.

31. For cabinet meetings, Blaine almost always arrived early: Muzzey, 192.

32. "the Spartan band of disciplined office hunters": Garfield diary, March 8, 1881.

33. "pursues his prey with the grip of death": Garfield diary, May 7, 1881.

34. "I told him I declined to be lectured at": Garfield diary, March 9, 1881.

35. the job of Private Secretary: See Cortissoz 41-42 and JSB file. The Private Secretary was the top-ranking White House clerk or professional staffer, a distant precursor to today's White House Chief of Staff but with no policy voice. Blaine, as cabinet head, served that role. Stanley Brown, at twenty four years old, was the youngest then to hold the position. Garfield had considered elevating the office's role by appointing the more experienced John Hay to the position, but Hay refused the offer.

36. "Well, my boy. I may have to give it to you": Stanley-Brown, 7-8.

37. scrapbooks to keep the President posted: These scrapbooks still exist in the Garfield papers at the Library of Congress and are a fabulous resource.

38. Garfield's White House: White House details mostly from Whitcomb, 174, and "A President's Daily Life," unidentified newspaper, March 18, 1881. Garfield papers. LC.

39. "Assassination can no more be guarded against": Garfield to Sherman, November 16, 1880; in Sherman, 789.

40. "magnificent dress of white brocaded satin": *Washington Evening Star*, March 12, 1881.

41. "The House was beautifully decorated with flowers": Lucretia Garfield diary. March 11, 1881.

42. "all men on equal footing" ... "the ladies generally appearing": Whitcomb, 166.

43. "exceedingly becoming, and her manner was quietly self-possessed": "Her First Reception," unidentified newspaper, March 14, 1881. Garfield papers. LC.

44. "Before the first hour was over I was aching": Lucretia Garfield diary. March 12, 1881.

45. "cynosure of interest" ... "stately figure and commanding presence": "Her First Reception," unidentified newspaper, March 14, 1881. Garfield papers. LC.

46. "I stood up with Mrs. Garfield": Harriet Blaine to M. March 14, 1881. Harriet Blaine, 195.

47. "It is noticed that many Republican and Democratic Senators": March 12, 1881 Star quoted in the *Chicago Inter Ocean*, Garfield papers. LC.

48. "We received your letter and were all glad": Lide Rudolph to Lucretia, March 13, 1881. Lucretia Garfield papers. LC.

49. "the social drinking usage of our times": H.B. Spelman, National Temperance Society, to Garfield, March 14, 1881. Garfield papers. LC.

50. Frances Willard had led a group of fifty ladies to the East Room: Peskin 546.

51. "freedom of individual judgment" ... "not in so narrow a sense": Ridpath 512-3.

52. the White House reception that Saturday: Probably the reception on March 12, 1881, which was open to the public, though Guiteau does not specify the date in his testimony.

53. In Milwaukee, he'd contracted ... to print copies of his book *New York Tribune*, July 3, 1881.

54. ushers ... recognized his familiar face: Entering a White House reception today requires not only an invitation, but guests must also provide social security numbers in advance for the Secret Service to run security checks, and must pass various security inspections. Even cabinet members must carry identification and pass security. A familiar face alone won't do it.

55. "I was one of the men that made Mr. Garfield President": Guiteau testimony, United States v. Charles Guiteau, 665.

56. "I had never anticipated going into black": Harriet Blaine to M. March 18, 1881. Harriet Blaine, 196.

57. "if any gentleman who was chosen to this body as a democrat": *Congressional Record*, March 14, 1881: page 21-22.

58. "I would rather have Mahone's chance": Garfield diary, March 14, 1881.

59. "grim row of clerks": *New York Times*, March 19, 1881.

60. "is not clothed by the Constitution" : *Congressional Record*, March 18, 1881; 33.

61. "I must resist a very strong tendency": Garfield diary, March 14, 1881.

62. "sense of annoyance and worry" ... "[v]exed with more thought": Garfield diary, March 16, 1881.

63. "An Associate Justice of the Supreme Court was infuriated": Stanley-Brown, 10.

64. "This must be changed".... "[I]f I know any way to change it": Garfield diary, March 18, 1881.

65. "I do not take kindly to this sort of life": Garfield diary, March 16, 1881.

66. "we were not among the lingering snow banks of our Mentor home": Lucretia Garfield diary, March 19, 1881.

67. Platt ... away to New York City ... Conkling ... had his colleague's proxy: Platt, 147-149.

68. These men didn't deserve "exile": Garfield diary, March 20, 1881.

69. "Well, Mr. President, I suppose I can go out into the lobby": *New York Sun*, July 16, 1883.

70. "the President's evident liking" for Robertson: *id*.

71. "Mr. Conkling, I am extremely anxious that you": *New York Herald*, May 11, 1881.

72. "We will leave that for another time": Boutwell, 273.

73. "in very good humor": Connery 154.

74. "it will not be necessary for me to delay the NY appointments": Garfield to Conkling, March 21, 1881. Garfield papers. LC.

75. He sent five nominations up to the U.S. Senate: They included Stewart Woodford and Louis Payn to be U.S. Attorney and Marshal of the Southern District of New York, Asa Tenney to be U.S. Attorney for the Eastern District, Clinton McDougall to be Marshal for the Northern District, and John Tyler to be customs collector at Buffalo.

76. "weakness," "surrender," and "ingratitude": Jordan, 325; Reeves 223.

77. "expressed great distress at the N.Y. appointments": Garfield diary, March 22, 1881.

78. In fact, Blaine launched into a tirade: Peskin, 559.

79. "A hush fell on all at the table"... "I have broken Blaine's heart": Lucretia Garfield diary, March 22, 1881.

80. "on account of [Mr. Blaine's] anxiety" ... "to send in another batch of appointments": *id*.

81. Merritt to be Consul-General to London, England: Newspapers later reported that Conkling, after his Sunday meeting with Garfield, had seen an opportunity to force Merritt out of the Custom House early and replace him with someone more friendly. They allege that Conkling wrote Merritt a letter suggesting that he apply for a foreign mission and Merritt, fearing he was about to be forced out of the Custom House, immediately wrote to Garfield suggesting London. The story, even if true, was unlikely to have affected Garfield's decisions on the Robertson appointment. See *New York Sun*, April 1, 1880 and *Chicago Tribune*, undated, both clippings from Garfield papers. LC.

82. Garfield ... kept them secret: At least that's what he'd tell people later. See Boutwell 274; *New York Tribune*, January 7, 1882; DS Alexander, 470.

83. "an attempt by the President to give control of New York": *New York Herald*, March 24, 1881.

84. Platt ... could only hang his head in silence: See Gosnell, 27

85. "Did you notice the nominations sent in yesterday?": Harriet Blaine to M., March 24, 1881. Harriet Blaine, 197.

86. "I spoke to the General [Garfield] about it": Guiteau to Blaine, March 11, 1881, United States v. Charles Guiteau, 124.

87. "The pressure has been so enormous on you": Guiteau to Blaine, March 17, 1881, United States v. Charles Guiteau, 127.

88. "I think the President feels well disposed": Guiteau to Blaine, March 21, 1881, United States v. Charles Guiteau, 127.

89. "He appealed to me for some assistance": Harrison testimony, United States v. Charles Guiteau , 947.

90. "less than sane": Harrison testimony, United States v. Charles Guiteau Guiteau, 946-7.

91. "I came in one way and he came in his private way": Guiteau testimony, United States v. Charles Guiteau Guiteau 588.

92. "[T]he doors [were] thrown open and everybody can come in": *Id.*

93. "alike in desire, and pretty nearly all alike in disappointment": Blaine testimony, United States v. Charles Guiteau Guiteau 131.

94. "We have not got to that yet": Guiteau testimony, United States v. Charles Guiteau Guiteau, 588.

95. "I could be Secretary of State easily enough": Cortissoz, 58.

12. The Senate *(pages 265–307)*

1.   "The War of the Roses has now begun": *Boston Daily Advertiser*, March 24, 1881. Garfield papers. LC.

2.   "open rupture" ... "the President and the Grant element": *Philadelphia Press*, March 31, 1881. Garfield papers. LC.

3.   "Conkling will fight the Robertson nomination" *St. Louis Republican*, March 31, 1881. Garfield papers. LC.

4.   "very lively bombshell": *New York Herald*, March 24, 1881.

5.   "an extreme man on our side": Chandler to Garfield, February 19, 1880. Chandler papers. LC.

6.   Robertson as Postmaster General or Interior Secretary: Reid to Elizabeth Mills. March 2, 1881, in Cortissoz, 55. , "[T]hat surely will not be done," Reid had confided to his fiancé. Still, enough people took the idea seriously that when a mysterious "official package" had arrived in Albany, New York for Robertson from Washington, D.C. that week and was forwarded unopened to his wife in Westchester, where Robertson was visiting a sick parent, it sparked waves of rumors that Robertson was about to be named Postmaster Genera in Garfield's cabinet. *New York Times*, March 4, 1881.

7.   "catastrophe": Boutwell, 273.

8.   "The change of [Adam] Badeau from London": Garfield diary, March 23, 1881.

9.   "I think the Senate will approve": *id.*

10. "It is said in some quarters that Mr. Robertson's appointment": *The Nation*, April 7, 1881; Reeves, 224.

11. "political change" ... "political office": *Harpers Weekly*, April 16, 1881.

12. Not all the reactions were negative: "James A. Garfield is no Rutherford B. Hayes... there will be no retreating now," the *Buffalo Express* opined, for instance. "There is a man in the White House who knows his own mind and has a mind worth knowing." March 24, 1881. Garfield papers. LC.

13. "This is a complete surprise": *New York Tribune*, March 24, 1881.

14. "This evens things up": *id.*

15. State Senate ...resolution backing the nomination: Resolution of New York State Senate, March 24, 1881. Garfield papers. LC.

16. "I have had the new Collector of the Port": Contissoz, 60.

17. "Under no circumstances... will I ask President Garfield": Robertson to Reid (date uncertain, but March 1881), in Cortissoz 63.

18. "confidential talk": Garfield diary, March 25, 1881.

19. He had no choice ... but "regretfully" to resign: *id.*

20. "I gave them both to understand": Garfield diary, March 24, 1881.

21. Garfield put his arm around Tom James: Whitelaw Reid had offered to help put some muscle on Tom James if Garfield needed his support. "If James shows signs of weakening in any way, I hope you will let me know at once," Reid had written, and offered to have Thurlow Weed "talk to him very emphatically" about it. Whitelaw Reid to Garfield, March 24, 1881. Garfield papers. LC.

22. "The appointment of Chandler may prove": Garfield to Hinsdale, April 4, 1881. Mary Hinsdale, 490.

23. MacVeigh ... fully intended to quit the cabinet: MacVeigh repeated the same message to Robert Lincoln the next day. Garfield diary, March 26, 1881.

24. Blaine himself were spreading these rumors: Blaine denied it and backed Garfield' story, at least after the fact to George Boutwell. "From Mr. Blaine I received the specific information that he had no knowledge of the nomination of Judge Robertson until it had been made." Boutwell 274.

25. "Some servant has leaked about the callers": Garfield diary, March 30, 1881.

26. Blaine ..."came in very pale and much astonished": Boutwell, 274.

27. "[t]he attempt to shift the fight to Blaine's shoulders": *New York Tribune*, January 7, 1882; DS Alexander, 470.

28. Merritt, for one, heard that Blaine had insisted: Merritt, 136; Jordan, 383.

29. "Your work of today... creates a splendid impression": Blaine to Garfield, March 23, 1881. Garfield papers. LC.; Peskin 560.

30. Garfield managed to ignore Blaine's flattery: Garfield diary, March 26, 1881.

31. Garfield ... had to "enforce discipline": Richardson, 269.

32. "sick of a perpetual row": Connery, 155.

33. "How are the envoys extraordinary tonight?": Connery, 156.

34. "I must remember that I am president of the United States": Connery, 157.

35. "We had only two days before this been informed from you": Arthur, Platt, James, and Conkling to Garfield, March 25, 1881. Garfield papers. LC.

36. "duplicity," "grave discourtesy": *New York Commercial Advertiser*, March 26, 1881. Garfield papers. LC.

37. "I wish to say to the President": Cortissoz, 60. A copy of Reid's letter was "stolen from the wires," according to Cortissoz, and later published by Garfield's enemies to suggest that he was just a puppet of the New York publisher.

38. "Robertson may be carried out of the Senate": Cortissoz 60. Blaine must have felt relieved at Garfield's sudden hard line, telling Reid in late March that a withdrawal would be "a deep damnation personally and politically." Blaine to Reid, March 31, 1881, in Jordan 385.

39. "Whether Garfield meant it or not": Ridpath, 505. Rutherford Hayes relates hearing of how Garfield, in yet another White House meeting around this time, found himself in a yelling match with Wayne MacVeigh, Senator Don Cameron, and a Pennsylvania group over the William Chandler nomination as Lucretia waited impatiently for him downstairs to start dinner. She had sent one of the clerks, Crump, to interrupt them, and Crump heard Garfield tell the group that it could not be done. One of the men "with an oath brought his fist down on the table saying the name must be withdrawn," Crump recalled. Garfield then slammed the table with his own fist: "By God, sir, it shall not be withdrawn!" He stormed out of the room to dinner, but was too angry to eat. Rutherford Hayes diary, October 29, 1881.

40. "I suppose you don't attend this Senatorial fight": Lide Rudolph to Lucretia Garfield, April 1, 1881. Lucretia Garfield papers.

41. "the two New York factions stood looking": Lucretia Garfield diary. March 23, 1881.

42. "much less disturbed": Lucretia Garfield diary, March 24, 1881.

43. "I am coming [to Washington from Philadelphia]": Lucretia Garfield diary, March 29, 1881.

44. "I am sorry that" the Senate fight "will probably alienate": *id.*

45. "I have despised him ever since I have known": *id.*

46. "They hate the situation": Harriet Blaine to M., March 28, 1881. Harriet Blaine, 198-9.

47. John Sherman ... to "take charge": Garfield diary, April 3, 1881.

48. "did not consult him": Garfield diary, March 27, 1881; Allison to Garfield, March 27, 1881.

49. "If yes, on what ground of reason": Garfield to Whitelaw Reid, March 30, 1881, in Cortissoz, 61-62. Garfield in this letter is referring to Tom Platt making the same argument, but the logic applied to Conkling as well.

50. "[S]hall the principal port of entry": Garfield to Hinsdale, April 4, 1881. Mary Hinsdale, 490.

51. "It better be known ... whether the President": Garfield to Reid, March 30, 1881. Cortissoz, 61-62. Garfield also now saw compelling political logic in his stance: "If I am right in my plan of adjusting N.Y. affairs, I may conquer a peace." Garfield Diary, March 26, 1881.

52. Grant bristled at Garfield's showy reward to William Robertson: Badeau 328.

53. "intended to be offensive": Badeau 329.

54. "See the President at once with my letter": Grant to Badeau, March 24, 1881, in Badeau, 532.

55. "disapproving my services or displeasing General Grant" ... "pleasant and easy diplomatic post": Badeau, 329

56. "I advise you to decline Copenhagen": Grant to Badeau, March 25, 1881, in Badeau, 532.

57. "I do claim that I ought not to be humiliated": Grant to Garfield, April 24, 1881. Garfield papers. LC.; Garfield diary, May 13, 1881, fn. 152.

58. "I am completely disgusted with Garfield's course ... Garfield has shown that he is not possessed": Badeau, 330.

59. "I have got the President and Gen. Logan worked up": Guiteau to Blaine, April 2, 1881, in United States v. Charles Guiteau, 128.

60. "I understand from Colonel Hooker": Guiteau to Blaine, March 28, 1881, in United States v. Charles Guiteau, 128.

61. "I think Mr. Blaine intends to give me": Guiteau to Garfield, April 8, 1881, in United States v. Charles Guiteau, 210.

62. "Mr. Guiteau, the President says it would be impossible": Guiteau testimony, United States v. Charles Guiteau, 589.

63. Guiteau even got close enough to the president to shout at him: Guiteau to Garfield, April 8, 1881, in United States v. Charles Guiteau, 210.

64. a regular at the Navy Department library: Ridpath 531.

65. "Would it not be well to withdraw": Guiteau to Garfield, April 29, 1881, in United States v. Charles Guiteau, 210.

66. "I stand by you" in the conflict: Guiteau to Garfield, May 7, 1881, in United States v. Charles Guiteau, 210.

67. "Run the presidency on your account": Guiteau to Garfield, May 10, 1881, in United States v. Charles Guiteau, 211.

68. "repeatedly about the hotel" ... "seemed to be rather discouraging": Storrs testimony, United States v. Charles Guiteau, 720.

69. Newspapers had rallied to his side, reflecting their readers: This newspaper count, though published by the anti-Conkling Albany Evening Journal on April 4, 1881, was not challenged.

70. Tenure in Office Act ... ruled unconstitutional: See Myers v. United States, 272 U.S. 52 (1926).

71. "Conkling seems to have a magic influence": Cortissoz, 62; Jordan 386.

72. "spend the next four years simply in wreaking his revenges": Reid to Garfield, April 11, 1881, in Cortissoz 63-64.

73. "Conkling makes a very strong case": Garfield diary, April 5, 1881.

74. "a test of friendship or hostility": Garfield diary; Welch, 102

75. a "principle ... as serious in result": Hoar to his son Rockwell Hoar, April 12, 1881, in Welch, 103.

76. "Committee of Conciliation": Members included Dawes, Rollins (R-NH), Cameron (R-Wis), Jones (R-Nev), Sewell (R-NJ), and Miller (R-Calif).

77. "The one wants to be watched like a child": Dawes to Mrs. Dawes. Dawes papers. LC.; Hoogenboom, 204-5.

78. Conkling "raged and roared like a bull": Dawes, 343.

79. "the man at the other end of the avenue": *New York Sun*, May 9, 1881. Garfield papers. LC.

80. "I have in my pocket an autograph letter of this President": Dawes 343.

81. a new-fangled petroleum-driven "air engine": Garfield diary, April 11, 1881.

82. books: "Everywhere- in every nook and corner": "The First Lady of the Land," from the *Detroit Evening News*. Unidentified newspaper, Garfield papers. LC.

83. "more regret... at being separated": Garfield diary, April 7 and 9, 1881.

84. "feeling as if I had been struck a light blow": Garfield diary, April 15 and 16, 1881.

85. "I have been thinking of suggesting Greek": *New York Herald*, April 22, 1881, in Garfield papers. LC.

86. "The number of coats he wears, the size of his hat": Ridpath 513.

87. "These people would take my very brain, flesh and blood": Peskin 551.

88. "I hope the mob infesting all the approaches to the White House" Reid to Garfield, March 21, 1881. Garfield papers. LC. After the death of a Baltimore postmaster that month, four different Baltimore delegations had arrived at the White House the following morning, each with its own favorite candidate, despite the fact that the funeral hadn't even occurred yet. "Gentlemen, I am delighted to see you, I have no doubt you have all agreed on a candidate and I shall be glad to hear his name," Garfield had said to their surprise. The interview lasted ten minutes; they icily huddled in a corner and came up with one. Stanley-Brown, 10.

89. Arthur ... he'd resign ... if it would help Roscoe Conkling: Ridpath 515.

90. "You spoke of calling this evening": Garfield to Blaine, April 15, 1881. Blaine papers. LC.

91. "Yes, if the leaders determine it shall." ... "Of course I deprecate war": Garfield to Reid, April 18, 1881, in Jordan 387, and Cortissoz, 64-65. Reid, trying to reassure him, wrote Garfield back: "absolutely you are the master of the situation... I really believe you have [Conkling] where there is a chance to make an end of him, and of the corrupt, insolent and bullying elements which he had carried into our politics." Reid to Garfield, April 11, 1881, in Cortissoz, 64.

92. "Oh, you allude to a letter": Dawes 343.

93. "Please say to [Assistant Postmaster General Thomas A.] Brady": Garfield to Hubbell, August 22, 1880. Garfield papers. LC.; Peskin, 568; Josephson, 299.

94. Two names topped the list of suspects: Stephen Dorsey: On March 4, 1881, during the height of the drama over cabinet appointments, Dorsey had written him frantically: "Mr. James of New York is not fit to be in your cabinet... He is all things to all men ... *You cannot trust him.....* I beg you not to do ii." Dorsey to Garfield, March 4, 1881. Garfield papers. LC. Garfield diary, April 14 & 19, 1881, footnote 14.

95. "base ingratitude and the worst of politics" Dawes, 344.

96. delay on Robertson "would not be just": "The President's Views," Unidentified newspaper, "from a Washington Special." Garfield papers. LC.

97. "The shortness and sharpness of [Garfield's] replies" *Albany Times*, May 11. Garfield papers. LC.

98. "The president is intoxicated by his power" *New York Sun*, May [unidentified date], 1881. Garfield papers. LC.

99. Garfield ... "obstinate" and "sullen": *New York Sun*, May [unidentified date], 1881. Garfield papers. LC.

100. "The Committee had been bull-dozed": Garfield diary, April 29, 1881.

101. "no peace by evading the NY contest": Garfield diary, April 30, 1881.

102. "I do not propose to be dictated to": Platt, 152. Tom Nicol, speaking for the president, downplayed the remark but didn't actually deny it; he said only that it had been made casually in a light moment and taken out of context. *New York Herald*, May 12, 1881.

103. Garfield ... cut off their patronage: Through the *Cincinnati Commercial*, he threatened to withdraw the nomination of a friend of Senator Platt named Mr. Elmer as Second Assistant Postmaster General if Platt opposed Robertson. *New York Sun*, May 10, 1881. Garfield papers. LC.

104. "trading and dickering with Senators for their votes": *New York Sun*, May 10, 1881. Garfield papers. LC.

105. "of whose great brainpower political sagacity": Dawes 342.

106. "it is probable the Republicans will accommodate him": *New York Times*, May 3, 1881.

107. "So binding are the influences of the Senatorial position": *The American*, May 14, 1881. Garfield papers. LC.

108. "Crete is severely ill. Please come by first train": Garfield to Boynton, May 8, 1881. Garfield papers. LC.

109. "My anxiety for her dominated all my thoughts": Garfield diary, May 8, 1881.

110. "Gentlemen, if you do not want to control a single nomination": *Trenton Times*, May 7, 1881. Garfield papers. LC.

111. "This will bring the Robertson nomination": Garfield diary, May 5, 1881.

112. "I *know* by inspiration that it will work": Blaine to Garfield, [late March, 1881, date unclear]. Garfield papers. LC. Blaine, in the letter, would claim that it was his idea.

113. "[S]tick and let the Senate squirm" Halstead to Garfield, May 11, 1881.

114. "I trust that you will not withdraw the nomination": Dingman to Garfield, May 6, 1881. Garfield papers. LC.

115. "all of its energy and enthusiasm was in the wholesome kick": *Trenton Times*, May 7, 1881. Garfield papers. LC.

116. "the tomahawk and scalping knife": Unidentified newspaper, May 8, 1881. Garfield papers. LC.

117. "malaria and overwork" with a "danger of cerebrospinal meningitis": Garfield diary, May 9, 1881.

118. "This will burn her out if not arrested": Garfield diary, May 13, 1881.

119. T.C. Connery ... "I am so glad you decided to come here": Connery, 147. The source for this meeting is Connery, 147 *et seq*.

120. "Garfield has not been square, nor honorable": *id*.

121. "The Wriggler": *New York Herald*. May 11, 1881.

122. "the absolute rejection of Robertson": *New York Herald*, May 12, 1881.

123. "Angry Boy!" ... "a man without convictions": *New York Herald*. May 11, 1881.

124. "danger of permitting the executive to influence the Senate": *Albany Times*, May 11, 1881. Garfield papers. LC.

125. And it all got worse from there: Democrats, hearing the Republican caucus travails from outside in the Capitol corridors, savored the chance to throw their votes whichever way would most embarrass their rivals. "I am not an arbiter of Republican differences," Democrat Dan Voorhees of Indiana said innocently. "They must settle among themselves." *New York Times*, May 10, 1881.

126. "Feudalism dies hard,"... "The Senatorial Barons insist": *Chicago Tribune*, May 12, 1881.

127. "I don't know for my part *why* so much attention" Ella Dawes to Henry Dawes, May 6, 1881. Dawes papers. LC.

128. Dawes .... "Fabricators of facts": *New York Times*, May 6, 1881.

129. "every Republican Senator desires peace in the family": Hawley to Garfield, May 11, 1881. Garfield papers. LC.

130. Conkling could expect only about one-fourth of the Republican Senators: *Chicago Tribune*, May 13, 1881.

131. "Garfield is all worn out and fairly broken down": Dawes to Ela Dawes, May 17[?], 1881. Dawes papers. LC.

132. "I will not compromise with traitors": *Chicago Tribune*, May 13, 1881.

133. "If the President would only see the danger": *New York Tribune*, May 14, 1881. Garfield papers. LC.

134. Henry Anthony ... too close to Roscoe Conkling: *id.*

135. "No committee will attempt to smother any nomination": *id.*

136. "Those laugh best who laugh last": *Philadelphia Times*, story datelined May 14, 1881. Garfield papers. LC.

137. "This is Conkling's Bull Run": *New York Sun*, May 14. Garfield papers. LC.

138. "Nothing but a failure on Robertson's part to appreciate": Hawley to Garfield, May 13, 1881. Garfield papers. LC.

139. "I think several things are working out right": Cortissoz, 66.

140. Guiteau ... on Saturday, May 14: Guiteau in his December 1881 testimony places this encounter in mid-April, but in a letter to Garfield dated May 16 he refers to its occurring the prior Saturday. This latter timing makes more chronological sense, coming two days before the Senate climax and his decision to take political affairs into his own hands.

141. "Never speak to me again on the subject of the Paris consulship": Blaine testimony, United States v. Charles Guiteau, 131.

142. "Well, if he will." ... "If the President wants to remove": Guiteau testimony, United States v. Charles Guiteau, 589.

143. "I should have had very decided objections": Blaine testimony, United States v. Charles Guiteau, 131-132.

144. It had "hurt my feelings": Guiteau testimony, United States v. Charles Guiteau, 589.

145. "I hope Mrs. Garfield is better": Guiteau to Garfield, May 13, 1881, in United States v. Charles Guiteau, 211-212.

146. "Until Saturday I supposed that Mr. Blaine was my friend": Guiteau to Garfield, May 16, 1881, United States v. Charles Guiteau, 211.

147. "out of curiosity ... to see what kind of church he attended": Guiteau testimony, United States v. Charles Guiteau, 695.

148. "see that Mr. Guiteau no longer troubled the office": Stanley-Brown testimony, United States v. Charles Guiteau, 209.

149. Conkling ... happened to see Henry Dawes on the sidewalk: Dawes, 344, for this incident.

150. Platt had visited Garfield in the White House repeatedly: Platt had visited Garfield days before the appointment and, when Garfield had to cut the meeting short, he said "I will see you again next week about those matters. When I am ready to talk about them, I will send you word or let you know." New York Tribune, March 24, 1881, clip attached to Reid to Garfield, March 24, 1881. Garfield papers. LC. Then, before leaving for New York City that weekend, Platt had sent word to Garfield asking that no action occur on the appointments until he returned: "I hope you will give me opportunity to be heard before action is taken." Platt to Garfield. March 18,1881, in Platt147-148.

151. the president had refused to listen: "I refused to take the initiative or make any suggestion to change Robertson," Garfield recalled of the meetings. Garfield diary, April 5, 1881.

152. Garfield "did not take kindly": Unidentified newspaper. Garfield papers. LC.

153. "self-respect" would "hardly allow him or the vice presiden": New York Sun, May [unidentified date], 1881, Garfield papers. LC.

154. Reid had only repeated his threats: "If Mr. Platt should undertake to make trouble, I think we can probably convince him that it is unwise," Whitelaw Reid had written to Garfield in late March, threatening to expose Platt's pledges in the New York Tribune. Reid to Garfield, March 24, 1881. Garfield papers. LC.

155. "I am directed to lay before the Senate the communication": New York Times, May 17, 1881. Congressional Record, May 16, 1881.

156. "Sir: Will you please announce ... my resignation": Conkling to Arthur, May 16, 1881; Congressional Record, May 16, 1881, 459.

157. "Sir: I have forwarded to the governor ... my resignation": Platt to Arthur, May 16, 1881; Congressional Record, May 16, 1881, 459.

158. "Conkling has made a fool of himself": New York Times, May 17, 1881.

159. "Senator Conkling acts like a boy" ... "It's bad enough without discussing it": Philadelphia Press, May 17, 1881, in Garfield papers. LC.

160. "A great big baby boohooing": Dawes to Ela Dawes, May 16, 1881, Dawes papers. LC.; Peskin, 572.

161. "the people will endure ill nature even to ugliness": Claflin to Hoar, May 19, 1881, in Welch, 103.

162. "[A] very weak attempt at the heroic": Garfield diary, May 16, 1881.

163. "Sometime, somehow I *knew* the end would come": Pierrepont to Garfield, May 18, 1881. Garfield papers. LC.

164. "great sensation" from America: *London, The Times*, May 17, 1881.

165. "I was in bed. I think I retired about eight o'clock": *New York Herald*, October 6, 1881.

166. "senatorial suicide": See, for instance, *New York World*, May 17, 1881.

167. "the idea flashed through my brain": *New York Herald*, October 6, 1881.

168. "the same impression came upon me with renewed force": Guiteau testimony, United States v. Charles Guiteau, 593.

169. "kept growing on me, pressing me, goading me": *id.*

170. "kept bearing and bearing and bearing down upon me": *New York Herald*, October 6, 1881

171. "I never had the slightest doubt as to the divinity": Guiteau testimony, United States v. Charles Guiteau, 593.

172. an "inspiration" ... "where a man's mind is taken possession": Guiteau testimony, United States v. Charles Guiteau, 590.

173. "[M]y getting an office or not getting an office... had nothing to do with": Guiteau testimony, United States v. Charles Guiteau, 587.

174. "Had Jefferson Davis and a dozen or two": *New York Herald*, November 15, 1881.

175. "I did not go near Mr. Blaine or near the President": *New York Herald*, October 6, 1881.

13. Stalwart of the Stalwarts (*pages 308–336*)

1. Celebrations erupted across upstate New York: *New York Times*, May 19, 1881.

2. "It is no time for timidity or palliations": *Cincinnati Commercial*, May 18, 1881. Garfield papers. LC.

3. "the President would [be] powerless to appoint anyone in New York": Sherman, 817.

4. "The proper sphere for him is the monastery": *The Nation*, May 19, 1881; Jordan, 395.

5. "What does this mean, marshal?": Platt, 158.

6. "no statesman ever wore a more winning smile": *New York Times*, May 25, 1881; Reeves, 234.

7. "I have been portrayed as a 'Me, too,'": Platt 159

8. "general impression" ... "Senators Conkling and Platt would be returned": *National Republican*, May 17, 1881. Garfield papers. LC.

9. "Huh, but you will be the first to desert us": Platt, 160.

10. "political privateer, armed with letters of marque and reprisal": Connery, 159. A growing number were "only too glad to abandon [Conkling] the moment they scented danger and began to feel the strong arm of the administration on them," he also observed. The *Utica Herald*, Conkling's own hometown paper, joked that many of his followers were genuinely surprise to learn "the world has not gone smash, nor the earth varied from the usual time of its revolution" due to Lord Roscoe's abdication. *Utica Herald*, May 17, 1881, in Jordan, 394.

11. "a freak of insanity on the part of a man": Hay to Reid, May 26, 1881, in Jordan, 396.

12. Conkling and Platt saw the bad news plainly: *London, The Times*, May 31.

13. "Her weakness is most pitiful": Garfield diary, May 28, 1881.

14. Senate adjourned *sine die* ..."a great relief" to Garfield: Garfield diary, May 20, 1881.

15. "Conkling and Platt cannot be reelected by the legislature": Hickman to Garfield, May 18, 1881. Garfield papers. LC. Before the Senate had left town, Garfield had sent back all the original pro-Stalwart New York nominations except for Louis Payn (who'd been too partisan with Conkling) and John Tyler (whom local Buffalo merchants had widely disliked).

16. "everything possible or impossible must be done": Blaine to Stephen Elkins, May 18, 1881, cited in Jordan, 400, and Reeves, 233.

17. Garfield didn't seem to mind Blaine's egging him on: Garfield diary, May 24 and 25, 1881.

18. Garfield got himself out on the water: Garfield diary, May 27 and 28, 1881. On Europe trip, see Garfield diary, July 13 through November 6, 1867.

19. "My services ought to be worth more to the government": Garfield diary, June 8, 1881.

20. "My day is frittered away by the personal seeking of people": Garfield diary, June 13, 1881.

21. "I am no expert on firearms at all": Guiteau testimony, United States v. Charles Guiteau Guiteau 636.

22. "just to get used to the outward act of handling the weapon": Guiteau testimony, United States v. Charles Guiteau Guiteau 637.

23. "a dull young man, with a loud voice": Garfield diary, June 12, 1881.

24. "remove" a man ... "at his devotions?": *New York Herald*, October 6, 1881

25. "The President's nomination was an act of God": *id.*

26. "I thought to myself, 'That would be a good chance to get him'": *id.*

27. "I never mentioned the conception to a living soul": *id.*

28. "I went to the depot all prepared to remove him": *id.*

29. Mexican Southern Railroad: Background on the Mexican Southern Railroad venture is from McFeely, 486-487.

30. "I hope that the Legislature will sustain our Senators": Quoted in *London, The Times*, May 28, 1881.

31. Conkling "has been shamefully treated, Sir": *New York Times*, June 4, 1881; Jordan, 404.

32. "while I am incapable of discriminating against any Republican": Garfield diary, May 17, 1881, fn. 156. The letter also corrected Grant's facts, reminding him that Robertson "did not, as you suppose, oppose your election in 1872" and had supported the Chicago resolution to back whichever candidate the convention nominated.

33. "very liberal terms made for us by the proprietor": Julia Grant, 322-323.

34. "very bitter on the administration" ... it "would be a disgrace": *Washington Evening Star*, June 18, 1881.

35. Grant ... "smokes and reads and receives his friends": "Special to *The Times*", dateline June 26. Garfield papers. LC.

36. "[I]n private conversation, [Garfield] spoke of Grant very contemptuously": *id*.

37. "bracing and invigorating salt air": Rockwell, 436.

38. "As yet, they have not met": *New York Times*, June 23, 1881; Garfield diary, June 22, 1881 fn. 190.

39. "It is now evident (what I had not supposed) that Grant": Garfield diary, June 21, 1881.

40. "The General "seems to have forgotten that he is only one citizen": Garfield diary, May 17, 1881. In fact, his temper had flared when Grant had arranged for Senator John P. Jones to give the newspapers a summary of the letter to print, in an attempt to avoid publication of Garfield's response—an "unmanly" tactic, Garfield grumbled. Garfield diary, May 17, 1881, footnote 157.

41. "what kind of scowl Grant would give Garfield": "Special to *The Times*", dateline June 26. Garfield papers. LC.

42. "This is his only courtesy to me since he came four days ago": Garfield diary, June 24, 1881.

43. Grant "approached Mr. Garfield and extended his hand": *New York Times*, June 26, 1881; Garfield diary, June 25, 1881, fn. 194.

44. "tardy recognition of the respect due to the office": Garfield diary, June 25, 1881.

45. "Argument is displaced by billingsgate": *Washington Evening Star*, June 18, 1881.

46. "most gorgeous colors of the Oriental and Egyptian types": *Id*.

47. "Senatorial criminals" ... "corrupt gangs": *Id*.

48. "I will not shake hands with you": *New York Sun*, June 24, 1881. Garfield papers. LC.

49. "He would hardly leave behind ... a single person": *New York Tribune*, June 10, 1881, Blaine papers. LC.

50. "the lizard on the hill": Jordan, 402.

51. "Do you not think it better to abstain": *Conkling* to Julia Conkling, June 29, 1881. Conkling papers. LC.

52. "I confess I feel dismayed that years of well tested loyalty": Julia Conkling to Conkling, cited in Jordan 411-412. See Ross, 261-262, on the divorce and Conkling's possible role in advising her on it.

53. Chet Arthur ... covering bar tabs: See Delavan House bill to Arthur, June 24, 1881, for three days' board, carriage, wine, bar, newspapers, so on, in Arthur papers. LC.

54. "the Vice President of the United States, lobbying like any": Hudson, 119.

55. "If General Arthur does not desire four years of public contempt": *New York Tribune*, May 26, 1881, cited in Reeves, 234. E.L. Godkin also chided Arthur now for his "subterranean politics," noting that the public should "not expect to change a man's nature by electing him to the Vice-Presidency." *The Nation*, June 9, 1881. Garfield's own goal was now finally being understood by the pub-

lic: "to wrest the civil service of the country from the clutches of boss politicians." *The Galveston News*, June 24, 1881. Garfield papers. LC.

56. "I did not engage you, Vice-President Arthur, to do this kind of work": *Harper's Weekly*, July 16, 1881.

57. "which justifies [Garfield's] removal in disgrace from office": United States v. Charles Guiteau, 726.

58. "How Long Will The Republican Party Last?": United States v. Charles Guiteau Guiteau, 726.

59. 'The President and Gen. Grant have not yet met" ... Grant, "trifled with by General Garfield": United States v. Charles Guiteau Guiteau, 730-732.

60. "Address to the American People": Guiteau, "Address to the American," June 16, 1881. Guiteau papers. Georgetown University. Rosenberg, 41.

61. "I wanted to see what sort of quarters I would have to occupy": *Philadelphia Inquirer*, July 3, 1881.

62. as jails went, this one was "excellent": Kingsbury, 9.

63. "I had a splendid sleep last night": Lucretia to Garfield, June 30, 1881. Shaw, 389.

64. "Is there anything you wish [David] Swaim": Garfield to Lucretia, June 30, 1881. Shaw, 390.

65. "How are you this morning? I hope there is no doubt": Garfield to Lucretia, July 1, 1881. Shaw, 390.

66. "And this is the 'vindication' he appealed for": Garfield diary, May 31 and June 9, 1881.

67. "You cannot imagine how uncomfortable": Harriet Blaine to M. June 7, 1881. Harriet Blaine 206.

68. lay out his ideas on civil rights and the South: Peskin, 595.

69. Frederick Douglas ... Blanche Bruce ...John M. Langston:: Doenecke, 49.

70. "united America, reciprocity, arbitration, trade, glory, and the rest": Josephson, 320.

71. "It will suffice to say that the couple were scantily attired": *Chicago Tribune*, July 1, 1881.

72. A "compromising" sight: *Springfield Republican*, July 1, 1881. Garfield papers. LC.

73. "peeping into his room over a transom": *Chicago Tribune*, July 1, 1881.

74. "A Disgusting Scandal" ..."The Shame of Albany" ... "a blunder and an outrage": Headlines from July 1, 1881, in Garfield papers. LC. Quote from *New York Times*, July 2, 1881.

75. "Platt evidently and unfortunately is a very weak man": *New York Sun*. July 1, 1881. Garfield papers. LC.

76. "Mrs. Baldwin" ... a "married woman": *Chicago Tribune*, July 1, 1881.

77. "shouts of laughter" and cries of "Oh, Oh": Associated Press Dispatch, July 1, 1881. Garfield papers. LC.

78. "For goodness sake, don't do it!" ... "I became satisfied on the night of June 30": Platt, 160-162.

79. "terrible hot sultry day": *New York Herald*, October 6, 1881.

80. "I was several yards behind him": *New York Herald*, October 6, 1881; Guiteau testimony, United States v. Charles Guiteau, 692, 693.

81. a "very handsome & happy looking man": Harriet Blaine narrative, 2-3. Blaine papers. LC.

82. "in the most delightful and cozy fellowship possible" ... "just as hilarious as two young school-girls": Guiteau testimony, United States v. Charles Guiteau, 694.

83. *"The President's tragic death was a sad necessity"*: Rosenberg, 41-42.

84. *"I have just shot the President"*: *New York Times*, July 3, 1881.

85. "These boys think they can do great things": Hayes diary, October 29, 1881; Peskin, 595.

86. "Don't have breakfast till I get back": Harriet Blaine narrative, 7. Blaine papers. LC.

87. "Both [Garfield and Blaine] were at their very best, with new gray spring suits": Stanley-Brown, 12.

88. "Little 'Me Too' Drops Out, Unable to Wag Any Longer": *Philadelphia Inquirer*, July 2, 1881.

89. "I will escort you to the car": Blaine testimony, United States v. Charles Guiteau, 121.

90. "How much time have we, officer?": *New York Times*, July 2, 1881.

91. Guiteau had awoken ... his mind "perfectly clear": *New York Herald*, October 6, 1881.

92. "straightened up and threw his head back and seemed to be perfectly bewildered": *id.*

93. "'My God! What is this?'": Blaine testimony, United States v. Charles Guiteau, 121.

94. "His lower limbs gave away, broke from under him": White testimony, United States v. Charles Guiteau, 141.

95. "a very loud report of a pistol discharge" ... "I touched the President": Blaine testimony, United States v. Charles Guiteau, 121.

96. "I have sent a letter to General Sherman" ... "Keep quiet, my friend": *New York Herald*, October 6, 1881.

97. "I did it. I will go to jail for it": Kearney testimony, United States v. Charles Guiteau, 187; Rosenberg, 2-3. See also *New York Times* and other newspapers, July 3, 1881.

98. "I thank you doctor" ..."but I am a dead man": Rosenberg, 3.

14. Bulletins *(pages 339–379)*

1. "should Garfield die, Arthur, Conkling and [Tom Platt]": Platt, 163.

2. "What is the latest report?": *New York Tribune*, July 3, 1881.

3. "I certainly trust so. It is a most shocking event." ..."Express to the President": *New York Tribune*, *New York Times*, and *Chicago Tribune*, July 3, 1881.

4. Platt ...reminded him of the ...1863 draft riots: Platt, 163.

5. Conkling "promptly shook his head in a decidedly negative manner": *New York Tribune*, July 3, 1881.

6. "Men go around with clenched teeth and white lips": Special to the *Chicago Tribune*, July 2, 1881.

7. "Chet Arthur President of the United States! Good God!": As described in a letter from Andrew White, in Jordan 406.

8. "The President of the United States was shot this morning": Blaine to Arthur, June 2, 1881. [10:20 am] Original in Blaine papers. LC. Typed copy in Arthur papers. LC.

9. he'd tell Senator Jones he'd never heard of the man: At least that's what Jones told the newspapers. *Chicago Tribune*, July 3, 1881

10. "Your telegram with its deplorable narrative": Arthur to Blaine, July 2, 1881. *New York Tribune*, July 3, 1881.

11. "The President wishes me to say to you": *New York Times* and other papers, July 3, 1881.

12. "almost frantic": *Boston Globe*, July 3, 1881.

13. "The President's wounds are not mortal": *Boston Globe* and other papers. July 3, 1881.

14. Grant's "quiet firm words": Letter from Lucretia Garfield to Julia Grant, 1888. Lucretia Garfield papers. LC.

15. The locomotive … took two full miles to reach a stop; a derailment would have killed them: *Chicago Tribune*, July 5, 1881.

16. "They have telephoned over to you [from the White House]": Harriet Blaine to M. July 3, 1881, in Harriet Blaine 210.

17. "Whatever happens I want you to promise to look out for Crete": Harriet Blaine to M. July 3, 1881, in Harriet Blaine 211.

18. "Mr. Secretary, the President's has been shot": Stanley-Brown, 12.

19. "an express wagon slowly drove up to the rear door": Stanley-Brown, 13.

20. "the upper story was unhurt; it was the hull": Peskin, 597. See also Rockwell, 437, with a variation: "It was only the hull that is staved in; the upper words are unharmed"

21. "Mr. President, your injury is formidable" … "Well, Doctor, we'll take that chance": Bliss, 300; Ridpath 519. The two sources have slight variations in Bliss's half of the exchange, the doctor claiming he said simply: "In my judgment, you have a chance of recovery." Ridpath's "one chance in a hundred" is more widely quoted and more likely.

22. "You know how well I love you": *Boston Globe*, July 4, 1881.

23. "Why did that man shoot me?" *Washington Evening Star*, July 2, 1881; *Chicago Tribune*, July 3, 1881; *Boston Globe*, July 4, 1881; Reeves, 239. Note slight variations in the wording; I've used all three versions.

24. Garfield said nothing; he never raised the issue again: See generally Bliss, 300.

25. "The surgeons, on consultation, regard his wounds as very serious": Blaine to James Russell Lowell, Minister to London, July 2, 1881. In *Philadelphia Inquirer* and other newspapers, July 3, 1881.

26. "My God, it is terrible": *Chicago Tribune*, July 3, 1881.

27. "At this hour (1 p.m.) the President's symptoms are not regarded as unfavorable": Blaine to Arthur, 1 pm. July 2, 1881. *Washington Evening Star*, July 2, 1881.

28. "Internal hemorrhage is taking place": Ridpath 521-521 and newspapers.
29. "The president's condition is alarming": Robert T. Lincoln to John Logan, July 2, 1881. Logan papers. LC.
30. "It is a sad state of affairs when the President of this country": *New York Times*, July 3, 1881.
31. "Scores of men were heard to say": *Chicago Tribune*, July 3, 1881.
32. "I have my own opinion as to where this originated": *id.*
33. "Arthur for President! Conkling the power behind the throne": Hayes diary, July 3, 1881. Hayes papers.
34. "This is the result of placating bosses": *New York Times*, July 3, 1881.
35. "Send C.O.D. that s___b that shot Garfield": *Washington Evening Star*, July 3, 1881.
36. German Americans were "indignant": *id.*
37. "can't stop our railway building": *Chicago Tribune*, July 3, 1881.
38. "Mother is so wrapped up in James" ... "Don't be alarmed by sensational rumors": *Philadelphia Inquirer*, July 4, 1881, including telegram from Harry Garfield to Eliza Garfield, July 2, 1881.
39. Irvin "has been my shadow, wanting to talk it over": Lide M. Rudolph to Lucretia Garfield, July 4, 1881. Lucretia Garfield papers. LC.
40. "They... examined me and took all my personal effects": Guiteau testimony, United States v. Charles Guiteau, 601.
41. "I have nothing to say" ... "Charles Guiteau, a theologian and lawyer": Kearney testimony, United States v. Charles Guiteau, 188.
42. "I want to go to jail": Guiteau testimony, United States v. Charles Guiteau, 601.
43. "I am a native-born American. Born in Chicago": *Philadelphia Inquirer* and other papers, July 3, 1881.
44. "I will catch cold on this stone pavement": *Philadelphia Inquirer*, July 3, 1881.
45. "I had not been so happy for weeks until the 2d day of July": Guiteau testimony, United States v. Charles Guiteau, 601. See also *Chicago Tribune*, July 3, 1881.
46. telegram ... saying that the president had died at 3:05 pm: *New York Tribune*, July 3, 1881.
47. Arthur ... was "overcome with grief": *id.*
48. "At the hour Six O'clock the condition of the President is very alarming": Blaine to Arthur, June 2, 1881. [6:00 pm] Original in Blaine papers. LC. Typed copy in Arthur papers. LC.
49. "Gens: We will hang Conkling and Co.": Platt, 163.
50. Lucretia ..."frail, fatigued, desperate, but firm": Harriet Blaine to M. July 3, 1881, in Harriet Blaine 211.
51. "Well, my dear, you are not going to die": Peskin 598.
52. doctors ... signs of "profound collapse.": Bliss Report, *New York Herald*, October 6, 1881.
53. "he will not probably live three hours": *New York Times*, July 3, 1881.

54. "Within the last two hours the President's condition": Robert T. Lincoln to John Logan, July 2, 1881. Logan papers. LC.

55. "I love my father" … "A Southern sympathizer would have you know" … "God preserve the President": Telegrams to Lucretia Garfield, July 2, 1881. Lucretia Garfield papers. LC.

56. Queen Victoria …"Please wire latest news": *Philadelphia Inquirer*, July 4, 1881.

57. "Go, now, and rest": Rockwell, 437.

58. "It is the judgment of the Cabinet that you should come": Blaine to Arthur, July 2, 1881, from *Chicago Tribune* and other papers, July 4, 1881.

59. "The President is no better, and we fear, sinking": Hunt and James to Arthur, July 2, 1881, in *Chicago Tribune*, July 3, 1881.

60. "Good-bye, Arthur, and God bless you" … "You have nothing to fear": *Chicago Tribune*, July 4, 1881, citing dispatch from *New York Sun*.

61. "thronged with people awaiting the issuing of bulletins": Sievers 199.

62. doctors issued six different official bulletins: Ridpath 522-523 and newspapers.

63. Doctors … haggling over patronage even now: See *New York World*, July 7, 1881 editorial on this "unseemly squabble."

64. "If I can't save him, no one can": *Chicago Tribune*, July 4, 1881.

65. 3 Independence Avenue, just across the street from the Capitol Building: The site of today's Longworth House Office Building.

66. "I was so nervous and depressed last night": *Chicago Tribune*, July 4, 1881.

67. "Gen. Arthur has been untrue" … "Grossly slanderous as it would be": *New York Times*, July 3, 1881.

68. entire cabinet … had come to … visit. … They "grasped each other warmly": *Chicago Tribune*, July 4, 1881.

69. Arthur looked "less depressed": *id.*

70. Arthur … looking "all anxiety": Sievers, 202.

71. words "greatly affected" her … she …"did not give way to her emotions": *Washington Evening Star*, July 4, 1881.

72. "I pray to God that the President will recover": *id.*

73. "Mrs. [Mary] Surratt [of the Lincoln murder conspiracy] was hanged": *Louisville Courier Journal*, July 3, 1881.

74. "I don't want to appear strained and awkward": *Chicago Tribune*, July 5, 1881.

75. Harrison … dismissed him as a "nuisance": Sievers, 199.

76. "He wanted me to sign a paper recommending him": *New York Tribune* July 3, 1881.

77. "He hung around Washington last winter, during the coldest weather": *Chicago Tribune*, July 3, 1881.

78. "The anti-Administration Republicans love their country": *National Republican*, July 2, 1881, reprinted in *Chicago Tribune*, July 3, 1881.

79. Old World and South America had suffered a plague of political killings: For full list, see *Washington Evening Star*, July 4, 1881. See also "Socialistic and other Assassinations," *Atlantic Monthly*, October 1880, 466.

80. "crazed mind, seeking infamous notoriety": *Chicago Tribune*, July 3, 1881.

81. "may have shown madness, but it was certainly": *Harpers Weekly*, July 23, 1881.

82. "insanity" ... "differed only in degree": Josephson, 319.

83. The law put "insanity" in a small box in the 1880s: See generally Rosenberg on the history of the insanity defense.

84. "If a man has an irresistible impulse": Rosenberg 54-55, 103. One state, New Hampshire, had adopted a more liberal standard, making insanity a factual question for the jury.

85. "All the facts point to a deliberately formed plan": *Washington Evening Star*, July 4, 1881.

86. "Fellow citizens! God reigns": *New York Herald*, April 16, 1881; *Washington Evening Star*, July 5, 1881; *Chicago Tribune*, July 6, 1881; Bartleby.com. See Peskin, 250-251, regarding questions over the authenticity of this famous quote.

87. "If the President should live two or three days": *Washington Evening Star*, July 5, 1881.

88. "Great surprise" at the absence of sympathy calls ..."nor any of the leading Stalwarts": *New York Times*, July 3, 1881.

89. "More than this is not necessary, unless the President dies": *Washington Evening Star*, July 4, 1881.

90. "to redeem some fancied public wrong by sacrificing a life": *New York Times*, July 3, 1881.

91. "outwardly, she holds herself with much composure": *Washington Evening Star*, July 4, 1881.

92. "If the President passes through to-day without losing strength": *id.*.

93. "We are hopeful, but there is great anxiety": *id.*

94. "You are so calm and brave yourself": Adelaide Rudolph to Lucretia Garfield, July 10, 1881. Lucretia Garfield papers. LC. Her sister Lide wrote later that summer marveling that "you, dear Crete, from whom I have taken many a lesson quietly, ... did your duty and spent no superfluous strength talking over it...." Lide M. Rudolph to Lucretia Garfield, July 17, 1881.

95. "Dear Lady. May the God of all grace sustain you" ... "A humble American wife and mother prays earnestly" ... "Dear Mrs. Garfield. Weeping may endure for a night": Telegrams to Lucretia Garfield, July 3,5, and 7, 1881. Lucretia Garfield papers. LC.

96. "Do not allow probing" ... "Saturate every thing": Patee to Lucretia Garfield, July 3, 1881. Lucretia Garfield papers. LC. It is interesting that a frontier doctor in Kansas would be more familiar with anti-septic medical practice than the president's own physicians from Washington, Philadelphia, and New York City.

97. "I do not believe there is another woman in the country": Sievers 199. Even among the cabinet wives, she emerged as spiritual leader. Hearing that Blaine had caught another summer chill, she sent a note to his wife Harriet: "if Mr. Blaine is not feeling as well as usual we shall insist that you go away as soon as possible. Our love to you all." Lucretia to Harriet Blaine, August 10, 1881. Blaine papers. A few weeks earlier she'd written: "Keep you your courage. I do mine." Lucretia to Harriet Blaine, July 5, 1881. Blaine papers.

98. "Gen. Arthur had received about fifty letters": *Washington Evening Star*, July 5, 1881.

99. "one of the most terrible incidents": *New York Sun* dispatch, contained in *Washington Evening Star*, July 4, 1881.

100. "The President has forced me to commit suicide or murder": *Indianapolis Journal*, August 54, 1881, carried in the *New York Times*, August 7, 1881. The original quote had occurred in the *Indianapolis News*, July 9, 1881; Conkling's denial was in a letter to W.H. Lamaster, July 28, 1881.

101. "seized a dark and dangerous hour": Conkling to Alexander T. Brown, July 9, 1881, in Reeves, 243.

102. "Please also give to Mrs. Garfield my most respectful condolence": Conkling to MacVeigh, July 5, 1881, in Ridpath 536 and newspapers.

103. "Please say to Mrs. Garfield for me that today's reports": Conkling to Arthur, July 7, 1881, in *Chicago Tribune*, July 9, 1881.

104. "There is no occasion for public apprehension or excitement": *The Nation*, July 7, 1881.

105. "faction fight" had "led this deluded assassin to believe": *New York Tribune*, July 4, 1881.

106. "his enemies might try to manufacture such a sentiment": *New York Sun* dispatch, in *Washington Evening Star*, July 4, 1881.

107. "That Mr. Roscoe Conkling and his friends": *New York Tribune*, July 7, 1881.

108. "Keep Quiet" and "withdraw at once": *Philadelphia Inquirer*, July 8, 1881.

109. Conkling "would be the controlling influence": *Chicago Tribune*, July 6, 1881.

110. his "utter insufficiency": *Toronto Globe*, July 4, 1881, in *Washington Evening Star*, July 4, 1881.

111. "With Garfield dead, Arthur would be President": *New York Times*, July 4, 1881.

112. "It is out of this mess of filth": *The Nation*, July 7, 1881.

113. "two or three times" ... "None that I know of": Arthur responses to written questions, United States v. Charles Guiteau, 896; *Chicago Tribune*, December 9, 1881.

114. "not in good health" ... "his head bowed and looking vacantly": *Chicago Tribune*, July 5, 1881.

115. "Tears stood in [Arthur's] eyes": *New York Times*, July 5, 1881. See Reeves, 242.

116. "No one deplores the calamity more than": *Chicago Tribune*, July 5, 1881. Marshall Jewell was one of many public figures to defend him, saying even Arthur's political enemies didn't "question their integrity."

117. "I wish to inform you, Mr. Arthur": *Chicago Tribune*, July 5, 1881.

118. "what can he do about it?" ... "General Arthur has told me that life": *Washington Evening Star*, July 6, 1881.

119. "He is now, six o'clock, still comfortable": Harriet Blaine to M., July 6, 1881. Harriet Blaine, 212.

120. "The President had a natural movement": Robert Todd Lincoln to John Logan, July 5, 1881. Logan papers. LC.

121. "The President passed a very comfortable night": Blaine to Lowell, July 6, 1661; in *Washington Evening Star*, July 6, 1881.

122. "The conditions reported by the surgeons give": Robert Todd Lincoln to John Logan, July 5, 1881. Logan papers. LC.

123. doctors ... most detailed diagnosis yet: Ridpath, 526 and newspapers.

124. doctors ... firing pistols at cadavers: *Chicago Tribune*, July 9, 1881.

125. "His physical strength keeps up wonderfully": Blaine to Lowell, July 11, 1881, in Ridpath 545 and newspapers.

126. "Arthur can go back to New York": Harriet Blaine to M., July 8, 1881, Harriet Blaine 216.

127. "The President is doing very nicely": Harriet Blaine to M., July 10, 1881, Harriet Blaine 216.

128. "His hair is white, and his florid color has changed": *Chicago Tribune*, July 5, 1881.

129. "I want you and Mr. Blaine": Chandler to Harriet Blaine, July 9, 1881. Blaine papers. LC.

130. "Garfield will now have a hold on the hearts": Hayes to John Hay, July 8, 1881. Hayes papers.

131. "I like him" ... "When things are going against him": *Chicago Tribune*, July 6, 1881.

132. "The whole country has been agonized": Chandler to Harriet Blaine, July 18, 1881. Blaine papers. LC.

133. "one thing is necessary now to clinch his popularity": Blaine to Lucretia Garfield, July 18, 1881. Lucretia Garfield papers. LC.

134. "I should think the people would be tired of having": Smith, 1197; Peskin 600.

135. "Strangulatus pro Republica": Rockwell, 298.

136. "I am glad it is over. I am sorry for Conkling": Bliss, 302.

137. Conkling had visited the White House one last time: *New York Times*, July 15, 1881.

138. "Very well; whatever you say is necessary must be done": Bliss, 301.

139. "[Y]our Father says an administration with a sick bed": Harriet Blaine to Children, August 19, 1881. Harriet Blaine, 230.

140. "trim his sails for places in Arthur's cabinet": Hayes diary, April 6, 1863. Hayes papers.

141. "The less Arthur has to do with Conkling" ... "Guiteau Stalwarts" and "Arthur Stalwarts": Hayes diary, August 28, 1881; February 24, 1882. Hayes papers.

142. "The hours of Garfield's life are numbered": Julia Sand to Arthur, August 27, 1881. Arthur papers. LC.; Clancy 264, Reeves, 245. Arthur's papers at the LC contain twenty-two letters that he saved from Julia Sand spanning the period from August 1881 through September 1883. Arthur as president finally met her personally in August 1882, paying an hour-long surprise visit to her New York City home. She was then a thirty-two year old spinster and it was a highlight of her life. Reeves, 295-6.

143. "I am most deeply grieved at the sad news of the last few days": Lowell to Blaine, August 27, 1881, in Ridpath, 600 and newspapers.

144. "Yes, go and ride; I want you to": Rockwell 437.

145. "Oh, no, send him my oatmeal": Dole, 128.

146. Garfield ... single act of state in August: Rockwell, 298.

147. "Dear Mother—Don't be disturbed by conflicting reports": Garfield to Eliza Garfield, August 11, 1881, in Ridpath 581 and newspapers.

148. "the heat is so great, and every particle": Harriet Blaine to M. September 1, 1881. Harriet Blaine, 234.

149. "Doctor, how soon do you think": Bliss, 302.

150. "We must get the President out of this": *Philadelphia Inquirer*, September 3, 1881.

151. "I think the president is doing very well today": *Philadelphia Inquirer*, September 6, 1881.

152. "I think [the President] will be immediately benefited": *id.*

153. "I hope you are coming to Elberon": Lucretia Garfield to Harriet Blaine, September, 1881. [Tuesday morning]. Blaine papers. LC.

154. "To this day I cannot hear the sound of the low slow roll": Stanley-Brown, 13.

155. "I can't understand how it is": *New York Times*, September 20, 1881.

156. "Oh, Swaim. I am in terrible pain here": *id.*

157. "Oh! Why am I made to suffer this cruel wrong?": Bliss, 304.

158. "It is over": Bliss, 304

159. "I hope—my God, I do hope it is a mistake": Howe 1-2; Peskin 608.

160. "He is sitting alone in his room sobbing like a child": *New York Times*, September 20, 1881.

161. "grave and critical": MacVeigh to Arthur, September 1, 1881, Arthur papers. LC.; Reeves, 246.

162. "The most frightful responsibility": *New York Times*, November 21, 1886; Reeves 246.

163. "It becomes our painful duty to inform you": Newspapers, September 20, 1881.

164. "I have your telegram, and the intelligence fills": *New York Times*, September 20, 1881.

165. proclamation summoning the United States Senate to ...choose a *President Pro Tempore:* Reeves, 247.

15. Arthur *(pages 380–400)*

1. "No man ever assumed the Presidency of the United States": *New York Times*, September 21, 1881.

2. "extremely embarrassing" circumstances ... acted as "a gentleman of the finest sensibility.": *Chicago Tribune*, September 21, 1881.

3. "I am done with politics now and forever,": *The Independent*, August 4, 1881, in Jordan, 410.

4. Friends kept his name alive in local politics ..." Reeves, 256.

5. "The topic is exciting and... will tend to stir up the old quarrels and dissentions ":*New York Times*, September 21, 1881.

6. "dressed with usual care and looking in the best of health.": *Washington Evening Star*, October 8, 1881.

7. "I came to see the President. He and I have long been friends….": *Washington Post*, October 9, 1881.

8. "you put it down for a fact that 'Conk' wanted 'Chet' to remove Robertson": Hudson, 127. See also Boutwell, 275, saying that Conkling wanted "one thing, and one thing only—the removal of [William H.] Robertson."

9. "outrageous,"…. He felt "morally bound to continue": Platt, 180.

10. "bound neither morally nor politically nor in any other way,": *id.*

11. "all our friends have turned traitor ":Hudson, 127.

12. "When I saw him *afterwards*": Kate Chase Sprague to Arthur, October 21, 1881. Arthur papers. LC.

13. Conkling could be a "tower of strength": *id.*

14. "suffering from his old malarial troubles,…. It is the general impression,": *Washington Post*, October 11, 1881.

15. … he "doesn't like to talk about it,": Hudson, 127.

16. "The President is right …. "He isn't 'Chet' Arthur anymore": Hudson, 126-7.

17. "For the Vice-Presidency I was indebted to Mr. Conkling…" : Jordan, 415.

18. Conkling turned it down even after the Senate had confirmed him: Jordan, 416.

19. "the organization was not disposed to forgive Arthur …": Platt, 178.

20. Arthur's "career would have been more agreeable …": Boutwell, 275.

21. "Madam, I may be President of the United States, but my private life …": Whitcomb, 185. See also Dole, 194—saying it came in response to rumors about eligible women.

22. He "passed his little finger": Stanley-Brown, 13.

23. "It is indeed humiliating to the historian,": Whitcomb, 180.

24. "the most ordinary precautions of medical surgery": *Chicago Medical Journal* in *New York Times*, August 23, 1881.

25. … they wouldn't see a dime … until well over a year: The drama is played out in newspapers over a year-long period starting shortly after Garfield's death. See, for instance, *New York Times*, August 28, September 11, September 19, October 20, December 30, December 31, 1881, and April 23, 1882.

26. "There is a better color in her face": *New York Times*, December 29, 1882.

27. … stood with President Grover Cleveland at the unveiling : *Program of Exercises at the Unveiling of the Statue of Gen. James A. Garfield*, at Washington, D.C. May 12, 1887. Lucretia Garfield papers. LC.

28. "For you personally, my dear friend": Lucretia Garfield to Harriet Blaine, November 18, 1884. Blaine papers. LC.

29. …Grant called on Blaine: Muzzey, 312; Stanwood, 287; Badeau, 346.

30. … Blaine would make an "excellent president.: Badeau, 346.

31. … lengthy biography …, letter to incoming President Arthur: *New York Herald*, October 6, 1881; Rosenberg, 49.

32. "The doctors did that. I simply shot at him": Guiteau, 1160.

33. ... reduced the courtroom to a circus: William Chandler complained about this phenomenon as early as July. "[Guiteau] has actually been allowed to give his views as to Arthur's cabinet, to name his men, & and have them printed by leave of the Dept. of Justice," he wrote to Harriet Blaine. "Can't you stop this?" Chandler to Harriet Blaine, July 18, 1881. Blaine papers. LC. See also George Edmunds, "The Conduct of theGuiteau Trial," *North American Review.* March 1882.

34. "the most interesting place, by all odds, in Washington": arriet Blaine to M. December 11, 1881, Harriet Blaine, 260.

35. "that vile room." ... she wanted to see Guiteau "out of the way....": Harriet Blaine to M., January 25, 1882. H. Blaine, 290-291.

36. *"I am going to the Lordy; I am so glad,..."* : Rosenberg, 237; Kingsbury, 52; newspapers.

37. "If you would like to come up-stairs to my office, Mr. Gould, ...": Connery, 162.

38. "The death of Garfield is a fresh grief to me.": Blaine to Elkins, September 30, 1881, in Stanwood, 240.

39. "never quite the same" ... "The flow of animal spirits..." : Stanwood, 240

40. "His Accidency" or "the stalled ox of the White House" : Jordan, 416.

41. "struck speechless ... egregious blunder": Platt, 181.

42. "Can Conkling be induced to speak for us? ...": Blaine to Elkins, July 27, 1881, in Stanwood 285.

43. "I am out of politics" : Summers, 273.

44. "No, thank you, I don't engage in criminal practice.": Muzzey, 307; Jordan 421. Summers suggests the famous retort might be mere rumor driven by the newspapers, though even he agrees that if Conkling didn't say it, he'd have wished he had; it was an exchange "that 'Lord Roscoe' would have given years off his life to have delivered." Summers, 273.

45. "How can I speak into a grave? ..." : Stoddard, 114; Clancy, 263; Jordan, 407.

46. "Don't you think I'm better?": Jordan, 429.

47. "having had my chance and lost....": Stanwood , 304.

48. "I have come to a time of life": Stanwood , 339-340.

49. "lost Americans ... gravely vacant ... faces..." : Whitcomb, 180.

50. "a sort of *delirium tremens* vision ...a nasty *chopping-sea* in politics.": Cater, 115-116; Doenecke, 54.

51. "A non-entity with side whiskers": Dole, 194.

52. "I am a poor hater": Garfield diary. April 26. 1876.

ACKNOWLEDGEMENTS

I happily give my warmest thanks to the many people who helped me in researching, writing, and finalizing this book. They not only made it possible for me to undertake and finish the project but also vastly improved its quality at every step. My manuscript benefited from the sharp eyes and careful comments of a host of knowledgeable people who read all or parts of the book, including: George Manno, Clyde Linsley, Sky Beaven, Ed Jaffe, George Vercessi, and Terry Davidson of the Washington Independent Writers history small group; Ellen E.M. Roberts of "Where Books Begin"; Jan Brunner and Bob Hahn of Olsson, Frank, and Weeda, P.C.; Don Ritchie, associate historian of the United States Senate; Joan Kapsch of the James A. Garfield National Historical Site in Mentor, Ohio; James Hershberg, my nephew and professor of history at the George Washington University; and Louis Peck, my old friend who also edits *Congress Daily* in Washington, D.C.

The Library of Congress was my principal research home for this project, and the excellent staffs at its Manuscript, Newspaper and Periodical, Prints and Photographs, and Photo Duplication rooms helped me at every turn. The publishing professionals who took my idea forward and turned it into a finished commercial product also have earned my highest thanks and respect, including my agent Jeff Gerecke at JCA Literary Agency; my editor Philip Turner, assistant editor Keith Wallman, and publicist Wendie Carr at Carroll & Graf Publishers; copyeditor Judith McQuown; and David Sheon of Sci Wards, LLC. I also particularly thank my colleagues at Olsson, Frank, and Weeda, P.C., where I practice law in Washington, D.C., for giving mw the greatest latitude and support during the many months it took me to complete the book. And, of course, Karen, my thanks and love.

Finally, for this new Viral History Press edition, I thank Catherine Zaccarine of Zaccarine Design, Inc., a very talented designer who has tranformed this book into an elegant new edition.

Thanks to all of you and to many more for giving me the chance and the wherewithal to write *Dark Horse*, and for making it come out as well as it has.

INDEX

Made in the USA
Lexington, KY
01 December 2012